Undocumented Immigrants in the United States

Undocumented Immigrants in the United States

An Encyclopedia of Their Experience

Volume 1: A–J

Anna Ochoa O'Leary, Editor

 GREENWOOD

AN IMPRINT OF ABC-CLIO, LLC
Santa Barbara, California • Denver, Colorado • Oxford, England

Library of Congress Cataloging-in-Publication Data

Undocumented immigrants in the United States : an encyclopedia of their experience / Anna Ochoa O'Leary, editor.
    pages cm
  ISBN 978-0-313-38424-0 (hardback) — ISBN 978-0-313-38425-7 (ebook)
1. Immigrants—United States—Social conditions.   2. Illegal aliens—United States—Social conditions.   3. United States—Emigration and immigration—Encyclopedias.
I. O'Leary, Anna Ochoa.
  JV6475.U48 2014
  305.9'069120973—dc23   2013024574

ISBN: 978-0-313-38424-0
EISBN: 978-0-313-38425-7

18 17 16 15 14   1 2 3 4 5

This book is also available on the World Wide Web as an eBook.
Visit www.abc-clio.com for details.

Greenwood
An Imprint of ABC-CLIO, LLC

ABC-CLIO, LLC
130 Cremona Drive, P.O. Box 1911
Santa Barbara, California 93116–1911

This book is printed on acid-free paper ∞
Manufactured in the United States of America

Contents

List of Entries   vii

Guide to Related Topics   xi

Preface   xvii

Introduction: The History of and Uncertain Future
for Unauthorized Immigrants   xix

Chronology of Undocumented Immigration in the United States   xxv

The Encyclopedia   **1**

Recommended Resources   797

About the Editor and the Contributors   803

Index   811

List of Entries

Acculturation
Acculturation Stress
Activism
Adult Education
Advocacy
Airports
American Civil Liberties Union (ACLU)
American Friends Service Committee
Amnesty
Amnesty International
Arizona
Arizona SB 1070
Assimilation
Asylum
Aztlán
Banking
Barriers to Health
Barrios
Bilingualism
Border Control. *See* U.S. Border Patrol
Border Crossing
Bracero Program
California
Canadian Border
Catholic Church
CC-IME (Consejo Consultivo Instituto de
    los Mexicanos en el Exterior)
Central American Civil Wars
Childcare
Children
Chinese
Citizenship
Citizenship Education
Civil Rights
Clinton Administration

Colleges and Universities
Community Activism
Community Concerns
Corridos
Counterfeit Documents
Counterterrorism and Immigrant Profiling
Coyotes
Crime
Cubans
Cultural Citizenship
Culture
Day Labor
Death
Deferred Action for Childhood Arrivals
    (DACA)
Department of Homeland Security. *See*
    U.S. Department of Homeland
    Security (DHS)
Deportation
Detention Centers
Devil's Highway
Dillingham Report (1910)
Discrimination and Barriers
Displacement
Domestic Violence
Domestic Work
Dominicans
The DREAM Act
Driver's Licenses
Drug Trade
East Asians
Eastern Europeans
Economics
Education
Elementary Schools

Emergency Quota Act of 1921
Employer Sanctions
Employment
Employment Visas
Enclaves
English as a Second Language (ESL)
  Programs
English Language Learners (ELL)
English-Only Movement
Exclusion
Expedited Removal
Faith-Based Organizations
Families
Family Economics
Family Reunification
Family Structure
Fernandez-Vargas v. Gonzales
Film and Television Representation
Flores-Figueroa v. United States
  No. 08-108
Foreign Consulates
Form I-9
Fourteenth Amendment
Gangs
Garment Industry
Gateways
Gender Roles
Globalization
Governance and Criminalization
Great Lakes Region
Green Cards
Guatemalans
Guestworker and Contract
  Labor Policies
Hart-Celler Act (1965)
Hate Crimes
Head Start
Health and Welfare
High Schools
HIV/AIDS
Homelessness
Home Town Associations
Hondurans
Hospitals
Hotel Industry
Housing
Human Rights Watch

Human Trafficking
Identification Cards
Identity Theft
Illegal Immigration Reform and Immigrant
  Responsibility Act (IIRIRA) (1996)
Illinois
Immigrant Workers Freedom Ride
Immigration Act (IMMACT) (1990)
Immigration and Customs Enforcement
  (ICE)
Immigration and Nationality Act (The
  McCarran-Walter Act) (1952)
Immigration and Naturalization Service
  (INS)
Immigration Reform, 2013–2014
Immigration Reform and Control Act
  (IRCA) (1986)
Inadmissibility
Incarceration
Indians (East). *See* South Asians
Indigenous People
Individual Taxpayer Identification
  Number (ITIN)
Informal Economy
International Students/
  Student Visas
Irish
Japanese. *See* East Asians
Johnson-Reed Act (1924)
Kanjobal Mayans
Koreans. *See* East Asians
Labor Supply
Labor Unions
Landscaping Industry
Lawful Permanent Residents
Laws and Legislation, Post-1980s
League of United Latin American Citizens
  (LULAC)
Legal Representation
Legal Status
LGBT Immigrants without
  Documentation
Limited English Proficiency (LEP)
Literature and Poetry
LULAC. *See* League of United Latin
  American Citizens (LULAC)
Marriage

McCarran-Walter Act. *See* Immigration and Nationality Act (The McCarran-Walter Act) (1952)
Meat Processing Plants
Media Coverage
Mental Health Care Access
Mental Health Issues for Immigrants
Mental Health Issues for Undocumented Immigrants
Mexican American Legal Defense and Education Fund (MALDEF)
Mexicans
Midwest
Migrant Farm Workers
Migration
Military Recruitment and Participation
Minutemen
Mixed-Status Families
Mobility
Mortgages
Morton Memo
Multicultural Education
NAFTA. *See* North American Free Trade Agreement (NAFTA)
National Council of La Raza (NCLR)
National Network for Immigrant and Refugee Rights (NNIRR)
Naturalization
New Jersey
New Mexico
New York
Nicaraguan Adjustment and Central American Relief Act (NACARA)
Nicaraguans
North American Free Trade Agreement (NAFTA)
Nutrition
Obama Administration
Operation Streamline
Operation Wetback
Overstayers
Passports
Patriot Act. *See* USA PATRIOT Act (2001)
Patriotism
Personal Responsibility and Work Opportunity Reconciliation Act (PRWORA) (1996)

Plyler v. Doe
Policies of Attrition
Policy and Political Action
Ports of Entry
Postville, Iowa Raid
Pregnancy and Childbirth
Proposition 187
Prostitution
Protests
Provisional Unlawful Presence (PUP) Waiver
Public Libraries
Racialized Labeling of Mexican-Origin Persons
Racial Profiling
Racism
Refugee Act (1980)
Refugees
Religion
Remittances
Repatriation
Restaurants
Salvadorans
Sanctuary Cities and Secure Communities
Sanctuary Movement
Select Commission on Immigration and Refugee Policy
Seniors
Shadow Population
Single Men
Small Business Ownership
Social Interaction and Integration
Social Security
South Asians
Southern States
Spanish-Language Media
Special Agricultural Workers (SAW)
Sponsors
Sports
State Legislation
Strangers from a Different Shore
Strangers in the Land
Student Visas
Suburbs
Taxes

Temporary Assistance for Needy
  Families (TANF)
Temporary Protected Status (TPS)
Tennessee Immigrant and Refugee Rights
  Coalition (TIRRC)
Texas
Theater
Trafficking Victims Protection
  Reauthorization Act (TVPRA)
Transnationalism
Transportation in the United States
Trauma-Related Symptoms
The "Undocumented" Label
Undocumented Students
United States v. Brignoni-Ponce
United States v. Roblero-Solis
The Uprooted
Urban Life
USA PATRIOT Act (2001)
U.S. Border Patrol

U.S. Census Bureau
U.S. Citizenship and Immigration
  Services (USCIS)
U.S. Customs and Border Protection
  (CBP)
U.S. Department of Homeland Security
  (DHS)
U.S.-Mexico Border Wall
U-Visas
Violence
Violence against Women Act (VAWA)
Wages
Welfare System
Women's Status
Workers' Rights
Workplace Injury
Workplace Raids
Work Visas
Xenophobia
Zapotec People (Oaxaca)

Guide to Related Topics

Following is a list of the entries in this encyclopedia, arranged under broad topics for enhanced searching. Readers should also consult the index at the end of the encyclopedia for more specific subjects.

Advocacy

Activism
Advocacy
American Civil Liberties Union (ACLU)
American Friends Service Committee
Amnesty International
CC-IME
Community Activism
Community Concerns
Faith-Based Organizations
Home Town Associations
Human Rights Watch
Immigrant Workers Freedom Ride
League of United Latin American
    Citizens (LULAC)
Mexican American Legal Defense and
    Education Fund (MALDEF)
Minutemen
National Council of La Raza (NCLR)
National Network for Immigrant and
    Refugee Rights (NNIRR)
Policy and Political Action
Protests
Sanctuary Movement
Tennessee Immigrant and Refugee Rights
    Coalition (TIRRC)

Crime and Violence

Domestic Violence
Drug Trade

Gangs
Human Trafficking
Identity Theft
Violence
Violence against Women Act (VAWA)

Cultural Representation in the United States

Corridos
Devil's Highway
Film and Television Representation
Literature and Poetry
Media Coverage
Spanish-Language Media
Sports
Theater

Culture

Acculturation
Assimilation
Aztlán
Barrios
Central American Civil Wars
Corridos
Cultural Citizenship
Culture
Enclaves
Exclusion
Faith-Based Organizations
Family Reunification

Family Structure
Gateways
Indigenous People
Kanjobal Mayans
Literature and Poetry
Media Coverage
Mixed-Status Families
Patriotism
Remittances
Single Men
Social Interaction and Integration
Sports
Strangers from a Different Shore
Strangers in the Land
Suburbs
Theater
Transnationalism
Urban Life
Zapotec People (Oaxaca)

Discrimination and Barriers

Barriers to Health
Community Concerns
Discrimination and Barriers
English-Only Movement
Film and Television Representation
Hate Crimes
LGBT Immigrants without Documentation
Minutemen
Mobility
Operation Wetback
Racialized Labeling of Mexican-Origin
    Persons
Racial Profiling
Racism
The "Undocumented" Label
Xenophobia

Education

Adult Education
Bilingualism
Children
Citizenship Education
Colleges and Universities
The DREAM Act

Education
Elementary Schools
English as a Second Language (ESL)
    Programs
English Language Learners (ELL)
Head Start
High Schools
International Students / Student Visas
Limited English Proficiency (LEP)
Multicultural Education
Public Libraries
Undocumented Students

Employment and Economics

Banking
Day Labor
Domestic Work
Economics
Employer Sanctions
Employment
Garment Industry
Globalization
Hotel Industry
Individual Taxpayer Identification Number
    (ITIN)
Informal Economy
Labor Supply
Labor Unions
Landscaping Industry
Meat Processing Plants
Migrant Farm Workers
North American Free Trade Agreement
    (NAFTA)
Postville, Iowa Raid
Prostitution
Remittances
Restaurants
Small Business Ownership
Special Agricultural Workers (SAW)
Taxes
Urban Life
Wages
Workers' Rights
Workplace Injury
Workplace Raids
Work Visas

Gender and Family

Childcare
Children
Family Structure
Gender Roles
Marriage
Pregnancy and Childbirth
Single Men
Violence against Women Act (VAWA)
Women's Status

Government Agencies and Administrations

Clinton Administration
Foreign Consulates
Immigration and Customs Enforcement (ICE)
Immigration and Naturalization Service (INS)
Obama Administration
Trafficking Victims Protection Reauthorization Act (TVPRA)
U.S. Border Patrol
U.S. Census Bureau
U.S. Citizenship and Immigration Services (USCIS)
U.S. Customs and Border Protection (CBP)
U.S. Department of Homeland Security (DHS)

Health

Acculturation Stress
Barriers to Health
Death
Health and Welfare
HIV/AIDS
Hospitals
Mental Health Care Access
Mental Health Issues for Immigrants
Mental Health Issues for Undocumented Immigrants
Nutrition
Pregnancy and Childbirth
Trauma-Related Symptoms

History

Barrios
Central American Civil Wars
Dillingham Report (1910)
Flores-Figueroa v. United States
Hart-Celler Act (1965)
Illegal Immigration Reform and Immigrant Responsibility Act (IIRIRA) (1996)
Immigration Act (IMMACT) (1990)
Immigration and Nationality Act (The McCarran-Walter Act) (1952)
Immigration Reform and Control Act (IRCA) (1986)
Plyler v. Doe
Proposition 187
Sanctuary Movement
Strangers from a Different Shore
Strangers in the Land
The Uprooted

Housing

Discrimination and Barriers
Homelessness
Housing
Mortgages
Suburbs
Urban Life

Laws and Policies

Amnesty
Arizona SB 1070
Asylum
Bracero Program
Citizenship
Civil Rights
Counterterrorism and Immigrant Profiling
Crime
Deferred Action for Childhood Arrivals (DACA)
Deportation
Detention Centers
Discrimination and Barriers
Displacement

Emergency Quota Act of 1921
Employment Visas
Expedited Removal
Fernandez-Vargas v. Gonzales
Flores-Figueroa v. United States
Form I-9
Fourteenth Amendment
Governance and Criminalization
Green Cards
Guestworker and Contract Labor Policies
Hart-Celler Act (1965)
Human Trafficking
Identification Cards
Illegal Immigrant Reform and Immigrant
    Responsibility Act (IIRIRA) (1996)
Immigration Act (IMMACT) (1990)
Immigration and Nationality Act (The
    McCarran-Walter Act) (1952)
Immigration Reform, 2013–2014
Immigration Reform and Control Act
    (IRCA) (1986)
Inadmissibility
Incarceration
Individual Taxpayer Identification Number
    (ITIN)
Johnson-Reed Act (1924)
Lawful Permanent Residents
Laws and Legislation, Post-1980s
Legal Representation
Legal Status
Morton Memo
Naturalization
Nicaraguan Adjustment and Central
    American Relief Act (NACARA)
North American Free Trade Agreement
    (NAFTA)
Operation Streamline
Operation Wetback
Passports
Personal Responsibility and Work
    Opportunity Reconciliation Act
    (PRWORA) (1996)
Policies of Attrition
Policy and Political Action
Provisional Unlawful Presence (PUP)
    Waiver
Refugee Act (1980)

Refugees
Repatriation
Sanctuary Cities and Secure Communities
Select Commission on Immigration and
    Refugee Policy
Social Security
Sponsors
State Legislation
Student Visas
Taxes
Temporary Assistance for Needy Families
    (TANF)
Temporary Protected Status (TPS)
The "Undocumented" Label
United States v. Brignoni-Ponce
United States v. Roblero-Solis
USA PATRIOT Act (2001)
U.S.-Mexico Border Wall
U-Visas
Violence against Women Act (VAWA)
Welfare System

Migration

Airports
Border Crossing
Canadian Border
Counterfeit Documents
Death
Devil's Highway
Migration
Mobility
Overstayers
Ports of Entry
Transportation in the United States
Urban Life

Nationalities and Regional Origins

Chinese
Cubans
Dominicans
East Asians
Eastern Europeans
Guatemalans

Hondurans
Indigenous People
Irish
Kanjobal Mayans
Mexicans
Nicaraguans
Salvadorans
South Asians
Zapotec People (Oaxaca)

Religion

Catholic Church
Faith-Based Organizations
Religion
Sanctuary Movement

Social Organization

Childcare
Exclusion
Families
Family Economics
Family Reunification
Family Structure
Housing
Marriage
Military Recruitment and Participation
Mobility
Seniors
Shadow Population

Single Men
Social Interaction
    and Integration
Transportation in the United States
Urban Life
Women's Status

States and U.S. Regions

Arizona
Arizona SB 1070
California
Great Lakes Region
Illinois
Midwest
New Jersey
New Mexico
New York
Southern States
Texas

Transportation

Airports
Coyotes
Driver's Licenses
Human Trafficking
Mobility
Ports of Entry
Transportation in the United States

Preface

Undocumented Immigrants in the United States: An Encyclopedia of Their Experience aims to offer a more complex, nuanced (and therefore more accurate) portrait of un-documented immigration than is often available. The work offers evidence-based information that can help promote rational assessment of the issues arising from irregular immigration in the United States. While most information available to the public is limited to news media sound bites, or already reduced information derived from statistical government reports, this encyclopedia presents a much broader view of the issues of undocumented immigration.

This two-volume reference work on the experiences of undocumented immigrants in the United States will address many of the historic changes we are witnessing today. Latino populations as a whole now comprise the largest minority groups in the United States, and with increased social and economic integration and with each generation, the nation will continue to undergo demographic changes that will change the way the United States embraces immigrants, the way it votes, and the way it sees itself *vis-á-vis* the rest of the world. The changes are electrifying, and there is no better time to consider having this reference work.

The audience for *Undocumented Immigrants in the United States: An Encyclopedia of Their Experience* includes high school and undergraduate students, teachers, researchers, and anyone interested in immigration and the reasons that people risk their lives to enter a foreign country without legal documentation, the issues that U.S. citizens face as a result, and the policies and legislation that politicians, policymakers, and the government respond with in order to address this complex subject.

Scope

The 239 entries in this work offer the accumulated insights of eighty-five scholars, graduate students, and writers, many of whom have dedicated years of study to the issues of undocumented immigration. The alphabetically arranged entries range in size from five hundred to approximately four thousand words. Each entry ends with cross-references to related entries and a selected list of recommended articles, books, websites, and videos covering the topic of undocumented immigration.

Although most of the entries in the encyclopedia present information on the past thirty years or so, historical information before that is given, especially in relation to immigration legislation, where relevant. To further help readers understand the historical context of the treatment of immigrants by the United States, a chronology at the front of the book extends back to 1790, with the first laws for acceptance of immigrants into this country, and extends to 2013. In the chronology, the reader will be able to trace the numerous laws and policies that were written both to keep out certain immigrants—especially those considered "non-white"—and the legislation that was written and passed to rectify those laws based on prejudice and ignorance.

Special Features

The front matter of each volume includes the list of entries included, as well as a "Guide to Related Topics," which groups all the entry names (or headwords) under broad topics, for easier consulting of certain issues of interest, such as "Education" or "Health" or "Legislation." Also at the front of the first volume are the extensive chronology, and an overview and introduction to the topic of undocumented immigration. Following the 239 entries is an extensive list of recommended resources, including online sources and documentary films, for better understanding the subject of undocumented immigration in the United States. A comprehensive index will further help the user to find specific topics of interest in the two volumes.

A Special Note about Terminology

In this book, the term *undocumented immigrant* refers to an individual who entered without inspection and is therefore without official authorization, who may have entered legally but has subsequently overstayed the term limit of the visa, or who may have entered legally and is legally present but is not a legal resident (and therefore not entitled to work nor to access public benefits). In the literature, other terms are occasionally used, such as *unauthorized immigrant* or *illegal immigrant*. U.S. government agencies most often use the legal terms *illegal alien* or criminal *alien.*

Introduction: The History of and Uncertain Future for Unauthorized Immigrants

The hope of comprehensive immigration reform energized many in 2013, stirring a certain amount of nervous anticipation among the nearly 11.1 million undocumented immigrants living in the United States (Pew Research, 2012). Within grasp was the elusive promise that some—if not many—might soon be on their way down the path to citizenship that would lead to the American Dream. Just seven years ago, in 2006, both citizens and noncitizens mobilized across the nation for immigration reform in what is widely heralded as the most significant political movement since the Civil Rights Era. The demonstrations were inspired by frustration that the newly proposed bill, the *Border Protection, Antiterrorism and Illegal Immigration Control Act of 2005* (H.R. 4437), offered no way out from living in the shadows to the estimated 11.3 million undocumented immigrants living in the United States at the time (Pew Research, 2012). Political pressure continued to build in the years following this unrest, as would greater backlash in the way of **Workplace Raids,** more policing of immigrant communities, more removals (deportations), and harsher, more punitive measures put into place that many believed would further criminalize, racialize, problematize, and stigmatize those in the country without authorization. In this reference work, *Undocumented Immigrants in the United States: An Encyclopedia of Their Experience,* readers should consult entries with headings such as **Advocacy, Activism, Faith-Based Organizations, Policy and Political Action,** and **Protests** for more information on important trends in the immigration rights movement in the nation's history. The mass demonstrations of 2006 marked only one of many tipping points in the long history of lawmakers, communities, interest groups, and the disenfranchised drawn together by the issue of immigration, at times coalescing, then clashing, but always reconstituting themselves in relation to one another.

Regardless of the outcome of efforts pledging to bring much needed reform to the country's "broken" immigration system, the history of undocumented immigration is not new nor will it end with any comprehensive immigration reform. However, what is certain is that the phenomenon has already left and will continue to leave an indelible and undeniable mark on the wider social fabric of the nation. Readers will find testament to this in this work, with entries that outline the history of America's ambivalence towards newcomers. Numerous legislative pieces described in entries such as the **Emergency Quota Act of 1921,** and the **Johnson-Reed Act (1924),** paved the way by which some hopeful immigrants gained admittance, while others were blocked. The long line of efforts—some with unpredictable outcomes—can be used to trace the nation's formulation of ideas and approaches to immigration and immigrants. Many decisions—often emerging amidst heated discussions about the nation's identity and its vision for its future—offer insightful evidence as to the struggle to come to terms with, and in one form or another, accommodate to some degree the "huddled masses" at the doorstep with the nation's needs. Entries such as **Bracero Program, Operation Wetback, Guest Worker and Contract Labor Policies** and **Special Agricultural Workers (SAW)** will shed light on the many considerations that went into the policies and programs intended to provide a balance between the nation's need for workers, and workers who need employment.

With greater frequency—and perhaps due to social media technologies and the twenty-four-hour news cycle—the contentious nature of undocumented immigration has unfolded and even been exacerbated before the nation's eyes, involving ever more a widening social sphere of individuals, communities, and political actors. Few in the country today can escape the fact that they have somehow been impacted by the presence of undocumented immigrants: as family, allies, or outsiders, or through language, political discourse, or socioeconomic exchange. In this way, this encyclopedia helps understand and contextualize many of the phenomenon's related facets and its salient contribution to the development of the nation as it moves forward in the twenty-first century. Often forgotten in the information about undocumented immigrants are efforts to understand current events through performance and literature. This work thus includes entries about literary, musical, theatrical, and film industry productions that have contributed to our understanding of undocumented immigration. Such a wider view helps fill in the gaps and provide depth to what we know about undocumented immigrants, offering a more complete and nuanced version of their experiences, and in this way inviting greater tolerance and reasoned discussion that might lead to more just and humane solutions in the interest of peace and harmony.

The selection of topics in *Undocumented Immigrants in the United States* marks the incipient but significant and perceptible demographic shifts that have been developing to solidify the United States' role within a global community of nations, many of which are less developed. Not surprisingly, an age-old solution by those suffering poverty in underdeveloped nations has been to follow a migratory path in search of better opportunities and a more dignified life. Indeed, the images of European immigrants arriving at Ellis Island helped permanently etch in the nation's psyche—both as symbol and reality—the United States as a land where dreams are realized. After immigration quota restrictions based on nationality and race were lifted with the Immigration Act of 1965 (also called **Hart-Celler**), the United States continued with its grand, albeit uncertain experiment with cultural and ethnic diversity.

However, the magnitude of recent and unprecedented immigration to the United States, especially from Latin America, has brought about new disquiet. The United States is part of a larger contiguous land mass often referred to the Americas: North America (Canada, the United States, and Mexico); Central America; and South

America. Thus, it should not come as a surprise that with economic and political crises in countries south of the U.S.-Mexico border, the natural geography would be the greatest ally of those seeking refuge from catastrophic poverty, armed conflict, and natural disaster. Entries such as **Migration, Mobility,** and **Refugees** can be used to identify some of the many causes that have brought the issue of undocumented immigration to the nation's forefront. Beginning in the 1970s, significant immigration to the United States began with those entering through its southern border, largely due to growing civil unrest and armed conflict. The entries on **Guatemalans, Salvadorans** and **Hondurans** aim to shed more light on this development. In response, U.S. administrations have endeavored to design and implement greater immigration restrictions. Entries related to immigration enforcement and border security elucidate this process further. In turn, desperate populations circumvented the growing obstacles to their movement, and a pattern that is all too common today was put into place. As the entries **Border Crossing, Counterterrorism, Xenophobia,** and **Racialized Labeling** demonstrate, such efforts coincide with the development of popular and demeaning notions of the "illegal immigrant," especially as the numbers of those entering the United States continued to rise. In the 1980s, the number of immigrants coming from Latin America surpassed the numbers of the decade before, and both decades combined were surpassed by immigrants entering the country in the 1990s. The surge in the number of immigrants coming to the United States was in part helped by the most significant immigration reform act since **Hart Celler,** the **Immigration Reform and Control Act (1986)** which legalized nearly 2.5 million immigrants out of the estimated five million immigrants that were in the country without documents at the time. However, other important developments must be taken into account, such as economic restructuring in the United States that resulted in the implementation of neoliberal economic plans in less developed countries, and the ensuing structural adjustments in these countries resulting in growing poverty and displacement. The entries such as **Globalization** and the **North American Free Trade Agreement (NAFTA)** are expected to broaden the readers' understanding of undocumented immigration as an issue that is embedded within broader changes in the global community of nations.

By the mid 1990s, immigrants and their children had become a visible presence in American schools and hospitals, and with their notable visibility, anxieties among immigration restrictionists resurfaced and gained momentum. Their concerns centered on the use of public welfare programs by those individuals not authorized to be in the country and the perception that the nation's border with Mexico was uncontrolled. Media reports that frequently and insistently depicted the border as uncontrolled and overrun by lawless drug runners and migrants seeking welfare benefits stoked the unease of a public already concerned about diminishing resources, taxes, and their economic future. Needless to say, many entries point out some of the common legal terms used to discuss the process used to systematically enforce immigration regulations with greater intensity (such as **Inadmissibility, Expedited Removal, Deportation, Repatriation**), pertinent court cases (e.g. *Flores-Figueroa v. United States, United States v. Roblero-Solis*), and authorities key in the process (e.g. **U.S. Border Patrol, Immigration and Naturalization Service**). It was also in this decade, the 1990s, that anxieties were translated into numerous laws, many of which were state-initiated such as California's **Proposition 187.** Although this one effort was later struck down as unconstitutional, the approach and political perspectives that it embodied would gain greater traction with the ***Personal Responsibility and Work Opportunity Reconciliation Act (PRWORA) (1996),*** and the most significant immigration reform bill since IRCA, the ***Illegal Immigration Reform and Immigrant Responsibility Act (1996)***.

The events of 9/11 not only doomed hopes of much needed immigration reform but reenergized counterterrorist strategies that began with formidable measures to close the border. The entries **Counterterrorism and Immigrant Profiling**, **U.S.-Mexico Border Wall** and **Ports of Entry** are expected to add to readers' understanding of this critical period of history. With circulatory migration patterns sealed off, the undocumented immigrant population grew in size, and became quasi-permanent. For this reason, many entries are devoted to the deluge of immigration regulation policies, whose stated goals included the reduction of undocumented immigration through attrition. The entries on **Arizona** and **Arizona SB 1070** are examples of this trend. These as well as other entries show that in fact the proposal and implementation of these laws, so-called "**Policies of Attrition**," would serve to push undocumented immigrants further into the shadows, making them more vulnerable to exploitation. While in some places enacted laws were benevolent, providing sanctuary for besieged immigrants, many promoted a generalized deterioration of conditions, especially for employment (see, for example, **Labor Unions**, **Workers' Rights**, **Workplace Injury**) and accessing needed benefits for those who are eligible out of fear of the negative consequences associated with a widening range of immigration enforcement tactics.

The U.S. population today is a historical amalgamation of social groupings that includes U.S.-born, foreign-born, naturalized citizens, dual nationals, and noncitizens. Those in this latter category include yet other categories of individuals distinguished by their lawful or unlawful status. Those who do not have the legal authority to reside or work in the country are popularly known as "undocumented." This last label deserves the detailed and competent introspection provided by the entry "**Undocumented**" **Label**. However, also important to consider is that with greater frequency families and households may be composed of a combination of individuals from any of the aforementioned categories, defying any simple legal solution to undocumented immigration. Many of the entries contained in this reference work are thus devoted to understanding the family and household dynamics that make existing in highly contested social spaces not only possible but sustainable. Highlighted in the collection are several entries dealing with the role of immigrant women, whose growing importance to **Economics**, **Family Structure**, **Acculturation**, and **Social Interaction and Integration** cannot be overstated. A patchwork of administrative efforts, for example, the entries **Deferred Action for Childhood Arrivals (DACA)**, **Provisional Unlawful Presence (PUP) Waiver,** and **the Morton Memo,** have helped address issues important to immigrant families, especially with respect to the education of their young. Embodied in the children of immigrants are the hard-fought struggles for educational equality and equal opportunity. As testament to these are entries such as ***Plyler v. Doe***, and the **English-only Movement, Elementary Schools,** and **English as a Second Language (ESL) Programs,** to mention only a few. Central to these efforts and in the absence of any long-awaited efforts to pass a **DREAM Act,** the steadfast hope for the future continues to hinge on the next generation of aspiring young adults waiting to strengthen the ideals and opportunities that will provide a bright economic future for all.

Anna Ochoa O'Leary

Reference

Pew Research. 2012. 11.1 Million Unauthorized Immigrants Were Living in the U.S. in 2012. Dec 6, 2012. Available at: http://www.pewhispanic.org/2012/12/06/unauthorized-immigrants-11-1-million-in-2011/

Chronology of Undocumented Immigration in the United States

Following is a timeline of important events in U.S. history, including laws, policies, and other events that reflect the U.S. attempts to contend with immigrants, and in particular, immigrants without proper documents or those considered "unsuitable" for citizenship.

1790   In one of its first official actions, the U.S. Congress establishes a uniform rule of naturalization that imposes a two-year residency requirement for "aliens" who are "free white persons of good moral character."

1798   President John Adams signs a series of four laws known as the Alien and Sedition Acts. One of the laws, the Naturalization Act, makes it more difficult for immigrants to obtain U.S. citizenship by raising the residency requirement from five to fourteen years; another, the Alien Act, authorizes the president to deport without proof foreigners suspected of carrying out subversive activities.

1802   Congress repeals the Naturalization Act of 1798.

1819   Congress enacts an "act regulating passenger vessels" requiring shipmasters to deliver a manifest enumerating all aliens transported for immigration and requiring the secretary of state to inform Congress annually of the number of immigrants admitted. This act, for the first time, keeps count of the number of immigrants who enter legally for the purpose of permanent immigration. In short, it is the first official immigration act.

1848   Treaty of Guadalupe Hidalgo guarantees citizenship to Mexicans remaining in the territory ceded by Mexico to the United States. This action sets the first base for the migration of Mexicans to the United States and provides for a citizen base from Mexico into which future immigrants, both legal and undocumented, can assimilate. It forges the first link into what develops as "chain migration" from Mexico and even Central America to the United States.

1849   The California Gold Rush spurs emigration from around the world, particularly China, of those seeking their fortunes.

1850   The influx of foreign workers as a result of the Gold Rush leads to ethnic tensions in California. The state enacts a monthly foreign miners' tax aimed at Asians and Mexican Americans.

1855   Castle Garden becomes New York's principal port of entry for legal immigration. Its volume of immigrants sets the stage for later development of "visa overstayers" who are able to remain because such extensive numbers overwhelm the ability of immigration authorities to keep accurate track of them.

1862   Congress enacts the Homestead Act, granting acres of free land to settlers who develop the land in frontier regions and remain on it for five years, spurring heavy levels of immigration.

California's "Anti-Coolie Act" aims to protect white laborers by imposing a monthly fee on Chinese immigrants seeking to work in the state.

1865   Central Pacific Railroad begins to recruit thousands of Chinese workers to build the western half of the first transcontinental railroad.

1868   The Fourteenth Amendment is ratified. It guarantees that all persons born or naturalized in the United States and subject to its jurisdiction are citizens, and states that no state may abridge their rights without due process or deny them equal protection under the law. The amendment ensures citizenship rights of the former slaves and thereby changes the "free white persons" phrase of citizenship to include blacks. It further establishes the supremacy of federal law over actions by state governments in matters pertaining to citizenship, naturalization, and immigration.

1870   Congress enacts the Naturalization Act of 1870 granting citizenship eligibility to persons of African descent.

1875   In *Henderson v. Mayor of New York,* the U.S. Supreme Court rules that state laws governing immigration are unconstitutional, arguing that they infringe on the federal government's authority to regulate commerce.

1882   Congress passes the Chinese Exclusion Act, barring the immigration of Chinese laborers for ten years and denying Chinese eligibility for naturalization. Its harsh provisions induce many Chinese immigrants to get around the law by using falsified documents—becoming "paper sons and daughters" of Chinese born in the United States. This sets a precedent for using phony documents by undocumented immigrants that persists to the present day.

1885   Congress passes the Alien Contract Labor Law making it unlawful for laborers to immigrate to the United States under contract with a U.S. employer who in any manner prepays passage to bring the laborer to the country.

1886   *Yick Wo v. Hopkins* overturns a San Francisco municipal ordinance against Chinese laundry workers as discriminatory and unconstitutional on the grounds that the

Fourteenth Amendment prohibits state and local governments from depriving any person (even a noncitizen) of life, liberty, or property without due process.

1888   The Scott Act expands the Chinese Exclusion Act by rescinding reentry permits for Chinese laborers and thus prohibiting their return.

1889   In the case of *Chae Chan Ping v. United States,* the Supreme Court upholds the right of Congress to repeal the certificate of reentry as contained in the Scott Act of 1888, thereby excluding *ex post facto* certain Chinese immigrants who had previously entered legally.

1891   In the Immigration Act of 1891, Congress expands the classes of individuals excluded from admission and forbids the soliciting of immigrants. It also establishes the Office of the Superintendent of Immigration (later the Bureau of Immigration) within the Treasury Department, the first of several such home departments for immigration services.

1892   Ellis Island is opened as the nation's leading port of entry. It becomes the source of many visa overstayers from European countries.

The Geary Act extends the Chinese Exclusion Act for another ten years and requires Chinese residents to carry a certificate of residence at all times or face deportation.

1896   In *Wong Wing vs. United States,* the U.S. Supreme Court holds that the penalty of hard labor for immigrants in violation of the Chinese Exclusion Act requires a jury trial.

1897   A federal district court decides the case *In re Rodriguez.* This west-Texas case affirms that Mexicans have the right to naturalize based on the 1848 Treaty of Guadalupe Hidalgo. However, they were still subject to the "scientific classification" of the races for the purposes of determining their citizenship rights, and nonwhites could not be citizens.

1898   In the case of *Wong Kim Ark v. United States,* the Supreme Court rules that a native-born son of Asian descent is indeed a citizen of the United States despite the fact that his parents may have been resident aliens ineligible for citizenship.

1902   The Geary Act of 1892, which extended and added restrictions to the Chinese Exclusion Act, is made permanent.

1903   Congress enacts a law making immigration the responsibility of the Department of Commerce and Labor.

1906   The Basic Naturalization Act codifies a uniform law for naturalization. With some amendments and supplements, it forms the basic naturalization law thereafter.

1907   In the Expatriation Act, Congress adds important regulations about issuing passports and the expatriation and marriage of U.S. women to foreigners. It continues to stir controversy until Section 3 of the act is repealed in 1922.

President Theodore Roosevelt issues an executive order, known as the Gentleman's Agreement, by which Japan agrees to restrict emigration of laborers from Japan and Korea (which was then under Japanese jurisdiction). Picture brides, however, are permitted to emigrate.

1911   The Dillingham Commission (1907-1910) issues its report, whose recommendations form the basis for the quota acts of the 1920s.

1915   The Americanization/100 Percentism campaign begins and is supported by both government and private enterprise. These social movements represent the first attempt at "forced assimilation" encouraging the adoption of the English language and social customs. After World War I, its perceived failure will contribute to the disillusionment that sets the stage for the quota acts of the 1920s.

1917   The United States enters World War I in April. Congress enacts the Immigration Act of 1917 that includes a literacy test and bars all immigration from a specified area known thereafter as the "Asian barred zone." The State and Labor departments issue a joint order requiring passports of all aliens seeking to enter the United States and requiring that the would-be entrants be issued visas by U.S. consular officers in their country of origin rather than seeking permission to enter the United States only when arriving at the port of entry. Puerto Ricans are granted U.S. citizenship. Substantive requirements on those coming from Mexico are imposed, including a head tax, a medical examination to check for lice, a literacy test, an an investigation to determine if the applicant for admission would likely be a "public charge." With so many restrictions that were not only unaffordable but also humiliating, many opted to forgo the inspection and cross surreptitiously into the United States.

1918   Congress gives the president sweeping powers to disallow the entrance or the departure of "aliens" (those who are not citizens) during time of war. Similar presidential declarations are used in virtually all periods of war thereafter.

1919   Congress enacts a law granting honorably discharged Native Americans citizenship for their service during World War I. In the summer, the Red Scare following the Bolshevik revolution in Russia leads to the summary deportation of certain specified "radical" aliens deemed thereby to be a threat to U.S. security. It serves as a precursor to the USA PATRIOT Act in that respect.

1921   Congress passes the first Emergency Quota Act, in which immigration from a particular country is set at 3 percent of the foreign-born population from that country based on the 1910 census.

1922   Congress passes the Cable Act, stating that the right of any woman to become a naturalized citizen shall not be abridged because of her sex or because she is a married woman unless she is wed to "an alien ineligible for citizenship." (Therefore, for example, any woman married to an Asian immigrant was not eligible for citizenship.) This latter provision is later amended in 1931 and the act repealed in 1936.

1923   The U.S. Supreme Court rules in *United States vs. Bhagat Singh Thind* that "white person" means those persons who appear and would commonly be viewed as white. Thus, Asian Indians, although Caucasians, are not "white" and are therefore ineligible for citizenship through naturalization.

1924   Congress enacts the Immigration Act, known as the Johnson-Reed Act, setting the national-origin quota for a particular country at two percent of the foreign-born population from that country as of the census of 1890. This new system drastically shifts the sources of immigration from South, Central, and Eastern Europe to Northwestern Europe. The act bars the admission of most Asians, who are thereby classified as "aliens ineligible for citizenship." Congress passes an act granting citizenship to those Native Americans who had not previously received it by allotments under the 1887 Dawes Act or by military service during World War I. Grounds for deportation change drastically by expanding the list of reasons to include "entering without inspection."

Congress establishes the Border Patrol, charged with policing the U.S. borders against undocumented entrants. It is also charged with finding and deporting "illegal aliens" from the interior who had managed to elude apprehension at the border.

1929   President Herbert Hoover proclaims new and permanent quotas in which national-origin quotas for European immigrants are based on the proportion of those nationalities in the total population as determined by the 1920 census. The total number of such to be admitted is fixed at just over 150,000.

1929–1939   U.S. immigration levels slow dramatically in response to the worldwide Great Depression.

Rising anti-immigrant sentiment as a result of the Great Depression leads to the repatriation of tens of thousands of Mexicans and Mexican Americans.

1933   The Immigration and Naturalization Service (INS) is established to administer the United States' immigration and naturalization laws.

1940   President Franklin D. Roosevelt signs into law the Alien Registration Act, or the Smith Act, which requires noncitizens to register and be fingerprinted.

1941   President Roosevelt issues a proclamation to control persons entering or leaving the United States based on the first War Powers Act.

1942   The Bracero Program begins through an agreement with Mexico that allows migrant farm workers to enter as temporary labor to satisfy wartime labor shortages in agriculture.

President Roosevelt issues Executive Order 9066, leading to the evacuation, relocation, and internment of Japanese and Japanese Americans into relocation camps.

1943   The Supreme Court rules, in *Hirabayashi v. United States,* that the executive orders for curfews and evacuation programs were constitutional, based upon "military necessity."

The Magnuson Act repeals the Chinese Exclusion Act, first established in 1882, sets quotas for Chinese immigration, and finally allows Chinese immigrants to become naturalized after sixty-one years of official prohibition.

1944   The Supreme Court decides *Korematsu v. United States,* again affirming the constitutionality of the executive orders excluding Japanese Americans from remaining in certain "excluded zones."

The court also rules, in *Ex Parte Mitsuye Endo,* that the internment program was an unconstitutional violation of the habeas corpus rights of U.S. citizens—namely, the Nisei.

1946   The Luce-Celler Act grants naturalization rights to Filipinos and Indians.

1948   President Harry S. Truman signs into law the Displaced Persons Act, which provides permanent residency and employment to a limited number of Europeans fleeing persecution after World War II.

1951   Public Law 78 formalizes the Bracero Program due to labor needs during the Korean War.

1952   The Immigration and Nationality Act, also known as the McCarran-Walter Act, overhauls U.S. immigration laws. While it ends Asian exclusion policies, it continues the quota system that favors immigrants from northwestern Europe. It also provides a basic framework for guest worker programs.

1954   In response to a national backlash against unauthorized immigration, the Immigration and Nationality Service commences "Operation Wetback," a mass arrest and deportation effort that targeted undocumented Mexicans but also included citizens of Mexican descent.

Ellis Island closes.

1956   President Dwight D. Eisenhower establishes a "parole" system for Hungarian freedom fighters. Two years later, Congress endorses the procedures in an act to admit Hungarian refugees.

1959   Congress amends the Immigration and Nationality Act of 1952 to provide for unmarried sons and daughters of U.S. citizens to enter as "non-quota" immigrants.

1960   Congress enacts a program to assist resettlement of refugees from communist countries who have been paroled by the attorney general (mostly Cubans).

1964   The Bracero Program (begun in 1942) ends.

1965 Congress passes the Immigration and Nationality Act, also known as the Hart-Celler Act. It amends the 1952 Immigration and Nationality Act by ending the quota system and establishing a preference system emphasizing family reunification and meeting certain skill goals, standardizing admission procedures, and setting per-country limits of twenty thousand across the world, with certain total limits for Eastern and Western Hemisphere migration.

1966 President Lyndon B. Johnson signs into law the Cuban Refugee Adjustment Act. This sets up the distinction between refugees based on anticommunist U.S. foreign policy goals and those based on economic refugee status.

1967 UN Convention and Protocol on Refugees; 130 nations sign the protocol accords. Refugees entering under its provisions (such as Cuban refugees) get resettlement assistance, whereas those entering based on economic grounds (Haitian refugees) are excluded.

1968 Bilingual Education Act is passed.

The Southwest Council of La Raza—now known as the National Council of La Raza—is established in Arizona to empower Latinos through community organizing.

The Mexican American Legal Defense Fund (MALDEF) is founded in Texas to help protect Latinos' legal and civil rights.

President Johnson issues a proclamation on the UN Protocols on the Status of Refugees, essentially endorsing the U.S. commitment to the multinational protocols.

1972 The House passes, but the Senate kills, a bill that would have made it illegal to knowingly hire an "illegal alien." It becomes the first of many attempts prior to 1986 to impose what becomes known as "employer sanctions" for hiring undocumented immigrants.

Haitian boat influx of unauthorized immigrants begins arriving on the East Coast, mostly in Florida. Haitian detention camps are set up in Miami.

1975 The fall of Saigon, then Vietnam along with Cambodia and Laos, precipitates a massive flight of refugees to the United States from the Indochina region. Vietnamese, Cambodians, and Laotians are classified as refugees from communist countries and are thereby assisted in resettlement and aided by "assimilation assistance" programs, many conducted by church-based organizations that assist immigrants.

President Gerald Ford establishes an interagency task force to resettle South Asian refugees following the fall of Saigon.

Soviet Jews begin fleeing in large numbers. Haitians continue arriving in large numbers.

In *United States v. Brignoni-Ponce,* the U.S. Supreme Court decides that it is permissible for law enforcement to use race as a factor in determining which vehicles to stop and search.

1976   Congress amends the 1965 Immigration and Nationality Act by extending the per-country limits of visa applicants on a first-come, first-served basis to Western Hemisphere nations as regulated by the preference system.

The U.S. Supreme Court rules, in *Matthews v. Diaz,* that an alien has no right to Social Security or Medicare benefits.

The Gerald Ford administration establishes a cabinet-level committee to study immigration options.

1978   President Carter and the Congress set up the Select Commission on Immigration and Refugee Policy (SCIRP).

1979   Civil war in El Salvador leads to beginning of their refugee movement.

Vietnamese and Southeast Asian "boat people" influx.

1980   Congress passes the Refugee Act to systematize refugee policy. It incorporates the United Nations' definition of refugee, accepting fifty thousand persons annually who have a "well-founded fear" of persecution based on race, religion, nationality, or membership in a social or political movement. It also provides for admission of five thousand "asylum seekers."

1981   An economic recession begins.

On March 1, the Select Commission on Immigration and Refugee Policy issues its final report, recommending many changes in policy that form the basis of the Immigration Reform and Control Act of 1986 and other subsequent reform acts, several of which underlie proposed reforms even after 2001.

President Ronald Reagan creates the Task Force on Immigration and Refugee Policy, which reports in July.

1982   A federal district judge rules the lockup of Haitians unconstitutional, ordering release of 1,900 detainees.

The first version of the Immigration Reform and Control Act, a major bill to amend the Immigration and Nationality Act, is introduced into the House by Republican senator Alan K. Simpson.

In *Plyler v. Doe,* the U.S. Supreme Court rules that a Texas law denying public education funding for the children of undocumented immigrants is unconstitutional.

1983   The Supreme Court rules, in *INS v. Chadha et al.,* that the use of the legislative veto to overturn certain INS deportation proceedings, rules, and regulations by the House of Representatives was unconstitutional.

1986   Congress enacts the Immigration Reform and Control Act's (IRCA) employer sanctions/legalization approach granting amnesty to about 1.5 million undocumented immigrants and more than 1 million special agricultural workers. IRCA requires all employers to complete Form I-9 to verify a worker's identity. It also includes additional specifications to the H-2 guest worker program established by the Immigration and Nationality Act of 1952.

The National Network for Immigrant and Refugee Rights is established as a nonprofit organization to advocate for the rights of immigrants and refugees, no matter their immigration status.

1987   In *INS v. Cardoza-Fonseca,* by a vote of 6 to 3, the Supreme Court rules that the government must relax its standards for deciding whether undocumented immigrants who insist that they would be persecuted if they returned to their homelands are eligible for asylum.

1988   The Senate passes, but the House kills, the Kennedy-Simpson bill, in what becomes the Immigration Act of 1990.

Canada-U.S. Free Trade Agreement Implementation Act is signed.

1989   In May, the International Conference for Central American Refugees is held in Guatemala City.

San Francisco declares itself a "sanctuary city" for all immigrants. The ordinance, one of the first of its kind, protects individuals arrested on non-felony charges from being reported to federal immigration authorities.

The Nursing Relief Act grants permanent resident status to certain registered nurses.

1990   Congress passes the Immigration Act of 1990, a major reform of the laws concerning legal immigration, setting new ceilings for worldwide immigration, redefining the preference system for family reunification and employment, and setting up a new category of preference called "diversity immigrants." It enacts special provisions regarding Central American refugees, Filipino veterans, and persons seeking to leave Hong Kong. Significant changes were included with respect to naturalization procedures. It also allows authorities to grant "Temporary Protected Status" to individuals unable to return to their home country because of armed conflict, epidemics, or other unsafe conditions.

1993   Congress ratifies the North American Free Trade Agreement (NAFTA), which goes into effect January 1, 1994.

The Government Accountability Office (GAO) publishes a report that estimates the number of undocumented immigrants in the United States at 3.4 million in 1990. The U.S. Census estimates the population for this same year to be 3.3 million, with an annual growth rate of 200,000.

Economist Donald Huddle issues his report "The Cost of Immigration," setting off the decades-long debate over the relative costs and benefits of immigration and unauthorized immigration.

1994   California passes Proposition 187, the "Save Our State" initiative that attempted to ban undocumented immigrants from accessing public services.

Congress enacts the Violent Crime Control and Law Enforcement Act, the "Smith Act," giving law enforcement agencies more authority to issue "S visas" to informants.

Congress passes the Violence against Women Act with provision to grant special status to immigrants who are victims of domestic abuse through cancellation of removal and self-petitioning provisions.

1995   Federal district court for California rules, in *LULAC et al. v. Wilson et al.,* that many of Proposition 187's provisions are unconstitutional.

The General Accounting Office (GAO) issues its first major and comprehensive report on the costs of undocumented immigrants to governments and to the overall economy.

A Human Rights Watch report is highly critical of the INS and alleged abuses.

The Immigration and Naturalization Service (INS) begins to systematically publish information by way of tables on the estimated size and characteristics of the U.S. "illegal" immigrant population.

1996   In June, the Board of Immigration Appeals (*In re: Fauziya Kasinga*) grants the first woman asylum on the basis of gender persecution (female genital mutilation).

Congress enacts welfare reform through the Personal Responsibility and Work Opportunity Reconciliation Act, with numerous immigration-related provisions. Congress essentially enacts aspects of the failed California Proposition 187 regarding welfare and other public benefits.

Congress passes the Illegal Immigration Reform and Immigrant Responsibility Act (IIRIRA), the sixty-plus immigration-related provisions of the Omnibus Spending Bill. It removes welfare and economic benefits to undocumented immigrants and to some legal resident immigrants. The law also authorizes the E-Verify program, an electronic verification system that enables employers to determine whether a worker is eligible for employment in the United States.

The Antiterrorism and Effective Death Penalty Act of 1996 is signed into law. Among its provisions, it gives INS inspectors the power to make "on-the-spot credible fear" determinations involving asylum. It takes effect on April 1, 1997, as part of IIRIRA reforms beginning then.

The Border Patrol makes a record 1.6 million apprehensions at the borders nationwide. Congress authorizes the addition of one thousand new Border Patrol agents annually.

1997   The Jordan Commission on Immigration Reform, set up by the Immigration Act of 1990, recommends restructuring of the INS in its final report.

The "Expedited Enforcement Rules" of the IIRIRA of 1996 take effect at U.S. land borders, international airports, and seaports to issue and enforce expulsion orders. Some 4,500 INS officers are added at 300 ports of entry.

The General Accounting Office issues its Report on the Fiscal Impact of Newest Americans.

In July, under the welfare reform legislation of 1996, the federal government implements the Temporary Assistance to Needy Families (TANF) program, which provides funds to underprivileged families while encouraging recipients to find employment. TANF replaces Aid to Families with Dependent Children (AFDC), a New Deal–era welfare program that had fewer work requirements.

On November 19, President Bill Clinton signs into law the Nicaraguan Adjustment and Central American Relief Act (NACARA), which provides a path to legal permanent residency and relief from deportation to certain groups of immigrants, mainly from Central America, affected by the strict immigration reforms enacted by the Illegal Immigration Reform and Immigrant Responsibility Act of 1996.

1998   President Clinton sends another immigration bill to Congress seeking, in part, a restructuring of the INS. It dies in committee when the Judiciary Committee begins hearings on impeachment.

The Agriculture Job Opportunity Benefits and Security Act establishes a pilot program for twenty thousand to twenty-five thousand farm workers.

The Social Security Board of Trustees Report is issued, documenting positive effects of immigration on the status of the Social Security fund but also the dire, long-term crisis in the Social Security account as the U.S. population ages and fewer active workers support ever-growing numbers of retirees.

Congress passes the American Competitiveness and Workforce Improvement Act, which expands the H-1B category to the computer industry.

California voters approve its Proposition 227, which ends bilingual education programs in state schools.

1999   The Carnegie Endowment for International Peace presents its International Migration Policy Program.

Twenty-one nongovernmental organizations concerned with immigration call for INS restructuring, separation of enforcement from visa and naturalization functions, and the sending of some functions to the DOL and HHS. INS provides Border Patrol/adjudication.

In *INS v. Aguirre-Aguirre*, a unanimous Supreme Court rules that immigrants who have committed serious nonpolitical crimes in their home countries are ineligible to seek asylum in the United States regardless of the risk of persecution when returned to their countries.

Rep. Christopher Smith (R-NJ) introduces the Trafficking Victims Protection Act of 1999.

With a restored economy, President Clinton's administration reenacts some of the benefits stripped away from legal immigrants by the 1996 acts.

On November 22, 1999, a five-year-old Cuban boy, Elian Gonzalez, is rescued off the Florida coast. He becomes the center of an international custody battle between relatives in Cuba and the United States.

The Office of the United Nations High Commissioner for Refugees issues guidelines related to Detention of Asylum Seekers in Geneva, Italy.

2000   In April, Attorney General Janet Reno approves a Justice Department "raid" on the Miami home to "return Elian Gonzalez" to his father in Cuba.

In *Gonzales v. Reno,* the Eleventh Circuit Court of Appeals rules that only the father of Elian Gonzalez can speak for the boy.

In October, President Bill Clinton signs into law the Victims of Trafficking and Violence Protection Act. It creates the "T visa" for victims of trafficking and the "U visa," which provides temporary legal status to noncitizens who are victims of certain crimes.

2001   In August, senators Dick Durbin (D-Ill.) and Orrin Hatch (R-Utah) introduce the Development, Relief, and Education for Minors Act (DREAM Act), which is designed to provide undocumented students access to legal residency and federal financial aid for higher education.

On September 11, terrorists attack the twin towers of the World Trade Center in New York and the Pentagon in Washington, D.C. Immediate calls for a crackdown on terrorists begin.

On October 24, Congress passes the USA PATRIOT Act, granting sweeping new powers to the attorney general, the FBI, and the Department of Justice regarding immigrants and the authority to detain "enemy combatants" involved in or suspected of terrorism.

The American Competitiveness in the Twenty-first Century Act is approved.

Texas and California become the first states to enact legislation allowing undocumented students to be eligible for in-state tuition at public universities. By 2011, 10 other states enact similar measures.

2002   In November, Congress establishes a cabinet-level Department of Homeland Security to assume the immigration service and enforcement functions of the federal government.

The United Nations issues its Protocols on Human Trafficking and Immigrant Smuggling in Palermo, Italy. The protocols are signed by 141 countries.

2003   In March, the INS is dissolved. Its functions are transferred from the Department of Justice to the newly formed Department of Homeland Security and divided into three new agencies: Citizenship and Immigration Services, Immigration and Customs Enforcement, and Customs and Border Protection.

In September, Immigrant Workers Freedom Ride (IWFR) is launched as several buses depart from U.S. cities to Washington, DC to draw attention to the social injustices faced by undocumented immigrant workers, and lobby the U.S. Congress for immigration reform.

2004   Unauthorized immigrants within the United States reach an estimated record of 11 million. Immigration and Customs Enforcement reports 1.1 million apprehensions at the nation's borders.

2005   The House passes the Border Protection, Anti-Terrorism and Illegal Immigration Control Act, also known as the REAL ID Act.

Virginia enacts a law prohibiting unauthorized immigrants 19 years of age or older from accessing non-emergency public benefits such as Medicaid.

Arizona enacts a measure, House Bill 2030, preventing cities from constructing day labor centers if such centers serve unauthorized immigrants.

Arizona enacts a law making human smuggling a state crime. The legislation leads to the arrests of thousands of people who are charged as conspirators for paying to be smuggled into the United States.

Nine states enact anti-human trafficking laws.

Nine states enact laws related to eligibility requirements for driver's licenses, including those that prohibit the issuing of such licenses to unauthorized immigrants.

Three states enact laws related to immigration and law enforcement.

The governors of Arizona and New Mexico issue "state of emergency" declarations, freeing state emergency funding for use in areas dealing with border crime and unauthorized immigration.

The federal government launches Operation Streamline in Del Rio, Texas, a tough border enforcement program aimed at criminally prosecuting every migrant who crosses the U.S.-Mexico border without authorization.

The U.S. House of Representatives proposes a comprehensive immigration reform bill, the *Border Protection, Antiterrorism and Illegal Immigration Control Act of 2005* (H.R. 4437). The proposals offered no path to citizenship for the nearly 11.3 million undocumented immigrants living in the United States at the time.

2006   In *Fernandez-Vargas v. Gonzales,* the U.S. Supreme Court rules that the reinstatement statute of the Immigration and Nationality Act, enacted as part of the Illegal Immigration Reform and Immigrant Responsibility Act, can apply to a noncitizen who illegally reentered the United States before the statute went into effect.

2007   The largest demonstrations since the civil rights protests of the 1960s take place as thousands of immigrants and their allies rally in major cities across the nation against the harsh "enforcement only" provisions HR 4437.

2008   On May 12, a raid at a meatpacking plant in Postville, Iowa, by U.S. Immigration and Customs Enforcement results in the arrests of 389 undocumented workers, most of them from Guatemala and Mexico.

The federal government launches Secure Communities. The program automatically sends the fingerprints of anyone booked after an arrest to the Department of Homeland Security, which checks the fingerprints against its immigration databases. If the person is flagged for removal, Immigration and Customs Enforcement proceeds with enforcement action.

2009   In *Flores-Figueroa v. United States,* the U.S. Supreme Court unanimously rules that in order to be guilty of "aggravated identity theft," undocumented workers who use a false identification card must know that it belongs to a real person.

The Ninth Circuit Court of Appeals in *United States v. Roblero-Solis* rules that the process of mass pleadings involving defendants criminally prosecuted for unauthorized entry into the United States, known as Operation Streamline, violates due process. However, the convictions in the case are upheld.

2010   On April 23, Arizona governor Jan Brewer signs Senate Bill 1070 into law. The controversial legislation would allow the police to detain individuals suspected of being in the country illegally, among other provisions.

In July, U.S. district judge Susan Bolton places a temporary injunction against four provisions in Arizona's Senate Bill 1070: the portions that deal with police enforcement of immigration laws; criminalize the failure to carry immigration papers; make it a crime for an undocumented immigrant to apply for or hold jobs; and authorize warrantless arrests if there is probable cause that a person committed a deportable offense.

After being reintroduced in the Senate, the DREAM Act is brought to a vote on December 18. It fails to garner the number of votes needed to move forward.

2011   The U.S. Supreme Court upholds a 2007 Arizona law which penalizes businesses for hiring undocumented workers.

Several states consider passing restrictive immigration bills, many of which include provisions similar to Arizona's controversial SB 1070. While many of these proposals fail to pass state legislatures, efforts to sign them into law succeed in Alabama (HB 56), Georgia (HB 87), Indiana (SB 590), South Carolina (S 20), and Utah (SB 497).

A memo was issued by Immigration and Customs Enforcement (ICE) Director John Morton, which outlined new guidelines recommending "prosecutorial discretion" to help immigration enforcement agents determine whether cases for removal are of a high or low priority, bringing some relief to undocumented immigrants with close family ties and same-sex binational partners.

2012   The Pew Hispanic Center reports that net migration from Mexico to the United States has fallen to zero or less (meaning the number of people moving to the country is equal to the number leaving it). Additionally, Asians surpass Latinos as the largest group of legal immigrants.

On June 15, President Barack Obama announces an executive action, the "Deferred Action for Childhood Arrivals," which would allow young undocumented immigrants who came to the United States as children to remain in the country and work without fear of deportation.

On June 25, the U.S. Supreme Court strikes down three of the four contested provisions of Arizona Senate Bill 1070, keeping in place the part that requires immigration status checks during law enforcement stops.

2013   In January of 2013, the Obama Administration announced a new rule that will allow thousands of American citizens to avoid long separations from immediate family members who are undocumented and want to initiate the process of becoming legal residents by applying for a Provisional Unlawful Presence (PUP) Waiver.

In April, a bipartisan group of senators nicknamed the "Gang of Eight" present a proposal for comprehensive immigration reform that includes a pathway to citizenship for undocumented immigrants and an overhaul of visa programs. It clears the Democratic-controlled Senate in June of the same year, and in the fall, stalls in the Republican-controlled House of Representatives.

On April 29, the U.S. Supreme Court by a vote of 8–1 refuses to hear the appeal by the state of Alabama, which had been blocked in 2012 by the U.S. Court of Appeals for the Eleventh Circuit, from enforcing a provision in Alabama's 2011 state law that had made it illegal for anyone in the state to transport or assist undocumented immigrants.

The U.S. Ninth Circuit Court of Appeals renders a decision in *United States v. Arqueta-Ramos* ruling the process of *en masse* pleadings involving defendants criminally prosecuted for unauthorized entry into the United States, known as Operation Streamline, is flawed, because it fails to ensure the judge determines, as legally required to do, that each person understands the charges and their rights if they plead guilty.

A

Acculturation

Acculturation is a process in which members of one cultural group adopt and learn the beliefs and behaviors of another cultural group, while still maintaining their own cultural practices. As one is immersed in the dominant culture, one tends to adapt to mainstream customs, values, and traditions over time. According to acculturation theory, there are different types of acculturation. Selective acculturation is when a person chooses specific values or beliefs to adopt while at the same time retaining one's

Angelica Medina, 17, of Baltimore, Maryland, whose parents are Mexican and Guatemalan, poses for a portrait at the end of the Rally for Citizenship, a rally in support of immigration reform, on Capitol Hill in Washington, on April 10, 2013. In the summer of 2013, a bipartisan group of Senators drafted a comprehensive immigration reform bill that included a proposed pathway to citizenship for the nation's 11 million undocumented immigrants. (AP Photo/ Jacquelyn Martin)

own cultural values. Structural acculturation depends on where a person acculturates in a particular context such as in a Mexican barrio or a white suburban neighborhood.

It is important to examine acculturation because it shows how, for example, immigrants from another country might adapt particular belief systems and values of their hosts. This impacts their behaviors, health, knowledge, and beliefs, but is associated with adapting to life in a different place. However, while most adaptation benefits the individual, often it does not. For example, there has been significant research about the effect of acculturation on immigrants and how acculturation affects health. The "healthy immigrant effect" looks at why immigrants appear healthier than the native-born, but as the length of time spent in the United States increases, their health status declines. Acculturation is presumed to be linked to this phenomenon. Studies have shown that more acculturated Mexican-Americans tend to have more health ailments due to poorer diet. Another problem that comes from acculturation is acculturative stress, which has been researched extensively as a stress that comes from the difficulty or anxiety immigrants may experience from trying to adjust to the new culture. The longer immigrants are exposed to life in the United States, the higher the propensity is to engage in risky behaviors. Studies show that new immigrants are less likely to engage in substance abuse, but after about ten years of living in the United States, there is an increase in the use of alcohol, tobacco, and drugs among them.

Because the process of acculturation is continuous and cumulative over time, generational differences may influence the level of acculturative practices. Immigrants who are first or second generations within the United States may practice more traditional cultural practices; however, third and fourth generations may tend to adopt more Westernized belief systems. As acculturation increases, traditional cultural values, language, and health beliefs may also decrease. "Heritage Consistency" is a concept that describes the degree to which one's lifestyle reflects his or her culture (Zitzow and Estes, 1981). The process includes how immigrants are socialized about their culture, and how they learn and practice cultural rituals, religion and ethnicity. The idea is that the longer immigrants are in the United States, the more likely they are to become acculturated into Western culture, and with each generation, there will be a greater degree of acculturation.

There are various ways by which acculturation takes place and becomes obvious. Some of the most well-known markers of acculturation are language preference, language spoken in the home, length of time spent in the United States, birth place, ethnic identification, and generational status. While some studies explore all of these factors combined, others explore just one or two. Such variation in methodology complicates the study of acculturation and its effects. Acculturation may also be measured at the behavioral, affective, and cognitive levels. The behavioral perspective examines influences in language use, including the frequency of the use of one's native language and the use of the language of the dominant culture. In the United States this is often gauged by one's ability and comfort level when speaking English. Other behavioral factors include customs such as holiday practices, dietary practices, listening and viewing habits for television or radio, and social behavioral practices in which one engages. Affective levels of acculturation can be gauged by how one chooses to identify (one example would be those who define themselves as Mexican-American versus Chicano), the symbols with which one associates, and meanings that people attach to items. Lastly, cognitive acculturation examines the personal beliefs, perceptions, values, and attitudes one expresses. Although these different measures can be used to define the acculturation process, researchers have difficulty in determining how long it takes and when the process is completed.

Immigrants are particularly susceptible to acculturative stress as they may experience discrimination from the dominant culture, experience frustration and humiliation related to language proficiency, as well as concern about the loss of one's culture or giving up one's own cultural identity. Immigrants going through the process of acculturation may experience decreased emotional/mental health and physical health. Research shows that substance abuse and affective disorders are more likely to occur once an immigrant has migrated to the United States. Social isolation is one of the main contributing factors to higher rates of depression and substance abuse. Differences in cultural norms and customs may vary between countries. The differences can lead to feelings of alienation or rejection from the host culture. If that becomes internalized, health and well-being of the immigrant may become jeopardized.

Discrimination may exacerbate risk factors for immigrant youth. Discrimination and racism have a negative impact on a child's sense of self-esteem, leading to depression and poor mental health as well as involvement in risky behaviors. Low self-esteem has been linked to lower academic achievement and higher dropout rates among minority youth (Delgado et al., 2009). Conversely, if a student is invested in academic achievement, doing well in school should contribute to his or her self-esteem. For youth who are undocumented and dealing with additional stressors that are unique to their situation, having low self-esteem as well could significantly impact their ability to perform academically. Discrimination at the institutional level may also play a role in a minority youth's education. Students have reported feeling left out of activities, being wrongly disciplined, and generally experiencing racial bias in an academic setting. Specifically, Latino/a youth may define discrimination based on their ability to speak English, immigration status, race, socioeconomic status, and stereotypes. A study on adolescents of Mexican descent showed that immigrant youth might experience higher levels of stress and discrimination when compared to youth of earlier generations. Not only do undocumented Latino/as face discrimination from outside groups, they may also face discrimination from within their own peer groups. Latino/as who are U.S. citizens or legal residents may target undocumented immigrants for discrimination in an effort to differentiate themselves from those who are out of status.

Researchers have looked at how having a strong cultural base and cultural strength may counteract negative feelings associated with discrimination. Values such as familism, where the role of the family is very strong, have been linked to minimizing negative behavior in the classroom and have been indicated to increase self-esteem in Latino/as. Additionally, studies have shown that the more positively adolescents feel about their ethnic identity, the higher their self-esteem (Phinney et al., 1997). Acculturation also has an impact on self-esteem. Immigrant groups that feel more acculturated to the majority group have exhibited higher self-esteem.

Language poses a significant barrier for undocumented immigrants. In the United States there remains a nationalistic ideology that suggests that immigrants' languages and cultures are threatening and that learning English results in progress and betterment of themselves and their children. In this way, immigrants have been pressured to give up their cultural identities, and assimilate, meaning they should speak only English and uphold American values. Immigrant parents may have experienced discrimination and violence and may fear that their children will also, so they encourage them to give up their cultural traditions and speak English. After only a few generations, the language and cultural traditions may be lost, resulting in a cultural divide.

Language is often used as an example of acculturation. Language barriers impede the adjustments to living in the United States if the immigrant is unable to speak English. The United States reflects a monolingual perspective, recognizing English as the only official language. For immigrants who have difficulty communicating because of language barriers, there is often a feeling of frustration and helplessness that follows. Children often respond to language barriers by withdrawing from social interactions, remaining silent, and may appear moody or fearful. Children learning a new language may be placed in English as a Second Language (ESL) classes. Studies suggest that isolation from English-speaking students does not foster positive social interactions. In the state of Arizona, students are often not tested for English proficiency but instead are placed into ESL classes because of their surnames. ESL courses focus on a four-hour block of English Language learning which limits the student's ability to participate in other classes such as geography, history, art and sciences. There also remains an expectation that immigrant students are to become English-proficient within two to three years, though studies indicate most languages take at least seven years to fully learn and understand.

Acculturation may also contribute to parent-adolescent conflict. Research suggests that children tend to become acculturated more quickly by adopting the host culture as one's own. This may increase tensions in the family, as cultural norms are perceived differently. This can cause significant miscommunication and stress within the family, pitting one set of cultural values against another.

Courtney Martínez

See Also: Acculturation Stress; Assimilation; Culture; Exclusion; Health and Welfare; Mental Health Issues for Immigrants; Nutrition; Social Interaction and Integration.

Further Reading

Delgado, M.Y., K.A. Updegraff, M.W. Roosa, and A.J. Umana-Taylor. 2009. "Discrimination and Mexican-Origin Adolescents' Adjustment: The Moderating Roles of Adolescents', Mothers', and Fathers' Cultural Orientations and Values." *Journal of Youth and Adolescence* 40:125–139.

Leow Mclean, Deborah, Marion Goldstein, and Lisa McGlinchy. 2006. "A Selective Literature Review: Immigration, Acculturation & Substance Abuse." Education Development Center.

Phinney, J.S., C.L. Cantu, and D.A. Kurtz. 1997. "Ethnic and American Identity as Predictors of Self-Esteem Among African American, Latino, and White Adolescents." *Journal of Youth and Adolescence,* 26.2:165–185.

Macias, T. 2006. *Mestizo in America: Generations of Mexican Ethnicity in the Suburban Southwest.* Tucson, AZ: University of Arizona Press.

Zitzow, Darryl, and George Estes. 1981. Heritage Consistency as a Consideration in Counseling Native Americans. ERIC Clearinghouse, available at: http://elib.uum.edu.my/kip/Record/ED209035.

Acculturation Stress

Acculturation stress refers to the psychological, physical, and social difficulties that may come from being introduced to a new culture. Acculturation is understood not only as the process by which individuals are exposed to new cultural surroundings, but everything that this experience may set into motion, including heightened awareness, and pressures to adapt and to conform to new places, new people, and new languages. The concept of acculturation stress reflects the anxieties and concerns about the sense of loss of familiarity that occurs when adjusting to or integrating into a new system of beliefs, routines and social roles. For many Latinos, acculturation and the stress that comes from it may be worsened if they are undocumented. Over the years, researchers (Caplan, 2007) have identified two particular dimensions of acculturative stress as a result of being undocumented.

The first dimension is referred to as instrumental and/or environmental, where stress to individuals and groups is related to the difficulty in obtaining the goods and services needed for one's day-to-day existence. This can be compounded with anti-immigrant laws that are in place that make obtaining basic goods and services even more difficult. The stress experienced by these situations may be alleviated by immigrants' reliance on cultural mechanisms such as social capital and the social networks that assist those in need so that they are able to become better integrated into the settlement communities and in this way resolve many of the problems that come with adaptation to new surroundings. With anti-immigrant sentiment growing, reliance on these cultural mechanisms may become even more important as more barriers designed to keep immigrants from accessing jobs and housing are implemented, making the survival of families more difficult.

The second dimension that Caplan refers to is social and/or interpersonal. Healthy acculturation requires strong social ties to community and familial support. Any loss of connection to either family or community threatens successful transition into a new culture. Social networks and familism have been shown to serve as a safeguard against moderate acculturative stress and are viewed as a major stressor in their absence. These stressors are related to changes in relationships, gender roles, behaviors, and cultural norms that occurred as a result of the immigration. For example, undocumented single migrant men who come alone to the United States often face isolation. Without families or a strong familial or social support, undocumented immigrants may have little choice but to suffer acculturation stress alone. This may have unhealthy consequences or provoke unhealthy responses such as substance abuse. Other signs of acculturation stress may include depression, sadness, and loss of appetite. Without the ability to access mental health care services, their health may be additionally compromised.

Caplan's study noted that the groups with the greatest number and severity of stressors were undocumented immigrants and migrant farm workers. This is due to the fact that many of these immigrants were recent arrivals to the United States and therefore experienced the greatest daily stressors, and more acculturation stress. Farm workers are also known to be highly mobile with harvest demands, and under this occupational category, undocumented migrant farm workers experienced elevated levels of acculturative stress. They reported higher anxiety as a result of feeling caught between the influence of traditional values and norms and the values, norms, and hardships experienced in the new society in which they lived. Feelings of achievement, fulfillment, and success associated with the immigration experience may alleviate acculturative stress with immigrants who feel that they have a sense of control over their lives. They experience greater resiliency to stress.

It is important to recognize that some scholars suggest that the concept of acculturative stress does have its limitations and may not completely account for the mental health illnesses experienced by undocumented migrants. Escobar and Vega (2000) argue that acculturative stress theory is limited because there is a poor understanding of what acculturation means and immigrants experience culture differently based on where they settle and where they come from. In their study, Escobar and Vega point out that often it is unclear what aspects of acculturation are actually being measured. Furthermore, other scholars argue that acculturative stress and marginalization theories of Latino mental health assume that after-migration circumstances or encounters in the United States are similarly experienced by all migrants regardless of reasons or circumstances for coming to the United States.

Anna Ochoa O'Leary

See Also: Mental Health Issues for Immigrants; Single Men.

Further Reading

Caplan, S. 2007. "Latinos, Acculturation, and Acculturative Stress: A Dimensional Concept Analysis." *Policy, Politics & Nursing Practice* 8.2:93–106.

Cuellar, I., E. Bastida, and S.M. Braccio. 2004. "Residency in the United States, Subjective Well-Being and Depression in an Older Mexican-Origin Sample." *Hispanic Journal of Behavioral Sciences,* 17.3:275–304.

Escobar, J.I., and W.A. Vega. 2000. "Mental Health and Immigration's AAAs: Where Are We and Where Do We Go from Here?" *Journal of Nervous Mental Disorders* 188.11:736–740.

Hovey, J.D., and C.G. Magaña. 2002. "Cognitive, Affective and Physiological Expressions of Anxiety Symptomatology among Mexican Migrant Farmworkers: Predictors and Generational Differences." *Community Mental Health Journal* 38.3.

Redfield, R., R. Linton, and M.J. Herskovits. 1936. "Memorandum for the Study of Acculturation." *American Anthropologist,* 38.1:149–152.

Zuniga, M.E. 2002. "Latino Immigrants: Patterns of Survival." *Journal of Human Behavior in the Social Environment* 5.3/4:137–155.

Activism

Undocumented migrants have often been referred to as living in the shadows. However, while undocumented migrants are strategic about the spaces in which they reveal their immigration status, they are not passive subjects. They are active members of their communities and resist against the oppression brought on by their immigration status. Migrant struggles have a number of fronts including worker's rights, housing rights, and schooling rights. Undocumented students in the university occupy a unique space as they are trained for positions promising social mobility, but given their immigration status, the likelihood that they can enter the labor force in such privileged positions is minimal. Furthermore, attending the university is a difficult endeavor. There are widespread racism, sexism, and xenophobia and as such, the cost of schooling is not just financial but also psychological. In order to resist these forces, undocumented students have created collective organizations aiming to create an easier context under which they live, work, and study.

Activism can take many forms ranging from everyday acts that resist and disrupt the status quo to concerted collective efforts aimed at creating change. In the United

A young woman wears a Mexican flag as a bandana as she carries an American flag while marching to the Capitol in Denver on May 1, 2006, for a rally on immigration reform. Wearing symbolic white and waving both American and Mexican flags, tens of thousands of activists marched through Denver, hoping to demonstrate the urgency of comprehensive reform, and the economic contributions to the nation made by immigrants from all walks of life. (AP Photo/Jack Dempsey)

Internationally recognized immigrant rights activist and public defender Isabel Garcia (right) of Tucson, AZ, attends a screening of CNN's *Latinos in America* (2009), a documentary exploring how Latinos are reshaping U.S. communities and culture, forcing a nation to rediscover what it means to be "a nation of immigrants." Interviewed for the documentary, Isabel Garcia is co-founder of the Coalición de Derechos Humanos in Tucson, AZ, an immigrant rights organization that emerged in the late 1990s in response to the dramatic rise in immigrants who died while crossing into the United States. (Mike Moore/WireImage/Getty)

States, university undocumented students engage in activism at different levels of society including activism at the national level as well as involvement in local communities. As such, undocumented students are a big part of the overall migrant rights movement in the United States, working within the spaces they inhabit to enact change while at the same time aiming for a broader end goal: comprehensive immigration reform.

Nationally, undocumented students have gathered collectively to form campus organizations in their respective universities aiming to combat the oppression brought on by undocumented immigration status. Organizations join coalitions aiming to pressure the federal government into adopting legislation that will improve the circumstances under which undocumented students live. This includes the improvement of the conditions under which they attend school, putting a stop on deportations, and increasing the level of access to public goods including driver's licenses and financial aid. One such piece of legislation is the "Development, Relief and Education for Alien Minors Act"

(DREAM Act) which would provide residence status to qualified individuals who enroll in higher education or join the military. To this end, students have engaged in hunger strikes, pilgrimages, marches and the occupation of senate offices. With full knowledge of the potential consequences including deportation, students have risked their well being in order to inform the wider public of their dismal situation and to become agents of change. For example, in July of 2013, nine young activists who have come to be known as the "Dream 9" exited the country and attempted to re-enter the United States at the Nogales, Arizona port of entry, claiming asylum from customs and border officials. They were arrested and detained in an immigration detention center in the state and were released a month later, but not before gaining the nation's attention.

On July 20, 2010 twenty-two undocumented students were arrested after staging sit-ins at the Senate Hart Office Building. These students engaged in acts of civil disobedience to bring visibility to the effects of immigration status on their everyday lives in order to provide an additional push to the passage of the DREAM Act. While appearing publicly as an undocumented migrant can be quite dangerous, these students engaged in such an act strategically. In their interviews, they are quoted as hoping that the release of information regarding their immigration status to the media, given the large coverage of the event, would grant them protection from immigration authorities. While most students were correct in this instance, at the time this essay was written eight still faced charges that carried the possibility of deportation. Because of this, it is important to note that safety is often determined by the political climate, and depending on the context, disclosing immigration-related information is a very dangerous action.

California is one of eleven states with legislation enabling undocumented university students to attend state-funded universities while paying resident tuition. In this state, campus organizations directed at bettering the experience and opportunities of undocumented students exist across three distinct public systems of higher learning (University of California, California State University, and community college campuses). These organizations are active in the advocacy for increased access for undocumented students to college education as well as an overall call for comprehensive immigration reform.

At the state level there are a number of organizations aiming to pressure the government into adopting comprehensive immigration reform as well as state-level policy benefiting undocumented migrants. One such organization is the Bay Area Dream Act Coalition (BADAC) which in 2010 organized a Northern California DREAM Mobilizing Summit aiming to "bring together all organizations and activists in Northern California for the DREAM Act with the purpose of collectively discussing a unifying Northern California Action." This is yet another example of concerted efforts at larger-scale mobilization in order to produce legislative change to benefit undocumented students.

Activism takes many forms in the local context. At UCLA, undocumented migrants decided to tell their stories through a book, *Underground Undergrads: UCLA Undocumented Immigrant Students Speak Out.* This book serves as a testament of their stories and experiences and aims to re-humanize the discourse of undocumented migrants who are often dehumanized in popular discourse. The book serves as an activist medium whereby undocumented university students counter the predominant misconceptions about their experiences, accessing higher education while at the same time informing the public about the barriers they continue to face despite the existence of state legislature providing entry into the university. While the pains and frustrations experienced by these students are evident in this manuscript, these accounts also display stories of resistance and resilience.

While some undocumented university students have chosen to write their individual stories, others have come together to engage in collective action. Villegas (2010) found that a campus organization in Northern California engaged in many forms of advocacy and organizing work. The organization, primarily made up of Latina/o students, follows a long tradition of student activism dating back to the Chicano movement. This tradition informs members of the need to not just advocate for their personal well-being but also to engage with the community and work at disrupting the institutional factors that lead to their multiple oppressions. As such, this group made the effort to inform community members of the state policy granting undocumented students access to the university; they liaised and coordinated community events with established grassroots organizations, and lobbied the local, state, and federal governments towards the creation of policies benefiting undocumented migrants, and ultimately leading to comprehensive immigration reform. The group was made up of undocumented students and allies and disseminated information to high school students about relevant policy through classroom presentations as well as a regional conference. The conference was funded by the student organization as they, like other recognized campus groups, also engaged in traditional fundraisers (food sales, tickets to sponsored events, etc.). The group also worked in conjunction with longstanding civil rights and migrant rights organizations in letter-writing campaigns, speaking events, marches, and press releases. In addition, members also received newsletters and joined listservs in order to become further engaged and to broaden their knowledge of similar efforts outside of the university context. Finally, like hundreds of other migrant rights organizations, this university group also marched in solidarity during the various May Day marches.

Another form of activism involves strategic invisibilization. In contrast to the students engaged in the sit-ins at senate offices who visibilized their presence, undocumented students in the student group mentioned above highlighted a different facet of their identity to hide their immigration status while still engaging in political activism. Given that undocumented university students are indistinct from their documented peers, at times they can use their identity as university students without divulging information about their immigration status in order to enact social change. This strategic invisibilization of their immigration status allows for safer access to influential institutions where lobbying and advocacy can occur. In the previously cited study, students attended business bureau meetings as university students and dialogued with business leaders about the importance of supporting undocumented migrant students and the need for the business sector to call for comprehensive immigration reform. This effort was duplicated at local politicians' offices such as U.S. representatives and California senators.

There have been a number of victories through the activism of undocumented students. Nationally, they have increased the visibility of undocumented migrants in the United States as well as furthered a political agenda towards eventual comprehensive immigration reform. Locally, migrant groups have succeeded in lobbying businesses and local organizations into dropping social security requirements to scholarships so that undocumented students can apply for them, they have increased awareness in the community about the possibility of attending higher education, and they have created a safer space on campus where they can share stories, seek mentoring, and find a sense of belonging.

Francisco Villegas

See Also: California; Colleges and Universities; Community Activism; Community Concerns; DREAM Act; Protests; Xenophobia.

Further Reading

Bahrampour, Tara. 2010. "Students disclose illegal status as part of push for immigration reform." *The Washington Post,* July 21.

Chavez, Leo. 1992. *Shadowed Lives: Undocumented Immigrants in American Society.* Fort Worth, TX: Harcourt Brace Jovanovich College Publishers.

Eyck, Tiffany ten. 2010. "Undocumented and unafraid students sit-in for their Dream at the Capitol." *Labor Notes,* July 21.

Madera, Gabriela. 2008. *Undocumented Undergrads: UCLA Undocumented Immigrant Students Speak Out.* Los Angeles: UCLA Center for Labor Research and Education.

Villegas, Francisco. 2010. "Strategic In/visibility and Undocumented Migrants." In George Dei and Marlon Simmons, eds., *Fanon & Education: Thinking through Pedagogical Possibilities.* New York: Peter Lang.

Adult Education

For undocumented immigrants, especially recent arrivals to the United States, Adult Education programs offer the means of adapting and acculturating to their new surroundings. The goal of Adult Education is to teach basic skills and literacy, including English to Speakers of Other Languages (ESOL), to adults over the age of sixteen. The Federal Adult Education and Family Literacy Act understands literacy to mean a person's ability to read, write, and speak in English, along with being able to solve math problems at levels necessary to be a functional participant in one's family, on the job, and in the larger society. Adult Education programs are funded by the federal government, as well as by individual states and agencies. While most states make Adult Education available to everyone, regardless of legal status, the state of Arizona passed legislation in 2006 that made Adult Education inaccessible to people without legal documents.

A hallmark of Adult Education instruction is that learning is put in real-life contexts such as shopping for groceries, balancing one's checkbook, and writing business letters, in order to make concepts immediately useful to learners. Adult Education, or Adult Basic Education, typically has six strands: adult literacy instruction, developmental education, General Educational Development (GED) preparation, English to Speakers of Other Languages (ESOL) education, citizenship education, and family literacy.

Adult Literacy Instruction

Adult Literacy Instruction focuses on the teaching of reading to adults, especially the development of comprehension skills as they relate to everyday life contexts. Those contexts might include reading bank statements, understanding medical information, or apartment leases.

Developmental Education

Developmental Education, previously known as remedial education, is education that is geared toward adults who score below an eighth-grade level on standardized measures. They study basic subjects, such as reading, history, writing, science, and math. Developmental education students may study these subjects in order to prepare themselves for GED test preparation classes, or they may study these subjects in order to become more functional in their daily lives. Typically, students in developmental education have not had success in other educational settings because of learning differences or interrupted educational experiences.

GED Preparation

GED preparation classes offer a non-traditional way for adults to complete high school by preparing them to pass the GED test. The GED test covers content that is typically taught in U.S. high schools, and it can be taken in English, Spanish, or French. Passing the GED is usually accepted by employers and U.S. universities in lieu of a high school diploma.

English to Speakers of Other Languages (ESOL)

Adult Education ESOL or English as a Second Language (ESL) classes are for adults who speak a language other than English, and who want to learn communication skills in English. Adult Education ESOL classes focus on teaching listening, speaking, reading, and writing in real-life contexts. Those contexts may include talking with teachers at a child's school, explaining symptoms to a doctor, or asking a landlord to fix a faucet. Most Adult Education ESOL programs emphasize speaking and listening skills first, and then more attention is paid to reading and writing at the advanced levels. Students range from those with limited formal education in their native language, to professionals born in other countries.

Citizenship Education

Adult Education programs offer Citizenship Education to help immigrants (foreign nationals) who are legal permanent residents of the United States to pass the test that can lead to their becoming naturalized U.S. citizens, the U.S. Naturalization or Citizenship Test. While people who are in the United States without legal papers can hypothetically take these classes in every state except Arizona, they are not eligible to take the test which can result in U.S. citizenship.

The prerequisites for naturalization were established by Congress in the Immigration and Nationality Act (INA). Applicants for naturalization must have had a green card, evidence of lawful legal residence in the United States, for no fewer than five years. People who are legally married to a U.S. citizen and are lawful permanent residents of the United States can apply for naturalization after three years. All petitions for naturalization must be made on U.S. soil, although there are exceptions for some members of the military and their families. After the extensive paperwork has been filed and fees have been paid, it may take several years before the applicant is called for the naturalization interview. The average time it takes to get to the interview stage is fifteen months.

The naturalization interview involves a test of English proficiency and a civics test. The English test has three parts: speaking, reading, and writing. There are one hundred possible civics questions on the civics test, and applicants are asked up to ten questions. They must answer at least six questions correctly.

Applicants over the age of fifty who have been lawful permanent residents of the United States for twenty years are permitted to take the citizenship test with the aid of an interpreter. Those who are fifty-five years old and have been lawful permanent residents for fifteen years have the option of taking the citizenship test in their native language. People over the age of sixty-five who have been lawful permanent residents of the United States for twenty years are able to take a short form of the citizenship test, and conduct the interview in their native language, with the help of an interpreter. There are special exemptions for people with disabilities as well.

Family Literacy

Family Literacy is a federally and state-funded program intended to increase the educational attainment of parents and their children. There are four aspects of family literacy:

- Adult education or ESOL classes for parents
- Early Childhood classes for children
- Classes for parents and children together
- Classes in parental support and development

The key idea behind family literacy is that parents are a child's first teachers, and the more parents know about how to develop language and literacy skills in their children, the more both parents and children will benefit.

Char Ullman

See Also: Arizona; Bilingualism; Citizenship Education; Education; English as a Second Language (ESL) Programs; Naturalization.

Further Reading

Imel, Susan. 2003. Youth in Adult Basic and Literacy Education Programs. EDO-CE-03–246. Clearinghouse on Adult, Career, and Vocational Education. http://www.calpro-online.org/eric/docs/dig246.pdf.

United States Citizenship and Immigration Service (USCIS). http://www.uscis.gov/portal/site/uscis.

Advocacy

Immigrant rights and immigration policy have been at the forefront of the national debate. Immigration policy provides the legal course of action used by people of other countries to migrate to the United States. Since the founding of the United States, immigrants have migrated to this country for various reasons, including the search for better employment opportunities, family reunification, and/or refuge or asylum.

Many immigrants, however, have faced fear, hostility, and discrimination, after they have entered the United States, especially during hard economic times. In spite of the fact that the U.S. Bill of Rights does not grant foreigners with a right of entry into the United States, it does prohibit discrimination based on race and national origins to both citizens and non-citizens. Undocumented immigrants are compromised in their ability to access the opportunities that they seek and to advocate for themselves the rights that they have, rendering them susceptible to discriminatory acts and/or policies. It is within this context that advocates for immigrant rights fight to ensure that policies pertaining to these individuals do not undermine fundamental rights immigrants have.

Advocacy is the process of supporting an issue or proposal that aims to change public policy or create systemic changes. Advocacy is also a critical tool for changing public opinion that can favor progressive and social change. There are several types of advocacy including self-advocacy, community advocacy, and legislative advocacy. Advocacy is taking action. Individuals and/or organizations participate in advocacy activities that include researching and providing educational information on a cause or issue, public speaking, lobbying, starting a signature petition, writing a letter to a local elected official, telephone campaigns, or organizing a rally or a march. With the emergence of the Internet, there has been an increase in "e-advocacy" efforts, which include electronic petitions and/or social media campaigns to build awareness of a particular issue or cause. With social media, e-advocacy can inform and mobilize a larger volume of supporters at a faster pace in order to facilitate civic engagement and collective action. In essence, advocacy is speaking up for, or acting on behalf of, yourself or someone else. Advocacy is best understood as a practice of empowerment. The result of successful advocacy is an improvement in policies or practice that benefits a group that has been susceptible to discrimination and systematic mistreatment.

Advocacy has led to changes in American society that have saved lives and strengthened American democracy. When government policies have denied equal rights and due process to an underprivileged group, advocates have worked to raise awareness about discrimination and unequal treatment against these vulnerable groups. For example, advocacy played a critical role in ending segregation and in the civil rights movement. Some well-known advocates in the long struggle for civil liberties include Harriet Tubman in the nineteenth century and Martin Luther King Jr. in the twentieth. The struggle for civil rights has shown that with raised awareness, public opinion pressures policy makers to enact laws to prevent future discrimination and unequal treatment. Cesar Chavez and Dolores Huerta advocated for the rights of Mexican and Filipino migrant workers. Their work helped in the formation of the United Farm Workers Union (UFW). Politicians such as Texas's Henry Cisneros have also proven to be staunch allies of Latino immigrants by championing housing development. Many grass roots organizations, such as the National Network of Immigrant and Refugee Rights, are also well-known advocates in their fight against social and racial injustice and their impact on the improvement of civil, labor, and human rights of immigrant communities and refugees from violence-ridden countries. Lately there have been several advocacy efforts surrounding immigrant rights, particularly of undocumented immigrants. These efforts have led to voter registration efforts, marches and rallies, and protests and educational campaigns to build support of immigrant rights.

Advocacy efforts had a major impact on the formulation of recent proposed legislation such as the Development, Relief, and Education for Alien Minors, better known as the "Dream Act" (yet to be enacted). The Deferred Action for Childhood Arrivals (DACA) Program, made possible by a Presidential Executive Order, which allows certain undocumented youth to remain in the United States without fear of deportation for a renewable two-year period and to apply for social security numbers and work permits, is also a result of advocacy. Advocacy efforts have also been successful in the increased awareness of immigrant rights, particularly of "Dreamers," undocumented immigrant youth who came to the United States as children. Dulce Matuz, a well-known Dream Act advocate, is president of the Arizona DREAM Act Coalition, a youth-led advocacy coalition for immigrant's rights. She and other undocumented immigrant students have already led many efforts in support for policy change at the state and federal level.

However, while progressive change can be credited to forms of advocacy, issues needing advocacy continue to surface. For example, many immigrant women continue to experience domestic violence in spite of many years of advocacy by numerous groups. Many also continue to fight state anti-immigrant laws such as SB 1070 in Arizona and similar copycat laws enacted in Alabama, Georgia, Indiana, South Carolina, and Utah. Attrition through enforcement policies, referred to as "policies of attrition," attempts to discourage illegal immigration by encouraging undocumented immigrants to "self-deport" by means of restricting their access to public services. At the federal level, advocates also campaign against policies such as the Secure Communities ACT, 287 (g) and for immigration reform.

In addition advocacy led by individuals and groups, advocacy organizations with the sole purpose to promote social change through legislative advocacy, continues to fight for immigrant rights. These organizations include the American Civil Liberties Union (ACLU); National Council of La Raza (NCLR); League of United Latin American Citizens (LULAC); National Network for Immigrant and Refugee Rights;

American Bar Association's Commission on Immigration; and the National Immigration Project. These organizations also advocate for due process of immigrants in detention centers who have been unjustly arrested and detained. Advocates continue to advocate for immigration reform at the state and federal levels to ensure that immigrant rights are not undermined.

Sofía Gómez

See Also: Activism; Community Concerns; League of United Latin American Citizens (LULAC); National Network for Immigrant and Refugee Rights (NNIRR); Protests; Sanctuary Movement; Tennessee Immigrant and Refugee Rights Coalition (TIRRC).

Further Reading

Cantor, Guillermo. 2010. "Struggling for Immigrants' Rights at the Local Level: The Domestic Workers Bill of Rights Initiative in a Suburb of Washington, DC." *Journal of Ethnic & Migration Studies.* 36.7:1061–1078.

Juby, Cindy, and Laura E. Kaplan. 2011. "Postville: The Effects of an Immigration Raid." *Families in Society.* 92.2:147–153.

Lyon, Beth. 2008. "Changing Tactics: Globalization and the U.S. Immigrant Worker Rights Movement." *UCLA Journal of International Law & Foreign Affairs.* 13.1:161–196.

Milkman, Ruth, Joshua Bloom, and Victor Narro, eds. 2010. *Working for Justice: The LA Model of Organizing and Advocacy."* Ithaca, NY: ILR Press/Cornell University Press.

Revilla, Anita Tijerina. 2012. "What Happens in Vegas Does Not Stay in Vegas." *Aztlan* 37.1:87–115.

Airports

Airports have an underestimated role in irregular migration, even though the widespread image of such migration is walking through deserts and fording rivers on land borders between ports of entry. The accurate term for most irregular migrants through airports is "unauthorized," for two interconnected reasons. They almost always have travel documents when entering through airports (thus, not being "undocumented"). Such documents might be visitor or student visas, or one of many other categories; pre-boarding inspections make it nearly impossible to board airplanes to the United States or other migrant destination countries without such documents, or to proceed past airport entry inspections upon leaving the plane. And these migrants go out of status later, by violating the terms of the visas by staying too long ("overstaying"), working without authorization, and so forth. (Some wealthy source countries do not require visas for entrants to the United States, just valid passports, but rules governing stays in the United States remain the same.) Strictly unauthorized or undocumented entry through airports is itself extremely rare (occurring via sophisticated schemes of corruption). Entry by hiding physically in international passenger planes (air stowaways) is dangerous, and arguably impossible. Little is known about entry via small planes and small airports.

The number and proportion of ultimately unauthorized migrants who have entered the United States through airports is unknown. Estimates of the proportion of visa violators in the overall irregular migrant population are 33 to 48 percent (as of 2006), amounting to 4 to 5.5 million people. However, we do not know what portion of this overall group arrived through airports, because entry via land border ports (with Mexico and Canada) is also a significant route for persons who later become visa violators. Airports are important in adding national origin diversity to the U.S. unauthorized population. The southwest land border, whether via undocumented entry or via land border ports, is most heavily used by Mexican nationals, and also Central Americans, though smaller numbers of nationals from all over the world transit to the United States via Mexico. The Canadian border entrants are nationally diverse. But airports are key for future unauthorized migrants from distant places such as Poland, the Philippines, Peru, and of course many others. Again, this is important because in the United States, the archetypical image of the "illegal" is Mexican by nationality, and the transits via airports are an important reason why this is misleading.

Entry at airports, even with proper documents, is not automatic. Customs and Border Protection inspectors have the discretionary power to turn away "applicants" for admission. This is rare, but certainly does occur. Inspectors might decide—fairly or unfairly—that clues such as visible nervousness, one-way tickets, vagueness as to destinations or plans, lack of financial resources for the declared purpose of travel, past travel history, or information on watch list databases merit turning a person away. As ports of entry, airports provide latitude for unwarranted searches, interrogation, detention, and removal without formal process ("expedited removal").

United States international airports have entry registration. This program is called US-VISIT. International visitors have biometric (digitized photographic and fingerprint) data recorded at airports at the time of entrance. This also results in turn-aways or questioning. However, the United States has never implemented a full scale, biometric exit registration program at airports. As a result, databases cannot determine which individuals have either departed or, in the case of overstays, failed to depart (entries are known, but not exits). That, plus lack of investigative resources to trace overstays and other visa violators within the U.S. interior (interior immigrant enforcement is vast, but almost entirely uses other mechanisms for identification and removal), has meant that airports are not effectively used as a mechanism to trace and deport irregular migrants, or to bottle them inside the national territory; their sole—if important—enforcement role is that of initial exclusion.

Airports are also the locales often for initial requests for asylum. Persons intending to seek asylum may travel internationally with standard passports and visas. Some of them produce these documents directly at the point of entry, when asking for asylum, but others destroy the documents in transit. The logic is that lacking such documents makes it more difficult for the United States to return people to the country of persecution. Those people have become undocumented migrants in the control of the government. Whether with passports and travel documents or not, the U.S. government initially has a policy of holding asylum applicants in detention at the port, until they are released by an immigration court. The logic is that application for asylum indicates an intention of remaining in the country different from the original declared purpose of travel, but obviously this is a punitive response to seekers of asylum.

Airports have been the main route by which international terrorists have entered U.S. territory (in one case, entry was a port at the Canadian land border). It is important to emphasize that terrorists make up an infinitesimal proportion of travelers through airports. The 9/11 terrorists all had U.S. government-awarded visas or other legal entry documents, though some later overstayed their visas. No Salafi terrorists have crossed the Mexican land border (Salafi is the term for the political-religious ideology associated with Al Qaeda and similar organizations). Actual and potential terrorist travel routes rely on standard transportation and ports of entry, not the difficult routes across land or sea outside such ports. The key point is that homeland security policy applies most rationally to airports, rather than either the Mexican border as a whole or the non-port land border in particular. This puts into serious question the "homeland security" justification for southwestern border immigration enforcement, even though the Department of Homeland Security puts the majority of its personnel and resources on that border. It also removes from rational policy discussion the linkage of terrorism with Mexican and Central American undocumented migration.

Josiah McC. Heyman

See Also: Ports of Entry; Transportation in the U.S.; U.S. Department of Homeland Security

Further Reading

Heyman, Josiah McC., and Jason Ackleson. 2009. "United States Border Security after September 11." In *Border Security in the Al-Qaeda Era,* edited by John Winterdyck and Kelly Sundberg, 37–74. Boca Raton, FL: CRC Press.

Pew Hispanic Center. 2006. "Modes of Entry for the Unauthorized Migrant Population." http://pewhispanic.org/files/factsheets/19.pdf. Accessed July 12, 2010.

Salter, Mark B., ed. 2008. *Politics at the Airport.* Minneapolis: University of Minnesota Press.

American Civil Liberties Union (ACLU)

American Civil Liberties Union (ACLU) is an organization that has addressed many issues confronting undocumented immigrants in the United States. Its Immigrants' Rights Project is dedicated to expanding and enforcing the civil liberties and civil rights of immigrants and to combating public and private discrimination against them. For example, ACLU and other civil rights groups have filed lawsuits challenging anti-immigrant laws such as Arizona's SB 1070, passed in 2010. The legal teams at the ACLU have also challenged the practices used by the U.S. Immigration and Customs Enforcement with respect to the detention conditions at ICE facilities in Arizona, California, Nebraska, Rhode Island, and Texas. In 2013, the ACLU was very vocal in promoting a certain set of priorities when the Obama administration and the U.S. Congress began to take up the issue of immigration reform, when they began to voice

Roger Baldwin, the principal founder of the American Civil Liberties Union (ACLU) in 1920 visiting the U.S. Supreme Court in Washington, D.C. on January 20, 1970. Baldwin's tenure as director lasted for 30 years. (Bettmann/Corbis)

their opposition to plans for greater immigration enforcement because of its potential for aggravating discriminatory actions against immigrants.

Established in 1920, ACLU operates in various aspects of human rights and tackles the most problematic issues in American society including racism, homophobia, torture, right to personal privacy, ethnic and racial profiling, and religious tolerance. For almost nine decades, the American Civil Liberties Union has been working to ensure the protection of civil rights and liberties guaranteed by the Bill of Rights, and it aspires to assure the extension of those rights to newly emerging areas. ACLU's areas of operation cover the following problematic issues: capital punishment, prisoners' rights, drug law reform, right to free speech, racial justice, HIV/AIDS, religion and belief, right to reproductive choice, human rights, immigrants' rights, technology and liberty, LGBT rights, voting rights, national security, and women's rights.

American Civil Liberties Union is a non-profit organization. It does not receive funding from any government institutions. Financial resources that are necessary to run the organization are generated through membership payments, contributions, and grants provided by private institutions. Today, ACLU is one of the largest law firms that works for the public interest with its over five hundred thousand members and offices spanned across the U.S. territory. With headquarters in New York City, ACLU operates with one hundred staff attorneys and around two thousand volunteer attorneys in order to handle about six thousand court cases annually. ACLU is organized across the nation and has offices and affiliates in every U.S. state and Puerto Rico.

ACLU's main operations include filing lawsuits (especially the ones that will drive wide public attention and stimulate important policy changes in the end), lobbying for policy reforms in the U.S. Congress (through the ACLU legislative office in D.C.), educating the public about issues of civil right violations, preparing briefings and organizing campaigns. The campaign organized in the realm of immigration is titled "Keep America Safe and Free." The campaign targets unlawful government acts that emerged in the aftermath of the September 11 attacks. The campaign calls attention to government spying, ethnic and racial profiling, midnight raids, unlawful arrests, indefinite detentions as well as torture programs initiated by the Bush administration. The major message behind the campaign is that concerns for national security should not result in the violation of civil liberties and individual freedoms protected by the Constitution.

ACLU has a long history of working for the betterment of civil rights and protection of liberties. In 1920s, when the organization was first established, the major activity conducted by ACLU was to advocate political immigrants' right to free speech, and trade unionists' right to hold meetings and organize. Religious intolerance was also a priority issue for ACLU since early 1920s. It ardently supported religious tolerance through various court cases. In 1942, ACLU argued against the government policy that sent around 120,000 Japanese Americans to concentration camps in the aftermath of Pearl Harbor attacks. During the 1950s ACLU worked towards the termination of the racially segregated education system. The right to free speech became a significant concern where ACLU participated in its protection not only through court cases but also organizing public campaigns from 1960s onwards. Abortion, a highly controversial issue in the United States, did not escape from ACLU's attention and from 1970s onwards, ACLU started to support women's reproductive rights.

ACLU's span of interest and attention increased as new issues and debates surfaced in the United States The emergence of the Internet as a vehicle of communication drove ACLU's attention to the issue of free speech on the Internet in 1990s. From 2000 onward, ACLU's realms of operation expanded to include issues such as the equal treatment of gays and lesbians and the protection of their rights, the injustices that took place in the wake of the September 11 attacks, torture programs justified under war-against-terrorism policy and provision of national security, and the protection of personal privacy.

Committed to the ideal of "free speech for all," ACLU has been questioned for its support to controversial groups such as the American Nazis, the Ku Klux Klan and the Nation of Islam in the past. For each incidence, ACLU asserts that the reason why they supported these organizations is their belief in the right to free speech and the right to assembly of each and every person. According to ACLU, the rights of extremist or controversial groups are threatened if not violated more often than any other groups. In addition to that, ACLU perceives it is dangerous to allow the violation of rights and liberties of any organization, extremist or not, since it may pave the way for the transgressing of other people's rights and liberties. Once a government starts to violate rights and liberties, there is no way to guess where those violations would stop.

Among many other issues, ACLU operates in the realm of immigrants and immigrant rights. Their motto reads as "No Human Being Is Illegal." ACLU's Immigrants' Rights Project, established in 1987, aspires to expand the protection of rights and liberties of non-citizens living in the United States and to prevent their discrimination both in the public and private spheres. While the program was launched in the late 1980s,

ACLU's concern for immigrants dates back to the early 1920s when the government supported a policy which detained and deported immigrants due to their political views. ACLU not only provides legal support to immigrants but also conducts lobbying activities at the Capitol on issues pertaining to immigrant rights and liberties. It also provides assistance to groups and organizations working on the protection of immigrant rights. In addition to that, ACLU undertakes public education programs in order to raise awareness and increase knowledge levels on these issues.

ACLU indicates that the government has an indisputable authority to control U.S. borders and regulate immigration but it has to do it in a humane and lawful manner. Protecting immigrants' rights is crucial because of the following two reasons. First, as non-citizens, they constitute the most vulnerable group to government actions. Second, violation of immigrants' rights demonstrates the possibility of government trespassing of rights and liberties of other groups, in other words, the wider American public.

Zeynep Selen Artan

See Also: Advocacy; Detention Centers; Discrimination and Barriers; Exclusion; Immigration and Customs Enforcement (ICE); Obama Administration.

Further Reading

American Civil Liberties Union (ACLU). www.aclu.org.

American Friends Service Committee

The American Friends Service Committee (AFSC) is an affiliated organization of the Religious Society of Friends (Quaker), headquartered in Philadelphia, Pennsylvania. Founded in 1917, the AFSC draws on its religious principles of faith and nonviolence to address the root causes of poverty, injustice, and oppression. In 1947, the Nobel Peace Prize was awarded to, and accepted by, the AFSC and the British Friends Service Council for its efforts in opposing war, relieving the tensions that lead to war, and establishing programs of social and technical assistance in developing nations. Among the wide range of issues, countries, and communities that the AFSC is involved in, its work in immigrant and refugee rights in the United States emphasizes the need to respect and protect the human rights of the approximately 12 million undocumented immigrants in the United States by addressing the causes for migration, while ensuring the integration of the undocumented population in all facets of U.S. society.

Beliefs and Values

Reflective of the Quaker spiritual belief that the light of God is within each individual, the AFSC is guided in its actions to respect the worth and dignity of all. Drawing on the transforming power of human and divine love and its ability resolve conflict, the AFSC works with all communities in order to advance towards a society that recognizes the dignity of each person. As no group holds sole possession of the guidance and the power of the Spirit or the principles of truth, the AFSC collaborates with communities and individuals of many faiths and backgrounds, believing that the Spirit can move amongst the poor and the rich, or amongst the disenfranchised and the powerful, in order to make social change possible. In this fashion, hostility can be transformed into friendship, conflict into cooperation, poverty into well-being, and justice into dignity, thus turning the goodness in each individual into a force for reconciliation.

Through their work at the community level, the AFSC seeks to provide immediate aid and long-term development in partnership with those who suffer the conditions they seek to change, while also learning by their strength and vision. As such, they regard no person or group as their enemy. While they often oppose specific actions and abuses of power by specific individuals and/or groups, they seek to emphasize the goodness and truth existent in each individual. For the AFSC, it is only though seeking opportunities to reconcile enemies that a peaceful and just resolution of conflict can be achieved.

Current Activities

Recognizing that most conflicts have their roots in injustice, the AFSC has had a prolonged interest and concern with the elimination of injustice at home in the United States. As such, it has been involved with the Native American, Mexican American, African American, migrant worker, prisoner, and poor community, as well as war refugees and displaced persons, to obtain tangible reflections of human rights—better schools, better housing, and better working conditions.

Today, AFSC community organizers work with refugee and immigrant communities throughout the United States by directly supporting those communities to self-organize. The AFSC divides their immigrant rights program into sixteen geographic regions, each with their own exclusive conditions and demands. For example, in the state of Iowa, the AFSC has played a role in the organization of undocumented meat-packing workers; in Houston, it has collaborated with the Border Network for Human Rights to organize immigrant communities along the U.S.-Mexico border; and in Newark, New Jersey, the AFSC has chronicled how lives are impacted due to legislation enacted to criminalize the undocumented population. By working within this region-specific framework, the goal is to find and give voice to the populations' goals and needs, and to assist them in continuing to make contributions to the nation.

Project Voice

The AFSC has utilized human rights documentation to challenge systemic abuses by the U.S. Border Patrol and other government agencies, demonstrating how such documentation can be a powerful tool for confronting abuses in employment, housing, education, services, and law enforcement. In the same vein, it spearheaded the Project Voice initiative in order to strengthen the voices of immigrant-led organizations in setting the national agenda for policy and immigrants' rights. Project Voice combines local and national organizing, education, and outreach campaigns to foster a fuller integration of immigrants and refugees in their new communities, and to achieve a strategic impact on U.S. immigration policy.

Nationwide, AFSC organizers provide numerous services to immigrant communities including leadership development, legislative updates, policy analysis on relevant public sector initiatives or proposals, how-to workshops, information resources, and organizing assistance.

Through education and media outreach, Project Voice helps the U.S. general public understand the immigrant experience and how immigrants have enriched the nation's cultural, scientific, social, and economic landscape.

The Project strengthens its work and that of immigrant organizations by making connections with allies including labor unions, faith communities, and communities of color, educators, as well as social service agencies and community centers. Project Voice also brings together immigrant-led organizations with experienced policy analysts and advocates for public policy goals that are practical and attainable and directly responsive to the concerns of the community.

A New Path

In February 2009, the AFSC published "A New Path: Toward Humane Immigration Policy," a policy report in which it highlights the need to have the basis of current U.S. immigration policy be focused on the protection of human rights, rather than on the immigration system designed to supply labor to employers. For instance, of the approximately 12 million undocumented people residing in the United States, 8 to 10 million are workers in a variety of industries and services vital not solely to the U.S. economy, but also to the survival of their families both in the United States and in their countries of origin. According to the report, humane U.S. immigration policy must include a mechanism for undocumented workers to gain permanent resident status in a fair and orderly fashion. In addition, U.S. immigration policy must be tied with economic policies that encourage and fund sustainable development in countries abroad, permitting people to earn a living wage in their home countries. Immigration policy should also foster a commitment to U.S. demilitarization that would then lead to the peaceful resolution of internal and international conflicts.

David A. Caicedo

See Also: Activism; Advocacy; Community Concerns; Faith-Based Organizations; National Network for Immigrant and Refugee Rights (NNIRR); Tennessee Immigrant and Refugee Rights Coalition (TIRRC); Violence.

Further Reading

American Friends Service Committee. American Friends Service Committee: Quaker Values in Action Website. http://www.afsc.org.

Fager, Chuck, ed. 1988. *Quaker Service at the Crossroads: American Friends, the American Friends Service Committee, and Peace and Revolution.* Bellefonte, PA: Kimo Press.

Jones, Mary Hoxie. 1937. *Swords into Ploughshares: An Account of the American Friends Service Committee, 1917–1937.* New York: Macmillan.

Amnesty

In 2013 and amidst a renewed national debate about comprehensive immigration reform, the idea of amnesty for undocumented immigrants has resurfaced. In essence, amnesty is a type of "pardon." However, amnesty is not only an ambiguous term, but it has become politicized by nativists and politicians who have grown apprehensive over the growing "Hispanization" of America and thus favor greater restrictions on immigration (Waldinger, 2006). Those wishing to restrict immigration have maligned the word by reminding the American public how the amnesty that was provided by the Immigration Reform and Control Act of 1986 (IRCA) promoted greater immigration to the United States and not less. Signed into law by a conservative Republican President, Ronald Reagan, IRCA initially provided amnesty to nearly three million undocumented immigrants already living in the United States, a process that allowed them to become lawful permanent residents, and then citizens. The newly amnestied then proceeded to sponsor family members to join them—spouses, minor children, and unmarried adult children—in what would be one of the most significant demographic transformations of all time (Waldinger, 2006). Before the 1986 amnesty, Mexican nationals (the largest group among undocumented immigrants) who had been historically slow to become naturalized citizens felt that they had a stake in U.S. society and soon became citizens. Mexican nationals account for the greatest share of all undocumented immigrants, accounting for almost 60 percent of the unauthorized population. The newly amnestied began receiving their green cards in 1989, with some of the first becoming eligible for U.S. citizenship in 1994. Between 1992 and 1996 there was a surge of immigration due to family reunification (Orrenius and Zavodny 2012). With renewed efforts to achieve immigration reform during the Obama administration, there have been attempts to rebrand the word and concept of "amnesty," making it less toxic to the immigration reform dialogue (NPR, 2010). More neutral substitutions for the word that are synonymous in meaning and not yet marred in controversy are "legalization," or "path to citizenship."

There are pros and cons to implementing a legalization program where those living in the shadows are offered a process that will eventually lead to legal residency or citizenship. The economic benefits are that with more people adjusting their status, they are likely to earn more and pay into the U.S. tax system, resulting in a net economic gain for the nation (Griswold, 2005). This is an important consideration in light of the partisan debate over the nation's mounting budget deficit. Another benefit of a legalization program is that the nation would be infused with a more youthful population. In a speech given by the director of the Center for Trade Policy Studies at the Cato Institute—a conservative think tank, Daniel Griswold notes that immigrants provide a source of labor that will fill the growing gap left by an aging American workforce. Moreover, Griswold also points out that legalization of undocumented immigrants would enhance national security by bringing them out of the shadows and into the open, and thus freeing resources to devote to border security and the war on terrorism (Griswold, 2005). Economic and security concerns arguments aside, legalization would facilitate assimilation and integration into the nation's social fabric, a long-standing value in America's psyche, history, and development.

The down side is essentially for those whose profits depend on and are advantaged by having a poorly paid and disenfranchised workforce (Orrenius and Zavodny, 2012). Unauthorized immigrants typically tend to be near the bottom of the wage scale. Moreover, with greater restrictions for accessing educational resources and training, they have little hope of upward mobility. A study by Rivera-Batiz (1999) shows that legalization provides such populations with increased opportunities and earning potential. The Rivera-Batiz research examined the validity of this commonly accepted logic by measuring the impact of legalization on the earnings of previously undocumented Mexican immigrant workers. An examination of the earnings of 1.6 million undocumented workers who were eligible to become legal residents after IRCA shows that changes in earnings can be attributed to the benefits of legalization. Furthermore, greater leaps in earnings were achieved by women who had become legalized. This study included a longitudinal study that surveyed a large sample (1,103 individuals) of previously undocumented workers who worked in 1987–1988 and worked after becoming legalized residents with IRCA in 1992. Not surprisingly, the results showed that there was a significant rise in earnings after legalization.

Another important dimension that came with the amnesty was the freedom to move outside of traditional gateway cities and regions where undocumented immigrants were concentrated. Less fearful of arrest and deportation, newly legalized immigrants were able to move to other regions in the United States in search for better opportunities. These new opportunities led to increased prosperity for immigrants and their families, allowing them to achieve middle class status (Crowley, Lichter, and Qian, 2006). Before IRCA's amnesty, poultry and carpet industry employers in the American South could not attract enough laborers and had been actively recruiting Latino immigrants, to the extent of placing job announcements in Mexican and Central American newspapers. However, after amnesty, and subsequent "chain migration" (whereby people from the same areas of foreign countries or from the same families tend to come after the first emigrants from the area have gone to the United States), southern states found themselves as the preferred destinations for an unprecedented numbers of newcomers (Levine and Lenbaron, 2011).

Anna Ochoa O'Leary

See Also: Counterfeit Documents; Economics; Gateways; Immigration Reform and Control Act of 1986 (IRCA); Shadow Population; Southern States.

Further Reading

Crowley, Martha, Daniel T. Lichter, and Zhenchao Qian. 2006. "Beyond Gateway Cities: Economic Restructuring and Poverty Among Mexican Immigrant Families and Children." *Family Relations* 55:345–360.

Griswald, Daniel. 2005. Mexican Migration, Legalization, and Assimilation. http://www.cato.org/publications/speeches/mexican-migration-legalization-assimilation.

Levine, Elaine, and Alana Lenbaron. 2011. "Immigration Policy in the Southeastern United States: Potential for Internal Conflict." *Norteamérica: Revista Académica del CISAN-UNAM.* Special Issue, 5–31.

NPR (National Public Radio). 2010. "A Reagan Legacy: Amnesty For Illegal Immigrants." July 4, 2010. Available at http://www.npr.org/templates/story/story.php?storyId=128303672.

Orrenius, Pia M., and Madeline Zavodny. 2012. "The Economic Consequences of Amnesty for Unauthorized Immigrants." *CATO Journal* 32.1:85–106.

Rivera-Batiz, F. L. 1999. "Undocumented Workers in the Labor Market: An Analysis of the Earnings of Legal and Illegal Mexican Immigrants in the United States." *Journal of Population Economics* 12.1:91–117.

Waldinger, Roger. 2006. "Immigration Reform Too Hot to Handle." *New Labor Forum* (Routledge) 15.2:20–29.

Amnesty International

Amnesty International is an international non-profit-seeking organization pursuing human rights advocacy all around the world. The major objective of Amnesty International is to bring human rights abuses taking place across the globe under the spotlight and conduct campaigns for the betterment of the situations. In the United States, this organization has actively campaigned to pressure the U.S. government to make sure that its laws, policies and practices do not place immigrants at greater risk of human rights

Some of several hundred demonstrators with Amnesty International, convened for the organization's annual conference, chant during a rally in Boston, Friday, March 27, 2009, protesting the treatment of immigrants detained without a judicial hearing. (AP Photo/Josh Reynolds)

abuses. In 2011, Amnesty International released a report, "Hostile Terrain: Human Rights Violation in Immigration Enforcement in the U.S. Southwest." The report accuses the United States of failing in its obligations under international human rights law to ensure the rights of immigrants. Some of the findings of this report place blame on the collaboration between federal, state, and local law enforcement for increased racial profiling. The report also points out that immigrant communities already face a range of barriers to justice as victims of human trafficking, domestic violence, or hate crimes. The report also finds that the contemporary immigration enforcement measures along the border have impacted the rights of indigenous communities, whose traditional lands lie on both sides of the U.S.-Mexico border.

Established in 1961, Amnesty International has contributed to the field of human rights through organizing various campaigns and awareness-raising activities, lobbying for public policy change and issuing of a number of reports on cases of human rights breaches.

In 1961, a British lawyer Peter Benenson published an article titled "The Forgotton Prisoners" in *The Observer* newspaper in England. The article points out the issue of political prisoners, in other words, people who are arrested and imprisoned because of their political opinions. The article was the initial step of a worldwide campaign—"Appeal for Amnesty 1961"—advocating either release or fair trial of certain political prisoners (including Constantin Noica, Ashton Jones, Agostino Neto, Archbishop Josef Beran, Toni Ambatielos, and Cardinal Mindszenty) held in prisons across different parts of the world. The campaign was accompanied by the opening of a small office by volunteers in Benenson's court chambers in London. A year later, at a meeting in Belgium, a decision was made to establish a permanent organization that would be known as Amnesty International.

While the organization's main focus was on political prisoners, prison conditions and torture during the period between the 1960s and early 1990s, human rights of refugees came to be regarded as a significant field of activity in the second half of the 1990s. Following a council meeting in 1999, Amnesty International decided to incorporate issues including empowerment of human rights defenders, advocating against impunity, rights of refugees, women's rights and enhancing grassroot activism into its areas of concern. From 2000 onward, issues such as arms trade, children's rights, counter-terrorism measures, the death penalty, LGBT rights, poverty, as well as refugees and migrants are all included in Amnesty International's agenda.

Amnesty International has published a number of reports regarding human rights violations since its establishment. The first report was on prison conditions in three countries: Portugal, South Africa and Romania, which was issued in 1965. Almost twenty years later, in 1987, the organization published a report stating that the death penalty in the United States is racially biased and arbitrary. In 1989, *When the State Kills,* a report on the death penalty, was issued. Amnesty International published *Cruel. Inhuman. Degrades Us All – Stop Torture and Ill-treatment in the "War on Terror"* in 2005. A year later, in 2006, *Partners in Crime: Europe's Role in US Renditions* came out.

Conducting campaigns to direct people's attention to human rights violations is part of the activities of Amnesty International. Some of the campaigns organized by Amnesty International include Monthly Postcards to Prisoners Campaign (1965),

Worldwide Campaign for the Abolition of Torture, which brought about a UN Resolution (1972), Campaign Against Torture (1984), Stop the Torture Trade Campaign (1995), Campaign for a permanent International Criminal Court (1996), Campaign for human rights of refugees (1997), Campaign Get Up, Sign Up! (1998) conducted in order to mark the 50th anniversary of the Universal Declaration of Human Rights, the Campaign to Control Arms, organized together with Oxfam and International Action Network on Small Arms (2003), and Stop Violence Against Women Campaign (2004).

Amnesty International played a significant role in the adoption of various international policies and regulations. One of them is: Resolution Denouncing Torture—UN Resolution 3059 in 1973. In 1977, Amnesty International received the Nobel Peace Prize for its meaningful contribution to peace and its defense of human rights. In 1978, Amnesty International received the United Nations Human Rights prize for their activities in the field of human rights.

Among other issues, Amnesty International conducts activities regarding immigrants, refugees and internally displaced people. Amnesty International organizes international campaigns in order to raise awareness of the breaches and failures regarding human rights of people who have left their homelands in search of a new, secure shelter. In addition to that, activists lobby in their respective countries in order to devise new policies that would prevent further violations and mistreatment. Amnesty International also warns governments about the dangers of returning asylum seekers who would face persecution in their home country. Regarding internally displaced people, Amnesty International opposes any forced relocation of people based on their ethnicity, race, religion, sex or language.

Zeynep Selen Artan

See Also: Advocacy; American Civil Liberties Union; Asylum; Detention Centers; Displacement; Hate Crimes; Human Rights Watch; Human Trafficking; Migration.

Further Reading

Amnesty International, www.amnesty.org.

Arizona

Beginning in 2004 Arizona led other state efforts to implement harsh, anti-immigrant legislation. Especially well known is SB1070, signed into law in 2010, which at the time allowed law enforcement officers to require documentation for anyone stopped for a legal violation and led to other states passing similar laws.

In 2004, Proposition 200 (Arizona Taxpayer and Citizen's Protection Act), commonly referred to as "Prop 200," evolved from unsubstantiated accusations that immigrants were fraudulently subverting the electoral system and amended the state's laws by requiring proof of citizenship to register to vote. With Prop 200, Arizona became one of over twenty states in the nation that have since passed restrictive voter identification laws. Although there is no evidence to date that Prop 200 was effective in halting electoral fraud, other provisions contained in the measure made it a requirement of agencies administering state and local public benefits, under penalty of law, to verify applicants' immigration status through the alien verification system administered by the U.S. Department of Homeland Security (DHS) and to report to federal authorities those applicants for public benefits whose legal status makes them ineligible.

The Mexican American Legal Defense and Education Fund subsequently filed a complaint against the law on behalf of a number of plaintiffs, contending that it preempted federal law, which governs matters of immigration. Arguments focused on the law's restrictions to "public benefits," regarding certain state-supported entitlement programs. Among these were domestic violence services, elder abuse prevention, and other services for the elderly. The plaintiffs also argued that the law's unclear language could result in the denying benefits to legal resident immigrants eligible under federal law. It was also argued that eligible children might not receive public benefits because their undocumented parents would be afraid to apply, or be denied services altogether, resulting in a "chilling effect" that would discourage many from applying for and using social services. Although the law was ultimately upheld, it is important to consider that while many immigrant families may indeed be entitled to public services, there is also considerable probability that because of their mixed-status composition, among them is a family member who is not. Therefore, to avoid additional scrutiny, even those who are eligible for public services may hesitate to participate in entitlement programs.

Anti-immigrant laws that were passed in 2005 included HB 2259, which made it an aggravating factor for sentencing to be in violation of federal immigration laws, the "Anti-Coyote Law" (HB 2539/SB 1372) that prescribed penalties for those caught smuggling immigrants, and the work center prohibition law (HB 2592) that prohibits a city, town or county from constructing and maintaining day labor centers "if any part of the center is to facilitate the knowing employment of an alien who is not entitled to lawful residence in the U.S." These bills served to further frame the immigration phenomenon as a "problem" and fostered attitudes that associated immigrants with crime.

Other bills were introduced and although they failed to pass in 2005, revised versions were reconsidered in subsequent legislative sessions, and then passed. One of these (HB 2030—"Public Programs, Citizenship") exploited common misconceptions of immigrants as welfare-seeking intruders by requiring employees of the Department of Economic Security (DES) to verify an applicant's immigration status with the DHS's Secure America with Verification and Enforcement (SAVE) program before providing services. This law affected family literacy and adult education programs as well as Arizona's public health program programs because of the perception that largely undocumented immigrants were taking English classes. Also affected was Arizona's health care program for low-income families, the Arizona Health Care Costs Containment System (AHCCCS).

Senate Bill 1167 (English as Official Language) was introduced in 2005, vetoed by Governor Janet Napolitano, only to be reintroduced and passed a year later. Like its 1988 predecessor, Arizona's "English Only" law, SB1167 requires all official actions to be conducted in English, but now protects residents or businesses from civil action arising from any injury that is caused from not being able to comply with the English Only law.

About thirty-seven immigration-related bills flooded the second regular session of the 47th Arizona State Legislature in the spring of 2006. These were but a fraction of the over five hundred anti-immigrant state bills that were introduced the same year across the United States, many of which replicate established federal immigration enforcement responsibilities. Among these was HB 2448, "AHCCCS eligibility for services," which amended ARS 36–2903.03 related to AHCCCS. This law replicated provisions already contained in the federal 1996 Personal Responsibility and Work Opportunity Reconciliation Act (PRWORA), which among other things, puts a five-year ban on eligibility for federally funded public benefits programs for recent legal immigrants. Another notable law was "Prop 300," which requires students to prove legal residency status to qualify for in-state tuition rates or to apply for state financial aid for education at public colleges and universities. Prop 300 does not consider how these restrictions will impact students who have resided in the United States for most of their lives and have completed most if not all of their schooling in the United States. Also, in a little known provision in Prop 300, the eligibility for childcare assistance to parents became restricted by prohibiting guardians and caregivers who are not citizens or legal residents of the United States from receiving child care assistance from DES.

An unsuccessful proposal in 2006, related to workers' rights, sought to amend ARS 23–901 to exclude "… any person who is not a citizen or national of the United States and who is unlawfully present or unlawfully residing in the United States." Arizona employment statutes currently do not make distinctions between workers' legal status, and this prevents undocumented immigrants from engaging in the legal process for bringing charges against unscrupulous employers who violate labor laws and from filing claims for wage theft with the state's Wage and Hour Division of the Department of Labor.

A year later (in 2007), the number of bills dealing with immigrants nationwide tripled to 1,562. In Arizona, the Legal Arizona Workers Act, commonly known as "the employers' sanctions law," was passed. The law targets businesses that "intentionally" or "knowingly" employ immigrants without proper employment visas. Again, it largely replicates provisions found in the 1996 PRWORA. Under the Arizona law, *any* public or private employer who employs unauthorized workers can have their business licenses suspended for up to ten days. A second offense could lead to a revocation of the license. The new law also requires that all employers in Arizona check the employment eligibility of those hired after January 1, 2008, through E-Verify, which is an online federal database through which employers can check an individual's eligibility to work in the United States. Use of the E-Verify system by employers is voluntary under federal law but under the new Arizona law, participation is mandatory.

In September 2008, the employers' sanctions act was unsuccessfully challenged in the Ninth Circuit Court of Appeals where a three-judge panel rejected claims that the law infringed on the rights of the federal government to control immigration by requiring employers to check the immigration status of all new workers through E-Verify. The judges defended the law by pointing out that federal law reserves the power of states to decide a company's "fitness to do business" based on its hiring practices. At the time of the ruling, no Arizona employer had been charged with violating the law.

A year after the law's implementation, the law had been largely unused, and only 5.6 percent of the total firms in the state had signed up to use E-Verify.

Arizona's anti-immigrant stance drew national attention in 2010 with the introduction of the Senate Bill, "Support Our Law Enforcement and Safe Neighborhoods," more commonly referred to as SB 1070. On April 23 of that year, Arizona Governor Jan Brewer signed into law what was at the time the harshest anti-immigrant bill in the nation. Eleven states followed suit shortly after with their own versions of the law, with proposals passing in Alabama, Georgia, Indiana, South Carolina and Utah. Arizona's SB 1070, also commonly referred to as the "Papers Please" law, or the "Show me your papers" law made it a requirement for enforcement officials to ask of those that they reasonably suspected of being in the country without authorization for proof of being in the country legally, if such individuals were detained for any other violation. Critics of the law argued that the law would embolden racial profiling and violation of civil rights. There were other provisions in the proposed law, among them making it a crime to provide shelter or assistance to undocumented immigrants. The law was ultimately challenged in *Valle del Sol v. Whiting et al,* and the U.S. Supreme Court decision struck down some of the provisions while upholding the harshest provision requiring police to determine the immigration status of someone detained if they have "reasonable suspicion" that they are undocumented.

In 2012, Arizona again made national headlines when its governor, Jan Brewer, signed an executive order to deny driver's licenses and other public benefits to young undocumented immigrants who obtain work authorizations under the Obama administration policy, Deferred Action for Children Arrivals (DACA). The governor defended her order by saying that the Obama policy did not confer lawful status on undocumented immigrants, and therefore they are still ineligible for Arizona public benefits, and a driver's license thus might result in some of those in the state without authorization obtaining access to public benefits. Similar to what happened with SB 1070, the state's executive order regarding licenses for those eligible under DACA is being challenged in the courts as of this writing.

Anna Ochoa O'Leary

See Also: Arizona SB 1070; Barriers to Health; Deferred Action for Children Arrivals (DACA); Education; Employment Visas; Mixed-Status Families; Personal Responsibility and Work Opportunity Reconciliation Act (PRWORA); Policies of Attrition; Welfare System; Workers' Rights.

Further Reading

Gans, Judith. 2008. "Arizona's Economy and the Legal Arizona Workers Act." Tucson, Arizona: Udall Center Immigration Policy Program Report. Available at http://udall-center.arizona.edu/immigration/index.php.

Harnet, Helen M. 2008. "State and Local Anti-Immigrant Initiatives: Can They Withstand Legal Scrutiny?" *Widener Law Journal* 17:365–382.

Kilty, Keith M., and Maria Vidal de Haymes. 2000. "Racism, Nativism, and Exclusion: Public Policy, Immigration and the Latino Experience in the United States." *Journal of Poverty* 4.1/2:1–25.

Levitts, Justin. 2007. "The Truth about Voter Fraud." Brennan Center for Justice at New York University School of Law. Available on line at: http://www.immigrationpolicy.org/index.php?content=fc080724.

O'Leary, Anna Ochoa. 2009. "Arizona's Legislative-Imposed Injunctions: Implications for Immigrant Civic and Political Participation." Washington, DC: Mexico Institute at the Wilson Center. Available on-line: www.wilsoncenter.org.

Santa Ana, Otto, and Celeste González de Bustamante, eds. 2012. *Arizona Firestorm: Global Immigration Realities, National Media and Provincial Politics.* New York: Rowman and Littlefield Publishers, Inc.

Arizona SB 1070

Protesters hold up signs protesting Arizona's immigration bill. The passage of Arizona's SB 1070 calls for police in that state to use reasonable suspicion to ask for proof of legal status of those detained for violating any other law. The law sparked protests throughout the nation, and a call for a national boycott resulted in hundreds of cancellations by conference organizers. (Daniel Raustadt/Dreamstime.com)

On April 23, 2010, Arizona governor Jan Brewer signed into law Arizona Senate Bill 1070, the Support Our Law Enforcement and Safe Neighborhoods Act. Popularly known as SB 1070 or the "Papers Please" law, the act provided for broader policing of illegal immigration by state and local law enforcement officials in Arizona. It also ignited a national firestorm of controversy in the wake of its passage. Just three years before, in 2007, the Prince William County, Virginia, board of supervisors had passed what many consider to be a precursor of Arizona's SB 1070 (Cleaveland, 2013). This anti-immigrant ordinance had directed police officers to inquire about the immigration status of those who had been detained for any other violation. This measure backfired in Prince William County when Latino residents fled the county, straining the county's economic base. Restaurants and other businesses closed. Homes were abandoned. Two lawsuits challenging the law and the costs of litigation began to strain the county's limited resources. Residents became divided amidst the fiscal and political turmoil. Compounded by the effects of the nation-wide construction industry downturn and mortgage crisis, Prince William County was forced to rescind the parts of the ordinance that required checking the papers of those detained. Lessons learned notwithstanding, Arizona's SB 1070 became widely regarded as the harshest anti-immigrant measure in the nation. However, subsequent "copycat" laws in other states, such as Alabama and South Carolina, would eventually surpass it in terms of punitive provisions.

It is important to understand the historical context that elevated Arizona into the national limelight. Scholars have pointed out that Arizona's history is one peppered by instances of racial oppression and discrimination. Shortly after admission into the union in 1914, a law designed to protect the "native born" from competition with other workers was passed. In 1934, Arizona passed a law prohibiting Asians from owning land. In the 1960s Arizona led some of the earliest efforts to deny public benefits to noncitizens, even though they were lawful residents. This law was invalidated by a U.S. Supreme Court ruling in 1971. Following party lines and before being appointed head of the U.S. Department of Homeland Security by President Obama, Arizona governor Janet Napolitano, a Democrat, prevented a number of measures coming from the state legislature from becoming laws. In 2005, she vetoed a law that would allow local officers to make arrests for federal immigration violations. In 2006, she vetoed two laws that would have made it a crime to be in the United States without documentation. In 2008, she also resisted a law that would have obligated local agencies to cooperate with federal authorities to enforce immigration. These laws came to be incorporated into SB 1070 after Janet Napolitano left the state for her new post as director of the U.S. Department of Homeland Security with the Obama administration, and after Republican Jan Brewer assumed the office.

SB 1070 attracted national attention because it was an attempt to create several new state crimes related to immigration. Although many of these were existing crimes according to federal laws, penalties for violation of the federal provisions were different, with the state penalties proposed by the state being more punitive. These new crimes were:

- Failure to complete or carry an alien registration document
- Impeding traffic while being hired to work
- Applying for work if the applicant is an undocumented immigrant
- Soliciting work in a public place
- Actual performance of work if the worker is an undocumented immigrant
- Impeding traffic to hire an individual for work
- Transporting, moving, harboring, or concealing noncitizens
- Encouraging or furthering the entry of noncitizens into Arizona

At the heart of the controversy were new provisions and greater policing powers, such as

- Allowing officers to arrest someone without a warrant, based on probable cause that the individual "has committed any public offense that makes the person removable from the United States."
- Requiring law enforcement to take reasonable steps to investigate immigration status, when a person has been lawfully stopped, detained, or arrested, and if there is

reasonable suspicion that the individual is an undocumented noncitizen, unless it is impracticable to do so.

• Requiring that law enforcement officers verify, by checking federal government databases, the immigration status of every arrested person.

There was significant public outcry against SB 1070 once it passed, particularly by advocacy groups concerned about how the law would embolden authorities and encourage racial profiling of Latinos. A boycott of Arizona was organized by various groups in an effort to bring attention to the issue and in this way bring public pressure to bear on political actors responsible for the law. In an unusual move, the Mexican government urged the courts to declare the law unconstitutional. Later in 2010, there was further evidence of how the law strained U.S.-Mexico relations when all six Mexican border governors refused to attend the 28th annual conference of border governors scheduled to be hosted by Arizona in Phoenix. The controversy followed political party lines when Democratic Governor Bill Richardson re-convened the meeting in his state of New Mexico, and all of the Republican governors stayed away. The controversy over SB 1070 also entered more local politics with major U.S. cities like Los Angeles and San Francisco adopting resolutions and issuing proclamations denouncing the law, and ending their contracts with Arizona-based firms. This strategy had in the past worked to pressure Arizona politicians when the governor and some legislators of the state had refused to recognize Martin Luther King Day after it was declared a holiday by the U.S. Congress in 1983. In this controversy, the National Football League boycotted the state by relocating Super Bowl XXVII from the Sun Devil Stadium in Tempe, Arizona to the Rose Bowl in Pasadena, California.

In response to SB 1070, various civil rights groups, the American Civil Liberties Union (ACLU), the National Association for the Advancement of Colored People (NAACP), and the Mexican American Legal Defense and Educational Fund (MALDEF), joined the U.S. Department of Justice in filing legal challenges to the law. Artists and musicians also responded with creative works and in social media and refused to perform in Arizona. Dozens of musicians, including Nine Inch Nails, Kanye West, Sonic Youth, Rage against the Machine and others boycotted Arizona. Kaftan (2013) reveals that this period of intense controversy gave life to different forms of contestation and expression, with a predominance of symbols and cultural themes emerging as new opportunities to examine national identity. Raul Antonio y Mexia, son of Hernan Hernandez of the renowned norteño group, Los Tigres del Norte, wrote "Somos Arizona." Poets Responding to SB 1070 and Artists against SB 1070 emerged. On the day that the law was scheduled to go into effect, protesters amassed in an act of civil disobedience to block a street near city hall in Phoenix, Arizona.

On July 6, 2010 after U.S. District Judge Susan Bolton issued an injunction in response to legal challenges, Governor Brewer threatened with an appeal. On July 28, 2010, a day before SB 1070 was scheduled to go into effect, U.S. district Judge Susan Bolton temporarily blocked key parts of the new law, including a provision that would require police to check a person's citizenship or immigration status at the time of a traffic stop, detention, arrest, or other police action if there was reasonable suspicion that the person was not a U.S. citizen or legal immigrant. Judge Bolton based her reasoning on the claim that the Arizona law conflicted with and usurped existing federal laws regulating immigration. Judge Bolton also put on hold a component that would make it a state crime for an immigrant to ask for work. The law also included several other controversial provisions such as the one that would make it a crime for anyone to harbor or transport anyone who was in the country without proper authorization. However, the part of the law that provoked the most controversy was the provision that obligated police to request papers that would prove legal presence. Failure to do so could be grounds for legal action against the policing agency. As with Prince William County, police officials argued that this provision would be virtually impossible to enforce, given their agency's limited budget. Other critics argued that this provision would potentially lead to unconstitutional infringement of the civil rights of many U.S. citizens. Supporters of SB 1070 maintained that because the federal government had failed to enforce federal immigration laws, states were obligated to address the economic and public safety of citizens.

Bolton's injunction was upheld by the Ninth Circuit Court of Appeals in April 2011, leading the state of Arizona to file an appeal with the U.S. Supreme Court with *Chamber of Commerce of the United States of America et al. v. Whiting et al.* On June 25, 2012, the U.S. Supreme Court struck down several of the contested provisions that were inconsistent with federal immigration laws, but kept in place Section 2(B), the most contentious provision of SB 1070, which obligated law enforcement officials to check the documentation of anyone who was detained for violation of any other law including traffic violations, if they had a "reasonable suspicion" that the person was in the country illegally. This is the so-called "Show me your papers" part of the law.

In sum, the portions of the proposed law that were struck down by the Supreme Court in 2012 were:

- Forbidding the release of anyone who is arrested pending the determination of their immigration status
- Requiring those in the country unlawfully to carry with them an "alien registration document
- Making it a crime for those who are unlawfully present to apply for work, seek work in a public place, or work as an employee or independent contractor in Arizona.

In addition, on October 9, the 9th Circuit Court of Appeals negated another part of SB 1070 that would bring criminal charges against those who knowingly transport or harbor someone in the country who is present unlawfully. This portion of the law, if allowed to be enforced, would have potentially brought criminal charges against those (such as parents and guardians) who transport and provide homes to young people who may be eligible for relief from deportation under the Deferred Action for Children Arrivals (DACA).

At the time the law was enacted in 2010, Arizona's SB 1070 reenergized the national debate over immigration and drew attention to a larger movement taking place in many states to expand their reach for combating illegal immigration and challenging the doctrine of federal preemption in such matters. Moreover, the laws that were considered in state legislatures came to reflect a growing partisan rift that has increasingly come to characterize fundamental difference between Republicans and Democrats and political approaches to immigration reform and immigrants in general. Many political analysts acknowledge that Republicans' support of the move towards harsher measures to regulate immigration raised the ire of Latino voters, resulting in an overwhelming 71 percent of them voting for the re-election of Barack Obama in 2012.

Anna Ochoa O'Leary

See Also: Arizona; Employer Sanctions; Exclusion; Policies of Attrition; Racial Profiling; Shadow Population; Southern States; State Legislation.

Further Reading

Arrocha, William. 2010/2011. "Arizona's Senate Bill 1070: Targeting the Other and Generating Discourses and Practices of Discrimination and Hate." *Journal of Hate Studies* 9.1:65–92.

Chin, Gabriel J., Carissa Byrne Hessick, and Marc L. Miller, 2012. "Arizona Senate Bill 1070: Politics through Immigration Law." In *Arizona Firestorm: Global Immigration Realities, National Media & Provincial Politics,* edited by Otto Santa Ana & Celeste González de Bustamante. Lanham, MD: Rowman & Littlefield.

Cleaveland, Carol L. 2013. "'I Stepped over a Dead Body …': Latina Immigrant Narratives of Immigration and Poverty." *Journal of Human Behavior in the Social Environment.* 23.1:1–13.

Heyman, Josiah McC. 2010. "Human Rights and Social Justice Briefing 1: Arizona Immigration Law SB 1070." Society for Applied Anthropology. Available at http://www.sfaa .net/committees/humanrights/AZImmigrationLawSB1070.pdf.

Kaftan, Joanna. 2013. "National Identity during Periods of Controversy: Celebrating Cinco de Mayo in Phoenix, Arizona." *Nations & Nationalism* 19.1:167–186.

Lopez, Tomas. 2011. "Left Back: The Impact of SB 1070 on Arizona's Youth." University of Arizona. Available at http://www.law.arizona.edu/depts/bacon_program/pdf/Left _Back.pdf.

United States Court of Appeals for the Ninth Circuit. 2010. Amicus Brief 2010. http://www .volokh.com/wp-content/uploads/2010/10/mexicoamicusbrief.pdf.

Assimilation

Assimilation in relation to migration can be loosely defined as the process by which people of a different background come to see themselves as a part of a larger national family. The process of assimilation includes economic and socio-cultural factors. As immigrants become more established in the United States, they are more likely to become more financially stable, allowing them to adapt—or acculturate—to their adopted community, and through this process they acquire what they need to blend into the larger society. This process may take years or more than one generation. Socio-cultural factors, such as learning English and behaving within what is considered the norm of the destination community, also allows immigrants to blend in. Assimilation is often viewed as a negative outcome of the homogenization of different cultures within the dominant national society, because languages and dialects risk being lost as are different customs, beliefs and knowledge that make for and enrich a multicultural environment.

Mixed-status Latino families (families containing at least one undocumented member) do not follow the same assimilation patterns to United States culture as did immigrants to the country dating back to the 1920s, and as recent as the late 1980s and early 1990s. Today's immigrants are subject to a more intense degree of racial profiling and marginalization in the United States which often prohibits normal trends of assimilation. Recent laws enacted and proposed that have the goal of excluding undocumented immigrants from their full integration into the social fabric of the United States have been blamed for disrupting the many paths towards assimilation. In this way, the power of the state has mounted challenges to assimilating, resulting in the permanent or quasi permanent stigma of illegality of those that are unlawfully present in the United States, as well as those who belong to immigrant families even though they may be U.S. citizens. For example, practices such as workplace raids by immigration enforcement agents may result in intimidating and stigmatizing entire mixed-status families. These practices have significant negative consequences on the ability of migrants to integrate themselves and their families politically, culturally, and socially into their communities. Ultimately, the basis for migrant identity, race, class, ethnicity, and gender is being defined by U.S. immigration policy and law enforcement practices. The new forms of racial profiling and discrimination experienced by immigrants (primarily Latino) in the United States significantly challenge theories of immigrant assimilation and pose challenges to assimilation not only for undocumented immigrants, but likewise for immigrants here legally and their children.

Most of the challenges in relation to immigrant assimilation can be linked to immigration policy and law after September 11, 2001 which has been radically reshaped by anti-terrorism policies. Post 9/11 immigration policy has rarely been created without an anti-terrorism policy in mind. As the management of immigration laws and policies in the United States moved from the Department of Labor to the U.S. Department of Homeland Security a strong merger between immigration and terrorism policy was formed. This merger promotes the idea that immigrants are to be seen first as "suspects" and only after passing the suspect stage can they be seen as "welcomed newcomers." Even though the Equal Protection Clause of the Fourteenth Amendment of the United States Constitution prohibits states from discrimination regardless of citizenship status, in recent years there have been many cases of direct discrimination in the United States by states such as Arizona against particular ethnic groups and communities. The discrimination seen in recent years is not equally experienced by citizens and noncitizens nor is it experienced equally between different ethnic groups. This can be seen as going against the Equal Protection Clause of the Fourteenth Amendment and, furthermore, significantly affecting immigrants' ability to assimilate to the culture and society of the United States.

The joining of terrorism and immigration policy also allows state governments to legitimize policies of attrition when attempting to reduce illegal immigration. Policies of attrition can be defined as those measures which intend to increase the probability that immigrants will return to their country of origin without the cost of government intervention, and forcible removal. The Center for Immigration Studies (CIS) further defines attrition strategies as including the following: mandatory workplace verification of immigration status, measures to curb misuse of Social Security and U.S. Internal Revenue tax identification numbers; partnerships with state and local law enforcement officials; increased non-criminal removals; and state and local laws to discourage illegal settlement. The highly discriminatory nature of attrition strategies is evident in events such as the 1997 Chandler Raids and laws such as SB1070 in Arizona. In both cases mixed-status Latino familie were deeply impacted.

The creation of the War on Drugs also impacts a migrant's opportunity to assimilate. This campaign further blurs the distinction between the act of entering the United States without documentation and a person committing a crime. Regardless of status, Latino immigrants are now viewed as part of a group of dangerous foreigners related to narco trafficking and not as people who come to the United States to work and contribute in a positive way to U.S. society. Today the degree of a person's "Mexicanness" can place one at risk when going about daily activities and interacting with law enforcement.

As a result, children in mixed-status families are also negatively affected by being socialized by law enforcement officers. Children may experience a form of imperialist treatment when they feel they must disassociate from the cultures of their parents and say they are only American to avoid being stigmatized. In addition, children may question their right to walk with an undocumented grandparent to the store, they may witness police treating their father as a criminal, and they may be afraid of knocking sounds on their door at home. Many children ultimately witness their parents' inability to protect them from the police, and instead of seeing the police as a source of security the children label them as a danger. It is clear that by simply not fitting the norms established by the host society and being seen as a threat to national security, mixed-status households will always have their citizenship questioned and will not be able to participate in society as freely as other racial groups.

There is a certain degree of coercion enforced by the state that defines parameters that immigrants can live within. To be more specific, Latinos residing in certain neighborhoods may feel restricted in terms of where they can shop, how they dress, how they speak, and also in terms of inter-familiar relations. This level of state coercion is increasingly moving from the federal level to the local level. Therefore, the surveillance of immigrants has become not only the job of immigration officials, but is now the job of local police, state officials, possibly public education administrators, housing managers, welfare administrators, and also private citizens in the way of employer verification of work authorization.

In certain communities it is evident that even more examples of local surveillance of illegality exist; college admissions, financial aid officers, and social services sometimes use immigration status as a qualifying factor in applying for aid. Citizens untrained in law enforcement are doing police work for the federal government and are at the same time upholding the idea of migrant illegality as a normal component of our society. The creation of a social space of illegality creates a space of exclusion, subjugation, and forced invisibility which surrounds the undocumented in every aspect of daily life.

It is clear that undocumented immigrants and members of mixed-status households are not able to follow historical patterns of assimilation. The space of illegality that has been created by immigration laws has created strict parameters restricting the daily freedoms of migrants. Understanding both the way in which the state is able to locate and control undocumented immigrants and use them as a source of cheap labor is crucial for future studies on the changing processes of immigrant assimilation. Likewise, this understanding is crucial to uncovering the seemingly invisible forces that control and restrict members of mixed-status households and stifle the assimilation process.

There is a need for research explaining an impeded assimilation, meaning immigrants are blocked from a healthy assimilation process by federal and state government actions. Impeded assimilation can be seen as a direct effect of state-sponsored attrition strategies and significantly aids in creating a new underclass in the United States. A large part of creating this underclass is the label of "illegality" put on undocumented immigrants. These actions are not only discriminatory in nature, but also violate the value of immigration to the development of the United States.

The implications of second-class citizenship for Latino immigrants are grave and must be considered not only in future research, but also by policy makers. The creation of a new Latino underclass which provides cheap labor to fuel capitalist interests in the United States is unacceptable as it also implies grave violations of the Equal Protection Clause of the Fourteenth Amendment where the state is blatantly discriminating more against non-citizens than citizens. The future of thousands of U.S.-born children is at stake when considering immigration and attrition policies. Policies of attrition and state-impeded assimilation not only affect immigrants, but also affect U.S. citizens who are a part of a mixed-status family or reflect the genetic traits shared with those deemed unworthy of citizenship. The consequences of attrition policies and impeded assimilation are a daily reality for thousands of immigrants and U.S. citizens residing in our cities and communities.

Christopher B. Yutzy

See Also: Acculturation; Arizona SB 1070; Citizenship; Discrimination and Barriers; Exclusion; Fourteenth Amendment; Mixed-Status Families; Policies of Attrition.

Further Reading

O'Leary, Anna Ochoa, and Azucena Sanchez. 2011. "Anti-Immigrant Arizona: Ripple Effects and Mixed Immigration Status Households under 'Policies of Attrition' Considered." *Journal of Borderlands Studies* 26.1:115–133.

Romero, M. 2008. "The Inclusion of Citizenship Status in Intersectionality: What Immigration Raids Tells Us About Mixed-Status Families, the State, and Assimilation." *International Journal of Sociology of the Family* 34.2.

Tumlin, K. C. 2004. "Suspect First: How Terrorism Policy Is Reshaping Immigration Policy." *California Law Review* 92.4:1173–1239.

Zhou, M. 1997. "Segmented Assimilation: Issues, Controversies, and Recent Research on the New Second Generation." *International Migration Review,* 31.4: 975–1008. Special Issue: *Immigrant Adaptation and Native-Born Responses in the Making of Americans.*

Asylum

Asylum, also known as the right to asylum or political asylum, is the protection given by one country to refugees from another country. One who seeks this protection is called an asylum seeker. In the United States, any foreign national regardless of immigration status who is physically present in the country or is at a port of entry can apply for asylum. When the application has been approved, the asylum seeker is then granted official "asylee" status. In compliance with the Refugee Act of 1980, based on the 1951 United Nations Refugee Convention, an individual granted asylum in the United States is entitled to a certain amount of rights and benefits, such as the right to remain in the United States and the right to find employment. Asylees are similar to refugees in that they are both foreign nationals who meet the formal definition set by the United Nations Convention Relating to the Status of Refugees of 1951 and the 1967 Protocol: "any person who, owing to a well-founded fear of being persecuted for reasons of race, religion, nationality, membership of a particular social group or political opinion, is outside the country of his nationality and is unable or, owing to such fear, is unwilling to avail himself of the protection of that country." The main difference between an asylum seeker and a refugee in the United States is the person's physical location at the time of application. Refugees are outside of the United States when they apply for refugee status, typically with the assistance of the United Nations High Commissioner for Refugees, while asylum seekers are already on United States territory or at a port of entry when they submit their application for asylum.

Foreigners that want to seek asylum in the United States can do so in two separate ways. First, an asylum seeker in the United States can submit an asylum application, Form I-589, Application for Asylum and for Withholding of Removal, with the United States Citizenship and Immigration Services (USCIS) asylum officer. If the asylum seeker has already been apprehended due to lack of authorization or documentation in the United States, he or she can also submit a request with an immigration judge as part of a hearing.

Another way to request asylum in the United States is at a port of entry through the Asylum Office Corps. The purpose of the Asylum Office Corps is to interview asylum seekers and evaluate if they are in fact eligible to apply for asylum. If the Corps determines that the asylum seeker has a "credible fear" of returning to the country of origin, the case is then referred to an immigration judge.

If an asylum officer determines that an individual is not eligible for asylum, but he or she currently has a valid immigration status (for example, a student visa), the asylum application will be denied by USCIS and the applicant will keep his or her previous immigration status. However, if the person does not have a previous valid status and is in the country unauthorized, and the asylum officer determines that he or she is not eligible for asylum, the individual is placed in removal proceedings with the Executive Office of Immigration Review (EOIR) of the Department of Justice, and the application is reconsidered. Furthermore, any foreign nationals who have not previously applied for asylum can be placed in removal proceedings by immigration enforcement officials if they are undocumented or are caught entering the United States without proper documentation. These individuals can apply for asylum with the EOIR as well. During the removal proceedings, the judge may either grant the request for asylum or deny the application. If the request for asylum is denied, the applicant can potentially appeal for another hearing with the Board of Immigration Appeals or the federal courts.

However, if the request for asylum is granted, the asylum seeker is now considered to be authorized and has the full rights and privileges of a refugee. One is entitled to certain rights and protections, the most important being non-refoulement, or protection against returning to the country of origin. Essentially, the host country cannot return or deport a refugee or asylee to the country in which he or she will be persecuted. They also qualify for other basic rights, including protection against physical threats in the host country, access to courts in the host country, freedom to move about the host country, with the exception of those that pose a public threat, and reunification with family members that also reside within the host country if possible. They are also given access to primary education for children, and assistance to cover basic needs, such as food, clothing, shelter, and medical assistance.

An asylee can also apply for a green card that authorizes him or her to remain in the country on a permanent basis. Eligible family members of asylees, or individuals that were granted asylum in the United States can apply for permanent resident status one year after the granting of the asylum status into the United States. For an asylee to be eligible, he or she has to also have physically lived in the United States for one year, continue to have asylee status, or be the spouse or a dependent child of an asylee, not have moved to another country, and continue to be admissible to the United States

In addition to the status of refugee and the status of asylum seeker, there are several other types of uprooted people. The definition of the 1951 Convention does not include general oppression, insecurity, or victims of economic deprivation. It also does not include those who are displaced within their country of origin, since the definition states that a refugee has to be outside the home country.

Furthermore, those who leave their country of origin due to economic factors are not considered to be refugees or asylees but rather economic migrants. They do not qualify for protection or assistance from the UNHCR. The main difference is that migrants flee to improve their economic standing while refugees/asylees flee to save their lives and avoid persecution. However, in many countries, economic hardship is often accompanied by political violence or is the result of a violent political system, and therefore it can be difficult to tell the difference between a refugee and a migrant. Typically, if an economic migrant crosses the border without proper authorization, he or she will not be granted asylum and cannot become a refugee.

The number of asylees in the United States decreased slightly from 22,090 in the fiscal year 2009 to 21,113 in the fiscal year 2010. The number of individuals that were granted asylum affirmatively, or through USCIS, also slightly declined from 11,904 in 2009 to 11,244 in 2010. Likewise, the number of people granted asylum defensively, either through an immigration judge or through the Board of Immigration Appeals of EOIR, dropped from 10,186 in 2009 to 9,869 in 2010. For the categories of overall asylees, the top ten countries for people who were granted asylum in 2010 were the People's Republic of China with 6,683 asylees, Ethiopia with 1,093, Haiti with 832, Venezuela with 660, Nepal with 640, Colombia with 591, Russia with 548, Egypt with

536, Iran with 485, and Guatemala with 465 asylees. Together, the top ten countries comprised 59.4 percent of all asylees in the fiscal year 2010.

The largest age demographic that was granted asylum through USCIS (affirmative asylum) was the age group twenty-five to thirty-four years, consisting of 3,743 out of 11,244 asylees, or 33.3 percent. The next largest age group was those eighteen to twenty-four years old at 22.5 percent or 2,529 asylees, followed by thirty-five to forty-four-year-olds at 19.8 percent or 2,230. Of the affirmative asylees, 52.2 were male and 47.8 percent were female. Exactly 50.0 percent of affirmative asylees were single, 44.4 percent were married, and 5.5 were divorced, separated, or widowed (and less than 0.1 percent had an unknown marital status).

Asylees diffuse throughout the country, with certain states containing larger populations than others. In 2010, the state with the largest new affirmative asylee population was California with 4,168 asylees, followed by New York with 1,722, Florida with 1,488, Virginia with 452 and Maryland with 393 asylees.

Jenna Glickman

See Also: Central American Civil Wars; Cubans; Nicaraguan Adjustment and Central American Relief Act (NACARA); Refugees; Salvadorans; Select Commission on Immigration and Refugee Policy.

Further Reading

Batalova, Jeanne. 2006. "Spotlight on Refugees and Asylees in the United States." Migration Information Source. http://www.migrationinformation.org/usfocus/display.cfm?ID=415#2.

Green Card Application Guide. 2013. U.S. Immigration Support. https://www.usimmigrationsupport.org/greencard.html.

Loescher, Gil, and Ann Dull Loescher. 1994. *The Global Refugee Crisis.* Santa Barbara: ABC-CLIO, Inc.

Martin, Daniel C. 2011. "Refugees and Asylees: 2010." Annual Flow Report—Office of Immigration Statistics, U.S. Department of Homeland Security.

Aztlán

With very public anti-immigrant rhetoric in the United States, the debate over undocumented immigration has at times brought negative attention to the concept of Aztlán, a debate often used to articulate and generate fears about the loss of a nation's identity in light of greater immigration, and particularly for those coming from Mexico and Latin America. Aztlán is the name given to the northern homeland and place of origin of the pre-Columbian people known as the *Mexica* (pronounced Meh-shee-kah), popularly known as the Aztecs. Anti-immigrant nativists in the United States have often and wrongfully accused Spanish-speaking populations and newly arrived immigrants of attempting a separatist movement in which Aztlán would be taken over to either form a separate country (called irredentism) or re-annexed to Mexico. Their arguments often refer to the pitfalls of "balkanization," a process associated with the fragmentation of a larger state into smaller ones (taken from the history of the states that make up the Balkan peninsula) based on culture or ethnicity—states that have been born out of historic hostilities towards each other and chronic displacement.

The creation stories of ancient Mesoamerican civilizations led many early scholars to think that the area referred to by the Aztecs may comprise modern-day California, Arizona, Texas, New Mexico, Nevada, Utah, and parts of Colorado, Wyoming, Oklahoma, and Kansas. Currently, these states are home to the largest number of Mexican-heritage populations in the United States and the continually inhabited regions that were understood to be the ancient Aztec homeland of Aztlán. In immigration research, these U.S. southwestern states have often been referred to as "gateway" states—places that have traditionally been settled by both modern-day documented and undocumented immigrants. Consistent with this development, California and Texas have the largest numbers of Mexican-heritage populations in the nation as traditional migrant destinations. With continued research in the modern era, archaeologists increasingly contend that the ancient homeland of the Aztecs, Aztlán, may have actually been a region known as Aztatlán, which encompasses the modern Mexican states of Nayarit, Colima, Sinaloa and Jalisco. Mounting empirical evidence notwithstanding, the popularized view of Aztlán as birthplace of Mexico's culture and identity continues to be embedded in Mexican and Mexican American thought, history, culture, and ties to the land.

There are many interpretations of the Aztecs' migratory journey to the central valley of Mexico from their northern origins. The most commonly known names associated with those origins are Aztlán and Chicomoztoc. Aztlán is said to mean the place of the herons, and Chicomoztoc means the place of the seven caves. However, most accounts suggest that Aztlán is the place of origin for the Mexica. Creation stories maintain that Aztlán is located on an island where the herons live. From Aztlán-Chicomoztoc, the seven original tribes that would later be the founders of the Aztec Empire, departed on their journey for a humble new beginning in the adopted homeland in the Valley of Mexico in about AD 1244.

The Mexicas' migration from Aztlán thus culminated with the formation of the historic city of Tenochtitlán, which was constructed on an island in the ancient lake of Texcoco. Currently, this is Mexico City. Once there and through the formation of alliances and conquest, the Mexica established an empire larger than any of its time, reaching its peak at about AD 1500. Though they had found a new home in Mexico's central valley, they continued to trade with peoples throughout the ancient Aztlán. Though there are many legendary codices mapping the migration of Mexica, the most famous is *La Tira de la Pereginacaion (The Strip of the Pilgrimage),* also known as the Codex Boturini. Various scholars have studied this sixteenth-century document, yet the exact geographical location of the Mexica homeland has not been found. For this reason Aztlán's location was highly debated in the sixteenth century.

The Spanish were informed of the Aztecs' northern homeland, and fueled by stories of gold and riches that could be found there, began to search for this ancient homeland. They were told that Aztlán was located on an island, which was home to the place of the seven caves. The Spanish had hoped to find a city similar to Tenochtitlán, and the search for the seven caves became known as the search for the "seven cities of gold."

The search for these riches thus took Spanish colonizers to the northern parts of Mexico, and into what is now the southwestern United States. However, the Spanish were unable to find the location of Aztlán, nor the gold. In their attempts to find the Aztec homeland, the Spanish ran into different indigenous settlements, resources, and riches. The search for Aztlán came to a halt in what is known as the current state of New Mexico, due to the harsh weather and continuous confrontations with the native Pueblo peoples.

Despite the uncertainty of the exact location of Aztlán, what is known is that the ancient trade routes through Aztlán continued to be traveled even after the Spanish colonization of Mexico. The Spanish not only knew of these trade routes but also utilized them and reshaped them to fit their own needs. The continuity of these routes can be seen today through commerce and migration, thought to have facilitated later and more modern migrations to the United States.

In addition to the migrations to and from Aztlán, large populations of Mexicans became displaced. In 1848 at the end of the Mexican-American War the United States gained the vast territories that are now known as the states of California, Arizona, New Mexico, and parts of Nevada, Colorado, Utah, Texas, and Oklahoma. The Mexican government tried to insure that the citizenship, language, culture, and property rights of the newly incorporated Mexican populations within the newly acquired United States territory would be respected through the treaty of Guadalupe Hidalgo. However, history would prove these efforts futile.

In 1961 Native American scholar Jack Forbes was the first scholar to place Aztlán not only in the U.S. Southwest, but also in the Mexican northwestern area. Due to the various different descriptions of Aztlán and the records of previous attempts by Spanish colonists to find Aztlán, Forbes felt this region was large enough to encompass the geography where the original Aztlán was thought to be located. Forbes also used a linguistic approach in redefining Aztlán's location. He focused on Uto-Aztecan languages, and other Native American languages, which extend past the U.S.-Mexican border. In addition, Jack Forbes's redefinition of Aztlán served as a unifying force behind Native American solidarity, despite geopolitical borders.

In 1969 as a part of the civil rights movements, Mexican American students held a conference to discuss their own needs as a community. This conference was named the Denver Youth Conference and was held in Denver, Colorado. Here, a reemergence of Aztlán as an idea and inspiration surged as a young poet, Alurista, read a poem entitled "Aztlán." This poem later became the beginning of a manifesto known as "El Plan Espiritual de Aztlán," which put forth the idea of the ancestral rights of all Chicanas/os to inhabit the region known as Aztlán in the U.S. Southwest. The student movement that would carry out these ideas for generations to come would identify with the name *El Movimiento Estudiantil Chicano de Aztlán* ("Chicano Student Movement of Aztlán").

Throughout the Chicano Movement of the late 1970s, Chicanos and Chicanas used the idea of Aztlán to lay claim to the region now known as the American Southwest, especially in light of attempts to displace Mexicans from the land through the legal system imposed on the region incorporated into the United States through the Treaty of Guadalupe Hidalgo in 1848. Articles VII, IX and X, which initially granted

Mexican citizens civil rights and landownership rights, were removed on March 10, 1848. Thus, Mexicans became territorially displaced. The Chicano movement helped produce scholars that have conducted extensive research into how the system of laws supported the often extra-legal encroachment by settlers of European descent to effectively uproot and disenfranchise existing populations as "foreigners," even though they had in reality been initially afforded citizenship, and the right to exercise their culture and language (Menchaca, 1995).

Thalia Marlyn Gómez Torres

See Also: Displacement; Indigenous People; Migration; Transnationalism; Zapotec People (Oaxaca).

Further Reading

Fields, Virginia M., and Victor Zamudio-Taylor. 2001. *The Road to Aztlán: Art from a Mythic Homeland.* Los Angeles: Los Angeles County Museum of Art.

Forbes, Jack D. 1973. *Aztecas del Norte: The Chicanos of Aztlán.* Greenwich, CT: Fawcett Publications.

Gutierrez de MacGregor, Maria Teresa, and Jorge Gonzalez Sanchez. 2011. "De Aztlán a Tenochtitlan: Cartografia de los Lugares Senalados en la Tira de la Peregrinacion." *Journal of Latin American Geography* 10.1:35–51.

Massey, Douglas S. 1987. *Return to Aztlán: The Social Process of International Migration from Western Mexico.* Berkeley: University of California Press.

Menchaca, Martha. 1995. *The Mexican Outsiders: A Community History of Marginalization and Discrimination in California.* Austin: University of Texas Press.

B

Banking

In the aftermath of 9/11, and the nation's war on terrorism, banking has become more problematic for undocumented immigrants who are not able to obtain many of the documents needed to conduct many bank transactions. After the attacks on the World Trade Center, the U.S. Congress passed the 2001 *Uniting and Strengthening America by Providing Appropriate Tools Required to Intercept and Obstruct Terrorism* (commonly known as the USA PATRIOT Act). Among other things, the legislation expanded the ability of government agencies to keep track of electronic communication and consumer purchases. This added more requirements for banks and other financial institutions to request information from potential clients. This added an immigration enforcement dimension to banking. Law enforcement authorities have always been able to request business records in criminal cases through grand jury subpoenas. Thus, enforcement agencies—through the Patriot Act—gave them additional tools for obtaining records of certain financial transactions from "third parties," meaning banks and other financial institutions. In line with this policy, banks adopted new policies that required everyone, not just undocumented immigrants, to provide residency and identification documents; but the policies impacted undocumented immigrants more severely. Currently, to obtain a bank account in the United States it is required to show a valid social security number.

In response, the Mexican and Guatemalan governments began to negotiate with certain banks to accept consulate-issued identification documents for banking transactions, such as the *matricula consular,* with limited success. When that is not possible, other forms of documentation to open a bank account may be accepted such as an international driver's license, a passport or a valid visa. This in itself is discriminatory as only *matricula consular* cards from two countries are accepted, Mexico and Guatemala.

Due to the foregoing, it can be argued that when citizenship becomes a criterion for service, banking establishments discriminate against certain minorities, and in particular Latinos regardless of status, because they share many attributes with immigrants. This barrier to becoming fully integrated into the fabric of society has broader implications for immigrants and those who are related to them by kinship ties. For example, in California after Proposition 187 was passed in 1994, many establishments, especially banks, refused services to many who they deemed were "illegal" based on appearance. Banks would not only ask individuals for multiple forms of identification, but specifically passports and green cards were required regardless of citizenship status. In contrast, during the "housing bubble" of the mid 2000s, banks were incentivized by the readily free flow of cash that became available to make loans to immigrants, regardless of their legal status. The research by McConnell and Marcelli (2007) shows that banks were so eager to make loans to immigrants that there was virtually no difference in the loans made to the different types of immigrants applying for loans: undocumented or legal resident immigrants.

Generally the U.S. Department of the Treasury allows for each individual business to decide what forms of identification they will accept. For Bank of America, an individual in the United States for less than two years must also sign an affidavit where they detail their reason for being in the United States.

Traditionally, when immigrants have been unable to access financial services from formal institutions, they rely on informal ways of financing their high-cost purchases. For example the *tanda* system present in the Mexican/Mexican-American community in the United States is one way that both undocumented and documented migrants can find ways around using or depending on established banking systems. The word *tanda* is said to mean "alternative order," which is fitting for a system used outside of the established traditional order of banking systems. A *tanda* is conducted with anywhere from eight to fifteen individuals. One person is assigned to be the collector of the money, and the number of individuals participating in the *tanda* determine the number of weeks that the *tanda* will last. The participants are most often family members, family friends, and neighbors, and especially coworkers. Every week each member of the group must give a small amount of money, such as twenty dollars, to the collector of the money and every week one member of the group gets the entire pot of money. This process continues until everyone in the group has received the pot of money at least once. This practice allows community members to make large payments at once that their minimal wages would not otherwise allow for, in addition to being a way to save money in general. This is a practice used often in Mexico, as well as by other ethnic groups both in the United States and abroad although under a different name.

The reason for practicing such a system is in part because of the unfamiliarity of the banking systems as well as general fear of discrimination from banking institutions. An ethnographic study by Ruth Horowitz in an immigrant community in the heart of Chicago examines briefly banking institutions within the community that charge more for services than their branches in other neighborhoods. This general avoidance of the banking system as well as a simultaneous underserving of the Mexican immigrant community is supported by another research study done in a similar neighborhood in Chicago by the Federal Reserve Bank of Chicago. When it came to being in need of finances, respondents of the study claimed to receive the needed funds predominantly from relatives (32 percent) followed by borrowing from friends (27 percent) and then gifts or assistance from friends (13.2 percent). The use of the formal banking system was 11.8 percent according to this study. This study shows how this community of immigrants preferred to seek assistance from family and friends before going to banking systems. For undocumented migrants this form of banking is especially important as many banks require social security numbers to open accounts or provide services. Additionally, another benefit of the informal systems is that banking systems usually charge large fees for their services, and for those with limited wages, avoiding additional charges is necessary.

Using alternative forms of financing institutions, migrants tend to pay more for services both for cashing checks as well as sending money back to their country of origin. This is an extreme disadvantage to the migrants as their already low wages take a hard hit when having to continuously pay these fees. Specifically, immigrant populations use banking systems primarily for cashing checks and savings as well as for sending remittances. The move away from formal banking practices was originally seen as the unwillingness of the banking institutions to service these communities and discriminatory practices within the institutions. Although discrimination is hard to prove, migrant's perception of anticipated discrimination also prevents individuals from seeking assistance from banks and banking institutions.

Additionally, migrants tend to have less money to put into saving accounts. The employment they have at times is not enough to live off, much less to save. When investing in their future most migrant families do not think of money or banking systems but instead think of their children as an investment in the family's future. The children of migrants have often been cited as the future of their families in that the parents depend on their children to care for them both physically and financially as they age.

The fact that migrants have been observed seeking alternative banking options affects newly developing migrant communities around the nation. In new gateway cities and states, many of the new immigrants tend to follow the path that has been set out by those who are already established in the community. A study in Virginia also showed migrants' unwillingness to venture out into more traditional forms of banking. The study established that those surveyed cited language barriers, lack of cultural understanding, and fear of discrimination as reasons why they steered away from banks. Additionally, lack of required documentation such as social security numbers also diminished their affiliation with banks and banking institutions. Even so half of the migrants who had bank accounts in their native country maintained those accounts when they were in the United States.

Yesenia Andrade

See Also: Counterfeit Documents; Counterterrorism and Immigrant Profiling; Economics; Family Economics; Foreign Consulates; Identification Cards; Identity Theft; Informal Economy; Shadow Population; Transnationalsim.

Further Reading

Bond, Philip, and Robert Townsend. July/August 1996. "Formal and Informal Financing in a Chicago Ethnic Neighborhood." Federal Reserve Bank of Chicago. *Economic Perspectives*.

Coyle, J. 2007. "The Legality of Banking the Undocumented." *Georgetown Immigration Law Journal* 22.1:21–56.

Horowitz, Ruth. 1983. *Honor and the American Dream: Culture and Identity in a Chicano Community.* New Brunswick, N.J.: Rutgers University Press.

Kurtz, Donald V., and Margaret Showman. 1978. "The Tanda: A Rotating Credit Association in Mexico." *Ethnology* 17.1:65–74.

McConnell, Eileen Diaz, and Enrico A. Marcelli. 2007. "Buying into the American Dream?" *Mexican Immigrants, Legal Status, and Homeownership in Los Angeles County* 88.1:199–221.

Rojas, Daisy Stevens. 2010. "Accessing Alternatives: Latino Immigrant Financial Experiences in Virginia." *International Journal of Business Anthropology,* 1.1:57–78.

Barriers to Health

Approximately one third of the United States immigrant population comprises undocumented individuals and families. In 2013, there are an estimated 11.1 million undocumented immigrants residing in the United States (Dann, 2013). Undocumented immigrants experience multiple barriers to healthcare and various forms of healthcare discrimination that affect their access to health services, as well as the quality of services.

Healthcare discrimination is a contributing factor in perpetuating health disparities within the United States. A health disparity is defined as differences in health outcomes that are unfair, avoidable and reflective of social disadvantages, such as poverty, low education level and group marginalization. The elimination of health disparities is a major goal of the National Institutes of Health, particularly within the National Institute on Minority Health and Health Disparities, which funds research and educational programs towards this goal (http://www.nimhd.nih.gov). Undocumented immigrants

Juana, who asked that her last name not be used, poses for a photo in her apartment in Conroe, Texas, 2004, with her 5-year-old son Christian who was born in the United States. Sometimes Juana, a 32-year-old undocumented immigrant, feels she has no choice but to send her two other school-age sons to classes sick, now that hospital districts in Texas are not required to provide non-emergency health care to undocumented immigrants under a new law. (AP Photo / Michael Stravato)

are more vulnerable to health disparities because they have a greater likelihood for social, educational and employment inequities compared to U.S. citizens. While there is a large body of scientific literature documenting the existence of health disparities in the United States (see Smedley, Stith & Nelson, 2003), less is known about the extent of health disparities affecting undocumented immigrant populations.

Barriers in Access to Healthcare Services

A major barrier that immigrants face in accessing healthcare is lack of health insurance. Estimates indicate there are more than 50 million people in the United States who lack healthcare insurance and approximately one-third of these are immigrants. An important distinction between U.S.-born citizens and immigrants is that immigrants are more likely to remain uninsured for longer periods of time (sometimes two decades longer). This is due, in part, to immigrants' overall lower education levels and employment in lower-paying jobs that do not offer healthcare insurance. Undocumented immigrants may experience even greater barriers than their immigrant peers who managed to obtain citizenship. Even though some health insurance programs may not require proof of citizenship for eligibility, national healthcare reform under the Affordable Care Act of 2010 restricts health benefits for undocumented immigrants. (Additionally, individual state-sponsored healthcare plans vary widely in eligibility requirements and in some states, such as Arizona, there has been increasingly restrictive legislation to eliminate healthcare and other social benefits to undocumented immigrants.) Because undocumented immigrants face greater unemployment, they have fewer resources to pay out of pocket for healthcare services. Fear of deportation may inhibit them from seeking necessary healthcare maintenance, such as immunizations for example, even when some of these services may be free.

Barriers in Quality of Healthcare Services

There are multiple factors that affect the quality of care when immigrant populations are able to access healthcare services. One of the most important factors that decrease the quality of care is language barriers between patients and providers. Despite federal mandates for healthcare systems to provide culturally and linguistically competent services (http://www.hrsa.gov/culturalcompetence/index.html), enormous gaps remain in meeting this mandate. The majority of U.S. healthcare providers speak only English, which presents serious challenges in their ability to communicate effectively with linguistically diverse patient populations. Further, immigrants who have lived in the United States for many years in segregated communities may experience persistent limited English proficiency. Inability to communicate effectively with healthcare providers impacts patients' perceptions of quality of care. For example, Spanish-speaking Latinos are less likely to rate their provider as respectful and concerned than are Whites or their English-speaking Latino counterparts, even when interpreters are available.

Another factor affecting the quality of care is bias from healthcare providers. Undocumented immigrants may perceive bias or disrespect from healthcare providers related to race, ethnicity, skin color, language spoken, citizenship status, or lack of income. These forms of interpersonal discrimination in healthcare settings tend to be subtle and may be unintentional on the part of the provider. Nevertheless, studies have demonstrated that patients are keenly aware of disrespectful attitudes when they occur. One way to improve the quality of care for culturally and linguistically diverse patients is through racial/ethnic concordance (same racial/ethnic background) between patient and provider. Studies have found that when the patient and provider are of the same race/ethnicity, the healthcare visits are longer and patients report feeling more positive about the relationship. Racial/ethnic concordance may increase the comfort level between patient and provider, while linguistic concordance is likely to increase both safety (quality of care) and comfort. Racial and linguistic concordance is difficult to achieve in most healthcare settings because the majority of healthcare providers are non-Hispanic White and English-speaking. However, a number of training initiatives have been offered to increase the availability of physicians and nurses from underrepresented minority groups (American Association of Colleges of Nursing).

Maureen Campesino

See Also: Health and Welfare; Laws and Legislation, post-1980s; Mental Health Care Access; Nutrition; Policies of Attrition; Trauma-Related Symptoms; Workplace Injury.

Further Reading

American Association of Colleges of Nursing. 2013. "Fact Sheet: Enhancing Diversity in Nursing," updated April 17. http://www.aacn.nche.edu/media-relations/diversityFS .pdf.

Blanchard, Janice, and Nicole Lurie. 2004. "R-E-S-P-E-C-T: Patient Reports of Disrespect in the Health Care Setting and Its Impact on Care." *The Journal of Family Practice* 53: 721–30.

Campesino, Maureen, Ester Ruiz, Johannah Uriri Glover and Mary Koithan. 2009. "Counternarratives of Mexican-origin Women with Breast Cancer." *Advances in Nursing Science* 32: E-57–67.

Dann, Carrie. 2013. "By the numbers: How America tallies its 11.1 million undocumented immigrants." NBC News, April 11. http://nbcpolitics.nbcnews.com/_news/ 2013/04/11/17691515-by-the-numbers-how-america-tallies-its-11.1-million -undocumented-immigrants?lite.

Henry J. Kaiser Family Foundation. 2004. *Missing Persons: Minorities in the Health Professions.* www.aacn.nche.edu/media/pdf/sullivanreport.pdf.

Henry J. Kaiser Family Foundation. 2008. *Summary: Five Basic Facts on Immigrants and Their Health Care.* http://www.kff.org/medicaid/upload/7761.pdf

"Immigrants and the Affordable Care Act" (2013). National Immigration Law Center. http://www.nilc.org/immigrantshcr.html.

Smedley, Brian, Adrienne Stith, and Alan Nelson, 2003. *Unequal Treatment: Confronting Racial and Ethnic Disparities in Health Care.* Washington: The Institute of Medicine.

Barrios

Barrios in the United States are urban, rural and suburban settlement spaces and neighborhoods of predominately Spanish-speaking peoples. In this article, the barrios under discussion are Chicano(a)/Mexican American and Mexican migrant-based. People in the barrios share an ethnic consciousness, a way of life, and a spatial identity that forms in time out of the mix of economic, social, cultural, and political conditions. Barrios are known by landmarks, streets, schools, public housing, places of work, churches, families, and so forth.

Barrios have a different history than European-based immigrant enclaves. They have their origins in the Spanish Empire's conquest of Mexico in the early sixteenth century and its northern expansion into New Mexico, Texas, California and Arizona. These Spanish-dominated settlements became part of independent Mexico in 1821. By 1848 the United States invaded, conquered and established its hegemony in those pueblos. Mexicans in the pueblos were pushed by legal and extra-legal means from their lands and into segregated spaces for political, economic and social control by Anglo elites.

From the 1880s with capitalist development of the region, Mexicans became the principal source of workers for the hardest jobs with the lowest wages along the border

Members of a tenants' organization in East Harlem gather outside the office of landlord developer Dawnay Day Group, as lawyers attempt to serve the company with court papers on behalf of tenants, during a press conference in New York, October, 2007. The tenants' group, Movement for Justice in El Barrio, filed suit against Dawnay Day Group, the London-based investment corporation, for harassing tenants by falsely and illegally charging fees in attempts to push immigrant families from their homes and gentrify the neighborhood. Barrios are places of social integration and support for recently arrived immigrants. (AP Photos/Bebeto Matthews)

region from Texas to California. Barrios had become the center of survival and resistance for Mexican American and Mexican workers. Especially in large urban cities, small businesses flourished, such as restaurants, shoe repair shops, groceries, bakeries, tortillerías, meat markets, tailors. Women took in wash, ironing, and sold food from their homes. People organized themselves in their churches, schools, social/civic/cultural groups, mutual aid societies and newspapers. This vibrant environment countered the Anglo repression with its racist narrative of "the other." Nevertheless in the barrios many problems surfaced as a result of concentrated poverty, little government services and discrimination.

From the early 1900s to the 1930s, Mexican migrants arrived in large numbers as a result of revolution and religious upheavals in Mexico. These war refugees were diverse, ranging from elites to radical organizers to the poorest of workers, including single women and children. Most of these refugees settled in urban/rural barrios throughout the border region, and some moved into the Midwest, such as Chicago and Kansas City, forming new barrios. Also Mexican American migrants from the border region traveled North following crops, returning home but leaving behind the foundations of barrios throughout the Northwest, the Plains and the Midwest. Barrios produced leaders and participants in the general struggles of the 1930s who founded civil rights organizations and unions.

The impacts of World War II and Korea led to a growing middle class in the Mexican American communities because of better wages for returning veterans whose job opportunities opened and women who remained in the workforce for a second income. A professional class formed from veterans using the GI Bill to acquire a university education. These gains did not assure Mexican Americans full citizenship rights because Anglo elites still held fast to their political, social and economic dominance. The Mexican American middle class moved out of barrios but they were excluded for the most part from areas closed to nonwhites. Therefore they moved into mixed areas whose landscape looked "American" but remained a middle ground of Mexican American middle class barrios. From those barrios came reformers who fought against discrimination from within the establishment where they occupied peripheral positions; they saw themselves as liberals in social and economic policies, strong anticommunist patriots who had fought in WWII and Korea and had earned full rights for themselves and their communities and who were at the same time proud of their Mexican heritage.

In the working-class barrios, however, a new generation was emerging that would question the effectiveness of these Mexican American reformers. The barrios in large part remained buried in substandard conditions, often with no sewers, unpaved streets, flooding problems, no recreation areas, inferior education, high unemployment and endemic poverty. The rural area barrios (also known as "*colonias*") were even worse off. Barrios at the same time remained viable with home ownership, a stable working class, businesses and a social cohesiveness. Nevertheless, barrios were destroyed by relocations to build freeways, community centers, sports stadiums, airports or whatever the Anglo elites believed to be in their best economic interest with little regard for the people in the barrios, now categorized as slum dwellers.

From the mid 1960s to the 1970s, the barrios everywhere became the centers of radical struggles for full civil rights. Known as the Chicano Movement, it was characterized by vocabulary, identity, music, dress, attitude, aspirations that exalted *el rasquachismo,* exemplified in the word Chicano(a), the ethos of the barrio working class. Middle class Mexican Americans were offended for they believed in a high culture approach, the *criolloismo* of proper speech, whether English or Spanish, and formalities. The Chicano(a) Movement made the barrio/colonia, whether urban or rural, the heart in the march for justice. Not everyone in the barrio agreed with the radical activists but the *movimiento* left a lasting legacy of achievements (and failures) visually seen in the murals and the living mythic aura of those times.

In the 1980s and 1990s, Latino growth, internal and from immigration, increased the populations in the established barrios in the border region states and Midwest states. With the civil wars in Central America and the economic devastation wrought by neoliberal policies, migrants forged new paths into the American South, the Southeast, and rural Midwest. Barrios were also found in suburbia. Many of the barrios now had concentrations of undocumented workers and their families. The undocumented workers became targets of anti-immigrant laws. Post 9/11 the migrant of color became a prime target for suspicion. With the creation of the Department of Homeland Security, migration, law enforcement and internal security became even more closely interconnected and repressive.

Again from the barrios came a political movement led by immigrant youth and their communities to demand justice. Millions marched against anti-immigrant laws aided by Mexican radio stations, Spanish-speaking TV, and new communication systems. Barrio churches, both Catholic and Protestant, provided sanctuary. The visibility of such large numbers of undocumented workers from the barrios standing up fearlessly led to more anti-immigrant legislation and hate. The barrios served again as the center and the heart of protest, even though in some areas there were tensions between native-born Mexican Americans and undocumented Mexicans. Those tensions lessened as all brown people came under attack, regardless of status and class, and demands for reforms surfaced from all directions.

Today's barrios are located throughout the United States as the Latino population has grown to be the largest minority. The vast majority of Latinos are Mexican Americans and Mexican migrants, and half live in two states, Texas and California, where the original pueblos were located. Barrios continue in their different ways to be the center of life for Mexican migrants and Mexican Americans with small businesses, restaurants, bakeries, bars, dance halls, churches, parks, social organizations, car clubs, political organizations, fiestas, sports, radio stations in Spanish and newspapers. Barrios remain *el Corazon del pueblo,* the heart of communities where struggles for justice are centered and have been since 1848.

Guadalupe Castillo

See Also: Aztlán; Community Concerns; Culture; Enclaves; Shadow Population.

Further Reading

Acuña, Rodolfo. 2002. *Occupied America: A History of the Chicanos.* 5th ed. New York: Longman.

Camarillo, Albert. 1979. *Chicanos in a Changing Society: From Mexican Pueblos to American Barrios in Santa Barbara and Southern California, 1848–1930.* Cambridge, MA: Harvard University Press.

Montejano, David. 2010. *Quixote's Soldiers: A Local History of the Chicano Movement, 1966–1981.* Austin: University of Texas Press.

Otero, Lydia R. 2010. *La Calle: Spatial Conflicts and Urban Renewal in a Southwestern City.* Tucson: University of Arizona Press.

Valdés, Dionicio Nodín. 2000. *Barrios Norteños: St. Paul and Midwestern Mexican Communities in the Twentieth Century.* Austin: University of Texas Press.

Bilingualism

Bilingualism means fluency in two languages. Immigrants living in the United States are expected to learn and use English. Access to work with higher wages and better working conditions, as well as the ability to function in mainstream U.S. society, is dependent on having a proficient level of English.

Language acquisition is not an automatic process and can be very challenging for adults who are not immersed in the language. Most undocumented immigrants live in a part of the United States where they know someone. Cities are segregated to the extent that entire neighborhoods speak a language other than English. Jobs are found through personal connections in workplaces where their native language is predominant. As immigrants settle into their new lives, English is not required in everyday communication. However, as the desire to earn more and have a better life grows, so does the urgency to learn English.

There are many options available to learn English. Many immigrant service organizations and community centers offer free English classes. However, these classes tend to be taught by volunteers rather than trained English as a Second Language (ESL) teachers. These classes are focused on helping people to communicate in everyday situations. They tend to prioritize conversation and a basic knowledge of English grammar and structure and are not intended to be a means to language fluency. Very rarely do these classes cover past tense and more advanced grammar topics essential to reading and writing on a proficient level.

Many community colleges and private language institutions offer classes in different levels of English. Some colleges and language schools require documents as part of registration, outright excluding undocumented immigrants. Tuition fees and fixed class schedules create obstacles for people with irregular schedules and inconsistent or low wages. In addition, unsuccessful attempts to learn English can be very demoralizing and lead to high turnover in all types of adult ESL classes. The majority of undocumented immigrants are preoccupied with having sufficient work, and learning English becomes less of a priority and more of a wish. Individuals are left vulnerable to higher rates of exploitation and to being taken advantage of financially via fraudulent contracts and business dealings, as well as by police and immigration officers.

Immigrant parents depend on their children to fill out forms and obtain important information. While learning English is a challenge for recent immigrants, 91 percent of second generation immigrants are bilingual. Children become proficient in English as a result of bilingual education programs in public schools.

Bilingual Education

Bilingual education was signed into existence with the passage of the Bilingual Education Act (BEA) in 1968. The law was passed on the heels of the Chicano Movement, which asserted that emergent bilingual students' language and cultural rights must be recognized in schools. The BEA also legalized the rights of emergent bilingual children to have instruction in their native language while they learn English.

Several different approaches to bilingual education have been developed since 1968. They can be divided into two categories: programs that include native languages in instruction of subject areas and those that use English-only for instruction of all subject areas. Programs centered on two languages maintain the goal of educating bilingual children who are fluent in both their native language and English. These are dual language or two-way immersion, maintenance bilingual programs, and developmental or heritage programs. Programs which use only English aim to transition the child from dependency on one's native language to communicate in English as the dominant language. English-only approaches include transitional bilingual programs, English as a Second Language programs, Sheltered English programs, English immersion, or "Sheltered English Immersion" programs; and the Null model. While there is debate amongst linguists on which model or approach is more effective, the introduction of bilingual education to public schools has been instrumental to foreign children learning English while at the same time recognizing the value of their native language and culture.

Specific regions of the United States, such as the South (Florida) and Southwest, are accustomed to having a sizeable English Language Learner (ELL) school population. However, over the past fifteen years there has been a surge in immigration, and as a result more school districts across the country have had to initiate bilingual programs. Increasing by over 110 percent, the emergent bilingual population is roughly 10 percent of the overall school population in preschool through grade twelve.

Beginning in the 1990s, politicians have begun to include bilingual education in their crusade against undocumented immigration. State laws have been passed aimed at eliminating bilingual education. In 1998, California passed Proposition 227 which greatly curtails bilingual education. Arizona approved a similar law in 2000, and again added more English-only provisions in 2006. Massachusetts followed this example and, in 2002, passed their own legislation, which replaced bilingual education with a one year complete immersion program. This discourse and legislative action have turned the debate on bilingual education from a pedagogical or linguistic issue to a political one with serious consequences for children.

Furthermore, recent changes introduced into education through the No Child Left Behind Act (2002) require that all students, including emergent bilingual students, pass city and state standardized tests printed solely in English. Those who do not pass the tests are not supposed to advance to the next grade. Additionally, there are harsh punishments for schools with high percentages of students with low test results, such as closure or ceding control to the city or state. As a result, schools are discouraged from having bilingual programs, and charter schools are not required by law to either include bilingual programs or accept emergent bilingual students. Without formal laws being passed, emergent bilingual students are being displaced and are no longer guaranteed a bilingual education as stipulated in the BEA. The changes in bilingual education present serious doubts about the future of immigrant children. Without the ability to become bilingual, truly proficient in English, children will have limited access to universities, scholarships, and secure jobs as adults.

Afsaneh Moradian

See Also: Adult Education; Assimilation; Citizenship Education; English as a Second Language (ESL) Programs; English Language Learners (ELL); and English-Only Movement.

Further Reading

Bale, Jeff. 2010. "Struggle for Bilingual Education." *International Socialist Review* 69. http://www.isreview.org/issues/69/feat-bilingual.shtml.

Bale, Jeff, and Sarah Knopp. 2012. *Education and Capitalism.* Chicago: Haymarket Books.

Shirin, Hakimzadeh, and D'Vera Cohn. 2007. "English Usage Among Hispanics in the United States." Pew Hispanic Forum. http://pewhispanic.org/reports/report.php?ReportID=82.

Border Crossing

Border crossing refers to the crossing of a country's border and is commonly applied to undocumented immigrants who enter the United States via the U.S.-Mexico border at a place other than a border inspection point, such as a port of entry. The way that they cross the border varies by region. Immigrants are known to enter by crossing the Rio Grande that separates Texas from Mexico, either by swimming, being carried across (where the water level permits it), or afloat on inner tubes. In the areas that have no river boundaries, such as Arizona and California, migrants are known to cross the desert on foot. Immigrants are known to climb the wall or fence that divides the United States from Mexico, or cross through underground tunnels and drainage pipes. In parts of the nation near the ocean, it has been reported that immigrants cross by rafting away from the shoreline, and rafting back to the mainland north of the border. The United States has a total of 317 official points of entry by land, air and sea as well as fourteen "pre-clearance stations" for United States entry located in Canada and the Caribbean. The U.S.-Mexico border has twenty-five ports of entry, and the

U.S.-Canada border has seventy-nine ports of entry. The border between the United States and Canada (including the continental United States and Alaska) covers over 5,525 miles, while the border between the United States and Mexico covers 1,989 miles.

During the 1990s undocumented border crossing changed drastically when the federal government invested billions of dollars to militarize the border and increase the number of border patrol agents. Along borders as throughout the interiors of the United States and Mexico, harsher and more visible measures to control immigration emerged (Andreas, 2003). The U.S.-Mexico border region evolved dramatically with greater militarization (Dunn, 1996), more border walls, virtual fences, surveillance and surveillance technology (Shirk, 2003). This trend can be traced to U.S. Attorney General Janet Reno and the commissioner of the Immigration and Naturalization Service (INS) of the time, Doris Meissner, who in 1993 launched a multi-year strategy of "prevention through deterrence" known as the "Border Patrol Strategic Plan 1994 and Beyond" (Andreas, 2003). This strategy involved the building of a rigid wall along the borders in California, Arizona and Texas. These wall-erecting efforts were known by the different names: Operation Hold the Line (1993) in El Paso, Texas, Operation Gatekeeper (1994) in San Diego, California, and Operation Safeguard in Nogales, Arizona.

In the same decade, the U.S. Congress adopted the North American Free Trade Agreement (NAFTA) between the United States, Mexico and Canada. NAFTA was touted as a measure that would reduce immigration because it would supposedly stimulate Mexico's economy, decreasing poverty and the need to migrate. However, it effectively made it more difficult for Mexican small holders to compete with U.S. subsidized corn on the market. No longer able to subsist on their lands, they were forced to migrate in search of jobs in greater numbers. For this reason, the Clinton Administration presided over one of the largest demographic changes in the United States due to immigration, documented and undocumented, However, with the fairly safe ports of entry closed off and with a saturation of border agents, the migrants fleeing poverty and starvation in their own country were forced to alter their migration routes away from urban areas and towards more remote areas where migrants have been subjected to greater isolation and dangers (Cornelius, 2001).

Many politicians heralded these border operations as a success in curbing undocumented immigration. However, as Andreas (2003) argues, the escalation of border enforcement was in effect only a symbolic effort to impress a public determined by nativism, rather than a rational response to the economic realities shared by the United States and Mexico. In short, the strategy did little to stop immigration, but rather made it more difficult and even deadly. For example, in 2005 alone, five hundred thousand immigrants were arrested along the border. However, the arrests and detentions were only part of the risk and hardship faced by migrants as they tried to evade detection and interdiction. In that same year more than four hundred people died from foul play, dehydration or starvation. With the ability to enter legally increasingly closed off to them, the militarization of the border has worked to make entry into the United States riskier and deadlier for migrants seeking entry. This development not only increases the suffering of family members left behind, but the millions of family members who live in the United States.

Regardless of higher arrest and detention rates, undocumented immigrants continue to cross the border and enter the United States in the hundreds of thousands each year. Rather than deter immigration, entry to the United States has been driven into dangerous mountain and desert terrain where many die trying to cross. In California, migrants are now forced to travel through the Otay mountains. The mountains have below freezing temperatures for a minimum of six months of the year and peaks of up to six thousand feet. Many immigrants cannot survive the hypothermia that commonly sets in at such low temperatures. In order to cross through Arizona's deserts, migrants must endure as much as 120 degree temperatures during the day and near freezing cold at night. Death by heat stroke and dehydration is common. Others drown trying to avoid the heat and border patrol agents. Hundreds of known deaths of presumed undocumented immigrants trying to enter the United States occur every year. In 2005 in Arizona alone, 472 deaths were reported (McCombs, 2011).

Because of poor economic conditions in Mexico and other Latin American countries, people continue to see crossing the U.S. border as their only option to work and provide for their families. The risks involved are more than death. Women are known to take birth control pills with them on the journey as they assume they will be raped during the journey which now lasts several days. People pay thousands of dollars to coyotes to lead them across the border. Many of these guides in turn abandon them to fend for themselves in the desert with no food, water or warm clothing. Furthermore, the border is a longtime home to drug smugglers, fugitives, corrupt policemen, rapists and murderers.

The heavy militarization of the border has also given birth to increased border vigilantism. As immigrants were pushed further into the mountains, they began to cross the border into U.S. towns that had no previous experience with undocumented immigrants. This sparked an increase in the number of vigilantes who either wanted to support the government's efforts, or felt that the government was not being effective enough. Individual vigilantes and organizations including the Minutemen and other groups aligned with hate groups began to use their guns to fire on immigrants who were crossing over the border into Arizona and Texan towns. In addition, individual ranch owners along the Arizona and Texas border entry points at times use violence as a response to migrants trespassing on their property.

In reaction, many activists, such as *Angeles de la Frontera* (in California) and No More Deaths and the Samaritans (in Arizona), have started leaving food and water in the desert. There have been a series of demonstrations and marches along the San Diego–Tijuana border (as well as other parts of the United States) demanding that undocumented immigrants be granted amnesty and that the U.S.-Mexico border be opened to end such avoidable deaths. They argue that the same people who watch children, clean houses and cook food should not have to risk their lives in order to perform these necessary services within the United States.

Even though undocumented immigrants contribute billions of dollars to the U.S. economy through taxes and purchases, they are forced to risk their lives in order to do so. The militarization of the border and the vigilantism that has grown out of it, have turned migrants into hunted criminals.

Afsaneh Moradian

See Also: Clinton Administration; Death; Devil's Highway; Globalization; Migration; North American Free Trade Agreement (NAFTA); U.S. Border Patrol; U.S.-Mexico Border Wall.

Further Reading

Akers Chacón, Justin, and Mike Davis. *No One Is Illegal: Fighting Racism and State Violence on the U.S.-Mexico Border.* Chicago: Haymarket Books, 2006.

Andreas, Peter. 2003. *Border Games: Policing the U.S.-Mexico Divide.* Ithaca and London: Cornell University Press.

Cornelius, Wayne A. 2001. "Death at the Border: Efficacy and Unintended Consequences of U.S. Immigration Control Policy." *Population and Development Review* 27.4:661–685.

Dunn, Timothy J. 1996. *The Militarization of the U.S.-Mexico Border, 1978–1992: Low-Intensity Conflict Doctrine Comes Home.* Austin: University of Texas Press.

Ellingwood, Ken. *Hard Line: Life and Death on the U.S.-Mexico Border.* New York: Vintage Books, 2004.

McCombs, Brady. 2011. "Yearly body count at the Pima County Medical Examiner's Office." *Arizona Daily Star,* Wednesday, July 6.

Shirk, David A. 2003. "Law Enforcement and Security Challenges in the U.S.-Mexican Border Region." *Journal of Borderland Studies* 18.2:1–24.

Bracero Program

The Bracero Program was a contract-labor, or "guest worker," program through which large numbers of Mexican nationals worked in the United States on a temporary basis between 1942 and 1964. It is estimated that as many as five million Mexicans worked in the United States as braceros, mostly as agricultural or railroad labor. In addition to the braceros, many more Mexicans worked outside of the auspices of the Bracero Program as unauthorized workers; it is estimated that there were as many as four unauthorized workers for any one bracero. Because the Bracero Program fortified economic and social interrelationships between workers from Mexico and jobs and people in the United States, it is identified as one of the main factors responsible for the growth in the unauthorized population from Mexico from the 1970s onward.

The labor of Mexican nationals in the United States did not begin with the Bracero Program, but by the 1920s, when major industries such as agriculture, construction, and railroads in the Southwest United States and in cities such as Chicago had become reliant on Mexican workers. However, the Bracero Program did institutionalize, expand, and fortify interdependence between Mexican workers and certain U.S. industries. As millions of Mexican workers became accustomed to employment practices, lifestyles, and consumption patterns in the United States, they established networks between jobs in the United States and friends and family members back home that allowed migratory worker patterns to become self-sustaining in the decades that followed the Bracero Program.

Mexican laborers prepare for work in the United States as part of the Bracero Program, one of the nation's first guestworker programs responding to the shortage of labor during WWII. After their work contract was explained to them, the braceros returned to sign the agreement. The Bracero Program is largely credited for accelerating migration from Mexico to the United States. (Howard R. Rosenberg, "Snapshots in a Farm Labor Tradition," *Labor Management Decisions*, Winter-Spring, 1993)

The Bracero Program was developed during the Second World War in order to relieve financial pressures in both Mexico and the United States. In Mexico, decades of modernization efforts had resulted in the consolidation of small land holdings into haciendas, the growth of agricultural technologies, and the undermining of local craft production by the importation of mass-produced goods. In spite of land redistribution after the end of the Mexican Revolution, in the 1940s millions of Mexicans, both with and without land, were in search of wage work. In the United States, entry into World War II had reduced the work force at the same time that demand for output of war materials increased; Mexican braceros were to ease shortages of inexpensive labor in agriculture throughout the U.S. Southwest. The food that braceros harvested would sustain the families of soldiers working abroad as well as the large industrial labor force in the north. During World War II, tens of thousands braceros were also used to build and maintain railroad tracks.

When the Bracero Program initially took effect in 1942, it was only supposed to last for five years and was to be jointly administered by Mexico and the United States. Growers who participated in the program agreed to provide certain wages, housing, and working conditions for braceros. Braceros agreed to work for the set wages and could not negotiate for higher wages or better conditions, nor were they allowed to change employers. Braceros were also required to leave the United States when their work visas expired. The program was extended a number of times and ultimately ended in 1964, twenty-two years after it began.

The wages offered by U.S. growers participating in the Bracero Program were often many times higher than the wages that agricultural workers could earn in Mexico. During the 1950s, bracero workers sent an average of 30 million dollars a year home to Mexico, making the bracero program Mexico's third largest revenue-generating "industry."

The program was, and continues to be, fraught with controversy. The importation of bracero workers allowed agricultural growers to avoid raising wages to attract citizen labor, helping to suppress the wages of agricultural workers overall. Braceros themselves were subject to widespread wage theft, mistreatment, and substandard food, housing, and working conditions. Between 1942 and 1948, ten percent was deducted from each bracero's pay with the guarantee that the money would be invested in a savings account and given to the bracero upon his return to Mexico, but many braceros never received this money. And while the Bracero Program was devised as an alternative to large-scale unauthorized migration, the program actually exacerbated unauthorized migration, both at the time and in the decades following the program.

While the U.S. government was trying to regulate the entry of Mexican workers under the Bracero Program, employers realized that they could circumvent the costs associated with the program by tapping into the social networks of their bracero workers. At their employers' behest, braceros could easily recruit brothers, cousins, and friends to come work in the United States outside of the auspices of the Bracero Program as unauthorized workers. According to some estimates, as many as four undocumented workers entered for every documented Mexican bracero. In addition, many bracero workers simply left their contracted positions in search of better opportunities elsewhere, becoming "illegal" workers in the process.

The program is also associated with persistent discrimination against ethnic Mexicans in the United States. Many Mexican Americans were worried that large-scale importation of low-wage Mexican farm workers would reinforce negative stereotypes that many Americans already had about Mexicans and would set back their ongoing struggle for equal rights. These fears were realized when, in 1954 in the midst of the Bracero Program, the United States launched a high-profile repatriation campaign, "Operation Wetback," that subjected ethnic Mexicans—citizens and immigrants alike—to heightened anti-Mexican sentiment and deportation. The term "wetback" itself was a slur, used because some Mexicans had to swim across the Rio Grande (or Rio Bravo del Norte in Mexico) to cross into the United States in Texas. Many Mexicans became angry, not only at the explicit racial orientation of the raids, but at the apparent hypocrisy of the U.S. government, which was condoning the use of Mexican labor while simultaneously deporting large numbers of so-called wetbacks.

By the 1960s, there was mounting public pressure to end the program. Civil rights advocates, union organizers, and Mexican American activists opposed the Bracero Program on the grounds that it legitimized the exploitation of Mexican nationals, degraded civil rights gains made by Mexican Americans, and undermined organizing efforts of U.S. farm workers. In addition, improved agricultural technologies had decreased the demand for migratory workers on U.S. farms.

In spite of the economic interdependence between Mexican workers and U.S. businesses that was fortified by the Bracero Program, the United States imposed immigration quotas on Mexican nationals for the first time ever when the program ended in 1965 (Calavita, 1992; Ngai, 2004:261). The initial cap of 120,000 visas for the entire Western Hemisphere was changed by additional legislation passed in 1976 that reduced the number of legal Mexican entries to twenty thousand annually (Ngai, 2004:261). That is, after encouraging labor migration from Mexico for the better part of a century, U.S. immigration policies slashed the number of visas allotted to Mexicans from an unlimited number to just twenty thousand per year in the fifteen years between 1965 and 1980 (Calavita, 1992).

In spite of these restrictions, the demand for immigrant labor from Mexico has persisted, particularly in agriculture and service sectors, and the appeal of guestworker programs has not gone away. In 2012, the United States granted 65,345 temporary agricultural work visas. Many U.S. farmers and business owners who have been affected by immigration raids and restrictive policies say that this is not enough, and they are advocating for an expansion of existing guestworker visa allotments.

Ruth Gomberg-Muñoz

See Also: Emergency Quota Act of 1921; Guestworker and Contract Labor Policies; Johnson-Reed Act (1924); Operation Wetback; Special Agricultural Workers (SAW).

Further Reading

Calavita, Kitty. 1992. *Inside the State: The Bracero Program, Immigration, and the INS.* New York: Routledge.

Gutierrez, David G. 1995. *Walls and Mirrors: Mexican Americans, Mexican Immigrants, and the Politics of Ethnicity.* Berkeley: University of California Press.

Ngai, Mae. 2004. *Impossible Subjects: Illegal Aliens and the Making of Modern America.* Princeton: Princeton University Press.

C

California

Today, California is one of the most diverse states of the United States with a population of over 38 million people, of which 9.9 million are immigrants. Of these 9.9 immigrants in California, 3.3 million of them are legal permanent residents. Although a significant portion of undocumented immigrants residing in California originate from Mexico, other nationalities of undocumented immigrants include Europeans, Asians and Central Americans.

California has been a land of immigrants since its early history. Originally the land of Native Americans, in the 1500s it began to be settled by Spain. In 1821, after gaining its independence from Spain, Mexico enjoyed California, along with other southwest states, as part of its country. As a result of the end of the Mexican-American War between the United States and Mexico in 1848, California along with present-day Arizona and New Mexico and parts of Utah, Nevada, and Colorado were given over to the United States through the Treaty of Guadalupe Hidalgo. Through this treaty, Mexico lost a total of 525,000 square miles of land in exchange for $15 million. Today the United States and Mexico are separated by a border reaching over 1,933 miles of land.

This same year, shortly after California was officially a new state of the United States, the discovery of gold in California was announced, and the "Gold Rush" began. People from all over the United States and the world rushed to California in search of gold. A couple of years later the transcontinental railroad was built in California in an effort to connect the state to the greater Midwest and East Coast, to increase the trade of goods. When the railroad had been completed in 1869, thousands of Chinese rail workers were laid off. Many white Californians began to blame the Chinese for the depressed economic conditions in the state; in the years to come an increase in anti-Chinese sentiment grew throughout the state. Many laws were passed throughout California to harass the Chinese, making for great hardships for the Chinese who were an established group living in California at the time. In 1882, the Chinese Exclusion Act was passed by the U.S. Congress. This law made it nearly impossible for more Chinese to enter California. Today Chinese and Asian people make up over 13 percent of California's total population.

Along with Asians, Hispanics have also a long complicated history with the state of California. They are primarily Mexicans, since California was part of the land that was ceded by Mexico as part of the Treaty of Guadalupe Hidalgo of 1848. Mexicans were living in this land when it was incorporated into the United States, and they were given the option of leaving their lands in California, to resettle in Mexico. But many people decided to stay in their houses and in their communities. This historical connection between the Mexican people in California is seen today, with the presence of over 37 percent of Californians who self-identify as Hispanic in census data. Relations between Mexico and California have been problematic since the treaty of Guadalupe Hidalgo. The influx of migration from Mexico and California's 140-mile border with Mexico has been the scene for much conflict in the twentieth and twenty-first century. Although not all those crossing the border into California are from Mexico, many of those individuals come from Latin American countries, since Mexico serves as the port of entry for these groups.

An example of the complicated history between Mexico and California can be seen by the massive influx of immigrants from Mexico who came in the early 1900s to work in the expanding economies of agriculture, mining, and railroads that California and the West Coast were experiencing during this time. Mexican immigrants were seen as contributors to the expanding industries of California and were even considered to be the backbone of California's agriculture sector. Things quickly changed during the Great Depression. Due to the terrible droughts taking place in the Midwest, many of those Americans moved to California in search of work opportunity and found that Mexicans were filling over 80 percent of the agricultural jobs. The shrinking job market resulted in resentment towards Mexicans from some Anglos, because Mexicans were now being blamed for taking the jobs that the Anglos felt they deserved. The U.S. government's solution was a repatriation program beginning in 1954, known as "Operation Wetback," which in cooperation with the Mexican government put pressure on Mexicans living in the United States to voluntarily return to Mexico, but at times resulting in outright deportation. Despite all this problematic history, California surpasses the rest of the United States in their ethnic diversity as well as being one of the most progressive states in the United States.

Along with the many struggles the people of California have had to face, there have been victories for ethnic minorities such as Hispanics. In 1945 when the segregation of public schools was taking a toll on the Mexican American communities of California, a group of five thousand parents led by Gonzalo Mendez filed a lawsuit against the Westminster school district of Orange County. The Mendez family took their case to the Supreme Court, demanding that the segregation of their children's education come to an end. The problem came about when the Mendez children were denied admission to a white school in the Westminster district of Orange County, California. During this time the United States had "separate but equal" laws, which resulted in children of Mexican descent, as well as African American children, being barred from attending schools with white children. The schools that the Mexican children had access to were not equal in facilities, resources, or books to their white counterparts' schools. In 1947, Mendez won the case, ensuring that Mexican children would be allowed to attend the same schools as white children in California. Seven years later in 1954 another historic case, *Brown vs. Board of Education,* overturned school desegregation in all United States schools.

Another law that has affected the immigrant population of California was Proposition 187 in 1994. Proposition 187 was a ballot initiative found unconstitutional in 1999.

The main idea behind Proposition 187 was to establish state-run immigration enforcement of undocumented individuals. Proposition 187 would prohibit undocumented individuals in the state of California from a public education and any health care and many other social services. This proposition would also allow local police departments to check immigration documents and require that people without them be reported to the appropriate enforcement authorities. School administrators would have been forced to report any child who was unable to show proper documentation and prohibit them from attending school.

In 2011, California made great strides towards the advancement of its immigrant population through the passage of the California DREAM (Development, Relief, and Education for Alien Minors) Act, signed into law by Governor Jerry Brown. This law would allow undocumented California students to apply for state financial aid and be eligible for many scholarships of which they were unable to take advantage of. California already offers in-state tuition to undocumented students who have graduated from a California high school, and this new initiative would be an additional help so that students could afford paying for college. This new law does not have a way to grant citizenship to these students, since citizenship is something that only the federal government can grant.

No national or state surveys can provide us with the most direct figures of the undocumented immigrant experience in California. The best estimates suggest that not only do immigrants in California help fuel the state's economy, but they also pay into the system and use fewer social services the longer they live in the state. Immigrants in California have a combined federal tax contribution of more than $30 billion annually, and pay approximately $5.2 billion in state income taxes each year ("Looking Forward," 2008). In 2011, it was estimated that they contributed about $600 billion to California's GDP ("Looking Forward," 2012). Immigrants in California and their children make up over 43 percent of California's population. California's immigrants play a major role in the state's economic development, particularly in the services, manufacturing and agriculture sectors. This is supported by figures that show that 91 percent of California's farm workers are immigrants, 76 percent of California's domestic workers are immigrants, 69 percent of California's restaurant cooks are immigrants and 66 percent of California's gardeners are immigrants. In 2005, the continents of origin for California's immigrant population were Europe (7.1 percent), Asia (34 percent), Africa (1.4 percent), Latin America (55.3 percent), North America (1.4 percent) and Oceania (0.7 percent) ("Looking Forward," 2008).

Carolina Luque

See Also: Arizona; Chinese; Home Town Associations; New Jersey; New York; Texas.

Further Reading

"Looking Forward: Immigrant Contributions to the Golden State, 2008." 2008. California Immigrant Policy Center. www.caimmigrant.org/document.php?id=231.

"Looking Forward: Immigrant Contributions to the Golden State, 2012." 2012. California Immigrant Policy Center. www.caimmigrant.org; https://caimmigrant.org/contributions.htmljavascript:void(0).

Menchaca, Martha. 1995. *The Mexican Outsiders: A Community History of Marginalization and Discrimination in California.* Austin: University of Texas Press.

Millman, Joel. *The Other Americans: How Immigrants Renew Our Country, Our Economy, and Our Values.* 1997. New York: Viking.

Canadian Border

The international border that separates the United States from Canada stretches across more than four thousand miles of land and bodies of water. The thirteen states bounded by this border include Alaska, Washington, Idaho, Montana, North Dakota, Minnesota, Wisconsin, Michigan, New Hampshire, Maine, and Vermont. Ohio and Pennsylvania are also bounded along the northern reaches of Lake Erie. This international border was first created by the Treaty of Paris in 1793 following the American Revolution and further defined by surveys conducted after the War of 1812 and the Webster-Ashburten Treaty of 1842. The exact reaches of the boundary continued to be debated by the Canadian and U.S. governments for several years, so in 1925, an official International Boundary Commission was created. This commission's sole responsibility is to survey and map the border.

Throughout early American history, the U.S.-Canadian border remained largely open. Passage through Canada to the United States has been a traditional migration pattern, particularly for Scandinavian, Russian, and other Northern European immigrants. It was not until the end of the nineteenth century that the United States began to perceive activity at its northern border as potentially problematic. This came mostly with the continued arrival of European and Asian immigrants through the U.S.-Canada border in the late 1800s. In 1882, the U.S. Congress passed the Chinese Exclusion Act. This act restricted the movement of Chinese immigrants into the United States to specific ports of entry, particularly San Francisco, California. Chinese migrants, however, continued to enter the United States illegally through other ports. A popular route was through Vancouver and Victoria, British Columbia and then southward into the United States via the railroad system. It was during this time that the United States became committed to implementing policies limiting the number of immigrants permitted to enter the United States and requiring approved certification of those immigrants.

In 1894, the Canadian Agreement was drawn to stymie immigration into the United States without limiting international trade or transport of goods from Canadian producers to U.S. distributors. It held Canadian carriers to stricter regulations and permitted the United States to assign inspection agents at ports of entry, though not all entries received agents. Enforcement was increased along the eastern reaches of the Canadian border, where there had traditionally been greater numbers of immigrants crossing. As a result, immigrants began to travel further west in order to enter into the United States at entries that were unmanned.

For many years, Canadian and U.S. citizens were able to cross the border without documentation in order to work, shop, or visit either country. In 1917 the government implemented the Border Crossing Card policy for people living within ten miles of either side of the international boundary. This policy was intended to ease the entry process for card holders by reducing the amount of time and personnel needed to confirm their legal status as they attempted to enter or leave the United States.

Following the Immigration Act of 1924, the U.S. Border Patrol was created to enforce the immigration policies, which required further documentation and focused on national origin of immigrants. Greater manpower was available through the new Border Patrol and agents were stationed at ports of entry that had previously been left empty. However, monitoring immigrant movement along the border proved to be difficult for the new agents as they struggled to deal with the amount of paperwork required of immigrants and Border Crossing Card holders alike. General Order 86 of the Immigration Act required that local visitors who had not received Border Crossing Cards now apply and pay fees in order to receive one. People who had previously traveled back and forth across the Canadian border with relative ease had to deal with challenges to their right to cross the border at all, or to return to one side of the border after having crossed to the other. This issue has persisted despite decades of attempts by both governments to resolve it and create both greater control over immigrant passage and less difficulty for local residents.

The ease of travel through the U.S.-Canadian border was conducive to solving labor needs in the United States As early as 1910, the Alien Contract Labor laws provided waivers for Canadian lumber workers to enter the United States and work in the timber industry. By 1929, over eleven thousand workers were issued waivers. Similar programs were created to bring Canadian laborers into the U.S. agriculture and railroad industries, as well as into the fields of nursing, insurance, athletics and more.

U.S. officials began to look more seriously towards the Canadian border in 1999. In December of that year, Border Patrol agents arrested an Algerian national who had been living in Canada when he entered the United States illegally via Washington. Explosive devises were discovered in the individual's possession and it was determined that he was a potential terrorist. The U.S. government began to turn its attention to its own presence along the border. However, while both the United States and Canada have acknowledged the problems of illegal activity at their shared border, it was not until the events of September 11, 2001 that security on both international borders of the United States was most noticeably increased. Although none of the individuals charged with the acts of terrorism were found to have entered the United States illegally through either of its international borders, the U.S. government initiated an intensive strategy to bulk security in both places. This included increased funds for personnel and equipment along the borders, more stringent immigration laws, and greater enforcement of existing laws and policies. In addition, five U.S. military bases have opened at various points along the border.

Despite increased border security, research indicates that illegal activities (such as the smuggling of humans and goods) along the U.S.-Canadian border have remained constant over the last decade. However, security has had an impact on U.S-Canadian trade. In the early 2000s, the nations conducted $1.3 billion in trade per day. Most of this trade was through commercial shipment across the border, and the daily movement of three hundred thousand people documented to work on the U.S. side of the border. With the increased security, processing time at ports of entry soared from just a few minutes to upwards of fifteen hours, and the local and national economies immediately began to feel the burden of labor and supply shortages.

In December 2001 the U.S. and Canadian governments created the NEXUS program. This program expedites travel across the border for people who have previously completed background checks. They are issued a specific type of identification card and permitted to travel through designated ports of entry. The Free and Secure Trade program with similar guidelines was created to facilitate speedier travel of commercial vehicles.

Most of the measures to increase security at the Canadian border in recent years have focused on determining the legality of documentation carried by immigrants crossing at official ports of entry. These methods have included the increase of personnel, but also the implementation of the highly technological tools such as biometric scanners and computerized photography to confirm the identities of individuals desiring to enter the United States.

Despite the U.S. desire and efforts to reduce undocumented entry into the United States through Canada, border control for almost one hundred years focused mostly on speedy passage through checkpoints to facilitate business and not heightened security. In 2001, for example, only 334 agents were assigned to the U.S.-Canada border while there were nine thousand agents assigned to the two-thousand-mile border between the United States and Mexico. However, researcher Peter Andreas argues that during the last several years, the U.S.-Canadian border has become a high-traffic area for illegal movement across the border in both directions of everything from drugs to arms to people.

Native American Reservations

The U.S.-Canadian border bounds a number of Native American reservations on the U.S. side, including the St. Regis Mohawk (New York), Mohawk of Akwasasne (New York), Blackfeet (Montana), Ojibway (Minnesota), and Grand Portage (Minnesota). The border transects the ancestral lands of most of these peoples and many others. As Border Patrol presence has increased, immigrant travel has been rerouted to avoid armed entry routes. Portions of these areas lie within Native American reservations. Consequently, those tribal nations are now experiencing an increased volume of illegal activity and related violence on their lands. Many tribes are ill-equipped to address these issues in terms of the necessary funds and personnel. In addition, questions of jurisdiction impede tribes' abilities to address such issues.

Andrea Hernandez Holm

See Also: Border Crossing; Indigenous People; Johnson-Reed Act (1924); Immigration and Naturalization Service (INS); Mobility.

Further Reading

Andreas, Peter. 2005. "The Mexicanization of the US-Canada Border: Asymmetric Interdependence in a Changing Security Context." *International Journal* 60.2:449–462.

Inda, Jonathan Xavier. 2006. *Targeting Immigrants: Government, Technology, and Ethics.* Malden, MA: Blackwell Publishing.

MacPherson, Alan D., James E. McConnell, Anneliese Vance, and Vida Vanchan. 2006. "The Impact of the U.S. Government Antiterrorism Policies on Canada-U.S. Cross-Border Commerce: An Exploratory Study from Western New York and Southern Ontario." *The Professional Geographer* 58.3:266–277.

Smith, Marian L. 2000. "The Immigration and Naturalization Service (INS) at the U.S.-Canadian Border, 1893–1993: An Overview of Issues and Topics." *Michigan Historical Review* 26.2:127–147.

Catholic Church

The Catholic Church is the largest religious institution within the United States. Within the United States, in 2006 approximately forty-two percent of all legal immigrants were Catholic, and it is estimated that by 2020 more than half of all Catholics will be immigrants (Miniter, 2006). The top immigration-sending countries hold large populations of Catholics. It is estimated that the Catholic Church will continue to acquire a significant amount of parishioners from documented and undocumented immigration. Since the turn of the nineteenth century, Irish migrants dramatically increased the number of Catholics residing within the northeastern part of the United States. Along with the dramatic increase of Irish immigrants, anti-immigrant sentiment also arose, but the Catholic Church worked to provide services and protect immigrants. By the same token, faced with precariousness and times of crises with few resources at their disposal, immigrants seek divine intervention and spiritual substance. Thus it is not surprising that by 1920 three out of every four Catholics were immigrants.

Historically the Catholic Church has held a strong stance on immigration due to its scriptural teachings, and its own experience as an immigrant institution. In addition the holy family, composed of the Catholic idols Mary, Joseph, and Jesus are the archetype of every migrant family. One of the most famous migration scriptures for Catholics, as well as for other Christians, is the migration of the holy family into Egypt. The holy family flees to Egypt from Bethlehem because Joseph has been warned by an angel of the persecution and killing of all male babies by King Herod. Thus, the Catholic Church holds immigration as an important part of their Catholic theology. In 1995 on World Migration Day Pope John Paul II stated that "The illegal migrant comes before us like the stranger in whom Jesus asks to be recognized." In this address by the Pope the Catholic faithful were asked to practice the teachings of the Bible, by acknowledging that Jesus is in every human being regardless of immigration status.

In 1988 the United States Conference of Catholic Bishops established the Catholic Legal Immigration Network Inc. (CLINIC). CLINIC serves community-based immigration programs and provides legal assistance to low-income immigrant and refugee families. CLINIC employees, attorneys, and paralegals provide legal aid support for immigrants and refugees who cannot otherwise afford it. In addition CLINIC serves all

Catholics take communion through the links of a fence during Mass celebrated by Pope John Paul II in Mexico City, Sunday, January 24, 1999. The top immigrant-sending countries hold large populations of Catholics, and Catholic leaders have called on the faithful to embrace the Church's message of hope and compassion for all migrants. (Associated Press)

immigrants and refugees regardless of religious affiliation and hosts and helps organize various workshops on immigrant and refugee rights.

In 2003 the United States Conference of Catholic Bishops issued a letter entitled *Strangers No Longer, Together on the Journey to Hope* in regards to immigration. This letter was drafted in conjunction with bishops from Mexico, the top migrant-sending country to the United States. This statement advocates for earned legalization, family-based immigration reform, and opposes enforcement-only immigration policies. It also petitions for the restoration of due process for immigrants, a right that had been weakened in 1996 through the Illegal Immigration Reform and Immigration Responsibility Act (IIRIRA). In addition the United States Conference of Catholic Bishops advocates for the United States Congress to address the root causes of migration. Some of the root causes identified are globalization, poverty, and underdevelopment in developing nations. In addition, the letter called for solutions to end to migration born out of necessity, and puts forth the hope that one day migration will be driven by choice.

Strangers No Longer: Together on the Journey of Hope also served to inspire the United States campaign entitled *Justice for Immigrants: A Journey of Hope* in 2005. This campaign looked to promote awareness on immigration policies and the Catholic Church's stance in the debate on immigration. The Catholic Church strived to positively influence voters to call for merciful and just immigration reform, as well as advocate for just policies and laws for immigrants. The Catholic faithful were called on to embrace the Church's message of hope, and to welcome migrants based on their contributions as human beings. In this way, the Catholic Church has followed similar pathways for immigrant advocacy as other faith-based organizations.

The campaign is driven by three pillars, which advocate and assist migrants. The first pillar is encouraging conversations on immigration within the Church. This advocates for pastoral lectures, pamphlets, multicultural activities, migration education programs, and the use of Catholic teachings relating to migration as the core. Secondly, it calls for an expressed solidarity with migrants. Due to their undocumented status, the Church recognized in this campaign that migrants are vulnerable to exploitation and other injustices. In addition to this the limitation of aid available for undocumented migrants also established the need for solidarity and assistance by the Church. Finally, the last pillar consists of a parish welcome plan and information to better serve newly arrived parishioners.

In 2005 religious institutions objected to H.R. 4437, *The Border Protection, Anti-Terrorism, and Illegal Immigration Control Act,* the failed attempt at comprehensive immigration reform because under the proposed legislation, aid given to undocumented persons would be deemed a crime. In this way, many church programs would be in jeopardy as they already engaged in assisting individuals, regardless of immigration status. The Catholic Church opposed this law because it felt it would only push an already underground population more into the shadows. In addition H.R. 4437's emphasis on enforcement was viewed by the Church as not addressing immigration comprehensively.

With shelters in both the countries of origin and in migrant destinations (Zwick and Zwick, 2010), the Catholic Church has become a witness to the plight of migrants as they move north from parts of Central America and Mexico. The work of Mexican priest Pedro Pantoja at Posada Belen, a migrant shelter just south of the border with Laredo, Texas, has been highlighted in many news accounts for his very vocal and very public advocacy in behalf of immigrants. Migrant shelters run by Catholic priests and social workers dot the border region to house, clothe, and feed weary migrants on their way to their destinations. In these shelters, migrants have the opportunity to heal their injuries and telephone relatives before moving on. Without the shelters, migrants would go thirsty, have to beg for food, sleep in the streets, and risk being victimized. Perhaps just as important, these shelters offer destitute migrants the opportunity to regenerate their spiritual fortitude with prayers for guidance and protection.

The Kino Border Initiative (KBI) is a bi-national organization that works in the area of migration and is located in Nogales, Arizona and Nogales, Sonora, Mexico. The KBI was inaugurated in January of 2009 by six organizations from the United States and Mexico: the California Province of the Society of Jesus, Jesuit Refugee Service/USA, the Missionary Sisters of the Eucharist, the Mexican Province of the Society of Jesus, the Diocese of Tucson, and the Archdiocese of Hermosillo (in Sonora). The KBI's Nazareth House provides shelter for migrant women and children, and its *comedor* serves meals. In addition to addressing basic humanitarian needs, KBI also enjoins efforts with networks to produce research that they hope will transform local, regional, and national immigration policies. For example, in November of 2011, they released the report, *Documented Failures: The Consequences of Immigration Policy on the U.S.-Mexico Border.* Based on surveys from nearly five thousand undocumented immigrants from Mexico and Central America conducted from March through August

2012, the report alleges systematic abuse of undocumented immigrants by the Border Patrol, including not allowing them to contact their consulate.

At yet another level of support for immigrants, Catholic Charities helps immigrants and refugees reunite with family members by helping them navigate through the legal immigration process and through the refugee resettlement process. Catholic Charities Community Services in New York City provides legal consultations, representation, and assistance to documented and undocumented newcomers regarding most immigration matters, including citizenship applications, family petitions, cases involving domestic violence, and cases that are in immigration court. Services are provided in a variety of languages.

Thalia Marlyn Gómez Torres

See Also: Advocacy; Border Crossing; Faith-Based Organizations; Migration; Religion.

Further Reading

Agren, David. 2011. "Mexican shelter is safe stop for migrants on a dangerous journey." Catholic News Service (April 5, 2011). Available at: http://www.catholicnews.com/data/stories/cns/1101357.htm.

Bedard, Ana T. 2008. "Us versus Them? U.S. Immigration and the Common Good." *Journal of the Society of Christian Ethics* 28.2: 117–140.

Groody, Daniel G. 2002. *Border of Death, Valley of Life: An Immigrant Journey of Heart and Spirit.* Lanham: Rowman & Littlefield Publishers.

Groody, Daniel G., and Gioacchino Campese. 2008. *Promised Land, a Perilous Journey: Theological Perspectives on Migration.* Notre Dame, Ind.: University of Notre Dame Press.

Miniter, Paulette Chu. 2006. "Is the Catholic Church pro-immigrant? You bet." *USA Today,* August 20. http://usatoday30.usatoday.com/news/opinion/editorials/2006-08-20-faith-edit_x.htm.

United States Conference of Catholic Bishops. 2011. "Welcoming Christ in the Migrant." Washington, D.C. Oct. 2011. Web. 13 Nov. 2011. http://www.usccb.org.

Zwick, Mark, and Louise Zwick. 2010. *Mercy without Borders: The Catholic Worker and Immigration.* Mahwah, N.J.: Paulist Press.

CC-IME (Consejo Consultivo Instituto de los Mexicanos en el Exterior)

In 2003, the Mexican government reached out to its communities abroad through the creation of the Institute of Mexicans in the Exterior (IME) and an advisory council composed of Mexican nationals living abroad: the *Consejo Consultivo, Instituto de los Mexicanos en el Exterior,* or the *CC-IME.* The goal of this national advisory body (the *Consejo*) is to coordinate efforts of Mexican nationals, Mexican Americans, and Mexican Canadians to improve conditions for Mexican immigrants living abroad, keep the Mexican government apprised of the experiences of Mexican nationals living abroad, and to help identify, analyze, and propose programs and services that might improve the conditions in U.S. settlement communities. In meeting these goals, CC-IME has increasingly taken on political roles in both the United States and Mexico. Members of the *consejo* (*consejeros*) are usually leaders elected by their own communities from the consular area where they reside. The number of *consejeros* that each consular area is entitled to depends on the size of the population that it serves. The first *Consejo* was organized in 2003. The 2009–2011 *Consejo* consisted of 101 of these elected *consejeros*. An additional twenty *consejeros* based on their specialized knowledge are elected in a plenary session by the other *consejeros,* and seven *consejeros* are selected by the executive committee from prominent national Latino organizations such as the League of Latin American Citizens (LULAC) and the National Hispanic Bar Association. The executive committee consists of the coordinators from each of the commissions, and the director and executive director of the IME. The entire body of *consejeros* is divided into seven commissions based on interest. These commissions in 2010 consisted of Politics, Health, Border Issues, Business and Finance, Education, Media, Legal Affairs.

The entire *Consejo* body convenes twice a year (usually in a large Mexican city) in regular plenary sessions called *"Runiones Ordinarias."* In these sessions, they attend informational presentations by scholars, political leaders, and representatives of agencies and institutions that may shed light on developments impacting a wide range of areas in the lives of Mexicans living abroad, for example, immigration reform or human rights. Other areas that might support the work of the *consejeros* living in the United States are addressed through these meetings and presentations, such as the range of consular services and educational programs that are available to families living in the United States. At these meetings, *consejeros* are expected to make recommendations and offer solutions that might improve the conditions faced by Mexicans living abroad, and engage in dialogues with those invited to present, including legislators, officials, and policy makers. The recommendations are then channeled to the proper federal and state government agencies so that these can be considered for adoption. The number of recommendations varies by *Consejo* but they can be found on the IME webpage (www.ime.gov.mx). In addition to the large plenary meetings of the entire *Consejo,* the smaller commissions also organize meetings to address the specific issues that are the focus of their commission. The smaller meetings are also ways for *consejeros* to expand their networks, gain knowledge, improve leadership skills, and devise strategies for empowering their local communities back home.

Anna Ochoa O'Leary

See Also: Advocacy; Citizenship; Community Concerns, Cultural Citizenship; Home Town Associations; Mexicans; Naturalization.

Further Reading

Alarcón, Rafael. 2006. "Hacia la construcción de una política de emigración en México." In *Relaciones Estado–diáspora: aproximaciones desde cuatro continentes,* Vol. 1, ed.

Carlos Gonzáles Gutiérrez. México: Instituto de los Mexicanos en el Exterior, Secretaría de Relaciones Exteriores y Miguel Angel Porrúa. Available at: http://www.ime.gob.mx/investigaciones/bibliografias_ime.htm. Accessed February 3, 2009.

Rivera-Salgado, Gaspar. 2006. "Mexican Migrant Organizations." In *Invisible No More: Mexican Migrant Civic Participation in the United States,* ed. Xóchitl Bada, Jonathan Fox, and Andrew Selee, 5–8. Washington, DC: Wilson Center/Mexico Institute.

Central American Civil Wars

Many undocumented immigrants in the United States come from Central American countries. Although many come fleeing the extreme poverty in these nations, the history of immigration from Central America is not complete without understanding how violent upheavals displace populations, causing them to seek refuge in neighboring countries such as Mexico. Thus, during the armed conflicts in Central America, millions of people from Guatemala, Nicaragua, and El Salvador were internally displaced or sought refuge in Mexico, the United States and Canada. Unable to enter the United

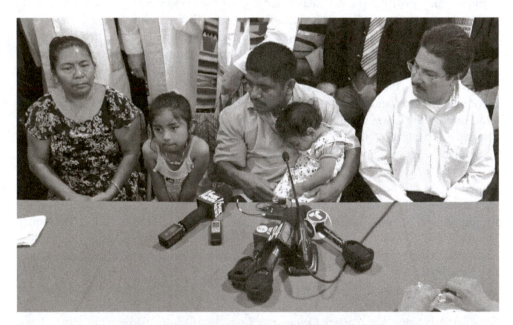

Juan, an undocumented immigrant from Guatemala facing deportation, holds his one-year-old daughter as he sits with his family, and Jose (right), an undocumented immigrant from Mexico facing deportation, before answering questions from the media after the public launch of the New Sanctuary Movement in Los Angeles. Calling for a moratorium on immigration raids and deportations that have separated hundreds of undocumented immigrants from their U.S.-born children, the New Sanctuary Movement is opening churches and places of worship to harbor families who risk being torn apart. (Danny Moloshok/X01907/Reuters/Corbis)

States legally, a robust social movement led by religious and secular groups developed in response to the Central American crisis. Known as the sanctuary movement, these religious advocates and aid workers throughout Central and North America publicly documented the human rights abuses and organized food and medical relief for victims and refugees. Many of these individuals fleeing the violence were targeted by political forces and had been killed. Advocates were also killed, the most notable being Archbishop Oscar Arnulfo Romero of El Salvador who was assassinated in 1980 shortly after asking the United States to withdraw military aid to El Salvador. In response to advocacy on behalf of Central American refugees, legal measures and policies were eventually passed to grant legal asylum to some refugees in Mexico, the United States and Canada. However, tens of thousands of Central Americans continue to migrate to the United States each year fleeing poverty and continued violence.

The Central American Civil Wars broadly refer to the era of armed conflict and political violence that plagued the Central American countries of Guatemala, Nicaragua and El Salvador in the second half of the twentieth century. To a lesser degree, Honduras also experienced violent repression and was a key political player in the conflicts. During the Cold War, Central America was an important region in global politics, and violence escalated in all these countries during the 1970s and 1980s. It is estimated that a quarter of a million people died during these conflicts, tens of thousands "disappeared" (missing victims of state terror likely tortured or killed), and millions more were displaced from their homes. People fleeing violence in Central America sought refuge in Mexico, the United States and Canada. While the political conflicts officially ended in 1996 when the last peace accords were signed, Central America is still plagued by widespread poverty, transnational gang violence and continued suffering. The history of war and violence in Central America continues to be a major factor in undocumented migration to the United States.

The United States played a significant role during the conflicts in Central America, supplying weapons, financial assistance and military training to Central American guerillas and right-wing governments. Under the Reagan doctrine, President Reagan sought to "rollback" the influence of Soviet communism around the world through supplying overt and covert aid to anticommunist guerillas and governments. The United States systematically trained Central American soldiers at the School of the Americas (now called the Western Hemisphere Institute for Security Cooperation), teaching counterinsurgency techniques, psychological warfare, military intelligence and interrogation tactics. The school was originally located in Panama at Fort Gulick but after the Panama Canal Treaty was signed in 1984, it moved to its current location at Fort Benning in Georgia. The U.S.-backed governments and guerillas in Central America killed and tortured hundreds of thousands of people during Reagan's eight years in office. For these reasons, some argue that the Cold War was largely played out on Central American soil.

Nicaragua

Civil war in Nicaragua, often called the Contra War, refers to the period between 1979 and 1990. After decades of rule and repression under the Somoza family and National

Guard (what is known as Somocismo) a broad class alliance formed under the movement known as the Sandinista National Liberation Front (FSLN). In July 1979 in the event known as the Sandinista Revolution, the FSLN overthrew the dictatorship of Somoza Debayle and opened a new period of revolutionary government. In 1982, counterrevolutionary guerrilla forces, popularly known as the Contras, opened warfare against the Sandinistas. The most notable of these contras was the Nicaraguan Democratic Force (FDN). The Contras worked out of bases in neighboring Honduras and Costa Rica and were heavily backed with arms from the CIA. In 1982, Congress passed the Boland Agreement which meant that the United States could no longer support the Contras. However, in 1984 the United States illegally mined the harbor in Managua and a second Boland Amendment was passed. From 1985 until 1990 the United States declared a full economic boycott of Nicaragua. Despite these policies, the Reagan administration continued to train the Contras, and finance their efforts with a secret slush fund amassed by sale of arms to Iran in exchange for U.S. hostages. Commonly known as the Iran-Contra affair, in 1986–1987, there are conflicting reports about how much President Reagan and his administration knew about these activities. United States Marine Corps Lieutenant Colonel Oliver North, who is credited for devising the plan, claims that Reagan enthusiastically supported it. The FSLN won the 1984 election in Nicaragua but was voted out in 1990 when the National Opposition Union (UNO) party was voted in. The UNO received strong financial support from the United States. During the conflict tens of thousands of people were killed or wounded and hundreds of thousands were displaced from their homes.

El Salvador

The civil war in El Salvador refers to the period of armed conflict between 1979 and 1992. However, social unrest and political violence and terror were rampant during the 1970s under the right-wing National Conciliation Party (PCN). The conflict was between El Salvador's military government and several left wing guerilla groups, most notably the Farabundo Martí Liberation Front (FMLN). The U.S. government trained Salvadoran military soldiers and police since the 1950s and continued to support the military government throughout the civil war despite widespread human rights violations. This culminated in a U.S.-supported military coup on October 1979 to oust President Carlos Romero. Despite the change in leadership, political violence continued under the military government and its intelligence service, the National Security Agency (ANSESAL) and a network of paramilitary groups known as the Democratic Nationalist Organization (ORDEN). These paramilitary death squads killed tens of thousands of people. Between 1979 and 1981 an estimated thirty thousand people were killed. In an event known as the El Mozote massacre, in just three days between December 11 and December 13, 1981 over a thousand people were murdered in six hamlets by the U.S.-trained and equipped Atlacatl Batallion. Throughout the 1980s the military government implemented a brutal counterinsurgency campaign. The conflict officially ended in January 1992 after twelve years of fighting and the signing of peace accords known as the Chapultepec Peace Accords. Over seventy-five thousand people were killed during the conflict, the second highest death toll after Guatemala.

Guatemala

The Guatemalan civil war, which was the bloodiest of all the wars in Central America, lasted for thirty-six years from 1960 until 1996 when the Peace Accords were signed. Throughout the conflict the United States had a heavy hand in the violence. In 1954, the CIA organized, funded and equipped a coup d'état that overthrew the democratically elected president, Jacobo Arbenz Guzman. The U.S. government feared Guzman's leftist leanings and his advocacy for social and political reform including land reform. The coup d'état, which put the anticommunist Guatemalan army in rule, instigated four decades of repression and violence. In the 1960s and 1970s the Guatemalan military modernized its weaponry, use of intelligence, paramilitary groups and torture techniques. In the early 1980s, in response to a rise in the insurgency movement and the formation of the Guatemalan National Revolutionary Unity (UNRG), the Guatemalan army stepped up its counterinsurgency tactics and warfare. Throughout the de facto presidency of ex-General Efrain Rios Montt in 1982–1983, the Guatemalan army initiated one of the most brutal and deadly periods during the thirty-six-year conflict. Rios Montt led a "scorched earth" counterinsurgency campaign that involved genocide, torture, rape and disappearances of men, women and children. Many of the victims were indigenous Mayans who lived in the rural highlands. The "scorched earth" campaign ultimately killed two hundred thousand people and tens of thousands of others disappeared.

Honduras

While Honduras did not erupt into full-blown civil war like its neighbors, it was revealed that the army was involved in repression, disappearances, torture and murder of suspected dissidents during the 1980s. In 1995, an award-winning series written by Gary Cohn and Ginger Thompson for the *Baltimore Sun* exposed the atrocities committed by the U.S.-backed Honduran death squad called Battalion 316. Battalion 316 was largely trained and equipped by the CIA and directed by General Gustavo Alvarez Martinez. The CIA trained members of Battalion 316 in surveillance and interrogation in the United States and later, along with Argentine counterinsurgency experts, on Honduran bases. In the report, which was based upon newly unclassified government documents, the Reagan administration purposely misled and minimized the violence to the American public and to Congress to maintain the flow of congressional funding to Honduras. In 1981, President Reagan appointed John Negroponte, who was known as a strong anticommunist, as the ambassador to Honduras, replacing Jack Binns who had complained about human rights abuses in Honduras. Negroponte denied knowing about human rights abuses and unsolved disappearances committed by the Honduran Army, but government documents suggest he was aware of them and played them down. Honduras played an important role in the Central American conflicts and fight against communism as a base for the United States and the Nicaraguan Contras, and from 1981 to 1985 the United States increased military spending in Honduras from $4 million to $77.4 million a year.

Wendy Vogt

See Also: Guatemalans; Hondurans; Human Rights Watch; Nicaraguans; Nicaraguan Adjustment and Central American Relief Act (NACARA); Salvadorans; The Sanctuary Movement.

Further Reading

Binford, Leigh. 1996. *The El Mozote Massacre: Anthropology and Human Rights.* Tucson: University of Arizona Press.

Chomsky, Noam. 1985. *Turning the Tide: U.S. Intervention in Central America and the Struggle for Peace.* Boston: South End Press.

Garcia, Maria Cristina. 2006. *Seeking Refuge: Central American Migration to Mexico, the United States, and Canada.* Berkeley: University of California Press.

Grandin, Greg. 2004. *The Last Colonial Massacre: Latin America in the Cold War.* Chicago: University of Chicago Press.

Pearcy, Thomas. 2006. *The History of Central America.* Westport, CT: Greenwood Press.

Schirmer, Jennifer. 1998. *The Guatemalan Military Project: A Violence Called Democracy.* Philadelphia: University of Pennsylvania Press.

Childcare

More than 5 million children are members of undocumented families in the United States, according to the Pew Hispanic Center. Most of these children were born in the United States and enjoy U.S. citizenship, but reside in mixed-status households with one or more undocumented parent, according to Urban Institute researchers. Like other children, they require attention, care, and supervision. In contrast to native-born and documented peers, undocumented children enjoy far less publically-funded or professional childcare. Though undocumented families are eligible to receive certain public childcare services (e.g., Head Start), laws such as the 1986 Immigration Reform and Control Act (IRCA) and subsequent anti-immigrant laws have fostered a climate of fear that dissuades undocumented parents from participating in these public programs. Further, undocumented parents often struggle to navigate local childcare bureaucracies and English-only registration procedures and service providers.

As a result of these issues, undocumented children are largely cared for by relatives or close friends of their families. The burden on these caregivers can be great, as undocumented parents often work long hours nearby or perform migrant labor. Childcare arrangements become particularly difficult when an undocumented parent is arrested, detained or deported, as Urban Institute researchers have documented (Chaudry et al., 2010). Increased immigration enforcement, unregulated work hours and conditions, and low pay force some undocumented parents to accept unsatisfactory childcare arrangements. These situations can put undocumented children at risk and disadvantage them educationally, physically, and socially. According to social scientists Lynn Karoly and Gabriella Gonzalez, poor childcare puts undocumented children at risk of developmental delays that continue throughout their childhoods and into adulthood. Since the late 1960s, researchers have documented the barriers that prevent many undocumented parents from obtaining quality childcare. In the 1970s, some federal lawmakers sought to address these barriers through federal legislation.

Barriers to Childcare: 1960s–1970s Research and Politics

In the early 1970s, InterAmerica Research Associates (IRA) paired with the Department of Health, Education and Welfare (DHEW) to undertake a comprehensive study of barriers to quality childcare for migrant farm workers, then the largest undocumented population in the United States. The researchers discovered economic obstacles, such as a lack of job security and economic exploitation; social obstacles, such as discrimination and a lack of bilingual childcare staff; and bureaucratic obstacles such as lengthy waiting periods for day-care spots and confusing eligibility requirements for free or reduced-price childcare. Migrant farm workers faced greater obstacles than other impoverished and undocumented groups, the authors concluded, as state and county agencies often refused services to these nonpermanent residents.

The IRA/DHEW report contributed to a broader debate about childcare for poor families. Given economic declines throughout the 1970s, the debate became highly politicized, eventually leading to a number of bills in Congress (i.e., the Comprehensive Child Development Bill of 1971). The movement for a national childcare safety net for the poor ultimately failed. According to child development scholars Edward Zigler and Mary E. Lang, bills proposed in Congress in 1971 and 1979 could have significantly improved the quality of childcare for poor families, but failed because conservative groups like the John Birch Society convinced lawmakers that childcare was a private, family issue. Further, opponents to the national childcare bills suggested that good families (e.g., wealthy, documented) were already able to provide quality childcare for their children. Thus, the childcare debates of the 1960s and 1970s failed to produce widespread reforms or comprehensive childcare supports for poor families. Still, undocumented parents gained some childcare assistance via 1960s and 1970s public welfare initiatives.

In the early 1960s, a few pilot programs served migrant families, according to the IRA/DHEW report. These state and federal childcare initiatives served tens of thousands of children, a fraction of the total number in need. Starting in the mid-1960s, migrant and non-migrant undocumented children benefited greatly from the opportunities afforded by the Johnson Administration "War on Poverty" programs, such as Head Start.

Head Start: General Results, Enrollments, and Targeted Benefits

In the summer of 1965, the first Head Start centers were launched at existing sites, such as the New Haven prekindergarten. Designed to nurture children's creativity and early learning, Head Start also provided valuable nutritional and social supports for poor families. Initially, the government program provided only a summer's worth of childcare prior to kindergarten. Head Start quickly expanded into a year-long program. In 1969, the first Migrant and Seasonal Head Start (MSHS) centers were launched to serve migrant families living below the federal poverty line. Questions about the effectiveness of traditional Head Start and MSHS programs surfaced almost immediately after the programs were launched.

In the decades following the launch of Head Start and MSHS, studies have failed to conclusively prove that participants perform better academically or socially than non-participants in the years that follow pre-kindergarten. In response to criticisms of Head Start, pilot programs, such as the nonprofit High/Scope Perry Preschool program have sought to demonstrate how to better implement pre-kindergarten education. Because these pilots are smaller and more geographically isolated, it is difficult to determine if they could more effectively serve diverse populations of poor children, especially undocumented immigrants. The limitations of the pilot studies are compounded by the fact that relatively few Latino children participate in these programs or in Head Start.

Latino children, who comprise the vast majority of undocumented children, are less likely to attend day-care centers or participate in Head Start programs than their Caucasian and African American peers, according to National Council of La Raza policy researchers Adriana D. Kohler and Melissa Lazarin. Currently, less than 3 percent of eligible Latino families participate in Early Head Start (EHS) programs, less than 20 percent of eligible families participate in MSHS programs, and less than half of all eligible Latino children attend day-care centers, according to Kohler and Lazarin. Researchers Karoly and Gonzalez suggest that these lower enrollments might result from Latino families' preferences for in-home childcare or discomfort with English-speaking or non-Latino childcare providers. They add that though recent researchers have questioned Head Start, sufficient evidence exists to support the value of well-designed early childhood education programs for children from non-English-speaking homes.

Karoly and Gonzalez and others also point to the value of consistent, high-quality childcare for struggling families, particularly Spanish-speaking undocumented families. Even if the long-term benefits of programs such as Head Start are difficult to statistically substantiate, they argue, the benefits of public childcare for undocumented families are immediate and wide-ranging. Enrollment in a childcare center, for example, provides undocumented children with an additional social safety net that might sustain them if their parents are arrested, detained, or deported. Additionally, pre-kindergarten and after-school programs provide undocumented children with safe places to play and additional nutrition, which many need due to family food insecurity. Recognizing these benefits, policy experts suggest a number of strategies for increasing access to quality, public childcare for these families.

Increasing Access to Existing Programs

Numerous public childcare programs exist and are available to undocumented families residing in the United States, but undocumented parents do not take full advantage of them. According to researchers from the National Council of La Raza, Pew Hispanic Center, RAND Corporation, and Urban Institute, the government should reform existing programs and outreach strategies to increase the participation of undocumented families. Karoly and Gonzalez suggest wide-sweeping reforms such as mandatory universal pre-school attendance and strategic subsidization of programs that address the social and linguistic needs of non-English-speaking parents and children. Karoly and Gonzalez support additional funding for English-access programs for children of all age levels. Urban Institute researchers suggest that the most effective way to support children would be to increase opportunities for their parents to obtain legal citizenship. They claim that such pathways would remove the attitudinal barriers that deter parents from seeking public services such as Head Start. Despite differences of opinion about the right path forward, all of the researchers agree that undocumented families are among the least likely to obtain consistent, high quality childcare, and that undocumented children face greater obstacles to success throughout their lifetimes as a result.

Sarah Elizabeth Ryan

See Also: Children; Families; Family Economics; Family Structure; Gender Roles; Head Start.

Further Reading

Capps, Randolph, Michael E., Fix, Jason. Orst, Jane Reardon-Anderson, and Jeffrey S. Passel. 2005. *The Health and Well-Being of Young Children of Immigrants.* Washington, D.C.: Urban Institute.

Cavanaugh, David N., Linda Jones Lynch, Sandra McClure Porteous, and Henry A. Gordon. 1977. *Migrant Child Welfare: A State of the Field Study of Child Welfare Services for Migrant Children and Their Families Who Are In-Stream, Home Based, or Settled-Out.* Washington, DC: InterAmerica Research Associates and Office of Child Development of the Department of Health, Education and Welfare.

Chaudry, Ajay, Randolph Capps, Juan Pedroza, Rosa Maria Castaneda, Robert Santos, and Molly M. Scott. 2010. *Facing Our Future: Children in the Aftermath of Immigration Enforcement.* Washington, D.C.: Urban Institute.

Karoly, Lynn A., and Gabriella C. Gonzalez. 2011. "Early Care and Education for Children in Immigrant Families." *The Future of Children* 21:71–101.

Kohler, Adriana D., and Melissa Lazarin. 2007. *Hispanic Education in the United States: Statistical Brief No. 8.* Washington, D.C.: National Council of La Raza.

Lang, Kevin. *Poverty and Discrimination.* 2007. Princeton: Princeton University Press.

Passel, Jeffrey S., and D'Vera Cohn. 2009. *A Portrait of Unauthorized Immigrants in the United States.* Washington, D.C.: Pew Hispanic Center.

Zigler, Edward, and Mary E. Lang. 1991. *Child Care Choices: Balancing the Needs of Children, Families, and Society.* New York: The Free Press.

Zigler, Edward, and Sally J. Styfco. 2010. *The Hidden History of Head Start.* New York: Oxford University Press.

Children

Millions of children are living as undocumented immigrants or as the children of undocumented immigrants in the United States. Approximately 1.5 million foreign-born children under the age of eighteen are living in the United States absent proper documentation, and over 4 million more U.S.-born children have one or more undocumented parents, according to demographers Jeffrey Passel and D'Vera Cohn of the Pew Hispanic Center. Mexican-American children comprise the largest group of U.S.-born children living in mixed-status households with undocumented parents, according to Passel and Cohn. Mixed-status Mexican-American families report median incomes lower than those for other undocumented immigrant populations, largely owing to lower parental educational attainment and employment in undercompensated occupations such as agriculture. The more than 5 million children living as members of undocumented families often lack access to quality medical care, nutrition, and childcare. Though they comprise close to seven percent of the elementary and secondary school population, according to Pew Hispanic Center researchers, these children are less likely to take full advantage of educational and social support programs than their documented peers. Today, these 5 million children are among the most vulnerable residents of the United States. That was not always the case.

Undocumented Children in the 1960s: The Golden Era

The 1960s were a time of greater opportunity for undocumented families, according to sociologist Ginny Garcia. Lax border controls, looser restrictions on Asian immigration, and limited stigma about hiring undocumented workers facilitated a rapid growth in the undocumented population of the United States. During this time, the United Farm Workers (UFW) organization was born, national origin quotas were abolished, and educational opportunities increased for undocumented and other vulnerable children.

Throughout the 1960s, educational possibilities expanded greatly for poor, rural, and other marginalized children. In 1954, the seminal Supreme Court ruling in *Brown vs. Board of Education* affirmed the right of all races to equal educational opportunity and commenced the slow process of school integration. Equally important, according to scholars Susan Morse and Frank Ludovina, a cultural shift emphasized the importance of a high school education, even for poor and rural students. Because migrant farm workers' children often completed only the early grades of elementary school, federal lawmakers created the Federal Migrant Education Program (FMEP), which raised both the attendance rates and educational achievements of migrant children, many of whom were undocumented or lived in mixed-status households. With laws such as FMEP and increasingly integrated schools, the 1960s were a golden era of sorts for undocumented immigrants and their children. This era was short-lived according to Garcia.

In the early 1970s, the post–World War II economic boom slowed significantly, wages stagnated, and native-born workers became increasingly disillusioned and nativistic, according to Garcia. Politicians responded by limiting services to undocumented immigrants, including children. In the spring of 1975, for instance, the state of Texas decreed that local school districts that continued to enroll undocumented children would be ineligible for state funds. In response, a class action law suit was filed on behalf of undocumented Mexican school children in Tyler, Texas. The case advanced to the Supreme Court as *Plyler vs. Doe* (457 U.S. 202). In 1982, on a 5–4 vote, the Supreme Court ruled that undocumented children have a Fourteenth Amendment right to equal education that cannot be denied by state governments. Though the *Plyler* ruling guaranteed seats in schools for undocumented children, it did little to quell growing animosity toward undocumented immigrants, particularly Mexicans.

Undocumented Mexican immigration was the focal point of many political debates in the late 1970s and early 1980s, and of the 1986 Immigration Reform and Control Act (IRCA). Though IRCA provided amnesty for families who had assimilated into farming communities during the late 1960s, its larger purpose was to reduce the inflow of undocumented Mexican workers. IRCA introduced employment verification, and increased the size and scope of the border patrol. IRCA also set in motion further attempts to exclude undocumented children from schools, according to Enrique Murillo, founding editor of the *Journal of Latinos and Education.*

IRCA paved the way for a spate of proposals aimed at preventing undocumented children from attending public schools. For example, Section 7 of California's Proposition 187, "Exclusion of Illegal Aliens from Public Elementary and Secondary Schools," intended to bar hundreds of thousands of undocumented children and U.S.-born children with undocumented parents from obtaining public school educations. The League of United Latin American Citizens (LULAC) and other nongovernmental organizations (NGOs) filed a lawsuit to stop the education ban. In the case of *League of United Latin American Citizens v. Wilson,* the U.S. District Court affirmed the right of the federal government to set immigration policy (i.e., upholding the *Plyler* ruling), and enjoined state officials from implementing Section 7 of Proposition 187. The district court's ruling fueled anti-immigration debates in the U.S. Congress.

In 1996, California Representative Elton Galley proposed an amendment to what became the Illegal Immigration Reform and Immigrant Responsibility Act (IIRIRA) that would have permitted states such as California to exclude undocumented children from local public schools. The amendment failed, partly because police departments worried it would create countless latchkey, or unsupervised, kids, according to Morse and Ludovina. Since the late 1990s, undocumented children have had relatively consistent access to public school educations. But during that same time, their parents have been at greater risk of arrest, detention, and deportation. Increased immigration enforcement has forced undocumented children and U.S.-born children of undocumented immigrants to live lives of fear and deprivation according to Urban Institute researchers (Chaudry et al.).

Impacts of Arrest, Detention, and Deportation on Children

During the early part of the twenty-first century, the United States invested heavily in immigration enforcement. According to the U.S. Department of Homeland Security (DHS), the number of border patrol agents nearly doubled from 2004 to 2010, and the number of U.S. Immigration and Customs Enforcement (ICE) agents increased significantly. In 2006, ICE agents conducted simultaneous raids at Swift and Co. meatpacking plants in six states, leading to the immediate deportation of thousands of undocumented workers. As Minnesota's *Worthington Daily Globe* and others reported, that immigration crackdown resulted in thousands of displaced children. According to the Urban Institute, more than one hundred thousand undocumented parents have been deported under similar conditions during the past ten years, leaving tens of thousands of children in limbo.

Undocumented children struggle greatly when their parents or caretakers are arrested, detained, or deported. According to Urban Institute researchers who conducted interviews with eighty-five undocumented families in six sites (Chaudry et al.), children experience long-lasting behavioral changes in the wake of immigration enforcement. Children who witness a parent's arrest have difficulty eating and sleeping. Children who are separated from a parent experience increased fear and anxiety as well, sometimes for long periods of time. Separation from parents can impose physical hardships, including homelessness and food insecurity. As researchers Kalina Brabeck and Qingwen Xu discovered, the relational and psychological impacts of detention and deportation increase in families with greater vulnerability to deportation (e.g., with a parent that has been deported before). As the Urban Institute documented, community-based organizations (CBOs) have responded to what some are labeling a "humanitarian crisis." Additionally, DHS has implemented some reforms, including monitoring arrestees with ankle bracelets so that they can remain at home. Urban Institute researchers and others suggest that more reforms are in order, particularly given the vulnerability of most undocumented children.

Vulnerabilities Among Undocumented Children

Undocumented children are more likely to live below the poverty line and lack access to important medical, educational, and social resources than their documented peers. According to Pew Hispanic Center researchers, more than half of undocumented immigrants are uninsured, whereas approximately one-quarter of legal immigrants and even fewer U.S. citizens are uninsured. Undocumented families can receive free emergency health services via Medicaid, but have to pay for non-emergency medical care, including preventative treatments. Undocumented children are not eligible for the State Children's Health Insurance Program (SCHIP), a joint federal-state program for families that earn too much to qualify for Medicaid but are still lower income and uninsured. As immigration policy specialist Alison Siskin reported for the Congressional Research Service, undocumented immigrants will not experience better care under the Patient Protection and Affordable Care Act of 2010 (PPACA), as they will be ineligible to receive health insurance subsidies or participate in most new government health care programs. Thus, undocumented children are likely to continue receiving only emergency care, even though they might require more care than their native-born peers.

Undocumented children are exposed to toxins and dangers that threaten their health and well-being at greater rates than their documented peers. Tens of thousands of undocumented children assist their migrant farm families in the fields, where they are exposed to pesticides and dangerous working and living conditions. Undocumented parents in other industries often struggle economically and are more likely to secure housing in poorer neighborhoods with insufficient health and social services.

Undocumented families are also more likely to face food insecurity and are ineligible for government programs such as SNAP (Supplemental Nutrition Assistance Program). Given their below subsistence wages, many of these families turn to CBOs and public schools for assistance (e.g., the U.S. Department of Agriculture's National School Lunch and School Breakfast programs). These and other programs provide basic social supports, but fail to resolve the inequities that make undocumented children more vulnerable than other children.

Sarah Elizabeth Ryan

See Also: Childcare; Education; Elementary Schools; English Language Learners (ELL); Family Reunification; Head Start; Migrant Farm Workers; Mixed-Status Families; *Plyler v. Doe*; Workplace Raids.

Further Reading

Borkowski, John W., and Lisa E. Soronen. 2009. *Legal Issues for School Districts Related to the Education of Undocumented Children.* Washington, D.C.: The National School Boards Association and the National Education Association.

Brabeck, Kalina, and Qingwen Xu. 2010. "The Impact of Detention and Deportation on Latino Immigrant Children and Families: A Quantitative Exploration." *Hispanic Journal of Behavioral Sciences* 32:341–361.

Chaudry, Ajay, Randolph Capps, Juan Pedroza, Rosa Maria Castaneda, Robert Santos, and Molly M. Scott. 2010. *Facing our Future: Children in the Aftermath of Immigration Enforcement.* Washington, D.C.: Urban Institute.

Coles, Robert. 1971. *Migrants, Sharecroppers, Mountaineers, Vol. 2, Children of Crisis.* New York: Little, Brown and Company.

Donato, Katherine M., and Ebony M. Duncan. 2011. "Migration, Social Networks, and Child Health in Mexican Families." *Journal of Marriage and Family* 73:713–728.

Garcia, Ginny. 2011. *Mexican American and Immigrant Poverty in the United States.* New York: Springer.

Morse, Susan C., and Frank S. Ludovina. 1999. *Responding to Undocumented Children in the Schools.* Charleston, WV: ERIC Clearinghouse on Rural Education and Small Schools.

Murillo, Enrique G., Sofia, Villenas, Ruth Trinidad, Galván, Juan Sánchez, Muñoz, Corinne, Martínez, and Margarita Machado-Casas. 2009. *Handbook of Latinos and Education: Theory, Research and Practice.* New York: Routledge.

Passel, Jeffrey S., and D'Vera Cohn. 2009. *A Portrait of Unauthorized Immigrants in the United States.* Washington, D.C.: Pew Hispanic Center.

Siskin, Alison. 2011. *Treatment of Noncitizens Under Patient Protection and Affordable Care Act.* Washington, D.C.: Congressional Research Service.

Chinese

Large-scale Chinese migration to the US began in the 1840s and 50s during the Gold Rush Era. A large Chinese, predominantly male labor force, came to mine for gold and

On September 2, 1885, white mine workers at Rock Springs, a coal mining operation in the Wyoming Territory, launched a withering attack on Chinese workers over access to a disputed work area. The mob ultimately killed 28 Chinese and destroyed the encampment in which all of the Chinese workers had been living. The attack reflected the extreme anti-immigrant sentiment and racism of the time, primarily against Asian people, including U.S.-born Asian-Americans, attitudes that were instituted and codified legislatively with the Chinese Exclusion Act of 1882, and the Oriental Exclusion Act of 1924. (Library of Congress)

also found employment constructing the transcontinental railroad, which was eventually completed in 1869. Given their industrious work ethic and commitment to seeking a better life, many Chinese were viewed as a threat by fellow European American workers. Due to this real and perceived threat of economic competition, sanctions were imposed upon non-native miners through the implementation of the Foreign Miners Tax of 1850. This law made it increasingly difficult for the Chinese and their Mexican miner counterparts to support themselves. Seeing the daily needs of their fellow miners, Chinese immigrants began to pursue other avenues to make a profit. By providing laundry services, finding employment as cooks and working in related industries, these migrants began the process of firmly establishing themselves in the United States.

By arguing that Chinese "coolies" who worked longer hours and for lower wages depressed the wages of native workers, labor leaders and government officials were successful in arousing significant anti-Chinese sentiment during the latter half of the nineteenth century. Passed in 1882 and lasting until its repeal in 1943, the Chinese Exclusion Act prohibited the entry of "skilled and unskilled laborers and Chinese employed in mining" under penalty of imprisonment and deportation. As a result of legislation barring Chinese entry into the United States, the federal government began encountering the issue of undocumented or unauthorized Chinese migration. Questions arose as to

The Chinese Exclusion Act and Its Legacy

The Chinese Exclusion Act was an immigration policy passed on May 6, 1882, by the U.S. Congress, which suspended the entry of Chinese laborers into the United States. It was one of the harshest and longest-lasting laws against a specific group of immigrants. The first U.S. immigration act to explicitly exclude a specific ethnic group, the policy targeted Chinese laborers, skilled and unskilled, who made up the overwhelming bulk of Chinese immigrants. The entry of merchants, students, diplomats, and tourists was not suspended. However, the 1882 act made all Chinese immigrants, regardless of the category under which they entered, ineligible for naturalization, the process of becoming a legal citizen of another country. Therefore, they could never become citizens.

In 1892 and 1902, the act was renewed. In 1904, Chinese exclusion was made a permanent feature of immigration policy. It wasn't until 1943 that the Magnuson Act repealed the Chinese Exclusion Act. It permitted Chinese immigrants to apply for naturalization and legally enter the United States. Passed by Congress during World War II, the Magnuson Act was a strategic gesture meant to counteract Japan's criticism of the United States as a racist society that officially excluded Asian immigrants and to appease China, which was an ally of the United States against Japan. The Magnuson Act, however, set an annual quota of 105 for all Chinese immigrants, a very low number. Further, to prevent people of Chinese origin from entering from another country, the 105 quota was enforced regardless of the country from which any Chinese immigrants originated. Finally, in 1965, the Hart-Celler Act, also known as the Immigration and Nationality Act of 1965, lifted the quota of Chinese immigrants from 105 to 20,000 immigrants, the limit for immigrants from any country at that time.

Tamara K. Nopper

---

the applicability of the newly passed Fourteenth Amendment to children of unauthorized Chinese immigrants, an issue that was the focus of the 1898 Supreme Court case, *United States v. Wong Kim Ark*. Other related technicalities included the admissibility of a native-born Chinese person after travel abroad or the ability of the Chinese to assimilate into mainstream American culture and be loyal to the American way of life.

Nevertheless, as the federal government began to impose more stringent immigration controls on the admission of the Chinese during the Exclusion Era, prospective Chinese immigrants also became more innovative in their tactics to circumvent this ban on migration. Through the process of "paper sons and paper daughters," many Chinese entered the United States illegally as the false children of native-born Chinese. In an intricately crafted process, prospective migrants paid large sums to "borrow" the identities of Chinese already residing in the United States or fabricated new identities of offspring of citizens. Upon arrival in the United States, Chinese claiming to be born in the United States or offspring of native-born Chinese underwent a rigorous interrogation by U.S. immigration officials. Chinese immigrants, however, were able to fabricate false identities as a result of the San Francisco fire and earthquake of 1906 in which many birth records and other key documents were destroyed. Under this scheme, many Chinese were able to enter the United States illegally. Later, in the mid-1950s, during the Cold War and amidst widespread hysteria and suspicion that Communist spies had infiltrated the U.S.

government, federal authorities initiated the Chinese Confession Program. As part of the program, Chinese who had entered the United States illegally were offered legal status in exchange for confession that they had entered the nation illegally.

Another method of unauthorized migration that the Chinese took advantage of during the Exclusion Era was smuggling, either as "in transit migrants" or through the U.S.-Mexico border via Latin America. As "in transit migrants," Chinese took advantage of their ability to pass through U. S. territory in transit to other nations, such as Cuba, Mexico or Canada. These migrants oftentimes were allowed to spend a few days in the port town (usually San Francisco, New York or New Orleans) to visit friends/relatives prior to continuing on their journey. During the visit with friends and family, "in transit migrants" would often exchange places with their native-born counterparts. These native-born Chinese not only received payment from the migrants, but also received a virtually "free" vacation to the train's or ship's destination. These individuals also were entitled, due to their birth on U.S. soil, to return at any time they wished. Other prospective Chinese immigrants utilized the extensive networks of Chinese shipping and labor contractors, such as the Chinese Six Companies. The Chinese Six Companies facilitated the unauthorized entry of migrants to the United States through the U.S.-Mexico border. Chinese would travel by ship to a destination in Latin America (most likely Mexico), and would receive training in the English language, in the skills of the profession in which they were to be employed, and in the customs and traditions of the United States. While many Chinese who were smuggled via the southern border were eventually caught, detained and deported back to China, a large percentage were never located and became subsumed by Chinese ethnic enclaves located throughout the nation.

The Chinese Exclusion Act was eventually repealed in 1943 during a period in which the Chinese were becoming a strong ally of the United States and the allegiance of the Japanese and Japanese Americans was quickly coming under intense scrutiny with the onset of World War II. The Immigration and Nationality Act of 1965, also known as the Hart-Celler Act, abolished the national origins quota system set in place as part of the Immigration Act of 1924. This act ushered in a new era in which restrictions were for the first time placed on migrants from nations in the Western Hemisphere, and federal immigration policy prioritized the migration of highly skilled laborers and family reunification. Through the preference for highly skilled labor, many educated, upper-class Chinese migrated to the United States from China and Taiwan, signaling the onset of the "brain drain," a situation where a nation is robbed of its intellectual elite as these individuals are attracted to more developed nations where they have greater prospects of economic success and opportunity. The prioritization of family reunification in U.S. immigration policy also led to mass migration not only of the Chinese and Taiwanese elite, but also of their immediate and extended families.

In recent times, as the People's Republic of China (PRC) has experienced increasing economic growth and prosperity as a result of the liberalization of its economic policy, moving toward a more capitalist-based model, undocumented migration has begun once more. In the past, where much of the documented and undocumented migration involved rural farmers and villagers from the Canton province of Southern China, present-day undocumented Chinese immigrants hail from the Fujian province, opposite Taiwan. Many of the residents of Fujian share similar characteristics with earlier Taishanese migrants given their working-class background and origin from a region with an agriculturally based economy. Just as the Taishanese men who migrated to the United States in the late nineteenth and early twentieth century were viewed as bringing prosperity and honor to their families through the sending of remittances, present-day Fujianese migrants are viewed by their communities in a similar light. Today's undocumented Chinese migrants, also predominantly male and overwhelmingly from Fujian, travel to the United States in cargo containers aboard freight ships bound for American ports. The migrants oftentimes pay inordinate sums of money (usually around $30,000 to $40,000 USD) to be smuggled, and are increasingly being caught and deported. Although deported and largely in debt to the "snakeheads" who smuggle these migrants, many return a second and even a third time if they are able.

Widespread, mainstream media attention to the issue of Chinese undocumented migration surfaced in the early 1990s when in June 1993 the ship *Golden Venture* ran aground just outside New York City. Approximately 286 undocumented Fujianese immigrants plunged themselves into the frigid waters below, swam ashore and soon found themselves detained by federal immigration officials. Due to the recent first bombing of the World Trade Center and economic recession, fear of illegal immigration was high. It had also been thought that those who had planned the first attempted bombing of the Trade Center were also undocumented immigrants. Half of the ship's passengers signed voluntary waivers of deportation and were sent back to China, while the other half waited in jail as they fought to remain in the United States. According to a documentary, today 220 of the ship's original passengers reside in the United States, but many have yet to receive permanent legal status. Though many have claimed to be asylum seekers fleeing the PRC's one-child policy, which the United States has recognized as a valid asylum claim, many still remain in a legal limbo status.

Today, there are new populations of Asian undocumented immigrants, in particular Korean and Filipino migrants, who have gained widespread media attention. While undocumented Chinese migrants were the first and longest sustained source of Asian undocumented migration, undocumented youth are now at the forefront of the immigrant debate. These youth have rallied around a piece of legislation, the Development, Relief and Education for Alien Minors (DREAM) Act, which would provide legal status for children brought to the United States at a young age by their parents. Though not an end-all solution to the ongoing debate around immigration reform, the role of undocumented Asian youth and the plight of undocumented immigrants are indeed becoming more pronounced. As the case of the undocumented Chinese illustrates, even in the very formative years of the American nation, Asians were highly involved in the battle to expand the civil rights of all immigrant newcomers.

Kevin Escudero

See Also: California; DREAM Act; East Asians; Emergency Quota Act of 1921; Human Trafficking; Hart-Celler Act (1965); Johnson-Reed Act (1924).

Further Reading

Cohn, Peter. 2006. *The Golden Venture.* New York: New Day Films.

Kwong, Peter. 1997. *Forbidden Workers: Illegal Chinese Immigrants and American Labor.* New York: Free Press.

Lee, Erika. 2003. *At America's Gates: Chinese Immigration During the Exclusion Era, 1882–1943.* Chapel Hill: University of North Carolina Press.

Ngai, Mae. 2004. *Impossible Subjects: Illegal Aliens and the Making of Modern America.* Princeton: Princeton University Press.

Romero, Robert Chao. 2010. *The Chinese in Mexico, 1882–1940.* Berkeley: University of California Press.

Citizenship

Citizenship is the dominant and valued category of belonging in the nation. The United States draws on liberal principles of democracy and equality in which it has generally invoked American citizenship as inclusive. However, citizenship is not a neutral category. Throughout history, it has upheld white supremacy. The Naturalization Law of 1790 required whiteness as a criterion for American citizenship. Yet, the state forcibly made an exception to this law when it extended citizenship to Mexicans in the 1848 Treaty of Guadalupe Hidalgo. This newly granted citizenship, however, did not protect Mexicans from racial discrimination and mistreatment. In 1870 the Naturalization Act extended naturalization citizenship to people of African descent.

The state has excluded groups of people from equal membership in the nation. It has monitored the boundaries of citizenship. The Nationality Act of 1907 revoked the citizenship of any American women who married "aliens ineligible for citizenship." The 1922 Cable Act revised the 1907 legislation; yet, American women still lost their citizenship if they married an Asian. This legislation maintained whiteness by penalizing white women for crossing racial lines. Furthermore, the 1924 Immigration Act categorized many Asian groups such as Chinese, Japanese, and Filipinos as "aliens ineligible for citizenship." The state maintained this ban for several decades until the Magnuson Act of 1943 (also known as the Chinese Exclusion Repeal Act of 1943) made Chinese eligible for citizenship. Legislation in the 1940s and 1950s extended citizenship eligibility to other previously excluded Asians.

The state not only defines American citizenship, but mainstream media also plays an influential role. It constructs who rightfully belong to the nation as citizens and under what circumstances. In 2010, Arizona Senate Bill 1070 gave license to the police to identify, prosecute, and deport the undocumented. Yet, the idea being American is generally defined by whiteness, middle-class status, and heterosexuality. This inevitably excludes people with a particular look from being deemed a citizen. Hence, the bill unfairly targets those looking "Latina/o," and it violates the rights of apprehended Puerto Ricans and other American citizens.

Notably, many undocumented youth and adults, who have resided in the United States for over half their lives, may easily be more familiar with American culture and practices. They may have poor knowledge and mastery of customs and languages of their countries of origin. These individuals may navigate their undocumented status without detection because of this heightened competency in mainstream American culture. Yet, suspicion of who does not belong in the nation is also determined by race, class, gender, sexuality, and other social categories. White bodies are believed to belong to the nation while darker, brown bodies allegedly do not fit in. Additionally, the state legitimizes students pursuing higher education versus laborers working in the informal economy. Other times, people expand the dominant idea of who is an American. Though the state ascribed American citizenship to Puerto Ricans in 1917, many continue to proudly preserve their language, food, and cultural traditions. Still others, regardless of citizenship, fervently identify with their countries of origin and maintain transnational identities and practices. Through these behaviors, they challenge the narrow terms of belonging in the United States.

Citizenship is an uneven category through which the government selectively determines which groups of people are to be valued and guaranteed full protection. The idea of second-class citizenship refers to people who are American citizens, but are not viewed as such by mainstream society and are not treated as such by the state. For example, the state interned many Japanese and Japanese Americans because they allegedly posed a major threat during World War II. In comparison, the state interned few Germans. This idea of second-class citizenship also describes the experiences of the Mexican Americans whom the government deported during the Great Depression and again under Operation Wetback in 1954.

Many groups have mobilized to demand equal and fair treatment as American citizens. Many African Americans led the civil rights movement and continue to fight for equality, dignity, and protection. Other racial groups, such as Asians previously denied U.S. citizenship, fought for inclusion, which the state gradually granted through new and revised legislation. Many groups of color continue to face discrimination that citizenship would presumably alleviate. The state, for instance, has violated the civil rights of citizens of Middle Eastern descent in the name of national security, particularly after September 11, 2001.

Not all groups residing in the United States can naturalize as American citizenship. People may not have the financial means to cover the required fees. Others may not have the necessary support to pass the exams on U.S. history and politics and English-language competency. However, naturalization is not the only means of gaining citizenship. In some cases, the government has awarded posthumous citizenship to immigrant soldiers. For the undocumented, there is no formal mechanism to secure citizenship. This is why people have mobilized and pressured the government to grant amnesty and to create a pathway for citizenship for the undocumented.

In contrast, people have rallied for harsher policies targeting the undocumented. Though the Fourteenth Amendment extends birthright citizenship to people born in the United States, politicians have pushed to amend this law. Officials have proposed that the state exempt children whose parents are undocumented from securing birthright citizenship. This sentiment is not new. In the 1880s and 1890s, the state did not necessarily extend birthright citizenship to Asian Americans born in the United States. However, the 1898 *United States v. Wong Kim Ark* federal court case ruled that the denial of birthright citizenship to any person born in the United States was unconstitutional.

Many in the United States deem citizenship as the ultimate means to belonging in society. Yet, citizenship is not a guarantee of equality especially within a capitalist system where the accumulation of wealth is valued over the equal distribution of resources. Because of racial discrimination, communities of color generally have less quality educational, health, and economic resources and are stigmatized as a result. People of color and the poor continue to face discrimination even though the state has instituted civil rights legislation in spite of their integration and contribution to the nation's development.

Myrna Garcia

See Also: Arizona SB 1070; Assimilation; Citizenship Education; Civil Rights; Cultural Citizenship; Fourteenth Amendment; Naturalization; Social Interaction and Integration; U.S. Citizenship and Immigration Services (USCIS).

Further Reading

Menchaca, Martha. 2011. *Naturalizing Mexican Immigrants*. Austin: University of Texas Press.

Plascencia, Luis F. B. 2012. *Disenchanting Citizenship: Mexican Migrants and the Boundaries of Belonging*. New Brunswick, N.J.: Rutgers University Press.

Citizenship Education

Adult Education programs offer citizenship education to help immigrants (foreign nationals) who are legal permanent residents of the United States to pass the test that can lead to their becoming naturalized U.S. citizens, the U.S. Naturalization or Citizenship Test. While test preparation is central to the curriculum, many adult education programs understand citizenship classes as a way for students to continue learning English. They organize the course so that learners can master the content, practice English, and learn to be confident and function well in the United States. Most citizenship classes are free to participants, and are funded by the federal government. The cost of filing the form to petition for naturalization has increased over the years, and as of 2011, it was $680 in order to file the N-400 form. While people who are in the United States without legal papers could hypothetically take these classes in every state except Arizona, they are not eligible to take the test that can result in U.S. citizenship. Because they must be involved in the legal process of applying for naturalization in order to take the citizenship test, if they were to try to take the test, they could possibly disclose that they are undocumented, and therefore risk deportation.

Prerequisites for Naturalization

The prerequisites for naturalization were established by Congress in the Immigration and Nationality Act (INA). Applicants for naturalization must have had a green card, evidence of lawful legal residence in the United States, for no fewer than five years. People who are legally married to a U.S. citizen and are lawful permanent residents of the United States can apply for naturalization after three years. All petitions for naturalization must be made on U.S. soil, although there are exceptions for some members of the military and their families. After the extensive paperwork has been filed and fees have been paid, it may take several years before the applicant is called for the naturalization interview. The average time it takes to get to the interview stage is fifteen months.

The Citizenship Test

The naturalization interview involves a test of English proficiency and a civics test. The English test has three parts: speaking, reading, and writing. United States Citizenship and Immigration Services (USCIS) officers decide if applicants can speak English based on whether they can answer the eligibility questions that are typically asked in the interview. Applicants are asked to read three English sentences aloud, and if they can read one sentence clearly, they are determined to be able to read in English. Applicants are not penalized for speaking accented English, but they do need to read without long pauses and they cannot leave out key words. The writing part of the test involves applicants listening to dictated sentences, and being able to write one of three sentences so that the USCIS officer can understand it. The meaning must be clear, but there can be spelling errors, and small words can be omitted.

There are one hundred possible questions on the civics test, and applicants are asked up to ten questions. They must answer at least six questions correctly. All one hundred questions and the acceptable phrasing of the answers are available for downloading on the USCIS website (www.history.com/images/media/pdf/100qENG.pdf). Applicants must be ready to answer any of the questions, and the test is administered orally. Some of the questions deal with who the senators and U.S. representatives currently are in the area where the applicant lives. Other questions require them to know how the federal government works, and to name the President, Vice President, Speaker of the House, and the Chief Justice of the Supreme Court. Still other questions require them to understand central issues related to the U.S. Constitution. Examples include: How many amendments are there to the constitution? Another is: There are four amendments to the Constitution about who can vote. Describe one of them.

People applying for naturalization have two chances to take the English and civics tests each time they apply. If they do not pass a portion of the test, they can retake that portion within ninety days.

Special Considerations

Applicants over the age of fifty who have been lawful permanent residents of the United States for twenty years are permitted to take the citizenship test with the aid of an interpreter. Those who are fifty-five and have been lawful permanent residents for fifteen years can have the option of taking the citizenship test in their native language. People over the age of sixty-five who have been lawful permanent residents of the United States for twenty years are able to take a short form of the citizenship test, and conduct the interview in their native language, with the help of an interpreter. There are special exemptions for people with disabilities as well. People who do not have legal documents seldom take citizenship classes, because the test is part of the process to become a naturalized citizen. Individuals who have entered the country without documents are "inadmissible," and if inquiry as to their status is made and they are found to be present in the country unlawfully, they can be deported.

Answers to the example civics questions asked in the citizenship test are: There are twenty-nine amendments to the U.S. Constitution. The four amendments to the Constitution about voter eligibility are:

1. Citizens eighteen and older can vote.
2. You do not have to pay a poll tax in order to vote.
3. Any citizen can vote, regardless of gender.
4. Any citizen can vote, regardless of race.

Benefits of Citizenship

For people who are eligible to apply for naturalization, which can result in U.S. citizenship, the benefits include:

- The right to vote.
- The right to travel internationally with a U.S. passport.
- The right to help relatives immigrate more quickly.
- The right to serve on a jury.
- The right to obtain employment with the U.S. government.
- The right to hold public office.

Char Ullman

See Also: Adult Education; Citizenship; Cultural Citizenship; Naturalization; U.S. Citizenship and Immigration Services (USCIS).

Further Reading

"Civics Education for Adult English Language Learners." N.d. Center for Adult English Language Acquisition. (CAELA). http://www.cal.org/caela/esl_resources/collections/civics.html.

"Civics (History and Government) Questions for the Naturalization Test." 2013. U.S. Citizenship and Immigrations Services. http://www.uscis.gov/USCIS/Office%20 of%20Citizenship/Citizenship%20Resource%20Center%20Site/Publications/100q .pdf.

Terrill, Lynda. 2000. "Civics Education for Adult English Language Learners." National Center for Literacy Education (NCLE). www.cal.org/adultesl/resources/digests/civics-education-for-adult-english-language-learners.php.

Civil Rights

The struggle for civil rights in the United States has encompassed organizers from various backgrounds and, increasingly so, has come to include advocacy for the undocumented. Competing, complementary, and overlapping ideologies have typified the civil rights movement. These philosophies included accommodation, communism, socialism, and others. Some civil rights groups such as the League of Latin American Citizens (LULAC) have found it critical to stress accommodation, or the social absorption of heterogeneous populations into greater society. They stressed the importance of adopting American practices that included mastering English proficiency and relinquishing ties to ethnic holidays, music, and food. Alternatively, communism and socialism influenced a sector of activists who believed in building an anti-capitalist movement. Whatever the underlying philosophy, the general quest for community empowerment has guided political movements and civic engagement. As activists moved forward in their respective agendas, they did so while navigating a complex web of political ideologies.

Throughout its history, the United States has deeply contradicted its principles of democracy in its unequal treatment of citizens and residents. Mainstream American perspectives have not always included the poor, women, gays, immigrants, and people

Many groups, predominantly African American, participated in the civil rights movement of the 1960s. Groups such as the National Association for the Advancement of Colored People, Southern Christian Leadership Conference, and the Student Non-violent Coordinating Committee organized acts of civil disobedience, boycotts, and sit-ins to draw attention to the scourge of racism. (Library of Congress)

of color. Even as the country fought fascism abroad during World War II, it failed to address discrimination domestically. For example, though U.S. Army soldiers of color fought for freedom abroad, they endured racism at home. Furthermore, they did not equally benefit from the G.I. Bill of Rights as their white counterparts did. Banks denied many veterans of color home and business loans. They had difficulty finding employment. Communities of color faced widespread poverty and many individuals could not afford to enroll in school.

Civil rights activism resulted in many important institutional changes. Building from the 1946 federal court case *Méndez vs. Westminster School District* that banned segregation of Mexicans in the public schools, the U.S. Supreme Court in the 1954 case *Brown versus Board of Education of Topeka, Kansas* outlawed segregation of African Americans in public schools. In 1956, a federal ruling made racial segregation in the public transportation system illegal in Alabama. This resulted from concerted efforts to coordinate the Montgomery bus boycotts and individuals, such as Rosa Parks, refusing to give up her seat to a white rider.

In the struggle for civil rights, activists fought for equal treatment and protection for all. Some used the language in the Universal Declaration of Human Rights, a 1948 United Nations document aimed to extend rights to all people. But the state did not easily concede to demands for equality if it sounded like communism, which the government considered a threat due to the Cold War and its strained relationship with the Soviet Union. The state used any hint of communism to repress activism. The state arrested many labor leaders because of their real and alleged affiliations with the Communist Party. Legendary entertainer Paul Robeson, one of the civil rights pioneers, challenged the state's contradictory practices so much so that he faced intense persecution. The government forbade him from performing in the United States and it revoked his passport. Though the state tried to erase him from the national narrative, many have resurrected his cultural politics.

This climate of anti-communism also attempted to squash immigrant rights activism and radical labor organizing. The government threatened to deport immigrant activists, and it did. The state forced labor leader Guatemala-born Luisa Moreno to leave the country in 1950. Moreno became a well-known labor leader and immigrant advocate in Southern California during the 1940s. Moreno's union organizing posed a threat to the politically conservative establishment because she advocated for citizens and non-citizens alike. The American Committee for Protection of Foreign Born (1933–1982), based in New York City, expanded the rubric of civil rights activism because it defended the rights of non-citizens, especially those labeled as communists. It fought state harassment, deportations, and other unjust state practices.

Many groups, predominantly African American, participated in the civil rights movement of the 1960s. Groups such as the National Association for the Advancement of Colored People, Southern Christian Leadership Conference, and the Student Non-violent Coordinating Committee organized acts of civil disobedience, boycotts, and sit-ins to draw attention to social injustices. Many used non-violent tactics to demand fair treatment. At the March on Washington, D.C. in 1963, Dr. Martin Luther King, Jr., delivered his famous "I Have a Dream" speech. The nation regularly summons his dream for the day where people are judged by their character and not skin color.

In contrast, the nation overlooks Malcolm X because of his militant ideas and tactics for self-determination. Yet, solely drawing on nonviolent tactics failed to produce the necessary changes.

During this turbulent period in the United States, many civil rights groups around the country firmly opposed the Vietnam War. Feminists demanded gender equality. Students for a Democratic Society and other groups disrupted the 1968 Democratic National Convention in Chicago. The American Indian Movement (AIM), a Native American civil-rights activist organization, was also founded in this period to encourage self-determination among Native Americans and to establish international recognition of their treaty rights. In 1972, members of AIM briefly took over the headquarters of the Bureau of Indian Affairs in Washington D.C. and the village of Wounded Knee to demand a review of the countless treaties broken by the U.S. government, resulting in native peoples, subjugation and marginalization. The National Chicano Moratorium Committee, a coalition of Mexican American or Chicano activists in Los Angeles, organized a march on August 29, 1970 to protest the Vietnam War abroad and to condemn racial discrimination. The police aggressively arrested, beat, and killed many Moratorium participants. Bobby Seale, Huey Newton, and other African Americans founded the Black Panther Party (BPP) in 1966. Popularly known for its slogan "All Power to the People!" the BPP designed initiatives to meet the needs of African Americans. Other militant groups also formed and launched community empowerment campaigns. A collective of Asian Americans created the East Wing in Los Angeles. Chicago's Puerto Ricans founded the Young Lords. One of the leading organizations for immigrant rights that emerged from this era was El Centro de Acción Social Autónoma— Hermandad General de Trabajadores Center for Autonomous Social Action—General Brotherhood of Workers or CASA. In 1968, Bert Corona and Soledad "Chole" Alatorre co-founded CASA in Los Angeles. CASA built on past generations of immigrant rights activism. It served as a community-based organization to meet the needs of immigrants, including the undocumented. CASA's objectives included unconditional amnesty, stopping deportations and raids, jobs for all, rights for all to organize, and respect for the rights of undocumented people. CASA had chapters in other parts of the American Southwest, as well as in Illinois and Washington. Though CASA folded as a national organization in 1978, it set a blueprint for future immigrant rights activism.

The U.S. Civil Rights movement paralleled the emergence of revolutionary ideas alive world-wide. Student protestors in Mexico City resisted state injustices. They faced death, torture, and kidnappings when paramilitaries violently attacked them, known as the 1968 Tlatelolco Massacre. Students and workers participated in widespread strikes and demonstrations in France in 1968, and successfully disrupted— through temporarily—the nation's economy.

Ultimately, the federal government instituted various affirmative action policies that would consider race, religion, gender, or national origin to make up for the historical legacy of racism and institutionalized discrimination. The Equal Pay Act of 1963 banned wage discrepancies based on gender. The Civil Rights Act of 1964 abolished discrimination in public places and in employment, and desegregated public schools. The Voting Rights Act of 1965 outlawed discriminatory voting practices. In 1974, as a result of Puerto Rican activism the Aspira Consent Decree mandated the right to bilingual education for limited English-proficient students in the New York City public school system.

Immigrants also reaped the benefits of the fight for civil rights and the struggle to end racial discrimination. The Hart-Celler Immigration and Nationality Act Amendments of 1965 lifted race-based restrictions and national-origins quotas and is widely recognized as the most progressive immigration reform in the nation's history. Most scholars acknowledge that it was a product of the predominating perspectives of the time that articulated values about inclusiveness, democracy and equality. However, the lifting of the quotas of Hart-Celler alone did not fuel immigration from Asia and Latin America. War, poverty, and U.S. intervention abroad also played a major role.

Many saw the passage of civil rights legislation as a victory, but inequalities persist today. Civil rights legislation did not remedy serious problems of de facto discrimination in education, health care, housing, and employment against women, gays, the poor, and people of color. The passage of civil rights legislation fostered the idea that equality is now possible because laws have changed. This logic places the responsibility on an individual to gain equality. However, this is not the case. For example, middle-class African Americans benefited from civil rights legislation while poor African Americans struggled to gain from the change in law. Schools are more segregated today than they were prior to the Supreme Court ruling that made it unconstitutional. Gays continue to fight for equal rights and protection. Civil rights legislation remains vulnerable. The state has repealed affirmative action programs. In 1996, California Proposition 209 prohibited public institutions from using race, sex, or ethnicity in its practices. In 2006, Michigan passed an affirmative action ban targeting public colleges and government contracting. These rulings adversely affect the retention and enrollment of students of color in higher education institutions.

Many immigrant rights activists today have expanded the traditional boundaries of civil rights to include the undocumented. Though the far right often argues that the undocumented should be entitled to no rights, the Constitution does provide protection for non-citizens. This legal protection, however, is also at risk. Though the Fourteenth Amendment extended citizenship to those born in the United States, politicians have proposed legislation to deny birth certificates to U.S.-born children of undocumented parents. However, this perspective neglects the complexity of today's struggle for civil rights. In 2006 both citizens and noncitizens mobilized in nationwide political demonstrations over immigration reform using this wide range of civic strategies. A broader view of political and civic participation thus recognizes that many immigrant families consist of individual members who have different legal statuses (citizen, noncitizen legal resident, or undocumented) and are therefore constrained or empowered in different ways. This broader view is useful for considering the future of a more inclusive political participation, as a growing number of younger activists— sons and daughters of current immigrants—learn and become inspired by older, politically active role models. Although the nation has much work to do to fulfill its lofty ideals as a nation where equality for all is attainable, the civil rights movement served as a critical turning point where the possibilities for an egalitarian society are within reach.

See Also: Activism; Advocacy; Community Concerns; Cultural Citizenship; League of Latin American Citizens (LULAC); Policy and Political Action; Protests.

Myrna García

Further Reading

American Indian Movement. 2012. *The Columbia Electronic Encyclopedia,* 6th ed. Columbia University Press. Available on line at: http://www.infoplease.com/encyclopedia/society/american-indian-movement.html.

Anderson, Carol. 2003. *Eyes Off the Prize: The United Nations and the African American Struggle for Human Rights, 1944–1955.* Cambridge & New York: Cambridge University Press.

Fraga, Luis, John Garcia, Rodney Hero, Michael Jones-Correa, Valerie Martinez-Ebers, and Gary Segura. 2010. *Making It Home: Latino Lives in America.* Philadelphia, PA: Temple University Press.

Johnson, Kevin R. 2012. "Immigration and Civil Rights: State and Local Efforts to Regulate Immigration." *Georgia Law Review* 46.3:609–638.

Johnson, Kevin R., and Bill Ong Hing. 2007. "The Immigrant Rights Marches of 2006 and the Prospects for a New Civil Rights Movement." *Harvard Civil Rights–Civil Liberties Law Review* 42.1:99–138.

Larralde, Carlos M., and Richard Griswold del Castillo. 1997. "Luisa Moreno and the Beginnings of the Mexican American Civil Rights Movement in San Diego." *Journal of San Diego History.* 43.3. Available on line at: http://www.sandiegohistory.org/journal/97summer/moreno.htm.

Ngai, Mae M. 2010. "The Civil Rights Origins of Illegal Immigration." *International Labor and Working Class History* 78.1:93–99.

Clinton Administration

The Clinton Administration (January 1993–January 2001) presided over the largest increase in immigration, documented and undocumented, the United States had experienced for seventy years. From 1990 to 2000, there was a 43 percent increase in immigration. By the decade's end, the 11.2 million immigrants who entered the United States during this time, an average of 1.2 million per year, constituted a substantial addition to the country's population. In addition, during this decade there were 6.4 million children born to recent immigrants, contributing to the growing number of mixed-status families. As a result, immigration, particularly undocumented immigration, was a key issue for the Clinton presidency.

Before 2000, immigration was concentrated in selected parts of the country. California accounted for 30.9 percent of the U.S. total immigrant population (almost 8.8 million people). New York had 12.8 percent, Florida 9.8 percent, Texas 8.6 percent, New Jersey 4.3 percent, and Illinois housed 4.1 percent of immigrants living in the United States. There were also dramatic increases in immigration population in Arizona, Colorado, North Carolina, and Nevada. Included in this period of increase was a sharp rise in the number of undocumented immigrants. A study done in 2002 reveals that there were 9.3 million undocumented immigrants residing in the United States. Of those 9.3 million, 57 percent were from Mexico; just under 25 percent were from the rest of Latin America; 10 percent were born in Asia; Europe and Canada combined made up 5 percent; and Africa and the rest of the world comprised the remaining 5 percent. With more than half of the undocumented immigrant population, Mexico was undoubtedly the greatest source of undocumented immigration.

As the numbers of Mexican immigrating to the United States began to rise from 1990 to 2000, the search for jobs led immigrants to settle outside of the traditional states. Work in meat processing and packing plants, light manufacturing and construction led Mexican-born workers to settle in the southeastern states, upper Midwest, and Utah and Colorado. Many states throughout the country began to see their demographics change dramatically. Immigration outside the four traditional states rose from five hundred thousand to 2.7 million from 1990 to 2002.

As politicians began to react to this drastic change in local populations, the Clinton Administration took notice and action as well. Nativist anxieties over these major demographic changes were increasingly expressed; and beginning in California with proposition 187 in 1994, laws began to be proposed that were anti-immigrant in nature. However, the growing nativist attitudes and the growing numbers of laws that were proposed threatened immigrant integration into the nation's economy by restricting their access to public programs. Although the California proposition was struck down by a U.S. district court as unconstitutional on the basis that it infringed on the federal government's exclusive jurisdiction over matters related to immigration, similar laws were to follow. The Clinton Administration thus presided over the passing of the *Illegal Immigration Reform and Immigrant Responsibility Act* of 1996, a piece of legislation that among other things succeeded in making it more difficult for legal residents and U.S. citizens to sponsor the legal immigration of noncitizen family members.

NAFTA

Among the Clinton Administration policies, perhaps none would have such dire long-term effects on migration as the North American Free Trade Agreement (NAFTA). A trade agreement between Canada, the United States, and Mexico, NAFTA was heralded as a way to increase trade and, therefore, boost the economies of all three countries.

However, the impact of NAFTA on Mexico has been severe. In order to enter NAFTA, Mexico had to devalue its peso (which caused an economic collapse in 1995) and renegotiate its debt with the International Monetary Fund (IMF). The United States offered Mexico a $20 billion loan with the condition that Mexico sell off many government businesses to private investors and that Mexico allow U.S. businesses and individuals to own land and factories without Mexican partners (in clear violation of Mexico's constitution).

With the doors wide open to foreign investment, the majority of entrepreneurial activity became concentrated in the north of Mexico where U.S. companies opened

80 percent of the existing *maquiladoras,* deregulated factories that operate as sweat-shops. While this created jobs, the low pay and poor conditions created incentives to move north into the United States.

NAFTA also had a massive impact on agriculture in Mexico. While imports of U.S. agricultural goods increased to Mexico, small farmers found themselves unable to compete. For example, U.S. corn imports to Mexico went from 2.7 to 6.1 million metric tons since 1997. In the same time, the price of corn dropped by 70 percent for Mexican farmers. The result is that over 2 million farmers have been driven off their land since the passage of NAFTA, mostly in Mexico's southern states, such as Chiapas and Oaxaca. In addition, upon signing NAFTA, the Mexican government repealed the law which protects communal indigenous land from being sold to private owners. This has resulted in the exodus north where most all but children, the elderly, and infirm leave their village in search of work and food. While the difficult conditions for Mexicans did not begin with NAFTA, the trade agreement greatly exacerbated the situation. Two-thirds of Mexican-born undocumented immigrants in the United States arrived in 1994 and later.

Border Walls

At the same time that the Clinton Administration worked to gain NAFTA's approval, the nation's attention turned to the country's immigration "problem." In the 1993 State of the Union address, the president stated that "our borders leak like a sieve," and proposed sending hundreds of more border patrol agents to the U.S.-Mexico border.

With the aim of curbing illegal entry into the United States, more police and border patrol forces were deployed to the border's common crossing routes so as to detain any immigrant attempting to enter, and deter others from following suit. The number of border agents was increased to 8,500. The annual budget for the Immigration and Naturalization Service or INS (now known as Immigration and Customs Enforcement or ICE) was increased to $4.6 billion, almost tripling its size.

However, the Clinton Administration went far beyond adding some more border agents. In addition to greater numbers of personnel policing the border, President Clinton oversaw the first significant effort in U.S. history to militarize the U.S.-Mexican border with the multi-year strategy of "prevention through deterrence" known as the "Border Patrol Strategic Plan 1994 and Beyond" launched in 1993. This strategy involved the building of rigid walls along the borders in California, Arizona and Texas known as Operation Hold the Line (1993) in El Paso, Texas, Operation Gatekeeper (1994) in San Diego, California, and Operation Safeguard in Nogales, Arizona.

The Operation Gatekeeper wall began at the Pacific Ocean and ran through San Diego all the way to the Otay Mountains in southern California. Along its route was a 73-mile, 10-foot-high steel wall, fifty-two miles of fences, stadium lighting, and a triple fence. At that time, this area had the most number of apprehensions of undocumented border crossers. Operation Gatekeeper counted on the most advanced military equipment such as night-vision telescopes, heat sensors, electronic vision–detecting devices, computerized fingerprinting equipment and Black Hawk helicopters. The merging of military type of technologies and tactics is what has been referred to "the militarization of the border."

In 1996, President Clinton praised Operation Gatekeeper, "Since 1992, we have increased our Border Patrol by over 35 percent; deployed underground sensors, infrared night scopes, and encrypted radios; built miles of new fences; and installed massive amounts of new lighting."

Border agent deployments, enhanced by fences as well as military equipment and training, arrested and repatriated thousands of immigrants attempting to cross the border via traditional routes. There was criticism raised as to how the detainees were being treated by the agents. Amnesty International issued a report in May 1998 condemning the operation. The Amnesty International report cited abuse of detainees including beatings with batons, fists and feet; sexual abuse of men and women; denial of food, water and blankets; and refusal to grant medical attention to detainees. In following years, other reports by civic organizations such as Border Action Network, No More Deaths, and the Kino Border Initiative, would continue to try to bring to light these abuses through similar reporting. Border patrol misconduct was also inflicted on members of a Native American tribe whose tribal land is situated on both sides of the U.S.-Mexican border.

The result of these massive, high-tech, expensive operations was to neither decrease nor deter the number of immigrants attempting to cross the border. Instead, by sealing off accessible entry points to the United States, entry points moved further east, through dangerous terrain. Forced to cross through desert and mountains, many people cannot survive the extreme heat during the day and extreme cold at night. By 2001, six hundred people had died trying to cross the San Diego–Yuma stretch alone, and 1,450 deaths occurred along the border from 1995 to 2001. In effect, the numbers of border deaths increased 500 percent in the seven years after Operation Gatekeeper was initiated.

Hailed by the Clinton Administration as a success, Operation Gatekeeper also invigorated vigilantism. As immigrants were pushed further into the mountains, they began to cross the border into U.S. towns that had no previous experience with undocumented immigrants. This sparked an increase in the number of vigilantes, such as the Minutemen, who either wanted to support the government's efforts, or felt that the government was not being effective enough. Other vigilante-type militia or paramilitary organizations affiliated with white supremacist hate groups including the Ku Klux Klan began to use their guns to fire on immigrants who were crossing over the border into their Arizona and Texan towns.

Conclusion

The Clinton Administration holds a historic place in the experience of undocumented immigration in the United States. The policies of the administration have permanently altered the continued influx of undocumented immigrants and subsequent deaths along the border, both of which are largely the result of the Clinton Administration's approbation of the North American Free Trade Agreement (NAFTA) and the militarization of the U.S.-Mexico border.

Afsaneh Moradian

See Also: Border Crossing; California; Death; Illegal Immigration Reform and Immigrant Responsibility Act (1996); Minutemen; North American Free Trade Agreement (NAFTA); Proposition 187.

Further Reading

Akers Chacón, Justin, and Mike Davis. 2006. *No One Is Illegal: Fighting Racism and State Violence on the U.S.-Mexico Border.* Chicago: Haymarket Books.
Camarota, Steven A. "Immigrants in the United States 2000." January 2001. http://www.cis.org/articles/2001/back101.html.
Ellingwood, Ken. 2004. *Hard Line: Life and Death on the U.S.-Mexico Border.* New York: Vintage Books.
Nevins, Joseph. 2002. *Operation Gatekeeper and Beyond: The Rise of the "Illegal Alien" and the Making of the U.S.-Mexico Boundary.* New York: Routledge.

Colleges and Universities

The US Latina/o Educational Pipeline

Latina/o students, regardless of immigration status or country of origin, continue to be underrepresented in institutions of higher education. To discuss colleges and universities and Latinos in the United States, we must first acknowledge that the educational pipeline and pathway to college begins as early as kindergarten. In states like California, overcrowded and deplorable classroom conditions, limited resources, along with low accessibility to college-track courses, all contribute to the low high school graduation rate of Latinas/os. The Latina/o students who graduate from high school are not entering colleges and universities in large numbers, and in fact, very few Latina/o students earn a doctorate or terminal degree. The staggering low numbers and representation of Latina/o students on college campuses is alarming and multiple factors contribute to this phenomenon, including but not limited to marginalization based on race, class, college preparation, language, and immigration status.

Undocumented Mexican children were the subject of a landmark U.S. Supreme Court decision in 1982 in *Plyler vs. Doe.* In this decision, the U.S. Supreme Court ruled that a state cannot deny a free public education from kindergarten through twelfth grade to undocumented immigrant students. However, acceptance into institutions of higher education is still an issue for this student population. The Illegal Immigration Reform and Immigrant Responsibility Act of 1996 (IIRIRA) and the Personal Responsibility and Work Opportunity Reconciliation Act of 1996 (PRWORA) are two federal statutes that mention immigration status in the context of higher education. However, neither the IIRIRA nor the PRWORA prevents nor prohibits an institution of higher education from enrolling or admitting undocumented immigrant students.

Table 1. The U.S. Latina/o Educational Pipeline, by Race/Ethnicity, Subgroup, and Gender, 2000

Latinas/os	Chicanas/os	Puerto Ricans	Cubans	Dominicans	Salvadorans
100/100 Elementary school students ↓	100/100 Elementary school students ↓	100/100 Elementary school Students ↓	100/100 Elementary school Students ↓	100/100 Elementary school Students ↓	100/100 Elementary school Students ↓
54/51 Graduate from high school ↓	47/44 Graduate from high school ↓	65/62 Graduate from high school ↓	63/63 Graduate from high school ↓	51/51 Graduate from high school ↓	36/36 Graduate from high school ↓
11/10 Graduate from college ↓	8/7 Graduate from college ↓	13/12 Graduate from college ↓	21/22 Graduate from college ↓	11/11 Graduate from college ↓	6/6 Graduate from college ↓
4/4 Graduate from graduate school ↓	2/2 Graduate from graduate school ↓	4/4 Graduate from graduate school ↓	9/10 Graduate from graduate school ↓	4/4 Graduate from graduate school ↓	2/2 Graduate from graduate school ↓
0.3/0.4 Graduate with doctorate	0.2/0.2 Graduate with doctorate	0.3/0.4 Graduate with doctorate	1.2/1.3 Graduate with doctorate	0.3/0.4 Graduate with doctorate	0.1/0.2 Graduate with doctorate

Note: The first column, in bold, represents Latinas/os as a whole. The first number in each box represents females, and the second, males.

Source: Data from the U.S. Bureau of the Census (2000) and adapted from L. Pérez Huber, O. Huidor, M. C. Malagón, G. Sánchez, and D. G. Solórzano, 2006. "Falling through the Cracks: Critical Transitions in the Latina/o Educational Pipeline: Latina/o Education Summit Report." UCLA Chicano Studies Research Center.

Beginning in 2008 and with the wave of anti-immigrant measures that were passed by state legislatures throughout the United States, greater restrictions for undocumented students who aspired to access institutions of higher education began to emerge. In general, these restrictions included denying those students who could not prove their legal residency the right to pay in-state tuition. Out-of-state tuition fees can be more than three times the in-state tuition rate. In addition, undocumented immigrant students do not qualify for government-sponsored financial aid until they have attained legal residency in the United States. For those undocumented students who were from economically disadvantaged households, these laws put higher education out of reach. According to the U.S. Department of Education, in 2010–2011 the average annual tuition for U.S. public universities was $13,297. By this time, there had been repeated attempts in the U.S. Congress to address what for many seemed to be a humane and reasonable solution to accommodate the educational goals of those children who as small children had been brought to the United States without legal authority by their parents. Known as the Development, Relief, and Education for Alien Minors Act (DREAM Act), as of 2013 no such act had been passed. In the meantime, several states such as California and Illinois began passing their own laws that followed the principles outlined in the DREAM Act, making it more plausible for all students to attend college if they meet the admission requirements of the institution. As of 2013, states that allow undocumented students to pay in-state tuition include: California, Colorado, Connecticut, Illinois, Kansas, Maryland, Nebraska, New Mexico, New York, Oklahoma, Oregon, Texas, Utah, and Washington. As a general rule, a student must have attended high school in the state for three or more years. Similar legislation has been under consideration in Florida, Hawaii, Massachusetts, Minnesota, New Hampshire, New Jersey, North Carolina, Oregon, South Carolina, Tennessee, and Virginia. Those that deny in-state tuition for undocumented students include Arizona, Georgia, Indiana, Ohio, and South Carolina. The Immigration Reform Bill (S744) proposed by the U.S. Senate "Gang of Eight" and approved by that chamber in June of 2013, included a DREAM Act provision for expediting citizenship for DREAM Act–eligible students. However, as of the fall of 2013, S744 had been stalled in the House of Representatives.

There are also specific college campuses that recruit, retain, and cater to the culturally specific needs of Latina/o students, Hispanic-Serving Institutions (HSIs). According to the Hispanic Association of Colleges and Universities (HACU), HSIs are defined as "colleges, universities, or systems/districts where total Hispanic enrollment constitutes a minimum of 25 percent of the total enrollment." "Total Enrollment" includes full-time and part-time students at the undergraduate or graduate level of the institution— the institution can be a technical school, a community college or four-year institution. All colleges and universities, not just HSIs, across the country must make a purposeful effort to recruit Latina/o students onto their campuses and institutionalize policies that retain this student population and graduates them in larger numbers. A bridge between colleges and universities, elementary schools, middle schools and high schools needs to be established to create a K-20 Latina/o educational pipeline.

Judith Flores Carmona

See Also: DREAM Act; Education; Elementary Schools; High Schools; International Students/Student Visas; *Plyler v. Doe.*

Further Reading

"Basic Facts about In-State Tuition for Undocumented Immigrant Students." 2013. National Immigration Law Center. http://www.nilc.org/basic-facts-instate.html.

Hispanic Association of Colleges and Universities (HACU). http://www.hacu.net/assnfe/CompanyDirectoryasp?STYLE=2&COMPANY_TYPE=1,5&SEARCH_TYPE=0.

Pérez Huber, L., O. Huidor, M. C. Malagón, G. Sánchez, and D. G. Solórzano. 2006. "Falling through the cracks: Critical Transitions in the Latina/o Educational Pipeline." Latina/o Education Summit Report. UCLA Chicano Studies Research Center.

United States Department of Education Lists of Postsecondary Minority Institutions and specifically, "Hispanic Serving Institutions" (HSIs). http://www2.ed.gov/about/offices/list/ocr/edlite-minorityinst-list-hisp-tab.html; http://www2.ed.gov/about/offices/list/ocr/edlite-minorityinst-list-pg4.html.

Community Activism

Community activism is a form of action engaged in by people who share a geography and/or experience. This community of people may be defined by a certain geographic region, e.g. East Los Angeles and/or could be defined based on similar or shared characteristics of a group, such as ethnicity or place of origin or a shared affront or discrimination. Immigrants who come to the United States from various Central and Latin American countries have a shared experience relative to their place of origin. This shared geographical and cultural origin serves to create bonds between people from the same place.

A main point about community activism is that it pertains to meeting the needs and concerns of members of a community. Why does it occur? Community activism occurs when people engage in some form of action designed to help or promote the community that they share. It is rooted in the notion that any individual or group of individuals can be proactive and work together to institute a social change. For a community to be mobilized to action, there first needs to be a sense of solidarity and shared experience felt by members of the community. This shared experience is usually tied to some shared inequality experienced by a collective of people. Sometimes the action is spontaneous, in which case it would be called collective action. At other times the actions are coordinated and persistent over time, which would represent a social movement. Spontaneous forms of collective action can occur in immediate reaction to a perceived atrocity, like, for example, the passage of California's Proposition 187, Arizona's SB 1070, Georgia's HB 87 and anti-immigrant laws in Alabama.

Being "undocumented" in the United States puts immigrants in a vulnerable position due to their lack of rights and protection. There is a great fear of being deported. Activism rooted in undocumented communities is a response to such inequality. When undocumented workers engage in active protest to try to improve unfair working wages and/or working conditions—they are routinely arrested and deported (Bacon, 2008). This represents the criminalization of undocumented immigrants and can serve as a major roadblock to community activism.

Undocumented immigrants and their supporters engage in community activism to try to promote necessary change that has not yet occurred. Examples of such changes could be the right to live, work, receive fair wages, save money, vote, go to college, serve in the armed forces, receive benefits and scholarships. Community activism is so central to the experience of undocumented immigrants in the United States because they are a group that has traditionally been used for their labor to power U.S. industry and agriculture. For undocumented immigrants there are many issues to be addressed such as: immigrant status, deportation, immigrant health and access to health services, lack of insurance, access to housing, fair wages, safe working conditions.

Different Forms of Community Activism

Community activism can involve written forms of protest such as writing letters to the editor of a newspaper or posting commentary in an online blog to expose an inequality. The sharing of information relative to a cause or an experienced inequality is a central part of any social movement because a movement needs to keep its members aware of recent happenings and inequalities experienced by members of the group. Most recently community activists are using social media to share information and organizing political and social actions. Social media (such as Facebook, Twitter) can also be used by activists to quickly highlight injustices as well that are experienced by their constituents and make a call for action. Because undocumented immigrants in the United States lack the same rights and protection as those of U.S. citizens, they are often a group that faces discrimination. To highlight this discrimination, constituents may choose from a variety of different forms of community action. These may include protest or boycotts of certain companies, marches, street theater, picketing and civil disobedience. Civil disobedience involves placing oneself or a group of people in a strategic location (e.g. city hall or the local police station) to highlight the issue of concern.

The goal of community action is to create some sort of a change. This change cannot occur without a general awareness being created of the issue or inequality faced. In any society there are many issues that need to be fixed, but for a community to rise up and take action, the issue has to rise above all other issues. Activists usually try to engage in peaceful protest. The fact is, however, that peaceful protests can turn violent depending on who else infiltrates the action. If people who choose not to participate peacefully enter into a street demonstration or protest march, that can quickly change the tenor of this action and lead to further criminalization. Community activists who seek to engage in peaceful protest have to guard against and take steps to curb violence so as not to negatively impact their cause.

The choice of the form of activism relates to the issue at hand. For instance, if the issue is lack of healthy foods provided by the stores, the form of activism may involve finding a suitable plot of land and planting a community garden. Similarly, if the issue is the issue of immigration status and the limitations to education imposed on the undocumented due to their status, the action may involve a more active protest. The protest may involve some sort of symbolism. For instance, when undocumented high school graduates who have gained admission to college are threatened with deportation, a strategy has been to stage a protest wearing the traditional graduation cap and gown regalia of a graduating student to highlight their situation. In this way, in July of 2013, nine young activists who came be known as the "Dream 9" were arrested and detained in an immigration detention center wearing their cap and gowns in a symbolic gesture to underscore and draw attention to the basic issue of access to education by undocumented students.

Within the label undocumented immigrants there are going to potentially be many different types of sub-communities. As mentioned above, these sub-communities may be based on geographic origin such as where the immigrants came from in their home country or their current situation or interest. Sub-communities can also vary from state to state depending upon the issue. Recently in the United States there has been focus amongst the undocumented immigrant communities on action related to deportations, the Secure Communities Program and limited rights of undocumented people in the United States. Undocumented immigrants do not enjoy the same privileges and opportunities afforded to U.S. citizens.

Roots of Immigrant Activism

The discrimination and inequality experienced by undocumented immigrants can involve the issues of access to housing, fair wages, working conditions. These are issues that Latino people in the United States and especially undocumented immigrants have historically faced. The movie *Salt of the Earth* released in 1954 is the only movie ever blacklisted by the United States government (Lorence, 1999). This movie was blacklisted in part because it exposed the inequalities experienced by Mexican-American mine-workers in New Mexico from a 1950 strike and perhaps more importantly because it illustrated the power and solidarity of effective community activism for this population. It is also a movie where the non-professional cast (or people from the local New Mexican community of Grant County) greatly outnumbered the professional cast. The movie was based on real-life events, and many of the people who starred in the movie, such as Juan Chacon, who played Ramon Quintero, the male lead, actually played himself in the movie as a local labor-union leader. The female lead in the movie, professional Mexican actress Rosaura Revueltas, was deported midway during the filming as part of an attempt to halt movie production. Issues faced by community members in the movie include gender inequality, inequality in housing, sanitation, safe working conditions and equal wages. Ironically, these are many of the same inequalities undocumented workers face today sixty years later. Undocumented people can be easily taken advantage of. Community activism can be a key means through which social change occurs for such populations—it is an example of power of the people.

A central issue for undocumented immigrants is a persistent concern around immigration status and deportation. These deportations often split families—families where perhaps the mother or father immigrated here from another country but whose children were born here or brought across the border to the United States when they were very young. Many of the immigrants lack the official documents to ensure them an official role and status in the United States. For many undocumented immigrants the challenges to immigration status, health, fair wages and safe working environments continue. Community activism will continue to be a central part of the undocumented immigrant experience in the United States. It is the glue that holds together communities of immigrant people who face uncertainty regarding their future. Community activism is a means for members of a community to be able to stand together and pro-actively challenge the status quo and indiscriminate mistreatment they face daily.

Sheila Lakshmi Steinberg

See Also: Activism; Advocacy; Community Concerns; National Council of La Raza (NCLR); National Network for Immigrant and Refugee Rights (NNIIR); Tennessee Immigrant and Refugee Rights Coalition (TIRRC).

Further Reading

Bacon, David. 2008. *Illegal People: How Globalization Creates Migration and Criminal- izes Immigrants.* Boston: Beacon Press.

Garcia, Jerry, and Gilberto Garcia, eds. 2005. *Memory, Community, and Activism: Mexican Migration and Labor in the Pacific Northwest.* East Lansing, MI: Julian Samora Research Institute.

Jonas, Suzanne, and Suzie Dod Thomas. 1998. *Immigration: A Civil Rights Issue for the Americas.* Wilmington, DE: SR Books.

Lorence, James. 1999. *The Suppression of* Salt of the Earth: *How Hollywood, Big Labor, and Politicians Blacklisted a Movie in Cold War America.* Albuquerque, New Mexico: University of New Mexico Press.

Minkler, Meredith. 2005. *Community Organizing and Community Building for Health.* New Brunswick, NJ: Rutgers University Press.

Ochoa, Enrique, and Gilda Ochoa. 2005. *Latino Los Angeles: Transformations, Communi- ties, and Activism.* Tucson: University of Arizona Press.

Community Concerns

Community concerns surrounding undocumented immigrants in the United States span a range of issues. Communities may be concerned about how immigrants are treated by authorities, resulting in the emergence of immigrant rights groups that advocate for changes in policies. In Arizona, for example, various groups concerned over the rise in the number of deaths of migrants who have crossed into the United States fleeing poverty and violence in their communities of origin have for many years worked not only to draw attention to the matter, but also made the effort to mitigate the loss of life by setting up water and humanitarian aid stations in the desert during the hot summer months. On the other hand, Arizona has also seen a rise of paramilitary groups such as the Minutemen Project, whose concerns reflect notions that the United States is being overrun by foreigners and who, because of its failure to deter their entry, stand armed and ready to repel them.

In other places, community concerns are not so openly expressed. There may be few concerns if the newly arrived assimilate to predetermined American ways, such as learning to speak English and adopting manner of dress and behaviors consistent with western culture. These expectations draw on the dominant idea that the United States is a nation of immigrants—that is, that immigrants flee their countries to pursue better opportunities in the United States and in this way become Americans. This narrative depicts a neutral landscape of opportunity, claiming that all immigrants can achieve the American Dream through hard work. However, this story neglects to account for the ways that state policies and practices shape the lives of immigrants. Throughout U.S. history, immigration and citizenship policies have perpetuated racial hierarchies in the United States. They have also shaped the terms of belonging in the United States that privilege assimilation. For example, Proposition 187, in 1994, popularly known as the Save Our State initiative, mobilized the idea that the community of citizens in California had to be protected from the undocumented. This idea evolved from the perception that undocumented immigrants did not respect the laws of the land and had surreptitiously gained access to the state's already depleted social welfare programs. Often also blamed for taking away jobs from citizens and the state's economic downturn, undocumented immigrants frequently face racial violence. In 1982 two men hurled racial epithets at and fatally beat Chinese-American Vincent Chin in Detroit. The offenders unjustly targeted Chin because as an Asian they believed he symbolized the economic hardship of a waning auto industry. In 2008, a group of high school students yelled anti-Mexican insults as they fatally attacked Luis Ramírez, an undocumented resident of Shenandoah, Pennsylvania.

On the other side of the spectrum, receiving communities sometimes adapt to immigrants, and their concerns may reflect a desire to see new arrivals prosper. Public and private institutions may implement bilingual and social services to meet the needs of the newly arrived. Businesses and restaurants may emerge to meet the needs of new immigrants, or current entrepreneurs may expand their offering of products accordingly. Reflecting these concerns, and at some moments, the state has moved in the direction of more support for immigrants. In 1982, for instance, the U.S. Supreme Court ruled in *Plyler vs. Doe* that undocumented children have the constitutional right to a public education at the elementary and secondary level. Moreover, cities, such as Chicago, New York City, and San Francisco, have declared themselves as sanctuaries for the undocumented. This generally means that the city prohibits police and officials from asking residents about their immigration or citizenship status when conducting municipality affairs.

In 1986, the Immigration Reform and Control Act adjusted the status for many groups, but it also stiffened policies. It provided amnesty and a pathway to legalization for the undocumented who met outlined criteria. The act also made it a crime for employers to knowingly recruit and hire undocumented workers. This legislation, however, did not halt undocumented immigration. Those who did not meet the criteria remained undocumented, and people continued to migrate. Since employers did not necessarily verify the authenticity of employees' documents, they could circumvent the law and hire workers with false papers.

Efforts to adjust the status of previously undocumented immigrants and U.S. dependence on immigrants' labor reflect realities that have remained consistent throughout history. For a whole variety of reasons, many people, by choice or by need, bypass the proper legal channels and risk their lives to migrate to the United States. For some, there is no way of accessing the proper authorization. Others face extenuating circumstances in their home countries, such as poverty, warfare, and social unrest.

Some face persecution in their home countries because of their political, sexual, or religious identities. They cannot wait the many years it takes to secure the proper authorization because their needs are immediate. Often it is a matter of life and death. Others immigrate to join family members residing in the United States. Some simply overstay their visas and become undocumented. Others risk their lives and embark on the treacherous journey to the United States because remaining in one's country is not an option. Undocumented immigration remains a major concern in the everyday lives of many people. Not having government authorization to live and work in the United States produces a great deal of emotional stress. The fear of deportation, for instance, runs deeply among citizens and non-citizens alike. The lives of the undocumented are very often intricately enmeshed in the United States. In mixed-status families, some members may be citizens or legal residents while others are undocumented. Parents may have no legal status in this country while their children have citizenship.

However, throughout history and with periodic downturns in the economy, community concerns have often focused on undocumented immigrants in negative ways. These concerns have translated into voter initiatives to restrict immigrant access to programs, or into the support needed for legislators to propose and/or enact anti-immigrant policies. Often, such measures also include the concerns over safety and national security. During the Great Depression, for instance, Immigration and Naturalization Services (INS) unjustly deported many American citizens, reflecting concerns over the economic downturn. In 1994, Governor Pete Wilson signed California Proposition 187, a voter initiative that proposed barring the undocumented access to public education, health care, and social services. However, a federal court deemed this measure unconstitutional.

Community concerns often reflect the national political climate, and in this way, offer support for some policies that in effect may adversely impact immigrants who are perceived as threats. For example, during World War II, the government unfairly targeted and interned many Japanese legal immigrants and Japanese Americans in the name of national security. In the twenty-first century, Immigration and Customs Enforcement (ICE) agents—formerly INS—have unfairly detained American citizens for terms ranging from a few days to several years. In some cases, ICE agents have wrongfully deported American citizens. The alarmist ideas that circulate among communities about the undocumented are often perpetuated by mainstream media by focusing on a racialized idea of the undocumented as Latina/o. The way anti-immigrant legislation is sometimes framed perpetuates anxieties about immigrants, resulting in more public support for harsher enforcement actions. People often declare outrage about undocumented immigration because the undocumented have broken the law. Concerns over undocumented immigration took a new form following September 11, 2001 because of the nation's fears of terrorism. This context fostered debates about border security and immigration. The nation worried that the undocumented, especially Latinas/os and Middle Easterners, could be potentially terrorists. In light of this fear, hate crimes directed at Muslims and Middle Easterners escalated.

In the same way that community concerns can articulate support for enforcement actions, they can also express criticism and perhaps, their revision. For example, the immigration enforcement arm of the Department of Homeland Security, the U.S.

Immigration and Customs Enforcement (ICE), has with greater frequency concentrated its efforts towards workplace raids where undocumented immigrants are known to be employed, reflecting a wave of anti-immigrant sentiment. But this has neither gone unnoticed by communities, nor has it occurred without a response. The case of Elvira Arrellano brought attention to the rights of citizen children with undocumented parents and highlighted how deportation frequently separates families. When ICE officials served Arrellano with deportation orders, she resisted and together with wide support of the community that had been her home, launched a campaign to educate the country about undocumented immigration. With support from Centro Sin Fronteras, Arrellano sought sanctuary in a Chicago church. While in sanctuary, Arrellano explained that her deportation would unjustly separate her from her son, Saul Arrellano. The argument followed that, as a U.S. citizen, Saul had a right to remain in the United States with his mother. In 2007, ICE deported Arrellano when she left sanctuary to participate in an immigrant rights rally in Los Angeles. Meanwhile, activists continued to advocate for Saul's citizenship rights. In the end, Saul joined his mother in Mexico and began a life in an unfamiliar country. The Arrellano case raised questions about the birthright citizenship outlined in the Fourteenth Amendment to the U.S. Constitution. Since then, there have been repeated efforts made to begin discussions about amending birthright citizenship. In a similar event, community concerns over the Postville Raids where nearly four hundred mostly undocumented Guatemalan immigrants were arrested came in the form of outrage with images of small children being separated from their mothers. Congressional hearings were called to examine the events. This resulted in ICE's reexamination of its tactics that were perceived by many as heavy-handed and violent.

In 2005, the U.S. House of Representatives passed HR 4437, the "Border Protection, Anti-Terrorism, and Illegal Immigration Control Act of 2005." Intended to be a comprehensive immigration reform bill, there was strong reaction to the enforcement-only sections in the bill, including a provision that would have made it a felony to aid the undocumented. Taken to its logical conclusion, the family members of undocumented immigrants risked becoming felons because they lived together and supported one another. In yet another manifestation of concern and support of undocumented immigrants, people mobilized across the United States to protest this bill. It died when the bill did not pass the U.S. Senate. The reelection of Barack Obama ushered in hope for much needed reform to the U.S. immigration system. In this way immigrant rights activists engage in a variety of overlapping strategies to address immigration concerns. They use current legislation to fight for rights. They lobby for new legislation. Activists also fight to hold the state accountable for unjust policies and practices, using strategies such as lawsuits, boycotts, and sit-ins. Furthermore, citizens and non-citizens alike participate in the political process. Although the undocumented may not have the right to vote, they frequently participate in political activities. They stand up for their civil and human rights, and for the rights of their undocumented family members and friends. The U.S. Constitution explicitly provides protection for all persons residing in the United States. It does not specify that the person must be a citizen.

Undocumented youth leaders, too, have mobilized for immigrant rights by openly sharing their life stories to inform others and to garner support. Tam Tran and Cinthya Felix were undocumented graduate students at Brown University and Columbia

University respectively. They fervently campaigned for the Development, Relief, and Education for Alien Minors (DREAM) Act, federal legislation that would legalize the status of those who are graduates of U.S. high schools and have completed at least two years of higher education or who receive honorable discharges from military service. Tran and Felix's lives tragically ended in 2010, but other students continue to rally support. In sum, immigrant rights activism continues to address pressing community concerns.

Myrna García

See Also: Activism; Advocacy; Barrios; CC-IME (Consejo Consultivo Instituto de los Mexicanos en el Exterior); Community Activism; Hate Crimes; Home Town Associations; LGBT Immigrant without Documentation; Minutemen; Protests; Sanctuary Movement.

Further Reading

Bosniak, Linda. 2007. "Being Here: Ethical Territoriality and the Rights of Immigrants." *Theoretical Inquiries in Law* 8.2:389–410.

Camacho, Alicia Schmidt. 2010. "Hailing the Twelve Million U.S. Immigration Policy, Deportation, and the Imaginary of Lawful Violence." *Social Text* 28.4:1–24.

Golash-Boza, Tanya Maria. 2012. *Immigration Nation: Raids, Detentions, and Deportations in Post-9/11 America*. Boulder, CO: Paradigm Publishers.

Hing, Bill Ong. 2006. "Misusing Immigration Policies in the Name of Homeland Security." *CR: The New Centennial Review* 6.1:195–224.

Ngai, Mae M. 2010. "The Civil Rights Origins of Illegal Immigration." *International Labor and Working Class History* 78.1:93–99.

Corridos

Corridos are a form of musical expression to tell stories. *Corridos* can be traced to about 150 years ago. They were a way to pass on knowledge across states in Mexico and later across generations, especially during the Mexican Revolution, before the existence of televisions. Inculcating knowledge orally and through *corridos* became a popular medium in Mexico and in the southwestern part of the United States. *Corridos* have served to convey news and events, to tell about the lives and deaths of famous men and women. More recently, *corridos* tell the narratives of immigrants who cross the Mexico-U.S. border. Generally, *corridos* consist of six parts: (1) a salutation from the singer (the *corridista*); (2) the setting and time period, dates of the events; (3) prologue to the story; (4) the story itself; (5) a moral message; and (6) a farewell from the singer, or "*corridista.*"

Corridos are the genre of music most frequently heard among people from low socio-economic status because *corridos* disclose the people's anxieties, their struggles, and, for example, their concerns with political figures, and their admiration for heroes and acts of valor. *Corridos* can also be humorous and can be sung as parodies, using double entendre, or as propaganda to organize people with different political views. Through their lyrics, *corridos* have served as the vehicle to inform people, to resist, and to organize masses via messages of injustice faced by marginalized people. Through *corridos* people can exert their discontent and disapproval of the status quo.

Corridos also have roots among Mexican transnationals and Mexican Americans in the United States. Throughout history, *corridos* have served to convey the people's voice and their experiences, their stories of resistance, the legends of revolutionary heroes and heroines, of drug traffickers and their crimes, tales of quotidian lives, love ballads, and the struggles of immigrants who cross borders in order to attempt to achieve the American Dream. *Corridos* that relate the border crossing experience describe the suffering and pain that it is experienced when crossing the United States *sin papeles* (without legal documentation). *Corridos* of undocumented immigrants also disclose how disheartening it is to leave one's land and family behind. *Corridos* are in a way like *testimonios*; through this musical genre people bear witness to their life experiences as heroes, as victims, or as people who might be undocumented in the United States but have dignity and a strong work ethic. Through *corridos* a person's story is told but many people can relate to that particular story, thus making *corridos* a representation of multiple truths and realities. *Corridos* have helped in the formation of national identity because a lot of *corridos* are imbued with messages of patriotism. Collective memory and an affirmation of a collective identity are reinforced through *corridos*.

Narcocorridos

Contemporary *corridos* feature more modern themes such as drug trafficking (narco*corridos*), immigration, politics, and migrant labor. In 1972, Los Tigres del Norte released "*Contrabando y Traición*" (contraband and betrayal). The song became an instant hit and provided Los Tigres their first big break into the music industry. Narcocorridos are a subgenre of *corridos;* they are ballads about drug traffickers outsmarting the border patrol and other authorities when smuggling drugs into the United States. Since the mid-nineties, with the growth in drug trafficking and the increase of murders along the Mexico-U.S. border, narcocorridos have been written for drug cartel leaders, for political leaders, and for women drug traffickers. A glorification of these acts of violence has exacerbated in recent years, through the media and especially through narcocorridos.

Los Tigres del Norte

Through the lyrics and music of Grammy Award winners Los Tigres del Norte, the experience of undocumented immigration has also been documented and crystallized in the minds of their followers. Patricia Zavella's interview with the eldest of the four brothers that make up Los Tigres in fact revealed that the name of the group came from an encounter with the U.S. Border Patrol when the oldest of the four brothers was only 14. The official was impressed by their youth and bravado and referred to them as "the little tigers" (Zavella 2011, 193). For several months, the young men made a living as undocumented in the United States. Living this life and watching others cross the border to work influenced some of their later *corridos,* and addressed larger issues such as the racism they experienced in the United States, the clash of cultures, border crossing (*Viva los mojados*/Long Live the Wetbacks, *Tres Veces Mojado*/Three Times a Wetback), social hostilities, injustice, and dual allegiance to both their country of origin and their new home in the United States (*Mis dos Patrias*/My Two Nations, *Somos Más Americanos*/We are More American). Perhaps their most famous of this type of *corrido* is "*Jaula de Oro*" (The Gilded Cage). The lyrics in this *corrido* narrate how after crossing into the United States without documents ten years ago as a "wetback," there is a growing anxiety about forgetting one's homeland, Mexico. The longing for a more socially cohesive context is not shared by family members as they become more absorbed into the American way of life. The children have lost their connection to their heritage and their language. The song narrates the pain and despair that comes with this loss of connection. When the father asks his son if he would like to return to Mexico, the son is contemptuous and answers by saying: "What are you talking about, dad? I don't want to go back to Mexico, No way, dad." The *corrido* speaks of the inability to leave the house without fear of deportation. The narrator reflects on this feeling of entrapment, aggravated by gendered expectations that usually privilege males as heads of household heads with greater mobility and autonomy. At the same time, he is resentful of those that deny their heritage in order to get ahead, in spite of their obvious ethnicity and race. What good, he questions, are earnings provided by working in the United States if one is relegated to living in a cage made of gold?

Judith Flores Carmona

See Also: Community Concerns; Drug Trade; Literature and Poetry; Migration.

Further Reading

de la Garza, M. L. 2007. *Ni Aquí, Ni Allá: El Emigrante en Los Corridos y en Otras Canciones Populares.* Fundación Municipal de Cultura, Excmo. Ayuntamiento de Cádiz, España.

Flores, R. 1992. "The Corrido and the Emergence of Texas-Mexican Social Identity." *Journal of American Folklore,* 105.

"History of El Corrido de los Perez." http://www.canadasdeobregon.com/losperez.htm.

Los Tigres del Norte Foundation. http://www.lostigresdelnortefoundation.org/research .html.

Zavella, Patricia. 2011. Chapter 6: "Transnational Cultural Memory." In *I'm Neither Here Nor There: Mexicans' Quotidian Struggles with Migration and Poverty.* Durham and London. Duke University Press.

Counterfeit Documents

A counterfeit document is a forgery of any document that is meant to be passed off as genuine. Unauthorized immigrants in the United States most often attain and use counterfeit documents in order to work there. The documents that are most frequently counterfeited for use by unauthorized immigrants are social security cards, state identification (ID) cards or driver's licenses, and green cards.

The United States has never had a national ID card, and no U.S. state mandates its residents to carry identification. That is, no one in the United States—whether citizen or non-citizen, immigrant or native born—is legally required to have or carry identification. However, the use of counterfeit documents by unauthorized immigrants is widespread and can be traced to policies that have tightened requirements for work eligibility. Prior to 1986, workers did not have to provide employers documents to provide proof that they were eligible to be hired. When the Immigration Reform and Control Act of 1986 (IRCA) made the employment of unauthorized people illegal, unauthorized workers were compelled to obtain counterfeit work eligibility documents in order to get and keep jobs. Acceptable documents for verifying a worker's identity and eligibility to work in the United States include a U.S. passport or green card, or a combination of a driver's license or state ID and a social security card, among others. Notably, IRCA does not require employers to determine whether these documents are genuine or not, and these same documents are often counterfeited for use by unauthorized immigrants. In fact, while the stated objective of this provision of IRCA was to quell unauthorized migration, IRCA's most enduring legacy has been a burgeoning black market in false documents.

The availability and cost of counterfeit documents can vary according to location and documents desired. The more difficult it is to counterfeit the document, the more expensive it is likely to be; thus, counterfeit social security cards are likely to be less expensive than counterfeit U.S. passports. In Chicago, for example, counterfeit social security cards can be purchased for thirty dollars or less and are readily available. In areas with fewer immigrants and fewer counterfeiters, the cost may be higher. Counterfeit documents are also much less expensive than genuine documents that are sold on the black market.

Although counterfeit social security cards in conjunction with a state ID or driver's license are acceptable as proof of work eligibility, the use of illegitimate social security numbers makes unauthorized workers vulnerable to "No Match letters." No Match letters are notices sent by the Social Security Administration (SSA) that inform employers and workers when employees' social security numbers cannot be matched to SSA records. Although the SSA notes that it cannot share this information with other federal agencies and has no enforcement authority, these letters are often used by employers to fire unauthorized workers. The other major drawback to using counterfeit documents is that the immigrant has no legitimate record of his or her tax payments.

Because of these drawbacks, unauthorized immigrants may choose to use an individual tax identification number (ITIN), an SSA-issued number that unauthorized immigrants can legitimately use to pay taxes. However, ITINs do not confer work eligibility. Some unauthorized immigrants have genuine documents that legitimately belong to them, such as social security numbers, driver's licenses, and green cards that they use to conduct a range of transactions, even though their authorization to be in the United States (usually through any among a variety of type of visas) has expired. Other unauthorized immigrants use genuine documents that belong to someone else or that have belonged to someone else. The advantage of using genuine documents is that the name and social security number being used match SSA records, protecting the immigrant from No Match letters. Genuine documents are also safer for use in travel. However, assuming someone else's name and using their social security number renders the immigrant vulnerable to charges of identity theft, a felony crime. Also, real documents are significantly more expensive than counterfeit ones. Because of the risk and the cost, many unauthorized immigrants prefer to use counterfeit documents rather than to fraudulently use genuine documents.

In order to make it more difficult for unauthorized immigrants to obtain employment using counterfeit documents, the federal government is promoting an online program called E-Verify. Employers can use E-Verify to determine the employment eligibility of new hires by verifying information provided on Employment Eligibility Verification forms (or I-9 forms) with the SSA and U.S Citizenship and Immigration Services (USCIS) databases. The use of E-Verify was authorized under the 1996 Illegal Immigration Reform and Immigrant Responsibility Act (IIRAIRA), though web-based accessibility was only implemented in 2004. In September 2009, federal agencies began requiring contractors to utilize E-Verify for employees on all new federal contracts, and the USCIS website boasts ever-increasing employer participation in the program. The impact that E-Verify will ultimately have on the counterfeiting of employment eligibility documents is not yet clear, though emerging evidence suggests a rise in the fraudulent use of genuine documents.

Ruth Gomberg-Muñoz.

See Also: Driver's Licenses; *Flores-Figueroa v. United States;* Identification Cards; Identity Theft; Legal Status; "Undocumented" Label.

Further Reading

Massey, Douglas, Jorge Durand, and Nolan J. Malone. 2002. *Beyond Smoke and Mirrors: Mexican Immigration in an Era of Economic Integration*. New York: Russell Sage Foundation.

U.S. Immigration and Customs Enforcement Web Site. http://www.ice.gov/identity-benefit -fraud/.

Counterterrorism and Immigrant Profiling

Over the past two decades, counterterrorism has become one of the main domestic and international security priorities for the United States, and these priorities have steadily and increasingly become merged with immigration. Although anti-terrorism legislation can be traced back before the terrorist attacks on 9/11, the connection between counterterrorism and immigration was entrenched by the 2002 Enhanced Border Security and Visa Entry Reform Act, and the Homeland Security Act in 2002. These also congealed the connection between counterterrorism and border security. However, questions have been raised about the effectiveness of what is criticized by

Accompanied by Chairman Thomas Kean (left) and Vice Chairman Lee Hamilton (right) of the September 11 Commission, President George W. Bush addresses the press during the presentation of the commission's report in the Rose Garden on July 22, 2004. 9/11 is considered to be a turning point in the nation's history with regard to immigrants, resulting in greater impetus to see all immigrants as threats, and the government's harsher measures to police them. (White House)

many as a heavy-handed approach, and in particular, of the forms of immigrant profiling that these policies have encouraged. As some critics have argued, counterterrorism operations that target immigrant communities run the risk of creating obstacles to the trust that is needed for effective information gathering. The tactics also cause undue stress by the threat they pose to civil liberties. The angst over this trend peaked with the proposed comprehensive immigration reform bill in 2005, *The Border Protection, Anti-terrorism, and Illegal Immigration Control Act.* Although it failed to pass the senate, this bill (known also as HR 4437, or the Sessenbrenner bill—named after the Wisconsin Republican congressman) caused outrage among immigrants and their supporters, resulting in mass demonstrations of hundreds of thousands across the United States in 2006.

It bears noting that only a small fraction of 1 percent of noncitizens who are removed from the United States each year are removed for reasons relating to terrorism or national security. In 2005, for example, this group accounted for less than 150 persons out of the over 800,000 individuals who were removed from the United States for immigration violations. At the same time, the goal of improving homeland security has become more focused on improving the government's ability to monitor all people who enter and leave the nation. These monitoring practices tend to place more emphasis on monitoring noncitizens than citizens. They also tend to use migrant legal status (or lack thereof) and even physical appearance as the basis for initiating a search or interrogation.

Counterterrorism and the Electronic Border

With counterterrorism increasingly linked to immigration, the U.S. government has intensified increased efforts to achieve operational control of the border. Conventionally defined, border control (including maritime security) involves the policing of the U.S.-Canada and U.S.-Mexico border and all naval ports. The attacks of 9/11, however, directed attention to airport security—resulting in the formation of a new federal department, the Transportation Security Administration, which was incorporated within the Department of Homeland Security. In addition to this, the US VISIT program has promoted the idea of creating a so-called electronic border that would allow the government to track noncitizens at all stages of their stay in the United States. The electronic border is a database that would store an immigrant's biometric data (finger prints) and other information such as photographic images, biographical information, legal status, and length of stay. All border entry workers such as customs and border enforcement officials would be able to enter data (collected from new entrants) into the system and crosscheck this data against other databases (notably, the National Crime Information Center database) that contain information on criminals, known terrorist suspects, noncitizens with outstanding orders of deportation, and so forth.

At present, this national database and tracking system is not as comprehensive as originally envisioned. Even so, the 2004 US VISIT program did push the federal government several steps in this direction, and subsequent legislation (including the 2006 Secure Fence Act and the 2007 Homeland Security Act) has increased funding for the development of border-control technologies that would make this system possible.

According to many of its proponents, this system would allow the government to be more selective in targeting terrorist suspects—despite the fact that it would also require more invasive forms of surveillance. As a result, the crude national origin profiles that were used to identify terror suspects immediately after 9/11 could be replaced by more refined indicators of likely terrorist activity (i.e. purchases of explosives, unauthorized visits to high security areas, suspicious deviations from travel plans and destination points, etc.). It is important, however, that this system—as envisaged under US VISIT—would primarily target noncitizens. Furthermore, it could still be used to track individuals by national origin, even if this is not its primary focus. However, an individual needs to already be recorded by the system in order to be tracked by the system, and therefore cannot be applied to those migrants who have entered the United States without documents.

Unauthorized Migrants as Security Threats

Since 9/11 new concerns have been raised about the possibility of terrorists entering the United States through the U.S.-Mexico border. The mere fact that a person is an unauthorized migrant does not make one a terrorist suspect, but the existence of unauthorized migration poses a problem for the seamless web of interior/exterior enforcement that has been proposed by some counterterrorism experts. Unauthorized migration is often referred to a security threat because it is creating a population that is almost entirely outside of the government's oversight. Another worrisome population is immigrants who are involved in transnational gangs.

Critics argue that counterterrorism should be kept distinct from immigration enforcement and that immigrant profiling adds very little to effectiveness to counterterrorism operations. Unauthorized migration provides evidence that the U.S. electronic border is not foolproof since, while uncontrolled, it continues to create social spaces and networks that are difficult to monitor with existing border-control technology. The unauthorized migrant population has doubled in size between the early 1990s and the present. Furthermore, anywhere between 25 and 40 percent of these persons entered the United States with some form of legal status (as a temporary worker, under a student visa, etc.) (Passel 2006). Many are undocumented because they have overstayed the limits of their visa.

This latter category of people with expired or revoked legal status could possibly be identified by the electronic border system, but persons who enter the United States without authorization and with no documentation are almost impossible to identify without resorting to invasive screening and enforcement practices. These practices are controversial because they require enforcement agents to use immigrant profiles to determine whom they should check for legal status. This encourages the targeting of individuals who are suspected of being undocumented immigrants simply because of where they work, where they are living, their appearance, or their accent.

These aggressive strategies are a typical component of immigration raids that are carried out by federal agencies—most often by Immigration and Customs Enforcement (ICE). These raids have targeted workplaces believed to employ unauthorized migrants. One in particular, Operation Tarmac, was explicitly defined as a counterterrorism operation. Shortly after the 9/11 attacks Operation Tarmac was carried out by federal agents who conducted a national sweep of airport workers with immigration violations on the grounds that such individuals were security risks. The vast majority of the individuals apprehended were unauthorized migrants, but none of the immigrants apprehended under Operation Tarmac were found to have any connection to terrorism. Immigrant-rights advocates have cited Operation Tarmac as an example of the inaccurate and unnecessarily punitive nature of the government's counterterrorism sting operations. It is telling, however, that ICE still treats Operation Tarmac as a best-practices model for the integration of counterterrorism and immigration enforcement. Subsequently these practices have been challenged by immigrant rights and civil liberties advocates. However, court decisions have upheld the practice of immigrant profiling. Most notably, the 2004 Supreme Court decision on *Muehler et al. v. Mena* affirmed the right of state and local police to use ethnic appearance as the basis for detaining and screening individuals for legal status if it occurs in the context of an ongoing investigation.

Concerns for national security have prompted the federal government to begin to take a similar approach toward asylum seekers as it has taken with unauthorized immigrants. In 2002 for example, the Bush administration adopted a new policy developed specifically for interdicting Haitian asylum seekers. Under this policy all Haitian asylum seekers—including individuals who managed to touch ground on U.S. soil—were to be summarily returned to Haiti. This policy was even more prohibitive than the wet foot–dry foot policy adopted by the Clinton Administration, which was criticized for using a more lenient standard for Cuban asylum seekers than Haitian asylum seekers. The Bush administration justified the unprecedented move on the basis of national security concerns. White House officials considered Haiti a haven for international terrorist networks. They also noted that a Haitian mass exodus could provide an entry point for terrorist operatives. Similar arguments have been used to justify the U.S. reluctance to admit Iraqi asylum seekers.

Many of the arguments used to strengthen counterterrorism measures have recast unauthorized migration as a security matter. According to this perspective both unauthorized immigrants and asylum seekers represent a potential risk. As a result and as the Haitian example demonstrates, it is also possible for this general suspicion to be reinforced by profiles based on national origin.

Proponents of immigration-focused counterterrorism operations see border control and national security as two sides of the same coin. By increasing the capacity to monitor who is entering and leaving the nation, the government is also restricting the mobility of terrorist operatives. Screening noncitizens (which may include the use of racial-ethnic profiles) is justifiable in their view because these populations (especially student visitors, tourists, and temporary workers) enter and exit the United States more frequently than most U.S. citizens. Although critics charge that the goal of screening all noncitizens is excessive, those in favor of screening say it is a necessary step if the government is interested in becoming more proactive in improving national security. The goal of creating such a wide-ranging system is not simply to identify possible terrorist suspects at points of entry (although this is one goal) but to introduce a paradigm-shift in the way that the United States regulates its borders and migration, and the way that counterterrorism priorities carry over into the debate over unauthorized migration.

Philip A. Kretsedemas

See Also: Airports; Border Crossing; Ports of Entry; U.S. Department of Homeland Security; Workplace Raids.

Further Reading

Chishti, Muzzafar, Doris Meissner, Demetrious Papademetriou, Jay Peterzell, Michael Wishnie, and Stephen Yale-Loehr. "America's Challenge: Domestic Security, Civil Liberties and National Unity after September 11." Migration Policy Institute. http://www.migrationpolicy.org/pubs/Americas_Challenges.pdf.

DeGenova, Nicholas. "Migrant 'Illegality' and the Metaphysics of Antiterrorism: 'Immigrants' Rights' in the Aftermath of the Homeland Security State." Social Science Research Council. Border Battles: The U.S. Immigration Debates. http://borderbattles.ssrc.org/De_Genova/.

Government Accountability Office. 2003. "Homeland Security: Overstay Tracking Is a Key Component of a Layered Defense." October 16.

Hines, Barbara. 2002. "So Near Yet So Far Away: The Effect of September 11th on Mexican Immigrants in the United States." *Texas Hispanic Journal of Law and Policy* 8.37: 37–46.

Koslowski, Rey. "Real Challenges for Virtual Borders: Implementing US VISIT." Migration Policy Institute. http://www.migrationpolicy.org/pubs/Koslowski_Report.pdf.

National Committee Against Repressive Legislation (NCARL). 2002. "Political Dissent and Union Organizing Called Terrorism." November Newsletter. http://www.ncarl.org/newsletter2002.html.

Passel, Jeffrey. "Size and Characteristics of the Unauthorized Migrant Population in the U.S. Estimates Based on the March 2005 Current Population Survey." Pew Hispanic Center. http://pewhispanic.org/files/reports/61.pdf.

Street, Paul. "Background Check: Operation Tarmac and the Many Faces of Terror." *Znet.* http://www.zmag.org/Sustainers/content/2003–01/11street.cfm.

U.S. Supreme Court. 2004. *Muehler et al. v. Mena.* Supreme Court Decision No. 03–1423, October term.

Coyotes

The term *coyote* is one of the most common terms to refer to a human smuggler in the U.S-Mexico border region. A discussion with almost any border resident will refer to commonalities between human smugglers and their four-legged namesake in that they are both sly and masters in the art of camouflage. Human coyotes seem to disappear when migrants are caught, much like how the desert creature easily blends into the environment. If per chance the coyote is apprehended with the group, unless identified by the others, he or she merges into the group. This frustrates officials' efforts to distinguish the coyote from the others.

Some definitions refer to the coyote as a coordinator or head of the human smuggling ring. In this way also they remain invisible and are rarely caught. Using this definition, coyotes are unlike the guides that lead migrants through the desert and assume the same risks of other migrants. Instead, as smuggling "organizers," coyotes coordinate the step-by-step migration process from a safe distance that often involves a range of actors, from those charged with recruiting migrants before crossing, to the guides who will lead them across, to the drivers who will pick them up and drive them to safe houses (locations where migrants are housed pending their transport to their final destination) in cities in the interior of the United States, to the managers of those safe houses. The remote management of the smuggling operation can be seen as a way of outsourcing of the more perilous activities like guiding migrants across a border where injury or even death can occur, and transporting smuggled migrants to their final destination where drivers are at risk of arrest or accidents, especially if engaged by law enforcement officials in high speed changes.

A term that is often used interchangeably with coyote is *pollero* (from the Spanish, "pollo," chicken). *Pollero* also has its analogous reference. In this analogy, migrants are much like chicks, and a guide who is responsible for keeping group members together through the trek through the desert is like a mother hen. Coyotes, *polleros,* and *guias* (a more neutral word and Spanish for guide) are often used interchangeably.

A variety of published sources can be used to argue that increased border enforcement measures have contributed to the spiraling costs of what migrants can expect to pay coyotes. Most observers and scholars agree that fees paid to coyotes have gone up as the United States has cracked down on its borders, especially after the September 11, 2001 attacks on the World Trade Center. Because migrating alone has become more complicated with harsher border enforcement measures, migrants have little choice but to pay coyotes these higher fees. Migrants have increasingly relied on human smugglers to cross into Arizona: 18 percent of migrants hired a human smuggler in 2000 and this grew to 55 percent in 2005 (Erfani, 2009). In the late 1980s, migrants crossing from Mexico to the United States were paying as little as $50–200 apiece. In 1996 the cost of smuggling migrants to the U.S. from Mexico was $150. Later, in 1999, the cost of crossing from Mexico at the Texas border at the Rio Grande and reaching Houston or Dallas was rising, from $500 to $700 per person to $1000. At that time, migrants reported that $1000 was not too much to pay. More recently, the reported amounts paid to human smugglers vary widely but are consistently higher. A 2004 study of 538 cases from papers, reports, journals, newspapers, magazines and conferences worldwide, reports that migrants to the U.S. from Latin America were paying an average of $2984 U.S. dollars. A significant share of this migration was from Mexico. This average amount paid is consistent with the approximately $3000 reported in 2006 by the Associated Press.

Coyotes are often demonized by the media and popular accounts of their activities. Indeed, lack of economic opportunities must be factored into understanding how coyotes are increasingly influenced and controlled by the lucrative human smuggling economy. Consequently, the lure of profits has resulted in the treatment of migrants as a cheap commodity by coyotes. In other words, the coyote's allegiance to powerful smuggling rings has worked to devalue human life. Numerous accounts by migrants surviving their abandonment in the desert because they were injured or slowed the group down contribute to the image of the coyote as heartless.

However, there is some evidence to suggest that the ruthless treatment of destitute migrants was not always so. Some research shows that fees may vary based on social relationships between migrants and known coyotes, *"coyotes comunitarios"* (coyotes from the community) (Castro Garcia, 2007). Based on the coyotes' relationship with clients (family members, former clients, friends or relatives of former clients), *coyotes comunitarios* offer discounted rates and in this way they help reduce the cost of migration. In addition, with these coyotes, the crossing process is not only an economic contract but rooted in a sincere desire to help and the sense of social obligation they may have to members of their social circles, and the desire to remain in good standing with them. Some research shows that a reliance on the human capital of family and friends assures lower costs of the coyote's services, provides guarantees for services rendered, and teaches migrants new to migration how to behave if and when they are apprehended and what to expect upon arrest. In this way, coyotes' help assures their safety amidst the many dangers of border crossing.

In recent years, coyotes have been subsumed under large-scale human smuggling rings with unparalleled influence and unprecedented inclination for violence. In response, Arizona passed House Bill 2539 and Senate Bill 1372 (Human Trafficking Violations) in March of 2005. This law, commonly referred to as the "Anti-Coyote Law," prescribes penalties for unlawfully obtaining the labor or services of a person, sex trafficking, trafficking of persons for forced labor or services, and smuggling of human beings. Arizona also initiated investigative campaigns to choke off human smuggling operations that bring into the state an estimated $1.7 billion a year. Some of these clandestine operations merge legitimate businesses with illicit human smuggling activities and are becoming one of the fastest growing informal economies on the border.

Anna Ochoa O'Leary

See Also: Border Crossing; Crime; Death; Human Trafficking; Ports of Entry; Trafficking Victims Protection Reauthorization Act (TVPRA); Transportation in the United States; U.S.-Mexico Border Wall.

Further Reading

Castro Garcia, Ismael. 2007. *Vidas Compartidas: Formación de una Red migratoria Transnacional. Aguacaliente Grande Sinaloa y Victor Valley California.* Sigfido Bañueles, México: Facultad de Estudios Internacionales y Políticas Públicas.

Conover, Ted. 1987. *Coyotes: A Journey Through the Secret World of America's Illegal Aliens.* New York: Random House/Vintage Books.

Erfani, Julie A. Murphy. 2009. "Crime and Violence in the Arizona-Sonora Borderlands." In *Violence, Security, and Human Rights at the Border,* edited by K. Staudt, T. Payan and Z. A. Kruszewski, 63–84. Tucson: University of Arizona Press.

Heckmann, Friedrich. 2007. "Towards a Better Understanding of Human Smuggling." IMIS-COE Policy Brief, Institut an der Universität Bamberg. http://www.efms.uni-bamberg.de/pdf/Policy_brief_Human_smuggling.pdf. Accessed on February 1, 2009.

Holstege, S. 2008. "Human-smuggling Rings from Mexico Turning to New Tactics." www.azcentral.com. *The Arizona Republic.* July 13, 2008. http://www.azcentral.com/news/articles/2008/07/13/20080713launder-main0713.html.

Lee, Jennifer. 2006. "Human Smuggling for a Hefty Fee." *New York Times.* http://www.nytimes.com/2006/05/28/weekinreview/28basic.html.

O'Leary, Anna Ochoa. 2009. "The ABCs of Unauthorized Border Crossing Costs: Assembling, Bajadores, and Coyotes." *Migration Letters* 6.1:27–36.

Petros, Melanie. 2005. "The Costs of Human Smuggling and Trafficking." Migration Research Unit/Global Commission on International Migration. http://www.iom.int/jahia/webdav/site/myjahiasite/shared/shared/mainsite/policy_and_research/gcim/gmp/gmp31.pdf.

Robbins, Ted.. 2007. NPR report. "Travel Agencies Tied to Human Smuggling Ring." http://www.npr.org/templates/story/story.php?storyId=9277364.

Singer, A., and D. S. Massey. 1998. "The Social Process of Undocumented Border Crossing among Mexican Migrants." *International Migration Review* 32.3:561–592.

Spener, David. 1999. "This Coyote's Life." North American Congress on Latin America (NACLA), *Report on the Americas* 33.3:22–23.

Crime

Undocumented immigrants, like any other member of a society, can be perpetrators or victims of crime. The experience of crime for undocumented immigrants is like that of other groups, but also has unique elements specific to immigrant groups. One such unique aspect is that they are commonly referred to as "illegal immigrants." This label of illegal immigrant reflects that the core identity associated with these groups of people is that both their entry and stay in the United States are against the law. This puts undocumented immigrants in an unusual situation since, even if they are otherwise law-abiding citizens, they are still considered criminals and can be prosecuted and deported because of their illegal or undocumented entry and stay.

Entry of undocumented immigrants has not only been associated with crime simply by the illegal nature of the entry but also with the crime of smuggling. Smuggling is bringing goods or people across prohibited areas, like borders, and violates or breaks laws. In the early twentieth century during the Prohibition era, undocumented immigrants were linked with the smuggling of alcohol. This smuggling of alcohol occurred especially with crossings at the Canadian border. Smuggling of goods occurring with immigration did not stop after Prohibition ended. Later in the twentieth century, and especially with greater efforts aimed at illegal entry of both immigrants and contraband through the U.S.-Mexico border, drug smuggling became the major crime associated with immigration and in particular undocumented immigration.

The Border Patrol is an agency that has been created to deal with immigrants illegally crossing the land border between the United States and Mexico and between the United States and Canada, but also the seacoasts. The agency tries to deter illegal entry and is charged with catching the smuggling that can occur with illegal entry. After the September 11, 2001 attacks, protecting against and the detection of acts of terrorism became a major focus of the Border Patrol. Immigrants, whether documented or undocumented who commit crimes can also be investigated by Immigration and Customs Enforcement, which is the investigative arm of the U.S. Department of Homeland Security. Before 2003, this was called the Immigration and Naturalization Service (INS). Investigations may result in felony convictions on an immigrant's criminal record and deportation. Agencies such as the Border Patrol and ICE try to stop criminals from entering the country but also attempt to prevent other crimes from occurring, such as smuggling and illegal reentry, with the overall goal of protecting and maintaining the security of the United States. In this way, because many immigrants share many phenotypical and linguistic traits with undocumented immigrants, they easily risk being mistaken for those thought to be engaged in criminal activity. For example, a well-known case of this is that of U.S.-born teenager Esequiel Hernandez, who while tending his herd of goats near his hometown of Redford, Texas, was mistaken for an undocumented immigrant and possible drug trafficker and was fatally shot by a member of the U.S. military Joint Task Force Six on May 20, 1997 (PBS.org, 2008).

Crime does not only occur with illegal border crossings nor does it stop at the border. The crimes that undocumented immigrants commit can be violent crimes such as murder or assault or can be property crimes such as burglary or robbery. Some undocumented immigrants participate in illegal activities or crime because they lack opportunities for legitimate or lawful employment. In this way, they are subject to the very same pressures that other impoverished groups suffer. The initial experience for most undocumented immigrants upon entering the United States very often includes settling down in neighborhoods or other areas with limited options and opportunities available to them both in terms of safe and affordable housing, and educational and employment opportunities. Furthermore, immigrants may lack fluency or a good command and grasp of the English language, and if undocumented, may find that the doors to learning English are closed if they cannot prove that they are legal residents. These factors add up and make it difficult for a number of undocumented immigrants to find and keep gainful and legal occupations. So, some undocumented immigrants turn to crime as a way to provide for themselves and their families. Crimes such as selling of illegal drugs, prostitution, and burglary provide such source for income.

Some immigrant groups have also created their own organized crime rings, similar in organizational structure and goals to the Mafia. These immigrant crime rings can offer some degree of protection from crime for immigrant groups and also can offer opportunities to earn an income. Selling of illicit drugs is only one way. Another is in providing fraudulent identification cards so that undocumented immigrants can be employed. Many consider this latter to be a victimless crime, but if caught, penalties may include removal from the country. However, the social and economic costs of belonging to crime rings greatly outweigh any potential benefits. They offer more opportunities to engage in black market economies, but also lead to more serious extortion of legitimate businesses and sometimes force those businesses to close. Moreover, crime rings usually generate other illegal enterprises such as selling drugs or creating prostitution rings, and entangle those who merely and often innocently seek the desired services and products they supply.

Technological advances have created new opportunities for immigrants to engage in crime. Identity fraud and telephone and credit card fraud have become major criminal enterprises or activities for some immigrant groups. Telephone fraud can include telemarketing scams to get credit card, bank, or personal information; credit card fraud can include the unauthorized use of credit card information for purchases or the creation of new fraudulent credit card accounts. Immigrant crime rings have also started participating in credit card fraud using handheld scanners to store credit card data. For example, within immigrant crime rings a member of the crime ring gains employment in a legitimate business and then steals credit card data from customers which can then be used to make unauthorized purchases. Other fraud schemes include using the internet to get bank account or credit card data, social security numbers, and other private, personal information using email or phishing scams. International crime rings have also fostered relationships with immigrants in the United States. This international cooperation has allowed for money laundering to occur and often targets large U.S. and international businesses. Fake businesses have even been set up to sponsor visas for more members of the crime ring or other criminal contacts to come over to the United States.

Undocumented immigrants may engage in crime but they can also be victims of crime. The number of undocumented immigrants who are victims of crime is difficult to accurately determine since the victims often do not report crimes that have happened to them. Undocumented immigrants do not usually report those crimes because the crimes may have been committed by someone connected to others in their communities, and the reporting of the crime to police may result in more acts of violence and retaliation. As well, undocumented immigrants may have had negative experiences with the police in their native country and do not trust police officials, believing that their reports will not resolve anything. Undocumented immigrants can also be targeted for crimes because of widely held stereotypes about immigrants. For example, undocumented immigrants and their households may be targeted for robberies because of the assumption that since they are illegally in the country they do not have bank accounts and so would keep a lot of money in their homes. Those who seek to rob them profit from the reality that the undocumented will be fearful of going to the police to report the crime. Furthermore, this targeting of undocumented immigrants may be done by other immigrant groups or by native-born Americans.

Cultural differences between the United States and the immigrant's home country also put undocumented immigrants in distinctive situations in regards to report of crimes. In some situations, what is defined to be a crime within the United States is not considered to be one by the immigrants, especially due to cultural views or understandings. Domestic violence and rape are such crimes. Those two crimes may be socially acceptable forms of punishment for acts of disobedience in some cultures and so may not be considered to be a crime by the victim, perpetrator, or both. Human trafficking is another example of a crime that undocumented immigrants may not report. Human trafficking involves tricking or coercing people to leave their country and then forcing them to work for no or low pay; this crime is a worldwide problem. Victims of human trafficking can be made to work within people's homes as maids or nannies, others may be forced into prostitution or sex trades. Many of the people brought over by human trafficking fear that reporting the crime will result in their deportation back to their home country. Victims of human trafficking are often psychologically, verbally, and/or physically abused by their captors and so fear being beaten or killed for even attempting to report the crimes. As well, the human trafficking victims are often dependent on their captors for necessary resources such as money, food, and shelter. All of these fears plus the lack of much needed resources often keep human trafficking victims stuck in the situation and prevent them from reporting the crimes.

There has also been robust scholarly debate on the criminal experiences of immigrants. Throughout history and to this day, there has been a fear that immigrants cause crime. Some people believe that immigrants are more likely to participate or engage in criminal activities than native-born Americans. Others contend that the longer immigrants are in the United States, and so the more Americanized the immigrants become, the more likely they are to participate in criminal activities, sometimes known as the paradox of assimilation. On the other hand, Pew Research has also found that immigrants do not participate in crime or criminal activities at higher rates than native-born Americans. In fact, it has been found that immigrants are equally likely or less likely than native-born Americans to participate in criminal activities. Many have argued that social misperceptions that immigrants are unethical (and therefore more prone to criminal behavior) predispose them to more scrutiny

(Inda, 2006), resulting in greater numbers being arrested and incarcerated as "punishment" for their behavior. Over the years, greater support has been given to the research showing that immigrants do not participate in crime more than native-born Americans do. However, the view that immigrants are criminals or are more likely to commit criminal acts continues to prevail even with compelling evidence to the contrary.

Amy Baumann Grau

See Also: Counterfeit Documents; Coyotes; Crime; Governance and Criminalization; Driver's Licenses; Drug Trade; Gangs; Hate Crimes; Human Trafficking; Identification Cards; Identity Theft; Incarceration.

Further Reading

Coutin, Susan Bibler. 2005. "Contesting Criminality: Illegal Immigration and the Spatialization of Legality." *Theoretical Criminology* 9.1:5–33.

Goldsmith, Pat, Mary Romero, Raquel Rubio-Goldsmith, Miguel Escobedo, and Laura Khoury. 2009. "Ethno-Racial Profiling and State Violence in a Southwest Barrio." *Aztlán: A Journal of Chicano Studies* 34.1:93–124.

Inda, Johnathan Xavier. 2006. *Targeting Immigrants: Government, Technology, and Ethics.* Malden, MA: Blackwell Publishing.

Martinez, Ramiro, Jr., and Abel Valenzuela, Jr., 2006. *Immigration and Crime: Race, Ethnicity, and Violence.* New York: New York University Press.

PBS.org. 2008. "The Ballad of Esequiel Hernandez." Available at: http://www.pbs.org/pov/pov2008/ballad/. Accessed April 4, 2009.

Stowell, Jacob I. 2007. *Immigration and Crime: The Effects of Immigration on Criminal Behavior.* New York: LFB Scholarly Publishing LLC.

Cubans

According to the U.S. Census, in 2011 there were 1,090,563 foreign-born Cubans in the United States, making up 2.27 percent of the nation's total foreign-born population. Cubans make up the third largest of the three major Hispanic groups in the United States, and according to the Pew Hispanic Center, they make up 4 percent of Latinos in the United States. The average age of forty-one for Cubans tends to be older compared with other Hispanic groups. Cubans are viewed as one of the most successful Latino groups in the United States in terms of their economic success and wealth, political and civic integration, and professional and educational achievement. However, different generations of Cuban immigrants have had different experiences.

As a general rule, many of the problems and issues associated with being undocumented in the United States have not applied to Cuban immigrants. The reason for this lies in the history of Cuba and U.S. relations with this island nation. The first wave of Cuban immigrants fled to the United States as political refugees in the 1960s shortly after the socialist Cuban Revolution led by Fidel Castro. Second-wave migrations of Cubans were primarily working-class and poor and were not as well socially situated as the first generation of immigrants who had more educational and economic resources (Portes and Rumbaut, 2001).

Most of the first generation of Cubans settled in Florida in the United States, just north of the island nation of Cuba. Referred to as "Golden Exiles," these refugees represented the business and professional classes of Cuba. They tended to have wealth and education and as refugees they were extended support by the United States government for accessing educational programs, for banking and investment opportunities, and for starting businesses. In terms of their racial characteristics, they were more likely to blend in with the United States' European stock of the eastern coast of the United States, and in this way, suffered less racial discrimination than other major Latino groups (Mexican and Puerto Rican) suffered. "The Golden Exiles" formed enclaves (areas of ethnic concentration) which have supported the arrival of new immigrants primarily to the state of Florida where they amassed great political clout (Stepick and Stepick, 2002). These enclaves are also known for their conservative family values, strong support for their national heritage, and strong civic engagement in all level of politics and governance.

As another general rule, United States immigration policies with regard to Cuba also have offered an advantage to immigrants from there, marking a distinction between immigrants from Cuba and other immigrant groups that contend with issues stemming from irregular or undocumented status. The general rule is that once an individual from Cuba reaches American soil and is out of American waters, they are allowed to legally remain in the United States as political asylees. This controversial policy is often referred to as the "wet foot, dry foot policy."

In the 1980s one of the largest mass refugee exoduses from Cuba took place, known as the Mariel Boatlift. This period in Cuban history was changing because of social and economic changes imposed by the revolutionary government (Diaz-Briquets, 1981). Johnetta B. Cole (1980) argues that the Cuban Revolution aggravated social inequalities and racism within social services, education and the legal system. Other authors such as Lourdes Arguelles and B. Ruby Rich (1984) believe that gender and sexuality played a role with oppressed groups in Cuba such as homosexuals. Until 1998 homosexuality was a crime a Cuba. During this period, the island nation was experiencing high unemployment and poor economic conditions. Those sympathetic to the Cuban condition have blamed its worsening economic outlook to the series of economic embargos against Cuba imposed by the United States to punish Cuba for what it considered to be a range of violations. The economic embargos began in 1960 in response to the revolution, and continue in some form even today. As a result, Cuban's economic progress has been stifled.

By the 1980s, relations between the United States and Cuba were strained. As the result of the economic downturn in Cuba, Cuban-Americans lobbied the U.S. government for assistance, and between April 15 and October 31, 1980, about 125,000 departed from Cuba's Mariel Harbor for the United States, arriving at the United States' shores in about 1,700 boats. Cuba's Fidel Castro agreed to temporarily lift the restriction that prevented people from leaving the island of Cuba. These refugees are often affectionately referred to as the *Marielitos*. On the Mariel boatlift were people from all economic classes, the majority of whom did not agree with the revolution. In this sense, they fell into categories of individuals that were supported and offered political asylum by the United States. Some larger families had also been separated from members in the United States because both the United States and Cuban governments only allowed a certain number of children to emigrate. In the story of Cuban immigrant Pedro Zamora from MTV's *The Real World* reality show, his family was split up. He had eight brothers and sisters. Zamora's parents were against the Cuban revolution and they were a very poor family. It took five days for their family to be processed, but there were five older siblings who were not allowed to immigrate because they were too close to draft age (Fisher & Verschoor, 1994). However, also among the Mariel refugees were those that would not have been allowed entry into the United States under ordinary circumstances. Many of the refugees, it was later discovered, had criminal records or mental health problems and had been released from Cuban institutions. Many were homosexuals, a reason to deny them entry by U.S immigration laws (Peña, 2007). In the end, all were granted political asylum by the U.S. government with all of the rights and privileges that this entailed. "Marielitos" in this way started a new life in Miami, Florida, but later fanned out to create lives for themselves in states like New Jersey and New York. Although public opinion of this rescue effort by the United States has been good, there have also been critics who pointed out that Cubans have in this way been given special treatment when immigrating to the United States not extended to other groups.

The next decade of Cuban immigration (the 1990s) involved immigrants known as "Rafters" because they traveled to the United States on small boats and rafts (Ackerman, 1996). The willingness of the United States to accept all comers further strained relations with the Cuban government and prompted Castro to test Washington's political resolve by opening Cuba's harbors in early August, allowing thousands more rafters to flee to Florida (Henken, 2005). Consistent with the "wet foot–dry foot policy," once they reached land on U.S. shores they were given refuge. However, many were caught steps before the shore and deported back to Cuba. From January to July of 1994, the U.S. Coast Guard rescued 4,731 "rafters."

As of 2012, the population of Cuba had increased to approximately 11 million people. In 2012 many families were experiencing housing shortages and poverty. During the administration of President Barack Obama, travel restrictions to Cuba were relaxed, as were limits to the amount of money that Cubans in the United States could send to support family members living in Cuba. Cubans are eligible to apply for admission to the United States through the refugee program, under what is known as the Priority 2 (P-2) category. The P-2 category is one in which the United States will accept both asylum seekers and resettled refugees.

Currently, two senators who are sons of Cuban immigrants, Florida Republican Marco Rubio, and New Jersey Democrat Robert Menendez, are part of the so-called "gang of eight," a group of eight senators from both parties working to craft a comprehensive immigration reform bill, which aims to provide a pathway to citizenship, especially for Latino immigrants.

Drew Berns

See Also: Asylum; Enclaves; Nicaraguan Adjustment and Central American Relief Act (NACARA); Nicaraguans; Refugee Act (1980); Refugees.

Further Reading

Ackerman, Holly. 1996. "Mass Migration, Nonviolent Social Action, and the Cuban Raft Exodus, 1959–1994: An Analysis of Citizen Motivation and International Politics." Ph.D. dissertation, Ann Arbor: UMI Dissertation Services.

Arguelles, Lourdes, and B. Ruby Rich. 1984. *Homosexuality, Homophobia, and Revolution: Notes toward an Understanding of the Cuban Lesbian and Gay Male Experience.* Chicago: University of Chicago Press.

Cole, J. B. 1980. "Race toward Equality: The Impact of the Cuban Revolution on Racism." *Black Scholar,* 1.8:1–22.

Diaz-Briquets, Sergio. 1981. *Cuba: The Demography of Revolution.* Washington, D.C.: Population Reference Bureau.

Fisher, R. J., and G. Verschoor. 1994. MTV's *The Real World*: Season 3, Episode 23. "A Tribute to Pedro Zamora." Los Angeles: MTV broadcast.

Henken, T. 2005. "*Balseros, Boteros, and El Bombo:* Post-1994 Cuban Immigration to the United States and the Persistence of Special Treatment." Baruch College, City University of New York. *Latino Studies* 3:393–416.

Peña, Susana. 2007. "Obvious Gays and the State Gaze: Cuban Gay Visibility and U.S. Immigration Policy during the 1980 Mariel Boatlift." *Journal of the History of Sexuality* 16.3:482–514.

Portes, Alejandro, and Ruben G. Rumbaut. 2001. *Legacies: The Story of the Immigrant Second Generation.* Berkeley: University of California Press.

Stepick, Alex, and Carol Dutton Stepick. 2002. "Power and Identity: Miami Cubans." In *Latinas/os: Remaking of America,* ed. Marcelo M. Suarez-Orozco and Mariela M. Páez. Berkeley: University of California Press.

U.S. Immigration Support. "Cuban Immigration to the United States." Cuban Immigration Support Webpage, available at http://www.usimmigrationsupport.org/cubanimmigration .html.

Wasem, E. 2009. "Cuban Migration to the United States: Policy and Trends." Congressional Research Service. Available at http://www.fas.org/sgp/crs/row/R40566.pdf. Retrieved February 25, 2013.

Cultural Citizenship

Discourses on citizenship tend to be limited to the legal/illegal binary and are very much about replicating the notion that some members of society have rights and others do not deserve them (Flores, 1997: 255). There is a clear distinction between those who should be treated as first-class citizens and those who should be relegated to second- or third-class citizenship status. Flores (1997) confers this distinction when he writes that "for nonwhites the link between membership and rights is a critical but vexing one, particularly since both rights and membership are restricted" (p. 257).

For Latinas/os it is troublesome to realize that even if they were to assimilate, the struggle to claim rights as citizens continues well after the Civil Rights movements of the 1960s and 1970s (p. 258). Cultural citizenship reframes "citizens" from individuals who have legal membership in a nation-state, to legitimate political subjects who contribute to society and claim membership and rights for themselves and their community.

Anthropologist Renato Rosaldo first developed and introduced the concept of cultural citizenship in the 1980s. Cultural citizenship refers to the right to be different (in terms of race, ethnicity, or native language) with respect to the norms of the dominant national community, without compromising one's right to belong, in the sense of participating in the nation-state's democratic processes.

Cultural citizenship focuses on claiming or affirming first-class citizenship (to have equal access to benefits that come from being a citizen of a particular country) without losing one's cultural identity[ies]. Cultural citizenship encourages the use of one's cultural practices to claim space and rights in the nation-state. Cultural citizenship has been defined as "the ways people organize their values, their beliefs about their rights, and their practices based on their sense of cultural belonging rather than on their formal status as citizens of a nation."

Cultural citizenship refers to the ways that Latinos, with or without a legal immigration status in the United States, organize and practice their citizenship rights while remaining grounded in their cultural Latina/o identities. Cultural citizenship moves from the legal definition of citizenship to include people who may not reside legally in this country. It also includes those who have historically been relegated to second-class citizenship and to society's margins. Latinas/os affirm their right to be different and carve out spaces of belonging in the "imagined community." The concept of the "imagined community" was coined by Benedict Anderson to convey the process by which displaced people, brought together in their new locations by a shared sense of history and belonging, will take steps to deliberately construct or reconstruct their sense of community through symbols, language, or identity politics. These help form a group consciousness that can produce social cohesion, which can help immigrants resist the hostilities and scapegoating they face in the United States (Flores, 1997).

Cultural citizenship has been useful in theorizing how the cultural practices of Latinas/os have kept them from assimilating fully into mainstream U.S. society and from claiming rights for their communities and families. In spite of a push to continue denying basic human rights to Latina/os, this population persists in affirming their identities to fight for their rights. Cultural citizenship provides foundational principles that position Latinas/os, and other groups viewed as second-class citizens in the United States, as de facto citizens, by exercising practices expected of citizens.

Latinas/os in the United States have experienced living as the "other": the perpetual foreigner in a land considered by many as home. Indeed, the limits Latinas/os have faced in being recognized as Americans (as exemplified by the case of Mexican-Americans) are part of the historical record (Flores, 1997: 257). This conceptual border, imposed by those who have struggled to perpetuate the Mexican American as the "other," has been the constant object of struggle embodied by the constant fight for equality and recognition in a variety of social and political spheres. Cultural citizenship allows for Latinas/os (transnationals and U.S.-born) to claim their right to be different and maintain their Latina/o identity and to use their cultural practices to claim rights. Latinas/os do not have to be "disowned" by the Mexican side or the Anglo side, for example, because they can live *en dos mundos* (to live, to straddle between two worlds, between cultures). Cultural citizenship recognizes that Latinas/os are "not fully accepted or welcome in either world; the hybridity forces us to claim our own space" (Flores, 1997: 257).

Cultural citizenship highlights how Latinas/os maintain their identity and claim first-class citizenship rights in the United States through the use of "multiple and innovative methodologies such as life histories, testimonials, and interviews, along with other forms of cultural productions such as narratives, *Corridos,* and visual arts." Cultural citizenship practices also include a range of activities of everyday life, which if taken together "claim and establish a distinct social space for Latinas/os in this country" (Flores and Benmayor, 1997: 1). Latina/o cultural citizenship reframes "citizens" from individuals who have legal membership in a nation-state, to legitimate political subjects who contribute to society and claim membership and rights for themselves and their community. Cultural citizenship acknowledges the cultural resiliency and rights-claiming agency of marginalized groups.

Judith Flores Carmona

See Also: Acculturation; Activism; Assimilation; Citizenship; Multicultural Education; Social Interaction and Integration.

Further Reading

Benmayor, R., R. M. Torruellas, and A. L. Juarbe. 1997. "Claiming Cultural Citizenship in East Harlem: '*Si esto puede ayudar a la comunidad mia…*'" In W. V. Flores and R. Benmayor, eds., *Latino Cultural Citizenship: Claiming Identity, Space, and Rights,* 152–209. Boston: Beacon Press.

Flores, W. V., and R. Benmayor, eds. 1997. *Latino Cultural Citizenship: Claiming Identity, Space, and Rights.* Boston: Beacon Press.

Rosaldo, R., and W. V. Flores. 1997. "Identity, Conflict, and Evolving Latino communities: Cultural Citizenship in San Jose, California." In W. V. Flores and R. Benmayor, eds., *Latino Cultural Citizenship: Claiming Identity, Space, and Rights*, 57–96. Boston: Beacon Press.

Rosaldo, R. 1997. "Cultural Citizenship, Inequality, and Multiculturalism." In W. V. Flores and R. Benmayor, eds., *Latino Cultural Citizenship: Claiming Identity, Space, and Rights*, 27–38. Boston: Beacon Press.

Culture

Defining Culture

Culture is made up of many parts, all integrated into the complex process of human adaptation. Knowledge about how a collection of cultural traits fit together helps those who study culture (anthropologists) distinguish different cultures and see how the

Before her 2002 wedding, Sonia Solares, a recent immigrant from Guatemala, receives a blessing from her mother in her modest rented house in Pico-Union, a bustling immigrant neighborhood in Los Angeles, California. Traditional family roles, although undergoing change with acculturation to the United States, are an important part of many cultures of Latin American immigrants. (Gilles Mingasson/Getty Images)

ideologies and practices make survival and adaptation possible in a whole range of environments. Widely accepted notions among scholars is that the many parts of culture include knowledge, beliefs and ideologies, art, laws, customs, inventions, and habits, all of which are acquired or learned by individuals as members of a larger group. The way that all of these parts work together into a culture that we can identify and label is commonly thought to be related to the larger sociopolitical and economic context in which it is found. We can also trace its evolution through time and across geographic areas.

For example, the persistence of economic instability and poverty among immigrant populations in the United States is useful in explaining the presence of cultural norms considered to be useful for adapting to difficult conditions. For Mexican immigrants living in the United States, many of their behavioral and symbolic practices are easily recognized as coming from Mexico or any one of its regions. In this way culture is seen as something that is shared with others of a larger group (i.e. other Mexicans), even if that culture and group originate elsewhere. Why the culture persists in other places and over time is not difficult to explain. When immigrants arrive in new destinations, they continue to depend on those systematic patterns of behavior that have been used by members of the group because these patterns of behavior have helped them survive in the past. In other words, the culture that has proven to be necessary and beneficial for adapting to conditions in another part of the world continues to be necessary and beneficial in new destinations. This is especially true when the conditions in sending communities (for example, poverty) are similar to those in destination communities. The chronic economic instability of many immigrant households in the United States—increasingly tied to erratic fluctuations in the global labor market and persistent discrimination—can therefore be used to explain the existence of supportive cultural practices among members of the affected group because these facilitate both the formal and informal procurement and exchange of goods, important information, or other resources. Indeed, what also proves to be consistent among socially stigmatized or economically vulnerable populations both in sending and destination communities is a pervasive loss of confidence that they will ever be fully absorbed by the existing economic order. Because of this, immigrants may be wary of abandoning older, proven cultural ways or traditions.

Thus, the logic of culture is that as the broader sociopolitical and economic conditions change, so will the culture of those who have to adapt to them. Given this logic, some cultures or traditions will inevitably be lost with time when they cease to be useful or meaningful. However, it should be noted that there have been times in U.S. history when cultural traditions were seen as backwards and forced into extinction (such as those of many Native American tribes). In the early part of the 20th century, organized efforts to assimilate millions of recent immigrants into the United States through English and American civics classes called "Americanization Programs" promoted the idea that the culture brought to the United States by immigrants retarded their assimilation into the United States. This idea perpetuated the idea that people from groups that were culturally different were inferior, and this resulted in their discrimination and segregation. In the case of Mexican children in particular, culture was blamed for their lack of educational progress, and this resulted in their being treated poorly by school teachers. As a result, many Mexican Americans grew up as mono language English speakers and ashamed of their cultural background. However, because culture by definition includes all those practices and traits that continue to help groups cope with poverty and discrimination (in other words, they continue to be meaningful and useful), Mexican culture persevered wherever descendents of Mexicans were found. In this way, Mexican culture continued to be transmitted over time by children of immigrants and subsequent generations who learned about their language and heritage from parents and elders and also learned to appreciate these for their usefulness in their daily lives.

George I. Sanchez was one of the first scholars of Mexican descent in the United States to challenge the notion that Mexican culture was to be blamed for the lack of progress suffered by Mexican populations. In his writings, he shifted the blame to the educational systems that neglected and discriminated against Mexican students. In a similar vein, it was another scholar of Mexican descent, Octavio I. Romano-V. who in the 1960s blamed the systematic misrepresentation of cultural groups in history and anthropology for the disrespect and discrimination that Mexican populations suffered. He defended culture in classic articles from *El Grito* that are considered by many scholars as pivotal in the development of a Mexican cultural renaissance. Similarly, with the U.S. Civil Rights Movement, cultural and quality of life issues such as poverty, racism, inequality, and the right to individual and cultural freedom became a central organizing theme. Historically discriminated groups (including blacks and Native Americans) were quick to grasp how a totalizing U.S. nation-state had nearly devastated cultural differences, ethnicities, cultural identities, and languages, and they politically reclaimed the right to defend them. Consequently, political and academic institutions were slowly transformed to reflect an appreciation of cultural diversity. The value placed on the nation's cultural plurality became more widespread and systematic during this period of unrest with the adoption of ethnic studies programs in colleges and universities throughout the nation. These programs renewed interest and pride in cultural heritage learning, bilingualism (resulting in Spanish-English bilingual education programs), black history and art, Mexican history, Mexican indigenous culture, and Mexican culture and art. In this way, shame about one's cultural background was replaced by the promotion of a positive ethnic identity and ethnic pride. For generations to come, this achievement continued to be a source of civic and political empowerment that led to further gains in the areas of education, housing, and politics. This sense of empowerment is still present in some Latino and immigrant neighborhoods where the exposure to this history in the schools has helped undermine the alienation and low self-esteem that students have experienced with pressures to forsake their heritage and language.

The Transmission of Culture

At the root of what we understand as culture are the social mechanisms that continually help individuals and families procure their most basic needs. However, the same social mechanisms are used to transmit the value of cultural practices to others in the group, across time (e.g. to future generations) and across space (e.g. across international borders). Central to this process is the idea of social solidarity among individuals who identify with the same culture. This sense of social solidarity not only helps to organize the distribution and exchange of resources, but also to promote ideas about who is entitled to those resources, and puts pressure on group members to develop a sense of obligation towards others. In other words, resources that are mobilized can be material in nature (such as goods, services, or information), but they can be symbolic (celebrations on cultural feast days), or emotional (such as sympathy and trust). All of these can help recent arrivals cope with acculturation stress. They also have adaptive properties.

To illustrate this process, we can examine how many Mexican immigrants and later generations of Mexican-American communities living in the United States have created and maintained social networks and other human relational ties that have helped in the process of social and economic integration, especially when problems associated with legal status or chronic, historical discrimination, and anti-immigrant sentiment dominate. Social networks can be defined as the informal mechanism for the redistribution of resources when the formal system of resource redistribution proves overly restricted. For example, laws and legislation (post 1980) like those passed in Arizona increasingly stress the household economy of immigrants and their families. Widely documented in the literature are cultural systems of material exchange based on family ties. However, family ties are not limited to those related by blood. Non-kin members are commonly incorporated into expanding webs of social relationships through ceremonial sponsorship known as *compadrazgo*. The reaffirmation of these relationships persists over time through exchanges of all types, many of which are symbolic. In this way, social networks have become a quasi-permanent feature among Mexicans living in the United States.

When the whole range of relational ties is considered, the logic of everyday reproductive activities, i.e. the provisioning and distribution activities, elevates women's status within culture, especially amid economic uncertainty. Specific examples highlight the importance of their role in social network formation and in the articulating of supportive ideologies. These can take place through ritualized celebrations (e.g. baptisms, weddings, funerals). In planning and preparing for year-round social gatherings, women actively create and reinforce a sense of belonging. Celebrations, such as birthdays and anniversaries, as well as important church holidays provide opportunities for members of extended families and their networks to reaffirm commitments towards each other. Participation in church and other community events might serve as the initial foundation for the expansion of social networks among immigrant women and thereby reduce the harmful effects of social isolation. Helping organize events for religious causes or advocacy also provides opportunities to express community concerns and in this way strengthen feelings of social solidarity and mutual support.

A Critical View of Culture

Not all of culture works in a positive way. Examined critically, culture also often works to aggravate existing social inequalities. For example, women in certain cultures may be expected to bear greater sacrifice and demonstrate greater altruism. In this way, cultural norms may disadvantage women because they reinforce dependencies and repress any real independence from controlling type of norms. By imposing more gender-specific burdens in this way, they may be excluded from accessing other resources or opportunities. In general, gendered norms that emphasize domestic responsibility for women subject them to greater scrutiny and parental control. Pressure to conform to cultural norms may come by way of sanctioning them for challenging traditional prohibitions concerning sexuality, mobility and self-promotion. Many studies point out that compared to women, men have additional opportunities to develop beneficial relationships *outside* the family and neighborhood. These extra-household relationships may include coworkers and members of other social groups. Thus, if cultural prescriptions for women limit their interaction to only those within a close-knit kin network, any attempt to access outside opportunities may be openly discouraged. Culturally-imposed limits to seek opportunities can thus result in diminished capacity. Moreover, a little known long-term benefit of broader social connections is the strengthening of children's scholastic progress. Research indicates that there is strong positive correlation between a woman's social network size and children's school performance. Other studies show that with more contact with kin and non-kin members, children learn the social skills needed to form friendships and construct social networks of their own, which helps them ne-gotiate their environments better. The conclusions in these studies agree for the most part that as long as networks and the means of social interaction are seen as resources, gendered patterns of discrimination will insure that women will continue to remain excluded from accessing the more powerful forms of resources that are readily available to men.

Cultural patterns emphasizing marriage and motherhood roles for women may also produce low educational expectations that may impede their educational progress. Relegated to primarily supportive, help-giving roles, women might exemplify the types of support-giving practices that the whole group finds routine and beneficial. It begins with the economic support they provide to families as daughters and as sisters. The pattern might be repeated after marriage as wives and mothers. Thus, a gendered em-phasis on parenting in which women are primarily responsible is often what keeps them from pursuing their own educational goals. Being primary caregiver to sick, aging parents and in-laws is consistent with these cultural expectations. In this way, little time is devoted to fulfilling her ambitions. In this light, socially supportive cul-tural practices can be seen as a liability for women because in fulfilling the needs of others, their own needs are deferred.

Cultural Change

With economically improved conditions, there is diminished need to depend on a larger group for material and emotional support. For example, with more women join-ing the labor force with migration, attitudes about gendered limitations placed on women appear to be changing. Increased stress on household economies has made it easier to accept women's changing roles. Thus, the cultural ideologies that have tradi-tionally suupressed women's mobility outside the domestic sphere necessarily have had to change. With opportunities to contribute with additional wages, women are exposed to new opportunities and the chance to widen their networks of support much in the same way that men have been able to do. In this way, changes in gendered norms can be observed.

The transformation from the kin-mediated society to one that is dominated by a corporate-style organization that privileges individualism is also associated with the loss of cultural values. An ideology of individualism socializes members of a commu-nity to the values that promote and prioritize the self over others. Individualism con-trasts with cultures that value mutual aid and group identity because these are more likely to prioritize group harmony and collective well-being for all. As such, impover-ished households or families that lose their members to a culture of individualism may also lose their battle for economic improvement that has traditionally come through the combined efforts of many—networks of kinfolk and grown children living together and working for the common good.

Shedding an affinity to culture—or loss of cultural identity—is often seen as inevi-table as more and more people migrate from kin-based economies to urban centers where there are more educational opportunities. Educational attainment provides the path towards economic success, and with this, traditional attitudes are also mediated.

This is especially true for women where where improved employment and educational opportunities also expose their children to other ideas and larger and more diverse groups of kin and nonkin, which is also beneficial. However, finding a balance between higher education and culture does not come without bicultural dilemmas for Mexican-origin women. The rising number of Latinas entering post-secondary education programs suggests that any hesitancy in adopting self-promoting behaviors may be undergoing some change. By resolving such dilemmas, the educational outcomes for a rapidly growing and increasingly educationally underserved population can be improved with future generations, as each continues to negotitate with their own set of obstacles and adaptations.

Finally, urban environments in the United States tend to devalue an individual's cultural heritage in what is popularly referred to as a melting pot of cultural differences. Moreover, with the replacement of local economies with corporately organized global economies, a high value on individualism and individual competitiveness is introduced. Moreover, long-distance interaction through technology may seem to make cultural groupings appear as nonessential. These trends de-emphasize social relationships that are fundamental to culture. With accelerated social integration in destination communities, we might expect immigrants to become transformed into highly individualized economic actors who are no longer incentivized by the rewards that collective behavior brings. The result will be the loss of historically powerful cultural mechanisms that have served groups in the past. The transformation of society promises to occupy generations of social scientists as they continue to examine the process of cultural breakdown and the result of pressures placed on individual members of cultural groups to assimilate into their new destinations.

Anna Ochoa O'Leary

See Also: Acculturation; Assimilation; Family Economics; Family Structure; Literature and Poetry; Social Interaction and Integration.

Further Reading

Alvarez, Robert R., Jr. 1991. *Familia: Migration and Adaptation in Baja and Alta California, 1800–1975.* Berkeley: University of California Press.

Chavez, Leo. 1985. "Households, Migration and Labor Market Participation: The Adaptation of Mexicans to Life in the United States." *Urban Anthropology* 14.4: 301–346.

Keefe, Susan Emily. 1980. "Personal Communities in the City: Support Networks among Mexican Americans and Anglo-Americans." *Urban Anthropology* 9.1:51–74.

O'Leary, Anna M. Ochoa. 1999. "Investment in Female Education as an Economic Strategy among U.S.-Mexican Households in Nogales, Arizona." PhD diss., University of Arizona, Tucson.

Selby, Henry A., Arthur D. Murphy, and Stephen A. Lorenzen. 1990. *The Mexican Urban Household: Organizing for Self-Defense.* Austin: University of Texas Press.

Sewell, William H., and Vimal P. Shah. 1968. "Parents' Education and Children's Educational Aspirations and Achievements." *American Sociological Review* 33.2: 191–209.

Stanton-Salazar, Ricardo. 2001. *Manufacturing Hope and Despair: The School and Kin Support Networks of U.S.-Mexican Youth.* New York: Teachers College Press.

Vélez-Ibáñez, Carlos G., and James B. Greenberg. 1992. "Formation and Transformation of Funds of Knowledge among U.S.-Mexican Households." *Anthropology and Education Quarterly* 23:313–335.

Willis, Katie. 1993. "Women's Work and Social Network Use in Oaxaca City, Mexico." *Bulletin of Latin American Research* 12.1:65–82.

Young, Gay. 1992. "Chicana College Students on the Texas-Mexico Border: Tradition and Transformation." *Hispanic Journal of Behavioral Sciences* 14.3:341–352.

D

Day Labor

Day labor is short-term contract work done with no promise that more work will be available in the future. Day labor centers are designated areas where day laborers congregate and wait for potential employers. In some cities in the United States, workers are provided a designated area for finding work. However, most of these hiring sites (79 percent) are informal (Valenzuela et al., 2006), that is, they are not formally designated as work centers. An example of informal areas can be in front of businesses (24 percent), home improvement stores (22 percent), gas stations (10 percent) and on busy streets (8 percent). Most of these sites are near residential neighborhoods. Only one in five (21 percent) day laborers searches for work at a formally sanctioned day-labor worker center.

In part this lower number of formal day labor centers may be due to the growing concerns about undocumented immigrants. For example in Arizona in 2005 legislation was passed (HB 2592: Alien Work Centers Prohibition) that prohibits a city, town or county from constructing and maintaining work centers if any part of the center is knowing by facilitating the employment of anyone who is not entitled to lawful residence in the United States. At the time that the National Day Labor Study was conducted (Valenzuela et al., 2006), there were 63 centers for day laborers throughout the country. These centers operate as a mediator between employee and employer. Those seeking employment arrive at the center and wait in line for any open positions, which are generally handed out on a first-come, first-served basis. These centers offer day laborers protection from the elements while waiting for work as well as restrooms and places to sit. While these conditions may be better than sitting on the street, the conditions of many labor centers are often subpar with no heat or air conditioning and unsanitary bathrooms. If selected for work, the day laborer is sent to the work site and returns to the day labor center at the end of the day to receive payment. The day labor center may deduct transportation, food, fees for safety equipment and other administrative fees from their checks. These centers do provide day laborers with some safeguards against workplace violations such as wage theft, discussed below, and sometimes provide resources for day laborers to bring legal action against employers who violate workers' rights.

Undocumented immigrants depend on day-labor centers or informal areas to seek informal hiring by employers. The Valenzuela study shows that day laborers are primarily used by homeowners (49 percent) and contractors (43 percent). Homeowners who are elderly or have limited resources find an advantage to day labor to help them with moving, gardening, landscaping, and a range of construction and home maintenance projects including painting, roofing, cleaning, carpentry and drywall installations. However, employers also have come to depend on such centers, both informal or formal. Construction contractors who are faced with a sudden unexpected demand to complete a job may also need to find additional labor with the right skills. The advantage of having a permanent or semi-permanent place for workers and employers to meet is that it saves time and resources that would otherwise be spent looking for workers. An advantage for workers in having a permanent or semi-permanent place to seek employers is that if they are new to the area, it saves the time needed to build connections needed to find work.

Many day laborers are part of the informal economy, accepting work that is performed outside the purview of the formal regulated economy. This aspect of the larger economy is widely held to be an advantage to employers who might expect to pay less in payroll taxes and employee benefits. Finally, day laborers find an advantage to having a place to seek work because as undocumented immigrants, they are prohibited from legally working in the formal economy. Valenzuela and colleagues found that 83 percent of the day laborers depend solely on this method as a source of income.

Finding places where workers congregate has enabled researchers to find out more about the conditions that day laborers encounter as they struggle to subsist and adapt to living and working in the United States. For example, in the National Day Labor Study done by Valenzuela and his colleagues (2006), they found that wage theft was the most common violation of employee rights reported among the 2,660 day laborers surveyed in their study, with half of all day laborers surveyed reporting at least one instance of wage theft within the two months of being surveyed. Another 28 percent of those surveyed reported having been insulted or threatened by their employers. Because most of the day laborers are undocumented, employers are emboldened to subject them to these abuses, including physical abuse. Employers often deter workers from reporting these abuses by threatening to turn them over to immigration enforcement authorities. The report also suggests that even when employers do not threaten them overtly, undocumented workers are mindful of their status and are reluctant to press charges against their employers using legal channels. Many day laborers believe that avenues for compelling their employers to abide by fair employment practices are closed to them. Because of this, the value of community education and advocacy is heightened (Valenzuela et al., 2006: 14), as is the role of documentation to better understand how abuse is carried out. This is an important first step in making visible the routine unfair treatment of a virtually invisible workforce.

Discussions centering on the rights of undocumented workers have been brought to the forefront of current legal and political debates in the United States at both the federal and state levels of governance. Organizations such as the National Day Laborer Organizing Network and the Day Labor Research Institute advocate for immigration and labor policy reform to help improve the work conditions for all day laborers. At the local level, community education about workforce abuses has been taken up by community-based organizations across the United States. The work they do to educate workers about their rights and the documentation that they generate help call attention to the human and economic rights of immigrant workers. The Coalición de Derechos Humanos (CDH) in Tucson, Arizona, is such an organization. Since 1994, the organization has been dedicated to promoting respect for immigrant and migrant rights. Most notably, it has worked actively to bring public attention to the increased militarization of the U.S.-Mexico border. An important service that they provide is assisting undocumented workers recuperate wages from unscrupulous employers. Although earnings can fluctuate greatly from month to month, the instability of this employment keeps most day laborers part of the working poor class with their annual earnings rarely exceeding $15,000.

Individuals with a grievance come to the organization's office because they trust the organization and feel safe from law enforcement interference. CDH staff members offer assistance in Spanish, help victims fill out complaint forms and negotiate the myriad of agencies in efforts to resolve their complaints. Many employers are unaware that employing immigrants, including those that are undocumented, subjects them to the same legal responsibilities as employing those with legal authorization to work. The fact that they have hired them through informal day labor centers does not exempt employers from fair employment standards. For example, employers are subject to paying back wages and overtime claims when they fail to pay their employees for work performed, regardless of their employees' immigration status. Employers may also be held liable by their immigrant employees for discrimination based on race, sex or national origin (Beerman, 2006).

The legal responsibility of employers to pay back wages and overtime claims has been the subject of recent law suits brought against Wal-mart by undocumented workers. On October 23, 2003, federal officers from the Department of Homeland Security's Bureau of Immigration and Customs Enforcement (ICE), formerly known as the Immigration and Naturalization Service (INS), entered sixty-one Wal-Mart stores in twenty-one states nationwide and arrested more than 250 undocumented immigrants. This plan of action was dubbed "Operation Rollback" as a pun on Wal-Mart's advertising campaign touting its "rollback of prices." Wal-Mart argued that it was not responsible because the workers were employed by independent contractors.

In the Wal-Mart case, all of the workers claimed they were paid weekly compensation of $350–$500 in cash. The plaintiffs in the case were undocumented immigrants who worked for at least 60 hours per week, and were obligated to work seven days a week. They also claimed they received no overtime compensation, in violation of fair labor practices, nor did they have taxes or Social Security (FICA) withheld from their earnings (Entelisano, 2003). The judge's ruling held for the workers, upholding the principle that all workers regardless of their legal status have rights to fair employment standards.

The Wage and Hour Division of the Department of Labor under the Arizona State Attorney General's office makes no distinction based on a worker's legal status and has an established process to help victims of wage theft to recover their earnings. Claims brought to organizations that assist workers can be forwarded to the Wage and Hour Division for processing.

Employers are also prohibited from retaliating against workers if there is a dispute, although research suggests that is a common tactic used against workers (O'Leary, 2007). Dismissals occurred after workers voiced objections about their treatment, their pay, or about a potential job hazard. Voicing objection is a straightforward way in which any worker at any job site might logically attempt to resolve problems as they arise. Yet for undocumented workers complaints may be routinely dismissed and the workers themselves may be threatened with dismissal. By maintaining a fear of dismissal, employers silence workers and sustain a systematic undercounting of employer abuse. The constant threat of unfair dismissal, the incessant and cumulative assaults on their performance and dignity, can take a toll physically, psychologically, and emotionally.

Valenzuela et al. (2006) show that day laborers tend to be active members of their communities with half (52 percent) attending church regularly and one-fifth (22 percent) involved in sports clubs. Many workers (11 percent) have been living in the United States for more than twenty years, and 29 percent have lived in the United States between six and twenty years. Twenty-nine percent of the children of the day laborers surveyed had been born in the United States. Chances are high that anyone living in the United States has had daily interaction and discourse with immigrants as employees, neighbors, or coworkers.

Kelli Chapman

See Also: Domestic Work; Employment; Employment Visas; Family Economics; Shadow Population; Single Men; Wages; Workers' Rights.

Further Reading

Beermann, Nick. 2006. "Liability in More Ways Than One: Employing Undocumented Workers." http://library.findlaw.com/2003/Sep/30/133064.html (accessed January 3, 2006).

Entelisano, Carol A. 2003. "The Woes of WAL-MART: A Lesson in Independent Contractor Practices and Immigration Law (Non)Compliance." http://library.findlaw.com/2003/Dec/29/133231.html.

O'Leary, Anna Ochoa. 2007. "Petit Apartheid in the U.S.-Mexico Borderlands: An Analysis of Community Organization Data Documenting Work Force Abuses of the Undocumented." *Forum on Public Policy: A Journal of the Oxford Roundtable.* Available at: http://www.forumonpublicpolicy.com/papersw07.html#crimjus.

Valenzuela, Abel, Jr., Nik Theodore, Edwin Meléndez and Ana Luz Gonzalez. 2006. "On the Corner: Day Labor in the United States," unpublished manuscript, UCLA Center for the Study of Urban Poverty. Available at: www.sscnet.ucla.edu/issr/csup/index.php.

Death

From the mid-1990s through the present, thousands of Mexican and Latin American immigrants have lost their lives while attempting to migrate to the United States. Although there is no complete and accurate count of these deaths, it has been estimated that over 5,600 bodies have been discovered on the U.S. side of the border between 1994 and 2009. Over two thousand known migrant deaths have occurred in Arizona alone since the year 2000 (Rose, 2012).

Juana Garcia Martinez poses next to a photo of her late husband, Ildefonso Martinez, in Vista, California, 2012. Ildefonso Martinez died from dehydration trying to cross back into the United States after being deported in 2011. The death of migrants crossing the Southwest border has long been a tragic consequence of increased poverty and the massive increase in U.S. border enforcement and border militarization. (AP Photo/Lenny Ignelzi)

The deaths are seen by scholars as a grave human rights crisis caused primarily by U.S. immigration policy. Studies have demonstrated the correlation between increased enforcement and a rise in deaths. During the Clinton Administration there were border enforcement policy changes predicated on the idea of *prevention through deterrence,* the goal of which has been to deter would-be unauthorized migrants by increasing the human costs of crossing. Undeterred migrants are routed through remote areas where U.S. authorities have a presumed tactical advantage due to geography. In a strategy of *segmented enforcement,* the traditional urban crossing-points were fortified, leaving open remote expanses of land and sea. The policy changes were enforced locally under the names "Operation Hold the Line" in El Paso (1993), "Operation Gatekeeper" in San Diego (1994), "Operation Safeguard" in Nogales (1995), and "Operation Rio Grande" in South Texas (1997). These policy changes created a "funnel effect" whereby migrants were effectively pushed into remote desert and mountain areas, where they perished in high numbers.

Border enforcement efforts have not stopped unauthorized crossings, but instead have made the process more clandestine and dangerous. Unauthorized migration is a complex social process that is influenced by various individual-, household-, regional-, national-, and global-level "push" and "pull" factors. Segmented enforcement efforts were designed to increase the individual-level physical and financial costs associated with unauthorized crossings to the point where they would exceed the benefits of expected earnings in the United States and therefore deter migration. However, this has not been the case. Market forces such as the structurally embedded demand for immigrant workers, neoliberal economic policies, and expansive social networks have all contributed to continued migrations despite increased border enforcement. Mexico's entry into neoliberal trade agreements such as the General Agreement on Tariffs and Trade (GATT) in 1986 and the North American Free Trade Agreement (NAFTA) in 1994 exacerbated the economic situation among the working poor in Mexico, and led to increased migration.

While migrant deaths date back generations, the increased prevalence of deaths seen today began in the late nineties in California and in Arizona. As enforcement in those areas increased, the deaths shifted to the U.S. Border Patrol Tucson Sector, which then experienced a twenty-fold increase in known migrant deaths between FY 1990 and FY 2005. Community-based organizations in these states began to draw the public attention to this human tragedy. In Tucson, Arizona, the Coalición de Derechos Humanos (CDH) began to make its mark in 1998 by publishing data on the number of deaths in Pima County, gathered from a range of sources, including the U.S. Border Patrol and the Pima County Office of the Medical Examiner (PCOME), in Tucson, Arizona, which provides medico-legal death investigation for the western two-thirds of the Tucson sector's southern border with Mexico. Between 1990 and 2010, the PCOME handled the remains of 1,887 migrants—more than any other jurisdiction in the nation.

The counting of migrant fatalities has been challenging and controversial. Two of the most common sources for approximating migrant fatalities, vital registry statistics and U.S. Border Patrol counts, are highly problematic. The former rely on death certificate data and do not determine whether the person died attempting to cross the border. U.S. Border Patrol counts are known to seriously undercount migrant fatalities by not including skeletal remains or those remains recovered on Native American reservations. The most accurate statistics come from medical examiners' offices, despite the fact that there are variations in the methods and systems used to determine whether a decedent is believed to be a migrant.

All body counts are limited to the number of human remains that have been found. Most researchers agree that there are far more border deaths than those which have been included in published counts. Because migrants are forced into remote desert and mountain areas, it can take months or years for their remains to be discovered. When they are discovered weeks, months, or years later, the remains may be skeletonized. In addition, many migrants never make it to the United States, but perish within Mexico as victims of violence or as casualties of the train used by many Central Americans to traverse Mexico.

The causes of death for migrants on the U.S. side of the border relate to the terrain they cross. Along the California portion of the border, migrants have died primarily by drowning in the All American Canal, by being hit by vehicles while attempting to run across Interstate highways, or by exposure. In Texas, migrants face the risk of drowning in the Rio Grande (Rio Bravo) or dying from exposure. Very little is known about New Mexico migrant deaths, but it appears that the deceased migrants found there have died primarily from exposure.

The Pima County Office of the Medical Examiner in Tucson, Arizona provides the most comprehensive demographic data on migrant deaths. The Binational Migration

Institute (also in Tucson as part of the University of Arizona) published a report utilizing this data in 2006 (Rubio-Goldsmith et al., 2006). Out of 927 decedents analyzed (remains recovered between 1990 and 2005), approximately 80 percent were male, and among those whose ages were known, the average age was around thirty years. In addition, the top four causes of death were exposure (59.7 percent), undetermined (21.2 percent), motor vehicle accident (12 percent), and homicide (3.6 percent). For remains listing the cause of death as "undetermined," the medical examiner was unable to determine a cause due to the extent of decomposition or skeletonization. Both conditions indicate a longer period of time between death and discovery, suggesting a remote area of death, and therefore a likely cause of exposure.

Within the crisis of migrant death there exists a secondary crisis in the number of unidentified remains and missing people. For Pima County, out of the 1,887 remains handled by the office between 1990 and 2010, more than 30 percent were unidentified as of November 2010. As of the same date, that office had records for over 850 missing migrants. The causes for this are primarily institutional: there is no centralized database of unidentified migrant remains and missing persons last seen alive crossing the border. Because so many of the bodies are found in a highly decomposed state, identification is difficult. Due to extreme poverty, many families of missing migrants do not have dental records or radiographs that can be used to identify their loved ones. To date, there is no comprehensive DNA comparison system that allows for blind-matches between samples submitted by relatives of missing migrants and samples taken from unidentified remains found on the border.

Families of missing migrants, whether they were left in the sending communities or live in the United States, experience complex grief and ambiguous loss. If they live in the United States, many are unable to effectively search for their loved ones because of their vulnerable status as undocumented immigrants. A number of immigrant rights organizations have stepped in to assist families and migrants in distress, including CDH, No More Deaths, Good Samaritans, Humane Borders, and the American Friends Service Committee in Arizona, *Angeles del la Frontera,* Border Angels, and Water Station in California, and *Paisanos al Rescate* in Texas. Countless others exist throughout Mexico that provide humanitarian services primarily to Central American migrants.

Robin Reineke and Daniel E. Martinez

See Also: Border Crossing; Coyotes; Devil's Highway; Human Smuggling; Immigration and Naturalization Service (INS); U.S.-Mexico Border Wall.

Further Reading

Cornelius, Wayne. 2001. "Death at the Border: Efficacy and Unintended Consequences of U.S. Immigration Control Policy." *Population and Development Review* 27.4: 661–685.

Eschbach, Karl, Jacqueline Hagan, Nestor Rodriguez, Ruben Hernandez-Leon, and Stanley Bailey. 1999. "Death at the Border." *International Migration Review* 33.2: 430–454.

Jimenez, Maria. 2009. "Humanitarian Crisis: Migrant Deaths at the U.S. – Mexico Border." ACLU of San Diego & Imperial Counties, and Mexico's National Commission of Human Rights, October 1.

Rose, Ananda. 2012. "Death in the Desert." *New York Times,* June 21. http://www.nytimes.com/2012/06/22/opinion/migrants-dying-on-the-us-mexico-border.html?_r=0.

Rubio-Goldsmith, Raquel, M. Melissa McCormick, Daniel Martinez, and Inez Duarte. 2006. "A Humanitarian Crisis at the Border: New Estimate of Deaths among Unauthorized Immigrants." Immigration Policy Center: 1–5.

Sapkota, Sanjeeb, Harold W. Kohl, Julie Gilchrist, et al. 2006. "Unauthorized Border Crossings and Migrant Deaths: Arizona, New Mexico, and El Paso, Texas, 2002–2003." *American Journal of Public Health* 96.7: 1282–1287.

Deferred Action for Childhood Arrivals (DACA)

Deferred Action for Childhood Arrivals (DACA) is a memorandum issued by executive order by President Barak Obama on June 15, 2012. The order directed agencies that form part of the U.S. Department of Homeland Security (U.S. Customs and Border Protection, the U.S. Citizenship and Immigration Services, the U.S. Customs Border Protection, and U.S. Immigration and Customs Enforcement), to practice prosecutorial discretion towards those who as children immigrated to the United States without proper authorization. Simply put, prosecutorial discretion means that administrative agencies (such as the ones mentioned above) have discretion as to whom they select to prosecute. Typically, individuals found to be in the country unlawfully risk removal. However, with prosecutorial discretion, deferred action will be granted on a case-by-case basis. In other words, DACA agencies can select those applicants for whom removal from the country will be suspended. DACA does not give undocumented youth lawful permanent resident status such as a green card or provide a path to permanent residency and citizenship. Rather, it gives temporary relief from deportation to undocumented youth and work authorization that can be renewed every two years to eligible applicants.

Under the executive order, in order to qualify for DACA individuals need to be at least sixteen years old and no older than thirty. Applicants need to prove that they were brought to the United States before they turned sixteen and have resided in the country for at least five continuous years at the time of their application. They also need to be currently in school, have received a high school or G.E.D. diploma, or have been honorably discharged from the military.

Deferred removal action does not grant lawful immigration status nor does it provide a path to citizenship. Applying for DACA is also a demanding process and there is a fee of $495.00 for a biometric background check that may be a hardship for many families. Other concerns stem from the fact that applicants must prove that they are in economic need of work to receive authorization to work. Moreover, the grant of deferred action will be given in two-year increments, and although it can be renewed indefinitely, it is uncertain how long this program will last. These concerns account for the lower number of applicants than expected. The *National Journal* reports that in the first eight months that the program has been in place, about a half million petitioners for the program have been accepted, reflecting about half of what was predicted. It is estimated that as many as 1.76 million individuals may qualify for DACA (Delahunty and Yoo, 2013). As of February of 2013, the state with the most number of applicants was California with 128,412, followed by Texas at 73,258, and then New York with 25,735. An overwhelming majority of applicants are from Mexico.

It is widely held that DACA came about only because of the repeated failed attempts to pass the Development, Relief, and Education for Alien Minors (DREAM) Act for immigrant children who are present in the country without papers. Many of the requirements to qualify for DACA are modeled from the bipartisan proposals that had been considered to be part of the DREAM Act. The prevailing arguments for those who have supported the DREAM Act, as they are for DACA, are that these children and young adults came to the United States with their undocumented parents through no choice of their own. The logical arguments that follows is that such children and young adults know little or nothing about their country of origin, they are American in every other sense, are highly motivated to come out of the shadows, and can be productive members of the United States if only they are given a chance.

For many years now, undocumented students in higher education have been the subject of scholarly inquiry. It is now well documented that these students reflect many of the values of U.S. society. They are civically engaged and have faith that their activism will have an impact on policy that will benefit the broader community. Research also consistently shows that undocumented students have overcome great odds against them by being resilient and persistent (Contreras, 2009). According to Dougherty and his colleagues (2010), every year approximately sixty-five thousand undocumented students who have lived in the United States at least five years graduate from U.S. high schools. However, they are less likely to go on to college than students that are citizens. It is also estimated that 48 percent of undocumented immigrants between ages eighteen and twenty-four who had graduated from high school had attended some kind of college by 2004, but at a much lower rate than those here legally (73 percent) and their native-born counterparts (70 percent). In many cases, they have done so while living in fear of deportation and family separation, and at times have had to deal with overt social hostilities (Contreras, 2009). They show a determination to excel in spite of the anxieties about their economic future and that of their families. Not surprisingly, they are concerned about how they will finance their education if they are not allowed to work or apply for loans. For those that do work, they fear that their undocumented status will be discovered and reported. In spite of all this, they have actively engaged in self-help activities to help them reach their goals, such as participating in campus organizations such as the MeChA (Moviemiento Estudiantil Chicano de Aztlán) or relied on peer networks for information about classes, jobs, and community activities. In short, while they may be considered victims of institutional barriers to success, many have also successfully navigated many of those barriers to improve their lives and those of their families.

Political analysts and immigration scholars have observed that the executive order issued by President Obama represents an important shift in the nation's attitudes towards immigrants. At the same time, fundamental divisions between the nation's two major political parties, Democrat and Republican, have been revealed. Supporters of DACA have hailed it as a just and practical remedy, and long overdue. Critics of the plan maintain that it undermines the rule of law. The political schism played out months after DACA went into effect with many young immigrants and applicants for deferred action encountering different reactions by their state legislatures, dashing any hope that the process will go smoothly. In several states dominated by Republican leadership, DACA hopefuls are finding that basic benefits available to legal residents, such as identification cards, health care, student financial aid, eligibility for in-state tuition, driver's licenses—are being denied. In other states, colleges and universities have rolled out the welcome mat. Not surprisingly, the numbers of those applying for deferment are lower in states hostile to immigrants, such as Arizona, where DACA-eligible students have been denied driver's licenses. In contrast, in Illinois, these students can apply and obtain driver's licenses. Michigan initially denied DACA students to apply for a license, but eventually conceded, perhaps in response to lawsuits brought against Arizona, Michigan, and Nebraska by the American Civil Liberties Union and National Immigration Law Center. Denying DACA students a license to drive makes many unable to exercise their new right to work or attend school. What appears to be true in how the politics of DACA play out at the state level is that in absence of any national litigation strategy to assure that the rights of young undocumented students are advanced, the fight for these rights seems to be heavily contingent on the relative power of the Latino community in those states (Dougherty et al., 2010).

Many states—Arizona, Alabama, Florida, Idaho, Oklahoma, Colorado, Georgia, and South Carolina—deny nonresident immigrants the right to pay in-state tuition. For example, in Arizona, in 2012, in-state tuition at a public university was approximately $10,000 per year, which is below average annual tuition for U.S. public universities of $13,297, according to the U.S. Department of Education. For out-of-state students in Arizona, the tuition is approximately $27,000 per year. In Florida, it is estimated that every year 2,000 undocumented high school graduates are shut out of Florida public colleges and universities because their status makes them ineligible for in-state tuition and fees averaging about $3,000 a year, compared to nearly $16,000 for out-of-state tuition. Some community colleges in Arizona consider DACA students as in-state residents. However, Arizona law prohibits undocumented students from applying for financial aid or government student loans. Paying substantially more for higher education in places where they are being denied in-state residency status is unattainable. In some states, such as South Carolina and Georgia, DACA eligible students are denied admission into some public universities altogether. In contrast, ten states have passed laws to allow undocumented students to pay in-state tuition: California, Texas, Washington, Kansas, Utah, New York, Illinois, New Mexico, and Nebraska (Contreras, 2009). After Texas HB 1403 granted undocumented students eligibility for in-state tuition in 2005, there was a seven-fold increase in the number of undocumented high school graduates who entered college (Dougherty et al., 2010).

Education policy and immigration law in the United States have for many years now intersected and with mixed results. Since the *Plyler v. Doe* case in 1982, the perception that there is a willful and sustained effort by xenophobes to make permanent an underclass made of ethnic and racial minorities has grown sharper and more focused. Those who continue to exert such repressive efforts have failed to prove how denying or blocking the education achievement of undocumented immigrants will help dissuade immigrants from coming or in fact remedy the economic issues that drive immigrants from their homelands in the first place. Opponents to Texas Proposition 1403 contested granting eligibility for in-state tuition to undocumented high school students because they were not seen as rightful members of American society. It was argued that undocumented immigrants were law breakers and in-state tuition eligibility would only encourage more illegal immigration at a cost to the state (Dougherty et al., 2010). Radoff (2011) further argues that the widening gap between rich and poor is increasingly reflecting the divisions that mark citizens and noncitizens, with more immigrants suffering disenfranchisement and exploitation. Regardless of whether they work in the fields or building homes, immigrants have become essential to the U.S. economy, and they and their children remain outside of the legal protection that comes with citizenship. Legal scholars Delahunty and Yoo (2013) argue that in light of such contentious political divisions, deep-seated ideologies, and a hostile Congress, the Obama Administration has resorted to the use of "prosecutorial discretion," on numerous occasions, and with this last executive order, virtually enacted a DREAM Act into law.

As of September, 2013, close to six hundred thousand individuals have applied for relief under DACA, and more than 430,000 people have received the status. However, the program has not reached all states and all immigrant groups equally, with Mexican immigrants overrepresented in applications and acceptances, and other groups, particularly Asian immigrants, underrepresented.

Anna Ochoa O'Leary

See Also: Activism; Adult Education; Advocacy; Colleges and Universities; DREAM Act; High Schools; Obama Administration; Undocumented Students.

Further Reading

Brannon, Jody. 2013. "Deferred-Action Counter: Number of Accepted Applications Exceeds 450,000." Available at http://www.nationaljournal.com/thenextamerica/immigration/deferred-action-counter-number-of-accepted-applications-exceeds-450-000-20121023.

Contreras, Frances. 2009. "*Sin Papeles y Rompiendo Barreras:* Latino Students and the Challenges of Persisting in College." *Harvard Educational Review.* 79.4: 610–631.

Delahunty, Robert J., and John C. Yoo. 2013. "Dream On: The Obama Administration's Nonenforcement of Immigration Laws, the DREAM Act, and the Take Care Clause." *Texas Law Review* 91.4: 781–857.

Dougherty, Kevin James, H. Kenny Nienhusser, and Blanca E. Vega. 2010. "Undocumented Immigrants and State Higher Education Policy: The Politics of In-State Tuition Eligibility in Texas and Arizona." *Review of Higher Education* 34.1: 123–173.

Radoff, Sara. 2011. "Crossing the Borders of *Plyler v. Doe*: Students without Documentation and Their Right to Rights." *Educational Studies* 47.5: 436–450.

Wong, Tom K., Angela S. García, Marisa Abrajano, David FitzGerald, Karthick Ramakrishnan, and Sally Le. 2013. "Undocumented No More: A Nationwide Analysis of Deferred Action for Childhood Arrivals, or DACA." Center for American Progress, available at: http://www.americanprogress.org/issues/immigration/report/2013/09/20/74599/undocumented-no-more/.

Deportation

Deportation is defined by the Department of Homeland Security (DHS) as the removal of an alien from the United States for violation of criminal or immigration laws. Deportation proceedings are handled by Immigration and Customs Enforcement, better known as ICE. In addition to deportation, ICE handles investigatory functions as well as intelligence and is under the Department of Homeland Security (DHS). In 1925, Congress established the border patrol, a group of officers who are still charged with policing the U.S. borders against undocumented entrants. The border patrol is also charged with finding and deporting undocumented immigrants from the interior who have managed to avoid apprehension at the border.

Historically, deportation laws have had several variations. In an effort to control the entrance of foreigners, particularly from Mexico, the United States has made several attempts at removing foreigners from the country. An example of such efforts is the repatriation efforts of the 1930s during the great depression. It is estimated that more than four hundred thousand Mexican and Mexican-Americans were pressured through job denials and raids to leave the country. Many of these adults and children leaving were U.S. citizens. Another wave of deportations that took place in the United States was in 1954 through Operation Wetback, in which an estimated 1.3 million undocumented farm workers were apprehended and deported to various locations far into Mexico, in an effort to make it harder for individuals to return. Deportation legislation has evolved since then, although current policy still results in very high numbers of deportations annually. As of fiscal year 2010, over four hundred thousand deportations from the United States have taken place.

There are various ways in which an individual can be deported from the country even as a legal resident. Common grounds for deportation can include but are not limited to: engaging in a fraudulent marriage with a U.S. citizen, committing certain crimes, and engaging in any activity that puts in danger the safety of the nation.

The majority of deportations are due to entry to the United States without valid entry documents through an unauthorized port of entry, or through overstaying an authorized period of time outlined on their visa. Individuals who hold green cards (not yet citizens of the United States) can also be entered into deportation proceedings if they commit a serious crime. If an individual is deported s/he may lose the right to return to the United States in the future, even as a visitor.

The deportation process is a legal proceeding, and the individual involved regardless of immigration status has rights. These rights include the right to challenge the removal itself on procedural or constitutional grounds. Individuals who are lawful permanent residents of the country are not at risk of deportation unless s/he has committed a serious crime, engaged in a fraudulent marriage to a U.S. citizen to gain citizenship, or it can be proven that s/he entered the country with fraudulent documents or through an unauthorized port of entry. Typically, the first steps in entering an individual into deportation proceedings is to issue a document called an "Order to Show Cause." This document tells the individual the time and location where the hearing will take place. At this time, the individual in question will have the opportunity to ask an immigration judge for relief. Although in immigration cases the individual is usually detained, s/he can be released by paying a bond fee determined by the immigration judge. The individual is then scheduled for a hearing with an immigration judge who will hear the case, and during this time the individual may ask the judge for relief from the charges against him/her. The individual has the right to an attorney who may represent him or her in court, so long as the attorney representation is of no cost to the government. There are in many areas attorneys who will work with individuals in these cases for reduced fees and at times pro bono (free of charge).

Once the immigration judge has heard the evidence on both sides, the judge will make a ruling, and this ruling can be appealed to the Board of Immigration Appeals (BIA). Although the decision regarding those in danger of deportation largely depends on their financial resources, they can take the case even further to the federal court of appeals. Once an individual has gone through these court proceedings, an alternative for some is "voluntary departure." Individuals who qualify for voluntary departure must possess good moral character and be able to cover their own transportation costs to their country of origin. They may be able to return legally to the United States.

Carolina Luque

See Also: Expedited Removal; Immigration and Customs Enforcement (ICE); Operation Streamline; Operation Wetback; Ports of Entry; Repatriation; U.S. Border Patrol.

Further Reading

Immigration Equality. Immigration Basics: "Voluntary Departure." http://immigrationequality .org/issues/law-library/lgbth-asylum-manual/voluntary-departure/.

LeMay, Michael C. 2007. *Illegal Immigration: A Reference Handbook.* Santa Barbara, Calif: ABC-CLIO.

U.S. Citizenship and Immigration Services. www.uscis.gov.

Detention Centers

Non-citizens in deportation proceedings are held in detention centers. A detention center is not a prison. Unlike imprisonment which is punishment for a criminal infraction, the law classifies detention as an administrative hold in preparation for deportation. The government is supposed to hold deportable non-citizens until final arrangements are made for their removal from the country. However, court appeals, delays associated with court docket overload, and other legal processes often mean that people spend weeks if not months and years in detention awaiting release or deportation.

The Transactional Records Access Clearinghouse (TRAC) has estimated that in 2011, the average wait for an immigration case to be decided was 302 days, an increase of 30 percent since 2009. Some courts have even worse backlogs: it takes Los Angeles 745 days and New York 646 days to decide on a case. For removal orders, the average for New York is 602 days and for Los Angeles 532 days (Rojas, 2011).

The majority of detainees (58 percent) are not criminal offenders and do not even have a criminal record (Kerwin and Lin, 2009). They are individuals who either crossed

Ecuadorian undocumented immigrant Miriam Lucia Rondona waits to be checked off an immigration list before being deported at a detention center in San Jose, California in 2007. The U.S. Coast Guard rescued a disabled boat abandoned by smugglers that was carrying 41 Ecuadorians and 13 Peruvian immigrants to the United States. (AP Photo/Kent Gilbert)

the border without authorization or who remained in the United States after the expiration of their visa. Detainees include not just adult men and women but also children and entire families. Since 1996, individuals who are seeking asylum in the United States are placed in mandatory detention until their asylum claim is adjudicated and they are either released into the United States or deported. Because asylum cases are complex, these individuals, many of whom have suffered persecution and torture, are held in administrative confinement for long periods of time.

According to Kerwin and Lin (2009), the average length of detention for individuals with pending removal cases was 81 days. The majority had been detained less than ninety days but 10 percent had been in detention between six months and one year and 3 percent had been detained for more than a year. Among those who did have a final removal order, average detention was seventy-two days. Non-criminal detainees are detained for an average of sixty-five days but more than four hundred have been detained for more than a year.

The standards for detention centers (National Detention Standards or NDS) were created in 2000 and are currently enforced by the Department of Homeland Security. In 2001, the United States held 209,000 detainees; by 2008 the number had grown to 378,000. According to the ACLU, today the United States holds approximately 429,000 non-citizens each year, including children. This means that the number of detainees has more than doubled in a decade, an indication of stepped-up enforcement by federal and also state and local authorities.

The total capacity of the American detention system is 33,400 beds. The Detention Watch Network has identified more than 350 detention facilities (Detention Watch Network, 2012). In 1994, the detention capacity of the United States was 6,785 beds but after the enactment of restrictive immigration reforms in 1996, the number of beds has increased annually. In 2006, the United States had a total of 20,594 detention beds but by 2008 the number had exceeded 33,000 (Kerwin and Lin, 2009). The increased demand for detention beds is the result of a renewed emphasis on non-citizen removal that started during the Bush Administration and has continued during the Obama Administration.

The increase in detention of non-criminal non-citizens has put pressure on the federal government to relieve some of the overcrowding in federally run detention centers. As a result, the Department of Homeland Security has outsourced detention to both private prison companies and to state and local jails. Overflow detainees are held in state and local prisons and jails which were not built to accommodate administrative detainees but rather to hold criminals. Federal authorities lease space from 312 county and local jails; about 67 percent of detainees are held in these facilities along with criminals (Detention Watch Network, 2012).

Running and expanding such a major detention system comes at a substantial cost to the American taxpayer. In 2008, Congress allocated $2.4 billion to non-citizen detention and removal as part of a $5.8 billion immigration enforcement budget. The Detention Watch Network estimates that the cost of detention is on average $122 per day for each detained non-citizen (Detention Watch Network, 2012). Alternatives to deportation are estimated to cost $13 per day (Kerwin and Lin, 2009). In February 2013, some undocumented immigrants were released by the Immigration and Customs Enforcement agency (ICE), with supervision, from detention centers to save money in anticipation of automatic budget cuts in the federal government, due to the so-called sequestration (Semple, 2013).

The costs associated with the detention system do not end with financial outlays. The decentralization, complexity and difficulties with management and oversight associated with the detention system have substantial human costs. As a result of lax oversight, at least 104 people have died in detention in recent years, and investigations have revealed significant lapses in the provision of medical and other basic care for detainees (Priest and Goldstein, 2008). Official documents obtained by the ACLU and the *New York Times* show that government officials were aware of deaths occurring in detention centers and "used their role as overseers to cover up evidence of mistreatment, deflect scrutiny by the news media or prepare exculpatory public statements after gathering facts that pointed to substandard care or abuse" (Bernstein, 2010).

Alexandra Filindra

Further Reading

Bernstein, Nina. 2010, January 9. "Officials Hid Truth of Immigrant Deaths in Jail." *New York Times.* http://www.nytimes.com/2010/01/10/us/10detain.html?ref=incustody deaths&_r=0.

Detention Watch Network. 2012. "About the U.S. Detention and Deportation System." http://www.detentionwatchnetwork.org/aboutdetention.

Kerwin, Donald, and Serena Yi-Ying Lin. 2009. "Immigrant Detention: Can ICE Meet Its Legal Imperatives and Case Management Responsibilities?" September. Migration Policy Institute. http://www.migrationpolicy.org/pubs/detentionreportSept1009.pdf.

Priest, Dana, and Amy Goldstein. 2008, May 11. "System of Neglect." *Washington Post.* http://www.washingtonpost.com/wp-srv/nation/specials/immigration/cwc_d1p1.html.

Rojas, Leslie Berestein. 2011, July 28. "Longer Immigration Court Wait Times, with Especially Long Waits in L.A." 89.3 KPCC—Southern California Public Radio. http://www.scpr.org/blogs/multiamerican/2011/07/28/7317/longer-immigration-court-wait-times-with-especiall/.

Semple, Kirk. 2013, February 26. "Mass Release of Immigrants Is Tied to Impending Cuts." *New York Times.* http://www.nytimes.com/2013/02/27/us/immigrants-released-ahead-of-automatic-budget-cuts.html?pagewanted=all.

Devil's Highway

In May 2001, U.S. Border Patrol officers encountered four undocumented immigrants in the far southwestern region of Arizona. The individuals, all men, had been wandering the Sonoran desert in temperatures soaring above one hundred degrees for at least five days. Dehydrated and delirious, the men were near death. It was soon learned that they were originally part of a group of twenty-six men who had crossed the U.S.-Mexico border together. Abandoned by their guides, the men attempted to find their way through unfamiliar terrain on their own. Between the time of their initial departure and their discovery by Border Patrol agents, the men encountered brutal circumstances that challenged their physical, mental, emotional and spiritual well-being. Of the original twenty-six immigrants, fourteen perished. They would come to be known as the Yuma 14. Luis Alberto Urrea captured the story of their journey in the widely-acclaimed novel, *The Devil's Highway.*

Urrea begins *The Devil's Highway* by introducing the reader to the area of Sonoran desert known as the Devil's Highway. This expanse of desert stretches from the U.S.-Mexico border in southwestern Arizona northward toward Gila Bend, Arizona. A few small cities and towns, some clusters of residences, a few ranches, tribal lands, and a U.S. Airforce base rest along various points of the outer reaches of the area, but they are small and far between. There are also Border Patrol stations in the area but the heart of the Devil's Highway is just desert, about one hundred miles of it.

The Sonoran desert is defined by mountain ranges with intermittent spans of rugged desert terrain. Common vegetation includes cacti such as the saguaro, ocotillo, cholla, and hundreds of small varieties that layer the desert floor. Trees and shrubs consist of thorny mesquite and palo verde, and creosote and sage. Wildlife in the Sonoran desert is diverse. It ranges from large animals such as mountain lions, bobcats, javelinas and coyotes; birds such as owls, eagles, hawks, and vultures; poisonous reptiles such as rattlesnakes, sidewinders, Gila monsters; and poisonous spiders and insects such as scorpions, black widow spiders, and recluse spiders, among many other creatures. In summer months, the daytime temperatures in this area typically reach above 110 degrees and, in winter months, nighttime temperatures may dip below freezing. There are natural river beds and *arroyos* (streams) through the desert, but they rarely run and then usually only briefly during monsoon season in late summer. Other natural bodies of water include wells and springs hidden deep within the mountains and known only to those intimately familiar with the Sonoran desert.

For those unfamiliar with the area, the desert can be very intimidating and even life-threatening. In just a matter of a few days, the extreme weather conditions combined with the harsh terrain can cause travelers to become disoriented, severely dehydrated, exhausted and injured to the point of serious health risk and even death. Urrea illustrates this in an overview of the history of human presence in the desert gathered from the oral traditions of the Tohono O'odham (a tribal group of people indigenous to the area), the experiences of the Spanish *conquistadors* and even the escapades of contemporary tourists. Many of the stories Urrea draws upon demonstrate the "unforgiving" nature of the desert and the fragility of humans attempting to survive in it. He shares, for example, the story of a pair of American visitors to the desert who, although they had experience traveling through the terrain and were well-equipped to do so, became disoriented and were unable to find their way back to their camp. Consequently, the pair died from dehydration just a short walk from safety.

In tandem with the description of the severity of the environment, Urrea establishes the desert as a space with a living history. He recounts stories of spiritual phenomena known for centuries, including the story of the restless ghost of a Spanish explorer. He also portrays the desert as a sentient entity, discussing its "language," "mood," and "energies." Rather than it just being a space or place where events take place, the desert is a primary "character" in the story that Urrea tells. He carefully details the type of treatment one can expect from the desert, from the intense burning of flesh and organs to the disorientation and delirium of dehydration and heat stroke. Urrea makes it clear to the reader that travel through the desert is a physically and emotionally violent and painful experience. The development of the desert and the fortitude required to survive it create an image of the area that helps prepare the reader to visualize the brutal experience of the twenty-six men who made that fatal journey.

Twenty-three members of the twenty-six man group who trekked into the Sonoran desert that May were from Veracruz, Mexico. Among them were smaller family groups—brothers-in-laws, cousins, uncles, fathers, and sons. Each had his own reasons for making the journey north, all motivated by the common desire to improve their financial situations to better provide for their families. Edgar Adrian Martinez, for example, was only sixteen years old. He worked at a Coca-Cola plant in Cuautepec, where he earned eight dollars a day. He hoped that in the United States he would earn enough to return home and build a house to share with his girlfriend. Martinez set out with his uncle, Jose Isidro Colorado, and his godfather, Victor Flores Badillo. Martinez died just as the Border Patrol found the group on their fifth day in the desert.

Urrea's retelling of the events leading to the death of the Yuma 14 reveals the multiple factors that are intricately woven into the process of immigration to the United States. He follows the stories of each of the men as closely as he has been able to determine from their hometowns into the Sonoran desert, but he also explores the perspectives of the Border Patrol units and the *coyotes* involved. *(Coyote* is the Spanish term commonly used to refer to the individuals who guide or transport undocumented immigrants across the U.S.-Mexico border.). In his treatment of the Border Patrol, he provides insight into their daily tasks, routines, policies, and the organizational structure and operational styles. Urrea's depiction of the Border Patrol serves to illustrate that while some policies are harsh and questionable, and some agents seemingly uncaring and irresponsible, there are many agents who work hard to fulfill their duties of "protecting" the border while still treating passers-through with the dignity and respect for life that all humans deserve. Urrea focuses his narrative on highlighting the fact that even the Border Patrol agents, who have a key role in the experiences involved in immigration, have individual stories that in turn inform the larger experience. Urrea does the same in his treatment of the young guide, Jesus Mendez (Jesus Lopez Ramos). Urrea gives the reader glimpses into Mendez's life as an undocumented immigrant himself, one who also wants only to earn a better life for himself. He becomes entangled in the smuggling industry and earns a reputation as a competent *coyote*. Mendez fails on his final trek, contributes to the death of fourteen men, and almost loses his own life.

Throughout *The Devil's Highway,* Urrea calls attention to the government policies and attitudes toward immigration. He points to the role of the North American Free Trade Agreement (NAFTA) in disturbing the economies of rural Mexican communities, and how that has in turn made it nearly impossible for rural Mexicans to make a decent living in their own communities. Urrea does not shy away from discussing the political agendas of both the United States and Mexico. He also addresses the growing industry of human smuggling and how it is also affecting the economies of both countries. He further describes the amount of money that is involved in undocumented immigration, including the soaring transport fees that immigrants are forced to pay to smugglers; the staggering costs to the U.S. government to detain, process, and deport immigrants; and the great costs that the Mexican government also assumes in the process.

Urrea's attention to the many and varied perspectives reveals more about the immigration process than many people may understand. From the father and son who set out in hopes of working long enough in the United States to earn extra money to help build their home in Veracruz, Mexico to the Border Patrol agents who spend countless hours cruising along desolate desert roads in search of immigrants, Urrea's accounts help the reader to understand that there is no simple or clearly defined "right" or "wrong" point of view and that, ultimately, the totality of undocumented immigration is rife with contradictions between human frailty and strength, indignity and respect, and suffering and survival.

Luis Alberto Urrea is an award-winning author and a professor of creative writing. He was born in Tijuana, Mexico and educated in the United States. He writes fiction, non-fiction and poetry and has had great successes in each genre. His titles include *Into the North, Across the Wire,* and *The Hummingbird's Daughter.* Urrea's works have earned him the Christopher Award, the 1999 American Book Award, Western State Books Award, the 2002 ForeWord Magazine Book of the Year Award and the 2002 Small Press Book of the Year Award. His poetry has been featured in *The Best*

American Poetry, and he is a member of the Latino Literary Hall of Fame. *The Devil's Highway* is the winner of the 2004 Lannan Literary Award and was a finalist for the Pulitzer Prize.

Andrea Hernandez Holm

See Also: Border Crossing; Coyotes; Death; Human Trafficking; U.S.-Mexico Border Wall.

Further Reading

Arizona-Sonoran Desert Museum Center for Sonoran Desert Studies. 2013. www.desertmuseum
    .org.
Couch, Nathan M., and Derek Hunziker. "The Devil's Highway Interactive Map." http://
    devil.ucdavis.edu.
Inda, Jonathon Xavier. 2006. *Targeting Immigrants: Government, Technology, and Ethics.*
    Malden, MA: Blackwell Publishing.
"Luis Alberto Urrea." 2013. www.luisurrea.com.
Urrea, Luis Alberto. 2004. *The Devil's Highway.* New York: Little, Brown and Company.

Dillingham Report (1910)

The Dillingham report, printed by the Government Printing Office in 1911, was a compilation of statistical and demographic data about immigrants in the United States. The report was completed by the Dillingham Commission, a commission created by Congress according to Section 39 of the Immigration Act of 1907. Composed of nine members, including senators, representatives, and presidential appointees, and headed by Senator William P. Dillingham of Vermont, the commission's job was to conduct a scientific investigation into U.S. immigration. The Dillingham report provided Congress with conclusions and recommendations, most notably the literacy test and quota system.

The creation of the Dillingham Commission and its resulting report arose at a time in U.S. history when Americans began questioning the assimilability of immigrants and advocating restriction. By the 1890s, the increase in the number of immigrants, particularly southern and eastern Europeans, the expansion of Ellis Island, and a greater number of urban ethnic enclaves all contributed to questions regarding assimilability. Within Congress, debates formed between restrictionists and anti-restrictionists over which immigrants posed the most serious danger and to what extent continued immigration was harmful to the nation. Advocates of restriction, such as Massachusetts Senator Henry Cabot Lodge, supported the passage of a literacy test as a way to exclude undesirable immigrants. The utilization of a literacy test passed in 1897 but was vetoed by President Grover Cleveland who doubted its effectiveness. After the veto, restrictionists and anti-restrictionists continued to disagree, making reform of immigration policy unlikely.

After the 1897 veto, Republican representative and anti-restrictionist Richard Bartholdt proposed the creation of a commission to investigate immigration. While

During his four terms in the U.S. Senate, William Paul Dillingham became the leading congressional authority on immigration. The report on immigration that bears his name fueled the movement to restrict immigration from countries considered culturally inferior, resulting in limits on immigrants originating from southern and eastern Europe, and a continuation of Chinese exclusion. (Library of Congress)

nothing came of it then, it aided the realization that a study could provide information that would minimize disagreement among re-strictionists and anti-restrictionists enough to result in a consensus on policy. Understanding the need for a comprehensive study on immigration, the U.S. Senate provided $1,000,000 in funds for the Dillingham Commission to complete its task.

The Dillingham report consisted of forty-two volumes most of which were compiled by the commission's two secretaries: W. W. Husband and C. S. Atkinson. The commission examined migration patterns from Europe, living conditions in European countries, and the socioeconomic status of recent immigrants. Members of the commission conducted field studies on immigrants' occupation, wage, and living conditions by obtaining data from 3,200,000 individuals. Scientists and anthropologists lent their expertise to the study, including Dr. Daniel Folkmar who created a *Dictionary of Races and Peoples* and well-known anthropologist Dr. Franz Boas. The *Dictionary of Races and Peoples* placed national groups into racial divisions such as Celtic, Iberic, or Slavic without clear parameters for classification. For example, while northern Italians were placed in the Celtic category, southern Italians were placed in the Iberic category.

One of the most contentious ideas promoted by the Dillingham Commission was the differentiation between old and new immigration. Many of the report's findings were used to validate differences between old immigration, which, according to the study, consisted of immigrants from northern and western Europe, and new immigration, which included immigrants from southern and eastern Europe. According to the report, individuals within the category of old immigration had settled throughout the United States, held a variety of occupations, and assimilated into American society. In contrast, the report concluded that individuals within the category of new immigration originated from less advanced countries, held unskilled labor positions, resided in urban ethnic slums, avoided trade unions, were less intelligent and unassimilable. The commission based these findings on three measures for assimilation: English competency, obtainment of citizenship, and abandonment of ethnicity. Other indicators of the undesirability of new immigrants were portrayed through the report's attention to the frequency with which immigrants engaged in crime or sought charity. One of the report's findings concluded that immigrants were disproportionately represented in insane asylums.

The report's findings on the flaws of new immigrants did not go uncontested. Jane Addams, known as the leader of the settlement house movement and co-founder of Hull House in Chicago, believed differences among immigrants were cultural, not racial. Through Hull House, Addams assisted immigrants with learning English and adapting to American society. Another skeptic, Grace Abbott, director of the Immigrants' Protective League in Chicago, disagreed with the Dillingham's Report's conclusion that new immigrants were less assimilable than old immigrants. Such opposing views were not of the majority and consequently did not affect the commission's report.

The report offered several recommendations to Congress to restrict the quantity of immigrants from southern and eastern Europe. First, the report recommended implementing tougher assessments of immigrants in their originating countries in order to prevent unwanted migrants from emigrating. The commission also advised a continuation of Chinese exclusion and reform of immigrant banks and employment agencies to reduce the quantity of single, unskilled male migrants. It also recommended that immigrants who became public charges, meaning disabled, financially destitute, or without family, within three years of immigrating be deported. Most of the report's recommendations addressed the migration of unskilled males from southern and eastern Europe. These suggestions included issuing a literacy test, setting preset quotas according to race, excluding unskilled workers without families, setting annual limits on the number of immigrants to be admitted, requiring immigrants to possess a minimum amount of money, and increasing the head tax.

The recommendations issued by the Dillingham Commission were a triumph for restrictionists and structured debates on immigration policy well into the 1960s. Many of the report's proposals were later incorporated into immigration policy. The literacy test passed through Congress in 1917, despite President Woodrow Wilson's veto, becoming part of the 1917 Immigration Act which also enhanced previous restrictions on Chinese and Japanese immigrants, nearly excluding them altogether. Additionally, the quota law, also recommended by the Dillingham report, became part of the 1921 Immigration Act which restricted immigration from any one nation to 3 percent of the number of individuals of that nationality living in the United States as documented by the 1910 U.S. Census.

Ashley M. Zampogna Krug

See Also: Assimilation; Chinese; Racism; Single Men; *Strangers from a Different Shore;* Xenophobia.

Further Reading

King, Desmond. 2000. *Making Americans: Immigration, Race, and the Origins of the Diverse Democracy.* Cambridge: Harvard University Press.

Zeidel, Robert F. 2004. *Immigrants, Progressives, and Exclusion Politics: The Dillingham Commission, 1900–1927.* DeKalb: Northern Illinois University Press, 2004.

Discrimination and Barriers

Discrimination, broadly defined as harmful or negative acts against a group deemed inferior, is a significant concern in the lives of undocumented immigrants. Whether due to actual experience being discriminated against or the perception that discrimination could occur, the undocumented face a unique set of barriers that have direct consequences on their socioeconomic status, potential for upward mobility, and physical or mental health.

Given their political status in American society, undocumented immigrants face a variety of barriers to full incorporation and participation that documented immigrants do not encounter. Among the undocumented, it is especially salient for non-Whites as they face discrimination based on their legal status and their skin color.

The first major barrier that undocumented immigrants entering from Mexico face is the danger in crossing the border. Of note, many undocumented immigrants (an estimated 40–50 percent) become undocumented due to overstaying their visas. This entry focuses on those entering the United States without legal permission. As the border has been increasingly militarized, migrants take ever more dangerous routes to gain access to the United States, resulting in death for some. Overall estimates by the U.S. Border Patrol show 5,570 have died while crossing the U.S.-Mexico border from FY 1998 to 2012. Deaths occurring during border crossings in the Tucson Sector alone have steadily risen from eight in 1990 to a high of 225 in 2010 according to a 2013 report issued by the Binational Migration Institute in 2013 (Immigration Policy Center, 2013). It has been widely acknowledged by both scholars and government officials that this rise in the number of migrant fatalities is a major consequence of border-security-focused immigration policy.

Generally, discrimination and the resulting barriers it creates are driven by the fear that somehow American democracy or the "American way of life" is threatened by an influx of new faces. The belief is that the undocumented are somehow exploiting the American economic and political system. This belief, although widespread, is false. The empirical record shows that the undocumented actually contribute more to the public treasury than they use in social services. In fact, due to their undocumented status there is an incentive to avoid using public services so as to not be discovered as undocumented. There are a variety of ways in which the undocumented actually help the U.S. economy; nonetheless the persistent view remains and, although based on incorrect information, creates a climate in which harassment and discrimination against the undocumented becomes somehow more warranted.

During economic downturns these nativist claims become more prominent as citizens are more likely to view the undocumented as "takers" of American jobs. These sorts of nativist views have been expressed by people such as former presidential candidate and current political analyst Pat Buchanan who warn that recent immigration encourages political and cultural disorder. The recent economic downturn led to more nativist claims similar to that of Mr. Buchanan and has inspired a series of strict immigration enforcement laws in many state legislatures, most notably in Arizona and Alabama. Critics of these laws note their potential for increasing harassment of immigrants, in particular, Hispanics, both documented and undocumented. Proponents argue that these laws are now needed as the federal government has shirked its duties of immigration enforcement. The major consequence, regardless of one's position on the matter, is to create a patchwork of immigration law in which each state determines its standards. In states with restrictive immigration policy, such as Arizona, undocumented immigrants are likely to move or go even farther underground. In the end, the problems associated with undocumented status simply get shifted to other states or exacerbated in high-volume immigrant-receiving places without rectifying the barriers that otherwise law-abiding immigrants face.

The major state bureaucracy that manages issues related to undocumented immigrants is the U.S. Immigration and Customs Enforcement agency (ICE). Over the last decade, ICE has been criticized for its treatment of the undocumented and in some ways has created a system in which their basic human rights are routinely violated. This has occurred in three main ways: through the use of private contractors with a corresponding lack of proper oversight by the agency, through the grouping of violent criminals with non-violent undocumented immigrants, and by neglecting to meet the medical needs of detained immigrants. The outsourcing of prison management to private contractors creates a major conflict of interest where social and moral objectives take a back seat to the profit motive. Put simply, private prisons have an incentive to detain people. With such a large number of undocumented immigrants already in the United States, the potential profits of imprisoning them have made the private prison industry a lucrative one. These measures have been legitimized by arguments from public sector employees that privatization eliminates bureaucratic red tape and lowers government costs, although studies on this topic have not been able to verify any significant cost savings. Policy makers promote the use of private prisons for the detainment of the undocumented not just through their decisions to outsource, but also by engaging in public rhetoric that frames the issue as a "war on the undocumented," with the implied goal being the implementation of control solutions that increasingly associates undocumented status with criminality and calls for harsh measures—such as walls, fences, and increased surveillance—to combat a so-called growing "problem." Furthermore, the fact that immigration enforcement is handled in bureaucratic space by ICE, the Department of Homeland Security, and the Department of Justice congeals and reaffirms the association between undocumented and "problem" that is in need of control. Interestingly, in the early parts of the twentieth century the Department of Labor was initially the department under which immigration enforcement occurred, a sure sign in the shift of perception from immigration as a labor issue to a criminal one under the Department of Justice. The physical safety of the undocumented is undermined in privatized prisons when they are mixed with violent criminals. This is especially a concern for women. Gender-based violence in U.S. detention centers is a serious issue that results from abuses committed by other inmates as well as detention officials. The experience of gender-based violence has serious negative consequences for the future of those that are victimized, which only exacerbates an already tenuous future that the undocumented have in the United States. Although ICE has detention standards explicitly stating that violent criminals shall not be mixed with undocumented inmates, independent third party analysts have found that this policy is rarely enforced and that a general lack of oversight of privatized prisons creates situations where abuses can go on unchecked. Also, pregnant women or those with young children report problems with accessing proper healthcare and nutrition while detained.

The federal government uses several methods to enforce immigration law, one being worksite raids, which is not currently used to the extent that it was during the George W. Bush administration. There has been a trend towards what is referred to as "silent raids," which occur when immigration officials scour employment records at sites suspected of using undocumented workers. The former tended to result in mass deportation and images of hard-handed treatment of immigrant women and children, while the latter, used more by the Obama administration, tend to result in the workers being fired without the media focus. Worksite raids resulted in many families being torn apart as the major breadwinners of families were sent back to their home country, leaving others behind in an even more economically burdensome situation. Silent raids tend to not result in the breakup of families, as deportation happens to a lesser extent. For otherwise law-abiding undocumented workers, criminal charges are not levied. Particularly problematic still is that undocumented workers with clean records who are fired are left without their chief way of providing for their families. Analysts note that this sort of strictly enforcement-based immigration policy results in shifting problems elsewhere without consideration for systemic push and pull factors that encourage the undocumented to come to the United States and employers to hire them. It also creates an environment in which the unique set of barriers that the undocumented face persists.

Immigrants with legal permanent status tend to follow a relatively normal pathway to citizenship. They may participate in civic life and use a variety of social welfare programs provided to them by the state that facilitate incorporation into American life. The undocumented encounter much more difficulty in becoming a part of their community. Their access to mechanisms facilitating social and political incorporation is severely limited. Although by definition many avenues of civic and community engagement do not require citizenship, the undocumented tend to avoid these paths so as not to publicly "outed." They also have limited access to mechanisms of economic and financial incorporation into U.S. society. For example, they have severely limited access to traditional banking methods due to their poor credit, lack of a social security number, and fear of apprehension by immigration authorities if they were to open an account. This fear is firmly grounded in recent trends as under the Obama Administration deportations have increased. Much borrowing for large purchases must be conducted informally, on the streets, or from family. As their financial options are constrained, undocumented immigrants become more attractive to predatory lenders. In addition, the undocumented are, by definition, considered criminals in the United States. This has important implications for how they are viewed and treated in their new communities. Even if law-abiding by any other measure, their undocumented status places them in a disadvantaged position, more easily manipulated and exploited by their employers, the unscrupulous, and prejudicial gatekeepers to educational and health care institutions and agencies.

Although a difficult population to collect data from, evidence suggests that the undocumented are a particularly vulnerable population at higher risk for disease and injury than either documented immigrants or native-born U.S. citizens. The major reason for this is their limited access to health care services, which have become more restricted over the last few decades as new provisions that increasingly bar the undocumented from obtaining publicly-funded health services gained in popularity. This creates yet another financial burden on the undocumented as many seek health care via emergency room visits, an exceedingly more expensive route, and one that does not provide the preventive care needed to keep health care costs down overall. Fear of government officials also contributes to delays in seeking care for the undocumented. These factors are major contributors to the poor physical and mental health of the undocumented. Not only do they avoid using health services, impacting their physical health, but they also expend much energy strategizing on how to avoid apprehension and discrimination, which has its own stressful effects on mental health.

Modern-day slavery continues to exist in the United States, and the undocumented face the most severe forms of discrimination in this regard. Forced labor is a major way that the undocumented are exploited. It occurs in poorly regulated industries with a high demand for cheap labor. Generally there is a lack of official monitoring, which allows for these types of work to persist. While forced labor occurs all over the United States, it is concentrated in major immigrant gateway states, such as California, Florida, New York, and Texas. Studies indicated in 2004 that approximately 47 percent of forced labor in the United States occurred in prostitution and sex work, while 27 percent were domestic workers and 10 percent worked in agriculture (Hidden Slaves: Forced Labor in the United States, 2004). These are sectors where, through either coercion or self-selection, migrant workers disproportionately find employment.

Undocumented immigrants face a unique set of barriers to full incorporation into U.S. society. This occurs when making the trip to their new society, while finding employment, when integrating into their local communities, when seeking to manage their physical and mental health, and while interacting with state agencies designed to manage their situations. The totality of these experiences creates a second-class status for the undocumented. They are welcomed to the extent that they fill a desired labor need (often low-skill and low-wage), but they are viewed as parasitic to the body politic in the public sphere. Complicating the matter even more is the fact that many undocumented immigrants face the realities of a system of racial categorization in the United States that increases the probability that they will face discrimination at work and in their communities. More recently, the economic downturn has created a context in which immigrants become scapegoats for much larger, more complex, macro-economic concerns. At the grassroots level the immigration reform movement is very active and effective in calling on the nation to reaffirm some of its core values and to address issues of discrimination, but it is yet to be seen if policy makers will respond in a direct material way to combat the challenges associated with second-class status or if they will react more symbolically, as they have in the past. The latter type of reaction does little to deal with the barriers faced by the undocumented, while the former is potentially a signal that human rights and fairness for the undocumented will be realized.

Aaron J. Howell

See Also: Barriers to Health; Deportation; Exclusion; Governance and Criminalization; Incarceration; Racialized Labeling of Mexican-Origin Persons; Racism; Social Interaction and Integration; State Legislation; "Undocumented" Label.

Further Reading

Herivel, Tara, and Paul Wright. 2007. *Prison Profiteers: Who Makes Money from Mass Incarceration.* New York: The New Press.

Hidden Slaves: Forced Labor in the United States. 2004. Free the Slaves and Human Rights Center, University of California at Berkeley. http://www.freetheslaves.net/document.doc?id=17.

Hirschman, Charles, Philip Kasinitz, and Josh DeWind. 1999. *The Handbook of International Migration: The American Experience.* New York: Russell Sage Foundation.

Immigration Policy Center. 2013. "The Cost of Doing Nothing: Dollars, Lives, and Opportunities Lost in the Wait for Immigration Reform." Available at http://www.immigrationpolicy.org/just-facts/cost-doing-nothing.

Lipman, Francine J. "Taxing Undocumented Immigrants: Separate, Unequal, and Without Representation." 2006. Chapman University School of Law Legal Studies / *Harvard Latino Law Review.* http://ssrn.com/abstract=881584.

Nandi, Arijit, Sandro Galea, Gerald Lopez, Vijay Nandi, Stacey Strongarone, and Danielle C. Ompad. 2008. "Access to and Use of Health Services among Undocumented Mexican Immigrants in a US Urban Area." *American Journal of Public Health* 98: 2011–2020.

United States Government Accountability Office. 2006. "Illegal Immigration: Border Crossing Deaths Have Doubled since 1995." www.gao.gov/new.items/d06770.pdf.

Villalobos, Jose D. 2011. "Promises and Human Rights: The Obama Administration on Immigrant Detention Policy Reform." *Race, Gender, and Class* 18:151–170.

Displacement

Displacement is the forced migration of people from their native place, typically because of armed conflict, persecution, or natural disaster. When displaced persons migrate within their own country, they are referred to as internally displaced persons (IDPs). IDPs legally remain under the protection of their own government—even though that government might be the cause of their displacement. When displaced persons cross an international border to seek sanctuary, they are referred to as refugees. Because of the devastation that drove refugees to cross into another country, their right to be there may have not been formalized in any way. Their lack of identification—a citizenship certificate, lost or destroyed in catastrophic events—can exclude them from accessing critical government services that may be available to them, including health care, education or employment. In this regard, they are considered to be "stateless." For such displaced persons, the United Nations High Commissioner for Refugees (UNHCR) is the only international organization that has a specific mandate to protect them, although other international agencies (such as the International Committee for the Red Cross) may assist. The UNHCR determines if an individual qualifies as a refugee and works to find the best possible solution: either safe return to the home country or third-country resettlement.

When it becomes obvious that a large number of displaced persons cannot return to their home country, commitments are made by other countries to admit them. For example, the United States Congress passed the Displaced Persons Act, which for a limited time admitted into the country certain European displaced persons fleeing persecution by the Nazi government of Germany because of race, religion or political opinions. Those that qualified were granted permanent residence and permission to work. The displaced person was allowed to bring family members under certain conditions. The act also made provisions that children under the age of sixteen who had been orphaned because their parents either went missing or died would be cared for by the United States. Although many countries accept refugees, the United States takes in more than all other resettlement countries combined. The United States is a signatory to the United Nations Protocol Relating to the Status of Refugees where it agrees to the principle of *nonrefoulement,* which means that it will not return a foreign national to a country where their life or freedom is threatened. Therefore, once in the United States, refugees can apply for permanent residence (commonly referred to as a green card) and after five years in the United States, they can apply for U.S. citizenship.

In some cases, persons may be determined to be displaced after they have entered the United States. While they are not refugees as defined by UNHCR, they might nonetheless be displaced because they cannot return to their country of origin. For example, a foreign state may request that their nationals who are in the United States without documents not be deported because the state temporarily cannot handle their return due to an environmental disaster. This is called deferred enforced departure (DED). In these cases, the United States will grant blanket Temporary Protected Status (TPS) to those from those countries, provided that it is consistent with U.S. national interests (Wasem and Ester, 2011).

Examples of blanket TPS for those displaced by natural disasters came in the aftermath of Hurricane Mitch in November of 1998, when U.S. Attorney General Janet Reno announced that the deportation of undocumented immigrants from El Salvador, Guatemala, Honduras, and Nicaragua would be temporarily suspended. Similarly, the devastation caused by the January 12, 2010, earthquake where thousands of Haitians died, resulting in the almost complete collapse of the infrastructure in the capital city of Port-au-Prince, led the Department of Homeland Security (DHS) to announce that it would halt the temporary deportation of Haitians who were present in the country without proper documents (Wasem and Ester, 2011).

In 2010, the dates for DED and TPS issued for those displaced by natural disasters were:

- El Salvador, March 2, 2001–September 9, 2010

- Haiti, January 15, 2010–July 22, 2011
- Honduras, December 30, 1998–July 5, 2010
- Nicaragua, December 30, 1998–July 5, 2010

It is important to note that grounds for inadmissibility are also enforced making many applicants ineligible for TPS, and there may be many more that apply and are denied, or that do not know that they are eligible and because of prevailing uncertainties fail to apply for TPS.

A blanket TPS does not come automatically with natural disasters. For example, as a result of other natural disasters in recent years that devastated Peru, Pakistan, Sri Lanka, India, Indonesia, Thailand, Somalia, Myanmar, Malaysia, Maldives, Tanzania, Seychelles, Bangladesh, and Kenya, some called for the U.S. Government to grant TPS to nationals from these countries. Proponents of these petitions argued that these countries could not handle the return of nationals due to the environmental disasters and that there were extraordinary circumstances preventing people from returning safely. Environmental disasters displace people but are seen as slow to develop, rather than unforeseeable and sudden. A position on these countries has yet to materialize (Wasem and Ester, 2010).

Blanket TPS for those displaced by political strife include

- Kuwait, from March 1991 to March 1992
- Rwanda, from June 1995 to December 1997
- Lebanon, from March 1991 to March 1993
- The Kosovo Province of Serbia, from June 1998 to December 2000
- Bosnia-Herzegovina, from August 1992 to February 2001
- Angola, from March 29, 2000, to March 29, 2003
- Sierra Leone, from November 4, 1997, to May 3, 2004
- Burundi, from November 4, 1997 to May 2, 2009
- Somalia, from September 16, 1991 to March 17, 2011
- Sudan, from November 4, 1997 to November 2, 2011
- Liberia, TPS from March 1991 to October 1, 2007, then DED from October 1, 2007 to March 31, 2010

Holders of TPS are then temporarily allowed to work and settle in the United States. However, some of the hardships associated with a TPS are that they cannot apply for permanent residence (commonly referred to as a green card), nor U.S. citizenship. Another critique of the TPS system is that those who fall under this status are not allowed to visit their home country without risking the loss of their status. Violating these terms may result in revocation of the TPS. In addition, if they fail to renew their TPS visa during the short window of time allowed (usually 60 days), they may fall out of status and thus become "undocumented." The period provided by the TPS may be extended beyond the initial period (12 to 18 months), as determined by the Secretary of Homeland Security. This determination depends on the changes in the conditions in the home country, and TPS beneficiaries experience anxiety waiting to hear the results of this decision (Wasem and Ester, 2011).

A case that illustrates the uncertainty that comes when displaced persons are granted TPS comes from Liberia. Liberians first received TPS in March 1991 following an outbreak of civil war. After their TPS expired September 28, 1999, approximately ten thousand Liberians in the United States were given DED, which was extended to September 29, 2002. On October 1, 2002, Liberia was again redesignated for TPS for twelve months, which was again extended. On September 20, 2006, the George W. Bush Administration announced that Liberian TPS would expire on October 1, 2007, and they were once again granted DED until March 31, 2009. On March 23, 2009, President Obama extended DED for Liberians until March 31, 2010 (Wasem and Ester, 2011).

Internally Displaced Persons (IDPs)

The issue of IDPs within the United States rose in the aftermath of Hurricane Katrina in 2005 where there was evidence that undocumented immigrants living in the United States were internally displaced by this environmental disaster. A Congressional Research Service report estimates that 20,000 to 35,000 unauthorized immigrants were victims of Hurricane Katrina (Wasem, 2005). The Congressional Research Service (CRS) report reaffirmed that refugees, asylees, and Lawful Permanent Residents (LPRs) were eligible for public assistance programs, and specifically pointed to the part in the law that also provided all noncitizens—regardless of their immigration status—short-term, emergency disaster relief and services that deliver assistance at the community level, provide assistance without individual determinations of each recipient's needs, and are necessary for the protection of life and safety (Wasem 2005, 6). Moreover, the Federal Emergency Management Agency (FEMA), which conducts disaster assistance efforts, requires nondiscrimination and equitable treatment in disaster assistance. In spite of these provisions, the CRS report noted that undocumented persons were hesitant to apply for assistance out of fear of deportation, and that DHS had discretion over the process, resulting in greater uncertainty about whether undocumented immigrants would receive assistance.

Immigrant-rights activists consistently point out that neoliberal policies that have spurred globalization have led to mass population displacement due to poverty. They increasingly point to the growing body of literature that explains how with the 1994 North American Free Trade Agreement (NAFTA) immigrants have had little choice but to leave their country for the United States in what is considered to be the largest movement of people of modern history. However, in the eyes of the U.S. government, displacement motivated by the quest for economic improvement rather than reasons associated with persecution, natural disaster or armed conflict, is not considered to be sufficient grounds for asylum, refugee resettlement, or TPS. Therefore, migrants displaced by economic policies are more likely to become undocumented as they seek the means by which they can support their families.

Anna Ochoa O'Leary

See Also: Asylum; Cubans; Inadmissibility; North American Free Trade Agreement (NAFTA); Refugees; Temporary Protected Status (TPS).

Further Reading

Chacon, Oscar. 2011. "Globalization. Obsolete and Inhumane Migratory Policies, and Their Impact on Migration Workers and Their Families in the North and Central American/Caribbean Region." *Journal of Poverty*, 465–74.

Cornelius, Wayne A., and Philip L. Martin. 1993. "The Uncertain Connection: Free Trade and Rural Mexican Migration to the United States." *The Center for Migration Studies of New York Inc.* 27.3:484–512.

Donato, Katharine, and Shirin Hakimzadeh. 2005. "The Changing Face of the Gulf Coast: Immigration to Louisiana, Mississippi, and Alabama." Migration Policy Institute/ Migration Information Resource. Available at: http://www.migrationinformation .org/usfocus/display.cfm?ID=368.

United Nations. 2013. "Refugees and Forcibly Displaced Persons." Available at http://www .un.org/en/events/refugeeday/background.shtml.

Wasem, Ruth Allen. 2005. "Hurricane Katrina–Related Immigration Issues and Legislation." Congressional Research Service/ The Library of Congress. September 19. Available at http://fpc.state.gov/documents/organization/53687.pdf.

Wasem, Ruth Allen, and Karma Ester. 2010. "Temporary Protected Status: Current Immigration Policy and Issues." Congressional Research Service/The Library of Congress. January 19. Available at http://fpc.state.gov/documents/organization/137267 .pdf.

Wasem, Ruth Allen, and Karma Ester. 2011. "Temporary Protected Status: Current Immigration Policy and Issues." Congressional Research Service/The Library of Congress. December 13. Available at http://www.fas.org/sgp/crs/homesec/RS20844.pdf.

Domestic Violence

Domestic violence is the exertion of intentional intimidation, assault, battery or other abusive behaviors over a household member or intimate partner in order to gain power and control over the individual. The abuse can be physical, verbal, sexual, emotional, psychological, or economic. Domestic violence is also commonly referred to as battering, relationship abuse, or intimate partner violence. Domestic violence is about power and control. The instigator of violence, also referred to as the perpetrator, seeks to dominate the victim in order to gain power and gain complete authority over her. In order to maintain control over time, the perpetrator will restrict the victim's outlets and social support system. This can be done by restricting the victim's activities outside the home such as employment, extracurricular activities as well as restricting time spent with friends or family. These restrictions isolate the victim while simultaneously creating dependency. Undocumented immigrants especially face tremendous obstacles when they are victims of domestic violence, as they are afraid to go to the police for help.

Domestic violence is a dynamic that can impact anyone regardless of gender, race, ethnicity, age, sexual orientation, socioeconomic status, educational level, physical ability, or religion. However there are certain characteristics that place people at greater risk than others. In intimate partner abuse, the majority of victims are women. Other risk factors include those individuals with physical or psychiatric disabilities, the elderly, teens in dating relationships, rural residents, persons in same-sex relationships and refugees and immigrants.

A victim of domestic violence who is not a legal resident and whose immigration status depends on her partner or other familial petitioner is at an increased risk of being abused or remaining in an abusive relationship. For the undocumented victim, the perpetrator has the capacity to utilize their immigrant sponsorship as a tool for abuse. Threatening to withdraw or withhold petition for legal resident status allows the perpetrator to intimidate, threaten, and control the victim. This is further exacerbated if the victim is unfamiliar with the local language or their legal rights. Fear and isolation are other increased risk factors for non-resident victims. Abusers intimidate their victims by threatening to report them to immigration authorities if they attempt to leave or terminate the relationship. Isolation for an immigrant is greater due to lack of a local social support network or possible language or cultural constraints. Fear of deportation for the undocumented individual is a strong motivator to endure abusive conditions.

Due to their undocumented status, victims may distrust any legal authorities or other possible available resources including shelters. Victims most often lack the knowledge of their legal rights. In the United States of America non-resident victims of domestic violence have legal rights. In 2013, the U.S. Congress reauthorized the Violence Against Women Act (VAWA). Initially passed in 1994, this landmark piece of legislation (crafted under the leadership of then-Senator Joe Biden), allows battered spouses, children or parents of sponsors or petitioners to separately petition for legal residency on their own. The purpose of the VAWA program is to allow victims to self-petition for legal immigration status independent of their abusive petitioner. This frees victims of their dependency on the perpetrator to sponsor their legal resident status. Despite the reference to women in its name, VAWA applies to both men and women. This self-petitioning model is limited to spouses, children or parents of U.S. citizens or Lawful Permanent Residents. However, a similar law was passed in 2000, the Victims of Trafficking and Violence Protection Act (VTVPA). This law further extends the rights of undocumented immigrants by allowing any victim of domestic violence or other crime to petition for a visa regardless of a relationship to resident or citizen sponsor. Under this law victims of human trafficking, crimes including domestic violence, can apply for either a "T"-visa or a "U"-visa. The T-visa is granted to victims of severe forms of human trafficking and the U-visa is for victims of crimes such as domestic violence, rape, assault, torture, kidnapping, and involuntary servitude on the condition that they aid in the detection, investigation and prosecution of the criminal activity committed.

Fleeing from an abusive relationship places the victim in a precarious situation and potential greater danger in the hands of retaliatory abusers. The victim requires aid from friends, family or community resources to be able to permanently leave her abusive home. Undocumented persons do not qualify for resources or aid that would otherwise be available to legal resident victims, in particular federally funded services. Their legal status further inhibits the victim's ability to seek employment, thereby limiting the ability to provide for herself or her children. Petitioning for an adjustment of status under either VAWA or VTVPA is a lengthy, detailed, and cumbersome process that requires much in the way of proof of abuse that often non-resident victims cannot provide if they avoided or were unable to file police reports or other documents that can be used to track the abuse. However, even successful petitioners under these acts are not alleviated of the burden and stress of the immigration system. Implementation and work authorization is often deferred, leaving the victim in limbo regarding her legal status for undetermined time periods.

Marcella Hurtado Gómez

See Also: Marriage; Trauma-Related Symptoms; U-Visa; Violence; Violence against Women Act (VAWA); Women's Status.

Further Reading

Alianza: National Latino Alliance for the Elimination of Domestic Violence. 2013. http://www.dvalianza.org/.

Bhuyan, Rupaleem, and Kavya Velagapudi. 2013. "From One 'Dragon Sleigh' to Another: Advocating for Immigrant Women Facing Violence in Kansas." *Affilia: Journal of Women & Social Work* 28.1:65–78.

Hancock, Tina. 2006. "Addressing Wife Abuse in Mexican Immigrant Couples: Challenges for Family Social Workers." *Journal of Family Social Work* 10.3:31–50.

"Immigrant Women and Domestic Violence." 2013. Futures without Violence. http://www.futureswithoutviolence.org/content/features/detail/778/.

National Network to End Domestic Violence (NNEDV). 2007–2011. Immigration section. http://www.nnedv.org/policy/issues/immigration.html.

National Network to End Violence against Immigrant Women. Accessed April 25, 2013. http://www.immigrantwomennetwork.org/.

Vishnuvajjala, Radha. 2012. "Insecure Communities: How an Immigration Enforcement Program Encourages Battered Women to Stay Silent." *Boston College Journal of Law & Social Justice* 32.1:185–213.

Domestic Work

Domestic work is an economic category that encompasses all work performed within the home, including childcare, eldercare, cleaning, cooking, laundry, shopping, and running errands. Domestic work is predominantly the responsibility of the woman of the household to either complete the work or hire a domestic employee. It is hard to ascertain how many undocumented domestic workers are currently working in the United States in this sector of the economy. Statistics on illegal domestic workers are unreliable because employers rarely report these workers to the Internal Revenue Service. Work performed but unreported and therefore impossible to regulate is considered to be part of the informal economy. However, the United States Census Bureau estimates there are currently 1.5 million domestic workers working in the United States.

Jessica Salsbury, center, a lawyer with CASA of Maryland, an immigrant advocacy group, hugs a domestic worker to celebrate the passing of legislation protecting the rights of domestic workers at a Montgomery County Council meeting in Rockville, Maryland in 2008. The legislation is believed to be the first of its kind in the nation. It aims to ensure the workers receive fair wages, overtime and other protections against abuse. (AP Photo/Jacquelyn Martin)

Domestic work is not always a fully recognized employment industry and therefore most U.S. labor laws do not extend to domestic work. Both the Occupational Health and Safety Act, which requires safe working conditions, and the National Labor Relations Act, which allows workers to unionize, exclude domestic work. While the Fair Labor Standards Act, requiring a federal minimum wage, does recognize domestic work, the act does exclude domestics from having the right to overtime pay. Despite its inclusion in this act, the minimum wage requirement is very rarely enforced in the employment of undocumented domestic workers.

Domestic work generally involves low status and poorly paid work that requires long hours. Because of this, domestic employees are often those from the lowest end of the economic spectrum who have few other employment options. Throughout United States history, immigrant women have held the majority of domestic work positions. Prior to the Civil War, domestic work in the south fell largely to slaves. In the north, large populations of Irish immigrant women filled the need for domestic workers. When former slaves began migrating en masse to the north following the Civil War, African American women began to take over the domestic work force in the North. In the Southwest, however, African Americans were never as large of a part of the employment sector as Mexican women. Currently, Latino and Caribbean-born immigrant women dominate the domestic work in the United States. An increasing demand for domestic workers has helped spark the feminization of migration. Currently almost half of all immigrants are women, many of whom are seeking employment as domestics in wealthier countries.

Many employers prefer that their domestic employee live within the home. In this situation, the employer can pay the domestic less because of the compensation of room and board. It also creates a more flexible working environment if the domestic is always available to work. Because they have fewer financial resources and fewer employment opportunities, undocumented immigrant women are often more willing to be live-in domestics than documented immigrants. While both employers seeking cheap labor and undocumented immigrants seeking employment seem to benefit from this situation, undocumented domestic workers often endure very little pay and hostile work environments. Domestics who live with their employers are often unable to decline work in the evenings or weekends, regardless of whether this time is designated as non-work hours. Because of their illegal status, lack of financial support and the language barrier that many domestics have, they are a very vulnerable population. Aside from low pay and long hours, undocumented domestics also frequently face sexual harassment, isolation from others, physical and emotional abuse, and threats of deportation or other legal repercussions. Besides the hostile environment in which they work, domestics often face the large emotional burden of raising children. Domestics often become very attached to the children in their care and yet have no rights to see the child if their employment is terminated.

More often than not, abuse and substandard working conditions remain undocumented because domestics fear they will face deportation if they report these occurrences to the authorities. The United States has responded to this problem by passing the Violence Against Women Act and the Victims of Trafficking and Violence Protection Act. These acts give undocumented women paths to legal residency if they have suffered domestic violence or other violent crimes. However, most domestics remain unaware of their rights under these laws.

Being a domestic worker can also cause tension with the worker's own family. Many domestics migrate to find work in order to support their own family and children, who often remain in the domestic's country of origin. Domestics then face the challenge of being separated from their own children while trying to mother from afar. They are often forced to leave their children in the care of other family members while they migrate for employment. This separation can also cause problems if the domestic tries to return home. Frequently family members have passed away and children have grown while they were away, making it difficult for them to readjust back into their country of origin.

Currently, there are many movements to raise awareness about these issues and to improve the work conditions and pay of domestic workers. Both Domestic Workers United and United Domestic Workers of America are advocacy groups that aim to organize domestic workers. Both groups are fighting for the expanded protection for domestic workers in U.S. labor laws and help workers. Currently, the United Nations Human Rights Council is working with domestic workers groups, including Domestic Workers United, to protect the rights of migrant workers in the United States. In a report prepared for the U.N. Human Rights Committee entitled "Domestic Workers'

Rights in the United States," these groups are demanding the United States enact special protections for migrant domestic workers, including protection from forced servitude, substandard working conditions, violence, and granting them the right to assemble. The report claims that migrant domestic workers need special protection under the law because of their increased vulnerability to their immigration status and the private nature of domestic work. The report calls for the expansion of the Fair Labor Standards Act, the National Labor Relations Act and Title VII as well as a reform of the visa system that would grant special visas to domestic workers who file reports of human rights violations.

Kelli Chapman

See Also: Domestic Violence; Family Structure; Gender Roles; Informal Economy; Trafficking Victims Protection Reauthorization Act; Violence against Women Act (VAWA).

Further Reading

Chang, Grace. 2000. *Disposable Domestics: Immigrant Women Workers in the Global Economy.* Cambridge, MA: South End Press.
Hondagneu-Sotelo, Pierrette. 2001. *Doméstica: Immigrant Workers Cleaning & Caring in the Shadows of Affluence.* Los Angeles: University of California Press.
Romero, Mary. 1992. *Maid in the U.S.A.* New York: Routledge.

Dominicans

The number of Dominican undocumented workers has been growing in the last five decades. Like most other undocumented immigrants that enter the United States, undocumented Dominicans flee poverty and lower wages in their homeland and seek to fill the demand for workers in the United States where they may find higher paying jobs. Although the number of Dominican immigrants nearly doubled in size since the 1990s, to 879,000 by 2010, according to the Center for Immigration Studies, compared to other Latino immigrant groups, they make up a significantly small share of the total. For example, in 2010, Mexican immigrants numbered 11.7 million. However, Dominicans make up a noticeable group of people in major cities along the East Coast, especially New York City. They are routinely employed in service and informal sector economies (Gurak et al., 1996). There are no reliable figures on the number of Dominican immigrants who are undocumented; the estimated numbers are low by comparison with estimates of Mexican undocumented immigrants. For example, the Department of Homeland Security estimates that Mexico adds to the undocumented population by over 150,000 a year, and by comparison, the Dominican Republic (along with other major Latin American groups, El Salvador, Guatemala, Honduras, and Haiti) add to the undocumented population at a rate of six thousand to twelve thousand each a year (Department of Homeland Security). Another way of gauging the proportion of

Dominicans compared to other undocumented groups is by looking at deportation rates. The Department of Homeland Security reports that in fiscal year 2011, 363,000 of the 396,900 people deported by Immigration and Customs Enforcement were from Mexico, Guatemala, Honduras and El Salvador. By comparison, seven other countries accounted for more than 1,000 deportations. Like virtually all other undocumented immigrants, Dominicans are susceptible to the three mechanisms the United States has to remove them from the country: they can leave voluntarily to avoid more severe penalties that come with deportation; deportation; and a process known as "exclusion." This third mechanism usually takes place at airports where individuals may be turned away before entering the United States (Santiago, 2011). Unlike the other major groups of undocumented immigrants that come from Latin America, Dominicans must reach the United States either by sea or air.

Like undocumented Mexican immigrants who risk their lives coming to the United States through areas of the Southwest, many Dominican immigrants also risk their lives trying to reach the United States in make-shift rafts across the Caribbean Sea. For many, the attempt to reach the United States begins by traversing Puerto Rico, often called the "backdoor pipeline" to the United States. From there they are at the mercy of human smugglers who often navigate the treacherous ocean straight in dangerously overloaded and ill-equipped boats.

Since the 1980s, there has been a notable trend from voluntary return towards more deportations for this immigrant group (Santiago, 2011). According to legal scholar Santiago, the enactment of the Immigration Reform and Control Act in 1986 and the Anti-Drug Abuse Act of 1988, which made drug addiction a deportable offense, are to blame. In part, this contributed to a second trend noted in 1991 when more Dominicans started to be deported for criminal offenses rather than non-criminal offenses. The shift in emphasis for which the Dominican population is deported has contributed to negative images of Dominicans as criminals. Moreover, a feature of the Dominican government is that those who are deported to their homeland are further stigmatized by their registration by an agency created especially for monitoring them, the Department of Deportees. This agency was created under pressure by and with financial support from the United States. Under the auspices of this agency, the Dominican National Police exerts social control of the Dominican deportees, treating them as criminals even though the reason for which they were removed from the United States is not a crime in the Dominican Republic.

Data from the registry of the Dominican Republic's Department of Deportees shows that the undocumented immigrants removed from the United States are very likely to be single males with family ties in the United States. There is some evidence that those who are removed are more likely to share phenotypic characteristics with African American males, including darker complexion. This suggests the influence of racial profiling in the enforcement of laws (Santiago, 2011). Most of those removed had entered the country legally, but had committed a deportable drug-related offense.

The longer a person stays in the United States, the less likely they are to ever return. One statistic from 1991 had a quarter of all Dominican undocumented workers living in the United States for at least ten years. However, transnational ties remain strong. Dominican immigrants living in the United States send nearly one billion dollars to help support families in the Dominican Republic (Rodríguez, 2009). The Dominican Republic constitution also allows U.S.-born children of at least one Dominican national the ability to claim Dominican citizenship in addition to U.S. citizenship. However, with the high rate of deportations for males, there are broad implications for both the families left behind in the United States and those back in the homeland who depend on remittances for support. Dominican social norms discourage the employment of women (Gurak and Kritz, 1996). Also, Dominican women residing in New York with children and no spouse or partner present are less likely to be employed than are either women who have their partners or spouses present. The lack of a partner or spouse brings new demands for the economic resources needed to meet the needs generated if children are in the household. By the same token, when young children are present in a household, caring for them represents a constraint on the time and mobility of the mother (Gurak and Kritz, 1996).

Dominican immigrants who eventually apply for citizenship or regular visa status typically have high levels of education. However it is difficult to get a tourist visa because the consulate in the Dominican Republic issues only to persons it feels can demonstrate accumulated assets and can travel legally. Once in the United States, there is the possibility of overstaying the limits of the visa. Thus, the majority of those overstaying their visas are actually professionals. This may account for a noteworthy number of more professional persons arriving without a visa status. In the Dominican Republic there is much insecurity about demand for educated, skilled professionals, and this also motivates many who can afford it to make the move. These are the same persons that take on blue collar jobs, disadvantaged by their inability to unionize and verify employment records. They take jobs considered to be lower-status because they want to acquire a level of comfort that falling wages in the Dominican Republic cannot provide.

Many also move to the United States because of chronic underemployment in the Dominican Republic. Few are members of organized labor. In New York, there is an especially large Dominican community where people work in the growing sector of small businesses with less than fifty coworkers. Many of those who are legal residents and owners provide jobs for their co-ethnics.

Ben DuMontier

See Also: Deportation; Drug Trade; Governance and Criminalization; New York; Transnationalism.

Further Reading

Department of Homeland Security. "Illegal Alien Resident Population." Available on line at http://www.dhs.gov/xlibrary/assets/statistics/illegal.pdf.

Grasmuck, Sherri. 1991. *Between Two Islands: Dominican International Migration.* Berkeley: University of California Press.

Graziano, Frank. 2006. "Why Dominicans Migrate: The Complex of Factors Conducive to Undocumented Maritime Migration." *Diaspora: A Journal of Transnational Studies* 15.1:1–33.

Gurak, Douglas T., and Mary M. Kritz. 1996. "Social Context, Household Composition and Employment Among Migrant and Nonmigrant Dominican Women." *International Migration Review* 30.2: 399–422.

Rodríguez, Tracy. 2009. "Dominicanas entre La Gran Manzana y Quisqueyal: Family, Schooling, and Language Learning in a Transnational Context." *High School Journal* 92.4:16–33.

Sagás, Ernesto, and Sintia E. Molina. 2004. *Dominican Migration: Transnational Perspectives.* Gainesville: University of Florida.

Santiago, Charles Venator. 2011. "Deporting Dominicans: Some Preliminary Findings." *Harvard Latino Law Review* 14:359–375.

The DREAM Act

The Development, Relief, and Education for Alien Minors Act, known as the DREAM Act, is a bipartisan federal legislation that would provide legalization of undocumented students who grew up in the United States and graduated from a U.S. high school, but whose future is restricted by their illegal immigration status. Under current immigration law, undocumented students' residency status is solely determined by their parents' immigration status; if their parents are undocumented immigrants, these students do not have a pathway to obtain legal residency status even though they have lived most of their lives in the United States To address this situation, the DREAM Act was first introduced in 2001. In 2009, it was re-introduced to the Senate (S.729) by Dick Durbin (D-IL) and Richard Lugar (R-IN) and to the House of Representatives by Howard Berman (D-CA), Lincoln Diaz-Balart (R-FL) and Lucille Roybal-Allard (D-CA) as the American Dream Act (H.R. 1751), but failed to receive necessary support by legislators to become a reality. In 2013, a DREAM Act provision was included in S.744, the version of the comprehensive immigration bill approved in the Senate. Hailed by many immigration rights advocates as one of the best DREAM Act versions that has been proposed to date, the provision would grant those who entered the United States before the age of sixteen, graduated from high school (or received a GED) in the United States, and attended at least two years of college or served four years in the military an expedited road to citizenship. DREAMers would be able to apply for registered provisional immigrant (RPI) status, and, after five years, would be eligible to apply for adjustment to Legal Permanent Residency status, after which they would then be able to apply for U.S. citizenship. Compared to a minimum of ten years for a green card and fifteen years for citizenship for most other undocumented people, this proposal has been lauded as one of the most generous compared to past proposals. In addition, young people who have been deported would be allowed to apply for inclusion in the policy if they would otherwise have been able to apply except for the fact that they had been deported. Previous DREAM bills offered no hope to those already deported, and explicitly declined to shield them from deportation. Moreover, the Senate version of the bill would repeal the state laws that make undocumented students ineligible for in-state tuition rates at

Supporters of the federal DREAM Act participate in a candlelight procession and vigil in downtown Los Angeles on December 7, 2010. In light of the failure of the U.S. Congress to adopt a federal DREAM Act, various states have adopted their own versions. (AP Photo/Damian Dovarganes)

public universities. Unfortunately S. 744 stalled in the Republican-controlled House when Virginia Republican Congressman Bob Goodlatte, chairman of the House Judiciary Committee, said that he would not allow an immigration reform bill that includes a path to citizenship to pass his committee, effectively killing any hope for immigration reform in the 113th U.S. Congress.

In an effort to mitigate the adverse outcomes for young people who are unlawfully present in the United States, the Obama administration issued an Executive Order on June 15, 2012, which directed agencies that form part of the U.S. Department of Homeland Security (U.S. Customs and Border Protection, the U.S. Citizenship and Immigration Services, the U.S. Customs Border Protection, and U.S. Immigration and Customs Enforcement), to practice prosecutorial discretion towards those who as children immigrated to the United States without proper authorization. Known as the Deferred Action for Childhood Arrivals (DACA), the order was intended to provide the legal mechanism for young undocumented immigrants to apply for relief from deportation if certain conditions and requirements were met.

Issues of Undocumented Students

According to the National Immigration Law Center, an undocumented alien student is a foreign national who (1) entered the United States without inspection or with fraudulent documents; or (2) entered legally as a nonimmigrant, but then violated the terms of his/her visa status and remained in the United States without authorization. Although undocumented students live in the United States illegally, most of them have been brought to the United States by their parents at a young age and experienced most of their K-12 education in the United States. As a consequence, these students share much in common with children born in the United States in that they think of the United States as their country. Youths that were brought to the United States as young children (often known as DREAMers) often have little attachment to their countries of birth, and tend to be bicultural and fluent in English. Oftentimes these students do not even know that they are undocumented immigrants until they apply for a driver's license or college. Yet, because of their undocumented immigration status, these students find it increasingly difficult to continue their education beyond high school, be legally employed, or join the military. Furthermore, they face restricted day-to-day living activities along with the fear of being deported to their countries of birth. Even worse, with future prospects truncated, these students may feel discouraged, become more at risk of dropping out of school and engaging in illegal activities. Without the hope of attaining the American Dream made possible with post-secondary education, students may have little incentive to complete high school.

Past failures to pass a DREAM Act have spurred protests and acts of civil disobedience by students, and most notably, students who were undocumented. A growing movement of undocumented student activism brought to the national forefront what many considered to be a great failure of the U.S. Congress to pass a commonsense remedy to the plight of young people who by any measure are American. However, by taking such action, these students, by making their identities public, open themselves up to possible deportation if arrested. In 2011, five undocumented Latino youth wearing graduation caps staged a sit-in at the Immigration and Customs Enforcement (ICE) offices in downtown Los Angeles. The sit-in was meant to urge the Obama administration to stop deporting undocumented youths.

In the United States, any undocumented students living in the United States may receive free public education through high school. However, these students may have difficulty in pursuing college education even if they are able to obtain admission because they are ineligible for federal financial aid under the Higher Education Act of 1965, and are likewise ineligible for state financial aid or in-state tuition under Section 505 of IIRIRA (Illegal Immigration Reform and Immigrant Responsibility Act) of 1996. Currently, however, eleven states (i.e., California, Illinois, Kansas, Nebraska, New Mexico, New York, Texas, Utah, Washington, Oklahoma, and Wisconsin) have passed state laws providing in-state tuition benefits to undocumented students, although the requirements for such benefits vary depending on the state. Generally, these states allow in-state tuition for undocumented students only if they have attended a high school in their state of residence for at least three or more years and obtained a diploma (or GED). Despite such laws, however, less than 10 percent of undocumented high school graduates are able to enroll in colleges throughout the United States, not due to a lack of desire for a college education but due to an inability to afford college tuition or to meet the legal residency status requirement of some colleges.

The DREAM Act Proposals

Although there have been various versions of a DREAM Act, in general provisions are made by which undocumented students would obtain legalization status through a two-stage process. The first stage is to obtain conditional Legal Permanent Resident (LPR) status by meeting the following requirements: (1) they entered United States at age sixteen or younger and have at least five consecutive years of residency, and (2) they have a high school diploma or its equivalent or an admission to an institution of higher education in the United States. The conditional LPR status is given for a period of time if the qualified student does not commit crimes and is not a security risk. Students with conditional LPR status may work, attend school, and engage in normal day to day activities like other Americans. Up to now, proposals continue to make students ineligible for Pell Grants or federal financial aid grants, although they are eligible for federal work study and student loans. The second stage is to obtain a full-fledged LPR status. Conditional LPR status is changed to a full-fledged LPR status if they have maintained a "good moral character" (in general, have not been convicted of a felony, though some misdemeanor arrests might count) and have met at least one of the following requirements: (1) acquisition of a degree from a two-year college or certain vocational colleges in the United States; (2) completion of at least two years in a bachelor's or higher degree program; or (3) service in the United States armed forces for at least two years and, if discharged, with an honorable discharge. If these students fail to complete educational or military requirements during the two-stage process periods, they lose either conditional or full-fledged LPR status and may be subjected to deportation.

Potentially Eligible Population

According to some research institutes (e.g., Pew Hispanic Center, Migration Policy Institute, National Immigration Law Center), approximately 2.5 million undocumented students under the age of 18 will be potential beneficiaries of the DREAM Act based on their physical presence in the United States and the age requirements. Annually sixty-five thousand to seventy thousand undocumented high school graduates would have been immediately eligible for conditional LPR status. In addition, 612,000 undocumented immigrants between eighteen and twenty-four years old who already have a high school diploma (or GED), and approximately 114,000 undocumented immigrants under thirty-five years old who have at least an associate's degree would be eligible for conditional LPR status. Of this total, an estimated fifty thousand undocumented college students are eligible for full-fledged LPR status. These eligible students are not only from Latin American countries but from various countries such as Iran, China, Russia, Ethiopia, and Turkey, etc.

Pros and Cons

The supporters of the DREAM Act argue that this act would be fair to both undocumented students and national interest because it enables undocumented students to continue their education in college and, in turn, bring socioeconomic benefit to the United States by increasing tax revenues, reducing the social costs for school drop-outs, and enriching cultural diversity. Also, the advocates of this act emphasize the humanitarian aspects that relief would bring to undocumented students because many of these students were brought into the United States at a very young age and should not be held responsible for their illegal entrance. However, the opponents of the DREAM Act argue that undocumented students and their families are in the United States illegally so they should face the consequences, including deportation. Moreover, opponents object to spending taxpayer money to subsidize college tuition of undocumented students by granting in-state tuition. They insist that expenditure of education for undocumented students should remain the responsibility of their parents and themselves. They state further that if this act passes, it would open citizenship to millions of families of the DREAM Act beneficiaries, encourage more undocumented immigrants and therefore undermine the U.S. immigration system.

Caleb K. Kim

See Also: Deferred Action for Childhood Arrivals (DACA); Driver's Licenses; *Plyler v. Doe;* Undocumented Students.

Further Reading

Batalova, Jeanne, and Margie McHugh. 2010. "DREAM vs. Reality: An Analysis of Potential DREAM Act Beneficiaries." Migration Policy Institute. Available at http://www .migrationpolicy.org/pubs/dream-insight-july2010.pdf.

Bruno, Andorra. 2010. "Unauthorized Alien Students: Issues and 'DREAM Act' Legislation." Congressional Research Service, RL33863, Washington D.C.: Congressional Research Service.

Corrunker, Laura. 2012. "'Coming Out of the Shadows': DREAM Act Activism in the Context of Global Anti-Deportation Activism." *Indiana Journal of Global Legal Studies* 19.1:143–168.

Galindo, René. 2012. "Undocumented & Unafraid: The DREAM Act 5 and the Public Disclosure of Undocumented Status as a Political Act." *Urban Review* 44.5:589–611.

Immigration Policy Center. "The DREAM Act." American Immigration Council Web Site. http.://immigrationpolicy.org.

National Immigration Law Center. "DREAM Act." hhtp.://www.nilc.org.

Zimmerman, Arely M. 2011. "A Dream Detained: Undocumented Latino Youth and the DREAM Movement." *NACLA Report on the Americas* 44.6:14–17.

Driver's Licenses

To drive in the United States, an individual is required to have a valid driver's license. Individual states are responsible for the issuance of driver's licenses and the requirements for obtaining a license vary by state. Typically, individuals obtain a driver's license from their state of residence. However, once a driver's license has been obtained, all states recognize the authority of licenses from other states. Guests driving in another state are subject to the driving laws and regulations of that state.

It is the responsibility of drivers to know and obey the laws of each state in which they drive.

In recent years, political debates over whether an immigrant present in the United States without authorization is allowed to obtain a driver's license have intensified. For example, in September 2003, then democratic governor of the state of California, Gray Davis, signed a bill that would have given undocumented immigrants the ability to lawfully gain a California State driver's license and as such be eligible for insurance as well. As in most all states, because a valid driver's license is the only way to obtain car insurance, many undocumented migrants cannot be insured. Supporters of this bill argued that because much of this population would be driving, the law would protect all Californians on the road. Proponents of the law believed that undocumented immigrants would drive whether or not they had a license or insurance, and in this way this would allow them the ability to legally do both, undergo exams, and thus reduce insurance premiums, which are more expensive when the pool of uninsured drivers is larger. Opponents of the law believed that by allowing undocumented immigrants to obtain driver's licenses they in fact were being rewarded for breaking the law by entering the country without authorization. Soon after being elected to office, Republican Governor Arnold Schwarzenegger repealed the law in California. Subsequently, he twice vetoed bills proposed by state Democratic legislators who repeatedly tried to reinstate the law. In a more recent example, after President Obama issued an executive order to stop deporting young, otherwise law-abiding undocumented immigrants (Deferred Action for Childhood Arrivals, "DACA"), most states have confirmed that they would be eligible for driver's licenses. Under this program, the Department of Homeland Security may grant permission for some who are unlawfully present in this country to stay. However, the governors of Iowa, Michigan, Nebraska, and Arizona responded by prohibiting this group of undocumented immigrants from obtaining licenses in their states. Subsequently, in September of 2013, attorneys for Arizona Governor Jan Brewer and the Arizona Department of Transportation filed a court order rescinding its own long-standing practice of granting licenses to those in other deferred-action programs, including the victims of domestic violence who the Department of Homeland Security has said can remain under the Violence Against Women Act (VAWA).

International visitors who have a valid driver's license from a country that has ratified the Convention on Road Traffic may use that license to drive in the United States. The Convention on Road Traffic is an international treaty agreed upon at the United Nations Economic and Social Council's Conference on Road Traffic in Vienna in November 1968. The treaty is meant to facilitate international road traffic and increase safety through the standardization of traffic rules.

Additionally, visitors to the United States from these countries who intend to drive need to obtain an International Driving Permit (IDP) from their home country before traveling to the United States. The IDP serves as an official translation of one's home license. This document facilitates the interpretation of the visitor's driver's license. An IDP only supplements a valid government-issued driver's license, and it will not serve as a replacement for a driver's license from their home country or the United States. The U.S. government or individual states will not issue an IDP to foreign visitors. Therefore, this document must be obtained before traveling to the United States.

The U.S. Federal Trade Commission has issued warnings about advertisements that claim to sell an IDP or international driver's license (IDL) that takes the place of a state-issued driver's license. These advertisements, which target non-native speakers including legal and undocumented immigrants, falsely claim that these documents will authorize recipients to drive legally in the United States without a state-issued license. Further, they claim this document can be used as valid identification. Importantly, an IDP does not replace a valid U.S. state driver's license and it is not a legal alternative to a state-issued license. If a law enforcement officer stops a driver in the United States and they present an IDP or IDL as proof of identity or authorization to drive, they could be arrested.

Therefore, those individuals who intend to stay in the United States for an extended visit or who plan to reside in the United States must obtain a driver's license from their state of residence. Each state has their own residency requirements for obtaining a driver's license, but most states require drivers to obtain a license issued by that state within a certain amount of time after they establish residence.

While each state has its own specific driver's license regulations, the Department of Motor Vehicles (DMV) in each state shares basic requirements for obtaining a driver's license. All states require applicants to present specific documentation. First, all states require proof of identity to obtain a license. Most states require two to three forms of identity proof that include the applicant's date of birth, such as a passport, birth certificate, or international driver's license. Second, an applicant must have proof of residency. In some states, an individual cannot obtain a license if he or she has a visitor's visa. Thus, applicants should be able to show proof of legal residency in the United States. Third, all states require proof of a social security number (SSN), a "letter of ineligibility" for a SSN because of visa type, or an individual tax identification number. Therefore, in order to receive a state driver's license, applicants are not required to be U.S. citizens, but must show proof of legal residence in the United States.

Once an applicant presents all necessary documentation, they must exhibit their ability to drive by passing an eye examination and passing both written and driving exams. Additionally, all states require minimum automobile insurance and some states will not issue a license without proof of insurance. All states also require applicants to be photographed for their driver's license. Since drivers' licenses are frequently used for age verification, standards set by the American Association of Motor Vehicle Administrators (AAMVA) require different photo orientation according to age: vertical for individuals under the age of twenty-one and horizontal for those over twenty-one. Finally, all states require the payment of a fee when receiving their driver's licenses, which varies for each state.

State DMVs also distribute official non-driver photo identification cards for those who are ineligible to drive or who choose not to drive. Photo identification card requirements also vary by state, but these requirements are basically the same as those for receiving a driver's license. A valid driver's license is a uniquely important document in the United States. Unlike many other countries, the United States does not distribute or require a national identification document. Thus, driver's licenses often serve as the de facto form of identification for most U.S. residents. U.S. driver's licenses and official non-driver identification cards are commonly used when completing business and governmental transactions. Because of the importance placed upon driver's licenses and non-driver cards for these additional purposes, they are particularly vulnerable to theft, counterfeiting, and acquisition using fraudulent documents.

The value of this document in the United States may persuade some undocumented immigrants, including individuals who have violated a non-immigrant visa, to use false documents or erroneous information to obtain a driver's license or non-driver card. Further, undocumented immigrants may be more receptive to using a stolen or fake driver's license in order to engage in activities that require valid U.S. identification, such as opening a bank account or gaining lawful employment.

As a result, states have enhanced driver's license and non-driver identification card security by making them essentially tamper-proof through various authentication measures, including fingerprints, bar codes, magnetic strips, holograms, and watermarks. Beyond protection against forgery, these measures also prevent identity theft. Additionally, state and federal government bodies have begun to crack down on falsely acquired driver's licenses by tracing identifying information, such as SSN and birth certificates, presented in order to obtain the license across databases.

States' DMV practices and the driver's license as a document have received more scrutiny following the 9/11 terrorist acts. Seven of the 19 airplane hijackers obtained drivers' licenses in Florida, New Jersey and Virginia by exploiting those states' license requirements. Furthermore, many of the hijackers had entered the United States under false pretenses; they were technically illegal immigrants. These findings and the catastrophic events that resulted have to some extent fueled public discourse about creating a national identification document in the United States.

In cities throughout the country that have experienced an high influx of undocumented immigrants, such as New York, Los Angeles, and Houston, government and community leaders have advocated granting identification documents to this population. These leaders argue that the distribution of state or national identification to undocumented immigrants will provide an account of this population as well as facilitate their access to services. The city governments in San Francisco and New Haven, Connecticut have both passed ordinances that allow identification cards to be issued to anyone living in the city limits, regardless of their legal status.

The discourse about creating national identification documents as well as allowing the issuance of documentation cards to undocumented immigrants has prompted heated arguments about public safety and individual freedom. At the heart of many concerns is if the public is safer at the expense of individual privacy. Concerns are also raised with regard to how large data bases of personal information may be used by the unscrupulous, or if information will be shared with government agencies that may tap into the information for other purposes. Regardless of one's position in this discourse, the linking of information databases belonging to a range of state agencies, such as the Department of Motor Vehicles, law enforcement, and the Immigration and Naturalization Service, has raised sufficient concerns and suspicions so that any linking between them in the name of public safety has been consistently met with much resistance.

In 2005, Congress passed the REAL ID Act. The intention of this act was to tighten the security of driver's licenses and non-driver identification cards and prevent undocumented immigrants from obtaining them by linking all state databases into a single national database. The Department of Homeland Security (DHS) was charged with bringing about the transformation of drivers' licenses into essentially national identification cards. However, in actuality, this act occasionally prevented legal immigrants as well as eligible citizens from attaining these documents. Further, states maintained that the requirements and timelines imposed by the REAL ID Act were unrealistic.

On July 29, 2009, the Senate Homeland Security and Governmental Affairs Committee passed the Providing for Additional Security States' Identification (PASS ID) Act of 2009. The National Governors' Association (NGA) led the passage of the PASS ID Act. This act amended the REAL ID Act. The PASS ID offered states more flexibility and reduced the implementation costs. Additionally, PASS ID strengthened the privacy of state and national databases by requiring procedures to prevent unauthorized access.

More recently, the debate over driver's licenses has taken a new turn.

Amanda Staight

See Also: Laws and Legislation, Post-1980s; Tennessee Immigrant and Refugee Rights Coalition (TIRRC).

Further Reading

Fischer, Howard. 2013. "State expands drivers' license denials for illegal residents." *Arizona Daily Star,* September 18, page 1. Available at: http://azstarnet.com/news/state-and-regional/state-expands-drivers-license-denials-for-illegal-residents/article_7a5b245c-65fa-5ace-826e-9f60c35227a7.html.

National Immigration Law Center. "Are Individuals Granted Deferred Action under the Deferred Action for Childhood Arrivals (DACA) Policy Eligible for State Driver's Licenses?" Available at: http://www.nilc.org/dacadriverslicenses.html.

Neuman, Gerald L. 2006–2007. "On the Adequacy of Direct Review after the REAL ID Act of 2005." *New York Law School Law Review* 133.

U.S. Immigration Support. "Driver's Licenses and Social Security Numbers for Illegal Immigrants." http://www.usimmigrationsupport.org/illegalimmigrant-driverslicense.html.

Drug Trade

The flow of illegal drugs into the United States from Mexico is a vexing problem for both nations. Demand for illegal drugs in the United States makes it one of the most profitable markets in the world. Complicating this problem is the growing interconnectedness of undocumented immigration to the United States and the drug trade. Both illegal drugs and cheap migrant labor are in high demand in the United States, and each moves across the Mexico-U.S. border with relative ease. Thus, the drug trade and undocumented immigration are often paired in both official U.S. policy and the popular imagination. Both issues are typically addressed as interrelated threats to national security.

To meet the growing demand for drugs, cartels of "narco traffickers" work tirelessly to bring cocaine, heroin, marijuana, MDMA, and methamphetamines into the United States for distribution. Most prominently, Mexican and Colombian cartels generate between $18 billion and $39 billion in drug proceeds annually. These illicit gains have been accompanied by increased violence. In 2008 alone, there were over six thousand drug-related killings in Mexico, and it is estimated that, from 2006 to 2012, an estimated 60,000 people were murdered in drug-related violence (BBC News, 2012).

While the American public has remained concerned about the drug trade for over a decade, new levels of violence and sophistica-

U.S. Immigration and Customs Enforcement agent guards an entrance to a tunnel found along the U.S.-Mexico border at a warehouse in Otay Mesa, California, January 30, 2006. The tunnel runs 2,400 feet and was used to funnel drugs into the United States from Mexico. With greater frequency, human smuggling rings have been co-opted by drug smugglers, exposing migrants to greater violence. (AP Photo/Denis Poroy)

tion on the part of the drug cartels have recast the drug trade as a significant national security problem for both the United States and Mexico. In 2008, outgoing Central Intelligence Agency (CIA) Director Michael Hayden claimed that Mexico could be "more problematic than [the war in] Iraq." In addition, the U.S. Drug Enforcement Agency (DEA) argues that Mexican cartels represent "the greatest organized crime threat to the United States."

During the 1990s, Mexico became the central point of transit for drugs into the United States. In 1991, 50 percent of U.S.-bound cocaine came through Mexico, and by 2004 that figure had increased to 90 percent. With this increase in business and sophistication came an increase in militancy. The Zetas, who were recruited from the Mexican army, grew into an independent and particularly ruthless enforcement and trafficking organization. With their newfound strength, the Mexican traffickers gained more power in Central American countries that provide cocaine, including Bolivia, Colombia, and Peru. They have also gained greater control over markets for heroin and methamphetamines in the United States.

The most recent escalation of drug trade–related violence along the U.S.-Mexico border began largely with the 2006 election of Mexican President Felipe Calderon. He declared a war on drug trafficking and sent some 45,000 troops to areas dominated by the cartels. In addition, the United States launched initiatives on both sides of the border to combat trafficking. These combined efforts have sent the old drug establishment reeling, and have led to more violence as new players seek greater shares of the market. The pressure on the cartels has led to open gun battles in many border cities, guerilla-style assaults on police stations, and the assassination of police officers, government officials, and journalists. It has also caused the Mexican cartels to diversify their operations, which now include kidnapping, extortion, contraband, and human smuggling. The election of Mexican President Enrique Peña Nieto in late 2012 has led to a new campaign, one that President Peña Nieto says will be based more on reducing crime and violence and less on hunting down drug lords.

The drug trade has created two additional problems for both the United States and Mexico: arms trafficking and money laundering. Over 90 percent of the guns seized in Mexico are traced back to the United States. Mexican police often find themselves outgunned by AR-15s and AK-47 semiautomatic rifles that were originally purchased in the U.S and smuggled into Mexico. In addition to the flow of guns, money also travels across the border. An estimated $15 billion to $25 billion flows out of the United States and into the hands of the Mexican cartels. These illicit funds fuel their criminal operations and violence on both sides of the border.

Official United States policy often includes undocumented immigrants in its assessment and strategy for combating the drug trade. According to the Department of State, U.S. drug policy seeks to "disrupt the trafficking of narcotics, money, people and arms across the border." This is reflected in the Merida Initiative, which was signed into law in 2008 by President George W. Bush. The Merida Initiative is a multi-year aid program that provides both equipment and training to Mexico, the nations of Central America, the Dominican Republic, and Haiti. The aid is intended to bolster their efforts to fight "criminal groups that traffic in drugs, arms, and persons." Included in the Merida Initiative is funding for the creation of a database on immigrants.

Many U.S. programs to increase border security seek to simultaneously stem the trafficking of both undocumented immigrants and illegal drugs. The Customs and Border Protection division of the Homeland Security Department uses Predator B drones, commonly used by the military in conflict zones, to monitor the Southwest border and the Canadian border. Between 2005 and 2009, the drones led to the seizure of more than 22,000 pounds of marijuana and to the apprehension of more than five thousand undocumented immigrants. In addition, the Secure Fence Act led to the construction of a fence along the Southwest Border that the Department of Homeland Security claims will make U.S. borders safer by "disrupting and restricting the smuggling of narcotics and illegal immigrants."

This marriage of undocumented immigrants and the drug trade in U.S. policy has forced the two into closer quarters. While the drug smugglers and migrants once occupied different worlds, tighter border enforcement has forced them into the same space as each seek new ways to cross the border. As their profits dip due to increased efforts by Mexico and the United States, the drug cartels are taking advantage of tightened border security by targeting these migrants. The cartels have moved into human smuggling, charging an average of $1,300 to $1,800 to be transported across the border. They also tax those who are attempting to cross the border on their own, taking inventory along transportation routes and charging fees to pass. The drug cartels have also expanded into kidnapping migrants for ransom. Currently, roughly 1,500 migrants are kidnapped each month trying to cross the border. This targeting of undocumented immigrants by drug cartels has created a more perilous journey for migrants and has contributed to their criminalization and victimization.

Ryan Strode

See Also: Border Crossing; Crime; Governance and Criminalization; Human Trafficking.

Further Reading

Andreas, Peter. 2009. *Border Games: Policing the U.S.-Mexico Divide.* New York: Cornell University Press.

BBC News. 2012. "Q&A: Mexico's drug-related violence." Dec. 24. BBC News Latin America and Caribbean. http://www.bbc.co.uk/news/world-latin-america-10681249

O'Neil, Shannon. 2009. "The Real War in Mexico." *Foreign Affairs,* August.

E

East Asians

East Asian populations in the United States notably include Japanese and Koreans. As a group, East Asians represent a significant number of undocumented immigrants, especially among newly arrived Koreans. The 2010 Census estimates that there are 230,000 Koreans living in the United States as unauthorized residents. Korea rates seventh in terms of the number of undocumented residents in the United States. Unlike undocumented immigrants who come from Latin America, most unauthorized immigrants from Korea come with some type of visa and overstay its limit. Many are elderly people who came to the United States to visit their children and did not go back, and some are international students who graduated from American institutions. Some came at an early age and have been in the United States for a long time, enough to call it their only home.

In the past, Japanese and Korean workers migrated in large numbers to the Pacific states region of the United States, primarily as agricultural workers. Koreans were also recruited to work as plantation workers to pick sugarcane in Hawaii. In 1902 an agreement was made between the U.S. Minister to Korea, Horace Allen, and the Hawaiian Sugar Planters' Association, and these men arranged a favorable business treaty in which Koreans would not be allowed to enter as contract laborers, in accordance with the Association's wishes to have control over workers' mobility and negotiating advantage. Those migrating did so with the understanding they would be provided lodging and medical treatment by the company, much like guest workers of the modern period. A basic obstacle was the need to bring "show money" before entering the United States—these were savings needed to show immigration officials they were not destitute and would not be public charges. To keep workers under control, U.S. Minister Allen threatened that these migrants were liable to be held under suspicion of treason by the Korean government if they left their registered residence in America.

As their numbers grew, they became the targets of anti-immigrant sentiment. As a result, they suffered discrimination and were unfairly exploited, and poorly paid. However, to counter the hardships that came with discrimination and exploitation, Japanese farmers and other workers often successfully organized strikes. They were not legally permitted to own or lease land, even though they often circumvented this restriction by entering unwritten agreements with sympathetic Anglo landowners.

However, their bargaining power was weakened as many could not immigrate to nor become citizens of the United States due to the Chinese Exclusion Act of 1882. Later, the 1924 Oriental Exclusion Act significantly codified the anti-Asian sentiment, and further reduced immigration from Asian countries. They remained as part of this exclusion until the Hart-Celler Act was passed in 1965 (Ngai, 2005).

The nativism, prejudice, discrimination, and the dehumanizing way in which Asians in general were depicted in the media (so-called "yellow journalism") became an object of contention between the United States and Japan. In their diplomatic relations with the United States, Japan saw this overt rejection and abuse of its citizens in the United States as damaging to its image in the eyes of the world and demanded greater respect. The result of this dialogue was a series of six diplomatic communiqués, referred to as "Gentlemen's agreements" between Japan and the United States from late 1907 to early 1908 in which provisions were made for some protection of Japanese citizens who were already in the United States from racist attacks and discriminatory treatment. In these agreements, Japan agreed to not issue passports to its citizens, thus eliminating new immigration to the United States. In exchange, the United States agreed to accept the presence of Japanese immigrants already residing there, to permit the immigration of wives, children and parents, and to avoid legal discrimination against Japanese children in California schools. The agreements were never ratified by the U.S. Congress.

The Japanese Empire restricted out-migration of Koreans after it made their country its protectorate in 1910, and in this way, Korean immigration to the United States was intertwined with Japan, Most migrants in this period went to Hawaii and became day laborers in ports as subjects of the Japanese empire. In the context of war with Japan in the 1940s, the most blatant action against Asian-Americans took place when President Franklin Roosevelt signed an Executive Order to incarcerate nearly 110,000 Japanese-Americans, the majority of whom were U.S.-born. The Supreme Court decision *Korematsu vs. United States* enshrined this decision in 1944. There were none ever relocated from Hawaii, because costs were deemed too great to move the entire population. The rationale and charge leveled against this population of residents and immigrants was that they would conspire with the enemy and commit espionage against the United States. There was never a case of a Japanese-American citizen convicted of treason, and many lost property and businesses they had built up over the previous forty years, unable to rebuild their lives after they were released.

In 1965 both the civil rights movement and the period of full employment helped push for the Immigration Act of 1965 (also called Hart-Celler) that year abolishing quotas based on national origins; this led to a more diverse population make-up. The maximum limit of 270,000 immigrants from the globe emigrating to the United States was reached in 1980. In theory there was no preference being given to any one nation, although in practice work visas were given out more selectively for various reasons. More opportunities were given to undocumented migrants and workers in the agricultural sector.

There have been many East Asians (similar to South Asians) who followed the high demand for skilled labor and professional services in the United States. U.S. firms expressed a desire to have more trained immigrants on their staff for various reasons. Asian scientists, nurses, and other professional workers took advantage of coming on "Schedule A" visas. Schedule A was a list of occupations that had low demand among

U.S. citizens. Asian migrants found they could overstay their temporary visas, and later decide to apply for permanent residency due to the unique nature of this skilled jobs list.

A perceived characteristic of Asian immigrant populations is that their settlement occurs in tightly-knit neighborhoods, and they are often referred to as a "model minority," because they work hard, are highly motivated to seek improved capacity through education, and ultimately attain a much desired level of higher per capita earnings than other populations. This generalization is often contested, even among scholars from the Asian-American community. In 1999, the median household income of all Japanese in the United States was $56,700, significantly higher than many groups including working-class Anglo-Saxons. Some have argued that the visible economic success of some glosses over how many others have had to contend with existing wage discrimination and racism that persists, although in more subtle ways. Asian-American scholars try to put statistics into perspective by noting that a family with a recent Asian background has on average more persons. Another thing that confounds the model minority theory is that in the 2000 Census Korean males earned less on average than other male groups.

There is much interaction of Korean migrants with black Americans and Latinos. Many Mexicans and others from Central and South American states are employed by Korean businesses. In this way, economic hardships and unequal structures affect both populations. At the same time, numerous news articles about the executive order issued by President Barack Obama that directs the Department of Homeland Security to use discretion in determining those who were brought to the United States as young children and grant them permission to stay in the country (Deferred Action for Childhood Arrivals, or DACA) point out the same hope and dreams for a better life that undocumented Korean students share with other students who are undocumented. It is estimated that thirty thousand undocumented Koreans nationwide are expected to benefit from deferred action.

Ben DuMontier

See Also: Chinese; Deferred Action for Childhood Arrivals (DACA); Hart-Celler Act (1965); Overstayers; South Asians; *Strangers from a Different Shore.*

Further Reading

Cheng, Lucie, and Philip Q. Yang. 2000. "The 'Model Minority' Deconstructed." In Min Zhou and James V. Gatewood, eds., *Contemporary Asian America: A Multidisciplinary Reader,* 459–482. New York: New York University Press.

Kim, Warren Y. 1971. *Koreans in America.* Po Chin Chai Co.

Oishi, Nana. 2007. "Pacific: Japan, Australia, New Zealand," in Mary C. Waters & Reed Ueda, eds., *The New Americans: A Guide to Immigration Since 1965,* 543–556. Cambridge: Harvard University Press.

Ong, Paul, and John M. Liu. 2000. "U.S. Immigration Policies and Asian Migration." In Min Zhou and James V. Gatewood, eds., *Contemporary Asian America: A Multidisciplinary Reader,* 155–174. New York: New York University Press.

Osajima, Keith. 2000. "Asian Americans as the Model Minority: An Analysis of the Popular Press Image in the 1960's and 1980's." In Min Zhou and James V. Gatewood, eds., *Contemporary Asian America: A Multidisciplinary Reader*, 449–458. New York: New York University Press.

Ngai, Mae. 2005. *Impossible Subjects: Illegal Aliens and the Making of Modern America*. Princeton: Princeton University Press.

Eastern Europeans

Since the fall of the Berlin Wall, the barrier constructed in 1961 to physically separate East Berlin in the German Democratic Republic (GDR) from West Berlin, many from the Eastern Bloc nations have found it easier to emigrate and enter other countries to settle and start new lives. Eastern bloc nations include those from an massive area in Eastern Europe that includes the states of the former Union of Soviet Socialist Republics (USSR) and former satellite nations, including Poland, the territories of Albania, the former country of Yugoslavia, Bulgaria, Romania, Hungary, the former Czechoslovakia, Poland, and the Baltic states.

The Cold War left a profound impact on the ability of Eastern Europeans to emigrate to the the West. The fall of the Berlin Wall in 1989 symbolizes the softening of relations between East and West. An amendment to the U.S. Foreign Operations Appropriations Act allowed Eastern Europeans from former communist bloc nations who had been denied refugee status to be "paroled" into the United States on an emergency or humanitarian basis. (Courtesy of NATO)

Immigrants in the United States who are from Eastern Bloc nations are a very small portion of the total immigrant population, about 3 percent. Most emigrants from these nations are more likely to leave their countries for nations that are closer. Great Britain has been a major destination for these emigrants. A major reason for the general lack of mobility of those from Eastern Europe in recent history is rooted in cold war politics and contrasting political and economic ideologies that distinguish Western nations (of which the United States is part) and Eastern Bloc nations dominated by communist regimes. Citizens from these latter, Eastern Bloc nations were restricted and in many cases prohibited from traveling to the United States while under the control of the former USSR. This was especially true if they were highly educated, in order to prevent a "brain drain" from those countries. Many who were able to escape to the United States or other Western nations often did so as "defectors." An additional, related reason has to do with U.S. immigration policies that were based on a quota system until 1965. During the time that the quota system was in place, Eastern Bloc immigrants were too few to generate a steady flow of petitions to bring family members to the United States.

The Lautenberg Amendment to the Foreign Operations Appropriations Act allowed certain individuals who were not eligible for refugee status and were denied, to be "paroled" into the United States on an emergency or humanitarian basis. Although the granting of this status is very rare, the Lautenberg Amendment provided for a very special category of people who had applied for but were denied refugee status in the former Soviet Union between August 15, 1988 and September 30, 2012. The amendment provided "parole in the public interest" of those individuals who were processed overseas in Moscow through the Moscow Parole Program before traveling to the United States, and was limited to those from the former Soviet Union, Estonia, Latvia, Lithuania, and included Jews, evangelical Christians, Ukrainian Christians of the Orthodox and Roman Catholic denominations, and others. After one year of residence in the United States, these individuals were then able to apply for a green card as a legal permanent resident, without regard to visa availability.

There has been scarce information about Eastern Europeans who have entered the United States illegally, or are present unlawfully as "overstayers." Undocumented immigrants from Poland have relied on social networks to primarily settle in industrial centers like New York, Chicago, and Detroit to work in labor in steel mills and stockyards. Undocumented immigrants from Poland make up the tenth largest group of undocumented immigrants living in the United States, numbering around seventy thousand. Like their undocumented immigrant counterparts, they too face discrimination and vulnerability. Unlike those who previously came to the United States legally, those that are undocumented are low-skilled and are fleeing conditions of economic decline and instability in former Soviet Bloc countries. They contend with racial discrimination and exploitation by unscrupulous employers who pay them below minimum wage. Many are afraid to approach the police or report crimes against them. In 2007, Eastern European countries rank among the top ten immigrant-sending countries. Moldova and Ukraine ranked among the top ten countries in the 2000s for numbers of undocumented migrants.

The Cold War left a profound impact on these Eastern Europeans and it also impacted their process of migration to the United States. Some one hundred thousand Czechs may live illegally in the United States. At least 110,000 from Poland arrived in the early 1990s and this number has gradually grown since then. Many came as refugees after the Balkan conflicts, but this number has dwindled lately. Seven hundred thousand Bulgarians have left their country because of economic recession and adjustment to the global economy. Some countries have been singled out for expedited process through laws such as the Nicaraguan Adjustment and Central American Relief Act of 1997 where aspiring immigrants were treated as political refugees and given residency.

Early in the history of immigration to the United States from Eastern Europe, many newcomers were educated in technical and scientific fields. An estimated 55.7 percent of them identified themselves as academics in the 1990s upon first arriving in the United States. This illustrated the high level of education they received before arriving, and suggests that they were fleeing underpaying jobs in their home countries for professions such as doctors and teaching, or the lack of employment in those sectors of the economy. Yet, once in the United States, many still had trouble applying to social service programs, perhaps owing to language problems, or discrimination. The countries least likely to have migrants with high levels of education were from the former Yugoslav Republic. The rate of those in poverty among total noncitizens for 2007 was 21.3 percent, including a high percentage of Eastern Europeans. Those that stay undocumented in the United States do so by overstaying work visas. Many Polish immigrants came initially as *wakacjusze,* roughly translated as "pleasure-seeking visitors." 80 percent of those arriving in the 1980s—during the decade of Polish Solidarity with the end of the Iron Curtain—came using this means.

A high percentage of women that both work and raise children come from the Eastern Europe region. Among the region's cultural groups, the extended family is often called upon to help raise children while the mother works. However this often is done in place of calling on state services. Roughly a quarter of all those who have grandparents living with them rely on them to help raise grandchildren. This speaks to the problems of bringing whole families over. It is harder to care for senior migrants if they make the journey, and many arrived in the United States only after the passage of years, when they were advanced in age. This number of family members that are able to care for their relatives is lower than numbers for migrants from Latin America, or Western Europe.

In a poll taken in 2011, Eastern European immigrants are still having issues finding equality and avoiding ethnic discrimination. Most associate only with other cohorts from their country of origin, yet roughly a quarter feel they have become acculturated to the social landscapes in Washington State, the East Coast, and other locales. However, most had networks of relatives before they came. Few migrants move to an area on their own without networks of support. Although not all feel discrimination, not knowing English is blamed for the discrimination against them.

Other concerns resulting in vulnerability of Eastern Europeans immigrants are that they often fall prey to unscrupulous employers. Work recruiters stationed both in East Europe and in the United States run false advertisements and colorful web sites to attract laborers with promises of tax-free earnings and possible overtime. Hidden fees, ranging from $500 to $2500, are collected by employers. Another concern exploited by nativist organizers—and not uncommon in other parts of the United States—is that these migrants compete with Americans and other established residents in the labor market.

On October 23, 2003, federal officers from the Department of Homeland Security's Bureau of Immigration and Customs Enforcement (ICE), formerly known as the Immigration and Naturalization Service (INS), entered sixty-one Wal-Mart stores in twenty-one states nationwide. This action was dubbed "Operation Rollback" as a pun on Wal-Mart's advertising campaign touting its "rollback of prices." These workforce raids on Wal-Mart in 2003 led to the arrest of 245 Russian workers suspected of overstaying their visas and working without legal authority. Fueling pressures for government to act against undocumented workers reflect common misperceptions that immigrants (especially undocumented immigrants) do not share the same rights as their U.S. citizen or permanent resident counterparts. However, employing immigrants, including those that are undocumented, subjects employers to the same legal responsibilities as employing those with legal authorization to work. For example, employers are subject to paying back wages and overtime claims when they fail to pay their employees for work performed, regardless of their employees' immigration status. Employers may also be held liable by their immigrant employees for discrimination based on race, sex, or national origin. The legal responsibility of employers to pay back wages and overtime claims has been the subject of recent law suits brought against Wal-Mart by several of the undocumented workers. Wal-Mart argued that it was not responsible because the workers were employed by independent contractors. Consistent with the practices of the legal investigating and prosecuting arm of ICE, the apprehended undocumented immigrants were recruited to help ICE in the enforcement of federal immigration laws; and on November 10, some of the arrested immigrants working as janitorial workers filed a federal racketeering class action lawsuit against Wal-Mart in a New Jersey federal court. The workers alleged that Wal-Mart violated the federal Racketeering Influenced and Corrupt Organizations (RICO) statutes. All of the plaintiffs were undocumented immigrants who worked for a contract cleaning service hired by Wal-Mart. All of these workers claim they were paid weekly compensation of $350–500 in cash, worked at least sixty hours per week, and were obligated to work seven days a week. They also claimed they received no overtime compensation, workers' compensation, nor did they have taxes or Social Security (FICA) withheld from their earnings. The case against Wal-Mart is clearly premised on the notion that undocumented workers have rights to fair employment practices.

Ben DuMontier

See Also: Family Reunification; Family Structure; Globalization; Immigration and Customs Enforcement (ICE); Workplace Raids.

Further Reading

Entelisano, Carol A. 2003. "The Woes of WAL-MART: A Lesson in Independent Contractor Practices and Immigration Law (Non)Compliance." http://library.findlaw.com/2003/Dec/29/133231.html (accessed January 3, 2006).

Gozdziak, Elzbieta M. 1999. "Illegal Europeans: Transients between Two Societies." In David W. Haines and Karen E. Rosenblum, eds., *Illegal Immigration in America: A Reference Handbook,* 254–271. Westport, CT: Greenwood Publishing Group.

Kole, William J. 2003. "East Europeans Find Jobs, Exploitation in U.S." *Los Angeles Times,* Nov. 2. http://articles.latimes.com/2003/nov/02/news/adfg-workersr2

Mehner, Shannon, and Brianna McClaine. 2010. "Exploited immigrants, unaware of labor laws, afraid to fight mistreatment." Medill Reports. Chicago. May 20. Available at: http://news.medill.northwestern.edu/chicago/news.aspx?id=164931

Mólnar, Judit. 2011. "The Integration Process of Immigrants in Scotland, UK and in Washington State, USA. Immigrants from Countries of the Former Soviet Union." In *Eurolines,* 201–215. Glasgow: University of Glasgow Press.

Robila, Mihaela. 2007. "Eastern Immigrants in the United States: A Socio-demographic Profile." *Social Sciences Journal* 44:113–125.

Economics

New arrivals in U.S. society are both culturally and economically diverse. The Immigration Act of 1990 (IMMACT) facilitated the immigration of any individual demonstrating substantial financial holdings. However, while these are for the most part welcomed, less welcomed are the poor and unskilled. There are two reasons why with greater frequency, the public gaze has been drawn towards those who fall into this second category, especially in terms of their impact on the U.S. economy.

First, their arrival marks a trend towards economic restructuring with companies geographically relocating, leaving many U.S. citizens without high-paying work and others in fear of displacement. Second, immigrants, especially the undocumented, are stereotyped as less skilled and less educated, which raises concerns about their net cost to taxpayers. In reality, immigrants are over-represented among both the less educated and the highly skilled. Pro-immigrant think tanks and nonprofits periodically release information on the lack of native-born workers needed to perform work considered too backbreaking or demeaning. Anti-immigrant, nonprofit organizations and activists also release their reports showing how undocumented workers take jobs away from American citizens. With so many contradicting arguments, it is no surprise that the public is divided on these issues, with attitudes likely to lean toward negative perceptions of immigrants during economic downturns regardless of research findings that frequently highlight immigrants' contribution to the nation's economy.

In times of economic downturn, immigrants are often blamed for the loss of jobs. Controversy over their impact on the economy boils at both local and national level. The business lobby supports immigration and has been known to be vocal in their opposition to legal restrictions that encumber their hiring of immigrant workers. For example, strong lobbyists for cotton, fruit and vegetable growers and packers representing the interests of agricultural states vigorously opposed including Western Hemisphere nations in the 1924 Johnson-Reed proposal for a national quota system because they heavily relied upon low-skilled, cheap workers from Mexico. More recently, in March of 2011 and nearly a year after Arizona SB 1070 was signed into law by Governor Jan Brewer, a letter from nearly seventy business executives and officers was sent to Senator Russell Pearce, president of the Arizona Senate, calling for a halt of the state's efforts to regulate immigration through punitive state laws, citing that such laws were adversely impacting the struggling economy and costing jobs. The letter pointed out that Arizona-based businesses saw sales decline and contracts cancelled as part of a boycott against the state for passing SB1070. The lawsuit that attempted to do away with the law was brought about by an alliance of civil rights and the national Chamber of Commerce. On the other hand, fiscal conservatives very often argue that immigrants are a drain on the economy and overburden public services paid for by citizens' tax dollars.

Lost in this controversy is what the U.S. economy would look like without the low-skilled immigrant work force that performs the hard tasks no one else seems to want: ranging from picking crops to house cleaning. The number of immigrants account for 15 percent of American labor. During the George W. Bush administration, the Council on Economic Advisors concluded that immigrants complement rather than substitute for native workers, making for a slightly favorable prognosis about the economic contribution of immigrants to the nation's economic growth.

Economic Restructuring

The growing role of undocumented immigrants in the contemporary U.S. economy has been sped by globalization and economic restructuring. Economic restructuring refers to the move of industrial sector jobs to other countries where the cost of production is lower. For example, the rustbelt states of the U.S. Midwest lost jobs when automobile assembly work was outsourced to places like Mexico to cut costs. Restructuring dramatically reduced employment in manufacturing, and now blue collar, skilled, native-born workers from states like Michigan, Ohio, and Pennsylvania earn less than they did at the peak of their careers. They are part of a shrinking middle class and may have learned to resent unskilled immigrant workers.

With economic restructuring, the United States entered a postindustrial economy—a bifurcated economy increasingly reliant on technology on one end, and service sector industries on the other. Service sector industries are not easily outsourced to other countries because the work needs to be carried out domestically. Examples of service sector jobs are domestics, maids, and janitors, child- and elder-care providers, landscapers, and bus boys, waiters, and cooks in the restaurants and fast food industries. These are occupations that undocumented immigrants fill. Another sector of the economy that is not easily outsourced is agriculture, including work in meat processing plants. This too is an economic sector that undocumented immigrants enter.

With the United States' growing advantage in technology fields, it produces high-paying jobs; but in so doing, it further devalues low-skilled work. Combined with global competition and a decline in unionization, the growing surplus of unskilled immigrant workers has placed downward pressure on wages and made it harder to get wage increases. Low-paying jobs often lack benefits and are characterized by poor working conditions. For example, in meat processing industries, assembly line cutting set-ups can result in serious injury and disability. In spite of all these disadvantages, when immigrants contemplate going to the United States to work, it is because the wage differential between the United States and their country provides the incentive. In Mexico, even skilled workers might expect to earn at most nearly $5.00 a day, when in the United States earning $10.00 an hour as a janitor allows them to live in the United States and send remittances home to their families. Business owners contend that filling low-paying jobs would be severely hampered were it not for undocumented workers.

Non-Gateway Destinations

Until the 1990s, immigrant destinations were primarily concentrated in Southwest states, although certain states such as New York also attracted immigrants. A Pew Hispanic Research report for 2010 indicates that traditional "gateway" immigrant destinations such as California and Texas continue to attract the most number of undocumented immigrants. However, as with economic restructuring, the southern U.S. states have also emerged as important immigrant destinations, especially when many former undocumented immigrants were able to become legal permanent residents and citizens through the amnesty provisions in the 1986 Immigration Reform and Control Act (IRCA). No longer fearful of venturing outside of safe communities and enclaves in gateway cities and states, the newly regularized immigrants and new citizens moved to areas in the United States that would provide them better wages and greater job stability. Later they were able to petition to bring family members to join them, among whom were additional undocumented immigrants (Crowley et al., 2006). In these southern states, undocumented immigrant workers have been concentrated in carpet mill factories, poultry farms, and agriculture. In this way, the number of immigrants is also becoming dispersed to nontraditional destinations, such as the southern states of Georgia, North Carolina, and Virginia, often with considerable political and social backlash.

Most southern states have right-to-work laws that inhibit labor union activity. Unions typically strengthen workers' demands for higher pay and better conditions. In the 1950s, almost one-third of the native-born labor force consisted of union members. In the age of the disappearing industrial sector, unions now only represent 13 percent of workers. Companies seeking to cut labor costs moved remaining manufacturing to the South. In former manufacturing centers, industries that have survived are increasingly nonunion, where garment factories increasingly resemble third-world sweatshops. However, in recent years there has been a notable shift in union organizing, reflecting the importance of undocumented workers to union organizing, such as UNITE-HERE, a merger between the Union of Needletraders, Industrial and Textile Employees, and the Hotel Employees and Restaurant Employees union. UNITE-HERE has been engaged in some of the most aggressive union-organizing campaigns in recent years where immigrant workers are key.

Public Opinion

The three important issues in the debate on undocumented immigrants are economic in nature: (1) whether immigrants compete for jobs with the native-born or complement their work in the labor force, (2) immigrants' likelihood of becoming a public charge (dependent on welfare and other government aid), and (3) how much educational and other social services for immigrants will cost taxpayers.

These issues have been the topic of many surveys and inquiries. The 2006 General Social Survey indicated that 60 percent of Americans believe that immigrants take jobs away from the native-born. In contrast, a May 2006 *New York Times*/CBS poll found that 53 percent of the public believe that undocumented immigrants take jobs that U.S. citizens do not want. A PEW Research Center poll indicated that 61 percent of Americans believe immigrants cost more than they contribute relative to education and health. Only thirty-one percent believed that immigrants contribute more in taxes than they may receive from the system. The Heritage Foundation published a report by Robert Rector that calculated that low-skilled, less-educated immigrants cost $89 billion more than they pay in taxes. He went on to claim that it would take three hundred years for this to be paid back. Such arguments have been countered by other reports showing that after the costs of immigrants' use of public services, there is a net gain to the economy (Gans, 2007). The proliferation of contradicting polls and studies illustrates the high degree of ambivalence in the U.S. public's views about immigration.

Low-Wage Immigrant Workers

Researchers estimate that 20 percent of low-wage immigrant workers are undocumented. They tend to be poorly educated, with 18 percent having less than a ninth-grade education. For this reason, they are more likely to be concentrated in low-wage and low-skill occupations—jobs that often lack benefits and opportunities for upward mobility. Only legal immigrants and the native-born workers have access to government job-training and education programs. Agribusiness and hotel and restaurant owners profit the most from immigrants who have few other options available. Consequently, the hourly wages of immigrants tend to be lower than the wages of the native-born with almost half of the immigrant population earning less than 200 percent of the federal minimum wage—as compared to one third of the native-born. However, research also shows that the length of time that immigrants live in the United States is associated with increased English-language acquisition and schooling, on the job training, and better knowledge of labor market conditions. When age and education are held equivalent for immigrant and native-born workers, immigrants catch up economically over a period of ten to twenty years. At issue are not necessarily the unskilled immigrants whose impact is questioned, but subsequent generations who may yet achieve the social mobility and the American Dream that define the United States as a nation of opportunities, where everyone who works hard can succeed. The American Immigration Law Foundation's Immigration Policy Institute has also acknowledged that the second generation invariably earns more and pays higher taxes than the first, showing that social mobility is still an important driver of the U.S. economy.

Unskilled Immigrants—Skilled Native-Born Complementarities

Few understand how unskilled undocumented immigrant labor complements higher-skilled American workers. The Council of Economic Advisors indicates unskilled immigrant construction workers allow skilled contractors and craftsmen to build houses at lower cost—making them more affordable. Economists believe that the period of economic expansion in the 1990s was related to economic complementarities that permitted a low rate of inflation. The native-born also gain from lower-priced goods and services provided. In this way, undocumented workers boost the consumer power of the native-born. The drawback is that the average consumer also becomes more dependent on undocumented immigrant labor for lower food prices. The surge in food prices caused by the 2008 oil shock reflects how economic change can suddenly hurt consumers. During this shock, the wages of agricultural workers did not increase, suggesting that without these workers, food costs and food shortages would have been worse.

Immigrant Labor Substitution and Native Job Loss

Overall, there is mixed evidence about the substitutability of less educated immigrants for similarly situated native workers. However, the number of native-born workers with less than a high school education has greatly declined over time and the U.S. economy still needs unskilled workers. In addition, the majority of the native-born workforce is becoming better educated. Even raising wages in sectors where immigrants have a foothold, such as agriculture, is unlikely to attract many closely substitutable, less educated, native-born workers who have higher expectations for a more dignified way to make a living. In 2005, immigrants offset a decline of 1.2 million in the number of low-wage native-born workers. Over 620,000 immigrants filled this gap, of which 460,000 were undocumented. Thus, it would be a fallacy to believe that legal or undocumented immigrants are taking unskilled jobs from the native-born when more of the native-born are becoming better educated and attaining degrees. Even where undocumented immigrants might compete with African American workers, the PEW Hispanic Center found no relationship between immigrant employment and native-born unemployment, even at equal educational levels. African Americans have often articulated concerns over new immigrants as competitors in the job market. However, leaders within the community have pointed out that this resentment may be caused by anti-immigrant rhetoric. What is overlooked is the way in which companies in the United States have sought out right-to-work states and ways to outsource production abroad—actions that have served to deepen inequality in the United States.

Immigrant Entrepreneurs

Latinos and Asians with some financial capital have also been active in starting businesses such as neighborhood grocery stores, restaurants, and services such as landscaping and home contracting. Immigrant business owners are likely to hire other immigrants. They often rely on family members as an unpaid source of labor. In 2002, the Current Population Survey counted 2.7 million Latino and Asian nonfarm businesses employing 3.7 million people and realizing $548 billion in income. President George W. Bush's Council on Economic Advisors issued a report indicating that foreign-born workers accounted for 50 percent of labor-force growth, generating work and increasing native-born earnings by $80 billion. Lower wages for immigrants decreased inflation. Immigrant households also contributed in additional taxation.

Conclusion

Federal government experts believe that a high level of immigration will have a positive long-term monetary impact. While many of the costs of immigrants have been felt at the state and local level, this is only a partial account of the potential benefits of immigrants for the economy. A misconception is that undocumented immigrants do not pay taxes while living in the United States. However, despite their low wages, undocumented immigrant workers in the United States are providing the U.S. economy with a subsidy of as much as $7 billion a year in uncollected contributions to Social Security and Medicare (Porter 2005). Shortly after the 1986 Immigration Reform and Control Act (IRCA) was passed and in keeping with the new law, there was an increase in false documents workers provided employers. Subsequently, the Social Security Administration received a flood of W-2 earnings attributed to undocumented workers. The earnings suspense file had grown to about $189 billion by the 1990's. This money has been deposited in an "earnings suspense file"—a fund growing on average by more than $50 billion a year—until the owners of those contributions can be identified.

Judith Ann Warner

See Also: Domestic Work; Education; Globalization; Johnson-Reed Act (1924); Labor Supply; Labor Unions; Landscaping Industry; Migration; North American Free Trade Agreement (NAFTA); Wages.

Further Reading

Borjas, George J. 2003. "The Labor Demand Curve Is Downward Sloping: Reexamining the Impact of Immigration on the Labor Market." *Quarterly Journal of Economics* 118:1335–1374.

Brimelow, Peter. 1995. *Alien Nation: Common Sense about America's Immigration Disaster.* New York: Random House.

Capps, Randy, Michael Fix, Jeffrey S. Passel, Jason Ost, and Dan Perez-Lopez. 2003. *A Profile of the Low Wage Immigrant Work Force.* Washington, DC: The Urban Institute. http://www.urban.org/UploadedPDF/310880_lowwage_immig_wkfc.pdf.

Capps, Randy, and Jeffrey S. Passel. *Trends in the Low Income Immigrant Labor Force: 2000–2005.* 2007. Washington, DC: The Urban Institute. http://www.urban.org/UploadedPDF/411426_Low-Wage_immigrant_Labor.pdf.

Council of Economic Advisors. 2007. "Immigration's Economic Impact." June 20. http://georgewbush-whitehouse.archives.gov/cea/cea_immigration_062007.html.

Crowley, Martha; Daniel T. Lichter, and Zhenchao Qian. 2006. "Beyond Gateway Cities: Economic Restructuring and Poverty Among Mexican Immigrant Families and Children." *Family Relations* 55.3:345–360.

Gans, Judith. 2007. "Immigrants in Arizona: Fiscal and Economic Impacts." Tucson, AZ: Udall Center for the Study of Public Policy, University of Arizona. http://udallcenter .arizona.edu/immigration/publications/impact_judy.pdf.

Kochhar, Rakesh. 2006. "Survey of Mexican Migrants, Part 3. Growth in the Foreign-Born Workforce and Employment of the Native-Born." PEW Hispanic Center. www .pewhispanic.org/files/reports/58.pdf.

Porter, Eduardo. 2005. "Illegal Immigrants Are Bolstering Social Security with Billions." *New York Times,* available at: http://www.nytimes.com/2005/04/05/business/05 immigration.html?_r=0.

Education

Regardless of legal status, all children in the United States must attend school until the ages of sixteen to eighteen, depending on the state. The United States has had compulsory education in all fifty states since 1929, and many states, such as Massachusetts, implemented these laws much earlier (1852). However, some jurisdictions have tried to make undocumented children pay a special tax for attending public school. But in the landmark legal decision of *Plyler v. Doe* (1982), the Supreme Court of the United States determined that undocumented children cannot be denied a public education. The court explained that undocumented children did not choose to come to the United States, but were brought to the United States by their parents, and preventing them from attending school would create an underclass of uneducated people, leading to increased social malaise.

Levels of Education

Head Start is a federal program for pre-school children (ages three to five) and their families. The program offers education, health, nutrition, and parental involvement aid to those with limited financial resources. While legal status is not a requirement for participating in the program, Immigration Control and Enforcement (ICE) officers frequently wait outside of Head Start and Migrant Seasonal Headstart Centers, creating a disincentive for undocumented people to use these services.

Public education, specifically in elementary and middle school, has been a legal right for all youth in the United States since the *Plyler v. Doe* decision in 1982. Even though this is the law, the U.S. Department of Education and organizations such as the Mexican American Legal Defense and Education Fund (MALDEF) have documented numerous instances of students being illegally required to show proof of citizenship before they are permitted to register for school.

Most undocumented students, at every educational level, are classified as English Language Learners (ELLs), or students who are learning English. While bilingual education and English for Speakers of Other Languages (ESOL) classes were once common in many public schools, they are no longer as widespread nationally as they once were. The Bilingual Education Act, mandated in 1968, was intended to make education accessible to immigrants who did not speak English. In 1974, the Supreme Court ruled in *Lau v. Nichols* that students needed to be able to comprehend what was being taught in the classroom, and if they could not understand the content of their classes, their rights were being violated. Together, these two laws led to the development of many bilingual programs. There are six models of English language instruction that have been used in the United States. They are:

- **Two-Way or Dual-Language Immersion Bilingual Education** has the goal of students becoming bilingual and biliterate. Half the students come from English-dominant households and half come from households where another language, such as Spanish, is spoken. Research indicates that Dual-Language Immersion programs are highly effective in helping students achieve in both English and another language, and they keep ELLs from being isolated from native English speakers.
- **Dual-Language Bilingual Education** has the goal of students learning content in English, while developing literacy in their native language. Students ask questions about content in the native language, and bilingual teachers answer in English. The focus is on content. Students also take classes in their native language, to develop writing and critical thinking skills.
- **Late-Exit Bilingual Education** has students learn literacy in their native language first, and then there is a gradual transition to English literacy. The idea is that students can transfer literacy from the native language to the new language.
- **Transitional or Early-Exit Bilingual Education** is intended to transition learners to English-only instruction within a three-year period. While the student's native language is used, the student does not receive instruction in order to develop in the native language. Rather, the native language is a tool for learning content and transitioning to English.
- **Sheltered English Instruction** has the goal of students learning content while they learn English. This approach uses the already established course content and employs techniques to help students practice English in the context of the subject matter.
- **Structured English Immersion (SEI)** is an approach used in Arizona, California, and Massachusetts, and it was adopted as a result of voter initiatives. SEI requires students to study English grammar intensively, with minimal content, for one year, and then move to content classes in English.

However, the introduction of No Child Left Behind (NCLB) in 2001 ended the Bilingual Education Act. NCLB states that students must be tested in English, each year, and this has led to the prevalence of approaches such as Sheltered English Instruction and in some states, Structured English Immersion. However, Transitional or Early-Exit Bilingual Education, along with Sheltered English Instruction and Structured English Immersion, are examples of subtractive bilingualism, approaches that erase the native language and replace it with English. Two-Way or Dual Language Immersion Bilingual Education, Dual-Language Bilingual Education, and Late-Exit Bilingual Education are examples of additive bilingualism, approaches that lead to students communicating fluently in two languages.

High school students who do not have legal documents face special constraints. They may be put into a non–college preparatory track, often without their knowledge, because teachers and counselors assume that they cannot attend college. At the same time, because they often are in the shadows, or invisible, counselors may not tell them about the ways in which they might be able to pursue a college education. Also, they will not be able to work legally, and in some states, although they have taken driver's education classes, they cannot apply for a learner's permit, because laws about whether or not undocumented people can obtain driver's licenses vary from state to state.

When it comes to attending university, undocumented students are in the same category with international students, and they have to pay international student tuition, which at public universities is usually three times that of in-state tuition. The Illegal Immigration Reform and Immigrant Responsibility Act (IIRIRA), passed in 1996, prevented states from providing educational benefits to undocumented students. However, states have interpreted the law in different ways. As of 2010, there are nine states that permit undocumented students to pay in-state tuition to attend state universities. They are: California, Illinois, Nebraska, New Mexico, New York, Texas, Utah, Washington, and Wisconsin.

Adult Education is funded by the federal government, as well as by individual states and agencies, and is available to adults over the age of sixteen. Its goal is to teach basic skills and literacy, including English to Speakers of Other Languages (ESOL). Adult Education programs provide an alternate route for adults to complete high school through preparation for the General Educational Development (GED) Exam, as well as for them to attain citizenship through preparation for the U.S. Citizenship/Naturalization Exam.

While most states make adult education available to everyone, regardless of legal status, in 2006, the state of Arizona made itself the one exception. A voter initiative called Proposition 300 made adult education inaccessible to people in Arizona without legal documents.

The DREAM Act

The legal constraints affecting undocumented youth have led to proposed federal legislation in the United States called the Development, Relief and Education for Alien Minors Act (The DREAM Act). The goal of the DREAM Act is to provide a path toward U.S. citizenship for young people without legal documents. The provisions of the DREAM Act would apply to students who have graduated from high school in the United States, have good moral character (have not been convicted of felonies), and who were brought to the United States as legal minors, under the age of eighteen. In order to qualify for the DREAM Act, a young person would have to have been living in the United States for five years without interruption and would have to have been between the ages of fifteen and thirty-five before the time the bill became law. For the young people who meet these requirements, the DREAM Act would allow them to earn temporary legal residence in the United States for six years if they complete two years at a community college, or two years at a four-year university, or if they serve two years in the military. They would be eligible for student loans and work study, but not for Pell Grants. If they complete one of these milestones, and are still in good standing after six years, they would have the right to apply for permanent legal residency in the United States.

The DREAM Act was introduced in the senate in 2001, and again in 2009 and 2010. Because some people see the DREAM Act as encouraging undocumented immigration, legislators have introduced the act attached to other bills, never by itself. Although it has bipartisan support in both houses of Congress, the Dream Act remains controversial. In 2013, a DREAM Act provision was approved as part of S.744, the U.S. Senate version of a new comprehensive immigration bill. This provision has been lauded by many immigration rights advocates as one of the best DREAM Act versions that has been proposed to date. Under this bill, eligible DREAMers would be on a fast track to registering for provisional immigrant (RPI) status, and, after five years, would be eligible to apply for adjustment to Legal Permanent Residency status, after which they would then be able to apply for U.S. citizenship. In addition, young people who have been deported would be allowed to apply for inclusion in the policy if they would otherwise have been able to apply except for the fact that they had been deported. In addition, the Senate version of the bill would repeal the state laws that make undocumented students ineligible for in-state tuition rates at public universities, enabling their ability to attain the American Dream. Unfortunately, in the fall of 2013, S. 744 was stalled in the Republican-controlled House when Virginia Republican Congressman Bob Goodlatte, chairman of the House Judiciary Committee, said that he would not allow an immigration reform bill that includes a path to citizenship to pass his committee, effectively killing any hope for immigration reform in the 113th U.S. Congress.

Char Ullman

See Also: Adult Education; Bilingualism; Colleges and Universities; DREAM Act; English as a Second Language (ESL) Programs; English Language Learners (ELL); *Plyler v. Doe;* Policy and Political Action.

Further Reading

Fortuny, Katrina, Randy Capps, Margaret Simms, and Ajay Chaudry. 2009. "Children of Immigrants: National and State Characteristics." The Urban Institute: http://www .niusileadscape.org/lc/Record/762?search_query=.

Morse, Susan C., and Frank S. Ludovina. 1999. "Responding to Undocumented Children in Schools." ERIC Digest, ED433172, http://www.ericdigests.org/2000-2/schools.htm.

Elementary Schools

Undocumented immigrants account for 28 percent of the nations' foreign-born population of 40.2 million (Pew Hispanic Center, 2011). It is difficult to determine the exact number of undocumented immigrants in U.S. elementary schools because schools do not collect information on the immigration status of students but, as of March 2010, experts estimate that 6.8 percent of the students in kindergarten through twelfth grade in U.S. schools were undocumented or were children of at least one parent who is an undocumented immigrant (Pew Hispanic Center, 2011). Because many students are born in the United States, they themselves are not undocumented. They are U.S. citizens and increasingly part of families with mixed immigration status.

Georgia Southern University senior Demetress Roberts, center, teaches Latino Outreach student Angel Leonardo, 12, about fractions using a computer program at Langston Chapel Elementary School in Statesboro, Georgia, Monday, March 20, 2001. Latino Outreach is a GSU program that uses college students to help Latino English Language Learner (ELL) students succeed in learning English. (AP Photo/ Stephen Morton)

The majority of these students, more than half, are in elementary schools which consist of kindergarten through sixth or eighth grades in the United States. Elementary schools are generally smaller than middle or high schools with enrollments ranging from several hundred to a thousand students, and a typical classroom is self-contained, that is, students are in one classroom with one teacher who teaches all the academic subjects of mathematics, science, social studies; most elementary schools also have physical education, art, and music teachers. Since Kindergarten is not mandatory in many states, percentages of undocumented immigrant students are smaller there than in the first through sixth or eighth grades.

According to the Pew Hispanic Research Center, the majority of undocumented immigrant students are Hispanic (76 percent), with most coming from Mexico (59 percent of the undocumented population). Other significant origins of students with at least one undocumented parent are other countries in Central America (11 percent), South America (7 percent), Asia (7 percent), Africa (3 percent), and Europe and Canada (2 percent). Historically, six states (California, Texas, Florida, New York, Illinois, New Jersey) enrolled more than three quarters of the undocumented student population, and that remains true as of 2011. In these six states the undocumented student population can account for up to 10 percent of the total student population. However, even though the majority of immigrant students are still enrolled in those six states, undocumented students have dispersed across the United States since the 1990s. States such as Georgia, North Carolina, Alabama in the South, Washington and Oregon in the Northwest, and Virginia in the East have experienced unprecedented increases. Further, undocumented students tend to be concentrated in large urban centers (47 percent) but increasingly are settling in suburban areas as well (Passel & Cohn, 2009).

States that traditionally enrolled immigrant students have well-established programs for them in elementary schools, but states receiving immigrants since the huge increase in the 1990s have struggled to incorporate the newcomers into their schools. Schools in the United States, elementary or secondary, do not ask for documentation status when children are enrolled in schools so procedures and programs are the same for immigrant students regardless of documentation status. School personnel, primarily teachers and principals, are sometimes made aware of documentation status when parents or children are detained or deported, but this does not affect academic placement or program. Over the years children in elementary schools have been relatively free from fear of deportation compared to adults in the workplace, but the specter of losing parents to deportation is still present for many immigrant elementary children. Experienced teachers of immigrant students tell stories of children going home to find their parents detained or deported while they were in school. Mexican-origin students in particular are feeling the effects of increased scrutiny and enforcement of immigration law since the economic downturn of 2008. In 2009 more than 70 percent of deportees were Mexican according to the Department of Homeland Security (U.S. Department of Homeland Security, 2010).

Since education is a responsibility of each state in the United States, the school experience of undocumented immigrants in schools varies across the country depending on the policies and resources of each state. In almost all cases though, students are accepted and enrolled in elementary schools without questions about their immigration status. Because most immigrants and children of immigrants are not proficient in English, they are placed in programs specifically for English language learners. After the Civil Rights movement of the 1960s, the Federal Government issued guidelines for all schools regarding identification and placements for children who were not proficient in English. Each state is still responsible for identifying students who need specific programs to teach English and for determining the type of educational programs for immigrant students, but the Federal government has influenced the actions of states relative to English language learners through federal funding and court decisions about the civil rights of students. An example of this is the procedure for identifying students for English as a Second Language programs. When any parent registers children in school, they are asked questions about home language background and which languages the student speaks. If there is another language in the child's background, the children are given an English proficiency assessment. If they score below the proficiency level, generally below 3 on a scale of 1–5, they are placed in specific programs for English Language Learners (ELL). If students score at a proficient level (above 3), they are placed in regular programs with the rest of the student population.

Another example of federal influence in education of undocumented elementary students is the decision in the Supreme Court case *Plyler v. Doe,* which prohibits schools from denying a public education to undocumented immigrants. Undocumented elementary students receive their schooling in classrooms with other children that include other immigrant children or children born in the United States who enter school not knowing English. The undocumented students are not theoretically segregated in elementary schools but in practice they are segregated from mainstream students because they spend many years in programs specifically for English Language Learners. These programs may be either bilingual education programs or English as a Second Language (ESL). By federal and state law, school districts must provide some type of ESL program but relatively few have bilingual education classrooms where teachers use both English and the native language of the children. Where elementary bilingual programs are available, they are primarily Spanish and English, with a few in California Chinese and English. Bilingual classrooms generally provide instruction in ESL and subjects such as mathematics, science, and social studies in two languages. However, the vast majority of English Language Learners are assigned to classrooms with monolingual English-speaking teachers, and they receive instruction in ESL from a certified ESL teacher who takes them from their classroom for a period of time ranging from several hours to a few minutes a day. Schools with large numbers of English Language Learners, especially in large urban districts, also generally have bilingual parent liaisons who help school personnel communicate with non-English-speaking parents.

The curriculum for all children in ESL programs revolves around the learning of English. Other academic subjects such as mathematics, science, and social studies generally are limited until the students are able to understand English well enough to join English speakers in regular classrooms. In some schools ELL students attend classes like music, art, and physical education with the non-immigrant student population, but they are not exposed to the same academic curriculum as non-immigrant students. In reality, schools are primarily interested in having immigrant students learn English and move into mainstream classrooms. This is the main measure of their success. Learning in other academic areas is either not assessed or tests are administered in English at levels the ESL students don't understand. When students achieve the desired proficiency level in English assessments, they are "exited" from ELL programs and placed in regular classrooms where they no longer receive special instruction in English. Unfortunately, the exit level of proficiency is generally low and immigrant students often flounder in English-only classrooms with no ESL support. In terms of school completion, not many elementary schools keep track of whether students go on to secondary schools, but because of mandatory schooling in the United States, undocumented students tend to go on to middle school. The status of undocumented students does not generally become an issue until they attempt to enroll in institutions of higher education where in-state or out-of-state tuition becomes an issue.

Traditionally, elementary schools in the United States have been safe, neutral spaces for undocumented immigrant children. This may be changing due to increasing anti-immigrant sentiment across the country. In some states there are proposals for schools to request documentation status, but as of 2011 only Alabama had adopted legislation requiring this. This type of legislation would have enormous implications for elementary schools, forcing them to collaborate with the Homeland Security Department in identifying undocumented children and/or parents. Further, it would greatly affect the school's ability to provide academic programs as well as relative safety for innocent children. Another hotly debated issue for elementary schools is the amount of money spent educating undocumented immigrant children. Some protest the extra state and federal funds given to schools for programs to teach English as a Second Language.

Toni Griego-Jones

See Also: Education; English as a Second Language (ESL) Programs; English Language Learners (ELL); Head Start; *Plyler v. Doe;* Policies and Political Action.

Further Reading

Passel, J., and D. Cohn. 2009. "Unauthorized Immigrants and Their U.S.-Born Children." Washington, DC: Pew Hispanic Center.

Pew Hispanic Center. 2011. "Unauthorized Immigrant Populations: National and State Trends." Washington, DC.

U.S. Department of Homeland Security. 2010. *2009 Yearbook of Immigration Statistics.* Washington, DC: Office of Immigration Statistics, Department of Homeland Security.

Emergency Quota Act of 1921

The turn of the twentieth century swept in a new era of federally controlled immigration policies. During this time period, limiting immigration from nations that were perceived as being undesirable was a key concern for the United States government. The Emergency Quota Act, also known as the National Origins Act of 1921, was passed by the U.S. Congress on May 9, 1921. The main objective of this legislation was to reduce the number of immigrants coming from Southern, Central, and Eastern Europe. It limited the number of immigrants to just 3 percent of the total number of foreign-born persons from that country recorded in the 1910 United States Census. The Emergency Quota Act had been proposed many times but had failed to pass. It succeeded in part as a response to the influx of destitute refugees from war-torn Europe. The new quotas limited the number of immigrants of any nationality entering the United States to 3 percent of the nationalities that lived in the United States according to the 1910 U.S. Census. Part of the motivation for greater restrictions was to ensure that communist-leaning Bolsheviks, anarchists, Jews, and other "undesirables" were kept to a minimum. It was originally intended to be a temporary piece of legislation. However, American employers had also found that immigrants from Mexico and the Caribbean were preferable, and this dramatically lessened the need for European labor that may have been radicalized by socialist ideas. This led to the later, more permanent National Origins Act of 1924.

Another important aspect of the Emergency Quota Act of 1921 is related to the supply and demand of cheap labor. During the early 1900s, massive numbers of immigrants were allowed to enter and work in the United States because the nation's expanding industries needed a large supply of cheap labor. The generous immigration policies of the late 1800s and early 1900s provided the labor market with abundant amounts of labor. A large surplus of cheap labor was needed so that the costs associated with industrialization would remain low. For example, Chinese laborers had been critical to the construction of the transcontinental railroad linking eastern ends of the United States to the west. Largely exploited, Chinese laborers were paid only one-fifth of what white workers earned for the same work. After completion of the railroad, the demand for Chinese laborers decreased, and in 1921 with the passage of the Emergency Quota Act, the U.S. Congress endeavored to further reduce the Chinese immigrant population (although Chinese laborer immigrants had already been banned through the Chinese Exclusion Act of 1882, which was renewed in 1892 and 1902 and made permanent from

1904 until 1943). Moreover, the 1920s ushered in a period of mechanization and labor-saving technologies, reducing the need for labor. The combination of anti-immigration climate, racism, and the slowing down of the nation's industries facilitated the Emergency Quota Act. With the passing of the 1921 Quota Act the foundation was set for the later 1924 National Origins Act, which further normalized more restrictive measures to curtail immigration based on race and national origins.

The Emergency Quota Act demonstrated that with increased acceptance, ethnicity and race could be used as ways to justify and to determine the entry and acceptance of certain classes of immigrants. This quota act was in line with previous immigration laws, such as the Chinese Exclusion Act of 1882, which was aimed at regulating and keeping out non–Western European immigrants from entering the United States. In this way the designing of immigration laws engaged a social process. To be sure, it was the result of the anti-immigrant climate and nativist movements of the time. Much of the anti-immigrant sentiment was fueled by fears of societal instability and the belief that the entry of non-Anglo immigrants would lead to the moral deterioration of American society. In public venues, politicians used arguments that would be considered offensive by today's standards. Non–Western European immigrants were thought to pollute and destroy the moral and social fabric of American society due to their inability to assimilate or become Americans. Eugenic scientists, whose main goals were to study and practice selective human breeding with the aim of improving human stock, helped construct and perpetuate theories about the supposed racial inferiority of non–Western European populations. Increasingly, scientists argued that racial mixture of Northern and Western Europeans with immigrants from Southern and Eastern Europe would deteriorate the white race.

It should thus come as no surprise that in the twenty-first century with the immigration debate raging in the United States, eminent scholars like Samuel P. Huntington would provoke great debate by arguing that immigration from Latin America threatens American identity and culture. In his 2004 book, *Who Are We? The Challenges to America's National Identity,* he challenges long-held notions that the United States is "a nation of immigrants." In his view, the problem lies with uncontrolled Mexican immigration. He points out that nearly 8–10 million undocumented immigrants were in the United States by 2003, 58% of whom were Mexican whose culture is incompatible with American values. He expressed concerns over the resultant "Hispanization" of regions of the United States, namely the west and California. He raised the ire of many Latinos by arguing that Mexicans lag other immigrants in their assimilation into American society, in part by their culture of Catholicism and lack of ambition.

Sahar Sadeghi

See Also: Exclusion; Hart-Celler Act (1965); Immigration and Nationality Act (The McCarran-Walter Act) (1952); Johnson-Reed Act (1924); Racism.

Further Reading

Gerstle, Gary. 2001. *American Crucible: Race and Nation in the Twentieth Century.* Princeton, NJ: Princeton University Press.

Holland, Kenneth M. 2007. "A History of Chinese Immigration in the United States and Canada." *American Review of Canadian Studies* 37.2:150–160.

Huntington, Samuel P. 2004. *Who Are We? The Challenges to America's National Identity.* New York: Simon & Schuster.

Ngai, Mae M. 2004. *Impossible Subjects: Illegal Aliens and the Making of Modern America.* Princeton: Princeton University Press.

Steinberg, Stephen. 2001. *The Ethnic Myth: Race, Ethnicity, and Class in America.* Boston, MA: Beacon Press.

Zolberg, Aristide R. 2006. *A Nation by Design: Immigration Policy in the Fashioning of America.* Cambridge, MA: Harvard University Press.

Employer Sanctions

The concept of employer sanctions, as the legal prohibition on employers against the hiring of migrants without employment authorization, has become firmly associated with the passage of the Immigration Reform and Control Act (IRCA) enacted on November 6, 1986 (P.L. 99–603) during the Ronald Reagan administration. When President Reagan signed the bill into law, he noted two important elements: it "is the most comprehensive reform of our immigration laws since 1952," and "[t]he employer sanctions program is the keystone and major element. It will remove the incentive for illegal immigration by eliminating the job opportunities which draw illegal aliens here." IRCA made it unlawful for an employer to hire "an alien, knowing the alien is an unauthorized alien."

For historians of migration policy, President Reagan's enactment of the law represented an interesting continuity and coincidence. On November 8, 1971, then Governor Reagan enacted the Dixon Arnet bill (Assembly Bill 528). The bill was the first state-level employer sanctions law aimed at penalizing employers who "knowingly employ an alien who is not entitled to lawful residence in the United States if such employment would have an adverse effect on lawful resident workers." The bill's supporters were diverse; included among these was the United Farm Workers of America (UFW). Shortly after its passage, the law was challenged in Federal court. The case moved through the courts and was reviewed by the U.S. Supreme Court (*De Canas v. Bica,* 424 U.S. 351, 1976). In *De Canas v. Bica* the court ruled that states had the power to regulate the behavior of employers, including the restriction to hire persons without formal authorization. Even though the 1976 ruling was a victory for California, the state did not pursue its enforcement, leading some observers to argue that the law was principally intended as a symbolic gesture toward employers and unauthorized migrants.

The Congressional adoption of the employer sanctions provision in IRCA was the product of a long-standing contentious debate. Central to the debate was the question of a balance between a provision authorizing sanctions for employers who hired persons without work authorization, and a provision to grant "amnesty/legalization" to qualified "undocumented" migrants. IRCA contained both provisions. The Senate and the House of Representatives had struggled with the idea of a national employer sanctions law for close to fourteen continuous years. During those fourteen years, an approved bill would pass one chamber, but not the other; thus the debate was carried over to the following session of Congress.

Although IRCA's employer sanctions provision marked a clear departure from what was in place, business and employer groups, such as the U.S. Chamber of Commerce, sought to prevent its passage, or reduce its impact on employers. In response to lobbying pressures, Congress softened a key concept in the law: the issue of whether employers actually "know" the migration status of persons they employ. To address this, Congress added an affirmative defense that excluded employers from having to prove the authenticity of documents presented by prospective employees as part of the new I–9 document required for employees hired after the law's enactment. The affirmative defense allowed employers to indicate that they did not knowingly hire persons without authorization, since they were not knowledgeable of the inauthenticity of the documents presented to them.

It would be beyond the scope of this entry to present an assessment of the implementation of IRCA's employer sanctions provision over the past twenty-four years; however, it can be noted that the inclusion of the affirmative defense, economic integration of migrant labor within the U.S. economy, varying national policy priorities from President Reagan to President Obama, the expansion of a lucrative market in false documents, and external political and economic factors have not led to the removal of the incentive for "illegal immigration." Migrants continue to enter without formal authorization, and employers continue to employ unauthorized workers.

Congress's approval of the employer sanctions provision in IRCA represented a major policy change. It reversed what was in place since 1952. The McCarran-Walter Act of 1952 (P.L. 82–414) was enacted and had the aim to deter the employment of "illegal aliens" through increased penalties for smuggling, transporting, and harboring such migrants. Yet, influential senators from Mississippi and Texas who sought to protect grower interests in their respective states inserted what became known as the "Texas Proviso." The Proviso noted: "Provided, however, that for the purposes of this section, employment (including the usual and normal practices incident to employment) shall not be deemed to constitute harboring." The language created an exception, and signaled that it was illegal and a federal felony to harbor "illegal aliens," but that it was not illegal to employ such persons, and protected employers from being criminally charged for harboring such persons at the workplace. The Texas Proviso protected the practice of employers who were providing job opportunities that were recognized as being part of the attraction to "undocumented" migrants, even while criminalizing the entry and presence of such migrants.

Academic scholars, public policy experts, media, and policy-makers commonly note the 1986 enactment of the employer sanctions provision as the start of the federal policy to regulate migration by penalizing employers. While the importance of the IRCA provision cannot be underestimated, it also should be noted that it was not the first time U.S. employers were penalized for a cause related to migrant employment. Three major policy actions predated the 1986 Immigration Reform and Control Act.

The first United States federal measure aimed at restricting migration to the nation—the 1875 Page Act (18 Stat. 477)—prohibited the entry of persons from China, Japan and other Asian nations. It also penalized employers who "knowingly and willfully" contracted for the entry and employment of migrants from Asia. Second, the 1885 Contract Labor Law (23 Stat. 332), until its repeal in 1952, prohibited employers from "knowingly assisting, encouraging, or soliciting the migration or importation of aliens" for employment in the United States. Employers violating the law were to be fined $1,000 for each offence. Although the provision in the act was in effect from 1885 to 1952, when it was repealed, very few employers had actually been fined. Moreover, along the Mexico–United States boundary area federal migration officials appeared to have interpreted the law as applying to coastal entries, and so ignored the illegal importation of Mexican migrants by agricultural, mining and other Southwest employers. Consequently, Southwest agricultural employers and others established a pattern of direct efforts in Mexico to identify, recruit, and transport Mexican workers for employment in the United States. This included major employers such as Goodyear, Tire and Rubber, which in 1916 recruited a sizeable number of workers from Mexico for its cotton farm in the Phoenix area.

The third important Congressional action to prevent the employment of unauthorized persons is Public Law 93–518 (Amendments to the 1963 Farm Labor Contractor Registration Act, FLCRA). The FLCRA prohibited farm labor contractors from recruiting unauthorized workers and providing such workers to farm operators. Farm labor contractors in violation of the law are subject to a $500 fine and imprisonment up to a year for the first offence.

A second broad area commonly overlooked in discussions of employer sanctions is the role that states have played in shaping the debate on employer sanctions. During the 1970s (prior to IRCA), California and nine other states (Connecticut, Delaware, Florida, Kansas, Maine, Massachusetts, Missouri, New Jersey and Virginia) enacted measures aimed at prohibiting employers from employing unauthorized workers. Moreover, the City of Las Vegas (Nevada) also adopted a parallel measure. Additionally, several other states (e.g., Illinois) considered adopting such a measure but the opposition prevented their passage.

More recently, states such as Arizona, Colorado, Georgia, Idaho, Mississippi, Oklahoma and others, have enacted state employer sanctions laws. Their specific foci however have varied. Some like Arizona and Mississippi target all employers, while others limit the scope to state contractors or state agencies. The specific case of Arizona has received much attention across the nation because of its scope (all employers), and the legal challenges it faced.

In 2007, Arizona's legislature passed the Fair and Legal Employment Act (FLEA), later renamed the Legal Arizona Workers Act (LAWA), and then Governor Janet Napolitano enacted the law on July 2, 2007. Shortly after its enactment, business interests and pro-migrant groups filed separate suits. The suits were combined and heard by Federal District Judge Neil V. Wake. On February 7, 2008, Judge Wake dismissed the suits on the grounds that the state had the right to regulate the business-operation licenses of employers, thus could void the licenses granted to employers who violated the law. He did not incorporate the aim of the law, which the authors and debate leading to its passage made clear: the sponsors of the bill wanted to regulate the presence of "illegal aliens" in the state; he focused on the licensing issue.

By the end of 2009, the law was in place but had resulted in less than a handful of convictions. The primary reason was that the focus of enforcement, principally led by

Maricopa County Sheriff Joe Arpaio and Maricopa County Attorney Andrew Thomas, had been on the apprehension of unauthorized workers through workplace raids or through traffic inspections. Even in the case of the workplace raids, the workers were apprehended and jailed, but few charges were brought against the employers who had been employing the arrested workers. The owner of a profitable granite countertop business who was arrested, was arrested not because of his violation of the FLEA/LAWA, but because he was an undocumented migrant from Brazil; he was thus charged with identity theft and unauthorized entry.

Whether the national or state-level employer sanctions laws are effective in removing the employment opportunities offered by employers remains an open question. Their assessment has become more complex due to the national recession and the impact that has had on unauthorized migration. Moreover, the subsequent passage of anti-migrant laws such as SB 1070 (Support Our Law Enforcement and Safe Neighborhoods Act) in Arizona seeks to expand the regulation of migration and migrants. However, SB 1070 also softened the FLEA/LAWA employer sanctions law. The law provides an affirmative defense for employers who hire unauthorized migrants if law enforcement personnel stimulated the hiring; in other words, in the case of a law enforcement sting operation, if the employer hired the unauthorized workers, the employer will not be sanctioned for such action.

Luis F. B. Plascencia

See Also: Arizona; Employment; Employment Visas; Green Cards; Policy and Political Action; State Legislation; Workers' Rights; Workplace Raids; Work Visas.

Further Reading

Calavita, Kitty. 1982. "California's 'Employer Sanctions': The Case of the Disappearing Law." Research Report No. 39, Center for U.S.-Mexican Studies, University of California, San Diego.

Fix, Michael, and Paul T. Hill. 1990. "Enforcing Employer Sanctions: Challenges and Strategies." The RAND Corporation and The Urban Institute.

Ndulo, Nchimunya D. 2008–2009. "State Employer Sanctions Law and the Federal Preemption Doctrine: The Legal Arizona Workers Act Revisited," *Cornell Journal of Law & Public Policy,* pp. 849–880.

Wishnie, Michael J. 2007. "Prohibiting the Employment of Unauthorized Immigrants: The Experiment Fails." University of Chicago Legal Forum, pp. 193–217.

Employment

Employing immigrants, including those that are undocumented, subjects employers to the same legal responsibilities as employing legal permanent residents or citizens. For example, employers are subject to paying back wages and overtime claims when they fail to pay their employees for work performed, regardless of their employees' immigration status. Employers may also be held liable by their immigrant employees for discrimination based on race, sex or national origin.

Common misperceptions that immigrants (especially undocumented immigrants) do not share the same rights as their U.S. citizen counterparts have grown with anti-immigrant politics and recently enacted employer sanctions laws in Arizona. This trend is in part due to post-9/11 political debates that have progressively attacked the rights of undocumented workers at federal and state levels of governance. Greater scrutiny of employers has thus been a strategy of those attempting to use laws and legislation to control immigration. In this way business firms have been placed in the crossfire of political debates over immigration.

A good example of this trend comes from recent law suits brought against Wal-Mart for failing to pay back wages and overtime claims for workers. On October 23, 2003, federal officers from the Department of Homeland Security's Bureau of Immigration and Customs Enforcement (ICE) entered sixty-one Wal-Mart stores in twenty-one states nationwide and arrested more than 250 undocumented immigrants. This plan of action was dubbed "Operation Rollback" as a pun on Wal-Mart's advertising campaign touting its "rollback of prices." Consistent with the practices of the legal investigating and prosecuting arm of ICE, the apprehended undocumented immigrants were detained to help ICE enforce federal immigration laws, and on November 10, a group of immigrant janitorial workers filed a federal racketeering class action lawsuit against Wal-Mart in a New Jersey federal court. The workers alleged that Wal-Mart violated the federal Racketeering Influenced and Corrupt Organizations (RICO) statutes. All of the plaintiffs were undocumented immigrants who worked for a cleaning service contracted by Wal-Mart. Wal-Mart argued that it was not responsible because the workers were employed by an independent contractor.

Independent contracting is a cost-saving measure used by companies to remain competitive in a global market, especially with growing market instability. With the globalization of markets with international free trade agreements, a variety of strategies used by firms have been designed to cut operational costs and increase profits. Moving operations abroad across national boundaries in search of cheap labor in less developed nations is one strategy. However, this has resulted in the loss of jobs in the more industrialized nations such as the United States. Another strategy that has been used domestically has been to use labor in flexible ways to make it less costly, such as contracting out services (also known as outsourcing). Flexible employment arrangements take advantage of growing poverty, human migration, and uncertainty in less developed nations. There are several types of flexible labor arrangements, but they usually refer to the freedom a firm has to regulate the level of wages it pays by adjusting the number of hours employees work or the size of its work force in response to production demands. In the United States, the loss of relatively stable full-time jobs and the adoption of flexible labor arrangements have expanded the number of low-wage, part-time jobs that immigrants are more likely to fill. Moreover, if they are fearful of expressing concerns about unscrupulous employers, they are especially subject to exploitation and unfair labor practices. For example, in the Wal-Mart case, all of these workers claimed they were paid weekly in cash, worked at least sixty hours per week, and were obligated to work seven days a week. They also claimed they received no overtime compensation, workers' compensation, as was their right. The case against Wal-Mart was clearly premised on the notion that undocumented workers have rights to fair employment practices. In the United States, the flexible use of employees through contract work, part-time, temporary, and short-term work, contributes to their unfair treatment and the economic instability of families. In response to the fluctuations in hours or wages, household economics among the undocumented invariably includes the deployment of more of their members into the workforce to make ends meet, and a reliance on cultural mechanisms of support such as social capital.

The tendency to undermine the legal rights of undocumented workers by employers can be traced to 2002 by a U.S. Supreme Court decision in *Hoffman Plastic Compounds v. National Labor Relations Board (NLRB)*. In the *Hoffman* case, a worker without the legal authorization as defined by the 1986 Immigration Reform and Control Act (IRCA) was denied back pay after he was fired by the company for union organizing. Attorneys for the undocumented worker who was illegally fired argued that under federal labor law an employer can be held liable for firing an employee who engages in union-organizing activities. In such cases the employer would be liable for any back pay for work not performed due to his termination. However, in *Hoffman,* the U.S. Supreme Court decided that the employee could not collect back pay for work not performed because he was an undocumented worker. The majority opinion argued that awarding back pay to those in the country illegally ran counter to the law set by IRCA. They further argued that the award would have condoned prior violations of immigration laws and would have condoned and encouraged future violations. The dissenting opinion argued the exact opposite: that the back pay award would penalize employers for hiring undocumented workers (a violation under IRCA) and in this way deter unlawful activity that immigration laws sought to prevent.

The effect this ruling will have on the implementation of state and local laws affecting employee rights is yet unclear. What is clear, however, is how employment laws and the common practices of employing undocumented workers continue to collide. Two years after the *Hoffman* decision, in *Celi v. 42nd Street Development Project, Inc.* (2004), a New York state court judge upheld a claim filed in behalf of an undocumented employee, Rodolfo Celi, who had been seriously injured while performing demolition when he fell through an opening in the basement floor and into a subbasement. In response to charges that the company was negligent and had violated labor law, company attorneys argued that under *Hoffman,* Mr. Celi's undocumented status prevented him from seeking lost earnings because payment of such wages violated federal immigration law. However, in *Celi,* State Justice David I. Schmidt argued that the *Hoffman* decision did not mandate a change in New York law so as to require the dismissal of the plaintiff's claim to *lost* earnings. Celi's claim for award, then, $26,000 in past lost earnings and $900,000 in future lost earnings was upheld. Two other decisions upheld the rights of undocumented workers to recover lost wages as a result of work-related injuries and in much the same way sidestepped the *Hoffman* decision. In *Sanango v. 200 East 16th Street Housing Corporation* and *Balbuena v. IDR Realty,* the New York state appellate court decisions ruled that the employers *were* liable for workplace injuries even though the workers were undocumented. The workers who were suing to recover wages lost as a result of workplace injuries were precluded by *Hoffman* from calculating their damages based on U.S. earnings, but they *were* permitted to seek damages including awards based on future earnings *based on the prevailing wage in their home countries.* The *Hoffman* decision suggests that workers who are later identified as "illegal" will be predisposed to lost wages and dismissals in retaliation for labor organizing, which will further predispose others, undocumented or not, to unsafe working conditions.

Finally, it should be noted that in spite of their average low wages, relatively low education, and the denial of many of the social benefits to which other U.S. workers are entitled, an estimated eleven million undocumented immigrant workers in the United States are now providing the U.S. economy with a subsidy of as much as $7 billion a year. In addition to consumer-related taxes that undocumented immigrants pay while living in the United States, workers pay contributions to Social Security and Medicare by way of employee wage deductions. Porter (2005) reports that these contributions added up to about 10 percent of the tax surplus in 2006, which is the difference between what the U.S. government currently receives in payroll taxes and what it pays out in benefits.

Anna Ochoa O'Leary

See Also: Family Economics; Labor Supply; Labor Unions; Policies and Political Action; Remittances; State Legislation; Wages; Workers' Rights; Workplace Injury; Work Visas.

Further Reading

Beermann, Nick. 2006. "Liability in More Ways Than One: Employing Undocumented Workers." http://library.findlaw.com/2003/Sep/30/133064.html (accessed January 3, 2006).

Entelisano, Carol A. 2003. "The Woes of WAL-MART: A Lesson in Independent Contractor Practices and Immigration Law (Non)Compliance." http://library.findlaw.com/2003/Dec/29/133231.html (accessed January 3, 2006).

O'Leary, Anna Ochoa. 2007. "Petit Apartheid in the U.S.-Mexico Borderlands: An Analysis of Community Organization Data Documenting Work Force Abuses of the Undocumented." Forum on Public Policy On-Line; available at: http://www.forumonpublic policy.com/papersw07.html#crimjus.

Porter, Eduardo. 2005. "Illegal Immigrants Are Bolstering Social Security with Billions." *New York Times;* available at: NYTimes.com (accessed April 5, 2005).

Sassen, Saskia. 1998. *Globalization and Its Discontents.* New York: The New Press.

Employment Visas

There are temporary and permanent nonimmigrant visas to work in the United States. Temporary non-immigrant visas are those issued to workers to enter in the United States temporarily for a specific purpose, and are restricted to the activity or reason for which their nonimmigrant visa was issued. Permanent-based immigrant visas are granted to individuals allowing them to live and work indefinitely in the United States. The more commonly emitted temporary-nonimmigrant employment visas are: H-1B,

H-2A and H-2B. The H-1B visa is a non-immigrant visa which is designed to be used for foreign workers in "specialty occupations," which require theoretical and practical application of a body of highly specialized knowledge in a field of human endeavor. For example, in 2011 the United States issued 14,805 H1B visas to computer programmers, 13,837 to computer systems analysts, 12,423 to computer software engineers, 3,171 to financial analysts, 3,036 to market research analysts, 2,363 to management analysts, 2,183 to accountants, 2,079 to physicians and surgeons, 1,795 to mechanical engineers, 1,680 to electrical engineers, among others. The H-1B visa has an annual numerical limit, or "cap" of sixty-five thousand visas. The states that issued the most of this type of visas were California, New York and Texas. The most prominent sponsors of H-1B visas were Microsoft Corporation, with 2,412 workers, IBM with 1,199, and Infosys Technologies with 1, 052.

The guest worker H-2 visa program was implemented after the Immigration Reform and Control Act of 1986 (IRCA) when they were separated into two types: H-2A visas for temporary agricultural workers and H-2B visas for non-professional and non-agricultural work. H-2A and H-2B both are an attempt to ban illegal hiring of undocumented workers. An H-2A visa (Temporary Agricultural Workers visa) allows a foreign national entry into the United States for temporary or seasonal agricultural work. In fiscal year 2010, U.S. Customs and Immigration Service (USCIS) received 64,071 applications for this kind of visa. The work categories for H-2A visas typically are: Farmwork for diversified crops; farm-worker and laborers; farm worker for farm and ranch animals and irrigation and sprinkling systems. In contrast, the H-2B visa is for non-agricultural temporary workers. The work categories for this visa are: landscaping and groundskeeping workers; maids and housekeeping cleaners; nonfarm animal caretakers; amusement and recreation attendants; helper production worker; forest and conservation worker; waiters and waitresses; cooks and restaurant workers, and street vendors. The H-2B visa is the only visa category that authorizes unskilled laborers to work in the United States. For this reason, this visa is highly in demand for individuals who may not be eligible to apply for any other types of U.S. visas. Currently, the H-2B cap set by Congress is 66,000 per fiscal year. This visa is also an invaluable resource that many U.S. employers rely upon to fill temporary or seasonal needs that would be impossible to fill with U.S. workers alone. Unfortunately, in 2010 the U.S. Government Accountability Office (GAO) detected some abuses of foreign workers by some recruiters and employers. These abuses involved non-payment of hourly wages or overtime or both by employers under the US H-2B visa program. The fraud cases in the H-2B visa program were associated with the submission of fake documents by employers in behalf of the prospective immigrant workers. Employers were also found to have charged excessive fees to workers under the US H-2B visa program for visa processing and for monthly rent in overcrowded places, and transportation charges. These abuses happened despite the H-2B visa program being overseen by agencies like the U.S. Citizenship and Immigration Services (USCIS), and the Department of State, and the Department of Labor (DOL).

Other types of temporary-employment visas are organized by categories E, I, L, O, P, Q, R and TN visas. The Treaty Trade (E-1) and Treaty Investor (E-2) visas are nonimmigrant visas for a national of a country with which the United States maintains a commercial treaty, for the purpose of travel to United States to carry on substantial trade activity, to develop and direct the operations of an enterprise, or to invest a substantial amount of capital. An I-visa is a non-immigrant visa for representatives of the foreign media temporarily traveling to United States to engage in their profession while having their home office in a foreign country. In fiscal year 2010, USCIS approved 15,344 such visas. An L-1 visa is a non-immigrant visa that allows a company operating both in the United States and abroad to transfer certain classes of employees from its foreign operations to the United States operations for up to seven years. The international company must have offices in both the country of origin and the United States, or intend to open a new office in the United States while maintaining office in the home country. L-2 Visas are for a spouse and unmarried children who are under twenty-one years of age. In fiscal year 2010, USCIS approved 74,719 of these visas. The O-1 nonimmigrant visa is for an individual who possesses extraordinary ability in the sciences, arts, education, business, or athletics, or who has demonstrated a record of extraordinary achievement in the motion picture or television industry, and has been recognized nationally or internationally for those achievements. O-2 is for individuals who will accompany an O-1 artist or athlete to assist in a specific event or performance, and O-3 is for individuals who are the spouse or children of O-1's and O-2's. In fiscal year 2010, USCIS approved 8,589 of these kinds of visas. The P visa is a non-immigrant temporary worker visa for athletes, artists, and entertainers, and their spouses and children. In fiscal year 2010, USCIS approved 25,186 P visas. The Q non-immigrant visa is for international cultural exchange programs designated by USCIS. R-1 visas are for non-immigrants who are foreigners working in the United States in a religious capacity on a temporary basis. An R-2 Visa is for a spouse or for unmarried children of religious workers under the age of 21. In fiscal year 2010, USCIS approved 3,390 R visas. The nonimmigrant NAFTA professional (TN) visa allows citizens of Canada and Mexico to work in the United States in a prearranged business activity for a U.S. or foreign employer as NAFTA professionals. NAFTA is the acronym for the North American Free Trade Agreement that was signed between the United States, Mexico, and Canada, to facilitate trade and commerce between these three nations. It became effective on January 1, 1994.

The H-1C is another type of visa that is no longer used as of December 20, 2009. This nonimmigrant visa was introduced in 1999 to address the shortage of nurses in the United States. The H-1C nonimmigrant temporary worker classification was for foreign nurses coming to the United States temporarily to fill a shortage of registered nurses as determined by the Department of Labor (DOL).

Permanent (immigrant) worker visas are issued to persons to live and work permanently in the United States. Approximately 140,000 immigrant visas are available each fiscal year for these foreign-born workers (and their spouses and children). Employment-Based immigration visas include the "First Preference, EB-1" visa that is reserved for persons of extraordinary ability in the sciences, arts, education, business, or athletics; outstanding professors or researchers; and multinational executives and managers. The "Second Preference" of this EB-2 type of visa is reserved for persons who are members of the professions holding advanced degrees or for persons with exceptional ability in the arts, sciences, or business. "Third Preference" Employment-Based immigrant visas are reserved for professionals, skilled workers, and other workers, and the "Fourth

Preference" EB-4 visa is reserved for "special immigrants," which includes certain religious workers, employees of U.S. Foreign Service posts, retired employees of international organizations, alien minors who are wards of courts in the United States, and other classes of aliens. "Fifth Preference EB-5" visas are reserved for business investors who invest $1 million or $500,000 (if the investment is made in a targeted employment area) in a new commercial enterprise that employs at least ten fulltime U.S. workers.

An important issue to be considered in the granting of temporary and permanent employment visas is that employers must verify that an individual whom they plan to employ or continue to employ in the United States is authorized to accept employment in the United States. Since the enactment of the Immigration Reform and Control Act (IRCA) in 1986, and until 2011, the employment-eligible verification system has had many modifications. Currently there is a federal database, known as E-Verify, through which employers can check whether or not an individual is authorized to work in the United States. The E-Verify system is equipped with the state of the art technology to identify persons through photo matching. Photo matching is the first step in incorporating biometric data into a web-based interface. Since 2003, this system has been operated by the U.S. Department of Homeland Security (DHS) in partnership with the Social Security Administration (SSA) of the U.S. government. For most employers, the use of E-Verify is voluntary and limited to determining the employment eligibility of new hires only. E-Verify is also mandatory for employers with federal contracts or subcontracts. However, under the laws of several states, some businesses may be required to verify a workers' eligibility

Erika Cecilia Montoya Zavala

See Also: Guestworker and Contract Labor Policies; Labor Supply; Legal Status.

Further Reading

Griffith, David. 2007. *American Guestworkers, Jamaicans and Mexicans in the U.S. Labor Market.* State College: Penn State University Press.

Payal, Banerjee. 2006. "Indian Information Technology Workers in the United States: The H-1B Visa, Flexible Production, and the Racialization of Labor." *Critical Sociology* 32.2–3:425, 445.

U.S. Government Accountability Office. 2010. "Closed Civil and Criminal Cases Illustrate Instances of H-2B Workers Being Targets of Fraud and Abuse." www.gao.gov/fraudnet/fraudnet.htm.

Enclaves

Over the past two decades, immigrant populations within the United States have not only grown, but they have become more dispersed. Undocumented immigrants are currently represented in every state across the country, although they are more concentrated in just twelve states.

The towns and cities where immigrants establish communities are often characterized by a collection of ethnic enclaves, or neighborhoods that are mostly comprised of

Chicago's Ukrainian Village neighborhood, December 8, 2004, is one of the country's largest and best-known enclaves of Ukrainians. Enclaves provide newly arrived immigrants a place to find familiar commodities, businesses, churches, newspapers, and services that help them reduce the effects of stress of acculturation. (AP Photo/Jeff Roberson)

one ethnic group embedded within a larger town or city that is predominantly of another group (i.e. white or black). Ethnic enclaves allow immigrants to be self-sufficient through network businesses, churches, newspapers, recreational sports teams, and services that appeal to their needs. These may also provide resources for immigrants that are more culturally appropriate than those provided in the surrounding communities, outside the enclave. Ethnic enclaves may also reflect desirable aesthetics, often displaying some of the symbolic reminders of their places of origin, such as national flags or the color schemes that are sensitive to the look and appeal of their native communities. In a way, enclaves serve as a home away from home for immigrants. Settlement in ethnic enclaves is not necessarily determined by the legal status of its residents as both documented and undocumented immigrants reside in these areas. However, for those insecure immigrants living in places where they may not be welcomed or viewed with suspicion, enclaves provide a place of social comfort where immediate needs may be met in relative safety.

A key factor underlying the development of ethnic enclaves is social networks. In fact, social networks provide access to needed resources of all types. Furthermore, social support networks can reduce the effects of anxiety and stress that accompany undocumented immigrant status for the carrying out of daily interactions.

Very often, members of ethnic enclaves can often go about their daily routine using their native language. They may even be able to completely avoid interaction with members of the host society. However, such a lack of integration can be detrimental to immigrants' new language acquisition. This is one argument for why ethnic enclaves may weaken immigrants' capacity for socioeconomic advancement.

In one study, immigrant participants claimed that they choose to self-segregate in ethnic enclaves because they experienced harassment and discrimination from the host culture, much of which is attributed to police. For these individuals, enclaves can serve as a buffer against those negative experiences. Considering the host of anti-immigrant legislation that has been proposed around state legislatures nationwide for the past two decades or so, immigrants' desire to remain in a comfortable and nondiscriminatory setting with other people like themselves is reasonable and expected.

Another potential way that ethnic enclaves may hinder society integration is the chronic poverty that many ethnic minority enclaves suffer. These neighborhoods are typically poorer than the surrounding communities in which they are embedded. They often lack public works infrastructure and public spaces (such as parks and recreational facilities) that are safe and inviting. Poverty can contribute to a lack of resources for immigrants, and crime or fear of crime can augment stress.

Ethnic enclaves can be largely homogenous, consisting of only one ethnic group, or they can be quite diverse in which several ethnic minorities are represented. For example, an ethnic enclave outside of Nashville, Tennessee is home to Latino immigrants as well as Kurds, Ethiopians, and Asians, all of whom are represented in numerous ways.

Some well-known examples of ethnic enclaves in large cities are Little Italy and Chinatown, which are situated in the major city of New York. In Chicago, communities known as Little Village and Pilsner have been home to numerous ethnic groups and immigrants over several decades. The current population of Little Village is 91,071, and is 83 percent Latino. Approximately 92 percent of the Latinos are Mexican. Little Village is a prime example of an ethnic enclave. Unfortunately though, its members claim to have a poor quality of life. Undocumented status is one factor that contributes to this claim. Undocumented immigrants have limited mobility and constrained job options. Additionally they must live in fear of deportation, as immigration raids have occurred in Little Village on a number of occasions. Although only a small portion of Little Village is undocumented, and in fact 51.2 percent of its population is U.S.-born, it is very likely that most of the community's residents know at least someone who is there without legal status. Thus, when the quality of life of the undocumented is compromised, the rest of the community suffers as well. The challenges that undocumented immigrants face, therefore, are the greatest challenges that the rest of Little Village faces.

While Little Village is concerned with gangs, criminal activity, and violence, some sources have noted that migration to ethnic enclaves among Latinos can promote social cohesion and trust, and therefore reduce community violence. The findings were also based on a Chicago community study (Almeida et al., 2009). These results demonstrate the diversity of ethnic enclaves and the range of positive to negative behavioral outcomes that are possible, and how they continue to evolve over time.

Courtney Waters

See Also: Barrios; Home Town Associations; Informal Economy; Small Business Ownership; Social Interaction and Integration; Suburbs.

Further Reading

Almeida, Joanna, Ichiro Kawachi, Beth E. Molnar, and S. V. Subramanian. 2009. "A Multilevel Analysis of Social Ties and Social Cohesion among Latinos and Their Neighborhoods: Results from Chicago." *Journal of Urban Health* 86.5:745–759.

Chaney, James. 2010. "The Formation of a Hispanic Enclave in Nashville, Tennessee." *Southeastern Geographer* 50:17–38.

Osypuk, Theresa L., Lisa M. Bates, and Dolores Acevado-Garcia. 2010. "Another Mexican Birthweight Paradox? The Role of Residential Enclaves and Neighborhood Poverty in the Birthweight of Mexican-Origin Infants." *Social Science & Medicine* 70:550–560.

Stodolska, Monika, and Kimberly J. Shinew. 2009. "La Calidad de Vida Dentro de La Villita: An Investigation of Factors Affecting Quality of Life of Latino Residents in an Urban Immigrant Residential Enclave." *Journal of Immigrant and Refugee Studies* 7:267–289.

English as a Second Language (ESL) Programs

Although the U.S. federal government has not legally designated English as the official language of the United States, the predominance of English in business, education, and mainstream society impels immigrants to learn this language in order to survive. The right to access English as a Second Language (ESL) programs is one of the few privileges available to undocumented immigrants in the United States. The Supreme Court case of *Plyler v. Doe* (1978) established the right to public education for undocumented K-12 students. This decision, coupled with Titles VI and VII of the Civil Rights Act of 1964, laid the legal groundwork to guarantee undocumented immigrant children the right to receive English-language instruction in school. While no corresponding laws exist guaranteeing this right to undocumented immigrant adults, the wide variety of community outlets providing such classes makes ESL programs generally accessible and affordable. However, despite the significant need for English language instruction in the United States, ESL programs for both K-12 students and adults face several challenges in effectively providing this service to immigrants.

Several states enacted laws in the nineteenth and twentieth centuries that have prioritized the public use of English over other languages, often with the goal of suppressing unwelcomed immigrant groups. State legislation and voter ballot initiatives established such laws as early as the 1920s and continued through the last decades of the twentieth century. Specifically in public education, Southwestern states such as Arizona, California, Texas, and New Mexico have passed English-only laws for public schools. These laws have functioned as part of an overall environment of discrimination against Spanish-speaking natives and immigrants who historically lived in large numbers in this area of the country. However, the suppression of a second language has not been confined to the U.S. Southwest. The United States' animosity toward Germany during World War I also motivated fifteen states to pass similar laws in the years during and after the war.

K-12 ESL Programs

Despite legal mandates requiring the use of English on the state level, no laws compelled K-12 schools to provide English-language instruction until the second half of the twentieth century. The Civil Rights Act of 1964 prohibited discrimination based on national origin and thus created the legal groundwork for future laws mandating English-language education in publicly funded schools. Federal court cases in the years that followed created standards for enforcing this right to English-language instruction programs. In *Lau v. Nichols* (1974) the Supreme Court used language in Titles VI and VII of the Civil Rights Act to rule that public school districts indeed were required to provide English-language instruction to students considered to be Limited English Proficient (LEP), referring to those students who speak English less than very well. This ruling subsequently led to the passage of the Equal Educational Opportunity Act of 1974, declaring that districts must provide ESL programs in order to afford equal access to educational opportunities for all students. Later, in *Castaneda v. Pickard* (1981) the court outlined explicit standards for assessing ESL programs in school districts, though debate still continued over how to fund the programs. Twenty years later, Title III of the No Child Left Behind Act firmly established federal funding for ESL programs for all LEP students in K-12 schools.

According to the National Clearinghouse for English Language Acquisition, there are approximately five million K-12 students classified as Limited English Proficient (LEP) in the United States. This group of students is the fastest-growing segment of the school-aged children in the United States, and increased at a rate of 57 percent between 1995 and 2006. LEP students at the K-12 level speak four hundred different languages, but 80 percent of these students speak Spanish. Although no statistics exist detailing what percentage of such students are undocumented immigrants, a significant portion (36 percent) of these students were born outside of the United States. However, an even larger proportion (64 percent) of LEP students were born in the United States to immigrant parents, and most of these U.S.-born students started school in the kindergarten or first grade. LEP students are more likely to be from low-income households than students who reported speaking only English or English very well.

The main task of ESL programs is to teach LEP students the skills necessary to learn the English language with the goal of using it in culturally appropriate ways and succeeding at all academic levels. As a result, ESL programs differ significantly from both foreign-language programs and English language arts programs at the K-12 level. While learning a foreign language is not always necessary for understanding material taught in other academic courses, ESL programs provide students with the language skills crucial for success in these other subject areas. English-language arts courses also differ from ESL programs in that language arts classes consist of native or proficient English speakers who are refining their language skills, while ESL students in general are learning a new language. Finally, language arts programs focus mostly on improving students' writing skills, while ESL programs require an integrated curriculum that consists of listening, speaking, reading, and writing.

K-12 ESL programs aim to help students gain enough proficiency in English to transition into the school's mainstream curriculum, but the timing of this transition varies by the program utilized in each school district. Some programs immediately place ESL students in the same academic courses as their English-proficient classmates and provide English-language instruction outside of normal class time. Other programs begin teaching academic material in the ESL students' shared native language and transition instruction to English as soon as possible. However, most ESL classes focus more on teaching the language skills necessary for social communication and survival and less on academic material. As a result, these courses do not typically cover academic content that is taught to English-proficient students who are taking classes as part of the mainstream curriculum. Oftentimes ESL students are excluded from mathematics and science courses until they have achieved sufficient language proficiency or, instead, are placed in remedial courses. Consequentially, ESL students often are not sufficiently exposed to the same academic material as their more English-proficient peers at the same grade level.

Adult ESL Programs

The U.S. Government Accountability Office estimates that at least 22 million immigrants across the country speak English less than very well, and little information is available on what percentage of these individuals are undocumented. English as a Second Language programs for adults appeared in the early decades of the twentieth century, but were usually associated with government programs intended to Americanize immigrants. These classes focused more on teaching immigrants about American customs and holidays and less on providing the language skills necessary to survive in the United States. A profound need for adult ESL programs emerged in the 1970s when a high number of refugees arrived from Southeast Asia. When three million undocumented immigrants applied for amnesty under the Immigration Reform and Control Act of 1986, thousands of immigrant students enrolled in English classes in order to navigate the paperwork process and eventually apply for citizenship.

Adult ESL programs differ in curricula and methodology, and this variety stems from a lack of standardization among educators and the wide range of outlets that provide English classes to adult immigrants. Affordable adult ESL classes are provided at a variety of locations, including community colleges, community-based organizations (CBOs), churches, and private employers. These programs differ in size and intensity, from private one-on-one tutoring to classes taught for academic credit. The curriculum of these programs also varies in focus, from generic literacy skills to communication skills in a variety of specific contexts such as the workplace, the community, the school, and the family. Despite a wide variety and large number of programs, demand for adult ESL classes consistently exceeds the capacity of the programs available. In 2000, the National Center for Education Statistics reported that nearly 3 million adults across the country wanted to but could not enroll in ESL classes, with programs reporting wait times of up to one year.

The education level of students in adult ESL classes also poses a problem for teachers and administrators. The 2001 U.S. Census reported that only 60 percent of non-citizens in the United States and 67 percent of immigrants overall have completed a high school degree. The lower levels of education among immigrants create conditions where some students in ESL classes lack literacy even in their first language. Other ESL students may have attended many years of school in their home country but are not familiar with the Roman alphabet. Beyond educational experience, undocumented immigrants face many obstacles in regularly attending classes, such as dealing with inflexible or unpredictable work schedules, the inability to find affordable childcare, a lack of reliable transportation, and a general fear of interacting with local police when traveling to and from class. In classes with students from a large number of countries or in a wide variety of economic and legal situations, this disparity in life situations presents challenges necessary to overcome in order to effectively provide English-language instruction to immigrants in the United States.

Emily Puhl

See Also: Bilingualism; Education; Elementary Schools; English Language Learners (ELL); English-Only Movement; Limited English Proficiency (LEP); *Plyler v. Doe;* Policy and Political Action.

Further Reading

Feinberg, Rosa Castro. 2002. *Bilingual Education: A Reference Handbook.* Santa Barbara: ABC-CLIO, Inc.

NCELA Publications. National Clearinghouse for English Language Acquisition website. http://www.ncela.gwu.edu/publications.

Office of English Language Acquisition. 2008. "Language Enhancement and Academic Achievement for Limited English Proficient Students." *The Biennial Report to Congress on the Implementation of the Title III State Formula Grant Program, School Years 2004–2006.* Washington, DC.

U.S. Government Accountability Office. 2009. *English Language Learning: Diverse Federal and State Efforts to Support Adult English Language Learning Could Benefit from More Coordination.* Washington, DC: Government Printing Office.

Valencia, Richard R. 2008. *Chicano Students and the Courts.* New York: New York University Press.

Wrigley, Heide Spruck, and Gloria J.A. Guth. 1992. *Bringing Literacy to Life: Issues and Options in Adult ESL Literacy.* San Mateo: Aguirre International.

English Language Learners (ELL)

Immigrant students who come to the United States without legal documentations are known as "undocumented students." Most of these immigrant students are learning English in addition to their native or first language. The term English Language Learners (ELLs) has been developed by scholars to replace the previous term of English as a Second Language (ESL) student. The change in term reflects the understanding that some immigrant students know more than two languages. Depending on the English proficiency of the student and the educational resources available from the school system, students may be placed into various models of Bilingual Education Programs. If the students have sufficient English proficiency, then they might participate in "mainstream" classes and education.

Historical Context of Bilingual Education

The United States public education system was originally established as a way to help students become successful members of society and help contribute to the progress of the United States. Federal law established that this education should be *free for all students* between kindergarten and the senior year of high school. Title VII under the Elementary and Secondary Education Act (ESEA) was established as the Bilingual Education Act (BEA) in 1968 (Ovando, Combs, and Collier 2006). Two major forces that helped establish the BEA were the civil rights movement and Cuban immigrants. Fundamental to the BEA idea was that while it was important to teach English to students, educators were to be mindful of students' first language as an asset to the educational system. The BEA has had many amendments leading up to the No Child Left Behind Act (formerly known as ESEA), which eliminated the word "bilingual" from the act. The act stated that programs should exist to help English language learners; however, it did not outline how to achieve English acquisition. For that reason, there are various models of Bilingual Education programs.

Bilingual Education Programs

Both documented and undocumented students should be able to take full advantage of Bilingual Education programs. According to the National Association of Bilingual Educators, the current goals for Bilingual Education are to (1) teach English, (2) foster academic achievement, (3) acculturate immigrants, (4) preserve a minority's linguistic and cultural heritage, (5) enable English speakers to learn a second language, (6) develop national language resources, or any combination of the above. Students who participate in the programs are now referred to as *English language learners* (ELLs).

Schools, districts, or states can choose from a variety of approaches towards Bilingual Education. Lynne T. Diaz-Rico and Kathryn Weed (2006) describe some of the approaches: In the "sink or swim" model students receive instruction only in English. Students need to have strong linguistic foundations in their first language to be able to succeed with such a model. There are various submodels of teaching English as a Second Language (ESL), including "pull out," "ESL period," "content-based ESL," and "sheltered instruction." The strategy with ESL is to teach English explicitly such as vocabulary, grammar, oral language, and spelling. The sub-model will determine the context and curriculum of teaching English. "Early Exit Transitional Bilingual Education" usually takes two to three years, and students are able to develop basic interpersonal communication skills (BICS). "Late Exit Transitional" or developmental bilingual education works on maintaining both English and the first language with emphasis on students' first language as well as heritage and culture. Finally, "Dual Immersion Bilingual Education" actively promotes bilingualism, biliteracy and biculturalism. Most of these programs work towards English proficiency.

Bilingual Education Standards

In order to have accountability for the programs, various organizations have developed standards. States and districts can select with which standards or organizations they will align themselves. The World-Class Instructional Design Assessment (WIDA) is one example of organizations that develop assessments for bilingual education programs. The WIDA consortium is a non-profit organization that extends over twenty-three states. WIDA was founded in 2002 and comes from the Wisconsin Center for Educational Research at the University of Wisconsin–Madison. WIDA has established English Language Proficiency (ELP) standards that help guide instruction for ELLs. The five standards focus on instructional language, language of language arts, language of mathematics, language of science, and language of social studies. WIDA also developed performance indicators to help determine appropriate level of instruction for ELLs; the levels are as follows: Level 1, Entering; Level 2, Beginning; Level 3, Developing; Level 4, Expanding; Level 5, Bridging; and Level 6, Reaching. Students have standards in four domains including writing, reading, speaking, and listening. School districts and states can adopt the WIDA standards.

English Only

There have also been propositions to directly attack the use of languages other than English in schools, with most of these coming from the English Only movement. This movement affected all students whose first language was not English including undocumented students. Ron Unz, Silicon Valley millionaire, believed that bilingual education wasn't effective because it used the students' first language. He also blamed bilingual programs for high dropout rates. Instead, he proposed to teach students only in English to learn English. He initiated three major campaigns to try to change Bilingual Education into English Only programs. In 1998, Unz sponsored proposition 227 in California called "English for the Children." Under this proposition, all instruction had to be delivered in English and no other language was allowed to be spoken or written in the classroom. Parents had an option to opt out of this program but were faced with many restrictions. Later in 2000, Unz was successful in passing Proposition 203 in Arizona. As in California, these laws affected students who had limited English proficiency. Two years later, in 2002, Unz succeeded in adding English Only to Massachusetts as a referendum in ballot question 2. Unz believed the best way for students to learn English was to be taught in English before teaching anything else (Ovando, Combs, & Collier 2006).

Anti-Immigrant Sentiment

More recently, there has been an anti-immigrant sentiment across the United States, made openly noticeable with Arizona's SB 1070 law. The law, which allows police to inquire about legal status if the person has been stopped for breaking another law, is considered by many to be anti-Latino immigrant., Although this law doesn't target English-language learners per se, it affects their families, which in turn affects them.

Furthermore, Arizona's Department of Education ordered school districts to remove non-native English-speaking teachers who had heavy accents or used improper English from classrooms with ELLs. Arizona's Department of Education has raised other concerns as pertains to ELLs. Arizona uses the Arizona English Language Learner Assessment (AZELLA) to evaluate English proficiency. Arizona has received much attention because Bilingual Education advocates have claimed that the AZELLA assessment would take ELL students who were not English proficient out of bilingual education programs, thus having students moved into English-only programs. The laws and initiatives that are taking place in Arizona reflect the anti-immigrant sentiment that is going across the United States. Some of these laws have direct impact on the teaching of English-language learners while others affect the families of ELLs.

Currently, there is the threat that more drastic measures will be taken in border towns, like Calexico, California. According to the local newspaper, the school district has considered the hiring of employees to verify the status of students prior to entering the school district (Nuñez, 2010). Other California districts are considering similar measures, such as the Mountain Empire School District east of San Diego. There are, however, some districts that are refusing to set resources towards this effort, including the Sweetwater Unified School District and the San Diego Unified School District. The anti-immigrant sentiment affects families and students alike.

Undocumented Students

English language learners (ELLs) who are undocumented are affected by the bilingual education programs and laws as well as the context of their education. According to federal law, all students are entitled to receive a free public education regardless of legal status. Also under federal law, it is illegal for school officials to ask students directly about their citizenship status. Some students may choose to self-disclose their legal status in efforts to find help and support to further their education. It may be common to find the students who are undocumented as students in Bilingual Education programs. Often, the students will trust their teachers with this information.

The greatest challenge with students who are undocumented may be motivation. When students know their legal status as undocumented, they may wonder what the future may have for them. If they don't see themselves as being able to access higher education or having the financial means to pay for higher education, they may give up at a younger age. One solution to this motivation may be the DREAM Act, which, if passed, would allow conditional citizenship for undocumented young people upon completing a college degree or two years of military service and fulfilling other requirements.

Gerardo Mancilla

See Also: Bilingualism; Deferred Action for Childhood Arrivals (DACA); DREAM Act; Education; Elementary Schools; English as a Second Language (ESL) Programs; English-Only Movement; High Schools; Limited English Proficiency (LEP); Policy and Political Action.

Further Reading

Diaz-Rico, Lynne T., & Kathryn Weed. 2006. *The Crosscultural, Language, and Academic Development Handbook: A Complete K-12 Reference Guide.* Chicago: Pearson.

National Association of Bilingual Educators (NABE). www.nabe.org.

Nuñez, Claudia. 2010. *La Opinion/News Report.* Translated by Jacob Simas and Elena Shore. "California Border Schools to Ask Students for Papers." http://newamericamedia.org/2010/08/california-border-schools-to-ask-students-for-papers.php.

Ovando, Carlos, Mary Carol Combs, and Virginia P. Collier. 2006. *Bilingual & ESL Classrooms.* New York: McGraw-Hill.

Teachers of English to Speakers of Other Language (TESOL). http://www.tesol.org/s_tesol/index.asp.

WIDA Consortium. http://www.wida.us/.

English-Only Movement

English-only philosophy argues that making English the official language of the nation will promote national unity, save tax dollars, and help immigrants to achieve the American Dream. The movement has been politically successful through legislation in more

Protesters carry signs and march in front of city hall in Farmers Branch, Texas, 2006, expressing their opposition to a measure that would, among other things, make English the city's official language. (AP/Wide World Photos)

than half of the states of the Union, where English has been established as the official language. Groups like U.S. English, Pro-English, and English First lobby to pass official English language legislation and advocate the elimination of bilingual programs and services. Nevertheless, supporters of this philosophy have found that it is easier to pass initiatives than to implement them.

It is deceptive to describe the United States simply as an English-speaking nation, since there are more than three hundred languages spoken throughout the country today. Nevertheless, the contemporary English-only movement has expanded mainly as a reaction to the spread of Spanish, which is by far the most widely spoken language after English. The growth of the Spanish-speaking population in the United States has been explosive in the past three decades in part due to immigration. Thus, the movement is perceived by some as anti-immigrant, and it is associated with the undocumented immigration debate. Currently, most undocumented immigrants come from Mexico and other Spanish-speaking countries in Latin America, but the majority of Hispanics in the United States are citizens or authorized residents.

Undocumented experiences and the diversity of languages in the United States have been closely related to three interrelated factors: historical developments, demographic trends, and the evolution of the market economy. The English-only movement and its prospects can also be viewed as a response to these forces and, in particular, as a reaction to the most threatening of all linguistic developments in U.S. history: the possibility of a de facto bilingual nation where Spanish becomes a widely operational language. For example, some English-only proponents critics have noted with alarm that, in cities with large Hispanic populations, bilingual households have a higher income than English-only households. Thus, a real dilemma for official English advocates is the growing number of Hispanic Americans and the enormous market they represent. Politicians want their votes and corporations want their dollars.

Ultimately, the English-Only Movement can be best understood in relation to the forces it opposes in the three abovementioned dimensions.

English-Only versus History

English is an immigrant language in the American continent and so is Spanish. However, it is inaccurate to say that Spanish is an immigrant language in the United States because it was spoken in what today is the southwestern United States centuries before the Anglo-Europeans arrived. Spanish was spoken in New Mexico when Santa Fe was first settled by Spaniards around 1610. Mexicans became the first official Spanish-speaking population of the United States by conquest, after the U.S.-Mexico War of 1846–1848. Amerindians living in the former Mexican territories also spoke numerous other languages and, unlike Native Americans in the United States, they had full citizenship rights under Mexican law. Ironically, Amerindians in the United States did not gain full citizenship until 1924, but U.S. government suppression of their political rights, religions and languages continued.

The Treaty of Guadalupe-Hidalgo ended the invasion of Mexico by the United States on February 2, 1848 and ceded half of the Mexican territory to the U.S. The treaty guaranteed that Mexicans who chose to remain in the land of their ancestors would have "the free enjoyment of their liberty and property," as well as "all the rights of citizens of the United States" (Article IX). Hence, since the former Mexican citizens did not speak English, they would rightly have the "liberty" and "rights" to speak and preserve their own language. Furthermore, since language is a form of cultural "property," Spanish and Amerindian languages from the former Mexican territories should be protected in consonance with this treaty.

The English-Only Movement faces many other historical challenges and moral dilemmas. Puerto Rico is a U.S. territory where Spanish is the majority language, while Puerto Ricans hold U.S. citizenship. New Mexico is a de facto bilingual state where 46 percent of the population is Hispanic. Hawaii is officially a bilingual state where Hawaiian is equal to English. Louisiana, a state with a unique multicultural and multilingual heritage, has a constitution that recognizes "the right of the people to preserve, foster, and promote their respective historic linguistic and cultural origins." These are examples of linguistic developments within the United States due to populations and languages that preceded the arrival of the United States. For the first time in history, one of these populations is growing faster than the English-speaking majority.

It is clear that Spanish is the only language that challenges the supremacy of English in the United States. Nevertheless, the importance of English as a U.S. language and as a lingua franca of the world is not endangered. On the contrary, Americans who speak Spanish and other languages represent invaluable "human capital" and reinforce our ability to understand and communicate with the world. The great majority of the states supporting English-Only laws have emerged in the past three decades as a response to astonishing demographic and economic transformations, while the forces of history silently continue to shape our future. In fact, some of the historical forces resisting the English-only movement emanate from the rights consecrated in the U.S. Constitution. The right of "free speech" involves language liberty as a tool of free expression, just as symbolic speech, which has been protected by the U.S. Supreme Court under the First Amendment. Additionally, the Equal Protection Clause of the Fourteenth Amendment can be violated when language is used as an excuse for discrimination based on national origin.

English-Only versus Demography

English and Spanish are the two most widely spoken languages in the Western Hemisphere. There are at least forty-three nations with substantial Spanish-speaking populations, where either Spanish is the majority language or where Spanish speakers constitute significant numbers. Spanish is the second most natively spoken language on Earth. It has been estimated that over half a billion people speak the language around the world. Native and bilingual speakers now make the United States the second largest Spanish-speaking country on Earth. Critics ardently argue that Spanish is not a legitimate language in the land of Faulkner and Hemingway. However, the U.S. Constitution does not establish an official national language, and a constitutional amendment establishing a national language appears continually more improbable.

For decades, Hispanics have been the fastest growing minority in the United States. In 2010, there were at least fifty counties in the United States where the majority population was Hispanic. Census projections show that, by 2050, Hispanic Americans will constitute 30 percent of the U.S. population with over 132.8 million people (U.S. Census Bureau, 2012). In the 2008 presidential election, Hispanic Americans who voted represented an increase of 47 percent from the previous presidential race, or a growth of two million voters. The U.S. Census has revealed that in only eighteen years, between 1990 and 2008, the U.S. population who speak Spanish at home increased from 17 to 35 million. By 2010, 37 million spoke Spanish (U.S. Census Bureau, 2012). This figure does not include Hispanic children younger than five, bilingual citizens, and Hispanics who prefer English. These changes are very significant and will have economic, political, and linguistic repercussions. As these trends evolve, English-only policies will appear increasingly hostile to a large portion of the U.S. population and contradictory to the U.S. civil and human rights tradition.

The U.S. news and entertainment media is a clear indicator of the demographic transformations in the country. Univision and Telemundo are among the largest Spanish television broadcasters in the world and compete with English broadcasters. Similarly, there are more Spanish radio stations in California than in all Central American countries combined. Furthermore, Spanish has rapidly transformed from a private language, only spoken at home, to a public one. A *de facto* recognition of Spanish as a public language in the United States is evident in political speeches, public services, and business practices. At the same time, large numbers of young non-Hispanics are learning Spanish, encompassing over half of all college enrollments in languages other than English. Meanwhile research shows that immigrants—both authorized and undocumented—are eager to learn English.

English-Only versus the Market

In 2001, it was estimated that undocumented Mexican immigrants alone contributed at least $154 billion to the U.S. Gross Domestic Product (GDP). Comparatively, this means that the size of the *undocumented Mexican economy* in the United States is larger than any Central American economy and many other small nations. Additionally, the buying power of all Hispanics in the United States is about one trillion dollars. In 2007, 500 major American companies spent $4.5 billion in Spanish advertisement. At the same time, according to the U.S. Department of Commerce, Hispanic-owned businesses grew by more than double the national rate between 2002 and 2007, generating economic growth and employment. For corporations, there is no doubt Hispanics will have a growing impact on American tastes, fashion, entertainment, communications, and other sectors of the economy. Language cannot be the exception.

The Spanish-speaking population in the United States not only represents a vast internal market, but a competitive advantage in the global economy as a link with the Hispanic world. Mexico not only is the third commercial partner of the United States, but it consumes more U.S. goods and services than China. In addition to the large international Hispanic market, there are important commercial allies of the United States that are not traditionally considered Spanish-speaking nations, but have large

Spanish-speaking populations, such as Belgium, Brazil, France, Morocco, Portugal, and the United Kingdom. Many Americans use Spanish as a lingua franca when English is not spoken in international markets. From this perspective, language skills are a form of human capital that we can use to our advantage, while a monolingual—English-only—population would be less competitive in global markets.

In 2010, a conservative gubernatorial candidate in Alabama who aggressively advocated English-only for his state had to learn a hard lesson. Alabama has 358 international firms that include Mercedes-Benz, Hyundai and Honda. Many foreign professionals working for these businesses, as well as their spouses, are multicultural and do not necessarily speak perfect English. Thus business people and politicians alike opposed the campaign as bad business for Alabama. The candidate lost in preliminary elections. Although his English-only campaign was in reaction to the growth of the Hispanic population in the state, it became clear that the global economy can be a challenge for this kind of movement. In contrast, California is a state that already resembles what the United States will look like in forty years. In October 2010, California's gubernatorial candidates engaged in the first ever Spanish-language debate, broadcast statewide by Univision with simultaneous interpretation. The political economy of demographics is inescapable.

Ultimately, the great majority of immigrants, whether authorized or undocumented, understand the economic value of the English language. The Pew Hispanic Center has found that about 90 percent of second-generation members of immigrant families speak English. Immigrants expect their children to learn English and, by the third generation, their preference for English is predominant, including immigrants from Spanish-speaking countries. At the same time, as Spanish gains legitimacy and is no longer treated as a foreign language, the United States will become a stronger nation in harmony with history, demography, and the free market economy.

Ricardo Castro-Salazar

See Also: Bilingualism; Economics; Enclaves; English as a Second Language (ESL) Programs; English Language Learners (ELL); Limited English Proficiency (LEP); Multicultural Education

Further Reading

Castro, Max J. 1997. "The Politics of Language in Miami." In Pierrette Hondagneu-Sotelo Romero and Vilma Ortiz, *Challenging Fronteras: Structuring Latina and Latino Lives in the U.S.* New York: Routledge.

Dueñas Gonzalez, Roseann, and Ildiko Melis, eds. 2000/2001. *Language Ideologies: Critical Perspectives on the Official English Movement,* Volumes I and II. Urbana, Illinois: National Council of Teachers of English.

Hinojosa-Ojeda, Raul. 2001. *Comprehensive Migration Policy Reform in North America: The Key to Sustainable and Equitable Economic Integration.* Los Angeles, CA: North American Integration and Development Center, University of California.

Lippi-Green, Rosina. 1997. *English with an Accent: Language, Ideology and Discrimination in the United States.* London: Routledge.

Peña, Maritza. 1997–1998. "English-Only Laws and the Fourteenth Amendment: Dealing with Pluralism in a Nation Divided by Xenophobia." *The University of Miami Inter-American Law Review* 29.1/2:349–371.

Schmid, Carol L. 2001. *The Politics of Language: Conflict, Identity and Cultural Pluralism in Comparative Perspective.* New York: Oxford University Press.

U.S. Census Bureau. 2010. *Facts for Features. Hispanic Heritage Month 2010: Sept. 15–Oct. 15.* http://www.Census.gov/newsroom/releases/archives/facts_for_features_special_editions/cb10–ff17.html

U.S. Census Bureau. 2012. *Facts for Features. Hispanic Heritage Month 2010: Sept. 15–Oct. 15.* http://www.Census.gov/newsroom/releases/archives/facts_for_features_special_editions/cb12-ff19.html

Wiley, Terrence G., Jin Sook Lee, and Russell W. Rumberger, eds. 2009. *The Education of Language Minority Immigrants in the United States (Bilingual Education and Bilingualism).* London: Multilingual Matters.

Exclusion

The term "exclusion" as it relates to immigration has been used in a variety of ways. Under the authority granted by the Immigration and Nationality Act (INA), any customs or border patrol officer may ask any person seeking entry into the United States for proof of that person's admissibility, either proof of citizenship or possession of a valid visa. If the authority fails to obtain such evidence, then there are "grounds for exclusion." Exclusion is different from removal (formal deportation) because with exclusion, there was no entry into the United States. One of the most famous uses of the idea of "exclusion" came with the Chinese Exclusion Act of 1882, where Asians were excluded from those groups determined to be eligible to immigrate to the United States, and from obtaining citizenship, even if they were born in the country. More recently, the proposed comprehensive immigration reform bill under consideration in the U.S. Congress in 2013 (S. 744) is predicted to "exclude" those who entered after December 31, 2011, from any path to citizenship. Whether the term "exclusion" is grounded in the nation's legal framework or not, there are far-reaching and long-term sociological repercussions for belonging to an excluded group, which can be based on legal status (i.e. undocumented), or race (Chinese, or Asian).

The concept of exclusion is used to characterize social disadvantage in contexts where certain groups of people, usually defined as "other" by socially dominant classes, are prevented from access to rights and resources. These rights and resources, such as voting, healthcare, education, or due process, are seen by social scientists as key to full social integration in a given society. Common socially excluded groups are defined in terms of race, gender, economics, language, religion, culture, nationality, age, sexual orientation, or physical ability. However, as practices of exclusion often have roots in xenophobia (fear of the other), many who are not undocumented but share phenotypic, linguistic, or cultural traits with undocumented immigrants also feel the effects of social exclusion.

The exclusion of immigrants can be seen on many levels of policy and society within the United States. The very definition of political borders can be seen as an act of exclusion—demarcating who is in, and who is out. Although this may seem innocuous, the barricading of certain borders over others may be evidence of the wish to exclude some more than others. The heavy fortification of the southern border of the United States versus the northern border can be understood as an effort to exclude those from the south more than those from the north.

Federally set quotas for the number of immigrants allowed into the country per year can be seen through the lens of exclusion, whereby the waiting line for the working poor can be decades longer than it is for the educated or for skilled laborers. Notable historic examples of exclusionary immigration policies include the Chinese Exclusion act of 1882, which was a race-based immigration act passed federally to halt Chinese immigration; the Anarchist Exclusion Act of 1903, which banned those deemed to be anarchists, epileptics, beggars, and importers of prostitutes; and the Johnson-Reed Act of 1924 which limited the annual number of new immigrants from any country to 2 percent of the number of people from that country who were living in the United States already as of the Census of 1890.

Undocumented immigrants living within the United States face classic examples of exclusion. In 1994, voters in California passed Proposition 187, banning undocumented immigrants from accessing public education, healthcare, and other social services in the state. The national healthcare legislation passed in 2010 (the Affordable Care Act, often referred to as "ObamaCare"), predicated on the idea of "health care for all," has in effect and for political reasons excluded undocumented immigrants from coverage.

The exclusion of immigrants from accessing healthcare, education, or welfare, while usually predicated on the idea that immigrants are outsiders, often has social effects that spill over into the society at large. The exclusion of immigrants from basic rights and services often denies them basic human rights. The denial of healthcare to immigrants can pose an epidemiological risk to the entire society. Children of undocumented parents often face extreme challenges although they may be full citizens. Healthcare providers and law enforcement personnel may be forced to choose between breaking the law and violating professional ethical or safety guidelines because of laws set up to exclude immigrants.

Those who experience social exclusion not only face practical and economic challenges, but are deprived of recognition and social value, even facing stigmatization. Though difficult on a personal level, these experiences are often damaging on a social level, and are passed down from one generation to the next. Social exclusion, like that of undocumented immigrants, can become a detrimental spiral whereby the original structural violence of exclusion can manifest generations later in the form of self-exclusion. Many traditionally excluded groups, such as African Americans and Hispanics, have very low voter turnout. Although a complex issue, it can be understood in part in terms of exclusion and its social effects.

The core issue in practices of exclusion is the creation of different rights for different sectors of a population. Exclusionary immigration laws and social practices intimately relate to projects of nationalism, defining who is part of the nation-state, and who is "other." These definitions are culturally constructed and tend to change through time depending on the contemporary concerns of the society in question.

Robin Reineke

See Also: Assimilation; Barriers to Health; Dillingham Report; Employer Sanctions; LGBT Immigrants without Documentation; Social Interaction and Integration; State Legislation; *Strangers in the Land;* Workers' Rights; Xenophobia.

Further Reading

Genova, Nicholas P. de. 2002. "Migrant 'Illegality' and Deportability in Everyday Life." *Annual Review of Anthropology* 31:419–447.

Inda, Johnathan Xavier. 2006. *Targeting Immigrants: Government, Technology, and Ethics.* Malden, MA: Blackwell Publishing.

Johnson, Kevin R. 2002. "Race and the Immigration Laws: The Need for Critical Inquiry." In *Crossroads, Directions, and a New Critical Race Theory,* ed. Francisco Valdes, Jerome McCristal Culp, and Angela P. Harris. Philadelphia: Temple University Press.

Quesada, James, Laurie Kain Hart, and Philippe Bourgois. 2011. "Structural Vulnerability and Health: Latino Migrant Laborers in the United States." *Medical Anthropology* 30: 339–362.

Expedited Removal

Section 235(b)1(A)(iii) of the U.S. Immigration and Nationality Act (INA) grants U.S. Border Patrol agents the authority to remove under certain conditions certain immigrants from the United States without a hearing or review by an immigration court. This is referred to as Expedited Removal, an administrative procedure that is different from court-ordered deportation. Through the expedited removal process, border patrol agents are authorized to determine an immigrant's admissibility into the United States. The most common way involves an investigation as to whether the apprehended immigrants possess any document (such as an immigrant visa or border crossing card) that would prove that they were legally admitted into the country. If a detainee has provided documents and those are determined to be false, Section 212(a)6(C) of the INA authorizes the agent to charge the immigrant with fraud or willful misrepresentation, and this makes the immigrant inadmissible and subject to expedited removal. Another reason for not granting admission into the United States is if the detainee has been previously deported or removed, or has a criminal record. Only those immigrants who have not been admitted into the United States prior to their apprehension, who have not been previously removed, and those encountered by a Border Patrol agent within one hundred air miles of the international border can qualify for expedited removal proceedings. Those with a criminal history or those with other immigration violations (such as multiple entries without authorization or smuggling violations) do not qualify.

There are several conditions specified under the INA that allow certain immigrants relief from the expedited removal proceedings. For example, if the detained immigrant

Expedited Removal is an administrated procedure that allows U.S. Border Patrol agents the authority to remove certain immigrants from the United States without a hearing or review by an immigration court. Here, a Customs and Border Patrol (CBP) officer uses high-tech equipment as she scans for fraudulent documents. The U.S. Border Patrol and the CBP are a branch of the Department of Homeland Security. (Department of Homeland Security/James Tourtellotte)

indicates to the agent an intention to apply for asylum, or expresses a fear of persecution, a fear of torture, or a fear of returning to their country of origin, an agent is prohibited from proceeding with the expedited removal.

The Border Patrol agent also needs to reasonably establish that the immigrants detained have not been physically present in the United States continuously for a fourteen-day period prior to the date of the arrest before proceeding with expedited removal. Hence, most of the expedited removals occur on the border or very close to the border. However, not all immigrants that fall under the above conditions qualify for expedited removal. Unaccompanied minors and Cubans are not subject to expedited removal proceedings, as well as certain Guatemalans and El Salvadorans who can be classified as refugees and entered the United States before 1990. Persons who appear to have mental health issues or a diminished mental capacity also do not qualify.

The goal of the expedited removal process is to accelerate the processing of those immigrants who, because they have entered the country without an immigrant visa or other official entry documents, are legally inadmissible. The process is a way of saving on the amount of resources it takes to formally bring charges against immigrants and process them through an already burdened legal system. The resources that would be affected are detention space, transportation that would be needed to move them between processing stations and detention centers, personnel needed in processing functions, and the cost of immigration court staff, attorneys, marshals, interpreters, and judges.

Once it has been determined that an immigrant detainee qualifies for expedited removal, a "Notice and Order of Expedited Removal" form is filled out. The form attests that the detainee has been found to be "inadmissible to the United States" for the lack of a valid immigrant visa, reentry permit, border crossing identification card, or other valid entry documents, and has "entered into the United States illegally with the intent to reside in the United States."

Criticism of the expedited removal procedure is that it is highly discretionary as the border patrol agent is often the only person who sees and interviews the detainee during the short period in which he needs to make the determination for expedited removal. In busy border patrol sectors (such as San Diego and Tucson where daily apprehensions can reach anywhere between six hundred and eight hundred), an overloaded immigration enforcement system and overworked officers may limit the time and training needed to recognize the circumstances that would require the referral of an immigrant's case for a credible fear interview or judicial review. In other words, an agent's determination in the field virtually takes the place of a hearing before an immigration court judge, and the conditions are far from ideal for making such a determination. Moreover, research on the border has confirmed that although immigrants may have a previous apprehension, making them ineligible for expedited removal, they are released.

It is a widely held belief that official apprehension numbers reported by the U.S. Border Patrol are commonly inflated due to repeat attempts on the part of destitute immigrants to cross into the United States in search of better life. In other words, any single migrant may try to enter any number of times, all of which are counted. Under the expedited removal process, many immigrants are caught and repeatedly released, only to be caught again in an endless game of "cat and mouse." The adoption of measures to seal the border such as expedited removal has been one of many ways that border enforcement agencies have tried to cope with the exponential growth of migrants crossing the border since the 1990s when neoliberal trade agreements between the United States and Mexico ruined subsistence-based agricultural economies in the rural parts of Mexico. For example, according to the Department of Homeland Security website, the Tucson Border Patrol sector in Arizona (which led all other border patrol sectors with 439,090 apprehensions in 2005) has also had the most number of expedited removals. Indeed, many migrants may be apprehended and released several times before being charged with "illegal re-entry after removal." When found guilty of this charge, migrants may serve sentences, after which they are deported. Even so, of those migrants who are removed or deported, it has been estimated that over one third reentered the United States without authorization. The vast majority of the detainees in Arizona's immigrant detention centers (roughly between 75–90 percent) are serving sentences for illegal re-entry after removal. Moreover, even through progressively longer prison terms are imposed on those who are re-apprehended based on the number of times they have been charged with this violation (Alvarado 2004), the economic hardships appear to outweigh the risk of serving longer prison terms if re-apprehended. As long as the economic conditions that prompted their migration to begin with remain the same, reattempting to cross will be a viable option for migrants.

Anna Ochoa O'Leary

See Also: Deportation; Operation Streamline; Ports of Entry; Repatriation; *United States v. Brignoni-Ponce;* U.S. Border Patrol.

Further Reading

Alvarado, Jeanette E. 2004. "The Federal Consequences of Criminal Convictions: Illegal Reentry after Removal." Unpublished manuscript prepared for the State Bar of Arizona.

Department of Homeland Security. 2005. *Yearbook of Immigration Statistics: Data on Enforcement Actions.* Table 36, available at http://www.dhs.gov/ximgtn/statistics/. Accessed 3/11/07.

Donato, Katherine M., Brandon Wagner, and Evelyn Patterson. 2008. "The Cat and Mouse Game at the Mexico-U.S. Border: Gendered Patterns and Recent Shifts." *International Migration Review* 42.2:330–359.

Nevins, Joseph. 2002. *Operation Gatekeeper: The Rise of the "Illegal Alien" and the Remaking of the U.S.-Mexico Boundary.* New York: Routledge.

F

Faith-Based Organizations

Faith-based organizations (FBOs) are a type of non-government organization that delivers services to multiple populations and operate under a religious framework. These organizations can be associated with a variety of religious traditions, and are often engaged in addressing a variety of pressing social issues. For example, many FBOs have come to engage in assisting undocumented immigrants with access to health care or other humanitarian needs out of a sense of religious obligation to help others. Religious discourses can also influence how some FBOs see poverty and injustice as a hindrance to access assistance. Catholic Charities, for example, has engaged in debates on healthcare reform, arguing that poverty and the way in which poverty—a condition that affects many undocumented immigrants—prevents all people from developing their full potential as human beings. American Friends Service Committee has been very vocal in drawing attention to the violence and injustice that immigrants are subjected to. Catholic Charities also provides assistance to refugees and has been vocal in advocating for immigration reform. Some FBOs, such as evangelical and Protestant organizations, provide direct services to undocumented immigrants as a way to increase proselytizing efforts. These organizations may provide clothing, shelter, food, health care screening and "free clinics," and referral services, as well as ask recipients of these benefits to participate and become part of the religious community. In this way, FBOs offer communities that may provide a sense of social solidarity and emotional support to those who may feel alienated and excluded from the wider society.

Because of the political nature of undocumented immigration in the United States, some of the work of FBOs ventures outside of what many might consider the role of providing spiritual guidance to their communities. For example, South Side Presbyterian Church in Tucson, Arizona follows a tradition set in the 1970s to provide sanctuary to refugees fleeing the wars in Central America by allowing and protecting day workers looking for work to congregate on their property in a state particularly hostile to undocumented immigrants. *Fe y Justicia* (Faith and Justice) in the immigrant sanctuary city of Houston, Texas organizes "know your rights" workshops to help day laborers protect themselves from arrest and from wage theft. They also work with agencies to help workers recoup unpaid wages from unscrupulous employers. Also in Houston, Casa San Diego offers shelter for the needy and homeless, many of whom are immigrants and their families (Zwick and Zwick, 2010). Yet others, such as Humane Borders (working under the auspices of First

Christian Church) and No More Deaths/*No Mas Muertes* (working under the auspices of South Side Presbyterian Church), both based in Tucson Arizona, have come under criticism from anti-immigrant groups and law enforcement agencies for their attempts to mitigate the risk of death for undocumented immigrants who have crossed into the United States through the area. Humane Borders is well known for putting out life-saving water tanks in the desert for immigrants to find, and No Mas Muertes conducts searches and provides first aid stations for migrants lost in the desert wilderness.

FBOs can operate both internationally and domestically. Examples of FBOs in the United States include Catholic Charities, the Salvation Army, the Jewish Federations of North America, and the Islamic Center for North American Relief. An example of a FBO with international reach in its efforts to alleviate migrant suffering is the Jesuit Network. Jesuit Refugee Service (JRS) International, whose mission is to accompany, serve and advocate on behalf of refugees and other forcibly displaced persons, works globally in 100 countries.

FBOs that specifically focus on immigrant or refugee services in the United States include Catholic Charities, Justice for Immigrants, and the Interfaith Immigration Coalition. FBOs are arguably adept at providing services to specific populations because they often have the necessary resources and infrastructure, and are also able to connect with some of their new parishioners' spiritual beliefs and integrate modern medicine with spiritual healing. However, some critiques of FBOs have arisen as they have gained influence in offering more social services to needy populations in the United States. These critiques range from their effectiveness in health care delivery services to larger examinations of how FBOs relieve governments of responsibilities to address coverage gaps in health care and various social services.

Since FBOs often consist of multiple congregations under an umbrella office, a sizeable number of people can be brought together through one FBO. This allows for FBOs to develop a large base of supporters, who may feel compelled to volunteer with the organization since it operates around their religious value system. Many FBOs are successful because of this access to an expansive network of willing volunteers, who are inclined to volunteer their time because of shared convictions. Furthermore, in some states, such as Florida, volunteering health providers can circumvent liability concerns when offering medical services in conjunction with a nonprofit organization that assists needy populations, demonstrating one of the ways in which certain policies encourage volunteerism through FBOs.

In the United States, the influence of FBOs has grown through other policy measures, including the establishment of the White House Office of Faith-Based and Community Initiatives in 2001 (later renamed the White House Office of Faith-Based and Neighborhood Partnerships in 2009), and through the charitable choice section of the 1996 Personal Responsibility and Work Opportunity Reconciliation Act. These two policies allowed for government funds to be directed to FBOs engaging in social services and encouraged FBOs to seek public funding and charitable donations to expand their roles as social service providers. These policies also represented new ways in which a secular government interacts with religious organizations to address social concerns.

FBOs provide an array of services to marginalized populations such as undocumented immigrants, including medical and dental care. Some FBO clinics that serve immigrant populations operate in multiple locations in one region. For example, an FBO clinic's staff may rotate and operate on different days of the week at farm labor sites, migrant housing sites, or other sites where immigrant labor is used. Many health-oriented programs from FBOs have a specific focus on prevention education, health maintenance, cardiovascular health, and cancer. Some organizations also provide screenings and diagnostic tests for hypertension or other detectible health problems. Oral health is not as well represented and may not be considered as much of a priority as other types of health care, but poor oral health can lead to greater systemic health outcomes, such as cardiovascular disease. Some organizations have invested in mobile dental clinics that have the ability to travel to specific communities where transportation may be a problem.

Like other non-government organizations, FBOs can fill service gaps that are not addressed by governments and can sometimes improve health outcomes for populations like undocumented immigrants. While filling service gaps may provide assistance and care to marginalized populations, the increased role of FBOs allows for governments to ignore the problem of lack of access to services rather than confront it directly. Other critiques of FBOs include some organizations' shortsighted engagements with providing care. In many ways, FBOs are ill equipped to recognize specific historical, political, and economic forces that impact immigrants' ability to access care. To become better adept at solving health disparities among immigrants, FBOs may need to focus their attention on how social factors influence health, such as living in environmentally harmful areas and earning low wages that constrain the ability to purchase nutritious food.

Nolan Kline

See Also: Advocacy; American Friends Service Committee; Amnesty International; Arizona; Community Concerns; Sanctuary Cities and Secure Communities; Sanctuary Movement.

Further Reading

Angrosino, Michael V. 1996. "The Catholic Church and U. S. Health Care Reform." *Medical Anthropology Quarterly* 10.1:3–19.

Brondo, Keri Vacanti, and Tara Hefferan, eds. 2010. Theme Issue: "Intersections of Faith and Development in Local and Global Contexts." *NAPA Bulletin* 33.

Castañeda, Heide. 2010. "Im/migration and Health: Conceptual, Methodological, and Theoretical Propositions for Applied Anthropology." *NAPA Bulletin* 34.10:6–27.

DeHaven, Mark J., Irvy B. Hunter, Laura Wilder, James Wlatron, and Jarett Berry. 2004. "Health Programs in Faith-Based Organizations: Are They Effective?" *American Journal of Public Health* 94.6:1030–1036.

Elisha, Omri. 2008. "Moral Ambitions of Grace: The Paradox of Compassion and Accountability in Evangelical Faith-based Activism." *Cultural Anthropology* 23.1:154–198.

Zwick, Mark, and Zwick, Louise. 2010. *Mercy without Borders: The Catholic Worker and Immigration.* Mahwah, N.J.: Paulist Press.

Families

Families are the most basic of social units. Families are groupings of individuals who may be but are not necessarily co-sanguinely related, that is, they may be related by virtue of marriage (e.g. in-laws, stepchildren) and ritual (e.g. *compadres and comadres, ahijados/as),* organized into the most basic of cooperative and decision-making structures.

Undocumented immigrant families encounter many challenges in the process of adjusting to daily life in their host culture, and more than those families that do not have to contend with immigration status. The migration process itself is stressful on the family regardless of the logistical methods chosen to enter the host country. The border crossing is risky and dangerous, which places all individual family members at heightened psychological and physical stress. The immigration experience or trauma associated with the migration process can place individual family members at risk for mental health or behavioral problems, which then affect family functioning.

For unauthorized immigrants, crossing the border most often includes hiring a "coyote" or smuggler (someone to assist) in the crossing and/or transportation from the border to a final destination. The majority of undocumented families crossing the border are low income or suffering from poverty in their home countries, which is often the impetus for migrating. The price of hiring "coyotes" is expensive, usually costing the family thousands of dollars, causing them to begin their new life under financial constraints. Financial stress can have direct negative effects on family dynamics and strained family relationships.

Due to the high cost of emigrating, families often do not migrate together but rather in stages. One or both parents will migrate first and after a period of time send for their children. However, research indicates that the traditional practice where women migrate to reunite with their husbands is drastically changing. In so doing, women leave other family members behind, primarily children, in an endless cycle. Thus, as women embark on the journey to spousal reunification, they are simultaneously being separated from other family members by migrating. Family reunification and family separation are thus often simultaneous experiences. This dynamic incorporates the additional stress of family separations and reunifications, bringing with it feelings of grief, guilt, resentment and loss. However, it also illustrates how the separation-reunification dynamic might over the years and several generations leave in its wake a transnational family form that facilitates movement between sending and receiving communities. The inability to move across borders due to greater immigration enforcement has the effect of keeping family members in the United States for longer periods, resulting in mixed-status families. Mixed-status families are those where the immigration status of at least one member is different from the others. Increasingly, immigrant families may be composed of U.S. citizen children of undocumented parents (Fix and Zimmermann, 2001).

Once in the United States, parents have the difficult task of raising their children within the context of an unfamiliar culture. Parents may not be familiar with local family laws that govern corporal punishment of children for example. Lack of knowledge of local laws can lead parents to being charged with domestic violence or child abuse and neglect, causing disruption in normal family functioning.

Undocumented immigrant families often experience social isolation due to their fear of deportation. This social isolation, coupled with a loss of extended family left behind in the home country, leaves families with little to no external help in coping with familial hardships. Combined with diminishing access to publically-supported safety net programs, immigrant families—including first generation immigrant children and second generation children of immigrant parents—also face critical challenges for overcoming dim prospects for reducing poverty and deprivation. Undocumented families are fearful of seeking any form of community aid including financial and social support services for fear of their undocumented status being reported to the authorities. At the same time, these conditions are both learning and emotional processes that rely heavily on family cohesion, and family connectedness can provide important resources, care, affection, and psychological support for these critical periods of adjustment and coping (Vidal de Haymes et al., 2011).

In adjusting to their host culture, immigrant families must reconcile the differences between the two cultures and redefine themselves accordingly. This process is known as acculturation and is critical in the formation of well-adjusted families. This adjustment process places stress on the family unit that often translates into negative behavioral expression, most often by the adolescents. Children who are being raised in a foreign country tend to experience high levels of acculturation but their parents, who often have limited interactions with mainstream culture, do not. This difference often causes conflict especially in terms of parent/child communication and bonding. The breakdown in communication places adolescents at greater risk of engaging in high risk behaviors. Different levels of acculturation compromise the family functioning, which can lead to adolescent behavioral problems. Research shows that more acculturated adolescents have more risk for externalizing behavior problems than their less acculturated peers. A traditional learning curve explains how youth acculturate at a more accelerated pace than their parents who tend to hold on to customs and traditions. This difference leads to a culturally diverse environment in the household where youth are pushing autonomy and parents family unity, resulting in children's loss of emotional/social support and parents' loss of authority. These intergenerational conflicts are compounded by intercultural conflict. Language brokering has been related to differential acculturation which in turn has been associated with compromised family functioning.

For immigrant families, having to make major adjustments to their new lives in the host country often involves changes in family roles and family structure. One instance where this occurs is when children learn English before their parents do and then are placed in situations where they must be the interpreters. The children in this case become the cultural broker for the parents. Parents rely on their children to help them with daily activities such as banking and grocery shopping or more complex situations such as doctor's appointments or meetings with attorneys. This language dependency disrupts the family hierarchy by placing children in a leadership position, resulting in a loss of parental authority that can contradict traditional family values. This dynamic can lead to increased rigidity and discipline by the parent to overcompensate and thus creates tension and often rebellion.

Another instance in fluctuation of traditional family roles is that women will work outside the home, often for the first time. In some cases, due to the nature of the man's work, the woman may at certain times be the sole wage earner, causing disruption to the traditional idea that it is the man's duty to be the breadwinner. Additionally, the fact that the woman is earning can be a source of empowerment for her that can lead to greater confidence and make her feel entitled to more power and/or responsibility in the home. In some families this dynamic can feel threatening to the male head of the family, causing negative reactions that disrupt the rest of the household.

Marcella Hurtado Gómez

See Also: Acculturation; Acculturation Stress; Assimilation; Children; Family Economics; Family Reunification; Family Structure; Gender Roles; Mixed-Status Families; Single Men.

Further Reading

Fix, Michael, and Wendy Zimmermann. 2001. "All under One Roof: Mixed-Status Families in an Era of Reform." *International Migration Review* 35.2:397–419.

Gonzales, N. A., J. Deardorff, D. Formoso, A. Barr, and M. J. Barrera. 2006. "Family Mediators of the Relation between Acculturation and Adolescent Mental Health." *Family Relations* 55:308–330.

Santisteban, D. A., J. A. Muir-Malcolm, V. B. Mitrani, and J. Szapocznik. 2002. "Integrating the Study of Ethnic Culture and Family Psychology Intervention Science." In H. A. Liddle, D. A. Santisteban, R. F. Levant, J. H. Bray, eds., *Family Psychology: Science-based Interventions* 331–351. Washington, DC: American Psychological Association.

Suarez-Orozco, Carola, and Marcelo Suarez-Orozco. *Children of Immigration.* 2002. Cambridge, MA: Harvard University Press.

Vidal de Haymes, Maria, Jessica Martone, Lina Muñoz, and Susan Grossman. 2011. "Family Cohesion and Social Support: Protective Factors for Acculturation Stress Among Low-Acculturated Mexican Migrants." *Journal of Poverty* 15:1–24.

Family Economics

Undocumented immigrant families have become among the most vulnerable populations in the United States subject to abuse by the state due to harsh immigration policies and state-enforced deportation regimes, by employers who exploit their labor, and co-ethnics who scam them for quick fixes to documentation problems. Families too have become sites of considerable conflict and vulnerability as undocumented men and women tend to live in mixed-status families creating complex hierarchies of privilege and subordination across their own nationality.

Traditionally, most scholars perceived the labor and wages of immigrant men as the primary source of family income, ignoring the emotional, reproductive, and wage labor that women do on behalf of their families. Today, we know that an understanding of

Mexican migrant family stands after been detained in the desert north of Sasabe, Arizona, October, 2003. The U. S. government estimates of the number of undocumented Mexican migrants in the United States rose from 2 million in 1990 to 4.8 million in 2000. In 2012, this population was estimated to be 11.7 million. Most immigrants come to the United States in search of better opportunities to support their families. (AP Photo/Jaime Puebla)

family economics must recognize the work of both men and women, and often children and other household members, who work for wages to provide for their families, and the work that many of these wage earners do in both sending and receiving communities. Family economic activity also includes participation in both formal and informal sectors of the labor market, and it is not unusual for any family member to have more than one job, since many immigrant and undocumented workers are underemployed.

To fully address the topic of family economics one must be aware of the vulnerabilities faced by immigrant families both prior to and post-migration as these issues are closely related to family economics.

Immigration scholars have observed that the twin forces of the state and economy shape family economics in a profound way. We know that the structural inequalities produced by a range of globalization policies—such as economic integration under trade agreements and neoliberal policies—have created the conditions for use of migration as a primary family survival economic strategy for families across the globe. Evidence suggests that migration as an income-generating strategy for families strapped for cash has been used by a range of social classes and groups in Latin America, Africa, and Asia. Different forms of migration are used to meet family needs. Some families may use internal migration as a way to increase diminishing family budgets. In Latin America, for example, there is evidence to suggest that families have allowed (some may say encouraged) young single women—working daughters—to leave peasant communities to procure income-generating activity. In China, internal migration is also an income-generating activity with severe repercussions for those who migrate, given strict laws about rural to urban migration. Men, women, and families that migrate, from the rural countryside to urban centers become "undocumented" workers within their own country because of strict state controls of internal immigration to cities. In other words, in order to avoid this, rural to urban migrants may lack the documentation necessary to provide the proof that they have followed the regulations (thus are "undocumented"), and as a consequence may be excluded from housing, education, and other social services that require this proof, thereby adding considerable stress to family life. Regional and international migrations are also used to address family economic needs in Latin America, Asia, and Africa. Women and men in different types of family arrangements migrate in search of employment, to provide emotional or family support for families already abroad, or simply in some cases to escape persecution and oppression.

Immigrant men and women in diverse family arrangements and from a range of nationalities have become part of what sociologists have called transnational families on the move. Researchers have documented that an important dimension of immigrant family economics (regardless of documentation status) is the multiple responsibilities falling on meager wages for immigrant families. Immigrant men and women must provide for themselves and for their families left behind, straining already meager family wages and resources. Because immigrant men and women find themselves in occupations that do not pay high wages, their ability to provide for themselves and the families left behind is seriously compromised. Failure to provide for the families results in marital and familial conflict creating instability and emotional stress. For example, research among Mexican undocumented immigrants has shown that long-term family separation of husbands and wives has led to a reorganization of gender roles between men and women. Husbands, once in the United States, must learn to do a lot of the gendered work to support their own living conditions. Wives who have been left behind become wage earners as a way to support their families. Some use migration as a way to keep their families together.

The family economics of single undocumented working mothers deserve some attention here as they too are vulnerable to exploitation and abuse. They, like other immigrant families, have to meet their own economic needs here and their family's economic and emotional needs in their countries of origin. Recent research has documented the struggles for working mothers to both provide economically and emotionally since women continue to see themselves responsible for the well-being of their children, adding a great deal of stress to an already fragile existence.

Securing the basic economic needs of shelter, food, transportation and health care places undocumented immigrant families in a precarious social condition with serious consequences for every family member. Research has shown how for undocumented families in agricultural work, children are seen as income earners for the family. As soon as they are able to help parents in some common agricultural task, they too become wage earners in order to meet family needs. This has serious consequences for the future educational prospects of immigrant children since some may be pulled from school to work alongside their parents. For migrant families who rely solely on seasonal crop labor, children are pulled from schools and moved around the country. The social consequences for children are many, but most principally early school desertion and lack of interest in school. For families in urban centers, once children reach working age, they too are encouraged to work and to help with family expenses. This survival strategy has exacerbated problems of retention and high school graduation rates of young Latinos around the nation.

There is another dimension of family economics that must be addressed here, namely the increasing role of immigrant women as primary breadwinners. We know that women's ability to earn wages gives them some measure of decision making power within their families and may demand more participation from men in parenting activities. For undocumented immigrant women, the result of their participation in the workforce is mixed, partly because their undocumented status adds vulnerability to their living conditions. Some are subject to exploitation in the labor force and thus are unable to bring home the wages to support their families.

Maura I. Toro-Morn

See Also: Economics, Employment; Family Reunification; Migration; Single Men; Wages; Women's Status.

Further Reading

Boehm. Deborah. 2008. "'For My Children': Constructing Family and Navigating the State in the U.S.-Mexico Transnation." *Anthropological Quarterly* 81.4:777–802.

Flores-Gonzalez, Nilda, A. R. Guevarra, M. Toro-Morn, and G. Chang. 2013. *Immigrant Women in the Neoliberal Age.* Urbana: University of Illinois Press.

Hondagneu-Sotelo, Pierrette. 1994. *Gendered Transitions: Mexican Experiences of Immigration.* Berkeley: University of California Press.

Hondagneu-Sotelo, Pierrette, and Ernestine Avila. 1997. "'I'm Here, but I'm There': The Meanings of Latina Transnational Motherhood." *Gender and Society* 11: 548–71.

Segura, Denise, and Patricia Zavella. 2007. *Women and Migration in the U.S.-Mexico Borderlands.* Durham: Duke University Press.

Family Reunification

Family Reunification is a term that has been referred to throughout the literature on immigration policy. It is both a value and a legal process that underlies the ability of U.S. citizens and legal foreign residents who live in the United States to have nonresident family members join them. Historically, U.S. immigration policies have held the value of reunification constant. However, laws regulating the process of family reunification have changed depending on a variety of political and economic factors, such as quotas based on country of origin and the U.S. demand for workers.

For immigrants living in the United States, especially those without proper residency visas (undocumented immigrants), the legal channels for family reunification have been increasingly restricted. In 1996, for example, the Illegal Immigration Reform and Immigrant Responsibility Act (IIRIRA) made family reunification more difficult for immigrants in general. However, an examination of the migration history shows that the process of family reunification is one that defies legislative remedies, in part because such remedies ignore the reason families are separated through migration in the first place. Reasons for migrating are varied, but many are rooted in the historical linkages between Mexico and the United States, in which Mexico has traditionally provided a much needed—and often cyclical—labor supply to the United States. In older patterns of migration, men migrated to the United States first, and after they settled, sent for their wives and children. The ability to maintain family connectedness is also rooted in geography, and the shifting border between the United States and Mexico. Much of the U.S. southwest region once belonged to Mexico, and the ties between former Mexican-Americans and their families in Mexico have long sustained networks of support that have facilitated family reunification across the border that separates them. In this way, the process of family separation is inextricable from its opposite: family reunification. Indeed, when laws and policies meant to curtail immigration from Mexico are considered together with those regulating the U.S.-Mexico relations, family separation and family reunification are opposite sides of the same coin.

For example, the North American Free Trade Agreement (NAFTA) between Mexico, the United States, and Canada, which went into effect in 1994, resulted in more poverty in Mexico and thus more migration to the United States. Not surprisingly, the number of undocumented migrants in the United States (the largest group of which is of Mexican origin) increased as more sought to relieve their growing poverty by better wages offered in the United States. It may be no coincidence that around the same time NAFTA went into effect, policies related to border security, such as Operation Gatekeeper in California, Operation Safeguard in Arizona, and Operation Hold the Line in Texas, also became harsher. These have worked to encourage migrants to avoid official ports of entry in more populated, urban areas, and to cross into the United States through isolated desert areas that are more dangerous. With the disruption of more established circular patterns of migration that comes with border enforcement, family reunification for immigrants has become even more problematic. Because of this, transnational family ties that facilitate reunification have become even more critical. Such ties reinforce social relations and support networks across households and international boundaries. Seen in this manner, family separation is inextricable from its opposite, family reunification. However, as migration is facilitated, border enforcement systems intended to restrict the movement across international boundaries are correspondingly challenged. In response, plans for border enforcement have become strengthened by the politics and policies that have resulted in more funding, more walls, additional enforcement technology, and militarization as solutions.

Family reunification has been particularly challenging for women since the mid-1990s with the feminization of migration, a condition characterized by increased job-related mobility by women. With the globalization of the U.S. national economy—policies intended to facilitate the movement of capital across international boundaries to take advantage of more favorable labor markets in less developed parts of the world—wages have declined and more and more women have found it necessary to help support their families. With the disruption of circular patterns of migration that comes from heightened border enforcement, more women are now either migrating alone to join their husbands, or are migrating for the same reasons as men: for better wages. If her attempt to cross into the United States is successful, a migrant woman's reunification with her husband or family members already living in the United States may in fact create separations of other kinds. Many women leave children behind in the care of grandparents or other relatives. Over the years, parents living in the United States may arrange for their children to journey to the United States to join them in "stages," a process of family reunification that can take years. In such cases, children may be entrusted to human smugglers who negotiate the crossing of the border through remote and less-enforced areas of the desert. Beyond the reach of border patrol agents and other enforcement measures, more migrants risk their lives every year, often with fatal results.

Internal immigration enforcement policies also work to create family separation through workplace raids. The threat of being arrested has motivated many women who have children in the United States to take them to Mexico where they will be safe with families. Upon leaving them there, they return to the United States. However, the steady increase in the number of deportations and repatriations of migrants every year—many of whom are repeat undocumented border crossers—suggests that as long as viable economic alternatives in sending communities remain elusive, the value of family reunification will be vigorously defended.

Anna Ochoa O'Leary

See Also: Deportation; Families; Family Structure; Mixed-Status Families; Repatriation.

Further Reading

Cerrutti, Marcela, and Douglas S. Massey. 2001. "On the Auspices of Female Migration from Mexico to the United States." *Demography* 38.2:187–191.

Cornelius, Wayne A. 2001. "Death at the Border: Efficacy and Unintended Consequences of U.S. Immigration Control Policy." *Population and Development Review* 27.4: 661–685.

Donato, Katherine M. 1993. "Current Trends and Patterns of Female Migration: Evidence from Mexico." *International Migration Review* 27.4:748–772.

Hondagneu-Sotelo, Pierrette. 1994. *Gendered Transitions: Mexican Experiences of Immigration.* Los Angeles, Berkeley, and London: University of California Press.

Manning, Robert D., and Anita Christina Butera. 2000. "Global Restructuring and U.S. Mexican Integration: Rhetoric and Reality of Mexican Immigration Five Years after NAFTA." *American Studies* 41.2/3:183–209.

McGuire, Sharon. 2007. "Fractured Migrant Families." *Family & Community Health* 30.3:178–188.

O'Leary, Anna Ochoa. 2008. "Close Encounters of the Deadly Kind: Gender, Migration, and Border (In)Security." *Migration Letters* 15.2:111–122.

O'Leary, Anna Ochoa. 2010. "Mujeres en el Cruce/Women at the Intersection: Mapping Family Separation at a Time of Global Uncertainty." *Journal of the Southwest.*

Rubio-Goldsmith, Raquel, M. Melissa McCormick, Daniel Martínez, and Inez Magdalena Duarte. 2006. "The Funnel Effect and Recovered Bodies of Unauthorized Migrants Processed by the Pima County Office of the Medical Examiner, 1990–2005." Immigration Policy Center Brief. Available at http://bmi.arizona.edu/sites/default/files/newsletter2_3.pdf. (accessed 2/18/07).

Thompson, Amy A. 2008. "A Child Alone and Without Papers: A Report on the Return and Repatriation of Unaccompanied Undocumented Children by the United States." Austin, TX: Center for Public Policy Priorities. Available at: http://www.aecf.org/~/media/Pubs/Topics/Special%20Interest%20Areas/Immigrants%20and%20Refugees/AChildAloneandWithoutPapersAReportontheReturn/Child_Alone_Papers.pdf

Wilson, Tamar Diana. 2000. "Anti-immigrant Sentiment and the Problem of Reproduction/Maintenance in Mexican Immigration to the United States." *Critique of Anthropology* 20.2:191–213.

Family Structure

Family structure is the way that a household or family is set up. For example, a family structure widely recognized as the "nuclear" family is made up of two parents and their children. Social theorists have long argued that types of family structures parallel economic needs and how households organize their members to address the family's needs. For example, an impoverished family may better survive by relying on "extended" family structures, where additional kin are brought into the family fold, and through the bonds that unite family members, pool a diverse range of resources together for everyone to share. In this way, the type of family structure also reflects the ideologies and value system of the wider social group to which the family belongs. For example, many cultures uphold the prominence of patriarchy and machismo, a privileging of male-dominated leadership, perspectives, and behaviors. Current data indicates that there are realities other than the nuclear family among undocumented immigrants and that these new realities are impacting and being impacted by changing values and views of individuals in ways which lead one to think that the structures of patriarchy and machismo are transitioning into new social structures for undocumented immigrant families.

Social structures, including patriarchy and machismo, need their values to be incorporated into the minds of people in order to be perpetuated. Therefore, when the values upheld by individuals functioning in a specific structure change, the social structure which was supported by them is necessarily transformed. However, the process of social transformation is complex, and also takes time. Changes in values at an individual level need to transcend from the private sphere to the public sphere, and they also need to become widely spread before the social transformations involved in the process become evident.

As mentioned above, there are several types of family structures. The nuclear family is understood as the one formed by a married heterosexual couple and their own children. Adopted children are considered as being at the same level of biological children. Therefore, the traditional notion of a nuclear family excludes single parents or a family with only one parent, children living with individuals other than their own parents, non-heterosexual couples, unmarried heterosexual couples, and heterosexual married couples living with children born out of wedlock. An important element is the the role of patriarchy that has been present in many societies for hundreds of years. Patriarchy is understood as an institutionalized set of beliefs leading to the systematic domination of women by men. It involves a strict sex role differentiation with unequal expectations for men and women. As an institution, patriarchy is reinforced through unequal opportunities, rewards, punishments, and the internalization of sex role differentiation. One of the expressions of patriarchy is machismo. Machismo is understood as "macho is best" or the idea that heterosexual men who behave as dominant and controlling in a more rational and less emotional way are better than women and better than men who are not heterosexual and/or do not behave as dominant, controlling, and rational.

Among the many concrete expressions of patriarchy and machismo, the work world and human sexuality are being particularly challenged by the new values being embraced by individual undocumented immigrants, impacting their understandings of the concept of family beyond the traditional nuclear family.

Two other major factors seem to be impacting the existence of the nuclear family and the values associated with patriarchy and machismo: one is the migrant process itself and the other one is the clash/mix of the cultures of undocumented immigrants with individuals from the dominant culture. The dominant culture refers to the one traditionally associated with the values of European-descended, heterosexual, Protestant men. The clash/mix of cultures refers to the interaction among undocumented individuals from different cultural backgrounds or with different levels of acculturation to the dominant culture.

The migrant process is affecting the traditional nuclear family in many different ways. The current trends in migration indicate that more individuals rather than couples or entire families are migrating. Among many migrant groups women are the majority of new, undocumented immigrants. They tend to come to the United States bringing their children with them or bringing them later on once they have become established. Hence, these women become the heads of their households.

The implementation of new policies related to undocumented immigrants and the enforcement of these new policies as well as some old ones in the United States are also affecting the traditional nuclear family. As a result of all these policies and their enforcement, more undocumented individuals are being deported and/or imprisoned, leaving their families broken. In many cases one or both parents have to leave and the children who were born in the United States are sometimes left in the country living with relatives. In some cases, the woman is the one leaving and the father becomes the sole head of the household. Regardless of how the family separation occurs, it is important to emphasize that family ties continue, resulting in transnational family structures, and their operation has important parallels with families that are not separated by borders.

The reality of transnational families existing as a result of the migration process is finally being acknowledged. Individuals may come to the United States alone but frequently form new families in the United States though they remain emotionally and financially connected to the families they left in their countries of origin. Many times this reality is known and accepted by both families. On occasions, children from the family in the country of origin are brought to live with the U.S. family.

Out of need, either because there is only one parent functioning as the head of the household or because both parents have to work and cannot care for their children, there is a growing number of grandparents called on to fulfill a parental role for those children. Often, these working parents are undocumented immigrants living in the United States who leave their children with their grandparents. The addition of grandparents to the organization of families has been referred to as the multi-generational family structure.

When members of undocumented immigrant families are forced to live in realities other than those reflected by the traditional nuclear family, they are also forced to re-think their allegiance to this view.

The clash/mix of cultures is also affecting the structure of immigrant undocumented families in multiple ways. When undocumented immigrant individuals are exposed to values other than those learned in a patriarchal, *machista* culture, it impacts their perceptions about topics such as the role of women in the work world and the family, the understanding of sexuality for men and women, the myth of virginity, and homosexuality.

Several reasons have propelled the entrance of undocumented immigrant women into the labor force, even those with little children. This is a radical change to the role traditionally assigned to women in many nonwestern and traditional societies. In some cases, this happens because women are the only providers. In other cases, this occurs because one income is not enough to support the family, and women need to work. When the need to support their families is great, social norms may adjust towards greater acceptance of women working outside the traditional domestic sphere.

Thus, among undocumented immigrants, there is a trend for men to be seen more as co-responsible partners in keeping the family together and for both men and women to become more accepting of the possibility of divorce, especially if the male provider proves irresponsible. This is a radical departure from the traditional view of women as being responsible only for providing stability to the family and therefore needing to endure even extreme circumstances such as emotional, physical and sexual abuse to achieve that goal.

Pleasure is being recognized by many undocumented immigrant individuals as a significant part of their sexuality and not only for men but also for women who are starting to claim some rights in making decisions in regards to their own sexuality. It has impacted the number of individuals having sexual relations without being married, which challenges the myth of virginity and has also impacted the number of undocumented immigrants functioning as single parents. Furthermore, in the case of many undocumented immigrant women, they live as single mothers with their child/children and their parents. The social stigma associated with being a single mother has also decreased among undocumented immigrant communities.

The visibility of homosexuals in the United States has dramatically impacted undocumented immigrant individuals. Many of them are coming out to their families and living openly as gay and/or lesbian people. More families are facing the overt reality of having a member who is homosexual, and in many cases it has led to greater tolerance. In addition, homosexuality is becoming a more common topic of discussion among undocumented immigrant communities. The secrecy surrounding it is fading.

One of the ultimate challenges for a patriarchy, *machista* culture occurs when men change their views about a system that in theory benefits them. This is the case with many groups of immigrants and has been documented in the case of Latinos, the largest and fastest growing minority in the United States and the main ethnic group among undocumented immigrants. In recent research, the vast majority of Latino men in a sample identified themselves with styles of masculinity more emotionally responsive, collaborative and flexible in regards to sex/gender roles than with the traditional definition of men as authoritarian, controlling, and emotionally restrictive "machos."

It will take time to see the specific ways in which undocumented immigrant families will negotiate their new realities and values in terms of family and social structure.

Mauricio Cifuentes

See Also: Acculturation; Assimilation; Children; Family Economics; Family Reunification; Gender Roles; Mixed-Status Families; Single Men; Transnationalism; Women's Status.

Further Reading

Anderson, Margaret L., and Patricia Hill Collins. 2009. *Race, Class, and Gender: An Anthology.* Seventh Edition. Belmont, CA: Wadsworth.

Torres, Jose B., Scott H. Solberg, and Aaron H. Carlstrom. 2002. "The Myth of Sameness among Latino Men and Their Machismo." *American Journal of Orthopsychiatry* 72.2:163–181.

Fernandez-Vargas v. Gonzales

Fernandez-Vargas v. Gonzales was a Supreme Court case decided on June 22, 2006 in which the high court upheld the deportation of Mexican national Humberto Fernandez-Vargas. The case was first brought to the Tenth Circuit Court of Appeals, which also upheld the removal. At issue in the case was a provision of the 1996 Illegal Immigration Reform and Immigrant Responsibility Act (IIRIRA) that allows for the reinstatement of prior removal orders if a migrant is found to have reentered the country illegally following deportation or voluntary departure. Unlike the legislation previously governing removal proceedings that the 1996 act replaced, IIRIRA prohibits the reopening or review of removal orders, leaving undocumented migrants with few options when removal orders are reinstated against them.

Because Fernandez-Vargas's 1981 deportation and 1982 illegal reentry occurred well before IIRIRA took effect on April 1, 1997, his attorneys argued that Congress had not intended the law to be applied retroactively. The Immigration and Nationality Act (INA) provides that any "alien" who has been ordered removed and subsequently seeks admission is "inadmissible." Additionally, his lawyers argued that even if Congress had explicitly made the law applicable to illegal reentries committed prior to the act's passage, it would in effect increase the punishment for a crime already committed and impair the rights of the perpetrator, thus constituting what is known in the legal profession as impermissible retroactivity. The Supreme Court has set very high standards for a bill to be able to apply retroactively to crimes already committed; and when a bill does not meet these standards, it is struck down as impermissibly retroactive. With a lone dissent from Justice John Paul Stevens, the court disagreed with both arguments and upheld Fernandez-Vargas's deportation 8-1.

Fernandez-Vargas first came to the United States in the 1970s and was deported and returned on several occasions. After his last illegal reentry in 1982, he settled in Utah where he worked as a truck driver, became the owner of his own trucking business, fathered a child in 1989 and married the mother of his child in 2001. For nearly twenty years he lived undetected by immigration officials and achieved an admirable degree of success for himself and his family. After their marriage, Fernandez-Vargas's new wife, who was a U.S. citizen, put in a petition for a relative visa for her husband. After the petition was submitted, Fernandez-Vargas filed paperwork to become a legal permanent resident (LPR), a fateful decision that alerted immigration officials to his unlawful presence in the country. Instead of processing his paperwork, the government reinstated his 1981 removal order, held him for ten months during deportation proceedings and deported Fernandez-Vargas to Ciudad Juarez, Mexico in 2004.

At the time of his 1982 illegal reentry, the 1952 Immigration and Nationality Act (INA) was the applicable law for Fernandez-Vargas's crime. While the INA allows for discretionary review of removal orders, the 1996 IIRIRA that replaced it states that removal orders are "not subject to being reopened or reviewed, the alien is not eligible and may not apply for any relief under this chapter, and the alien shall be removed under the prior order at any time after the reentry." Referring to this discrepancy between the two laws in his dissent, Justice Stevens wrote that "the laws in place at the time of [the] petitioner's entry and for the first 15 years of his residence in this country would have rewarded [his] behavior, allowing him to seek discretionary relief from deportation on the basis of his continued presence in and strong ties to the United States. . . . Given these incentives, [Fernandez-Vargas] legitimately complains that the Government has changed the rules midgame."

This was the backbone of the defense's argument that the 1996 law imposed additional punishments and burdens on Fernandez-Vargas that he was not subject to at the time of his crime in 1982. As Fernandez-Vargas's attorney David Gossett argued before the court, "applying [IIRIRA] to aliens who reentered before [the bill's] effective date would give the statute an impermissibly retroactive effect. Before IIRIRA, such aliens were entitled to seek, and eligible to receive, discretionary relief from deportation. Now if the provision is applied to them, they are not."

Another difference between the two pieces of legislation is that retroactive applicability of removal order reinstatements is laid out explicitly in INA, while never being mentioned in IIRIRA. The INA clearly states that a removal order can be reinstated for an illegal reentry "before or after the date of enactment of this Act." However, this "before or after" language was intentionally removed from IIRIRA's revision of this provision. This deliberate silence was the basis of Fernandez-Vargas's argument that Congress had intended the law to apply exclusively proactively to illegal reentries after the bill's effective date. Delivering the court's majority opinion, Justice David Souter rejected this argument by saying "[the petitioner] points out that the predecessor of [the provision] had some language that made it clear that the old law was retroactive, but Congress took that language out when it passed the new law. But we do not think that helps Fernandez-Vargas' argument, both because the old language did not refer to the date of re-entry and because the force of any inference of potential that might be drawn from its removal is weakened by the fact that IIRIRA made other provisions expressly applicable to only post-effective-date re-entries."

Justice Souter then went on to reject the defense's argument of impermissible retroactivity: "The provision does not penalize an alien for a past act that he is helpless to undo; it is the conduct of remaining in the country after re-entry that is the predicate to application of the statute, conduct that the alien could end by voluntarily leaving. Thus, it is the alien's choice to continue his illegal presence that subjects him to the new and less generous legal regime."

The Supreme Court's decision has far-reaching implications. Because the 1996 statute prohibits appeal or review of removal orders for migrants found to have reentered the country illegally and the high court decided that removal orders can be reinstated for illegal reentries before or after the statute's 1997 effective date, migrants have essentially no legal ground to contest removal orders after reentering the country illegally; without legislative action, their removal orders will follow them forever in the United States, making any adjustment of status or application for legal status an impossibility. In Fernandez-Vargas's case, the facts that he had spent much of his life in the United States, contributed to his community as a business owner and was a husband and father now have no legal value as removal orders are no longer subject to discretionary review.

Murphy Woodhouse

See Also: Deportation; Expedited Removal; Family Reunification; Illegal Immigration Reform and Immigrant Responsibility Act (IIRIRA); Immigration and Nationality Act (The McCarran-Walter Act) (1952); Inadmissibility; Mixed-Status Families.

Further Reading

Asseff, Brent. 2007. "Notes—Reinstatement of Removal and IIRIRA Retroactivity after *Fernandez-Vargas v. Gonzales:* Restoring Section 212(c) Discretion and Fairness to Immigration Law." *Brandeis Law Journal* 46.1:157.

Hawran, Gregory R. 2006/2007. "Taking Fairness and Retroactivity from Immigration Law: Casenote on *Fernandez-Vargas v. Gonzales." The University of Miami Inter-American Law Review* 38.2:431–455.

Film and Television Representation

Representations of undocumented immigrants are increasingly common in commercial film and television (also in documentaries) in the United States, but such portrayals are still rare and most instances are stereotypical: Latino, poor, and usually involved in

The stereotype of the undocumented immigrant made its way into commercial film and television with the television show *My Name Is Earl* with the portrayal of Catalina Rana Aruca (played by Nadine Velazquez, an American actress of Puerto Rican descent). Though the show was cancelled in 2009, examples of a prime-time television recurring character who is an undocumented immigrant are rare. (NBC/Photofest)

criminal activities. There are very few instances in modern film and television representing non-Latino immigrants who are specifically identified as undocumented. Early representations of immigrants, usually European or Asian, did not focus on undocumented status because the United States had more flexible immigration policies and the social problems surrounding immigrants did not specifically link with their undocumented status. The focus on undocumented immigrants has only been more recent, with Latinos filling the stereotypical portrayal. Popular culture and media in general are battlegrounds of meaning, where identity and race/ethnicity are assigned and reassigned significance. When not being ignored, fictional representations of undocumented immigrants tend to be based on stereotypes.

The stereotypical undocumented immigrant in commercial film and on television is exemplified in the portrayal of Catalina Rana Aruca on the television show *My Name Is Earl*. She is both domesticated and sexualized, playing a housekeeper and a stripper. Jokes about her illegal entry into the United States by being mailed in a crate are ongoing in this sitcom. Additionally, she fakes a marriage with one of the other main characters in order to obtain a green card and she speaks in heavily accented English. Played by Nadine Velazquez, an American actress of Puerto Rican descent, the character is revealed to be from Bolivia, after she is assumed to be Mexican by many of the characters on the show. Though the show is a comedy and the stereotypical portrayal of Catalina can be said to be a satirical comment on the state of undocumented immigrants today, it provides a very striking example of the undocumented immigrant stereotype. Though the show was cancelled in 2009, to date Catalina is the only example of a prime-time television recurring character who is an undocumented immigrant.

Other fleeting television portrayals usually are stereotypical and negative, where differences and conflict are emphasized instead of the more positive aspects such as mutual challenges and cooperation. Often, popular images of undocumented immigrants are not seen as competent or well-rounded people with ideas beyond their own ethnicity, culture, and citizenship status, but rather as tokens of a minority categorized as uneducated, low-wage workers. Despite there being some social and historical truth to these stereotypes (immigrants do struggle with English, low-wage jobs, acculturation, etc.), the lack of other images of immigrants perpetuates and hardens any prejudice that may be present in society against immigrants. Even a neutral stereotype, when left unchallenged, becomes prevalent over other, less-available impressions of a category of people.

The narrowly defined portrayal of undocumented immigrants, particularly Mexicans, has two important consequences. First, many scholars suggest that these predominant stereotypes hinder the immigrant's ability to be accepted by other Americans. The negative portrayal of Latinos in entertainment programming is fuel for hostile anti-immigration movements that seek to deny a sense of belonging to immigrants. Film and television are not just reflections of how society is, but also can serve as instructions for what society could be. The role of undocumented immigrants in these popular mediums can thusly serve as either a gateway to new possibilities for cultural understanding or as a barricade to social opportunities for undocumented immigrants.

Secondly, popular media representations affect the self-image and identity of immigrants, just as they do for other minority and marginalized groups. Most minority media consumers feel they are simply misrepresented. Constantly seeing immigrants as poor criminals can take a mental toll on those who are trying to form a more positive self-identity. Many studies suggest these negative media portrayals affect the individual self-esteem and identity work of minority groups, including both documented and undocumented immigrants.

Media representations of immigrants fluctuate based on the political and economic concerns with immigration and minority issues within mainstream U.S. culture. There is a larger precedent for the portrayal of immigrants (in general) in film. Hollywood productions about turn-of-the-century immigrants (from the late 1800s to early 1900s) tend to build on stereotypes of Italian immigrants as Mafia members (for example in *Godfather II* [1974]) or Irish immigrants as turning to boxing to survive (for example, in *Gangs of New York* [2002] and *Far and Away* [1992]). Immigrant portrayals during more troubling economic times are often portrayed as gang members, teen mothers, drug dealers and traffickers, and common criminals. Consistently showing immigrants as "bad guys" contributes to the dehumanization and criminalization of certain immigrant groups and can make discrimination more common.

A Day Without a Mexican (2004) is a satirical "mockumentary" that was written and directed by Latinos. The film focuses on a hypothetical day where all the Mexicans in the United States, legal and otherwise, suddenly disappear. Though the film takes place in California, by extension the rest of the United States sees the overall chaos that would come if there were suddenly no more Mexicans. The film begins by depicting the multitudes of agricultural labor, restaurant workers, and maids not showing up for work. It then presents the disappearance of professional workers, baseball athletes, musicians, etc. The overall message is seen in the utopist return of the Mexicans at the end of the film, who are now appreciated and accepted by the rest of the American population. The film was embraced by many in the Latino community and even resulted in political mobilization of many immigrants—raising their own consciousness of their position in society.

The stereotype of the Latino as the typical undocumented worker also figures into larger debates on media representation. Many depictions of Latinos do not associate them with the United States, but perpetuate the idea of "Latino/as as foreigners." Latin Americans are overrepresented as immigrants, especially undocumented, and later-generation Latinos, particularly as professionals, are conspicuously absent in media representations. This focus on the stereotype of recently immigrated Latinos does not represent the demographic truth for the United States, where only about 15 percent of Latinos are immigrants and where many Latinos can trace their ancestry for generations to the United States. This overrepresented group of media characters continues to support a more foreign model of Latinos. These characters are often asked what country they are from, instead of its being assumed they are U.S. citizens.

The popular reception of *A Day Without a Mexican* leads to questions about the role of mainstream film production as compared to films with Latino producers. There is a considerable lack of Latino employees in high-level positions such as producers or directors, which leads to lack of immigrant representations on TV and in film. It has been suggested that there is a systematic variation in representation when the product is from Latino directors. Many of the more sympathetic films about Latino undocumented immigrants are from Latino producers and directors, which is particularly evident in educational documentaries about Mexican immigration. The potential for these producers to diversify film and television images may combat degrading, insensitive and inaccurate representations of immigrants.

The following is a non-comprehensive list of portrayals of undocumented immigrants in popular film in the last three decades. The descriptions of these films demonstrate the points made above and show examples of ways undocumented immigrants have been portrayed frequently as Latinos or been secondary to non-Latino characters.

Borderline (1980) focuses on a white border patrol officer who is generally sympathetic to the plight of undocumented immigrants. However, when his best friend is killed by a smuggler, he must seek justice against the real enemy: the *coyotes* who take advantage of undocumented immigrants and defy law enforcement.

The Border (1982) similarly focuses on a white border patrol agent, played by Jack Nicholson, who is confronted with corrupted border enforcers who are in cahoots with smugglers. The agent becomes the champion for a victimized undocumented crosser named Maria.

El Norte (The North) (1983) empathetically follows two siblings on a journey from their Guatemalan village (fraught with military violence and *campesino* uprisings) through the crossing of both Mexico's southern and northern borders to a poverty-stricken life in Los Angeles.

Born in East L.A. (1987) shows the irony of Mexicans being cast as undocumented immigrants when comedian and U.S. citizen Cheech Marin is wrongfully deported and left in Mexico to fend for himself, despite having been born and raised in Los Angeles and not speaking Spanish.

A Million to Juan (1994) tells the humorous/fantastic tale of an undocumented widower who, only through the angelic gift of one million dollars, is able to conquer the many obstacles faced by undocumented immigrants.

My Family/Mi Familia (1995) follows one family over several decades as they seek a better life for succeeding generations. The first generation successfully crosses into Los Angeles, only to be broken up when wife and mother Maria is illegally deported. We then follow her trials and tribulations to return to her family in Los Angeles with her newborn son.

Bread and Roses (2000). This is a story of two Latina sisters who work as cleaners in a downtown office building and fight for the right to unionize. One of them crosses the border without papers to the home of her older sister, who gets her a job as a janitor. She suffers at the hands of her abusive supervisor who can fire workers while winning contracts by paying workers the lowest possible wages with no job security or benefits. The workers struggle to unionize in the Justice for Janitors movement, while management intimidates and tries to divide workers.

Maria Full of Grace (María llena eres de gracia) (2004) tells the tale of a young Colombian girl drawn to the drug-trade by promises of travel, adventure and a new life in America. She witnesses the death of a travel companion and must deal with the trauma of her choices.

The Beautiful Country (2004) is a story set in the 1990s that begins in Vietnam with the reunification of Binh with his mother in Ho Chi Minh City. A tragedy forces Binh to flee from Viet Nam to America in search of his American father, a Vietnam War veteran who disappeared years ago without explanation, and who now lives in Texas. The story develops as he is smuggled to the United States as an undocumented immigrant and experiences inhuman conditions through the journey in the hands of ruthless smugglers, called "Snakeheads."

Fun with Dick and Jane (2005) is a general satirical view of corporate America. At one point in the film, when the white protagonist has lost his job as a vice president for a major corporation, he is forced to look for day labor by waiting on a corner with a number of stereotypically portrayed undocumented workers. He is then caught in a raid and eventually deported to Mexico. His wife is able to help him re-enter the United States.

The Three Burials of Melquiades Estrada (2005). This story is about the loyalty of a hard-working Texas rancher (played by Tommy Lee Jones) who hires an undocumented Mexican immigrant named Melquiades Estrada. Melquiades is killed by a rookie Border Patrol agent. When the rancher finds out that the incident was covered up, he takes matters into his own hands. Out of honor and respect for his friend, he exhumes Melquiades from the pauper's grave where he was unceremoniously buried, to return him to his family in Mexico. He takes the rookie agent with him, in the learning experience of a lifetime.

Fast Food Nation (2006) is a film adaptation of Eric Schlosser's 2001 novel by the same name. The setting is a meat processing plant where undocumented immigrants eke out a living amidst cattle being slaughtered and eviscerated, and unsafe and unsanitary conditions. The stories of immigrant families are intertwined with those of industry managers and fast food workers. Depicted are the grueling conditions of their work, including the sexual harassment of women by unscrupulous supervisors, workforce injury, and the day to day stomach-turning images of the "kill floor," where cows are brutally slaughtered and workers often lose their limbs.

The Visitor (2007) moves away from the theme of Latinos as undocumented immigrants. When a professor returns to an apartment he has had in New York he finds two undocumented immigrants, a Syrian musician and a Senegalese street vendor, have been living there as squatters. The film shows his growing attachment to these immigrants, which is disrupted when one of them is arrested and detained for deportation.

La misma luna (*Under the Same Moon*) (2008) is a sympathetic portrayal of a Mexican mother forced to immigrate illegally due to economic concerns and to leave her nine-year-old son in Mexico. The son eventually crosses after her when his caretaking grandmother dies. The film shows the multiple trials of crossing the border, though the family is ultimately reunited at the end.

Jessie K. Finch

See Also: *Corridos; The Devil's Highway;* Literature and Poetry; Media Coverage; Spanish-Language Media; *Strangers from a Different Shore;* Theater.

Further Reading

Herrera-Sobek, María. 2009. "Transnational Migrations and Political Mobilizations: The Case of *A Day Without a Mexican*." In Kevin Concannon, Francisco A. Lomelí, and Marc Priewe, eds., *Imagined Transnationalism: U.S. Latino/A Literature, Culture, and Identity*, 61–73. New York: Palgrave Macmillan.

Maciel, David, and María Herrera-Sobek. 1998. *Culture Across Borders: Mexican, Immigration & Popular Culture.* Tucson: University of Arizona Press.

Flores-Figueroa v. United States No. 08–108

Ignacio Flores-Figueroa, a Mexican citizen, in 2000 gave his employer a false name, birth date and Social Security number. In 2006, Flores again gave his employer a new Social Security card; this time the card used his name but again used a social security number that was assigned to another person. Consequently, Flores-Figueroa was convicted of entering the United States without inspection, of misusing immigration documents and of aggravated identity theft. Flores argued that the government failed to prove that he knew the Social Security numbers belonged to someone else.

U.S. Statute 1028A(a)(1) required proof that the "defendant knowingly transfers, possesses, or uses, without lawful authority, a means of identification of another person; that defendant shall, in addition to the punishment provided for such felony, be sentenced to a term of imprisonment of two years." The government argued that the term "knowingly" did not apply to the words "of another person" but only to the elements to the crime. The Eighth Circuit Court agreed and affirmed. The Supreme Court granted certiorari as to the defendant's conviction under 1028A(a)(1). The Supreme Court came to a 9–0 decision, reversing the decision of the Eighth Circuit Court, with Justice Breyer delivering the opinion of the court. Justice Scalia, joined by Justice Thomas, filed a concurring opinion in part and in judgment. Also, Justice Alito filed a separate concurring opinion in part and in judgment.

Justice Breyer's opinion first rejects the government's position "as a matter of ordinary English grammar." The government claims that the word "knowingly" applies to the elements of the crime but not to the last three words of the statute, "of another person." This interpretation does not require the government to show that the defendant knowingly used identification that belonged to another person. Justice Breyer concludes that the term "knowingly," in ordinary English, applies to the entire action. He further gives examples of previous cases, such as *United States v. X-Citement Video Inc.* and *Liparota v. United States,* which used the ordinary English usage. Secondly, Justice Breyer breaks down the government's argument into four steps. Step One: We should not interpret a statute in a manner that makes some of its language superfluous. Step Two: A person who knows that he is transferring, possessing, or using a "means of identification" "without lawful authority must know that the document either (a) belongs to another person or (b) is a false identification document" because there are no other choices. Step Three: Requiring the offender to know that the "means of identification" belongs to another person would consequently be superfluous in this terrorism provision. Step Four: We should not interpret the same phrase "of another person" in the two related sections differently. Justice Breyer finds flaws in the argument. Primarily, if the two listed circumstances in Step Two are the only two circumstances possible when the defendant unlawfully used the identification, then why list them all? He asks, "Why not just stop after criminalizing the knowingly unlawful use of a means of identification?" Finally Justice Breyer ends his argument with the "greatest piratical importance," which is proving beyond a reasonable doubt the knowledge of the defendant. He goes on by giving an example of an "alien" who unlawfully gives an employer false identification. How is the government to go about determining whether the defendant knew the documents were false? The defendant does not care if they are real and belong to another person or if they are "simply counterfeit." The court concluded that 1028A(a)(1) "requires the Government to show the defendant knew that the means of identification at issue belong to another person."

Justice Scalia's concurring opinion can be summarized by his closing statement, "The statute's text is clear, and I would reverse the judgment of the Court of Appeals on that ground alone." While Justice Alito writes separately because of a concern that the Court's opinion "may be read as adopting an overly rigid rule of statutory construction." Justice Alito's concurrence first points out the overstated usage of ordinary English. Secondly, he determines that *mens rea* should apply to all the elements of the case. Lastly, he states that the government's interpretation leaves the defendants liable to chance whether the documentation belonged to a person or was false entirely. He joins the court in judgment "insofar as it may be read to adopt an inflexible rule of construction that can rarely be overcome by contextual features pointing to contrary reading."

Alfredo Estrada

Further Reading

Flores-Figueroa, Ignacio Carlos. Petitioner v. United States no. 08-108 Supreme Court of the United States; 129 s. Ct. 1886; 173 l. Ed. 2d 853.

Foreign Consulates

An estimated 214 million people currently live outside their country of origin. As populations become more mobile many nations are increasingly responding with an active consular presence in the main destination countries for their respective diasporas (Rannveig Aqunias and Newland, 2012). Consulates are of significant importance to individuals living abroad, including undocumented immigrants, because through their consular offices, governments interact with émigrés to provide help in destination countries and facilitate ongoing connection with their countries of origin.

Currently, 181 of the 195 independent nations recognized by the U.S. government have a chancery in Washington D.C. (U.S. Department of State, 2012). A chancery is a diplomatic office in the capital of the host country. Furthermore, 166 of these nations have one or more consulates in the United States (U.S. Department of State, 2012). Consulates are also diplomatic offices, but are typically located outside of the host country's capital and focus on providing services to their citizens residing in the host country. Since the United States does not have diplomatic relations with Iran, Cuba, and South Korea, these countries do not have chanceries or consulates in the United States. However, Cuba and Iran maintain an Interests Section in the Washington, D.C. chanceries of Switzerland and Pakistan respectively (U.S. Department of State, 2012). While they are not formal diplomatic missions, the Interest Sections serve as de facto embassies.

History and Legal Basis

While consular functions can be traced back to ancient Greece, the foundation for contemporary consular functions lies in the Vienna Convention on Consular Relations (VCCR), the Optional Protocol concerning Acquisition of Nationality and the Optional Protocol concerning the Compulsory Settlement of Disputes. The Convention and both Optional Protocols were adopted April 1963 and came into force on 19 March 1967 (Gómez Robledo, 2008). The Vienna Convention is comprised of 79 articles, which provide for the operation of consulates; outline the functions of consular agents; address the privileges and immunities granted to consular officials when posted to a foreign country; and specify consular duties when citizens of their country face difficulties in a foreign nation. Among the 79 articles, Article 36 is one of the most significant, as it delineates obligations for authorities of the host country in the case of an arrest or detention of a foreign national, in order to guarantee the inalienable right to counsel and due process through consular notification and effective access to consular protection (Gómez Robledo, 2008).

Consular Services

The breadth of services offered and geographic accessibility varies by country and consulate. Not all countries have a consulate in the United States, and those that do may only have one or a few to cover the whole country and may not provide a wide range of services. For example, Burkina Faso has a chancery in Washington, D.C., but no consulates in the United States In contrast Mexico has a chancery in the nation's capital and forty-five consulates throughout the United States.

As previously stated, the VCCR outlines the specific functions of consulates, with a focus on the protection and the interest of the state and its nationals abroad. However, more recently consulates have been expanding the array of programs provided to diaspora communities to include services that may not have been contemplated in the drafting of the VCCR (Laglagaron, 2010; Rannveig Aqunias and Newland, 2012). These new and expanded services and programs include the provision of consular identification cards, immigrant integration programs and community well-being and building programs. Thus, contemporary consulates can offer a wide range of programs, yet there is broad variation in what specific foreign governments and consulates can offer to their nationals residing in the United States. Some of the major programmatic areas include: services for migrants in distress, legal assistance, consular identification cards, health assistance, cultural programming, immigrant integration services, and programs aimed at maintaining ties between the migrant and his/her homeland (Laglagaron, 2010; Rannveig Aqunias and Newland, 2012).

Services for Migrants in Distress

One of the primary roles of consulates is to assist distressed nationals, represent their interests, and protect their rights in receiving states. Some of these functions are manifested in consular programs and activities that focus on assisting and advising their nationals on U.S. laws and their legal rights while in the United States. Consulates offer legal assistance to nationals in detention, provide safe repatriation, counseling and information about deportations to prisoners and their relatives, assist in locating missing persons, aid hospitalized persons, protect minors, help with the repatriation of the remains of deceased nationals, and assist with workplace rights, including help in situations of wage theft (Laglagaron, 2010; Rannveig Aqunias and Newland, 2012).

Legal Assistance: The VCCR specifies the mandatory notification of an immigrant's consulate in all cases involving the detention or death of a foreign national, or in cases where the appointment of a guardian or trustee may be required. Consular officers and programs help to acquaint their nationals with the basic rights, procedures and penalties applicable under the local legal system. Consulates can provide legal referrals, arrange for legal representation, or initiate legal interventions on the behalf of nationals to ensure that they receive fair and equal treatment under the laws of the arresting state (Gómez Robledo, 2008).

Health Assistance: Some consulates offer health care referrals through their *Ventanilla de Salud* program, and community health promotion fairs, such as the Semana Binacional de Salud (Binational Health Week), touted as the largest mobilization efforts in the Americas to improve the health and well-being of the underserved Latino population. These programs can consist of health kiosks in the consulates (as in the *Ventanilla de Salud*) that can offer a range of services. The fair during Binational Health Week held in October every year, federal, state and local government agencies, community-based organizations and thousands of volunteers come together to provide a range of resources that can include basic medical advice, vaccinations, health screenings, health education workshops, and insurance and hospital referrals. Some countries offer an emergency hotline for citizens who are distressed, including those who are hospitalized, and almost all countries provide medical visitations and guidance to their nationals (Laglagaron, 2010; Rannveig Aqunias and Newland, 2012).

Consular Identification Cards: Several countries offer consular identification cards, CIDs (e.g. *matricula consular, carte d'identité consulaire,* National Identity Card for Overseas Pakistanis—NICOP) to immigrants. While some consulates may issue CID cards, these cards have no bearing on the cardholder's legal residence status in the host country. Thus, CID cardholders can be either undocumented aliens or legal residents living in the United States. These identification cards can be used for transactions that require a secure form of identification and can be used in a very limited number of states to apply for a driver's license. Consular identification cards are particularly useful to undocumented immigrants, as they can be used to identify themselves to law enforcement, to access financial services such as opening a bank account and securing a mortgage, to remit money and provide identification needed to establish accounts with utility companies and other institutions. The CIDs can also help in alerting U.S. law enforcement officials of their need to advise an immigrant of his/her right to request that consular officials be immediately notified if they have been detained for immigration or criminal offenses (U.S. Government Accountability Office, 2004).

Cultural Programming

Some consulates in the United States help connect migrants to other diaspora community members and reaffirm homeland culture through cultural events and community gatherings. Some have developed community houses or centers that host community gatherings, cultural events, and provide information and services (Laglagaron, 2010; Rannveig Aqunias and Newland, 2012).

Maintaining Connection with Homeland: An important function of consulates is to foster and maintain connections between the émigré and his/her homeland. They do this in a number of ways, such as providing information on developments in the country of origin, posting news updates regarding their homeland on consular websites; offering programs on culture, education, and economic development; providing a space for hometown associations and federations to meet; coordinating overseas voting; marking important homeland holidays with celebrations and recognitions; providing language classes for children of émigrés; and facilitating the exchange of remittances (Laglagaron, 2010; Rannveig Aqunias and Newland, 2012).

Immigrant Integration Programs: A relatively recent development in consular services is the promotion of immigrant integration in the host country through an array of services. Immigrant integration has typically been a function of the receiving community institutions, but Mexico is taking the lead in providing such services to their nationals residing in the United States. These services are coordinated through their Institute for Mexicans Abroad, IME (Instituto de los Mexicanos en el Exterior). A recent study of IME concludes that its "mission is premised on the belief that a better integrated immigrant—one who has access to quality K-12 or adult education, learns English, is healthy, understands his or her rights, and is politically active—benefits the individual immigrant, the sending country, and the receiving country" (Laglagaron, 2010, 3). At each of the forty-five Mexican consular offices in the United States, there are between one and five community affairs staff charged with carrying out IME's mission. Towards this end, IME serves as the implementing or coordinating agency for some of the following integration-focused programs: assistance to U.S. school districts in determining appropriate grade placement for migrant children in the United States through transcript analysis and diagnostic assessments in Spanish; low-cost culturally and linguistically appropriate distance-learning instruction for adult immigrants that is aligned with instruction received in Mexico; and financial literacy workshops that encourage the understanding and use of formal banking institutions in order to establish a credit history in the United States to qualify for a home or car loans (Laglagaron, 2010).

Stephen Haymes and Maria Vidal de Haymes

See Also: CC-IME; Culture; Home Town Associations; Identification Cards; Legal Status; Passports.

Further Reading

Gómez Robledo, Juan Manuel. 2008. *Vienna Convention on Consular Relations.* United Nations, Retrieved from: http://untreaty.un.org/cod/avl/pdf/ha/vccr/vccr_e.pdf.

Laglagaron, Laureen. 2010. "Protection through Integration: The Mexican Government's Efforts to Aid Migrants in the United States." Washington, DC: Migration Policy Institute. http://www.migrationpolicy.org/pubs/ime-jan2010.pdf.

Rannveig Aqunias, Dovelyn, and Kathleen Newland. 2012. *Developing a Road Map for Engaging Diasporas in Development: A Handbook for Policymakers and Practitioners in Home and Host Countries.* Geneva, Switzerland: International Organization for Migration and Washington, D.C.: Migration Policy Institute. http://www.migrationpolicy.org/pubs/thediasporahandbook.pdf.

United States Department of State. 2012. *Foreign Consular Offices in the United States.* Washington, D.C.: U.S. Government Printing Office. http://www.state.gov/s/cpr/rls/fco/.

United States Government Accountability Office. 2004. *Consular Identification Cards Accepted within the United States, but Consistent Federal Guidance Needed.* Washington, D.C.: U.S. Government Printing Office. http://www.gao.gov/new.items/d04881.pdf.

Form I–9

The Form I-9, the Employment Eligibility Verification Form from U.S. Citizenship and Immigration Services, was a component of the Immigration Reform and Control Act (IRCA) of 1986. It is a form used by employers to check the identity of an employee as well as verify his or her immigration status.

IRCA required employers to verify that every employee hired on or after November 6, 1986 was legally authorized to work in the United States. The instrument used for compliance is the Form I-9, which every new employee must complete. Therefore, if someone is not authorized to work in the United States, they cannot complete the Form I-9 because they will not be able to provide the necessary proof, and thus are not eligible to work in the United States. Every new employee must complete the form on or before the first day of work and provide the proper documentation within three days of work. Exemptions from Form I-9 include employees hired before November 6, 1986, unpaid volunteers, intermittent domestic workers, and workers not physically working in the United States. The form was also not required for contractors, but nevertheless, under IRCA, a company cannot knowingly hire unauthorized workers. If an employee is continuing employment after an acceptable leave, this is not considered a new hire and a new Form I-9 is not necessary. Acceptable leaves include promotions, layoffs, a strike or labor dispute, reinstatement after wrongful termination, a transfer, or seasonal employment. However, if this occurs more than three years after the initial hire, a new Form I-9 must be filled out. All employers are required to keep a record of the I-9 for at least three years after the completion of the I-9 or for one year after the termination of work, whichever one comes later. Unlike some government documentation, there is no filing fee for the Form I-9.

The Form I-9 comprises three pages of instruction and one page that contains a list of acceptable documents to establish identity and verify employment authorization in addition to the one page of the actual form. The form itself has three sections. Section 1 requires basic employee information such as name, address, date of birth, social security number, signature and date. It also has a section for self-identification as either a citizen, noncitizen national, lawful permanent resident, or alien authorized to work. It also includes a subsection for a preparer/translator certification if someone who is not the employee completes section 1. In that case, the translator's signature is needed in addition to the employee's signature.

Section 2 requires the employer to list the documentation provided. All new hires must present proper documentation that establishes the worker's identification as well as evidence of work authorizization. A list is given at the end of the form of acceptable documents. According to the Form I-9 Lists of Acceptable Documents List A, the six documents that establish both identity and employment authorization are: a U.S. passport or passport card, a permanent resident card or alien registration receipt card, a foreign passport that contains a temporary I-551 stamp or printed notation, a foreign passport with form I-94 or I-94A and an endorsement of the alien's nonimmigrant status, or a passport from the Federated States of Micronesia or the Republic of the Marshall Islands with Form I-94 or I-94A.

Under List B, the nine documents that establish identity are: a driver's license or state-issued ID card, ID card issued by federal, state, or local government agency, school ID card with photograph, U.S. military card or draft record, voter's registration card, military dependent's ID card, U.S. Coast Guard Merchant Mariner Card, Native American tribal document, or a driver's license issued by the Canadian government. Furthermore, minors who do not have any of the above documents also have the option of providing a school record or report card, clinic, hospital, or doctor record, or a daycare or nursery school record.

However, if the new hire only provides a document under List B that establishes identity, they must also provide proper documentation under List C that establishes employment eligibility. These documents are: social security account number card, certification of birth abroad, certification of report of birth, original or certified copy of birth certificate issued by a state, county, or municipal authority, or territory of the United States with an official seal, a Native American tribal document, U.S. citizen ID card, identification card for use of a resident citizen in the United States, or an employment authorization document issued by the Department of Homeland Security. All of the above documents must be valid and not have expired.

Section 3, also completed by the employer, is utilized whenever there is an update or reverification necessary. Reasons for an update include a new name, a date of rehire, or a reestablishment of employment authorization if the employee is not permanently allowed to work in the United States

An important aspect of the I-9, also a provision of the Immigration Reform and Control Act of 1986, is the Anti-Discrimination Notice. The notice states that it is illegal to discriminate in hiring or discharge due to national origin or immigration status. Furthermore, it states that employers cannot say which of the documents they will accept, that is, employers must accept any/all documents included in the list of acceptable documents. If employers are shown to deny certain acceptable documents or have the intent to discriminate, they can face the consequences of loss of government contract, bad public image, and several fines. Likewise, employers can face fines for paperwork violations as well as hiring unauthorized workers. The Form I-9 also states that imprisonment for false statements is a provision of federal law.

Jenna Glickman

See Also: Counterfeit Documents; Employment; Small Business Ownership; "Undocumented" Label; Wages.

Further Reading

Form I-9, Employment Eligibility Verification. 2013. U.S. Citizenship and Immigration Services. www.uscis.gov/i-9.

Form I-9 Regulations and Requirements. 2013. University of Minnesota Office of Human Resources. http://www1.umn.edu/ohr/payroll/i9regs/index.html.

I-9 Central. U.S. Citizenship and Immigration Services. 2013. http://www.uscis.gov/I-9 Central.

Fourteenth Amendment

With the wave of anti-immigrant proposals in the nation, some of the national debate about immigrants in the United States has turned towards the U.S. children born of undocumented immigrants. On August 3, 2010, prominent Republican Senator Lindsey Graham announced on the national Fox cable news network that it was time to reconsider how current interpretations of birthright citizenship place an unfair financial strain on the nation's social safety net, Senate Republican Minority Leader Mitch McConnell and other leading Republicans, including Arizona Senators Jon Kyl and

John McCain, also indicated an openness to exploring the Fourteenth Amendment as a way to curb undocumented immigration. Then on March 30, Diane Black (R-Tennessee) along with twenty-four other Republicans sponsored the Birthright Citizenship Act of 2013. This proposal—filed by Rep. Steve King, R-Iowa—seeks to define a key phrase of the Fourteenth Amendment. These legislators contend that the Fourteenth Amendment to the U.S. Constitution has been misapplied and was never intended to automatically grant citizenship to children born of undocumented immigrants. Consistent with previous patterns, these debates about changing the Fourteenth Amendment come on the heels of nativist sentiment (Ngai, 2007).

The Fourteenth Amendment to the United States Constitution is most familiar as the one that confers citizenship to those born in the United States. Its adoption in 1868 during the Reconstruction Period following the Civil War was an affront to a powerful idea that race could be a criterion for exclusion (Ngai, 2007). After the war, national debates raged over which, if any, civil rights should be accorded to recently freed slaves and whether federal or state legislative entities could grant or deny such rights. The amendment was a direct response to reactionary violence directed toward freed slaves and abolitionists that ensued after the war, to the Supreme Court ruling known as the *Dred Scott* decision of 1857 (in which blacks were declared noncitizens ineligible for protection within the U.S. Constitution), and to the passage of the restrictive and discriminatory Black Codes in Texas in 1866.

The drafters of the Fourteenth Amendment sought to define eligibility for U.S. citizenship and limit jurisdiction over which governmental powers were responsible for protecting the rights of citizens. The 1868 amendment granted citizenship to all people born or naturalized in the United States and placed the federal government in charge of protecting citizens from state laws that threatened to violate their civil rights. In addition, the Fourteenth Amendment granted all persons residing in the United States the right to due process of the law as well as equal protection under the nation's laws. While the federal government has at different points changed its criteria for which immigrant groups were allowed to enter the United States and become eligible for citizenship (for example, the Immigration Act of 1924 denied citizenship to Chinese and Japanese immigrants until it was repealed by the McCarran-Walter Act of 1952), the Fourteenth Amendment remains the relevant constitutional clause used to protect the rights of citizens and *all other* persons residing within the nation's borders.

The Fourteenth Amendment also provided an advantage to the United States as a nation and sovereign. It was intended to and had the effect of encouraging assimilation and a building of a citizenry with children of immigrants as they settled in the United States. It was hoped that by conferring citizenship on the children of recent arrivals, those children would break allegiances to the country of their parents and grow up to be loyal and productive members of the United States (Ngai, 2007).

This amendment has particular significance for undocumented individuals living in the United States for two reasons: first, it grants migrants residing in the United States due process and equal protection under the law; and second, it automatically grants U.S. citizenship and its attendant rights to U.S.-born children of undocumented parents. With increased immigration from Latin America, eliminating birthright citizenship for the children of undocumented immigrants would create a caste-like structure in U.S. society, where one class of U.S. children would be subjected to a different set of laws from other U.S. citizens, and perhaps one of the most extreme cases of exclusion and disenfranchisement that would not only endanger the well-being and education of this category of second generation American citizens, but subsequent generations as well as they would start from a less advantaged situation, and more so than any other racialized group in the nation (Ngai, 2007).

Arguably, the most important case in which the Fourteenth Amendment was used to uphold the rights of undocumented individuals was the 1982 Supreme Court ruling in *Plyler v. Doe*. This case, like other key cases argued on the basis of the Fourteenth Amendment (see school desegregation cases, *Westminster v. Mendez* and *Brown v. Board of Education*) upheld the rights of all children residing in the United States to attend public school.

In the *Plyler* decision, the U.S. Supreme Court struck down a Texas law withholding funds from public schools that admitted undocumented Mexican children. The court argued that the state law violated the equal protection clause of the Fourteenth Amendment pertaining to persons of all races and nationalities residing within U.S. borders. It ruled that undocumented children had both the same right to attend public school and protection from decisions made by state legislators who had overstepped their jurisdiction. Moreover, the court concluded that denying public education to undocumented students would result in the creation of a permanent underclass comprised of members of this group and asserted that this was precisely the kind of injustice that the Fourteenth Amendment was meant to protect against.

The *Plyler* decision set an important precedent for federal intervention when laws passed at the state level violate the right of undocumented persons—rights jeopardized fourteen years later when California voters passed Proposition 187 in 1994. This proposition, passed by 59 percent of the voters who participated in the statewide referendum, established a system for determining individuals' citizenship status before providing services, thereby implicating local law enforcement, social service providers, and public school teachers in the process of identifying and reporting undocumented migrants. A district court judge delayed the implementation of most provisions in Proposition 187 after determining that it was unconstitutional for the state to have infringed on the federal government's exclusive jurisdiction over immigration and citizenship. In 1999, a newly elected state governor decided not to appeal the decision, effectively accepting the district court's ruling and dismissing the proposition.

At the time of writing, the protections afforded by the Fourteenth Amendment are facing a number of significant threats. Prominent Republican senators have recently called for the repeal of the Fourteenth Amendment in the hopes of deterring undocumented adults believed to migrate to the United States in the hopes of having U.S.-born children—derogatively referred to as "anchor babies"—from crossing the border. In addition, the recent passage of restrictive laws in Southern and Southwestern U.S. states such as SB 1070 in Arizona, HB 87 in Georgia, and HB 56 in Alabama have attempted to involve public school teachers, law enforcement officers, and other state employees in identifying and reporting undocumented migrants, reinvigorating national debate over which governing bodies have the power to regulate the presence of noncitizen persons and interpret and dictate the constitutional rights granted to them. Lastly, the American Civil Liberties Union and other civil rights organizations have reported recent violations of the *Plyler* ruling in which school officials have requested proof of U.S. citizenship from parents enrolling their children in public school. These advocacy groups have filed a number of briefs detailing the ways in which anti-immigrant state laws violate the equal protection clause of the Fourteenth Amendment. A national conversation about the historical and contemporary role of the Fourteenth Amendment is underway, and it remains to be seen whether this constitutional clause will continue to serve as a key provision for the protection of civil rights and liberties in the United States.

Ariana Mangual Figueroa

See Also: Children; Discrimination and Barriers; Exclusion; Mixed-Status Families; Pregnancy and Childbirth.

Further Reading

Barton, Paul C. 2013. "Birthright Citizenship Contested on Capitol Hill." *USA Today,* March 30. Available at http://www.usatoday.com/story/news/politics/2013/03/30/birthright-citizenship-constitution/2036095/.

Key Issues, Immigration Discrimination. American Civil Liberties Union. http://www.aclu.org/immigrants-rights

Meyer, Howard N. 2000. *The Amendment That Refused to Die: A History of the Fourteenth Amendment.* 3rd ed. Baltimore: Madison Books.

Ngai, Mae. 2007. "Birthright Citizenship and the Alien Citizen." *Fordham Law Review* 75: 2521–2530.

Preston, Julia. 2010. "Citizenship from Birth Is Challenged on the Right." August 6. *The New York Times.* http://www.nytimes.com/2010/08/07/us/politics/07fourteenth.html?scp=1&sq=birthright%20citizenship&st=cse.

Undocumented Immigrants DO Have Legal Rights (Video). 2008. Mexican American Legal Defense and Education Fund. http://www.maldef.org/truthinimmigration/undocumented_immigrants_do_have_legal3192008/index.html.

Varsanyi, Monica. 2008. "Rescaling the 'Alien,' Rescaling Personhood: Neoliberalism, Immigration, and the State." *Annals of the Association of American Geographers* 98.4:877–896.

G

Gangs

Gangs have been present in the United States for decades. The existence of Latino gangs, which are among those that have been the subject of most recent media attention, dates back to the 1930s. Originally, the gangs were concentrated in New York where they were mainly Puerto Rican and in the Southwest where they were mostly Mexican American. These demographics still predominate today, but gang activity has also become more widespread. Undocumented immigrants have an interesting relationship with gangs because they may be affiliated or, on the contrary, they may be negatively affected by them.

The 18th Street Gang (*Mara* 18 or M-18) and *Mara Salvatrucha* (MS-13) are two immigrant gangs that originate from Los Angeles but have expanded throughout the United States and beyond to Central America and Mexico. MS-13 has subgroups, or cliques, in over 42 states. Unlike most street gangs, M-18 and MS-13 have penetrated rural and suburban regions in addition to traditional urban areas. Both gangs operate in nontraditional locations such as Maryland, Virginia, and Tennessee. In 2005, M-18 had approximately thirty thousand active members throughout the United States while MS-13 had eight to ten thousand (Franco 2007: 3). Both gangs can be considered transnational because they operate in more than one country.

M-18 was formed in the 1960s by a group of Mexican immigrants. Mexican-American gangs existed during that time but did not welcome immigrants. M-18 members recruited other ethnic and racial minorities and became the first multiethnic gang in Los Angeles. MS-13 came about when three hundred thousand Salvadoran immigrants fled civil war in their home country and settled in Los Angeles during the 1980s (Franco 2007: 4). The gang was composed of former soldiers, which is believed to be a source behind its notoriously violent practices. A majority of the gang's current members are Salvadoran although there are also Mexican, Guatemalan, and Honduran members.

Some sources claim that M-18 and MS-13 became international phenomena when their undocumented members were deported to Central America and Mexico during the 1990s as a result of changing U.S. immigration laws. The gangs remained active in the Central American and Mexican destinations, and cliques began to grow as later deportees were recruited. It is unclear whether or not gangs were already operating in Central America and Mexico prior to the arrival of the deportees. The deportees may have continued the gang activity they had adopted in the United States in order to compete with the existing gangs. However, it is more likely that they mobilized for the purposes of social and financial security since many young deportees were considered foreigners in their country of origin.

It is unknown how many members of M-18 and MS-13 in the United States are undocumented immigrants. One method to disrupt gangs and remove undocumented gang members has been stricter immigrant enforcement. A series of laws were proposed in the 110th Congress (1989–1991) which would have made undocumented immigrant gang members more easy to deport, placed them in mandatory detention, maximized criminal punishment for violence and drug trafficking, and denied them eligibility for Temporary Protective Status (TPS) or asylum.

The latter point is troublesome considering that many gang members from Central America or Mexico enter the United States illegally in an effort to seek refuge from violence in their home country. These individuals may face life-threatening conditions upon deportation. Individuals who can prove that they will be persecuted if they return to their country of origin may be eligible for asylum. However, gathering the evidence to provide U.S. authorities to prove that the petitioner faces a credible danger if deported is extremely difficult if not dangerous if a formal denouncement involves corrupt officials in the service of the perpetators. The threat of death by gang violence in the home country is not a valid criterion for asylum-seeking.

In order to remove undocumented gang members, Immigration and Customs Enforcement (ICE) conducts gang raids. Because not all gang members are undocumented immigrants, this enforcement tool may be implicated in racial profiling. Furthermore, deported gang members show patterns of recidivism (repeated returns to the United States after deportation) Thus, deportation is not entirely effective.

In the United States, gang activity is more prevalent in disadvantaged neighborhoods where immigrants, especially undocumented populations, tend to reside. Undocumented teens are easy targets for gang recruitment. MS-13, for example, recruits members through glamorous depictions of the gang lifestyle. Social media are becoming an increasingly popular method for glorifying gang behaviors. In Santa Fe, New Mexico a seventeen-year-old member of the Barrio West Side gang used his MySpace page to publicly advertise his gang affiliation (Maas, 2009). Law enforcement was able to use MySpace to identify this young man and two others for their involvement in a fatal shooting. For undocumented teens who face unique pressures and who may feel vulnerable or socially misplaced due to their legal status, gangs can offer what appears to be an improved lifestyle, safety and protection from law enforcement, and a sense of belonging.

Females are often compelled to join gangs as a form of protection from abusive families. Up to 29 percent of females in one Mexican American gang had a history of sexual abuse in the home. Females in gangs tend to adhere to conservative gender roles. Women in Latino gangs may adopt submissive roles that are traditional in Latino culture. Males, on the other hand, are expected to exert dominance. Female gang members are stereotyped as being either "sex objects" or "tomboys" (Moore and Hagedorn 2001: 2). In one investigation, male gang members claimed that group sex was part of the initiation ritual for female members, yet females in the same gang refuted these claims. However, sexual exploitation of female gang members has been known to occur. Female members of an immigrant Salvadoran gang in San Francisco reported being sexually abused by male members. Traditional gender beliefs coupled with females' vulnerability raise the likelihood of sexual victimization for female gang members.

Little protection is available for undocumented immigrants who have trouble with gangs. Underreporting of gang and criminal activity is common among undocumented populations because immigrants fear deportation if they contact police. This is especially common in states such as Arizona and Alabama where Senate Bill 1070 and House Bill 56, respectively, have placed enormous pressures on undocumented immigrants.

Courtney Waters

See Also: Crime; Drug Trade; Incarceration; Violence.

Further Reading

Franco, Celinda. 2007. "CRS Report for Congress. The MS-13 and 18th Street Gangs: Emerging Transnational Gang Threats?" http://fpc.state.gov/documents/organiza tion/94863.pdf.

Maas, Dave. 2009. "Gang Signs of the Times." *Santa Fe Reporter*. http://www.sfreporter .com/santafe/article-4634-gang-signs-of-the-times.html.

Moore, Joan, and John Hagedorn. 2001. "Female Gangs: A Focus on Research." Office of Juvenile Justice and Delinquent Prevention, *Juvenile Justice Bulletin*.

Garment Industry

There are a large number of both Asian and Latina undocumented immigrants that are working the garment industry in the United States. Beginning in the mid-nineteenth century, the New York City garment industry has long provided an example of workplace exploitation that is dependent upon a workforce of mostly poor, immigrant women working in poor conditions and for low wages. More recently and since the 1970s, the garment industry grew in the city of Los Angeles because of the wide availability of undocumented immigrants from Mexico. Many of these garment industry shops are owned by Korean immigrants. Throughout history there have also been Irish, Italian, Polish, and Jewish immigrants who have worked in the garment industries.

A 1993 study found that there were 3,642 garment factories in Los Angeles County alone, with the overwhelming majority of its workers Latino, and mostly immigrant (Light et al., 1999). Although the exact number of garment industry workers is nearly impossible to ascertain given the informal nature in which they are often employed, the research by Soldatenko (1999) reports an estimated 120,000 workers formed part of this economic sector in the 1990s. Spener and Capps (2001) have argued that with globalization and neoliberal trade policies adversely impacting the economies of Latin America and Asia, more and more impoverished and displaced populations are uprooted, resulting in more exploitative conditions wherever they can find jobs. Free trade agreements are one reason that the wages are low and the workers are exploited. Aguascalientes, Mexico, was a big export partner to the United States

Former Seo employees Faviola Munoz Aguirre, 20, left, and her sister Maria Aguirre, 23, jot down addresses of mid-town Manhattan garment factories on Wednesday, June 12, 1996, before searching for work in New York's garment district. The sisters lost their jobs when the Seo factory, where they were employed closed after it was found to be producing garments for Kathie Lee Gifford's clothing line while violating state and federal labor laws. (AP Photo/ Kathy Willens)

during the 1990's. Later, many of these factories were moved to northern cities in order to cut down the costs of transportation of the finished products, resulting in job losses in the central and southern part of Mexico that contributed to growing migration to the north.

The number of jobs in the garment industry may decline as operations are moved offshore, such as when American-owned clothing and textile companies search for the lowest cost for wage labor in other countries. The movement of industries to other countries in order to optimize production and lower the cost of production is part of what is known as globalization. This happens when operations are exported into more impoverished countries, such as China, India or Cambodia, where workers have little option but to work for less pay. The garments produced in these factories are then exported to places where the factories originated, such as the United States and Mexico, resulting in the loss of jobs for those who used to work there. In this way, when factories abruptly move abroad, local workers are displaced. With greater frequency, the impact is felt by women and minority workers. As factories and sweat shops continue with this strategy, continually closing down operations in one place in search of more cost savings, the newly unemployed become increasing impoverished because they have little choice but to accept lower wages and underemployment. In other words, garment industry workers in one country compete with those in another, resulting in less wages for everyone. In the literature, this phenomenon has been referred to as "the race to the bottom." With extreme poverty and economic instability at the local level, migration increasingly becomes a viable option.

In this way, globalization brings a level of hopelessness for impoverished populations caught in the web of negotiations between big industries and those governments in countries eager to attract investors by offering them access to a labor force that is made powerless by the lack of opportunities, and because of it is less likely to complain about their conditions. In addition, governments become more willing to help large companies by not enforcing laws that favor workers' rights. This empowers large big-box U.S. companies such as Wal-Mart to pressure the companies they contract to produce their goods. Because big-box stores compete with each other for customers, striving for lower prices to attract a greater share of consumers becomes a driving force in finding the lowest costs for producing them. In turn, as consumers become more impoverished, they scour for ways to save money, forcing them to patronize those stores that provide the cheapest prices for goods—made possible by exploiting others.

Not all garments are produced abroad, as there are still many garment shops left in the United States, found in New York and Los Angeles. These produce high-end quality fashion merchandise. In contrast to the rest of the United States, apparel employment has been growing in Los Angeles. Between 1993 and 1997 the LA industry added an estimated 26,000 new jobs. The LA industry is now the largest apparel employer in the United States. Although New York still remains the chief fashion center of the nation, jobs have shifted away from that city. Apparel is the largest manufacturing industry in Los Angeles since the post–Cold War military cutbacks. The city is not as well known for its apparel and fashion districts that employ an estimated 150,000 skilled labor workers.

However, the U.S. garment industry has experienced job losses as companies relocate to other countries to maximize profits. Thus, in the United State too, many workers have been displaced as corporations turn to places in Asia where workers might be paid even less, such as the research in El Paso, Texas by Spener and Capps (2001) shows. The North American Free Trade Agreement (NAFTA) has caused sweatshops to move into Mexico. NAFTA's purposes, in part, were to enable U.S. apparel manufacturers and retailers to rely less on Asian countries and to develop their own wages in the western part of the world. As a consequence, apparel imports from Mexico have soared, overtaking the major Asian exporters to the United States, and they have continued to promise rapid growth.

In this way, more and more impoverished people end up in garment industry factories working under exploitative conditions, also known as "sweat shops," facing difficult, "third world" working conditions, and often occupational hazards, where they may work ten to twelve hours a day in hot and dusty, and often vermin-infested conditions (Soldatenko, 1999). According to firsthand accounts obtained by research by

Soldatenko (1999), women often work alongside their children, and at times there is interethnic conflict as those who have been working at the shop are replaced with more recent immigrant arrivals. Latina employees often express resentment of their supervisors or factory owners, who tend to be Asian—in particular Korean, leading to the racial overtones of the experience (Soldatenko, 1999). The research corroborates claims made by immigrant rights and union organizers about the industry's widespread violations of many U.S. labor laws. Indeed, a Department of Labor notice reports that 93 percent of the investigations of Los Angeles' garment manufacturers uncover violations (U.S. Department of Labor, 2012).

There is some variation in the conditions in the garment contracting shops of Los Angeles, but overall conditions are similar. Garment workers usually work on one piece at a time and are paid by each piece that is sewn or assembled. Both California and federal law require that workers be paid minimum wage and overtime, even if they are paid by piece. Employers are required to keep accurate time cards and ensure that the hourly minimum wage is paid and that the appropriate rate for paying overtime is followed when employees work over eight hours a day, or more than 40 hours a week. These employer requirements are according to the Federal Fair Labor Standards Act (U.S. Department of Labor, 2012). Common violations are poor record-keeping, not paying overtime, and poor reporting practices. Employers are found to devise schemes so that overtime is not paid, such as pressuring workers to work from home and on weekends, in violation of the law (Soldatenko, 1999). In sum, violations of the laws that regulate fair employment standards continue to be a problem.

Apparel workers have often attempted to unionize but this effort is challenged on several levels. Encouraging the American public to support local industries by buying American products would keep the depression of wages at bay, but the idea of paying more for clothing is generally an unpopular idea. High job insecurity that comes with globalization undermines workers' ability to create a culture of resistance that would allow them to network and organize (Soldatenko, 1999). Also, although immigrant men also work within the industry, most workers are women, and the union movement has been dominated by men. Without a union, calling attention to workplace conditions thus makes workers vulnerable to employer retaliation (Sullivan and Lee, 2008). Finally, as with all undocumented workers, employers may threaten to deport them or replace them if they unionize or complain about working conditions or low pay.

Drew Berns

See Also: Globalization; Labor Supply; Labor Unions; NAFTA; Workers' Rights.

Further Reading

Bonacich, Edna. 1998. "Organizing Immigrant Workers in the Los Angeles Apparel Industry." *Journal of World-Systems Research* 4:10–19.

Chin, Margaret. 2005. *Sewing Women: Immigrants and the New York City Garment Industry.* New York: Columbia University Press.

Collins, Jane. 2003. *Threads: Gender, Labor, and Power in the Global Apparel Industry.* Chicago: University of Chicago Press.

Jacobson, David. 1998. *The Immigration Reader: America in a Multidisciplinary Perspective*. Malden, MA: Blackwell.

Light, Ivan, Richard B. Bernard, and Rebecca Kim. 1999. "Immigrant Incorporation in the Garment Industry of Los Angeles." *International Migration Review* 33.1:5–25.

Louie, Miriam Ching Yoon. 2001. *Sweatshop Warriors: Immigrant Women Workers Take On the Global Factory*. Cambridge, MA: South End Press.

Soldatenko, María Angelina. 1999. "Made in the USA: Latinos/as, Garment Work and Ethnic Conflict in Los Angeles Sweat Shops." *Cultural Studies* 13.2:319–334.

Spener, David, and Randy Capps. 2001. "North American Free Trade and Changes in the Nativity of the Garment Industry Workforce in the United States." *International Journal of Urban & Regional Research* 25.2:301–326.

Sullivan, Richard, and Kimi Lee. 2008. "Organizing Immigrant Women in America's Sweatshops: Lessons from the Los Angeles Garment Worker Center." *Signs: Journal of Women in Culture & Society* 33.3:527–532.

U.S. Department of Labor. 2012. "US Labor Department Conducts Enforcement Initiative to End Sweatshop Conditions in Los Angeles' Fashion District, Southern California Garment Industry." Available at http://www.dol.gov/whd/media/press/whdpressVB3.asp?pressdoc=Western/20120808.xml.

Gateways

Immigrant gateways are communities where immigrants settle upon arrival in the United States. Gateways have undergone rapid and profound change over the past century. Whereas immigrants have traditionally settled in urban metropolitan areas, they are also now establishing communities in nontraditional suburban and rural locations. The changes can be attributed to several factors, most of which are related to shifting immigration policies and economic opportunities. Regardless of their evolving characteristics, gateways are and will continue to be important centers of cultural exchange.

Immigrant gateways are defined as "metropolitan areas with Census 2000 immigrant population of over 1 million" (Stodolska & Shinew 2009, 268). Most of the traditional Mexican immigrant gateways are situated in the west and southwest United States, while nontraditional locations have been emerging primarily in the Southeast and Midwest. Undocumented immigrants are currently present in every state throughout the nation, yet they are most heavily concentrated in certain regions.

Prior to 1995, six states were gateway communities for 70 percent of Mexican immigrants. Since 1995, immigrant populations in nontraditional gateways such as North Carolina and Kansas have grown by more than 50 percent. For example, the undocumented population in Texas, Louisiana, and Oklahoma rose by 240,000 between 2007 and 2010. Meanwhile, between 2007 and 2010, the undocumented population in Florida, New York, Virginia, Colorado, Arizona, Utah, and Nevada decreased by 230,000.

Immigrant gateways have been classified under six categories depending on the period of time in which they were most prominent. In the early years of the twentieth century, Cleveland and Buffalo were popular immigrant destinations. These cities are now considered "former gateways" as immigrants do not typically initially settle there anymore. Los Angeles and Miami are termed "Post–World War II" gateways because they were popular immigrant destinations in the second half of the twentieth century. "Continuous gateways" such as New York and Chicago are destinations that have endured as immigrant settlement communities for many years and continue to fit this role. Together, these three types of gateways are called "established gateways."

The cultures in established gateways are continuously evolving as different immigrant groups come and go. In 2005, Chicago's foreign-born population was over 1.6 million. A majority, or 79 percent, of the Latino immigrants who settle in the city are Mexican. A Chicago community known as Little Village has been home to a number of ethnic enclaves (communities comprised primarily of certain ethnic groups) over many years and currently consists of 83 percent Latinos. Immigrant groups who reside in continuous and post–World War II gateways have a longer presence in these communities, average poverty rates that do not differ significantly from the native population, and high rates of naturalization. Immigrants' English proficiency in these communities is relatively low. As a settling point for ethnic enclaves, gateways often lack diversity and as such, can hinder immigrants' assimilation into American culture.

Gateway cities such as Washington D.C., Atlanta and Dallas are considered "emerging," as their immigrant populations have grown rapidly over the past 20 years. Seattle is an example of a "re-emerging" gateway, a city that was a popular immigrant destination in the past but became less desirable for a number of years, and is now attracting immigrants again. "Pre-emerging" gateways are those such as Raleigh–Durham whose immigrant population has seen substantial growth throughout the 1990s. These three types of gateways are called "twenty-first-century gateways."

Beyond the standard definition, continuous, post–World War II, emerging, and re-emerging cities must also have a foreign-born population and/or a growth rate among the foreign-born that exceeds the national average.

Several factors have contributed to the emergence of nontraditional immigrant gateway communities. After the Immigration Reform and Control Act (IRCA) was implemented in 1986, gateway destinations began to change dramatically. Under IRCA, undocumented immigrants residing in the United States at the time were granted amnesty. With legal status, immigrants were no longer reliant on ethnic enclaves in traditional gateway destinations for protection and support. Instead, they had the freedom to move elsewhere where labor opportunities were more abundant and an improved quality of life was possible.

Labor opportunities in nontraditional gateways are an important factor pulling immigrants away from common destinations. In many metropolitan areas within cities and along the U.S.-Mexico border where migrants typically settle, the labor markets have been completely saturated. Beyond limited job opportunities, these communities also have poor schools, high crime rates, and expensive and crowded living conditions. In nontraditional settings, there is a demand for low-wage work. In particular, the poultry, fish, and meat processing industries in the Midwest are attractive options for immigrants, including the undocumented. These industries offer consistent work year round as well as steady wages. While low, the wages earned by working in food processing are enough to support a modest lifestyle. The potential to earn a good living along with more job options for women has led immigrant families to settle in nontraditional locations, whereas in the past, migrants were mostly men who lived in the United States and sent money to support their families abroad.

While some factors serve as favorable conditions that pull migrants to nontraditional locations, anti-immigrant legislation is one factor that pushes migrants away from traditional gateway communities. The implementation of the North American Free Trade Agreement (NAFTA) in 1994 and ensuing border enforcement, such as the construction of the border wall, are also believed to be important contributors to the growing prevalence of nontraditional gateways. These locations are favorable for undocumented immigrants because Border Patrol and Immigration and Customs Enforcement (ICE) are less likely to patrol them.

Overall, NAFTA did little to curb problems related to undocumented immigration. In fact, it can be argued that NAFTA worsened conditions. Without assistance from the federal government, several states have recently taken undocumented immigration into their own hands. The first state to propose severe anti-immigrant legislation was California with its Proposition 187 in the early 1990s. As the most prominent Mexican immigrant gateway, thousands of Mexicans were made to feel unwelcome and subsequently left California for other states.

More recently, a growing number of state laws related to immigration have been proposed. In 2005, 300 immigration-related bills were introduced nationwide. By 2009, that number had risen to 1,500. In the first quarter of 2011, more than 1,700 immigration-related bills have been introduced across fifty states and Puerto Rico.

After Senate Bill 1070 was passed in Arizona in 2010, the state's immigrant population was drastically reduced. However, it is unclear if undocumented immigrants moved back to their home country, as the bill intended for them to do in a process called self-repatriation, or if they moved further inland into the United States. It is more likely that the latter has been occurring. The same question remains for the reduction of Alabama's immigrant population after passage of House Bill 56 in 2011.

Immigrants' movement to nontraditional locations often causes drastic and rapid changes in the nontraditional destinations' current population. Immigrants who have recently arrived in the United States are mostly from Asia and Latin America. They tend to be poorer than the native population and usually have lower English proficiency. Additionally, most immigrant groups have complex social networks which play an important role in facilitating their establishment in the United States. For undocumented immigrants, this is especially true. Without social networks, undocumented immigrants' opportunities for success are greatly diminished. With these social networks, large groups of immigrants may settle in a new destination at one time; or a small group may attract and support the movement of other social network members to their recent destination.

Emerging and pre-emerging gateways with little prior exposure to immigrants are often not equipped to meet the needs of the new and growing population. For example, these cities may lack culturally-appropriate resources including bilingual or bicultural health care providers. Non-traditional communities may also exhibit stronger discrimination and racism than common gateways. Furthermore, there is concern that immigrant gateways shoulder a heavy burden as a result of undocumented immigrants.

States will need support from the federal government in order to accommodate and facilitate the integration of their growing immigrant populations.

Despite the growth of the immigrant population in nontraditional settings, traditional gateways are still heavily populated with immigrants, and new immigrants continue to join these communities. Up to 77 percent of the undocumented population currently resides in twelve states; California, Texas, Florida, New York, New Jersey, Illinois, Georgia, Arizona, North Carolina, Maryland, Washington, Virginia. California is home to the largest number of undocumented immigrants at one quarter, followed by Texas.

Courtney Waters

See Also: Enclaves; Globalization; Illinois, Mobility; Suburbs.

Further Reading

Cohn, D'Vera, and Jeffrey Passel. 2011. "Unauthorized Immigrant Population: National and State Trends, 2010." Pew Hispanic Center Web Site. http://www.pewhispanic.org/2011/02/01/iv-state-settlement-patterns/.

Crowley, Martha, Daniel T. Lichter, and Zhenchao Qian. 2006. "Beyond Gateway Cities: Economic Restructuring and Poverty Among Mexican Immigrant Families and Children." *Family Relations* 55: 345–360.

Reid, Carolina. 2006. "Crossing Borders, Creating Communities: Immigration Trends and Their Implications for Community Development." *Community Investments* (2006): 3–8.

Singer, Audrey. 2004. "The Rise of New Immigrant Gateways." *Immigration, Demographics, Ethnicity, Race.* The Brookings Institution.

Stodolska, Monika, and Kimberly J. Shinew. 2009. "La Calidad de Vida dentro de La Villita: An Investigation of Factors Affecting Quality of Life in Latino Residents of an Urban Immigrant Residential Enclave." *Journal of Immigrant & Refugee Studies* 7: 267.

Gender Roles

The study of immigrant women as an area of research and scholarly attention has come a long way. Initially, stereotypical and andro-centric biases on the part of researchers in the field deemed women's experiences as less important in the process of migration. For years research was conducted as if immigration did not affect women and/or families that were left behind or those that accompanied immigrant men. In the late 1980s and early 1990s, a vast and robust body of literature, primarily written by feminist scholars, has challenged these assumptions through rich empirical research. Feminist scholars across a range of fields have shown not only what happened to immigrant women and families left behind, but more importantly, the range of reasons and conditions that have pushed immigrant women to become part of global migration processes. Researchers have also deepened our understanding of migration processes by looking at how gender matters in the migration process and the social consequences of movement for families, communities, and children. It is in this body of work that we can find evidence of the rather fragile social status of immigrant women, in particular undocumented immigrant women.

Researchers have shown that undocumented immigrant women frequently become vulnerable to abuse and loss of social status within their families, at work, and within their communities. Although reliable statistics about undocumented immigrant women are hard to come by, researchers have documented that since the middle decades of the twentieth century the number of women joining the ranks of undocumented immigrants to the United States has steadily increased. Social scientists have also placed the current policies of neoliberal globalization as the main culprit shaping the migration of women. Women from diverse social classes and groups—including a significant share of working mothers and poor single women—leave their countries of origin seeking employment opportunities in the United States and Canada. Latin American migration to other post-industrial economies such as Europe, Asia, and the Middle East (Israel) has been noted as well. Regardless of destination, immigrant women without documentation become vulnerable and are subject to abuse as workers, as mothers, and as racialized/ethnic minorities. This triple form of vulnerability makes immigrant women's experiences all the more significant to social scientists and policy makers.

Within the family, it is their roles and responsibilities as mothers that push women to migrate abroad. Some seek to reunite with husbands who have left earlier, while others migrate leaving their husbands and children behind. Although the family is frequently assumed to provide security and shelter, for some undocumented women, the family is a site of abuse and vulnerability. Once in the receiving communities, women may be afraid to leave their homes for fear of being apprehended. A study conducted in Los Angeles found that undocumented Latinas were more likely to be homemakers when compared to documented Latinas and Anglo women. As mothers, undocumented immigrant women may be subject to some isolation from other community members if fear of being apprehended and deported discourages them from leaving the safety of their home.

We know that undocumented women tend to work in occupations that are high risk, low pay, and frequently unregulated. Again, research from Los Angeles indicates that the majority of undocumented Latinas tend to work in service jobs, mostly housecleaning, child care, waitressing, hotel maids, and kitchen workers. As workers, women face abuse from employers and coworkers. Newspaper reports of abuse in the agricultural industry have found that undocumented women in this sector are among the most vulnerable to sexual exploitation, harassment and rape. Since many undocumented women work in occupations that are not regulated by the state (domestic work and child care), employers take advantage of their vulnerability. We know that historically and in general, domestic workers in the United States have been subject to abuse—underpaid and rampant exploitation. They also suffer a life of exclusion and invisibility, while assuring that the various forms of the privileged and affluent are passed on from one generation to the next. The works by Romero (2002) and Hondagneu-Sotelo (2007) demonstrate how the hidden costs of paid domestic labor, in the way of domestics and nannies, are filled by immigrant women in the United States. These studies shows how work itself and the way work gets done are shaped by gender, class, race and immigrant status.

The following stories of two undocumented immigrant women in the Midwest, Elvira Arellano and Flor Crisostomo, may shed further light on the vulnerabilities that undocumented women face as women, mothers, and workers. These stories also exemplify how these vulnerabilities pushed them to become activists on behalf of themselves and other women in similar predicaments.

Elvira Arellano and Flor Crisostomo represent the experiences of two working mothers who prior to 9/11 worked and lived in Chicago "under the radar," a term used by anthropologist Ruth Gomberg Muñoz to describe the experience of undocumented workers in the city. Prior to moving to Chicago, both women's lives had already been disrupted by the forces of neoliberal globalization in Mexico. Elvira grew up in a small village in the state of Michoacan and like other working daughters of Latin Americans upon reaching adulthood, she had joined the labor force to support her family. Flor, an indigenous woman, from the state of Oaxaca, supported herself and her family through meager wages in the informal economy. They found themselves unemployed for different reasons and both viewed migration to the United States as the only alternative for their families' needs and survival. They crossed the border without documentation, revealing yet another dimension of the dangers and vulnerabilities that women face in the migration process. Women who cross the border alone expose themselves to state violence enforced by border patrols harassment and potential rape in the hands of smugglers, and even death in the desert areas, the new routes of movements in the post-9/11 era. After several failed attempts, Elvira crossed the border and followed the migrant route of work that took her first to Washington and eventually to Chicago. Flor crossed the U.S.-Mexico border by foot—nearly costing her life—and made it to Chicago where she had family. Both women had arrived in the city within years of each other and knew each other through the work they did organizing on behalf of undocumented immigrant families. As workers in Chicago's low-wage labor market, they were vulnerable to abuse, exploitation, and sexual harassment. Flor has spoken publicly about the sexual harassment she encountered in the workplace and her inability to be able to denounce the perpetrators because she could lose her job or, worse, face deportation. It has been shown that undocumented women's vulnerability is forged in the context of not only the profound stereotypes about immigrants and racism, but more significantly sexism. Yet their responsibility as working mothers drove them to persevere and become voices for social change.

In 2007, Elvira Arellano was catapulted to national headlines when she defied a deportation order and sought sanctuary in a local church in the heart of the Puerto Rican community of Chicago. Elvira represented the vulnerabilities that undocumented working mothers with U.S.-born children face in the United States. Through her frequent press conferences and public statements, Elvira spoke eloquently about her plight as a working mother trying to provide for her son, Saul. She also raised her voice to call for immigration reform and to end the separation of families underlying the emerging deportation regime. During Elvira's year-long refuge in the United Adalberto Methodist Church (August, 2006–August, 2007), her friendship with Flor, and their solidarity, and activism grew exponentially. When Elvira left her sanctuary in August, 2007, an act that resulted in her arrest and deportation to Tijuana, Mexico, Flor Crisostomo took her place at the United Adalberto Methodist Church. Like Elvira, she too had exhausted all her legal appeals and had been issued an order of removal. Unlike Elvira, Flor's claim to remaining in the United States was based on her right to work as a transnational working mother displaced by neoliberal policies. Eventually, Flor left sanctuary and today continues to live in the shadows yet still engaged in activism through her frequent post on her facebook page and other internet forums. Elvira, too, continues to be ever more vocal but her sphere of influence is now Mexico, where she lives and continues to be critical of the ongoing deportation and separation of families and continues to push for widespread immigration reform. She has also become part of marches and activities with the ever growing number of Central American mothers searching for their disappeared sons and daughters in Mexico. She is still connected to Chicago's efforts and sends frequent press releases voicing her concerns about the growing number of deportations, the need for the DREAM Act, and the ever growing need for immigration reform. Flor's sphere of activism has also expanded with her departure because now her blog has gone global and she is part of the larger transnational struggle to bring about change to indigenous communities across the Americas.

Maura Toro-Morn

See Also: Activism; Culture; Dream Act; Families; Family Economics; Family Structure; Marriage; Violence against Women Act (VAWA); Women's Status.

Further Reading

Chavez, Leo R., Allan Hubbel, Shiraz I. Mishra, and R. Burciaga Valdez. 1997. "Undocumented Latina Immigrants in Orange Country, California: A Comparative Analysis." *International Migration Review* 31.1:88–107.

Gomberg-Muñoz, Ruth. 2010. *Labor and Legality: An Ethnography of a Mexican Immigrant Network.* New York: Oxford University Press.

Hondagneu-Sotelo, Pierrette. 2007. *Domestica: Immigrant Workers Cleaning and Caring in the Shadows of Affluence.* Berkeley: University of California Press.

Romero, Mary. 2002. *Maid in the U.S.A.* New York: Routledge.

Toro-Morn, Maura, and Nilda Flores Gonzalez. 2011. "Transnational Latino Mother-Activists in the Americas: The Case of Elvira Arellano and Flor Crisostomo." *Journal of the Motherhood Initiative for Research and Community Involvement* 2.2:111–126.

Toro-Morn, Maura I. 2013. "Elvira Arellano and the Struggles of Low-Wage Undocumented Latina Immigrant Women." In *Immigrant Women in the Neoliberal Age,* eds. N. Flores-Gonzalez, A. R. Guevarra, M. Toro-Morn, and G. Chang, 38–55. Urbana: University of Illinois Press.

Globalization

The term globalization has been increasing in popularity since the mid-1980s. In general terms, globalization can be defined as the movement of ideas, people, and trade across the borders. However, although these kinds of movements have been present for many centuries, the term assumed new significance in the twentieth century with the

Maria Guaman receives 100 dollars sent by her husband, a U.S. immigrant, at a bank in Nabon, Ecuador, March 18, 2009. The country adopted a U.S.-dollar-based system in 2000. The vast majority of undocumented immigrants come to the United States because of economic necessity, and send remittances to family members left behind. Remittance flows to developing countries around the world increased from $285 billion in 2007 to $328 billion in 2008. During the 2008-2009 economic recession, remittances to these countries declined. (AP Photo/ Dolores Ochoa)

growth of transnational linkages that tie the fate of people and their local economies to distant macroeconomic policies and practices. In other words, globalization is what makes the local more dependent on the global: on the trade transactions, capital investments and speculations that take place in other parts of the world. Because of this increased interconnectedness, decisions and events have macro-level consequences when they impact even the most remote corners of the world. The growth of displaced persons and migrants is the most visible sign of how those decisions that often take place in remote parts of the world impact local decisions and activities. Knowledge of how such macro-level economic policies impact the local is fundamental to understanding how and why immigration—especially undocumented immigration—has increased in recent years.

The macro-level policies that have made our world more economically interconnected are grounded in certain economic philosophies that make the policies operational. Most scholars agree that at the root of many of these policies are neoliberal economic philosophies. Neoliberalism is a market-driven approach to economics that is based on a strong private enterprise sector that is allowed to operate unrestricted by government regulations and control. Although there are many, one example of a neo-liberal policy is the North American Free Trade Agreement (NAFTA) that was signed in 1993 by the governments of the United States, Canada, and Mexico. Although NAFTA was touted as an economic plan that would reduce immigration to the United States from Mexico, it proved to be the opposite. It did this in at least three ways. First, it resulted in the disruption of rural and agricultural-based economies because small holders who subsisted on corn production could not compete with the lower prices of subsidized corn production in the United States. When NAFTA provided for the lifting of international trade restrictions, Mexico was flooded with cheap corn from the United States. Rural land holders who did not have subsidies were unable to sell their own corn on the market. Unable to subsist, they were forced to migrate in search of jobs. Many sold their land to help pay for the cost of migrating. Others used their land as collateral to secure funds needed to migrate. In the mid-1990s, more undocumented immigrants from Mexico started to enter the United States than at any other period in history. The great majority of immigrants coming to the United States after NAFTA was signed have come from Mexico's southern and central states where the economic plan worked to undermine subsistence economies in already poor communities.

The second reason that NAFTA failed to reduce immigration to the United States is rooted in the neoliberal philosophy that promotes fiscally conservative approaches to spending and the belief that governments should not run large economic deficits to maintain social welfare programs. Offhand, this sounds like a sound fiscal policy. However, to reduce economic deficits neoliberal economists for the most part consider government-subsidized entitlement programs such as services for the poor, primary education, public transportation, and publically funded health care programs to be wasteful, and believe that these place undue tax burdens on individuals and businesses. The most significant change in the nature of migration after NAFTA was implemented was the greater number of women driven into the wage labor force (Marcelli and Cornelius, 2001). Facing increased poverty and less social support, the unprecedented number of women entering the labor market through migration has resulted in the feminization of migration.

The third reason that NAFTA failed to reduce immigration to the United States is related to the conditions through which less developed nations obtain large-scale loans to help develop their economies. A neoliberal approach to the economy is premised on the procurement of large investment loans that can help less developed countries that are struggling to remain competitive with other nations around the globe. Many of these loans are available from the International Monetary Fund (IMF) and the World Bank. However, obtaining such loans is often contingent on the adoption of neoliberal princi-ples, including reducing the nation's financial deficits. This results in the curtailing of expenditures for social welfare programs, referred to as structural adjustment programs (SAPs). Also known as the Washington Consensus, some of these free-market-oriented conditions include cutting public assistance programs, the deregulation of labor rela-tions, and the devaluation of a nation's currency to remain globally competitive. In this way SAPs resulted in harsher conditions for México's poor, especially for women who increasingly contend with rising education and health care costs for their families, diminishing employment opportunities, and declining purchasing power. Together with the reining in of expenditures for social welfare programs, conditions in poor communities worsened, forcing them to migrate for survival.

Neoliberal policies decided at the macro level have undermined local economies so that those who depend on social programs no longer can—a clear example of globalization. Unable to derive a living from the local economies, immigrants are driven into the global labor market. A great many of them may first move to larger cities until over-crowding and the lack of jobs force them to move to another country. Migration thus becomes a matter of survival. It is because they have no choice but to cross borders without the legal authority to do so that they risk arrest and even death. Although immigrants come to the United States from all over the world, the largest number of undocumented immigrants come from Latin America and in particular Mexico. In this way, globalization is central to the process that drives people from their native lands and towards those lands that are unfamiliar and at times hostile to immigrants. These environments have additional consequences for immigrants. Seeking out better opportunities splinters domestic units and their nurturing social contexts. As immigrants are dislodged from their land and family units, they may become alienated or isolated. Industries profit from this. The more alienation and isolation immigrants feel, the greater the likelihood that they will return to their country of origin after they become older and less productive. Furthermore, as nations compete with each other, they adopt different forms of employer-employee relationships resulting in more flexible forms of employment—underemployed, part time and seasonal employees—and additional dependencies. Global economies in this way disadvantage immigrants more, and even when they find themselves in more developed and wealthier destination countries such as the United States. Through immigration, wealthy nations are undeniably connected to the less wealthy, less developed nations.

Globalization also has impacted immigrant women in unique ways. Forced to migrate, women often become more independent from spouses and families. As they become wage earners, they also become distanced from their reproductive roles. Changes that come with globalization thus include choosing to have fewer children and marrying later in life, and having less time to devote to other reproductive activities such as the socialization of family members and caring for and monitoring dependent children, the elderly, and the sick.

Anna Ochoa O'Leary

See Also: Displacement; Families; Family Economics; Family Reunification; Family Structure; Gender Roles; Migration; North American Free Trade Agreement (NAFTA); Transnationalism.

Further Reading

Barndt, Deborah. 2001. *Tangled Routes: Women, Work, and Globalization on the Tomato Trail*. Lanham, MD: Rowman & Littlefield Publishers.

Canales, Alejandro I. 2000. "International Migration and Labour Flexibility in the Context of NAFTA." *Social Science Journal* 52.165:409–419.

Hing, Bill Ong. 2010. *Ethical Borders: NAFTA, Globalization, and Mexican Migration*. Philadelphia: Temple University Press.

Marcelli, Enrico A., and Wayne A. Cornelius. 2001. "The Changing Profile of Mexican Migrants to the United States: New Evidence from California and México." *Latin American Research Review* 36.3:105–131.

Stiglitz, Joseph E. 2002. *Globalization and Its Discontents.* New York: W. W. Norton.

Governance and Criminalization

Since the 1970s, crime and punishment have become an increasingly central means through which political authorities in the United States seek to govern the conduct of individuals and populations, and in particular, undocumented immigrants. Jonathan Simon refers to such development as "governing through crime." This way of governing is clearly visible in such measures as quality of life campaigns and zero tolerance policing, harsher penalties and the extensive utilization of imprisonment, three strikes and compulsory minimum sentencing policies, redress in juvenile court and the incarceration of minors, immigrant detention centers, and more extensive parole restrictions. It is further visible in the common practice of securitizing private spaces as a way of dealing with crime risks and insecurities. The most notable manifestations of this practice are undoubtedly gated communities. These fortified enclaves are segregated spatial enclosures designed to provide a safe, orderly, and secure environments for those who dwell within them. The rationale for governing through crime seems to be twofold. On the one hand, the thinking is that irresponsible individuals must be held accountable for their misdeeds. And on the other, it is that responsible citizens must protect themselves and be protected from the throngs of anti-citizens who threaten their security and quality of life. The containment of the few therefore becomes a prerequisite for the freedoms of the many.

This contemporary emphasis on governing through crime has had a significant impact on how undocumented migration is problematized and managed. In fact, undocumented migration has come to be seen largely as a law and order issue in the United States. Since the early 1990s, the United States has witnessed a rather strong wave of anti-immigrant sentiment—a trend that has only intensified in the post-9/11 context. From social scientists, immigration officials, and policy analysts, to immigration reform organizations and the public at large, it has been common for individuals and groups to cast unauthorized migrants—typically imagined as Mexican—as threats to the overall well-being and security of the social body. The fundamental problem with the undocumented has been deemed to be their illegality—the "fact" that they do not have a legal right to be in the United States. Thus, for some people, to be an "illegal" immigrant is to be inherently a lawbreaker. It is to be necessarily a criminal. In addition to being constructed as lawbreakers, the undocumented have routinely been linked to a host of other problems. For example, they have been associated with such cultural, social, and economic maladies as overpopulation, deteriorating schools, urban crime and decay, energy shortages, and national disunity. Furthermore, they have been accused of displacing American workers, depressing wages, spreading diseases, and burdening public services. All of these problems are seen as compounding the fundamental problem of immigrant criminality.

Given that undocumented migrants have largely been constructed as criminal "illegal aliens" who harm the well-being of American citizens and threaten the security of the nation, the measures employed to govern them have been extremely exclusionary and punitive. Put otherwise, undocumented migrants have largely come to be governed through crime. Governing immigration through crime has taken numerous forms in the United States. The most notable form it has undoubtedly taken is that of enhanced border policing. Since the early 1990s, the U.S. federal government has undertaken a major boundary control offensive, one that aims to shape the conduct of unauthorized immigrants in such as way as to deter them from entering the United States. Federal authorities have essentially determined that one of the best ways to deal with the "problem" of undocumented immigration is through expanding border policing operations. The expansion of the border policing as a way of governing unauthorized immigration has been most conspicuous along the U.S.-Mexico border. It is this border that has historically been seen as the primary source of the undocumented immigrant "problem." This expansion actually dates back to the late 1970s. But it really burgeoned in the early 1990s. That's when the Immigration and Naturalization Service (INS) put into effect a broad plan to gain control of the southwest border and reduce illicit immigration. This comprehensive border control scheme was based on a strategy of "prevention through deterrence." The objective was to increase fencing, lighting, personnel, and surveillance equipment along the main gates of illegal entry—such as San Diego, California and El Paso, Texas—in order to raise the probability of apprehension to such a high level that unauthorized migrants would be deterred from crossing the border. Now, in the post-9/11 context, the policing of the border as a way of managing unauthorized migration has only accelerated as the fight against immigrant illegality has become conflated with the "war on terror." A primary solution to the undocumented immigration problem, then, has been to turn the United States into a fortified enclave of sorts. It has been to cast a wide net of control and surveillance over the border in order to discourage illegal incursions and thus keep troublesome individuals out of the body politic. As with the government of crime more generally, the rationale for managing undocumented migrants through crime is that the public must be protected from the would-be criminals who threaten their security and contentment.

While the policing of the border continues unabated, the Federal government has since the early 2000s intensified its policing of the nation's interior. Indeed, interior policing, led by the Department of Homeland Security's (DHS) Bureau of Immigration and Customs Enforcement (ICE), has become a central component of the border fight against "terror" and "illegal" immigration. What has basically happened is that the border, as a focus of security and immigration control, has been deterritorialized and projected into the nation's interior. As part of this border respatialization, certain spaces of everyday life—most notably workplaces but also individual homes and a variety of public spaces—have been identified as strategic sites and become subject to intensified policing. As such, numerous locales across the interior of the United States have been turned into border zones of enforcement.

One of the main mechanisms ICE has employed to carry out its interior policing mission is the raid. A raid is a practice whereby immigration authorities, sometimes with the help of other policing agencies, descend en masse on homes, places of work, and other spaces with the express purpose of apprehending individuals believed to be in the country without authorization. Like border policing, the raid is a practice that seeks to securitize the nation through the abjection and exclusion of individuals and populations deemed threatening to the social body. ICE's initial targets were people whose criminal or other actions had rendered them deportable. But it soon focused on worksite enforcement. Indeed, in the period between 2006 and 2008, this agency pursued an aggressive program of policing of the nation's workplaces, with ICE apprehending about fourteen thousand undocumented migrants through worksite raids between 2006 and 2008. This compares to only about 2,700 arrests between 2002 and 2005. However, after a revised worksite strategy by ICE in 2009, the numbers are beginning to decrease. In 2012, the Homeland Security Investigations of ICE yielded 520 arrests, of which 240 were owners or managers of the workplaces ("Fact Sheet: Worksite Enforcement," 2013).

While the number of migrants caught in worksite raids is rather small in relation to the estimated 11.1 million undocumented migrants residing in the United States (in 2012), the effects of the raids have nevertheless been rather profound. The most palpable impact of the raids has been on the families, particularly the children, of the individuals who have been apprehended and deported. In 2007, the Urban Institute released a report titled *Paying the Price: The Impact of Immigration Raids on America's Children.* The report focuses on the aftermath of large-scale ICE raids in three communities: Greeley, Colorado; Grand Island, Nebraska; and New Bedford, Massachusetts. The authors detail how, by removing a parent and bread winner from the home, worksite operations have significant consequences for families and children. Not only does the removal of a breadwinner reduce a family's income and increase their material hardship, it also creates a rather unstable home environment. Moreover, the fear and stigma produced by a raid often lead to the social isolation of immigrant families and can have an adverse psychological effect on children, inducing depression, separation anxiety, and post-traumatic stress disorder.

Worksite raids, and the broader anti-immigrant climate that has spawned them, have also had a significant impact on the larger migrant community in the United States, Latinos in particular. A survey by the Pew Hispanic Center paints a rather grim picture of the psychological state of U.S. Latinos – legal residents, U.S. citizens, and unauthorized migrants alike (Lopez and Minushkin, 2008). Latinos generally report feeling anxious and discriminated against amid public immigrant bashing and enhanced immigration enforcement. Furthermore, the survey found that a majority of Latinos worry about deportation. Approximately 40 percent report being worried a lot that they, a family member, or a close friend could be deported, while 17 percent say they worry some. Not surprisingly, immigrants are particularly concerned about deportation, with 72 percent reporting being worried either a lot or some (Lopez and Minushkin, 2008). Immigrant raids, then, and the governing of immigration through crime more generally, have helped to create a sense of unease among Latinos, immigrants in particular. As such, the significance of raiding has less to do with the number of migrants arrested and more with the creation of apprehension and fear amongst migrant communities. These tactics are also known as "policies of attrition" or "attrition through enforcement." They are designed to erode the desire of immigrants to live and work in the United States.

The picture is not all bleak, however. Migrants and their allies have forcefully fought back against the governing of immigration through crime. For one, they have gone to court and filed lawsuits to stop ICE from conducting large-scale workplace raids. Furthermore, undocumented migrants themselves have taken to the streets and marched to claim rights and voice their rejection of the dehumanizing effects of workplace raids and border policing. While the enforcement climate might have been stepped up, then, migrants and their allies have kept hope alive and mounted political campaigns bent on gaining rights and recognition for the undocumented.

Jonathan Xavier Inda

See Also: Arizona SB1070; Counterterrorism and Immigrant Profiling; Crime; Incarceration; Operation Streamline; Policies of Attrition; Policy and Political Action; State Legttislation; "Undocumented" Label; Workplace Raids; Xenophobia.

Further Reading

Capps, Randy, Rosa Maria Castañeda, Ajay Chaudry, and Robert Santos. 2007. *Paying the Price: The Impact of Immigration Raids on America's Children.* Washington, DC: The Urban Institute and the National Council of La Raza.

Chavez, Leo R. 2008. *The Latino Threat: Constructing Immigrants, Citizens, and the Nation.* Stanford, CA: Stanford University Press.

"Fact Sheet: Worksite Enforcement." 2013, April 1. ICE. http://www.ice.gov/news/library/factsheets/worksite.htm.

Inda, Jonathan Xavier. 2006. *Targeting Immigrants: Government, Technology, and Ethics.* Malden, MA: Blackwell Publishing.

Lopez, Mark Hugo, and Susan Minushkin. 2008. *2008 National Survey of Latinos: Hispanics See Their Situation in US Deteriorating; Oppose Key Immigration Enforcement Measures.* Washington, DC: Pew Hispanic Center.

Simon, Jonathan. 2007. *Governing Through Crime: How the War on Crime Transformed American Democracy and Created a Culture of Fear.* Oxford, UK: Oxford University Press.

Great Lakes Region

The Great Lakes area in the northern United States has experienced much broadening of diversity in the last few decades. This region includes the states of New York, Pennsylvania, Ohio, Indiana, Michigan, Illinois, Wisconsin and Minnesota. Due to post-9/11 laws there has been increasing enforcement in this region bordering with Canada, including workforce raids and verification checks by border patrol in transportation hubs one hundred miles inland. States in this region have not experienced much turbulence with the nation's immigration debate yet the populace has its own competing groups to help shape their attitudes and policy regarding undocumented migrants. It will remain to be seen how states in this area react to recession and unemployment, and how the migrants weather the changing political and economic tides.

The area was never unfamiliar with newcomers, owing to the fact it has always had European settlers from France and Britain coming down the St. Lawrence River since the earliest waves of colonization in the seventeenth century. In the nineteenth century, cities like Chicago and Milwaukee received huge numbers of Eastern and Central Europeans, and recently many have moved to this region owing to its traditionally high offering of employment opportunities (less than 4 percent unemployment in 1996). The demographics have changed rapidly as Hispanics and Asians have moved to this area. In the 1990s, twelve thousand Asians alone migrated to Minnesota. Persons have migrated there because of new opportunities coming from legalization efforts in the 1980s. They moved to sites beyond the traditional destination of Chicago, often to rural areas of Michigan, Indiana, Wisconsin, Ohio and New York.

Undocumented workers have immigrated to some rural areas and driven population growth. The rise in population due to immigration has exceeded population growth due to increased fertility rates of established migrants. Destination communities have experienced initial cultural shock, as in the case of immigrants coming from rural villages in El Salvador, Laos and Vietnam. Hmong, a group of forest settlers on the border of Laos and Vietnam, moved in with 110,000 up until the 1980s, as refugees from the violence in Southeast Asia. After living in traditional societies and low-technology settings, many were exposed to a dominant culture of individualism and high-tech devices that westerners may take for granted.

Many immigrants have moved to the Great Lakes region to do low-wage jobs. They also came because of declining manufacturing jobs in other parts of the country and rising demand for restaurant and service industry workers. This movement integrates them into a larger part of the working class and aging population. Many businesses also offered potential employees starting bonuses and limited medical insurance plans in the 1990s as prosperity grew.

As more immigrant networks were created, some migrants, especially from Mexico, began to also build networks that attracted younger workers. As connections within cross-border networks between homes in Mexico and in the Great Lakes strengthened, these immigrants increasingly came because of seasonal work and new jobs related to small farms or megafarms.

Agriculture is one of the most important economic activities of the region. Following a south to north trajectory, the southern part of this agricultural region is the northern tip of the U.S. Corn Belt. Here, corn, soybeans, hogs, and cattle are major commodities. Dairy and associated alfalfa production are common in southeastern Minnesota and southwestern Wisconsin, as well as in scattered areas across central and northern sections of the region. Vegetable production is centered in the Central Sands area of central Wisconsin. In this way, seasonal migrant workers have become integrated into the region and the Midwest economy. The 1990s were marked by a period of growth, owing in part to the influx of undocumented workers, as they were paid low wages and in general were able to meet the demand of new businesses.

The influx of many undocumented workers presently causes some communities to hold town-hall meetings with the new residents, trying to see how more services should meet the needs of Spanish speakers. These are also ways to get migrants to comply with the established order. However, some towns have not increased social services, and local politicians and citizens' groups cite strained local funds as a reason why these workers do not deserve public housing or special educational accommodations. Migrants cope by joining churches that have bilingual services and provide some support services and resources. In many ways, migrants can be seen as self-sufficient by accessing critical social support services outside of government services.

Another community concern that has garnered recent attention is with regard to the Border Patrol stopping and detaining riders on the Lake Shore Amtrak line and other public transportation lines. In 2010, there were complaints filed accusing the U.S. Border Patrol of questioning persons based on their racial profile, and then detaining many. These actions have been harshly criticized by the American Civil Liberties Union (ACLU). Since the hasty enactment of the USA PATRIOT Act soon after the 9/11 attacks during the George W. Bush administration, there are fewer requirements on the part of the government to prove that there is just cause for detainment. The official title of the USA PATRIOT Act is "Uniting and Strengthening America by Providing Appropriate Tools Required to Intercept and Obstruct Terrorism (USA PATRIOT) Act of 2001." With the Patriot Act, all the government needs to do is make the broad assertion that their investigation of an activity is related to an ongoing terrorism activity. As a result, foreign students, their parents, and visiting professors have been jailed for irregularities in their visas. Moreover, because these are not criminal arrests, some persons have waited up to three weeks before getting a hearing. One case included a Taiwanese exchange student being detained. He sued the U.S. Border Patrol because they had picked him up for his "Chinese American" appearance.

Ben DuMontier

See Also: Community Concerns; Illinois; Labor Supply; Migrant Farm Workers; New York; USA PATRIOT Act (2001).

Further Reading

Bernstein, Nina. 2010. "Border Sweeps in North Reach Miles into U.S." *New York Times* web site; www.nytimes.com.

Faruque, Cathleen Jo. 2002. *Migration of Hmong to the Midwestern United States.* Lanham, MD: University Press of America.

Millard, Ann V., and Jorge Chapa. 2004. *Apple Pie and Enchiladas: Latino Newcomers in the Rural Midwest.* Austin, TX: University of Texas.

Green Cards

A "green card" is the informal name given to the identification card that declares lawful permanent residency in the United States. It is officially known as the United States Permanent Resident Card (Form I-551) and is administered by U.S. Citizenship and Immigration Services, an agency of the Department of Homeland Security. Until 2003, it was administered by Immigration and Naturalization Services under the Department of Justice. The term can also refer to the process of becoming a permanent resident and the subsequent authorization to live and work in the United States. Having a green card entitles the holder to certain benefits, such as the right to live permanently in the United States, the right to work in the United States, the ability to travel outside the United States, and the right to petition for a green card for a spouse or unmarried children under the age of twenty-one years old. In turn, the green card holder has certain responsibilities, such as obeying the laws of the United States, filing income taxes, registering with the Selective Services (for males ages 18–25) and keeping the green card at all times.

The Immigration and Nationality Act (INA) established the rules and regulations regarding the number of visas for green cards every year. Currently, there are 226,000 visas available for family-sponsored preference categories and 140,000 for the employment-based preference categories. There are also limitations on the percentage of visas allowed per country per year. Typically, there is a greater demand for visas than the allotted amounts above, and therefore a waiting list forms, which can last from a couple of months to a couple of decades.

There are several ways to become eligible for a green card, the first being through an immediate family member. U.S. immigration law permits U.S. citizens to petition for certain qualified family members to obtain a green card and live permanently in the United States. Eligible relatives include a spouse, an unmarried child under the age of twenty-one, or a parent if the citizen is over the age of twenty-one. Due to the fact that immediate relatives receive priority, there is no cap on the number of these types of visas issued annually, and therefore no wait time or backlog. There is also an option for U.S. citizens to petition for certain non-immediate family members, which is placed under the category of "family preference." Relatives that qualify for this category include unmarried children over the age of twenty-one, married children regardless of age, and siblings, provided that the petitioner is over the age of twenty-one. However, unlike the "immediate relatives" category, the "family preference" category does not have an unlimited number of visas and there is typically a waiting period.

In addition to U.S. citizens having the ability to petition for relatives, permanent residents (green card holders) can also petition for certain qualifying relatives to come and live permanently in the United States. A green card holder can petition for his or her spouse as well as unmarried children, and these relatives also fall under the "family preference" category; there is a waiting period before a visa number becomes available.

Furthermore, green cards are available to relatives who do not fit under any of the previous categories but are considered special cases. This category allows battered children, spouses, or parents to petition for permanent residence status if the abuser is a U.S. citizen or permanent resident. This is allowed under the provisions of the Violence Against Women Act (VAWA), which permits both men and women to seek protection and independence from their abuser. Another special category is the K nonimmigrant visa, which allows fiancés and their minor children to travel quickly to the United States and continue to apply for an immigration visa after the marriage occurs. This is eligible under the Legal Immigration and Family Equity Act (LIFE) provisions of 2000, which were intended to prevent long periods of separation between a non-permanent resident fiancé and a U.S. citizen. In addition, the LIFE provisions also created the V nonimmigrant category, which allows the spouse or unmarried child of a U.S. permanent resident to live and work in the United States while the immigration status is pending. Another special category is for children born in the United States to foreign diplomats such as ambassadors and ministers. While they cannot be considered U.S. citizens, they may be eligible for permanent resident status. Finally, there is eligibility for widows (women who have lost their husbands by death) and widowers (men who have lost their wives by death) of U.S. citizens. To immigrate as a widow or widower, she or he must prove that she or he did not enter into the marriage for immigration benefits and that the marriage was legal.

The second major way to obtain a green card is through a job or job offer. Depending upon the type of employment, the U.S. Department of Labor may require that there is a lack of U.S. workers for the specific job and that by taking this job, the immigrant will not replace or displace any American workers. Typically, highly skilled workers or workers with extraordinary skills are given priority for green cards.

Usually, an employment green card is obtained through a direct job offer, which signifies that an employer in the United States wants to sponsor someone on a green card and will file the petition for the worker. It is possible to not have a secure job offer and still apply for a green card, which is called a self-petition. In order to be eligible for a self-petition, the applicant must have an extraordinary skill in art, science, education, business, or athletics, or be an individual who was granted a National Interest Waiver (someone with an advanced degree or an exceptional ability). Examples include Nobel Prize winners or professional athletes.

There are also other, less common ways to obtain green cards through jobs. Foreign investors can secure a green card as long as they invest either $1,000,000 (or $500,000 in a rural or high-unemployment area) in commercial enterprise and create ten full time jobs for U.S. workers. Finally, there is a special category for those with specific skills and qualifications that are in high demand by the United States. These jobs include an Iraqi or Afghan translator, armed forces member, international organization employee, and a religious worker among other special-interest employments.

Another method of obtaining a green card is through refugee or asylee status. Eligible refugees, family members of asylees, or individuals that were granted asylum in the United States can apply for permanent residence status one year after entry (or the granting of the asylum status) into the United States. For a refugee to be eligible, he or she needs to not have applied for a green card previously, have current refugee status, and has to have been physically present in the United States for at least one year. For an asylee to be eligible, he or she has to also have physically lived in the United States for one year, continue to have asylee status, or be the spouse or a dependent child of an asylee, not have moved to another country, and continue to be admissible to the United States.

Finally, there are several special circumstances and programs through which an individual can apply for a green card. According to U.S. Citizenship and Immigration Services, the current special circumstances under which people can apply for permanent residence are if the petitioner is: an Amerasian child of a U.S. citizen, an

American Indian born in Canada, an armed forces member, a Cuban native or citizen, or a Haitian refugee. Programs that eligible applicants can use to apply are: Help HAITI Act of 2010, Indochinese Parole Adjustment Act, the Informant (S Nonimmigrant) visa program, Lautenberg Amendment Parolee Registry, Section 13 (Diplomat), Victim of Criminal Activity (U Nonimmigrant visa), or Victim of Trafficking (T Nonimmigrant visa).

Additionally, there is also an opportunity to get a green card through the Diversity Immigrant Visa Program, held through the Department of State, which grants a random selection of fifty thousand visas to qualified individuals applying from countries with low rates of immigration. However, this method has been subject to many online and email scams, asking for money to be wired with the promise of a visa or increased chances of obtaining a visa.

After a green card application and authorization is granted, a green card will be issued to all permanent residents, and it is a requirement to keep the green card at all times, in compliance with the Immigration and Nationality Act. They are valid for up to ten years, or two years for conditional residents, and it must be renewed before the expiration date. It is possible to replace a green card if it is lost, stolen, or damaged by filing Form I-90 with U.S. Citizenship and Immigration Services. It is important to note that only U.S. citizens, and not permanent residents, have the right to vote in all federal and most local elections.

Jenna Glickman

See Also: Inadmissibility; Provisional Unlawful Presence (PUP) Waiver; "Undocumented" Label; Work Visas.

Further Reading

The Beacon: Official Blog of USCIS. 2013. U.S. Citizenship and Immigration Services. http://blog.uscis.gov/.

Green Card Application Guide. 2013. U.S. Immigration Support. https://www.usimmigrationsupport.org/greencard.html.

Green Card (Permanent Residence). 2013. U.S. Citizenship and Immigration Services. http://www.uscis.gov/greencard.

Immigrants to the United States. 2013. Bureau of Consular Affairs, U.S. Department of State. http://travel.state.gov/visa/immigrants/immigrants_1340.html.

Guatemalans

Although Mexicans remain the largest group of undocumented immigrants in the United States, migrants today are increasingly from Central America. Migrants from Central American nations are increasingly fleeing violence, environmental disasters, as well as poverty. In 2011, the estimated number of undocumented Guatemalan immigrants was 520,000, the third highest national group after Mexican and Salvadoran.

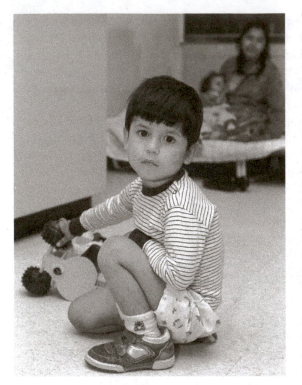

Marco Grijalba, 3, plays on the floor of a Red Cross shelter in Brownsville, Texas, as his mother and infant sister sit on a cot in the background, February 24, 1989. The Guatemalan family was part of a massive influx of Central Americans seeking asylum in the United States, fleeing civil war and armed conflict. (AP Photo/Pat Sullivan)

This number represents a growth rate of 82 percent since 2000 (Hoeffer et al., 2012). Increases in the deportation of Guatemalans have been equally dramatic, with from 19,061 deported in fiscal year 2011, to 32,486 in 2012. In 2008, the nation's attention and sympathy turned to the mass raid by dozens of Immigration and Customs Enforcement (ICE) agents who descended on Postville, Iowa, to raid the meat processing plant, Agriprocessors Inc., resulting in the arrest of over 400 undocumented workers, of whom 290 were Guatemalan.

Guatemala is a country in Central America that has a history of migration to other Central American countries and the United States throughout the second half of the twentieth century. This country shares a border with Mexico to the North and El Salvador and Honduras to the South. The primary source of income for the country as a whole is derived from crop exportation, primarily from the harvesting of coffee and bananas. Spanish is the primary language spoken in Guatemala, although there are over twenty-four indigenous languages spoken across the country. Its literacy rate is currently at 70.6 percent, and the majority of the population works in the service sector followed by industry and commerce workers. Agricultural work, which may often go hand in hand with peasantry and poverty, is a common condition of rural inhabitants, primarily indigenous people. These indigenous populations are of Mayan descent and have a long history of colonization, genocide and discrimination in Guatemala and Central America as a whole.

With three bordering countries, Guatemala has experienced many forms of military tensions and internal armed conflict emanating from civilian groups called guerillas and government groups whenever violence arises in the area. This causes a high number of casualties. Before the civil war in Guatemala (1960 to 1996), immigration was virtually nonexistent, with only a few thousand Guatemalans leaving the country each year. During civil war and beyond, migration has escalated, pushing individuals to leave their homeland as they escape torture, rape, and death.

For most *guatemaltecos,* their journey to the United States begins at the westernmost Mexican port of entry at the town of Suchiate, where 95 percent of Mexico's commercial traffic with Central America also takes place. After crossing, they hope to hop on a freight train known as La Bestia (The Beast), to make the clandestine journey through Mexico to the U.S. border. If Mexican authorities arrest them, they may be beaten, further exploited, and robbed before being deported. Many consider this a far worse fate than being arrested by the U.S. Border Patrol (Menjívar, 2006). Once in the United States, Guatemalans who lack a permanent legal status tend to work in low-paying, low-skilled jobs. As the research of Menjívar (2006) finds, among these immigrants there may be highly educated former teachers, business owners, nurses, students, or accountants working as dishwashers, domestics, or cleaning office buildings at night. Guatemalans who do not speak Spanish but rather any one of several Mayan dialects, find more difficulties in integrating into their new communities. Families may be occupied with finding homes and working in the hope of a better life, and parents risk becoming alienated from children as they adopt the customs of their new homeland. Additionally, many refugee youth come to the United States after early and repeated exposure to violence, itself a known risk factor for future antisocial behaviors (Sivan et al., 1999).

During the 1960s there were approximately 6,700 immigrants leaving the country. During the earlier years of the Civil War, few Guatemalans felt inclined to rise up against the forces oppressing them. Large-scale migration from Central America accelerated in the late 1970s, in the context of the turbulent civil conflicts in the region. For thirty-six years the U.S.-backed military regimes in Guatemala who committed crimes against civilians operated with impunity. While many who migrated during the political strife in their country might have fit into the classic profile of political refugee, every Washington administration during the two-decade period during which most arrived in the United States—from Reagan to Clinton—refused to grant them blanket refugee status. Once on U.S. soil, Guatemalans (like Salvadorans) can apply for political asylum, but historically they have not fared too well in obtaining it. Throughout the 1980s less than 3 percent of these applicants were granted asylum.

In the 1980s, faith-based communities in the United States formed the sanctuaries movement through which networks of activists sought to shield Salvadoran and Guatemalan refugees from being arrested and deported to the life-threatening conditions in their homelands. These religious groups were critical to championing the legal struggle for temporary protected status for refugees from Central American civil war violence. However, although in 1992 the U.S. government began granting temporary protective status (TPS) to Salvadorans towards the end of the Salvadoran civil conflict, this dispensation was not extended to Guatemalans. They were not judged as deserving of this protection, even though the U.S. State Department had pointed out on different occasions the brutality of the political conflict there, and the atrocious human rights record of the Guatemalan government (Menjívar, 2006). During the civil wars which ended in 1996, more than two hundred thousand Guatemalans disappeared. In these ways, the United States interventionism has figured prominently in the lives of the Central Americans who have migrated, as well as in the affairs of those who have stayed (Menjívar, 2012).

After the conflict, many former soldiers found themselves unemployed, raising the potential for a new kind of violence. Former soldiers had access to weapons and were easily lured into the gangs established by youngsters deported from the United States. Combined with fewer economic opportunities, gang crime and violence has risen exponentially, resulting in more migration. Guatemaltecos have increasingly migrated to Los Angeles, and more recently, Phoenix, Arizona as one of the newest points of destination. Here, religious institutions—Catholic Church and Protestant—have played an important role. They provide these immigrants assistance and a measure of protection as they attempt to adapt to their new environment. Faith-based organizations work to fill the vacuum of government assistance especially in places where greater restrictions based on citizenship status are in place. Immigrant newcomers also have established churches and have opened up their new temples to assist their compatriots in need. These spiritual communities allow immigrants to remain connected to their communities of origin, serving a critical function especially because they cannot go back easily. Unlike many other undocumented immigrant groups, newly arrived Guatemalan immigrants may be traumatized after the violence they may have suffered in their homelands or on their way through Mexico towards the United States, and a sense of community stands to mitigate the alienation of newcomers from mainstream institutions such as schools and social service agencies because of language and cultural differences.

Isabel Martinez and Bianca Guzman

See Also: Central American Civil Wars; Kanjobal Mayans; Nicaraguan Adjustment and Central American Relief Act (NACARA); Nicaraguans; Postville, Iowa Raid; Salvadorans; Sanctuary Movement; Temporary Protected Status (TPS).

Further Reading

Hoeffer, Michael, Nancy Rytina, and Brian Baker. 2012. "Estimates of the Unauthorized Immigrant Population Residing in the United States, January 2011." Office of Immigration Statistics, U.S. Department of Homeland Security. Available at http://www.dhs.gov/xlibrary/assets/statistics/publications/ois_ill_pe_2011.pdf.

Kinzer, S., and S. Schlesinger 2005. *Bitter Fruit: The Story of the American Coup in Guatemala.* Cambridge, MA: Harvard University Press.

Menjívar, Cecilia. 2006. "Liminal Legality: Salvadoran and Guatemalan Immigrants' Lives in the United States." *American Journal of Sociology* 111.4: 999–1037.

Menjívar, Cecilia. 2012. "Transnational Parenting and Immigration Law: Central Americans in the United States." *Journal of Ethnic & Migration Studies* 38.2:301–322.

Sivan, Abigail B., Lisa Koch, Claudia Baier, and Mala Adiga. 1999. "Refugee Youth at Risk: A Quest for Rational Policy." *Children's Services: Social Policy, Research & Practice* 2.3:139–158.

Guestworker and Contract Labor Policies

The history and experience of migrant contract labor, also known as "guestworker" or "*bracero*" policies in the United States, are topics for which there is a significant academic literature. Yet they are topics that have not been comprehensively addressed.

There are two major reasons for this. The first of these is a definitional issue. A substantial part of the literature has applied a narrow definition and focus; consequently much has been written about the World War II contract labor efforts between Mexico and the United States that covered the period from 1942 to 1964, what is commonly referred to in the literature as the "Bracero Program." The focus on this effort has produced a significant foundation for understanding the politics and economics of the implementation of the twenty-two-year effort that involved close to five million contracts across more than half of the continental states. However, the substantial attention to the 1942–1962 migrant contract labor efforts has been accompanied by limited attention to important predecessors, concurrent actions, and subsequent policies. Some of these are discussed below. The second reason is linked to a geographic dimension. Most of the academic research has focused on the experience of the 1942–1964 efforts in California. The result of this is that we have a fairly solid understanding of the use of migrant contract workers from Mexico in California's agricultural sector, but have no comparable analyses of similar workers in about twenty-five of the thirty states that participated in the efforts. Thus when viewed nationally, we have a limited understanding of the diversity in the implementation of the program and the experiences of the individuals who were contracted.

A key issue in examining migrant contract labor programs is deciding how broadly or narrowly to define what constitutes such a program. This issue involves deciding whether to only include programs formally negotiated by the United States and a second nation-state, or to broaden the scope and include unilateral decision by the United States, as well as arrangements made by employers who directly recruit migrant workers. A related dimension is whether there must be a written work contract, or whether situations involving verbal arrangements qualify. In the case of the 1942–1964 arrangement, the effort began by executive action and then was ratified by Congress, but in the last phases of the effort it was largely guided by unilateral congressional action. Throughout the twenty-two years, formal contracts were issued and signed by the workers. Prior to this, under the 1885 Alien Contract Labor law, it was illegal from 1885 to 1952 for U.S. employers to "contract" foreign workers with promises of work in the United States. Employers were able to circumvent the law by relying on verbal agreement and thus avoiding a paper trail. From 1885 to 1952, an unknown number of foreign workers migrated to the United States who were contracted but did not have a written contract. Employers on the East Coast as well as in the Southwest recruited such workers. In the case of Southwest agricultural interests, employers in the Imperial Valley and cotton producers in Arizona and Texas, as well as others, found it easy to dispatch recruiters into Mexico and illegally contract workers. While most scholars readily recognize the 1942–1964 effort as a contract program, they do not discuss the 1885–1952 contract labor arrangements as part of the long-standing "guestworker/contract labor" efforts in the United States.

The substantial literature on the 1942–1964 efforts tends to give limited or no attention to efforts that took place before the World War II Emergency Farm Labor Supply Program. And among those who have written about previous efforts, the starting point varies significantly. Thus there is no consensus among scholars about what the starting point should be, and the literature describing historical examples tends not to be necessarily framed as migrant contract labor actions, though workers may have migrated to the United States to work under a contract. In the colonial period, settlers came to rely on English, German, Irish, and Scottish "indentured servants" (also referred to as "White cargo") who contracted for three to seven years. Their passage was paid from their respective home and so they constituted migrant contract labor. In the same period but continuing until the nineteenth century, the African-descent population that was enslaved and brought involuntarily to work in the United States shared some features with migrant contract labor, though in this particular case the contract was a property contract. The above example of the 1885–1952 contract labor was initiated before 1942, but it overlapped ten years with the 1942–1964 efforts.

With reference to Mexico, there are two important precursor migrant contract labor arrangements. The first is the agreement reached between Presidents Porfirio Díaz and William H. Taft in 1909 as a result of their historic meeting in Juárez and El Paso. The arrangement was made despite the prohibition in place under the 1885 Alien Contract Labor law. The second example is the World War I "Bracero Program." The effort was made possible by an interpretation of a provision in the generally restrictive 1917 Immigration Act. Section 3 of the act contained the following provision: "*Provided further* [9] That the Commissioner of Immigration and Naturalization with the approval of the Attorney General shall issue rules and prescribe conditions, including exaction of such bonds as may be necessary, to control and regulate the admission and return of otherwise inadmissible aliens applying for temporary admission." This provision became known as the Ninth Proviso. Agricultural interests in Arizona, California, and Texas, as well as other states, convinced the Secretary of Labor (as the head of the agency containing the Bureau of Immigration) that he had the authority under the Ninth Proviso to waive the restrictions of the 1885 Alien Contract Labor law, and the literacy and head tax requirements under the 1917 Act, in order to allow the recruitment and entry of temporary migrant contract workers, principally from Mexico, to meet the emergency "labor shortage" faced by agribusiness as they sought to provide the food and fiber that "will win the war." Close to 73,000 workers were allowed entry into the United States; most of them were employed in agriculture. It should be noted that the figure of close to 73,000 is an approximation of contracts, and contracts represented principally the male "head-of-household." One unique feature of the WWI effort was that wives and children, and some single women, participated in the program. Some employers gave preference to families, knowing that all able-bodied children and adults would work, and this allowed them to pay only the one contracted worker.

An important policy that was implemented initially to address a Canada–United States border labor issue, but one whose legacy continues to the present is Department of Labor (DOL) General Order 86. The DOL order was an administrative policy adopted in April 22, 1927 to address a tense transborder labor issue in the Detroit-Windsor border cities. It was an issue regarding the daily movement of Canadians residing in Windsor to jobs in Detroit during the day, and then returning to Canada after work, and the strong opposition of some labor unions in Detroit to the commuting. General Order 86 created what one scholar labeled the "amiable fiction." The DOL created, without prior Congressional authorization, the commuter "green card," which granted permanent residency status to persons not residing in the United States, but allowed them to formally enter and work, and return to their place of residence after work. Because the order would have had political problems if limited to Canada, the order also applies to Mexico. Although several lawsuits sought to challenge the commuter provision, courts have upheld it and Congress has tacitly left it in place. Consequently, thousands of Mexican workers have acquired the commuter "green card" and are able to live in Mexico and work in the United States. The single largest group of Mexican commuters are employed in the Yuma fields in Arizona, and California's Imperial Valley. Most are recruited and transported by Farm Labor Contractors who supply the workers to the growers they contract with. Such workers represent a variant of migrant contract workers.

A final example of migrant contract workers are those granted one of the employment-based visas such as H-1A, H-2B, H-2A, H-2B, L-1, NAFTA-TN, O-1. Each of these designates a level of "skill/education," and they vary in the range of rights that they grant the visa-holder (e.g., transition to permanent residency). The 1952 Immigration Act, the 1986 Immigration Reform and Control Act, and the 1990 Immigration Act are the three principal statutes that have established and redefined the employment visas. Although most of the media and public attention has been devoted to the H-2A (temporary agricultural work), H-2B (temporary non-agricultural work), and H-1B (high-tech/specialty occupations), these constitute only about half of all the employment-based visas granted annually. Between 1998 and 2005, the annual number of visas granted ranged between 570,000 and 947,000. Since 2006, over a million such visas have been granted each year; even during the recent years of the Great Recession and 9 percent unemployment levels, U.S. corporations (e.g., Microsoft, Intel, Ernst and Young, Citi-Group, Motorola, General Electric, JP Morgan Chase) and institutions such as universities have been able to argue that U.S. workers are not available to fill vacancies.

In conclusion, the United States economy has had a long and sustained reliance on migrant contract labor to achieve the growth and prosperity it has achieved. Since World War II, U.S. agricultural and non-agricultural corporations have been able to garner the political support that has allowed the continuation of a discourse about the intrinsic need for both low- and high-wage labor from abroad, irrespective of actual unemployment or economic growth. And while much of the debate has focused on the recurrent call for a "new guestworker" program, particularly in low-wage sectors, the debate has overlooked the inherent problems in such programs, as evident in the WWI program, the 1942–1964 effort, or the 1952-to-the-present H-2/H-2A visa program, as well as the large number of higher-skilled/higher-wage migrant contract workers who have become a permanent and expanding part of the U.S. economy. The contemporary granting of over a million employment-based visas annually is an issue that merits greater discussion.

Luis F. B. Plascencia

See Also: Bracero Program; Employment Visas; Immigration Act (IMMACT) (1990); Immigration Reform and Control Act (IRCA) (1986); Johnson-Reed Act (1924); Migrant Farm Workers; Operation Wetback; Policy and Political Action; Special Agricultural Workers (SAW).

Further Reading

Allen, Ruth. 1939. "The Capitol Boycott: A Study in Peaceful Labor Tactics." *Southwestern Historical Quarterly* 42.4:316–326.

Calavita, Kitty. 1984. *U.S. Immigration Law and the Control of Labor: 1820–1924.* Orlando: Academic Press.

Calavita, Kitty.1992. *Inside the State: The Bracero Program, Immigration, and the I.N.S.* New York: Routledge.

Harper, Marjorie. 1992. "Emigrant Strikebreakers: Scottish Granite Cutters and the Texas Capitol Boycott." *Southwestern Historical Quarterly* 95.4:465–487.

Orth, Samuel P. 1907. "The Alien Contract Labor Law." *Political Science Quarterly* 22.1:49–60.

U.S. Supreme Court. 1892. *Church of the Holy Trinity v. United States,* 143 U.S. 457.

H

Hart-Celler Act (1965)

On October 3, 1965, President Lyndon Johnson signed into law the Immigration and Nationality Act Amendments, commonly known as Hart-Celler (PL 89–236: Immigration and Nationality Act Amendments of 1965 [October 3, 1965, 79 Stat. 911]) for its cosponsors in the U.S. Senate and House of Representatives. Hart-Celler was more pro-immigrant than any previous legislation, and many consider it a milestone of American foreign and domestic policy. Hart-Celler created for the first time a streamlined system by including refugees, by including Western Hemisphere immigrants, and by giving all countries the same numerical limit. In addition, it eliminated race as a legally relevant factor in deciding eligibility and by altering the category of people who could immigrate without counting against a country limit. Before Hart-Celler, individual refugees were considered no different from regular immigrants and groups were dealt with via ad hoc legislation. After the legislation they received six percent of the annual quota. Prior to Hart-Celler, country limits were allocated according to the percentage of the U.S. population that originated there. After the legislation each country had the same annual maximum. Before Hart-Celler, quotas were based on national origin (which has historically been equated with race). This was the principle behind the Chinese Exclusion Act of 1882 and the 1924 Oriental Exclusion Act (part of the Immigration Act of 1924). After Hart-Celler, race disappeared as a legal category for exclusion. Before Hart-Celler, the only immigrants not counted against a country quota were citizens' spouses. After the legislation spouses, children, and parents were all outside the quota, as were many professionals.

Hart-Celler's immediate origins are found in the enormous demographic changes that occurred in the United States during World War II. McCarran-Walter and Jim Crow laws labeled many of those fighting in and alongside the U.S. military as racially inferior. However, members of the Civil Rights Movement fought against race-based barriers to military service, and in 1943 Congress removed the race-based barriers to the immigration of America's allies in the Pacific Theater, the Chinese. As World War II ended, the United States started the Cold War, a strategic conflict with the USSR for control of the world. Many Americans began to see all restrictive, race-based policy as inconsistent with and undermining postwar foreign and domestic policy goals. They worried that newly independent African and Southeast Asian countries would reject an alliance with a United States whose laws they considered racially derogatory and align instead with the Soviet Union.

Race and Refugees

In 1945 President Harry Truman decided that to win the Cold War, America needed to make allies of those who had been, and still were, excluded by reason of their supposed unlikeness to Americans' national origin and race. The first problem he faced involved displaced persons in Europe. People displaced during World War II had to be settled before Europe could stabilize and provide secure and self-sufficient allies for the United States in the Cold War. In 1946, the wealthy and secure United States had an unmatched capacity to accept the displaced—but a great many of them were from ethnic groups and/or countries whose immigration the United States limited on historical or racial grounds. Albania, Bulgaria, Estonia, Finland, Greece, Hungary, Latvia, Lithuania, Romania, and Yugoslavia all faced Soviet occupation or control, but their combined quota was 3,823. China had been an important ally in the war, but its allocation was merely 105. A still-isolationist Congress compromised with presidential demands by allowing refugees to enter the United States if they drew down their country's future quota. The so-called mortgage system meant, for example, that Estonia's full quota of 116 could enter the United States in 1947, with the result that the entire quota for 1947 was used up, and then as more Estonians were admitted, each would be charged against part of the future Estonian quota—in the Estonian case, up through the year 2146.

Mortgaging proved insufficient because refugee crises became more frequent as the Cold War developed. Moreover, the Soviet Union upped the stakes in this rivalry by refusing to allow people to leave the countries it controlled. This increased pressure on the United States to admit anyone who could get out. In 1956, a failed anti-communist revolution in Hungary led to the flight of two hundred thousand people, of whom only 6,500 were initially authorized entry to the United States. National quotas could only be circumvented by presidential action. Only ad hoc legislation allowed 185,208 Cuban refugees to register in the years after the Cuban revolution. Until 1965 and the passage of Hart-Celler, the United States handled refugee crises by using the executive's ability to admit immigrants in this ad hoc, supposedly exceptional, way.

During the early years of the Cold War, scores of former colonies in Africa and Southeast Asia gained independence. The United States and the Soviet Union competed for the new countries' allegiance. Racial provisions in American immigration policy became a propaganda tool for the Soviets. The national origins quota system had not traced African Americans' ancestors to specific places, so under the quota system, African countries could claim no one. As a consequence, as each colony became independent, a U.S. Presidential Proclamation gave it the legal minimum: one hundred. The USSR also made the new countries aware of U.S. immigration policy's racial restrictions against Asians.

Global Scope and the Western Hemisphere

Like earlier immigration acts, Hart-Celler provided a numerical limit on annual immigration, but altered the way that immigrants got counted within those limits. Instead of basing percentages within the overall limit on Americans' ancestry, Hart-Celler gave an equal amount to all countries. Past policy had limited immigration from Europe and banned it from Asia, but had allowed unrestricted population movements within the Americas, reflecting a sense that North Americans were more or less part of the U.S. political economy. Hart-Celler excluded Western Hemisphere migrants from the set of unrestricted immigrants and included them in regular immigration policy. One reason was the country's new sense that, for principled and political reasons, it ought to treat countries equitably. A second arose from America's wartime experience. Labor shortages during World War II had prompted the U.S. and Mexican governments to establish a system whereby workers from Mexico would travel to the United States for a defined period to work in agriculture or industry at set wages and under decent working conditions. Known as the Bracero Program, this system engaged about four million workers from 1942 to its end in 1964, when it became clear that a great number of immigrants had been undocumented and illegally employed and worker abuses came to light. This experience bolstered legislators' sense that immigration from all countries should be allowed, but also be regulated. In 1964, actual immigration from the Western Hemisphere was 158,644. Hart-Celler set the Western Hemisphere cap at 120,000. Each country in the world faced an annual maximum of twenty thousand.

Preferences and Non-Quota Immigrants

Within each country cap, a system of preferences determines which immigrants will have priority. In addition, some immigrants have always been able to enter the United States without counting at all against the quota of their country of origin. Hart-Celler altered these preferences and non-quota categories. Spouses, children, and parents were no longer preferred within the cap but were exempt from the cap, as were many professionals. Preferences within the ceiling were given to other categories: married and unmarried adult children, brothers and sisters, needed workers. Before Hart-Celler, countries with the largest quotas, such as the United Kingdom and Germany, did not fill them, but small caps elsewhere led to pent-up demand. As an example, the national origins formula gave Turkey a quota of 761. Before 1965, should a Turk apply, become one of this 761, gain entry, and become a U.S. citizen, his or her spouse would get preference in a future year's quota of 761. After Hart-Celler, the same Turk faced a cap not of 761 but of twenty thousand, and after becoming a U.S. citizen could bring his or her spouse without reference to a quota at all. Indeed the new citizen's brothers and sisters would be given preference within the twenty thousand limit. Taken together, these changes allowed immigration from areas untapped for decades and eased entry for immigrants' extended as well as nuclear families, mainly outside numerical limits.

This legislation was cosponsored by Philip Hart, U.S. Senator (D-MI) and Emanuel Celler, U.S. House of Representatives (D-NY). Philip Hart was active in Michigan state politics before and after his 1959–1976 tenure in the Senate. After his retirement, Congress voted to name a new congressional office building in his honor. Emanuel Celler represented a district in Brooklyn and Queens in the House of Representatives from 1923 to 1973. His activism on immigration issues began his first year in Congress with debate over the National Origins Quota Act, which passed against his vote in

1924. The 1960s had ushered in new perspectives about immigration, in part infused by emerging theories on assimilation and the social value of pluralism and civil rights (Ngai, 2013). During this time, the writings of public intellectual Oscar Handlin were influential in shaping America's identity as "a nation of immigrants," exalting their contributions to the nation's economic and democratic development. Like Handlin, Celler opposed discrimination on religious and ethnic grounds and was especially vocal about the American refusal to accept refugees from Nazism during World War II. In his capacity as chair of the House Judiciary Committee from 1949–1953 and 1955–1973, he kept immigration legislation alive.

Region rather than party explains the final votes. In the House, Hart-Celler passed 320 to 69 (42 not voting), of which 46 nay votes were from the South. The East, Midwest, and West all supported the bill by large margins. The same was true in the Senate, which passed the legislation 76 to 18 (6 not voting), a full 16 of the nay votes coming from the South. Each party, in each chamber, voted in favor of the bill: 63 percent of House Democrats and 92 percent of House Republicans, 78 percent of Senate Democrats and 88 percent of Senate Republicans. This was an especially notable level of Republican support given that Republicans created the national origins system, and the bill was sponsored by Democrats in a Democrat-controlled Congress. Hart-Celler passed soon after two other major pieces of legislation, the Voting Rights Act of 1964 and the Civil Rights Act of 1965.

Cheryl Shanks

See Also: Bracero Program; Emergency Quota Act of 1921; Immigration and Nationality Act (The McCarran-Walter Act) (1952); Johnson-Reed Act (1924); *The Uprooted.*

Further Reading

Bosniak, Linda. 2006. *The Citizen and the Alien.* Princeton, NJ: Princeton University Press.

Calavita, Kitty. 1992. *Inside the State: The Bracero Program, Immigration and the I.N.S.* New York: Routledge.

Ngai, Mae M. 2013. "Oscar Handlin and Immigration Policy Reform in the 1950s and 1960s." *Journal of American Ethnic History* 32.3:62–67.

Shanks, Cheryl. 2001. *Immigration and Politics of American Sovereignty, 1890–1990.* Ann Arbor: University of Michigan Press.

Hate Crimes

Hate crimes against undocumented and other immigrants have increased substantially since the 1990s, as a fear of foreign or unknown people and cultures (known as xenophobia) has infiltrated United States society (Southern Poverty Law Center [SPLC], 2013). Hate crimes stem from anti-immigrant sentiment which is openly promoted through radio and television media.

The Federal Bureau of Investigation (FBI) defines a hate crime as "a criminal offense committed against a person or property which is motivated in whole or in part by an offender's bias against race, religion, someone with a disability, their sexual orientation, their ethnicity or national origin" (Seabrook, 2007). In 2005, a government report estimated that nearly 191,000 reported and unreported hate crimes occur annually (Seabrook, 2007). These crimes range in severity from intimidation to murder, while vandalism and assault are also common. Beyond violent crime, the activities of hate groups can include speeches, meetings, marches, rallies, and publishing documents with hateful messages. As of 2010, there were 1,002 hate groups operating throughout the United States, with the largest concentrations in California, Texas, and Florida (SPLC, 2013). Some common ideologies of hate groups are anti-gay, anti-Muslim, neo-Nazi, racist Skinhead, black separatist, and anti-immigrant.

The activities of anti-immigrant hate groups are among the most extreme of the hate group classifications. In 2010, 13.7 percent of reported hate crimes were related to ethnicity/national origin, affecting 1,122 victims. More than half of these hate crimes

Rosario Lucero, escorted by her son Joselo Lucero, left, walks in a hallway at the Suffolk County courthouse in Riverhead, New York, April 2010, during the third day of jury deliberations at the trial of a former high school athlete accused of killing her son, Marcelo Lucero, an immigrant living on Long Island, in a case that has led to a federal investigation of hate crimes in the area. Jeffrey Conroy, 19, had pleaded not guilty to murder and manslaughter as hate crimes, as well as other charges, in the November 2008 death of Lucero. The growing number of hate crimes across the nation has paralleled growing anti-immigrant sentiment. (AP Photo/Craig Ruttle)

(66.6 percent) were tied to anti-Hispanic bias. Some anti-immigrant groups are typically in opposition to Mexican immigration, as two conspiracy theories govern many of their beliefs (SPLC, 2013). The first theory is that Mexico seeks to reclaim the American Southwest in a scheme known as "Plan to Aztlán." The second theory is that the United States, Mexico, and Canada are plotting to unite and become the "North American Union." Anti-immigrant hate groups largely comprise white nativists who fear that the growing Latino population in the United States poses a cultural threat to "white America" (SPLC, 2013).

An example of nativist mentality was evident in November 2008 on Long Island, New York, when seven white teenagers who were members of a gang called the Caucasian Crew deliberately sought out a Latino whom they would assault in an activity they called "beaner-hopping" (SPLC, 2013). The assault resulted in the murder of Ecuadorian immigrant Marcelo Lucero. As of 2009, one of the young men pleaded guilty to gang assault. The others six were still awaiting trial.

Lucero's killer, Jeffrey Conroy, was convicted of manslaughter as a hate crime and gang assault as well as attempted assault against three other Latino men. Conroy was acquitted, however, of murder as a hate crime, a more serious charge, but was sentenced on May 26, 2010, to 25 years in prison ("Marcelo Lucero/Times Topics" 2010).

From 2003 to 2006, the FBI noted a 35 percent increase in hate crimes against Latinos, regardless of their immigration status (Seabrook, 2007). No other vulnerable groups experienced an increase in hate crimes during that period. The demonstrated growth of hate crimes against Latinos is even thought to be an underestimate because undocumented immigrants are unlikely to report incidents due to fear of deportation or ignorance of their rights (Costantini, 2011). Amongst the public, an association has developed between legally residing immigrants, undocumented immigrants, Latinos, and Mexicans. Many people mistake each of these distinct groups for being synonymous, which fuels negative sentiment toward the collective whole.

Indeed, it is believed that the rise in hate crimes against Latinos is largely related to a growing anti-immigrant sentiment that has been promoted in public media outlets such as radio and television (Media Matters, 2008). Anti-immigrant sentiment has been a persistent trend throughout U.S. history. The Chinese Exclusion Act of 1882 and the mass deportation of thousands of Mexican immigrants in the 1930s are just a few historical examples of policies and movements designed to expel immigrants. Anti-immigrant sentiment also shows a pattern of worsening during economic downturn, as immigrant groups receive the blame for the nation's problems. However, the current climate around immigration has entered a new dimension of hysteria that has not been witnessed since the 1920s (SPLC, 2013).

Some sources claim that American cultural depictions of morality, responsibility, and ethics are the root of unfavorable attitudes toward undocumented immigrants (Inda, 2006). Under these assumptions, individuals who enter the United States illegally are considered unethical, immoral, and irresponsible because they have broken the law. The presence of individuals lacking moral integrity serves as a threat to other law-abiding citizens. Thus, efforts to remove or demean these individuals are acceptable.

In the past, hate groups demonstrated the strongest objection to immigrants. Recently though, television personalities such as Lou Dobbs, Glenn Beck, and Bill O'Reilly as well as politicians are openly expressing negative regard for immigrants, particularly the undocumented (Media Matters, 2008). These public figures, as well as other forms of media, employ powerful fear-based language to describe undocumented immigrants and migrant movement. Terms such as "illegals," "aliens," "invasion," and "waves" perpetuate violence by degrading undocumented immigrants to less-than-human status (Inda, 2006). In Los Angeles, two radio show hosts, John and Ken of KFI AM640's *John and Ken Show* have been known to blatantly insult discriminated populations including African Americans, Asian Americans, members of the Jewish and Lesbian Gay Bisexual Transgender (LGBT) communities, and Latinos. On one occasion, the hosts encouraged listeners to place phone calls to Jorge-Mario Cabrera, the Director of Communications and Public Relations at the Coalition for Humane Immigrant Rights of Los Angeles (CHIRLA). As a result, Cabrera received over four hundred abusive and threatening phone calls.

Numerous other factors condone violence against undocumented immigrants. Two particularly influential factors are immigration enforcement and legislation directed at the undocumented population. In 1925, the Department of Labor handled immigration enforcement. By 1940, the Department of Justice took over, and in 2003, the responsibility shifted to the Department of Homeland Security. Placing immigration within Homeland Security assumes an association between immigrants and national security. Moreover, governmental efforts to secure the border further portray undocumented immigrants as a threat to public safety.

Although the United States Border Patrol is not a designated hate group, acts that have been committed by this entity indeed fit the definition of hate crimes. For example, numerous incidents of racial slurring as well as inhumane treatment through physical and psychological abuse and denial of food, water, and medical treatment have been documented in immigrant detention centers when detainees are under the control of enforcement agents.

Undocumented immigrants are also accused of burdening the welfare system. This belief supports laws and legislation that are designed to exclude undocumented immigrants from publically funded programs. For example, California's Proposition 187, proposed in 1994, aimed to deny undocumented immigrants access to education, health care, and other social services. It also endeavored to force public agencies to confirm the legal status of individuals seeking services and report those whose status is in question. Although Proposition 187 was later ruled unconstitutional by a federal court, subsequent state proposals, such as those passed in Arizona, were affirmed by court rulings. The public debate that accompanied the deliberations around Proposition 187 was characterized by discrimination and hate. More recent legislation such as Arizona's Senate Bill 1070 and Alabama's House Bill 56 has worsened the situation for not only the undocumented, but all immigrants.

In the weeks following the enactment of Arizona's SB 1070 in April, 2010, three members of a Minuteman vigilante group entered the home of a U.S.-born family of Mexican heritage where they killed Raul Flores and his nine-year-old daughter Brisenia (Costantini, 2011). The leader of the attack was a woman named Shawna Forde, who believed that Flores was smuggling drugs. She wanted to use his supposed profits to support an organization that would help secure the U.S.-Mexico border. Forde faces the death sentence after she was found guilty of first degree murder in 2011.

Anti-immigrant legislation also provokes dissent toward undocumented and other immigrants by criminalizing those who are associated with them. Under the aforementioned laws, legal residents may face criminal charges for offering transportation or housing to an undocumented immigrant. These policies thereby force regular citizens to assume a policing role. While many hate crimes are committed by people who define themselves as white supremacists, most perpetrators are in fact regular citizens. For example, in 2008, Derrick Donchak and Brandon Piekarsky, two white teenage football players, were charged with beating Mexican undocumented immigrant Luis Eduardo Ramirez Zavala to death in a well-known hate crime in the rural town of Shenandoah, Pennsylvania. The case was further complicated when local police attempted to cover up evidence supporting the men's involvement. As of 2011, each man faces nine years in jail and over $200,000 in fines.

In contrast to the numerous groups and individuals that express hate, there are also organizations that resist it. The National Hispanic Media Coalition has petitioned to remove the *John and Ken Show,* a Los Angeles-based radio show, and organizations such as the National Institute of Justice and the Pew Research Center have researched and published information on hate crimes in an effort to educate the public. Other advocacy organizations include the National Council of La Raza (NCLR), the Mexican American Legal Defense and Educational Fund (MALDEF), and the Southern Poverty Law Center (SPLC) whose sole mission is addressing hate crimes.

SPLC is a prominent civil rights organization that advocates for populations that are commonly the victims of hate crimes. The organization also tracks the activities of hate groups and promotes tolerance and justice through initiatives such as its Teaching Tolerance program, which is implemented in schools throughout the United States. SPLC's priorities include addressing hate and extremism, advocating for children at risk, defending LGBT rights, teaching tolerance, and fighting for immigrant justice.

Courtney Waters

See Also: Crime; Laws and Legislation, Post-1980s; LGBT Immigrants without Documentation; Minutemen; Racism; Violence; Xenophobia.

Further Reading

Costantini, Cristina. 2011. "Anti-Latino Hate Crimes Rise as Immigration Debate Intensifies." Huffington Post Latino Voices Web Site. http://www.huffingtonpost.com/2011/10/17/anti-latino-hate-crimes-rise-immigration_n_1015668.html.

Inda, Jonathan Xavier. 2006. *Targeting Immigrants: Government, Technology, and Ethics.* Malden, MA: Blackwell Publishing.

"Marcelo Lucero/Times Topics." 2010, June 4. *New York Times.* http://topics.nytimes.com/topics/reference/timestopics/people/l/marcelo_lucero/index.html.

Media Matters. 2008. Fear & Loathing in Prime Time: Immigration Myths and Cable News. Media Matters Actions Network Web Site. http://mediamattersaction.org/reports/fearandloathing/.

Seabrook, Andrea. 2007. "Latino Hate Crimes on the Rise." National Public Radio [NPR] Web Site. http://www.npr.org/templates/story/story.php?storyId=17563862.

Southern Poverty Law Center. 2013. http://www.splcenter.org/?ref=logo.

Head Start

As the nation's oldest poverty-fighting program, Head Start has helped over 27 million children since its inception in 1965. Head Start takes a holistic approach in order to provide comprehensive developmental services for this country's low-income, pre-school-aged children (three to five years old), and social services for their families. In this way, Head Start has proven to be beneficial to small children of undocumented immigrants in promoting cognitive development and critical learning skills. However, in recent years, some Head Start programs have been targeted in some states (Florida, Kentucky, Tennessee, Georgia and New Mexico) as a way to track the use of public services by undocumented immigrant families. For example, in Kentucky in 2011, a state bill that was proposed would have required Head Start officials to ask about a parent's immigration status to avoid losing federal grant funding for the program. U.S.-citizen born children are eligible for Head Start as part of several public assistance programs (such as Temporary Assistance for Needy Families—TANF, and the nutritional program, Women, Infants, and Children—WIC) available for the impoverished. Chronic poverty among undocumented immigrants and the growing number of immigrants settling in the United States to live make the children of these parents a growing demographic feature of the Head Start programs throughout the nation (Neidell and Waldfogel, 2009). In addition, immigrant children make up 20 percent of all school-aged children in the United States. Children of immigrants are more likely to come from lower socio-economic backgrounds where English is not regularly spoken, which puts them at greater risk of falling behind in school (Neidell and Waldfogel, 2009).

In spite of the well-known benefits of enrolling children in early childhood education programs such as Head Start, both U.S.-born children of immigrants and immigrant children are less likely than their native peers to be enrolled in Head Start and other early childhood education programs (Neidell and Waldfogel, 2009). Entering these programs requires parent involvement. In other words, small children cannot by themselves apply and need transportation to attend. Moreover, because parents may not know of the programs that their children may be eligible for, they may not apply for them. Many immigrant parents find out about them through networks of supportive relatives and friends. Even so, Head Start centers often face an excess demand for services. Like many publically financed programs, Head Start is subject to the ebbs and flows of federal funds. Also, parents may be hesitant to enroll their children in Head Start, fearing detection by authorities and service agency workers who might identify them as "public charges," and in this way inadvertently inhibit their children's development (Yoshikawa, 2011).

The Head Start program has a different approach to accomplishing their goal of fostering children's development; the program achieves this through parental involvement in the classroom, program operations, and through direct services through decision making and evaluation. Head Start's innovative approach is explained through the idea that a child's first and most important teacher is always one's parents. Head Start provides an array of services to help to meet their goals for: education, health, parent involvement, and social services. These goals reach into different programs that Head Start offers such as American Indian Head Start, Migrant Head Start, and Early Head Start.

Throughout the country, Head Start is offered in every state of the country. Head Start programs are located in areas where funds have been awarded to local private, nonprofit, or for-profit agencies that host the program. Children and their families can take advantage of the benefits of Head Start programs by applying and meeting the qualifications. In order to be accepted a child from birth to age five must be from a family that has an income below the poverty line. The Early Head Start program provides services to children from birth to age three and pregnant women. Children of families who qualify for public assistance (TANF or SSI) are eligible for both programs regardless of family income. Head Start also provides these services to foster children below the age of five regardless of the foster families' income level. Each Head Start program is also allowed to enroll up to 10 percent of their participating children from families that may not necessarily meet the above-mentioned requirements.

The Head Start program originated as an effort from the League of United Latin American Citizens (LULAC) in 1957, originally called the 400 School. This started as an effort to teach preschool-aged children 400 English words to prepare them for life in an English-speaking country. This small effort in Texas quickly turned into the federal funded Head Start program that reaches every state in the United States today. Head Start is a program under the umbrella of the United States Department of Health and Human Services, Administration for Children and Families (ACF).

There are a series of various programs that Head Start offers to low-income families and children. Family and community partnerships offer Head Start parents opportunities and support for growth to work with the strengths and knowledge of these parents, and their interest to find their own solutions. The objective of family partnerships according to Head Start is to support parents as they identify and meet their own goals, nurture the development of their children in the context of their family and culture, and advocate for communities that are supportive of children and families of all cultures. The collaboration between Head Start staff is essential to the success of their programs due to the emphasis Head Start places on parental involvement in their children's learning process. Another program of Head Start is their early childhood development and health initiatives. The objective of this initiative is that through a collaboration of Head Start staff and parents, a child's health and developmental concerns can be addressed and the child's basic health needs met.

The Migrant Head Start program is another program that Head Start has created in an effort to meet the changing needs of the country's population. The Migrant Head Start Program works primarily with children and their families of seasonal farm workers. This program was established in 2005 by the Bush administration and secured $35 million dollars to serve the children of migrant workers in the United States. Migrant Head Start programs currently serve more than 33,000 low-income children. The purpose of this service is to provide child care and comprehensive health programs and social services for preschool-aged children of low income migrant and seasonal farm workers. Low-income seasonal migrant families may qualify for these services so long as they have a child under the age of six years old. The services that are offered through this program are: transition services, health services, special services, child development programs, and family and community partnerships.

Something particular to the Migrant Head Start program is its cultural sensitivity to the population it serves. The programs are individualized, especially for children whose first language is not English: they are encouraged to build upon their first language and English is slowly introduced to their curriculum. Because these families move throughout the country following the crops they farm, the program is very creative in the ways in which they serve these families and their children. One example of this is conducting meetings at the camps where the families may be staying in order to ensure family participation. This helps demonstrate to these families that the program really does want the parents to be involved and it helps establish the relationship and trust that are of the utmost importance for successful outcomes.

Carolina Luque

See Also: Children; Education; Elementary Schools; English as a Second Language (ESL) Programs; English Language Learners (ELL); Mixed-Status Families; Policies of Attrition; Temporary Assistance for Needy Families (TANF).

Further Reading

Cantu, Virginia D., Frank Fuentes, and Robert Stechuk. 1996. "Migrant Head-Start: what does it mean to involve parents in program services?" *Children Today*, Summer-Fall 16+. Health Reference Center Academic. Web.

Musgrave, Beth. 2011. "Immigration Bill Could Hurt Head Start in Kentucky, Officials Say." January 20. Available at http://www.kentucky.com/2011/01/22/1606856/immigration-bill-could-hurt-head.html#storylink=cpy.

Neidell, Matthew, and Jane Waldfogel. 2009. "Program Participation of Immigrant Children: Evidence from the Local Availability of Head Start." *Economics of Education Review* 28.6:704–715.

Yoshikawa, Hirokazu. 2011. *Immigrants Raising Citizens: Undocumented Parents and Their Young Children.* New York: Russell Sage Foundation.

Zigler, Edward, and Sally J. Styfco. 2010. *The Hidden History of Head Start.* New York: Oxford University Press.

Zigler, Edward, and Jeanette Valentine. 1979. *Project Head Start: A Legacy of the War on Poverty.* New York: Free Press.

Health and Welfare

Medical choices are complex and determined by social, political, historical and economic processes. The term "medical pluralism" describes how people navigate through numerous choices and incorporate multiple medical systems simultaneously as a means of managing their health and treatment of illness. While many members of mainstream American society may choose to complement conventional (allopathic) medicine with homeopathy, or other forms of alternative medicine such as acupuncture or massage therapy, marginalized undocumented immigrants' medical choices are uniquely tied to state and federal health and immigration policy decisions.

Marginalized immigrants often seek health care in the shadows of U.S. cities rather than go to mainstream biomedical clinics or hospitals.

Research on undocumented Latinos in the United States suggests that they are less likely to seek and obtain physician visits as compared to other Latinos or the U.S. population as a whole. While the lack of insurance coverage and fear of deportation are some of the reasons these marginalized individuals seek health services outside the realm of biomedicine, they are not the only ones. Language can be a huge barrier for undocumented Latino immigrants. Translators are scarce, and when they are accessible, they still might not be equipped to translate culturally specific health syndromes, such as *susto,* fright sickness, or *empacho.*

In some cases, it is more advantageous for undocumented Latinos to seek the assistance and expertise of lay practitioners such as *parteras* (midwives), *hueseras* (bonesetters), *curanderas* (healers) and *sobadoras* (massagers). These local healers form a niche economy within the undocumented Latino immigrant population in the United States. U.S. Latino immigrants continue practicing forms of their medicine even after immigrating to this country. Immigrants arrive in the United States with discernible cultural traditions. People do not just throw away their cultural understandings of the body, healing, birthing, and illness, when they cross international borders. Instead, these understandings are adapted in this new transnational context. Immigrants to this country not only bring rich cultural foods and language to their new locations, but they also bring with them a rich history of medicinal, herbal, and healing knowledge.

Undocumented immigrants have responded to restricted access to formalized medical care in the United States by establishing and continuing intricate social networks that allow for the transnational flow of personnel, equipment, and supplies to support lay healing traditions in the shadows of the U.S. health delivery system. Studies in anthropology, sociology and international studies detail the negotiated process of healthcare social networking among immigrant populations. To gain access to practitioners in this niche economy, undocumented immigrants rely on intricate systems of kinship and community networks that include word-of-mouth references.

Some practitioners work from their homes receiving unannounced and scheduled clients. While others own stores where they sell prayer candles, herbs, and religious icons upfront while attending to patients in backroom treatment offices. Many of these practitioners hold many concurrent titles within the community such as *partera* (midwife), *huesera* (bonesetter), and *curandera* (healer). Some common forms of treatment by lay *parteras* include the *sobada*, a practice of massaging a woman's abdomen during pregnancy to feel out the health status of the baby as well as the progression of the birth. Another form of treatment is binding the abdomen after a birthing event with a *faja,* or tightly wound cloth. The binding assistants displaced organs and bones back into place after birth.

Culturally specific health syndromes commonly treated by Latino lay practitioners include *susto,* fright sickness, *mollera caída,* fallen frontanel, *aire,* bad air and *empacho. Empacho* is described as an illness caused when food becomes compacted in the stomach or when the patient eats something causing the stomach to stick to itself. *Empacho* is treated by pulling the skin around the spine until a snapping sound occurs. Afterwards the healer does a deep tissue massage of the back and the intestinal area to clear the blockage and has the patient drink a prepared herbal and oil tea. The process of healing this illness is referred to as *desempachar.*

Payment for these services can vary within different communities. Average treatment costs for legitimate healers in the Midwest typically are around $30–$40. Charlatans, or people who pretend to be healers, have swindled unsuspecting community members out of hundreds of dollars on healing methods that do not work. Respected healers caution clients not to pay these exorbitant prices and to be on guard for these counterfeit healers.

In addition to Latino lay healers many undocumented immigrants will seek assistance from community health clinics that promise a safe and anonymous care, regardless of an individual's documentation status or ability to pay. In the city of Milwaukee, one such clinic, Aurora Healthcare Walkers Point Clinic, a privately funded community health clinic, collaborates with CORE-El Centro, a community alternative health clinic. This unique partnership, located in a predominantly Latino neighborhood, provides services ranging from biomedical primary healthcare to reiki, acupuncture, and massage therapy for free or at reduced costs to patients.

As more and more state and federal funding diminishes and anti-immigrant rhetoric increases in this country, the need for both lay practitioners and community health clinics will increase. Part of the rhetoric circulating among anti-immigrant policy makers and their supporters includes the assertion that undocumented immigrants are a strain on the U.S. healthcare system and that they overuse medical care services, or overburden the system through high birthrates. To be sure, undocumented immigrants do utilize higher cost medical care such as private clinics and hospitals because these are measures of last resort. Consequently a number of state legislatures have passed measures to keep many undocumented immigrants from applying for health care programs available to the indigent, such as Medicaid. In some states, such as Arizona, the simple act of applying for such assistance when one is ineligible is punishable by law with fines and jail time. Finances force undocumented immigrants to exhaust a plethora of health care strategies including home remedies before seeking professional help. It is very common for individuals first to treat themselves and family members before seeking biomedical attention from a medical professional. When home treatment is not sufficient, a lay practitioner may be sought.

Ramona C. Tenorio

See Also: Acculturation Stress; HIV/AIDS; Hospitals; Mental Health Issues for Immigrants; Mental Health Issues for Undocumented Immigrants; Policies of Attrition; Trauma-Related Symptoms.

Further Reading

Menjívar, Cecilia. 2002. "The Ties That Heal: Guatemalan Immigrant Women's Networks and Medical Teatment." *International Migration Review* 36.2:437–466.

Sack, Kevin. 2008. "Illegal Farm Workers Get Health Care in Shadows." *The New York Times.* May 10. http://www.nytimes.com/2008/05/10/us/10migrant.html.

Zavaleta, Antonio, and Alberto Salinas Jr. 2009. *Curandero Conversations: El Niño Fidencio, Shamanism and Healing Traditions of the Borderlands.* Bloomington: AuthorHouse.

High Schools

The high school to college transition can be difficult for any student. Undocumented students experience additional challenges because of their legal status. It is estimated that about sixty-five thousand undocumented students graduate from high school every year. Many of these students belong to the "1.5 generation," that is, they were born outside of the United States but were raised in the United States, attend U.S. schools and learn English. By the time they graduate from high school many undocumented students are bilingual and bicultural; some, however, may not find out about their legal status until they start planning for college. About 5 to 10 percent of the undocumented students who graduate from high school every year actually go to college. Several factors affect undocumented students' ability to successfully enroll in college and obtain a college degree. These factors include: 1) state and federal policies, 2) college costs, 3) lack of incentives and support, and 4) stigma and fear. Even when undocumented students successfully navigate the high school to college transition they still face many challenges as college students. In many cases, these challenges ultimately prevent undocumented students from finishing their college education.

Federal and state initiatives have created pockets of educational access for undocumented students. Other policies have added additional legal barriers. Ten states, beginning in 2001, passed bills that allow undocumented students who meet certain criteria to pay in-state tuition. Among the ten are Texas and California, two states with the largest percentages of the undocumented population in the United States and the first to provide in-state tuition. The bills approved in these states were followed by Utah and New York in 2002; Illinois, Oklahoma and Washington in 2003; Kansas in 2004; New Mexico in 2005, and Nebraska in 2006. These bills have various criteria for eligibility. To qualify for in-state tuition under most of these bills undocumented students have to reside or attend a school in the specified state for a certain number of years, graduate from a local high school or obtain a GED, and complete an affidavit stating the intention to become a legal resident. Many undocumented students as well as high school and college counselors are not aware of the existence of these bills or their requirements. Despite the opportunities that these state initiatives created most undocumented students do not meet current federal criteria to legalize their status. Several states have introduced legislation to prevent undocumented students from receiving in-state tuition or are attempting to repeal existing bills that provide in-state tuition. Examples include Arizona and Georgia.

The cost of college is also a challenge for undocumented students who want to enroll in college or who are already college students. While state initiatives help defray some of the costs, only two states, New Mexico and Texas, provide access to state financial aid. Undocumented students are ineligible for federal financial aid, and scholarships are also limited. Thus many undocumented students already in college are not able to afford other expenses associated with college attendance such as books, housing, and student-fees. For many undocumented students community college is a more affordable alternative to four-year public institutions. For example, in California about thirty thousand students eligible under their in-state tuition bill are enrolled in community colleges in comparison to less than five thousand who are estimated to attend public universities.

Undocumented students also lack incentives and support to enroll and complete college. The incentive for professional employment after college is not a reality for many undocumented students since earning a college diploma does not change their legal status. The DREAM Act (Development, Relief and Education for Alien Minors Act) is a proposed federal legislation that would allow undocumented students who enroll in college or serve in the military to earn conditional permanent residency. It was first introduced to the U.S. Senate in 2001 and re-introduced various times. As of 2013, it still has not passed. Some undocumented students feel that the lack of job prospects after college and limited financial resources available to pay for college outweigh the benefits of a college education. Many undocumented students experience frustration because they feel that despite their academic achievements the prospects of going to college and obtaining professional employment after college are extremely limited. In most cases, high school and college counselors are not able to provide the advice undocumented students need to successfully navigate the high school to college transition. They are often not familiar with the unique challenges experienced by undocumented students and are unable to assist them through the process of enrolling and also staying in college.

Undocumented students also face stigma and experience fear particularly during the high school to college transition. Many students find out about their status during the process of applying to college. Those who are aware of their status are afraid to disclose it to high school administration, college counselors, teachers or other individuals because of the potential consequences for them and their families. These students are afraid that revealing their status may result in deportation or other forms of retaliation against them and their families. Deportation is actually a lived experience for many undocumented students as the number of non-criminal deportations experienced a steady increase between the years of 2003 and 2013.

In response to these challenges a youth-led movement began to take shape starting in 2006. Since then undocumented students have created grassroots organizations in colleges and cities around the United States and have partnered with existing groups in national campaigns that aim to educate the public about their experiences while helping undocumented youth navigate the challenges of a college education. Many of these groups actively endorse the DREAM Act. On January 1, 2010 four undocumented students initiated a 1,500-mile walk from Florida to Washington, DC known as the Trail of Dreams. In addition, other groups such as the United We Dream Network and Dream Activist created a coalition of organizations around the country that provide resources and mobilize students in support of new legislation. At colleges and universities the youth chapters of LULAC (League of United Latin American Citizens) as well as local groups such as the University Leadership Initiative at UT-Austin and FIEL (Immigrant Families and Students in the Struggle) in Texas also address the various challenges faced by undocumented students. In many cases, undocumented students involved in these groups disclose their status, as part of a "coming out" strategy.

The challenges that undocumented students experience as high school graduates and college students, despite some of the support available, ultimately lead many undocumented students to give up on a college education. Facing the inability to change their status, pay for college costs, and obtain legal employment after they graduate undocumented students ask if the sacrifices involved in getting a college degree are ultimately worth it.

Mariela Nuñez-Janes

See Also: Colleges and Universities; Deferred Action for Childhood Arrivals (DACA); DREAM Act; Elementary Schools; Education; Undocumented Students.

Further Reading

Chavez, Maria Lucia, Mayra Soriano, and Paz Oliverez. 1997. "Undocumented Students' Access to College: The American Dream Denied." *Latino Studies* 5:14–263.

Perez, William. 2009. *We ARE Americans: Undocumented Students Pursuing the American Dream.* Sterling, Virginia: Stylus.

Rincón, Alejandra. 2008. *Undocumented Immigrants and Higher Education: Si Se Puede!* El Paso, Texas: LFB Scholarly Publishing.

"Undocumented Student Tuition: State Action." 2012. National Conference of State Legislatures. http://www.ncsl.org/issues-research/educ/undocumented-student-tuition-state-action.aspx.

HIV/AIDS

The human immunodeficiency virus (HIV) is the virus that can eventually lead to a diagnosis of acquired immune deficiency syndrome (AIDS). HIV affects the body by destroying specific blood cells that help the body fight illnesses. HIV is primarily transmitted from one person to another through any of four body fluids: blood, vaginal fluid, semen (including pre-ejaculate fluid), and breast milk. HIV is not transmittable through casual contact (e.g. hugging, sharing utensils, hand shaking). HIV is most commonly transmitted through unprotected sexual intercourse (i.e. sex without the correct use of a condom), sharing injection needles, and mother to child transmission (in utero, during delivery, and breastfeeding).

There is currently no cure for HIV or AIDS; however, advances in health care have made it possible for some people living with HIV/AIDS to live relatively healthy, long lives. Access to culturally sensitive health care, stable housing, social support, nutritious food, and other basic needs contributes to the ability of people living with HIV/AIDS to stay healthy. On the other hand, misconceptions, stigma, and discrimination surrounding HIV/AIDS, in the United States and Latin American countries alike, can negatively impact people infected or affected.

Latinos in the United States are disproportionately affected by HIV/AIDS and often have poorer health outcomes if infected when compared to the broader U.S. population. Latinos in the United States, especially those who are immigrants, undocumented, or newly arrived to the United States, may not have equitable access to HIV prevention messages, safer sex supplies, harm-reduction materials for injection drug use, or prevention and education messages that are culturally or linguistically relevant.

Some undocumented immigrants may have emigrated from areas that have limited resources for HIV/AIDS education, and few resources for HIV care. Some immigrants living with HIV may have emigrated in response to HIV-related discrimination and stigma encountered in their home countries (Cheng, 2006). Undocumented Latino immigrants in the United States are also more likely to wait and seek out health care only when they are seriously ill and in the later stages of HIV infection. Consequently they receive AIDS diagnoses later than other groups of people. In addition, Latino and other immigrants living with HIV have historically had few opportunities to immigrate to the United States legally. The ban on travel or immigration to the United States by people living with HIV/AIDS was not officially lifted until 2010 under the Obama administration. For the undocumented, those with young children introduce even more complexity. They are vulnerable to threats of exposure (and therefore deportation) if they access care, and for those who are parents, returning to their home countries with their children would limit their ability to seek out health care. At the same time, returning to their homelands without their children is a painful and difficult decision (Pivnick et al., 2010).

Undocumented Latino immigrants who are sexual and gender minorities experience significant risks for HIV and poorer health outcomes if infected. Social stigma and homophobia, in both their home countries and the United States, may make it difficult for them to find social and family support, find or maintain employment, and place them at risk for experiencing bias-based crimes and other traumas, developing mental health problems, substance use, and consequent high-risk sexual behavior and risk for HIV. Transgender immigrants are often targeted for sexual violence, and the need to fund hormones and sexual reassignment surgery, or inability to find employment, may lead to commercial sex work, and incarceration, which contribute to an increased risk of HIV exposure.

HIV risk among heterosexual Latino migrants, especially young male urban day laborers and those working in agriculture (who are often undocumented), has also grown. They often have limited access to health care, and HIV prevention programs that are culturally or linguistically relevant. Social isolation, limited social supports, and separations from their primary partners often lead to high risk sexual behaviors and exposure to HIV in the United States. They may also have partners, in their home countries or the United States, with whom they do not use condoms, and unknowingly transmit HIV or other sexually transmitted infections.

Undocumented Latina immigrant women, given their often-subordinate roles in their relationships and communities, experience significant rates of interpersonal violence, forced human trafficking, involvement (often coerced) in the sex industry, and nonconsensual sex, which makes them vulnerable to HIV exposure. Some may also feel uncomfortable or unable to negotiate condom use with their partners given their cultural, religious, or social expectations. Immigrant women living with HIV/AIDS are also at high risk of living in abusive relationships.

Undocumented Latino/a immigrants living with HIV/AIDS in the United States are often unable, or experience barriers, to access medical or other supportive services from certain government-funded programs and other service organizations. They may also experience greater difficulty in finding culturally or linguistically competent health care providers. Shame, stigma, or fear of deportation may also keep them from seeking or engaging in preventive services or health care. Poverty and stressful work and living conditions may also make it more difficult for those living with HIV to stay healthy and take their medications as prescribed.

Adrian Sanchez

See Also: Barriers to Health; Exclusion; Health and Welfare; Hospitals; Mental Health Issues for Immigrants; Mental Health Issues for Undocumented Immigrants.

Further Reading

Jih-Fei Cheng. 2006. "HIV, Immigrant Rights, and Same-Sex Marriage." *Amerasia Journal* 32.1:99–107.
Pivnick, Anitra, Audrey Jacobson, Arthur Blank, and Maritza Villegas. 2010. *Journal of Immigrant & Minority Health*. 12.4:496–505.
Stowers Johansen, Pamela. 2006. "Human Trafficking, Illegal Immigrants and HIV/AIDS: Personal Rights, Public Protection." *California Journal of Health Promotion* 4.3:34–41.

Homelessness

Homelessness is defined as the condition in which people have no fixed or permanent dwelling. Undocumented immigrants may be more susceptible to becoming homeless due to difficulties in locating adequate, affordable housing. Deteriorating economic circumstances contribute to the difficulty in finding and maintaining adequate housing as does limited financial means because of work restrictions, the inability to apply for housing loans and the exclusion from participating in federally funded housing programs such as Section 8 of the Department of Housing and Urban Development (HUD) program, which provides assistance in the form of housing vouchers. The *Guide To Federal Regulations Concerning Public Housing* specifically addresses restrictions on assistance of the HUD program to non-citizens. Such regulations include prohibiting financial assistance to persons based on ineligible immigrant status, lack of proof of citizenship and/or legal permanent residency eligibility status. Though state requirements vary, those that remain eligible for the housing vouchers include refugees, victims of trafficking, victims of domestic violence and persons granted withholding of deportations. Additionally, undocumented immigrants may not be aware of their legal rights regarding housing and renting policies. If an immigrant is not eligible for one type of assistance, one may be eligible for another. For example if at least one member of the household meets the eligible criteria for housing assistance, then the family may be able to obtain a subsidy that is prorated.

Homeless immigrant Luis Hernandez, originally from Puebla, Mexico, walks past another homeless person, as he goes to work, September 2005, in the Skid Row area of downtown Los Angeles. Among the estimated 14,000 people who live in Skid Row there exists a small shadow population of homeless immigrants who bed down each night in parks or abandoned buildings and find refuge in camouflaged encampments under freeway overpasses and bridges. (AP Photo/Damian Dovarganes)

The fear of having one's immigration status questioned or detected may be another barrier to obtaining housing. Undocumented immigrants may fear speaking with housing officials for fear that they be reported to Immigration and Customs Enforcement (ICE). This fear is not unjustified. In recent years, there have been many proposed ordinances and laws intended to discourage undocumented immigrants from settling down, known as policies of attrition. One of them in particular, a local, municipal ordinance passed in 2006 in Hazelton, Pennsylvania (Ordinance to Establish a Residential Rental Property Tenant Registration Program, Ordinance 2006–13) in August of 2006 attempted to keep undocumented immigrants from renting housing units. The law threatened landlords with severe penalties and fines if they were found renting to anyone who could not provide proof of legal residency or citizenship. The proposed anti-immigrant ordinance would have required landlords to have potential tenants complete an "occupancy permit application," where they would produce identification and proof of U.S. citizenship or legal residency (Harnett, 2008). A review of this ordinance showed that it omitted 11 categories of lawfully present immigrants under federal law. Conceivably, it might have forced legal residents and children of immigrants out of a living space. The proposed ordinance was later legally invalidated because it clearly conflicted with federal law and potentially affected not only the undocumented but also legal immigrants. Though housing laws vary widely across states, housing officials cannot report someone based on their inability to produce a social security card, but it is important to check with specific state laws prior to disclosing one's immigration status. It should be noted that providing a fake social security number is a federal offense and should be avoided.

Undocumented immigrants may experience additional barriers to housing due to discrimination on the basis of financial income, lack of credit history, ethnic or racial identities, and immigration status. In certain cities, such as Fremont, Nebraska, there are new housing requirements that one must meet in order to rent a house or an apartment. In order to receive a permit, one must provide a social security number and immigration status. This law specifically targets and discriminates against undocumented immigrants. Landlords are not required to give a reason for determining to whom they decide to rent their property; thus issues of racism or personal bias may continue to contribute to the problem. Other laws in place may prevent friends or family from helping another, known as "harboring laws." Although difficult to enforce, these laws propose to make it illegal to knowingly house an undocumented immigrant, which places not only the immigrant at risk but also their friends and family. Harboring laws have been proposed as parts of harsh anti-immigrant measures such as Arizona SB 1070 and its copycat laws in several states throughout the nation.

Some of the most vulnerable populations include young immigrants who travel alone as they are especially susceptible to becoming homeless once they arrive in the United States. Advocates suggest that youth may come to the United States to seek work, escape violence or reunite with loved ones. However, they may be subjected to taking low-paying jobs due to their age and immigration status. Low-wage jobs may not provide one with enough income to meet all the financial needs and can force both youth and adults into homelessness if there is little or no support system in place.

The office of Refugee Resettlement reported that 8,244 children entered the United States unaccompanied by an adult and without the proper immigration documents and were taken into custody by U.S. immigration authorities in 2011. Children under the age of 18 may be subjected to living in shelters or detention facilities while they await immigration hearings and apply for asylum or visas. Certain nonprofit homeless youth shelters such as Solid Ground La Casa Norte in Chicago provide assistance to the increasing number of undocumented youth. Additional advocate groups such as The Young Center for Immigrant Children's Rights, based in Chicago Illinois, provide assistance in legal matters and advocate on the children's behalf. Their mission is to advocate for the best interest, safety and well-being for immigrant and refugee children that are alone in the United States.

Some studies suggest that there may be an over-representation of immigrants in the homeless population but they remain hidden because they are absorbed by social networks and supportive communities. Undocumented immigrants are often referred to as the hidden homeless, because they are often not represented in social service agencies. Fear of detection may also be a contributing factor in avoiding social services, especially if these are supported by public, taxpayer-funding sources. To avoid them, undocumented immigrants have been known to find shelter in churches or community-based organizations as they move from one place to another. Staff members in these places of refuge will not in principle report those that they suspect to be undocumented, making it difficult to estimate the accurate number of undocumented immigrants that are homeless.

Limitations on income have been determined to be one of the greatest barriers for undocumented immigrants to obtain housing, which in turn may lead to homelessness. Relying on social networks is one way of resolving the need for shelter, at least temporarily and until they are able to find adequate housing independently. For this reason, many new immigrants rely on the support of family and friends to assist them with their housing needs. Strong social networks provide a support system, which reduces the risk of undocumented immigrants becoming homeless. Most research indicates that because of social capital and strong support networks, undocumented immigrants tend not to rely on social services or homeless shelters. However, pooled resources and shared accommodations may at times lead to overcrowding and unsafe living conditions. Financial difficulties such as the inability to find work due to immigration status may greatly contribute to the need for shared resources. This oftentimes forces families to live in substandard housing and inadequate living conditions and may eventually lead to homelessness.

There are limited resources available for homeless undocumented immigrants, as most social services require a social security number. Those that do not have strong support networks may be more reliant on community-based or faith-based organizations for their survival, and this keeps them hidden within the social services system. Undeterred from the public discourse about providing aid to undocumented immigrants, the faith-based Catholic organization Casa San Diego in Houston offers shelter for the needy and homeless, many of whom are immigrants and their families (Zwick and Zwick, 2010). In this regard, this organization stands out as a beacon of both Christian doctrine and practice by providing shelter, food, and basic medical care to the homeless and destitute. According to one report (Freemantle, 2005), in 2005 about 10 to 15 percent of the Catholic Church's charitable budget went towards aiding immigrants and refugees, of which probably two-thirds would go to undocumented immigrants. However, though homeless shelters are an option, once one becomes homeless there are few services that can provide a way out of homelessness.

Courtney Martinez

See Also: Arizona SB 1070; Families; Family Economics; Housing; Mortgages; Policies of Attrition; Shadow Population.

Further Reading

Freemantle, Tony. 2005. "At Casa Juan Diego, there are no borders." *Houston Chronicle*, December 4. Available at: http://www.chron.com/news/houston-texas/article/At-Casa -Juan-Diego-there-are-no-borders-1502987.php.

Harnett, Helen M. 2008. "State and Local Anti-Immigrant Initiatives: Can They Withstand Legal Scrutiny?" *Widener Law Journal* 17:365–382.

La Casa Norte: http://www.lacasanorte.org/.

Middleton, Richard, IV, Candace Howell, Stacy Peebles, and Kendra Powell. 2011. "Unsafe Harbor: An Analysis of Local Government Use of Harboring Ordinances to Restrict Illegal Aliens' Access to Housing." *Journal of Immigrant & Refugee Studies* 9:127–138.

The Young Center for Immigrant Children's Rights (University of Chicago). Found at: http://www.theyoungcenter.org/ourwork.shtml.

Zwick, Mark, and Louise Zwick. 2010. *Mercy without Borders: The Catholic Worker and Immigration.* Mahwah, N.J.: Paulist Press.

Home Town Associations

For years, immigrants from Mexico living in the United States lobbied the Mexican government heavily for the right to participate politically in their country's elections while they lived abroad. Over decades of living in the United States, they emerged to wield growing economic leverage by sending campaign contributions, remittances, and investments to Mexico. Led by a growing number of migrant-formed "hometown associations" (HTAs) and migrant-led clubs (*clubes* or *federaciones*), immigrants have exerted political pressure and forced Mexican policy makers to acknowledge their country's condition as a nation of emigrants and to devise ways to empower their compatriots, especially those who were contending with U.S. anti-immigrant legislation, like Proposition 187 in California (Alarcón, 2006) or advocating for supportive legislation such as a state-based DREAM act such as the one approved by that state in 2011.

The Zacatecan Federation, one of the largest and most active of the HTA organizations, includes approximately sixty local clubs that span across the United States. Individual clubs mobilize the voluntary time and financial resources of hundreds of fellow migrants from the same locality to raise money for social infrastructure projects, to fund sports, scholarships and other philanthropic needs. Individual *clubes* have memberships that range anywhere from fifty to two thousand each. Thus, not only are individual remittances sent from immigrants to their families in communities of origin—helping address the needs of families in Mexico—but an increasing number of migrants and members of the clubs wish to do more to contribute to the development of social infrastructure projects in these sending communities. For example, funds have been used for projects to improve water and sewage systems that would benefit the overall well-being of sending communities. They have aided in the financing of electrical and transportation infrastructure projects that facilitate development of the private sector industries in Mexico. Initially the Zacatecas State Government provided a matching funds program to encourage collective remittances for improving infrastructure in sending communities.

In 1992 the federal government of Mexico also became involved by creating a program where funds sent to Mexican sending communities were matched two dollars for every one. Then in 1999 this program was expanded to include municipal funds to create the 3x1 program. Thus, for every dollar of immigrant remittances for community infrastructure projects, an additional three dollars is matched by combining the contributions for the projects provided from the three levels of government: the state, federal, and municipal. The funds raised now go into a fund for development projects in HTAs' hometown communities.

The examples set by early *clubes* in the United States encouraged the establishment of more than two thousand by 2013 throughout the United States and the world. A list of these clubs is periodically updated on the website of the Instituto de Mexicanos en el Exterior (IME) at http://www.ime.gob.mx/DirectorioOrganizaciones/. Although initially organized to help fund community and social projects, others evolved to include more comprehensive engagement with the political and economic process in both the United States and in Mexico. For example, as part of the larger *Federación de Clubes Michacanos en Illinois,* Casa Michoacán in Chicago, Illinois offers a wide range of programs and services that provide support for its local Mexican immigrant community, such as citizenship and education programs, workshops about applying for public services, and art and cultural events. For this reason, they are often seen as political and community-building catalysts that have only begun to realize their full potential as sources of immigrant empowerment. The organization of *clubes* through the United States is also credited with bringing about reforms in Mexican policies such as those that led to immigrants' absentee voting in the 2006 Mexican elections.

Anna Ochoa O'Leary

See Also: Advocacy; Community Concerns; CC-IME (Consejo Consultive Instituto de los Mexicanos en el Exterior); Foreign Consulates; Small Business Ownership; Social Interaction and Integration; Transnationalism.

Further Reading

Alarcón, Rafael. 2006. "Hacia la construcción de una política de emigración en México." In *Relaciones Estado – diáspora: aproximaciones desde cuatro continentes.* Vol. I. Edited by Carlos Gonzáles Gutiérrez. México: Instituto de los Mexicanos en el Exterior, Secretaría de Relaciones Exteriores y Miguel Angel Porrúa. Available at: http://www.ime.gob.mx/investigaciones/bibliografias_ime.htm.

"Directorio de Organizaciones y Clubes de Oriundos." ["Directory of Clubs and Organizations."] 2013. Instituto de los Mexicanos en el Exterior. http://www.ime.gob.mx/DirectorioOrganizaciones/.

Rivera-Salgado, Gaspar. 2006. "Mexican Migrant Organizations." In *Invisible No More: Mexican Migrant Civic Participation in the United States,* ed. Xóchitl Bada, Jonathan Fox, and Andrew Selee, 5–8. Washington, DC: Wilson Center/Mexico Institute.

Hondurans

Honduran migration to the United States is best described as a series of migrations. Each has distinct historical roots and push-pull factors. The following time periods are approximations of major Honduran migrations: the first occurred from the early 1900s to 1963; the second, from 1963 to the 1970s; the third, in the 1980s, during the civil wars in Central America; and the fourth runs from the 1990s through the present.

Migration up to the 1965 Immigration Act

The second migration, occurring from 1963 into the 1970s, began after the 1963 coup d'état, when dictator Oswaldo Lopez Arellano ousted Ramon Villeda Morales from the presidency, a power struggle that left Liberal party members and workers in jail or without work. The second migration is characterized by male political exiles leaving the country during a politically unstable period, a continued migration by company *empleados de confianza* for work or pleasure, and a small but significant migration of women to work in the service industries. The Liberal party activists left Honduras, some to work in the United States and others to nearby countries to work for low wages. Many of these exiles were teachers and local activists; many were also working-class railroad workers and technicians and other laborers who worked for the fruit companies on the North Coast and had been disenfranchised because of their allegiance to the Liberal party. The second migration points to the diversity and challenges of migration and exodus. State violence made it hard for local Liberal party activists and leftists to remain, but it also made it nearly impossible to leave. Workers devised creative clandestine paths to exit the country and re-enter whenever necessary. The ousting of Ramon Villeda Morales formed a class of dissidents and disillusioned Liberal party members who fled Lopez Arellano's military regime.

The small Honduran community from the second migration provided a support network for other immigrants. One of the ways in which this small community may have been obscured was that in larger working-class Los Angeles, Hondurans were confused for Mexicans (Argueta, 2007). The second migration was made up mostly of men, who often migrated for shorter periods due to political exile. There were also a growing number of women migrants to the United States who tended to remain in the settlement country to work in the service industry.

Immigration Act of 1965 and Succeeding Legislation

The third period of Honduran migration to the United States, during the 1980s, is marked by the carnage created by the wars in neighboring Guatemala and El Salvador. Hondurans migrated in large numbers during this period, but this migration was overshadowed by the large Salvadoran and Guatemalan migrations. The Sanctuary Movement of the 1980s was concerned with helping Salvadorans and Guatemalans obtain asylum and refuge from torture and brutality. True horror stories about the poor treatment and abuse of refugees by the contras and Honduran authorities were ubiquitous. Honduras was then seen by local activists of the Sanctuary Movement as complicit in the U.S.-backed campaign, and many believed their migration stories had perhaps been obfuscated. The reality is that Hondurans also had organized revolutionary movements during the 1980s. These movements, though small and localized, supported many of the organized movements of nearby El Salvador and Nicaragua (Hamilton and Stoltz Chinchilla, 1991)

Economic instability intensified as the banana companies began to threaten union stability and militancy with violence and massive firings. Workers' livelihoods were threatened as well as their lives in the North Coast. A reluctance to confront this paradox of state-supported repression and worker resistance of the period further obscures Hondurans and their history of migration. Migration during the 1980s was difficult. People made their way however they could, riding on buses or on top of trains, or paying *coyotes* (who help bring people across the border) to smuggle them into the country (Escobar, 2007). Honduran migrants sought out *coyotes* to bring them from Honduras directly to the Tijuana border (Velasquez, 2007; Rodriguez, 2007; Escobar, 2007).

Honduran migrants, mostly economic migrants but also some fearing the political destabilization, migrated alongside Salvadorans and Guatemalans, traveled north and found a niche within the already existing Central American and Mexican communities in cities such as Los Angeles and New York. This generation of immigrants struggled side by side with Salvadoran and Guatemalan and Mexican undocumented immigrants, all of whom shared few options for legalization.

In 1986, the U.S. government passed the Immigration Reform and Control Act (IRCA), which imposed employer sanctions for hiring undocumented workers. This period was a formative one for Honduran immigrants who arrived then, many of whom became active in the immigrant rights movement and in their labor unions, including those for janitors, garment workers, and domestic workers. The shared space with other Central Americans and Mexican undocumented immigrants created an opportunity for coalition building, but, at the same time, it marginalized Honduran voices due to their smaller numbers compared to the large Mexican and Salvadoran populations. The shared work and living experiences, IRCA, and the constant deportations brought Hondurans to work collectively (Rodriguez, 2007). These migrants were able to enter into Central American networks being formed at the time even though Hondurans were still lower in numbers. Hondurans learned to work under larger umbrella groups.

Honduran Migration: 1990s to Present

The most recent Honduran migration to the United States, occurring from the 1990s to the present, is marked by growing instability created by natural disasters, the closing of banana plantations, the loss of stable union jobs in the North Coast, and neoliberal policies that have made it hard for subsistence farmers. At the same time, due to the decline of the banana industry, the North Coast has become the prime area for the development and proliferation of the export-processing zones that employ many young women and men from the interior. This period is marked by significant migration to the United States, Mexico, and Spain. According to Honduran newspaper *La Prensa* (2006), one Honduran leaves the country every five minutes. The forms of migration are brutal, with men and women leaving the country with little money, expecting to work en route, and hopping trains for undetected and free passage.

The well-known tragedy of Hurricane Mitch, which devastated Honduras, prompted the United States to pass the temporary protection status (TPS) policy, which answered Honduran advocates' original requests to be included in the Nicaraguan and Central American Relief Act (NACARA), a program for asylees or potential asylees left out during the 1980s—mainly Guatemalans and Salvadorans and also controversially Nicaraguans. While Hondurans did not gain entry into NACARA (and all the benefits and resources this program provided), they gained TPS, which is essentially a one-year renewable work permit that allows Hondurans to work legally, process their taxes, and open bank accounts in the United States. While a step in the right direction for the short time allotted may prove difficult and they may fall out of status. It is this set of circumstances that prompted the organization of HULA (Hondurans United in Los Angeles), taking the example of other Central American and Mexican groups to organize around immigration reform and services.

After Hurricane Mitch, U.S. immigration policy changed to include Hondurans in the TPS program; this change increased Honduran applicants to the program. While immediate relief and temporary aid alleviated dire conditions, longer-term changes to address the fundamental causes of economic hardship and migration were elusive in the disaster response.

Demographic Profile

Hondurans have been fairly "invisible" in the United States due to their relatively small documented population size. There were an estimated 731,000 Hispanics of Honduran origin residing in the United States in 2010, according to the Census Bureau's American Community Survey (Motel and Patten, 2010). The largest numbers of the Honduran population are spread out in three regions, the South, the Northeast, and the West. The majority of Hondurans (54 percent) reside in the South, in the states of Florida, Texas, and Louisiana (Pew Hispanic Center, 2009). In the West, there are 93,000 Hondurans, with California boasting 69,000 Hondurans (Pew Hispanic Center, 2009). According to the American Community Survey (ACS) 2006–2008, 41.2 percent entered the country in the year 2000 or later, 34.2 percent entered between 1990 and 1999, and 24.6 percent entered the United States before 1990. According to figures held by the Honduran Consulate in Los Angeles, in 2007 there were 350,000 Hondurans in Southern California, including Los Angeles County and the surrounding counties of Orange, San Fernando, and San Bernardino.

Adjustment and Adaptation

Immigrants from different periods of migration have different levels of involvement in the current immigration movement and reflect different levels of integration into U.S. society. The immigrants from the 1960s tend to be more acculturated; their incorporation may have happened in the 1960s and 1970s, when it was easier to adjust their status. On the other hand, the very recent Honduran migrants are still at the margins of society and the immigrant rights movement—facing the everyday uncertainty that has come from the current anti-immigrant climate and the threat of workforce raids. Visibility is contingent on each immigrant period's particular relationship with immigration status, acculturation to U.S. society, the size and history of the migration trajectory, and degree of involvement in the immigrant rights movement. Undocumented migration has as much to do with exit factors as it does with pull conditions and information flows from the new country. Tropes about life in the United States are deployed in a variety of ways depending on the time of arrival of the family member or friend. Immigrants that arrived during the Central American exodus of the 1980s, alongside Guatemalan and Salvadorans, tend to be more involved and participate in activism networks established by Central Americans and other Chicano and Mexican groups.

Paths toward Citizenship

Hondurans are able to retain their Honduran citizenship when becoming citizens in the host country. This means that they are able still to participate in civic life in Honduras, retaining the right to vote in Honduran presidential elections. Many Hondurans, however, are not becoming U.S. citizens, as the most common but limited way to legalize their status in the United States is via the TPS program. An estimated 374,000 Central Americans are on TPS status; it is estimated that eighty thousand of them are Hondurans (Migration Policy Institute, 2006). Although immigrant Honduran organizations dedicate themselves to helping Hondurans process TPS, they also help by advocating and insisting that government authorities grant residency status to these Hondurans. Their reasoning is that many Hondurans pay the fees to file TPS every year, and for many years, they have filed taxes and reported their stay to the government. Their lawful behavior should at least be rewarded with a path to legalization. Few Hondurans have gained permanent residency when compared to the rest of Latinos in the nation.

The most common scenario Hondurans face is to live and work with undocumented status facing entrapment and detention by Homeland Security. The entrapment and deportation scenario for Hondurans is grim in the United States. Rates of deportation have increased drastically since 2000. In 2000, 4,768 people were deported to Honduras; by 2005, the rates of Honduran deportees had climbed to 15,572; by 2008, the numbers were at a staggering figure of 28,851; and by 2009 Homeland Security reported 19,959 Honduran deportees (Department of Homeland Security 2012). The Honduran government has entered into an "expedited Honduran removals" agreement with U.S. Homeland Security so that Honduran nationals facing deportation will only be held 15 days. This process involves video teleconferencing to advise detainees in order to issue them proper travel documents (Department of Homeland Security 2012). The Honduran government encourages Hondurans in the United States to apply for TPS. Many who arrived before 2001, however, may not be eligible for TPS, as this temporary program is hardly a catch-all response to the massive Honduran migration.

For the recent and growing Honduran community, the process of naturalization and permanent residency is an increasingly viable option through intermarriage and family petition.

Political Associations and Organizations

In 1997 Honduran organizers, as part of HULA, lobbied for TPS alongside Salvadoran activists in CARECEN (Central American Resource Center) but were stalled in their efforts until 1998, when Hurricane Mitch devastated Honduras. In the aftermath of Hurricane Mitch, the Clinton administration granted the inclusion of Honduran immigrants in the Temporary Protected Status (TPS) program in 1998. Hondurans in Los Angeles attended meetings at CARECEN to learn about the required paperwork, but many still feared exposure as undocumented immigrants. Nevertheless, enough acquired TPS status so that it has given Hondurans more of a presence within the local Los Angeles multiethnic immigrant rights and organizing communities. The energy and interest the meetings and the process generated helped Honduran activists and CARECEN organizers begin to conceive of a newly organized Honduran group. Sponsoring organizations, such as CARECEN, and hometown associations created the infrastructure for the development of leadership among Honduran activists.

Suyapa G. Portillo Villeda

See Also: Central American Civil Wars; Guatemalans; Mexicans; Nicaraguans.

Further Reading

Argueta, Marina. 2007. "Immigrant and merchant in banana plantations of the United Fruit Company." Interviewed in Los Angeles, California.

Benjamin, Medea, ed. 1989. *Don't Be Afraid, Gringo: A Honduran Woman Speaks from the Heart: The Story of Elvia Alvarado.* New York: Harper Perennial.

Department of Homeland Security. 2012. "Immigration Statistics." http://www.dhs.gov/files/statistics/immigration.shtm.

Escobar, Julio. 2007. "Member of Honduran United in Los Angeles (HULA)." Interviewed in Los Angeles, September 23.

Hamilton, Nora, and Norma Stoltz Chinchilla. 1991. "Central American Migration: A Framework for Analysis." *Latin American Research Review* 26.1:75–110.

Hamilton, Nora, and Norma Stoltz Chinchilla. 2001. *Seeking Community in a Global City: Guatemalans and Salvadorans in Los Angeles.* Philadelphia: Temple University Press.

"Hispanics of Honduran Origin in the United States, 2007." 2009. Pew Research Hispanic Center. http://pewhispanic.org//files/factsheets/55.pdf.

Migration Policy Institute. 2006. "The Central American Foreign Born in the United States." http://www.migrationpolicy.org/.

Motel, Seth, and Eileen Patten. 2010. "Hispanics of Honduran Origin in the United States, 2010." Pew Research Hispanic Center. http://www.pewhispanic.org/2012/06/27/hispanics-of-honduran-origin-in-the-united-states-2010/

Rodriguez, Cecilia. 2007. President of Alianza Hondureña de Los Angeles (AHLA). Interviewed in Los Angeles, California, August 10.

Velasquez, Leoncio. 2007. President of Honduran United in Los Angeles (HULA). Interviewed in Los Angeles, California, September 1.

Hospitals

Hospitals that receive federal Medicare funding are required by law to have emergency treatment facilities and must treat anyone in need of emergency medical care. Under the 1986 Emergency Medical Treatment and Active Labor Act (EMTALA), hospitals receiving federal funds must provide medical treatment to all individuals requiring emergent medical care regardless of insurance coverage or immigration status. However, the EMTALA act only covers treatment within the emergency room (ER) and does not cover hospital admissions or hospital stays once the patient is stabilized, nor rehabilitation treatments. In some states, undocumented immigrants injured on the job who require emergency treatment and follow-up care are covered under state workman's compensation laws.

Once a patient is no longer in critical care and no longer needs emergency care, hospitals have the ability to transfer the patient out to another facility for follow-up, often long-term care. However if a patient does not have insurance, other facilities are not obligated to accept the patient and the patient will remain in emergency care, until hospital administrators find a way to discharge the patient either to another facility or to the family, called "patient dumping," so that the hospital is no longer responsible for the expenses incurred for long-term care or rehabilitation. Consequently "anti-dumping" laws have been put into place in some areas in an effort to insure that those that need critical, post-emergency care receive it regardless of their ability to pay. Hospitals that do not follow these regulations run the risk of incurring a civil monetary penalty for each violation.

The imposition of the Professional Responsibility and Work Opportunity Reconciliation Act (PRWORA) in 1996, passed under President Bill Clinton to reform welfare programs, terminated all non-emergency health care to undocumented immigrants. Without insurance coverage, undocumented immigrants may be turned away from hospital admission or rehabilitation services within the hospital as well as through other agencies. Denial of care may increase their vulnerability and contribute to the deterioration of their physical well-being, thus requiring them to be readmitted to the emergency room.

Lack of medical assistance does not just affect undocumented immigrants but may also impact certain legal permanent residents. Most legal permanent residents are not eligible to receive Medicaid assistance until seven years of residency. Lack of health care may cause undocumented immigrants to be more susceptible to recurring health aliments, because of the inability to receive constant medical treatment. For example, if immigrants are unable to receive hospital care and treatment due to immigration-related restrictions, consequential health risks (including disability and death) may impact those dependent on them, such as young children. Though statistically Latino immigrants tend to be healthier than the general population, their health tends to deteriorate as they become more acculturated, which is known as the immigrant paradox. This may be attributed to factors such as a poor diet, increased alcohol and drug use, and inability to receive regular health care.

Undocumented immigrants are not eligible for most private insurance plans and unable to apply for any kind of government medical assistance programs such as

Medicaid or Medicare. This makes it very difficult to find medical treatment and care for those that are ill. Undocumented immigrants may avoid health care clinics due to fear of deportation and denial of health services because of their immigration status. Hospital emergency rooms have become one way to access health care for undocumented residents. At the same time, there are reports of U.S. Border Patrol agents staking out hospital wards awaiting the release of patients so that they can detain and remove them from the country. Spokespersons for the Border Patrol admit that at times there are agents at the hospital because they need to detain someone they have in custody. In Tucson, Arizona, activists accused a Border Patrol agent of staking a hospital for an undocumented woman, Miriam Aviles-Reyes, who went into labor after being detained for an alleged traffic violation. She publically testified that the agent remained by her side until she had given birth to her child, waiting to deport her and her newborn to Mexico—along with her husband and three other children.

There has been much concern about the overcrowding of emergency rooms with non-emergency ailments, and the spiraling costs of emergency medical care that often go uncompensated. In 2008, uncompensated care for hospitals and physicians was almost 56 billion dollars; the Federal government covered only 75 percent. Undocumented immigrants are often considered to be the main drain on hospital resources; however, seventy-six percent of uninsured people are U.S. citizens.

Hospital repatriations also known as deportations occur when hospitals transfer undocumented patients back to their countries of origin, as they are unable to secure a more long-term plan of medical treatment. As medical costs for admitted patients in critical care may cost upwards of thousands of dollars, hospital or medical repatriation has become an increasingly common practice. The American Medical Association estimates that it happens on a limited basis, once or twice a month, but other sources suggest annual repatriations are in the hundreds (Stead, 2010). One hospital in Arizona admitted to repatriating ninety-six immigrants in one year. An Associated Press news report (April 24, 2013) reported that two undocumented immigrants were involved in an automobile accident resulting in emergency treatment at Iowa Methodist Medical Center in Des Moines. After the patients were stabilized, the hospital administrators consulted with the patients' families and sent the two comatose men via a private jet to their community of origin, in Veracruz, Mexico. The report reveals that hundreds of undocumented immigrants make their way back to their homeland in this way through a little-known removal system run not by the federal government trying to enforce laws but by hospitals seeking to reduce the cost of treating uninsured patients, effectively removing them from the country outside of and without consulting any court or federal agency.

Sometimes, hospitals have repatriated patients without the consent of the family or patient, as was the case in *Montejo v. Martin Memorial Medical Center.* In this case, a drunk driver in a stolen van injured Luis Jimenez, an undocumented immigrant, in a head-on collision. Jimenez sustained multiple injuries and suffered severe head trauma. Due to a patchwork of policies, the patient's health was jeopardized and the burden of payment landed primarily on the hospital. Martin Memorial Medical Center provided treatment to Mr. Jimenez for approximately two years at a loss of over one million dollars. Martin Memorial Hospital sought and received permission to return Jimenez to

Guatemala in a Florida trial court in 2003. Mr. Jimenez was flown by private plane to his native country without consent or notice to his cousin and legal guardian Montejo Gaspar Montejo. Luis Jimenez was not able to receive the type of medical care he needed in Guatemala, and his condition continued to deteriorate. The decision to repatriate Luis Jimenez was reversed in the court of state appeals; however, Jimenez had already been deported. In 2008, Martin Memorial Medical Center was providing uncompensated care for at least six other uninsured immigrant patients and was investigated for repatriating another brain-injured patient back to Mexico without the country's permission. Instances such as these are increasing as the cost of uncompensated care for medical treatment in hospitals rises. As of 2010, Jimenez remained in the care of his seventy-two-year-old mother and suffers violent seizures, vomiting blood and suffering loss of consciousness.

Socioeconomic conditions play a significant role in the limited health care options for undocumented immigrants. Undocumented immigrants are over-represented in low-wage jobs including farming, construction, and in the food and hospitality service industry. These types of jobs provide limited access to health care insurance. Because the majority of these jobs remain in the low-wage arena with a median income of approximately $36,000, most cannot afford to purchase private insurance.

Access to health care is a public health and societal issue. If undocumented immigrants have no access to health care facilities, they are forced to rely on emergency rooms for primary care, which is costly, or receive no health treatment at all. Many believe that it is in the public's best interest to support healthcare availability for all people regardless of immigration status. Others, however, argue that it is not the responsibility of the U.S. hospitals to care for free for those who are in the country illegally.

Courtney Martínez

See Also: Barriers to Health; Health and Welfare; Laws and Legislation, Post-1980s; Mental Health Issues for Immigrants; Mental Health Issues for Undocumented Immigrants; Policies of Attrition; Trauma-Related Symptoms; Workplace Injuries.

Further Reading

Akincigil, A., R. S. Mayers, and F. H. Fulghum. 2011. "Emergency Room Use by Undocumented Mexican Immigrants." *Journal of Sociology & Social Welfare* 38.4:33–50.

Associated Press. 2013. "Hospitals 'repatriate' hundreds of seriously injured immigrants." *Arizona Daily Star,* April 24. Available on line at: http://azstarnet.com/news/local/border/hospitals-repatriate-hundreds-of-seriously-injured-immigrants/article_ecf81cd5-3748-58b9-a576-d6850f732e5f.html.

Procaccini, D. I. 2010. "First, Do No Harm: Tort Liability, Regulation and the Forced Repatriation of Documented Immigrants." *Boston College Third World Law Journal* 30.475:445–495.

Stead, K. 2010. "Critical Condition: Using Asylum Law to Contest Forced Medical Repatriation of Undocumented Immigrants." *Northwestern University Law Review* 104.1:307–333.

Tovar, Cindy. 2012. "Border Patrol Stakes out Hospitals." *Being Latino.* http://www.beinglatino.us/politics-2/border-patrol-stakes-out-hospitals/.

Hotel Industry

Hotels are service-producing businesses, employing anywhere from tens to hundreds of workers. A large hotel with two thousand rooms may employ up to 1400 employees (Waldinger, 1992). The largest concentration of workers is in housekeeping where menial work is performed, and to a lesser degree, in food service. Each day, a typical hotel employee undertakes a wide range of jobs. Organizationally, a hotel is a hierarchically ordered business enterprise where highly skilled workers are employed to answer telephones, register guests, solicit sales, and manage lower-level employees and accounting. Less skilled workers may engage in other tasks such as making beds, changing light bulbs, folding laundry, parking cars, washing dishes, and waiting tables. Immigrants are a vital source of low-skilled labor for the hotel industry the world over. In the United States, hotel service industry jobs are one of the few labor sector jobs that cannot be outsourced. In other words, these jobs must take place domestically. By the same token, because of the generally low barriers to entry in many of the low-skilled jobs, hotels provide an important source for work for undocumented immigrants seeking temporary or permanent employment once they come to the United States. In

Protesters hold hands as they wait to be arrested by Los Angeles police officers after refusing to leave a busy thoroughfare near Los Angeles International Airport while demanding unionization of mostly immigrant workers at a dozen high-end hotels in Los Angeles, Thursday, September 28, 2006. Hotel service industry jobs are one of the few labor sector jobs that cannot be outsourced, and many of the low-skilled jobs are filled by immigrants. (AP Photo/Damian Dovarganes)

recent years, there have been changes in employment laws that have made it more difficult for hotels to find legal workers they need for their operations, and they have resorted to hiring undocumented workers.

American workers tend to be more educated, and therefore they have more opportunities at their disposal and are less likely to compete with undocumented workers for jobs that pay poorly, are difficult, and not without hazards. Moreover, American industries increasingly undergo "restructuring," that is, opt out of hiring employees for full-time work and resort to flexible employment patterns such as part time, temporary and seasonal employment. In this way, hotels can adjust to slow or peak seasons. The result of restructuring is that service employee work has grown increasingly precarious, resulting in high turnover rates and less attraction for native workers. Because of this, and in addition to the increase of available immigrants, immigrants have slowly but surely replaced blacks in the lower-skilled and lower-paid ranks within the industry (Waldinger, 1992). However, some researchers argue that managers prefer immigrants because they are easily exploited and compliant and are more willing to accept the demands and instability of hotel employment (Zamudio and Lichter, 2008).

Immigrant women prominently fill housekeeping jobs. Housekeeping chores include daily cleaning of the guest rooms, vacuuming, making sure guests have necessary towels and accessories. Other duties usually include changing the linens on the beds, cleaning restrooms, and dusting. A housekeeper on a standard eight-hour shift may clean between fifteen and twenty rooms a day. In a study of hotel management in Los Angeles, Zamudio and Lichter (2008) found that 93 percent of the managers interviewed said that the job could be done by someone without any prior experience. None listed reading, writing, or English language ability as the most important skill for the job. At the same time, employers interviewed in this study complained about the inability of immigrant men and women to speak English and communicate with guests. This is in spite of the fact that one of the most important criteria for hiring employees was that they exhibit the right skill sets that would keep customers coming back to the hotel. These are referred to as "soft skills," and include the ability to interact with customers and coworkers, attitudes that can be characterized as nurturing and amenable, a deference to authority, and a "sunny disposition."

Because so many workers employed by the hotel industry have been undocumented, they have experienced difficulties in demanding from their employers better working conditions and pay to align them with the fair employment standards offered to legal workers. Some of the patterns that structure inequality have surfaced, such as:

- Immigrant workers are likely to remain in low-skilled and lower-paid positions in the hotel industry.
- Promotion and career development opportunities for immigrant workers are limited at best, and inaccessible at worst.
- Immigrant workers face particular vulnerabilities in terms of health and safety in hotel work and are more likely to be involved in workplace accidents.

Great unionizing efforts have been made by the Hotel and Restaurant Employees Union that helped organize labor to demand remedies to conditions experienced during the economic downturn during the 1980s when industry restructuring took hold. More recently, and in response to growing numbers of both legal and undocumented immigrants and growing inequality, in 2004 the Union of Needletraders, Industrial and Textile Employees and the Hotel Employees and Restaurant Employees union merged into UNITE-HERE and together they have waged very public organizing campaigns where immigrant workers have played a key role. UNITE-HERE's *Hotel Workers Rising* campaign launched strikes in cities such as Boston, Chicago, New York, and San Francisco in support of a largely female immigrant workforce (UNITE-HERE 2009).

Anna Ochoa O'Leary

See Also: East Asians; Garment Industry; Immigrant Workers Freedom Ride; Labor Unions; Workers' Rights.

Further Reading

Baum, Tom. 2012. *Migrant workers in the international hotel industry.* International Labour Office, International Migration Branch, Sectoral Activities Department. Geneva: ILO. Available at: http://www.ilo.org/wcmsp5/groups/public/@ed_dialogue/@sector/documents/publication/wcms_180596.pdf

Choi, J. G., R. Woods, and S. K. Murmann. 2000. "International Labor Markets and the Migration of Labor Forces as an Alternative Solution for Labor Shortages in the Hospitality Industry." *International Journal of Contemporary Hospitality Management* 12.1:61.

Durazo, Maria Elena. 2005. "Making Movement: Communities of Color and New Models of Organizing Labor." *Berkeley La Raza Law Journal* 16.2:187–193.

UNITE-HERE. 2009. "Hotel Workers Rising! About the Campaign." http://www.hotel workersrising.org/Campaign/.

Waldinger, Roger. 1992. "Taking Care of the Guests: The Impact of Immigrants on Services—An Industry Case Study." *International Journal of Urban and Regional Research* 16.1:97–112.

Zamudio, Margaret M., and Michael I. Lichter. 2008. "Bad Attitudes and Good Soldiers: Soft Skills as a Code for Tractability in the Hiring of Immigrant Latina/os over Native Blacks in the Hotel Industry." *Social Problems* 55.4:573–589.

Housing

Until recently, housing for undocumented workers and families as a whole has not been a target of anti-immigrant laws and ordinances. However in the past few years many local ordinances have sought to target undocumented immigrants through regulations pertaining to housing building codes and rental unit regulations.

In general, undocumented individuals and families face many of the same issues that other disadvantaged populations contend with in regard to housing. If they own their home, they are also responsible for violations of local housing codes for assuring that residences are safe and in compliance with public safety standards. If they rent their dwellings, they, like many other resource-poor tenants, have limited financial means so tend to settle in low-income neighborhoods. With few options but to seek units available for the least amount of rent, they also are vulnerable to neglect and poor management of living quarters, and unsafe spaces or buildings. However, immigrants who are also of undocumented status are additionally vulnerable to a range of violations by landlords who seek to cut maintenance costs of rental units, and may be tempted to take advantage of them due to their being out of status. Abusive landlords may discourage immigrants from making demands for improvements and registering complaints about negligent landlords for housing violations with housing authorities. Often, unscrupulous landlords may take advantage of immigrants' poor English proficiency and a lack of financial resources that hinder their ability to make changes to their living conditions, or to move elsewhere. As such, landlords can resort to scare tactics to refuse to fix units and to request high rents and minimal services. Landlords have been known to turn off water and heat on undocumented individuals when they complain about conditions or threaten to take up action against their landlords.

There has been research that links poor living conditions to building toxicity levels, with poor health outcomes for both children and adults regardless of race or status. Health hazards such as asthma are linked specifically to living environments and not to life style choices or eating habits as had been previously thought (Adelman, 2008). Research shows that when new immigrants arrive in the United States, their health is often better than more wealthy U.S. citizens; but within five years of living in the United States, their health deteriorates. This has been linked directly to the poor living conditions that immigrants are forced into due to their financial limitations.

Along with the barriers to adequate housing in recent years, there have been various laws and ordinances that are aimed at taking away the current housing options that immigrants have available to them. Sharing living quarters with family and friends that are already in the United States is a way to pool resources and save money on rent, utility, food, and transportation. Laws limiting the number of persons that can live in one unit is a way to undermine this strategy that is vital to the survival of the immigrant community.

For example one housing option for single men in the United States alone is group living. Undocumented workers who come into the United States without their wife or children often live in a housing unit with many other men in the same situation. Day laborers, as they are often referred to, rent one room or one apartment and split the rent and other expenses among them; it is not uncommon for groups up to twenty men to live together. In this manner they are able to maximize their earnings by sharing the housing expenses with others. Often these men spend most of their time at work or out looking for work so they do not spend much time in their apartment or room.

Although these men find that multiple occupants in one unit alleviates their housing and other financial obligations, so that more money can be sent to families back home, it has also been increasingly common for the town or city where these men labor to see this way of living as a blight, or threat, or an affront to the dominant culture. Consequently, proposing new housing regulations or ordinances to restrict or eliminate altogether this living arrangement has been a way to make immigrants invisible or unwelcomed. For example in Morrison, New Jersey there was a move in 2006 to try to get rid of the day laborers by enforcing the town's "anti-stacking ordinance" specifically in areas where day laborers were known to reside, by increasing fines for landlords who were found renting to undocumented individuals. Anti-stacking ordinances, also known as anti-crowding ordinances, are housing policies that have been enacted to facilitate the eviction and removal of unwanted housing occupants such as Mexican immigrants. These ordinances are enacted in towns and cities that are known for being hubs for Mexican immigrants and the town or city wishes to push out these groups indirectly. These policies have been known to put an even stricter restriction on the number of people who can live in one place, as well as limiting residency to immediate family members only. These policies come with fines for both the occupants and the landlords and tend to be enforced unequally in the towns and cities. Additionally more housing inspectors may be hired to ensure the success of these types of tactics of instilling fear in both migrants and landlords, such as in the Morrison case.

In recent years various local and state courts have passed laws and ordinances that target undocumented immigrants by putting further barriers on their ability to attain housing in the United States. The first of these anti-immigrant sentiment laws has been credited to the mayor of Hazelton, Pennsylvania, Lou Barletta. In 2006, Barletta passed the Illegal Immigration Relief Act, an ordinance that aimed at targeting undocumented immigrants in their work and home. This ordinance was put in place to discourage both the hiring and renting to undocumented immigrants. In the first stages of the ordinance the section that was specifically about housing was the Tenant Registration Ordinance which states that all potential tenants over the age of eighteen are required to fill out an "occupancy permit application" before being allowed to rent or stay in any rental unit. This application would require that the applicant present documented proof of legal citizenship/residential status within the United States. In this ordinance the landlords could be fined $1,000 per unlawful tenant with $100 for each day the tenant occupied the unit after receiving the violation notice (Harnett, 2008).

This ordinance would later prove to be unconstitutional on the grounds that only the federal government (not local or state governments) has jurisdiction over the determination and consequences for being unlawfully present. This ordinance threatened to prohibit many legal residents or citizens from the right to housing for lack of proper documentation (Harnett, 2008). However, although the proposed ordinance failed to become law, it still proved to instill fear and anxiety in many people. Half the town's Hispanic population was said to have left after the ordinance was put in place, in anticipation of the havoc it would provoke.

A similar law to that of Hazelton, Pennsylvania was signed in 2010 by Governor Jan Brewer: the Support Our Law Enforcement and Safe Neighborhood Act known as Arizona Senate Bill 1070 or more commonly as SB1070. This anti-immigrant bill was signed on April 23, 2010 and listed various restrictions aimed not only at undocumented immigrants, but anyone else who aided in any way an undocumented immigrant. Regarding issues of housing this law proposed that anyone—not just landlords—who in any way assisted an undocumented immigrant by providing them with any short-term or long-term housing would be charged with "harboring" a criminal. This broadening of housing restrictions caused heightened controversy throughout the nation. Although on October 9, 2013, the 9th Circuit

Court of Appeals negated this part of SB1070 that would have brought criminal charges against those who knowingly harbor someone who is present in the country unlawfully, the idea that simply making available any type of property to undocumented immigrants is a crime has brought about great consternation for families who feel morally bound to provide shelter to those undocumented immigrants even if they are here lawfully.

Although these laws aimed at instilling fear in individuals and potentially causing undocumented individuals difficulty in securing a place to live, they also put additional stresses on the individuals, families, friends, and landlords who are sympathetic and feel that they have a moral obligation to provide shelter to those in need. There has also been a move toward raiding private homes to apprehend individuals in or around their home. Such was the case for a young Honduras woman who was detained after U.S. Immigration and Customs Enforcement (ICE) agents broke into her home and took her and her infant daughter in for lack of documentation (Murguia, 2008).

Another instance of this occurred in September, 2007 in Chaparral, New Mexico. Police officers conducted raids of private homes along with ICE agents. These unwarranted raids were based on the physical appearance of the individuals or speaking Spanish, and in neighborhoods where undocumented individuals were thought to live. They would find reason to stop or question individuals who looked Latino or spoke Spanish and would then have ICE agents ask for proper documentation. ICE agents would also enter the home either by force or invitation of individuals they suspected of being "illegal." After the apprehension of parents, ICE agents would accompany the parents to their children's schools to pull them out and detain them as well.

After such raids many families are afraid to return to their home. Some will turn to local churches that may provide temporary shelter and food. Families aware that ICE agents are still surveying the neighborhood will not return to their homes.

After 2006, policy changes provided that children would only be removed when there was no adult present to care for them, and they would be placed in the care of Child Protective Services instead of being held in a detention center (Murguia, 2008).

With various laws that seek to charge people or organizations that aid immigrants with "harboring illegal immigrants" many religious organizations, most notably churches and charity organizations, have spoken out against such laws. Many insist that this law and others like it go against their religious freedoms to act out of religious convictions and that regardless of the laws, they will continue to shelter as well as feed, clothe and aid people in need regardless of citizenship status (Rieser-Murphy, 2011).

Yesenia Andrade

See Also: Acculturation; Assimilation; Barriers to Health; Family Economics; Family Structure; Health and Welfare; Policies of Attrition; Suburbs.

Further Reading

Adelman, L. (Executive Producer). 2008. "In Sickness and in Wealth" [Television series episode]. In *Unnatural Causes*. California Newsreel.

Harnett, Helen M. 2008. *State and Local Anti-Immigrant Initiatives*.

Murguia, Janet. 2008, May 20. *The Implications of Immigration Enforcement on America's Children*. Hearing on ICE Workplace Raids: Their Impact on U.S. Children, Families, and Communities. Submitted to: U.S. House of Representatives Committee on Education and Labor, Subcommittee on Workforce Protections. Washington, DC.

Ong Hing, Bill. 2009. "Institutional Racism, ICE Raids, and Immigration Reform." *University of San Francisco Law Review* 44:1. Available at: http://works.bepress.com/billhing/4.

Rieser-Murphy, Elizabeth, and Kathryn DeMarco. 2011. "No Good Deed Goes Unpunished?" Alabama's New Immigration Law—A Threat to Conservative Values. Available at Social Science Research Network: http://ssrn.com/abstract=1926447

State of Arizona, Senate. 2010. *Senate Bill 1070: An Act*. Forty-ninth Legislature, Second Regular Session. Phoenix, AZ.

Human Rights Watch

Human Rights Watch is an independent organization that focuses on the protection of human rights across the world. The activities of Human Rights Watch began in 1978 with the establishment of the Helsinki Watch, which would become a component of the wider Human Rights Watch organization that would be founded in the late 1980s. The major objective of the Human Rights Watch is to drive international public attention to any region in the world where human rights are violated. It aspires to stimulate change by placing abusive governments under a spotlight through the methodology of "naming and shaming." The operation areas of Human Rights Watch include arms trade, business in human rights, women's rights, children's rights, LGBT rights, domestic violence, terrorism and methods of counterterrorism, torture, rape as war crime, health, freedom of press, migrants and refugees, trafficking, and child soldiers.

In 2011, Human Rights Watch became a vocal advocate for respecting the rights of undocumented immigrants. In a report titled "No Way to Live: Alabama's Immigrant Law" (available on its website), the organization reported on first-hand accounts given by 57 state residents, including citizens and permanent residents, who reported abuse or discrimination. Considered a law that copies most of the provisions of the proposed Arizona SB 1070, parts of the proposed Alabama law, HB 56, took effect September 28 after a federal judge ruled that most of it was constitutional. Among other things, the measure prohibits undocumented immigrants from entering into "business transactions" with the state; denies bail to any undocumented immigrant arrested for any offense; requires police to check immigration status during traffic stops; and denies court protection to immigrants who have had a contract, such as an employment contract or a lease, violated.

Human Rights Watch is an independent, non-profit and non-governmental organization that does not receive funding from any government institutions. It generates resources through the contributions of private individuals and foundations across the world. While its headquarters are in New York City, Human Rights Watch has offices in major cities worldwide: Chicago, Los Angeles, San Francisco, Toronto and

Washington D.C. in North America; Berlin, Brussels, Geneva, London, Moscow, Paris in Europe; Johannesburg in Africa and Tokyo in Asia. Aside from experts and consultants hired for temporary projects, the actual full-time staff of the organization consists of over 280 people.

Helsinki Watch was established in 1978 with the objective of observing Soviet bloc governments' compliance with the 1975 Helsinki Declarations. Three years later, in 1981, Americas Watch was founded to closely investigate the civil wars erupting in Central American countries. The establishment of region-based Watch organizations continued throughout the 1980s with Asia Watch (1985), Africa Watch (1988) and Middle East Watch (1989). Finally, the Watch organizations were united under the roof of the Human Rights Watch in 1988. While the initial areas of concern were mainly human rights violations during warfare, or violations by undemocratic governments, Human Rights Watch gradually expanded its horizon and now conducts research on issues including women's rights, gay and lesbian rights, refugees, migrants, children, arms trade and counterterrorism policies. Human Rights Watch publishes news releases, commentary articles, and reports. *World Report*, covering human rights violations in six regions (Africa, Americas, Asia, Europe and Central Asia, Middle East and North Africa and the United States), has been published annually since 1989. The publication of reports on immigration-related issues dates back to the early 1990s.

In the realm of migration, Human Rights Watch focuses on the following topics: asylum seekers, refugees, internally displaced people, women and girls, children, workers, forced labor and trafficking, and policy developments. Various reports touch upon the issue of undocumented immigration, yet there are reports specifically produced on this issue. In March 1998, Human Rights Watch published a report on undocumented immigrants in South Africa, entitled "Abuse of Undocumented Immigrants, Asylum Seekers, and Refugees in South America." The report looks at the treatment of undocumented immigrants by South African officials, the conditions of detention centers in the country, and abuses faced by refugees and asylum seekers. In November 2009, Human Rights Watch produced the report entitled "No Refuge: Migrants in Greece," which focuses on Greece's treatment of undocumented immigrants. The report is a follow-up to the "Stuck in a Revolving Door: Iraqis and Other Asylum Seekers and Migrants at the Greece/Turkey Entrance to the European Union" published in November 2008, and analyzes the migration routes of Iraqi undocumented immigrants and the ways in which they are treated by officials from both Turkey and Greece, the two countries they have to cross in order to enter the European Union.

Zeynep Selen Artan

See Also: Advocacy

Further Reading

Human Rights Watch. 2011. *No Way to Live: Alabama's Immigrant Law.* Available at: http://www.hrw.org/news/2011/12/13/usalabama-no-way-live-under-immigrant-law
Human Rights Watch. www.hrw.org.

Human Trafficking

Human trafficking refers to the illegal trade in human beings for purposes of exploitation and profit. It is often referred to as a modern-day form of slavery. It is the third most lucrative crime in the world behind drug and arms trafficking. The United States (U.S.) Department of State estimates there are anywhere from 4 to 27 million human trafficking victims globally. Every country in the world is involved in human trafficking as a country of origin, transit or destination for victims. The human trafficking industry generates $32 billion dollars worldwide in profit per year. Estimates range from 14,000 to 50,000 victims trafficked from abroad into the United States each year with many more tens of thousands of victims trafficked inside the country (International Labour Office, 2008).

The 2000 United Nations Protocol to Prevent, Suppress and Punish Trafficking in Persons, especially Women and Children, to the UN Convention against Transnational Organized Crime defines trafficking as:

> Trafficking in persons shall mean the recruitment, transportation, transfer, harbouring or receipt of persons, by means of the threat or use of force or other forms of coercion, of abduction, of fraud, of deception, of the abuse of power or of a position of vulnerability or of the giving or receiving of payments or benefits to achieve the consent of a person having control over another person, for the purpose of exploitation. Exploitation shall include, at a minimum, the exploitation of the prostitution of others or other forms of sexual exploitation, forced labour or services, slavery or practices similar to slavery, servitude or the removal of organs.

This protocol is called the Palermo Protocol and is considered the global standard for defining human trafficking. Domestic legislation on human trafficking throughout the world draws on the three Ps of the Palermo Protocol: prevention, criminal prosecution, and victim protection.

Efforts to combat human trafficking in the United States are guided by the Trafficking Victims Protection Act (TVPA) of 2000. The U.S. Department of State points out that the TVPA defines severe forms of trafficking as "sex trafficking in which a commercial sex act is induced by force, fraud, or coercion, or in which the person induced to perform such an act has not attained eighteen years of age" or " the recruitment, harboring, transportation, provision, or obtaining of a person for labor or services, through the use of force, fraud, or coercion for the purpose of subjection to involuntary servitude, peonage, debt bondage, or slavery." The third reauthorization of the TVPA happened through the William Wilberforce Trafficking Victims Protection Reauthorization Act of 2008. Each reauthorization aims to clarify definitions to make it easier to prosecute traffickers and better protect victims.

Human smuggling and human trafficking are not the same. The differences revolve around three main issues: consent, final destination, and exploitation. A smuggled person agrees to be transported from one place to the other across an international border. Furthermore, once the smuggled person arrives at his/her destination, the relationship with the smuggler ends.

Human trafficking, on the other hand, involves deceit or fraud; a person does not agree to get trafficked. Humans can be trafficked across international borders or within the same country. Human trafficking involves the continual exploitation of a human being. The person does not have to be physically moved to be a victim of trafficking, though victims may be moved from one place to another. The exploitation of the victim continues day after day.

Even though human smuggling and human trafficking are not the same, they can be connected. Human smuggling can turn into human trafficking. A person who agrees to be smuggled can be turned into a trafficking victim at any point in the smuggling process because the smuggler can decide to not deliver the person to the agreed-upon destination and instead keep the person for exploitation, or sell the person to human traffickers. Therefore, though an individual may give consent to be smuggled, whether or not an individual ends up a victim of traffickers depends on extraneous factors, including the ethics of the smuggler and the presence, or not, of traffickers along the smuggling route.

Collecting reliable and accurate data about human trafficking is difficult for policymakers and practitioners for many reasons. Victims are often hidden or are so scared they often go undetected or, when seen, do not report their situation. In addition, policy discussions, training of personnel and statistics tend to focus on undocumented immigrants. Officials charged with immigration policy enforcement often do not receive training on how to distinguish between smuggled and trafficked persons. Trafficking victims usually do not get the support they need when discovered because they get classified as undocumented immigrants. Since many victims are children, they tend to be voiceless and powerless in society. Furthermore, large, transnational organizations involved in trafficking use their resources to make sure that victims do not get discovered. Finally, it is difficult to trace victims when they are trafficked through various cities and countries.

Despite the difficulty in collecting data, organizations such as the United Nations do publish statistics on human trafficking worldwide. According to the United Nations, 79 percent of victims are trafficked for reasons related to sexual exploitation, nearly 18 percent for labor exploitation, and the remaining 3 percent for other reasons. Sexual exploitation includes working as a prostitute and being used to produce pornographic films or websites. Labor exploitation includes being forced to work for no pay or low pay and not having rights as a worker. Other reasons can include organ trafficking, illegal adoption, and recruitment into military service. Regardless of the reason why a person gets trafficked, the process always includes coercion and exploitation. Human trafficking exists because of the demand for sexual commercialization, low-cost labor, and other services provided by the victims.

Females make up the largest percentage of trafficking victims worldwide. Sixty-six percent of victims are women, thirteen percent are girls, twelve percent are men, and nine percent are boys. This means that over one-fifth of trafficking victims are children.

Traffickers use a combination of intimidation, physical and emotional violence, deceit, drugs, and barriers to keep their victims in captivity. Traffickers make it impossible for victims to escape by stealing vital documents such as passports, visas and other forms of identification from their victims. They threaten to kill family members or to deport the victim. They drug their victims. They trap laborers in a system of debt bondage in which the victims are expected to pay off with their work a debt to their employer or even the traffickers they knew nothing about. The emotional, psychological and physical burdens placed on victims by those who exploit them make escape very difficult.

Restrictive immigration policies tend to increase the money that can be made by human traffickers. As it becomes more difficult for individuals to cross into the United States, the price charged for migrant smuggling increases as does the price of trafficking victims sold into exploitation.

2010 marked the tenth anniversary of the enactment of the TPVA and the Palermo Protocol. Also, in 2010, for the first time, the United States appeared on the U.S. Department of State's Human Trafficking Report. The report divides countries into four tiers based on the effort of their government to combat trafficking. A country in Tier 1 recognizes human trafficking exists, takes steps to combat it and meets the minimum standards established in the TVPA which include punishing acts of trafficking. For example, in 2010, Canada and the United States were categorized in Tier 1. A country in Tier 2 has not met the minimum standard but is making an effort to do so. For example, in 2010 Mexico and Peru were categorized in Tier 2. A country in Tier 2 Watch List may have made promises to do better over the next year or is a country with significant trafficking activity that it tries to combat. In 2010, Guatemala and Panama were on the Tier 2 Watch List. A country in Tier 3 has not met the minimum standards and has not made an effort to do so. For example, in 2010, Iran and North Korea were categorized in Tier 3.

In 2009, the United Nations Office on Drugs and Crime (UNODC) initiated the Blue Heart Campaign against Human Trafficking. Symbolized by a blue heart, the campaign aims to raise awareness about human trafficking, generate a sense of urgency around the issue, and create a basis of community support to fight against human trafficking wherever it occurs. Signs that a person may be a victim of human trafficking include: comments about frequent travel out of town or having lived in several cities; malnutrition; lack of control over identification documents; references to sexual abuse; and an unpredictable schedule.

Moira A. Murphy-Aguilar

See Also: Border Crossing; Coyotes; Crime; Drug Trade; Migration; Trafficking Victims Protection Reauthorization Act; U.S.-Mexico Border Wall.

Further Reading

Hepburn, Stephanie, and Rita Simon. 2010. "Hidden in Plain Sight: Human Trafficking in the United States." *Gender Issues* 27.1/2:1–26.

"Human Trafficking." 2013. "The Polaris Project: For a World without Slavery." http://www.polarisproject.org/human-trafficking/overview.

International Labour Office. 2008. "ILO Action against Trafficking in Human Beings." http://www.ilo.org/wcmsp5/groups/public/@ed_norm/@declaration/documents/publication/wcms_090356.pdf.

McCabe, Kimberly A. 2010. *Sex Trafficking: A Global Perspective.* Lanham, MD: Lexington Books Office to Monitor and Combat Trafficking in Persons.

U.S. Department of State Web Site. 2013. http://www.state.gov/g/tip/.

Identification Cards

Identification (ID) cards have become a common and valid form of identification for residents from other countries who are living in the United States. Identification cards are small, portable, and durable documents that are issued to individuals to establish their identity. They are commonly needed in many day-to-day tasks such as conducting financial transactions such as cashing checks, opening a bank account, and applying for credit. They are also necessary for obtaining a driver's license, a business license, and applying for a job. Identification cards validate one's identity as authentic and true, which in itself presents problems for undocumented immigrants who may make use of counterfeit documents or claim the identity of another in order to qualify for employment. Since the Immigration Reform and Control Act of 1986, employers are required to verify that any employee is lawfully entitled to work in the United States. In this way, identification cards have become critical for applying for work.

Each identification card varies in the type of information it carries but will usually contain a photo of the individual along with other identifying information such as current residence and birth date. An identification card may also include other information such as issue date, and expiration date. ID Cards may combine several features such as photographs, bar codes, and holograms to prevent false replication of such documents.

Unlike most countries the United States does not have a national ID card. A bill proposed in Congress known as the "REAL ID" act (Public Law 103–13, 119, Statute 302, enacted May 11, 2005), would require that everyone in the United States possess a national ID card beginning in 2013. However, the nation has been steadily evolving in a way that makes achieving this goal increasingly untenable. The research by Barkin (2003) using different polls conducted between 1982 and 1998 showed that the push towards laws that would require the use of national identification cards tended to come from nativists who sought to use such laws to curb undocumented immigration. Arguments used in favor of such an approach reflected the perceptions that undocumented immigrants were taking jobs away from U.S. citizens. A 1993 Gallup poll showed that a majority of the nation across different sectors of society based on religion, income and ethnicity, favored the use of national ID cards. Low-income earners were more likely to favor ID cards for everyone, while high-income earners were likely to oppose them.

If passed, A REAL ID law requiring the use of a national ID card for everyone will force states to develop a system for authenticating birth certificates or passports as part of the application process. This will make it difficult if not impossible for undocumented immigrants to apply for such a card. A REAL ID would also contain biometric data, such as fingerprints. However, although the law was originally scheduled to take effect May 11, 2008, most all of the states have filed for extensions to come into compliance. Most judicial analysis indicates that by the new deadline in 2013, little or no action will have been taken on the part of the states in order to comply, so the future of the law remains uncertain. Writing for the libertarian-leaning CATO institute, Harper (2012) argues that a national ID card such as the proposed REAL ID card impedes the freedom of movement for workers and employers and effectively transfers the ability of individuals to control their own lives to the government.

Immigrants in the United States attempt to comply with laws requiring proof of identification through consular services. For example, the Government of Mexico dispenses identification cards known as the *"Matricula Consular"* to foreign nationals living in the United States with the goal of providing a means of identification for its citizens. The terms "Certificate of Consular Registration" and "Matricula Consular Card" are used to refer to the same document. The Mexican consulate has provided this service since 1871. Only recently in the post-9/11 era have these identification cards been accepted as a valid form of identification. Undocumented immigrants are often not able to obtain any other types of identification cards, such as driver's licenses. Prior to 9/11 state-issued driver's licenses did not have a "lawful presence" requirement of applicants; therefore undocumented immigrants and residents could obtain a driver's license, which was considered the only form of valid identification. Due to increased post-9/11 security measures, forty-seven states now require a valid social security number to obtain a driver's license. Having a driver's license offer proof of residency has assumed new importance in light of laws such as Arizona's SB1070 where those stopped for any violation of the law must prove that they are in the country legally. Additionally, a coordinated effort to crack down on the misuse of drivers' licenses by legal permanent residents in twenty-six states will have their licenses expire the same date that their immigrant visas expire.

Without the ability to obtain a driver's license or identification card, undocumented residents become targets for crime and theft. There are accounts from the Austin, Texas police department of increasing numbers of undocumented immigrants being robbed on their way home from work or their houses being broken into. Because they did not have a valid form of ID they were not able to open bank accounts. There was a great need for other forms of valid identification. Local and federal businesses recognized this and started to recognize other valid forms of identification for those unable to obtain a license.

The "Matricula Consular" is to be used exclusively for Mexican citizens. Its purpose is to serve as a form of registration and identification in government offices, at the police department, at the hospital, and at the library to name a few. It does not, however, give permission for the individual to travel to other countries nor does it establish any form of naturalization.

Wells Fargo Bank began accepting the Matricula as a form of identification for new account openings and other daily bank transactions. As a result, several financial services become available to people with a Matricula Consular Card, and also the need to carry large amounts of cash is eliminated through the use of bank checks and debit cards. Mexican citizens are suddenly able to make purchases online as well as safely and securely manage their finances. By 2004, over 178 banks accepted the Matricula Consular as a valid form of ID when opening a new account.

There are strict requirements that must be met in order to obtain a consulate identification card. An appointment with the nearest consulate office must be made and the individual must appear in person at the established time. A signed application must be submitted at that time along with the requirements for the issuance of a Matricula Consular. The three requirements are: proof of Mexican citizenship, proof of identity, and proof of current physical address. Proof of Mexican citizenship can be fulfilled with either a birth certificate or a current passport. As proof of identity, a current Mexican passport, voter registry ID with photo, work permit, school ID, United States driver's license or permanent resident card issued by the United States government can be used. Proof of physical address can be established with a rental agreement, utility bill, car insurance, or a United States driver's license with the current physical address. A small fee is required before a consulate ID can be issued.

Though falsified ID documents do exist, they are often created because undocumented immigrants are not able to obtain IDs in most states. As stated earlier, they may become a target of crime if they are unable to open a bank account and are forced to carry their money with them at all times. False documentation is declining as technology has become more sophisticated. The use of digital holograms, fingerprints, watermarks, and barcodes is making it almost impossible to fake any form of identification.

With the implementation of the E-verify system, false identification cards and social security cards are becoming less frequent. The E-verify program is a system that verifies new employee's work eligibility. It is an Internet-based system that compares information from an employee's Form I-9, Employment Eligibility Verification, to data from U.S. Department of Homeland Security and Social Security Administration records to confirm employment eligibility. This system detects if someone is providing a false identification or social security number and prohibits them from working. More than 288,000 employers, large and small, across the United States use E-Verify to check the employment eligibility of their employees. Employers that utilize the E-verify program must display posters in the window of the business advertising that they use it. If an employee's information does not match, they will receive a notification of Tentative Non-Confirmation or TNC Notice. However, there is a large margin for error within the E-verify system, and an estimated 2.5 million legal residents risk losing their jobs if the errors go undetected. E-verify is not mandatory for all employers; however, federal employers and employers in the states of Arizona and Mississippi are required to use the program. E-verify and the Department of Homeland Security recognize that some employers may violate the program rules and conduct discriminatory practices; thus they request that such practices be reported to DHS in order to protect the rights of the employees.

Other forms of identification include any of the different types of nonresident visas, such as the kind that are used to secure employment in the United States and Legal Permanent Resident (LPR) green cards. Green cards, or permanent resident cards, are a form of identification given to an immigrant once legal permanent status is attained. A green card includes much of the same information as the identification card, but also includes the USCIS number and category status of how the Green card was obtained (i.e. through marriage, conditional residency).

All forms of identification must remain with the immigrant at all times. Legal charges may be imposed if they do not have their identification cards with them at all times. In the event that the ID is stolen, there is a process that one must go through to get a duplicate copy. It is also very important to pay attention to the expiration dates of the cards. There are lengthy processing times for paperwork and it is suggested that one file ninety days prior to the expiration date; otherwise the holder may "fall out of status" and may be deported. Additionally, Overstayers, or those who do not renew their visas for travel or work, are considered to be in the country unlawfully and their visa may be automatically voided, making them "undocumented."

Courtney Martínez

See Also: Arizona SB 1070; Counterfeit Documents; Driver's Licenses; *Flores-Figueroa v. United States;* Identity Theft; Passports; "Undocumented" Label.

Further Reading

Barkin, Elliott R. 2003. "Return of the Nativists." *Social Science History* 27.2:229–284.
Harper, Jim. 2012. "Internal Enforcement, E-Verify, and the Road to a National ID." *CATO Journal* 32.1:125–137.
Matricula Consular web source: http://www.ime.gob.mx/agenda_migratoria/matricula.htm
Requirements to Obtain a Mexican Consulate ID web source: http://consulmex.sre.gob .mx/tucson/index.php/documentacion.
Wells Fargo Accepts Consular Cards web source: https://www.wellsfargo.com/press/ matricula20011109b.

Identity Theft

Many citizens and legal permanent residents are tracked by numerical systems developed by federal and state agencies. For this reason, unique identity numbers are assigned to individuals' Social Security and Medicare cards, work authorization papers, visas, passports, driver's licenses, among other documents. A Social Security number is required for jobs in the formal economy, and for immigrants, a green-card work-authorization permit is needed. Immigrants who do not have any of these are "undocumented." For those who are undocumented, obtaining an identity number is the key to finding employment. For this reason the crime of identity theft, stealing the numbers and other information that tracks an individual's identity, is on the rise among document-counterfeiting rings that have ready customers in the form of undocumented immigrants seeking to secure legitimate employment in the United States.

Identification numbers of both citizens and legal permanent residents can and have been stolen for the purpose of gaining jobs. While there are many ways of acquiring a fictitious or stolen identity, including simply having one's wallet or purse stolen, employers share some of the responsibility for preventing identity theft. The Department of Homeland Security (DHS) set up a pilot social security number verification program called E-verify for this purpose. Employers are able to, but are not obligated to electronically check and validate the Social Security numbers presented by job applicants to verify their eligibility for employment.

Background

The obtaining and fraudulent use of someone else's Social Security number carries a prison term of up to five years and a $250,000 fine. It is not known if immigrants purchasing fraudulent documents know if the numerical ID is fictitious or real, but certainly, counterfeiters and thieves know. Counterfeiting rings produce counterfeit identification documents ranging from Social Security cards to driver's licenses. One Chicago counterfeiting ring employing twenty-two people was raided. The operators were Mexican, as were many of the customers; but individuals of other ethnicities and United States citizens patronized the business (Sanders, 2007). For $200 to $300, fraudulent identification could be purchased. The ring was thought to operate in several cities including Denver and Los Angeles, generating $2 to $3 million in profits per year. The types of documents produced included Social Security cards, driver's licenses, and green cards. In some cases, customers provided fictitious or real information about identities to be merged with their own identification. Eight individuals were indicted for counterfeiting IDs based on their matching Puerto Rican birth certificates and Social Security cards. These were used to provide customers with information to obtain identification cards in the state of Ohio. In the United States, counterfeiters can be tried for violating federal immigration law, conspiring to commit identity fraud, and aggravated identity fraud. Conspiring to commit identity fraud and committing aggravated identity fraud can carry twenty years imprisonment and/or a fine of $500,000.

However, the federal government is often slow to catch up with sources of information that can lead them to cases of identity theft. For this reason, there has been growing pressure to pass the REAL ID Act, which would incorporate the use of biometric data in a national identification card that could be used simultaneously as a driver's license. Biometrics, which is literally the measurement of life, refers to the technology of measuring, analyzing and processing the digital representations of unique biological data such as fingerprints, eye retinas, and voice recognition. Following the 9/11 attacks on the World Trade Center in New York City, biometric technology has become central to the development of border control and management technologies. However, the American public is wary of cards that might be used in any number of ways without their full awareness. Proponents of a national identification card argue that it would be a stronger means of protecting personal identity against the various risks present in a high-tech world (Ajana, 2010).

Notable Cases of Identity Theft

Until recently, identity theft and document fraud were unusual charges made against undocumented immigrants captured in workplace raids. Since the 1986 Immigration Reform and Control Act (IRCA), there has been a dramatic proliferation of fraudulent documents produced in order for those who do not have proper authorization to work to have the opportunity to provide the papers in order to do so. In 2003, Department of Homeland Security Immigration and Customs Enforcement (ICE) established an Identity and Benefits Fraud unit to work with U.S. Citizenship and Immigration Services to locate identity violators and reduce fraudulent benefit applications. The task forces are operative in ten cities (U.S. Immigration and Customs Enforcement Factsheets, 2008). In 2004, 2,334 investigations were conducted and in 2005, 3,591 were conducted. Criminal indictments were issued in 767 cases in 2004 and 1,052 in 2005.

The U.S. Supreme Court Case *Flores-Figueroa v. United States* (2006) provided the U.S. government a powerful tool for enforcement by cracking down on those employers who hire undocumented workers; an accused immigrant can be convicted of identity theft. As Immigration and Customs Enforcement (ICE) stepped up enforcement efforts in the U.S. interior, more incidents of identity theft have been prosecuted. In 2006, a series of immigration raids were carried out against Swift Company meat processing plants. In the case of Swift, the operation revealed that despite the company's participation in the U.S. government's Basic Pilot program to verify employment eligibility with the Social Security Administration and other government databases, over 1,200 undocumented workers were employed without proper documents (U.S. Immigration and Customs Enforcement Fact Sheets, 2008).

In 2007 and 2008, the federal government targeted meatpacking plants in a series of raids. Pilgrim's Pride poultry process plants were raided in Mount Pleasant, Texas; Live Oak, Florida; Chattanooga, Tennessee; Batesville, Arkansas; and Moorfield, West Virginia. The AgriProcessors (the nation's largest processor of kosher meat) kosher meat plant in Postville, Iowa, was raided and the Waterloo, Iowa, plant was raided. Of the 389 undocumented immigrants taken into custody in Waterloo, Iowa, 270 were arrested for identity theft used in gaining jobs at an Agriprocessor meatpacking plant. Instead of utilizing expedited removal procedures, 260 undocumented immigrants were sentenced to five months detention while two received sentences of a year and one day and a felony charge for identity theft. The immigrants were tried, with their hands and feet shackled, in groups of ten in courtrooms. They pled guilty, receiving five months detention for either using false social security cards or other forged immigration documents. These pleas were in exchange for avoiding the more serious charge of felony identity theft that carries a mandatory penalty of two years minimum. Many of those charged were in procession of real Social Security card numbers or resident immigrant visas, known as green cards, that belonged to other people. Those who pled guilty were subjected to removal with few concerns over what many have come to characterize as a terrorizing and traumatic event (Buff, 2008).

If anything, this information reveals the scope of the problem, and the evolving nature of identity theft. Before the pilot program, thieves were simply inventing nine-digit social security numbers. Attempts to discover these with the pilot program provided an impetus for more complicated identity theft techniques.

Prosecution Against Identity Theft by Immigrants

In 2007, ICE apprehended 863 on criminal charges in worksite investigations and arrested 4,077 workers on immigration violations. Although not all of these cases involved identity theft and statistics are not available, there was a substantial increase in misdemeanor and felony charges for it. In a 2007 case involving the nation's largest pallet manufacturing company, five defendants pleaded guilty and were given expedited removal; seven defendants were to be tried for counterfeit alien registration (up to a seven-year penalty), illegal use of Social Security numbers (five-year penalty), two years for identity theft, and all could receive six months to a maximum of twenty years for illegal reentry after deportation. ICE efforts increased through August 2008, with more than one thousand criminal arrests, including 116 owners, managers, or business administrators. An additional 3,900 administrative arrests were of unauthorized entrants for immigration violations (U.S. Immigration and Customs Enforcement Fact Sheets, 2008).

Although the federal government has had the sole responsibility for regulating immigration and enforcing immigration laws, many states have assumed a greater role for enforcing state identity theft laws as a method to control immigration. For example, in Arizona several laws have been passed in recent years that require agents administrating social services to use E-verify to check on an applicant's legal status. In Arizona, agents neglecting this duty are themselves subject to penalties in the way of fines and jail time. In 2001, California passed a model law restricting companies from placing an individual's social security number on cards required for private transactions to prevent identity theft. Thirty-one states have laws protecting social security numbers and many have begun requiring private health insurers not to put social security numbers on their cards.

Immigration enforcement measures have increasingly added jail time to the deportation of undocumented workers. Immigrant advocates often argue that identity is very often a victimless crime because immigrants use identity numbers (such as social security numbers for employment) and most likely make payroll contributions to Social Security and Medicare. However, undocumented immigrants who obtain fraudulent credentials may damage the wage, taxation, and credit histories of the individuals whose numerical identity was obtained. ICE investigations have uncovered many identity theft victims. Criminal activities wrongfully attributed to victims of identity theft have included: (1) owing up to $17,000 in Internal Revenue back taxes on unreported employment wages, and (2) arrests on warrants issued for individuals using their identity.

Undocumented immigrants convicted of the crime of identity theft are jailed or imprisoned for periods ranging from five months with expedited removal to up to twenty years. U.S. prisons and jails are already over capacity and the costs of immigrant detention are straining federal budgets.

Judith Ann Warner

See Also: Driver's Licenses; *Flores-Figueroa v. United States*; Identification Cards; Immigration and Customs Enforcement (ICE); Incarceration; Postville, Iowa Raid; Social Security; Workplace Raids; "Undocumented" Label.

Further Reading

Ajana, Btihaj. 2010. "Recombinant Identities: Biometrics and Narrative Bioethics." *Journal of Bioethical Inquiry* 7.2:237–258.

Associated Press. "Oregon, More Than 165 Workers Are Detained After Raid." *New York Times.* http://www.nytimes.com/2007/06/13/us/13brfs-immigration.html.

Buff, Rachel Ida. 2008. "The Deportation Terror." *American Quarterly* 60.3:523–551.

Preston, Julia. "270 Immigrants Sent to Prison in Federal Push." *New York Times.* http://www.nytimes.com/2008/05/24/us/24immig.html.

Sanders, Libby. "Officials Raid Illegal Document Operation." *New York Times.* http://www.nytimes.com/2007/04/26/us/26immig.html.

Saulny, Susan. "Hundreds are Arrested in U.S. Sweep of Meat Plant." *New York Times.* http://www.nytimes.com/2008/05/13/us.13immig.html.

U.S. Immigration and Customs Enforcement. "ICE and Department of Justice Joint Operation Targets Identity Theft at Poultry Process Plants in Five States." 2008. http://www.ice.gov/pi/news/newsreleases/articles/articles/080416dallas.htm.

U.S. Immigration and Customs Enforcement. "ICE Immigration Enforcement Initiatives." http://www.ice.gov/pi/news/factsheets/immmigration_enforcement_initiatives.htm.

Illegal Immigration Reform and Immigrant Responsibility Act (IIRIRA) (1996)

The Illegal Immigration Reform and Immigrant Responsibility Act (IIRIRA) was signed into law by President Bill Clinton in 1996. Intended to reduce illegal entry into the United States, increase interior enforcement, streamline deportation processes, provide stricter sanctions for employers who hire unauthorized workers, and increase requirements for legal immigration, IIRIRA was a major shift in policy and has made a significant impact on undocumented immigration to the United States since its passage.

Several parts of IIRIRA dealt with the reduction of illegal entry to the country. This included money for the construction of a fence near the San Diego/Tijuana crossing and the purchase of high-tech equipment for increased surveillance of the border. The law also increased funding to hire one thousand active-duty border patrol agents and three hundred support staff in the five years after its passage. IIRIRA also increased penalties for those caught attempting to enter the United States illegally. The law increased the number of crimes which lead to deportation and made detention mandatory for many more non-citizens than had previously been the case.

A separate provision of IIRIRA required the implementation of a system to better track entries and exits of those coming to the United States. Border crossing identification cards with biometric identifiers such as fingerprints were to be given to those entering the country in order to keep closer tabs on who was in the country at any point in time.

IIRIRA also sought to increase interior enforcement of immigration laws among the undocumented within the United States. It did so by increasing cooperation between local authorities and the Immigration and Naturalization Service (INS, later renamed Immigration and Customs Enforcement or ICE). The 287g section of the legislation codified this cooperation by giving federal immigration officials the authority to deputize local police officers to check the immigration status of those arrested. These so-called 287g agreements have resulted in the deportation of many undocumented immigrants arrested for non-immigration-related offenses.

IIRIRA also streamlined processes for the removal of non-citizens from the United States. It allowed for expedited removal procedures for many undocumented immigrants and made them ineligible to legally reenter the United States for five years. It also provided for voluntary departure, a procedure that allows undocumented immigrants to avoid deportation and the associated restrictions on eligibility for reentry. IIRIRA also increased sanctions on those deemed to have been unlawfully present in the United States. Those deported after spending 180 to 365 days in the United States without documents are barred from reentry for three years. Those whose time in the country was greater than one year are barred from the United States for ten years. There is also a permanent ban on reentry for those who file a frivolous asylum application.

Other provisions of IIRIRA dealt with sanctions for employers who hired undocumented workers. The law stated that employers were immune from negative consequences if they unintentionally hired undocumented workers as long as they had made a good faith attempt to check their legal status on hiring. IIRIRA also reduced the number of documents that were deemed eligible to prove legal status on I-9 forms. Funding within the law also increased the number of federal staff tasked with investigating issues surrounding employment eligibility.

While much of IIRIRA focused on reducing undocumented immigrants in the United States, one provision of the law increased the requirements for the legalization process. This provision increased the fee that those seeking to legalize their status have to pay to do so. It also sought to make eligible for legalization only those who were unlikely to use social services of the federal, state, and local government. In addition to making it virtually impossible for undocumented immigrants to receive federal welfare assistance, IIRIRA made those who legalized their status ineligible for federal welfare during the first five years as permanent residents. In addition, those applying for permanent resident status were forced to find a sponsor, who was tasked with ensuring the newly legalized person did not become a public charge. This was done so by requiring the sponsor to earn at least 125 percent of the federal poverty level. In the event of the newly legalized person violating the conditions of their legalization, the sponsor could be held responsible.

Several major effects of IIRIRA have become very visible in the time since it was passed. Although it, as well as subsequent legislation, has increased border enforcement measures, their impact on overall rates of unauthorized entry is limited. While these measures have not reduced overall numbers of crossings, they have forced those seeking to enter without legal paperwork to cross in increasingly distant locations (to avoid patrols and law enforcement surveillance in more urban areas) and to rely increasingly on people smugglers to cross (to navigate the treacherous terrain through which they must now maneuver). The impact of cooperation between federal immigration authorities and local police, however, has been clearer. 287g agreements throughout the country have led to a large increase in deportations. Once minor offenses that led to fines and/or short jail sentences now can— and often do—lead to the deportation of many undocumented immigrants in the United States. The provisions of IIRIRA intended to increase sanctions on employers for hiring undocumented workers have had little impact. With little enforcement mechanism in place, IIRIRA had little impact on the employment of undocumented workers.

David Keyes

See Also: Clinton Administration; Expedited Removal; Governance and Criminalization; Immigration Reform and Control Act (IRCA) (1986); Policy and Political Action; Proposition 187; Sponsors.

Further Reading

Fragomen, Austin T. 1997. "The Illegal Immigration Reform and Immigrant Responsibility Act of 1996: An Overview." *International Migration Review* 31:438–460.

Haskins, Ron. 2009. "Limiting Welfare Benefits for Noncitizens: Emergence of Compromises." In *Immigrants and Welfare: The Impact of Welfare Reform on America's Newcomers,* ed. Michael Fix, 39–68. New York: Russell Sage Foundation.

Meyers, Deborah Waller. 2006. "From Horseback to High-Tech: US Border Enforcement." *Migration Information Source,* February. http://www.migrationinformation.org/Feature/display.cfm?ID=370.

Illinois

The state of Illinois, located in the Midwest United States, is one of the states with the greatest number of undocumented individuals outside of the border region. The state, and within it, Chicago specifically, are considered to be traditional destinations for undocumented even as many recent undocumented migrants have begun to settle in non-traditional states.

Illinois became a traditional receiving state for migrants, in particular Mexican migrants, from traditional sending states in the early part of the century and has maintained this status even today. With the railroads needing employees especially during the wars, Mexican migrants were recruited to fill the need for workers. During this time and after, the vast array of factory work available in Chicago drew Mexican migrants to return and settle in the Chicago area. Factory work often paid more than field work and posed less immediate physical hardship, and was less risky in respect to border patrol or INS fear of apprehension. Additionally, though Illinois is often a secondary location in relation to undocumented migrants, Illinois has continuously been

Immigration rally at Grant Park in Chicago, Illinois, on April 28, 2006. Cities across the country held marches and rallies in protest to proposed changes to the nation's immigration laws. The failed 2005 proposal, HR 4437, was an enforcement-only bill, proposing measures to further criminalize immigrants and those who came to their aid, and offered no "pathway to citizenship" for the undocumented. (Chad Magiera)

one of the top three states that have the highest number of cases where false social security numbers are being used. California and Texas were the two other states that held this title from the years 1997 to 2001 when the report was released.

In general the distance from the border is in part what allowed the Mexican immigrant community to grow and flourish in the Chicagoland area while also promoting a hyper sense of nationalism. As a Midwestern state the climate of Illinois, most notably Chicago, is vastly different from that of many of the undocumented migrants that reside here. As the majority of the undocumented immigrants tend to be of Mexican origin followed by other Latin American migrants, the extreme change in climate is one other factor that migrants must deal with when they arrive.

According to the PEW Hispanic Center in 2010 the estimation of undocumented migrants living within state lines rose from 450,000 in 2008 to 525,000. Illinois has consistently been the home of some half a million undocumented migrants and consistently finds itself in the list of states that house the majority of the United States undocumented population. California and New York are considered first tier states regarding influx of undocumented migrants; however, Texas and Illinois are second tier, although together with Florida, New Jersey, Arizona and now Georgia these states contain 68 percent of the country's undocumented population as of 2009.

Illinois is one of only ten states that have allowed undocumented students who have graduated from in-state high schools to pay in-state tuition as opposed to elsewhere where students and families must pay out-of-state tuition. This policy in Illinois is known as HB 60; other states that have a similar policy are California, Kansas, Nebraska, Texas, New York, Utah, Washington, Wisconsin, and New Mexico as of 2010.

Additionally, Illinois is one of the states that has rejected the Real ID Act stating that proof of legal residency or citizenship needs to be shown before receiving a state ID card or a driver's license.

Also in the court case *Illinois Migrant Council v. Pilliod,* a federal court of appeals upheld a trial court opinion in Chicago that the United States Immigration and Naturalization Service (INS) agents could not stop and question individuals simply because they appear to be Latino. This is significant as similar cases closer to the border still allow for racial profiling to occur, stating that the proximity to the border allows that to be probable cause for stopping and searching vehicles.

Chicago is the city with the third highest population in the nation and makes up 68 percent of the entire population of Illinois according to the U.S. Census Bureau. The towns, cities, and counties that surround Chicago are known as the Chicagoland area and include the northwestern region of Indiana. However, as is the trend to move to rural areas, migrants that historically went into the city to find work and housing are now finding housing and work in nearby suburbs and rural locations. Part of the reason is the gentrification that was occurring within Chicago city limits in recent years which forced out many immigrant families.

During the anti-immigrant sentiment that was raging through the nation Chicago was one of the major cities to conduct protests against the anti-immigrant sentiment laws and raids that were occurring in both businesses and private homes throughout the country.

Chicago is the second largest gateway city for Mexican immigrants (Los Angeles is the largest gateway city). There are approximately 1.6 million Mexican-heritage individuals in this Midwestern city. As a gateway community there is a large population of newly arrived Mexican individuals and families while it is also home to many first and second generations of families. Historically this population has settled in the worst parts of the city due to financial limitations. In these neighborhoods there is a lack of public transportation, satisfactory schools, and recreational or green areas.

The predominately Mexican neighborhood of Pilsen on Chicago's Southside has a history of significant Mexican occupancy since the early 1970s and since then has come to represent the heart of the Mexican-American community in Chicago and the Midwest. In 2000 Pilsen's Mexican-American population was at 98 percent. This significant number is in part due to historically discriminatory housing policies and banking institutions. This coupled with the self-isolation practiced by the Mexican-American population within the neighborhood has led to the Pilsen of today. As an immigrant community the neighborhood struggles with economic hardship and political underrepresentation. Although there are many NGOs and institutions such as the Catholic Church that constantly advocate for the needs of the community, their efforts are met with little or no action by politicians or government officials.

Pilsen is also the home of the renowned National Museum of Mexican Art, formally known as the Mexican Fine Arts Museum, which not only functions as a non-profit art gallery and museum but also is involved in community issues and especially invested in the future of the children in the community and their families. The museum is known for the commission of murals both in the museum but also all over the neighborhood. Local artists are commissioned to paint murals that depict historical Mexican events as well as the everyday life, struggles and aspirations of the Mexican community. It is the only museum of its kind to date. Pilsen was also the setting for Chicano writer Sandra Cisneros' book *House on Mango Street.*

However, in recent years Pilsen has found itself undergoing heavy gentrification forcing longtime residents of the community to move out and many to lose their homes due to rising rents and property taxes. As a result there are many suburbs that are considered Mexican migrant communities just outside the Chicago city limits. Such examples are Cicero, Berwyn, Aurora, Elgin, Romeoville, and Plainfield that now serve to house the Mexican immigrant community and subsequent generations.

Chicago and the Midwest at large have been cited as the home and birthplace of the Mexican music genre known as *Durangnse,* and the coordinated dance form *el pasito durangense.* One reason for this is the large market available for this genre because of the large marketable audience located in Chicago. Many of the popular *bandas* currently in the genre started playing locally in the Chicago music scene. The first group to be credited with adhering to this style of music is the Grupo Montéz de Durango. Other popular Chicago-based durangense groups are Alacranes Musical, K-Paz de la Sierra, and Los Horóscopos de Durango.

Although not a border state Illinois has continuously been a safe haven in recent years for Mexican immigrants both documented and undocumented. The state continues to support immigrant rights and reject anti-immigrant legislation. Illinois not only holds historical significance for the Mexican and Mexican-American community as a place that opens doors for most migrants but is very relevant in today's migrant community. Outside the border region Illinois is one of the most significant locations for migrant migration from the south and has historically been more favorable to undocumented workers than states with similar demographics closer to the border.

Yesenia Andrade

See Also: Barrios; Gateways; Great Lakes Region; Midwest; Sanctuary Cities and Secure Communities; Social Interaction and Integration.

Further Reading

Dahm, Charles W. 2004. *Parish Ministry in a Hispanic Community.* Chicago: Paulist Press.
Horowitz, Ruth. 1983. *Honor and the American Dream: Culture and Identity in a Chicano Community.* New Brunswick, N.J.: Rutgers University Press.
Kattari, Kim. 2008. "From Quebradita to Duranguense: Dance in Mexican American Youth Culture." *Latin American Music Review* 29.2:283–285.

Johnson, Kevin R. 2010. "How Racial Profiling in America Became the Law of the Land: *United States v. Brignoni-Ponce* and *Whren v. United States* and the Need for Truly Rebellious Lawyering." *Georgetown Law Journal* 98.4:1005–1077.

Ong Hing, Bill. 2009. "Institutional Racism, ICE Raids, and Immigration Reform." *University of San Francisco Law Review* 44. Available at: http://works.bepress.com/billhing/4

Immigrant Workers Freedom Ride

With the 2003 Immigrant Workers Freedom Ride (IWFR), immigrant rights activism took a page from the 1961 Freedom Rides, which a little over forty years before had challenged segregation in the South. The goals of the Immigrant Workers Freedom Ride were similar. It aimed to raise awareness to social injustice by focusing on the plight of undocumented immigrant workers, who in addition to being relegated to low paying, mostly non-union jobs, were facing discrimination in the labor and housing markets, and demonization by anti-immigrant nativists. In late September of 2003, buses filled with riders departed from nine major U.S. cities for a cross-country ride to converge in Washington D.C. to meet with members of Congress to press them for political action.

The idea for the Immigrant Workers Freedom Ride was conceived by the staff of the Hotel Employees and Restaurant Employees (HERE) International Union Local 11 in Los Angeles. The president of Local 11 took the idea to HERE's 2001 national conference, where unionists' imaginations developed a plan that involved multiple buses from several U.S. cities carrying approximately a total of eight hundred activists, immigrants, and allies. In September of 2003, buses departed from Seattle and Portland, San Francisco, Los Angeles, Las Vegas, Houston, Minneapolis, Chicago, Miami, and Boston for the eleven-day ride. Each one of the routes made stops in close to one hundred cities as they went through different parts of the country. Included in the numerous groups who supported this campaign were representatives from civil rights organizations, immigrant rights organizations, the AFL-CIO (a federation of 60 labor unions), elected officials, religious organizations, and the American Immigration Lawyers Association (AILA) (Sziarto and Leitner, 2010).

The stated short-term goal of the IWFR was to publicize a broad agenda for immigrants' rights and U.S. immigration policy reform, including:

1. granting legalization status to working, tax-paying immigrants
2. clearing the path toward citizenship
3. restoring rights on the job
4. reunifying families torn apart by immigration laws
5. respecting and upholding civil rights and liberties for all

The riders on any IWFR bus were from the originating city (or nearby), but had not necessarily met each other before. They were recruited from the local organizations for their experience and potential as organizers, or had been activists in the 1960s. They were encouraged to share their stories with others on the bus, and keep journals. For example, Jerry Akin's journal recounts the story of forty-seven Freedom Riders that rode the bus from Portland, Oregon, to Washington DC, then on to New York City for a mass rally to celebrate the culmination of the ride. On his bus were immigrants from Mexico, Guatemala, the Dominican Republic, China, Taiwan, Palestine, the Philippines, and Siberia. Anglos and African Americans rode along to support immigrant workers' rights (Akin, 2005).

Before departing, riders were trained to respond to possible encounters with nativists and police, which was put to the test in the bus coming from Los Angeles on the fifth day of the ride. At a permanent checkpoint seventy miles southeast of El Paso, Texas, they were stopped by border patrol agents who boarded the bus demanding identification from individuals of color, while ignoring white riders. All refused in an act of civil disobedience, for which they were, for a brief time, treated as potentially undocumented immigrants by ordering them off the bus and detained in cells at the station. Subsequently, each of the riders was taken out for individual questioning and threatened with arrest unless they revealed their names and citizenship. For one rider, the experience was particularly personal because he had passed through the very same checkpoint when he first entered the United States years ago (Wong and Muñoz, 2004). After about three and a half hours of detention, the riders were released (Sziarto and Leitner, 2010). Along the way, other riders in other buses had to weigh the different levels of risk, experience, and willingness to confront the authorities if the occasion should arise (Akin, 2005).

In addition, a group made up of students, professors, and professionals from around the country were to deliver the "Petition for Academic Visa Reform" to the members of Congress while in Washington. The petition came from the International Student Committee of the Graduate Employees and Student Organization (GESO). The group hoped to show Congress what changes they would like to see in the visa process for students, removing some of the restrictions that had been implemented since 9/11. The number of student visas issued by the State Department decreased from 226,465 in October 1999 through August 2000, to 174,479 in October 2002 through August 2003, according to the department (Bland, n.d.).

In Arizona, riders on the Los Angeles buses participated in memorial services for immigrants who died trying to cross the Mexico-U.S. border. Activists in Tucson provided the riders with wooden crosses, each marked with a name, age, and the date their body was found—or simply the word *desconocido* (unknown) (Sziarto and Leitner, 2010). In Des Moines, riders attended a memorial service for eleven immigrant workers discovered dead in a railroad car (Akin, 2005).

Once in Washington, the riders made more than three hundred congressional visits, sharing their stories of immigrant strife in the United States. Some spoke on behalf of workers and immigrants from all over the country. Immigrant workers who had journeyed on the bus were encouraged by the opportunity to meet their congressional representatives face to face (Wong and Muñoz, 2004). Freedom Rider Jerry Akin noted in his journal that his group had been assigned a visit with a Republican congressman from Oregon. He planned on telling him about some of the issues that undocumented immigrants suffered: unpaid overtime, unsafe working conditions, sexual harassment, or discrimination, and the job insecurity that comes with the ability of employers to call immigration agents at any time, and because of their status, they have no right to workers' compensation if injured, nor unemployment, nor retirement funds to pay into. However, the congressman's schedule changed, making it impossible for the group to meet with him.

The IWFR concluded with a rally in Flushing Meadow Park in Queens, a borough of New York City where thousands of people came together to address the issues of civil liberties, labor protections, family unification, visas and legalization for immigrants. Queens is considered one of the most diverse areas in the country, home to over 100 ethnic groups. The AFL-CIO and other labor and advocacy groups that help put on the event included the New York City Immigrant Rights Coalition.

Mizrahi (2004) places the Immigrant Workers Freedom Ride within the broader global movement for social justice that often does not get too much attention in the United States. However, at the core of the messages conveyed by these political actions are the issues of poverty and growing injustice when governments neglect the working poor and privilege corporations that benefit from their labor.

Anna Ochoa O'Leary

See Also: Activism; Advocacy; Domestic Work; Economics; Hotel Industry; Labor Supply; Labor Unions; Protests; Workers' Rights.

Further Reading

Akin, Jerry. 2005. "We Make the Road by Riding (Se Hace el Camino al Viajar): Stories from a Journal of the Immigrant Workers Freedom Ride—Portland to New York." September 23 to October 4, 2003. *Radical History Review* 93:200–216.

Bland, Siskind Susser. N.d. "Immigrant Worker Freedom Rides." Available at http://www .visalaw.com/03sep4/16sep403.html.

Mizrahi, Terry. 2004. "Are Movements for Social and Economic Justice Growing? Reports on Protest and Social Action in the United States and Israel." *Journal of Community Practice* 12.1/2:155–160.

Sziarto, Kristin M., and Helga Leitner. 2010. "Immigrants Riding for Justice: Space-time and Emotions in the Construction of a Counterpublic." *Political Geography* 29.7:381–391.

Wong, Kent, and Carolina Bank Muñoz. 2004. "Don't Miss the Bus." *New Labor Forum* 13.2:61–66.

Immigration Act (IMMACT) (1990)

The Immigration Act of 1990 (IMMACT 90) modified and made changes to the previous Immigration and Nationality Act (1965). And, although this piece of legislation attracted much less attention than the 1986 Immigration Reform and Control Act (IRCA), it can be viewed as a cornerstone of the modern immigration system of the United States (Boswell, 2010). The IMMACT 90 significantly increased the total level of immigration to 700,000 for 1992–1994, and lowered it to 675,000 for subsequent years. An important component of the IMMACT 90 was to make family reunification the main path for entry into the country. Another goal was to double employment-related immigration, and to provide for the admission of immigrants from underrepresented countries to increase the nation's diversity through immigration. The act significantly amended the work-related nonimmigrant categories for temporary admission. The act thus established a three-way preference system for family-sponsored, diverse, and employment-based immigrants.

Significant in this Act was Section 131, which provided for a diversity program and a new class of visas for "diversity immigrants." Those awarded the visas are chosen by a lottery, which is why this program is also known as the "Green Card Lottery." The Diversity Immigrant Visa program makes 55,000 visas available each year to countries with low immigration rates to the United States. As such, not every country is eligible for this program. Those invited to apply are drawn from random selection among entries of individuals. About half of these visas go to immigrants from Africa. Those born in any territory that has sent more than fifty thousand immigrants to the United States in the previous five years are not eligible to receive a diversity visa. There are also other requirements making it necessary for green card lottery winners to have at least a high school diploma, or its equivalent, or two years of work experience in an occupation requiring at least two years training. The U.S. secretary of state is in charge of issuing these visas to qualified applicants through random selection. The spouses and children of the admitted immigrants are also granted visas and then become eligible to obtain permanent residency. In addition, the 1990 act also established a brief amnesty program that granted legal residence to up to 165,000 minor children and spouses of immigrants who had legalized their status through the previous 1986 Immigration Reform and Control Act (IRCA). The country with the highest number of green card lottery winners in 2012 was Nigeria, followed by Ukraine, Iran, Venezuela, Australia, and the Bahamas. Since 2007, Republican Congressman John Goodlatte (R-VA) has attempted to eliminate the green card lottery. As head of the House judiciary committee, he has also blocked the progress of S. 744, the comprehensive immigration reform bill that was passed in the Senate in July 2013.

The Immigration Act of 1990 thus made changes to the system of legal immigration by raising overall limits, creating a process to admit immigrants from more countries, which had been previously underrepresented, and increasing employment-based immigration. However, the act also made modifications to the grounds for excluding and deporting undocumented individuals and enacted a system of measures to ensure a better system of removal of immigrants convicted of crimes. More importantly, IMMACT 90 barred the deportation of spouses and children of those in the United States legally and allowed them to work, as long as they were present in the country by May 5, 1988.

Additional modifications of the act provided for strengthening the U.S. border patrol. There were also changes made to the previous restrictions based on certain diseases, removing acquired immunodeficiency syndrome (AIDS) from the list of illnesses that made applicants ineligible to enter the United States. Other modifications include the removal of homosexuality as grounds for exclusion from entering the country. The 1990 act also made important changes to the employment-related "nonimmigrant" categories, under which people were allowed to enter the country temporarily rather than as permanent residents.

The Immigration Act of 1990 restructured the immigration system by reallocating visas based on family ties with U.S. citizens or permanent residents. Separate ceilings were established for each of the immigrant categories. Family-sponsored visas received a maximum of 480,000, employment-based visas were set at 140,000, and diversity visas had 55,000. Immediate relatives of U.S. citizens were exempt from a maximum number of visas.

These changes came about due to a number of reasons. One of the reasons was the concern over the great number of immigrants admitted on the basis of family reunification as the result of the 1986 Immigration Reform and Control Act (IRCA) (Glick, 1993). The amnesty provided by IRCA had failed to reduce immigration. Other concerns were over the growing visa waiting lists, the small number of available visas for certain countries under the current preference system, and the admission of immediate relatives of U.S. citizens outside of the numerical limits previously established. These concerns led to the signing of this eight-title act to be signed into law on November 29, 1990 by then-president George H. W. Bush.

Carolina Luque

See Also: Immigration Reform and Control Act (IRCA) (1986); Johnson-Reed Act (1924).

Further Reading

Boswell, 2010. "Crafting an Amnesty with Traditional Tools: Registration and Cancellation." *Harvard Journal on Legislation* 47.1:175–208.

Glick, Paul C. 1993. "The Impact of Geographic Mobility on Individuals and Families." *Marriage & Family Review* 19.1/2:31.

Leiden, Warren R., and David L. Neal. 1990–1991. "Highlights of the U.S. Immigration Act of 1990." *Fordham International Law Journal* 14.328.

Immigration and Customs Enforcement (ICE)

ICE is the acronym for Immigration and Customs Enforcement, the agency responsible for the enforcement of immigration law in the U.S. interior. ICE was formed in 2003 as a result of a governmental reorganization that merged the Immigration and Naturalization Service (INS) and the U.S. Customs Service and gave the newly formed Department of Homeland Security (DHS) oversight over immigration matters. With a $5.8 billion annual budget (as of 2012) and more than twenty thousand employees across the United States and in 48 other countries, ICE is the second largest investigative agency of the U.S. federal government.

The Department of Homeland Security was established in the wake of the attacks on the World Trade Center and the Pentagon on September 11, 2001. Those attacks gave rise to fears about the security of U.S. borders and the presence of foreign-born people in the U.S. interior, which helped galvanize support for the formation of DHS in 2003. In addition to immigration and border regulation, DHS houses the Secret

Family members and allies of those arrested for immigration violations face off with ICE agents at the Swift & Company meat processing plant in Greeley, Colorado, 2006. Agents arrested nearly 1,300 people in an unprecedented coordination of immigration raids at Swift plants in six states. (AP/Wide World Photos)

Service, Transportation and Security Administration (TSA), and Federal Emergency Management Association (FEMA).

DHS operates four agencies that oversee immigration matters. The first two, Customs and Border Protection (CBP) and the U.S. Coast Guard, are responsible for policing the nation's borders and ports of entry. The third, U.S. Citizenship and Immigration Services (USCIS), processes applications for temporary visas, legal permanent residence, asylum, refugees, and naturalization, and it regulates employment eligibility of the foreign-born. The fourth agency, ICE, is the immigration enforcement arm of DHS and is responsible for identifying and deporting "removable aliens," who may be unauthorized immigrants or legal permanent residents who become deportable, for example, through a criminal conviction.

ICE operations are divided into two main components: Homeland Security Investigations (HSI) and Enforcement and Removal Operations (ERO). HSI is dedicated to tracking illicit movements of goods and people, such as human trafficking or weapons smuggling, across U.S. borders and throughout the U.S. interior. ERO is dedicated to finding and deporting removable aliens. ERO is also responsible for managing the Secure Communities and 287(g) programs, in which local law enforcement agencies partner with ICE to identify and detain suspected removable aliens.

The association of immigration matters with threats to national security can be understood as part of a long-term shift in U.S. immigration policy toward restriction and enforcement. Prior to 1924, U.S. borders were largely unregulated and the immigration of Europeans and Latin Americans was unrestricted. The Immigration and Nationality Act (INA) of 1924 established a quota system that restricted the entry of immigrants from Europe, particularly from Southern and Eastern Europe, and reinforced earlier laws that essentially prohibited Asians from immigrating to the United States altogether. While people from Western Hemisphere countries, including all of Latin America and Canada, were exempted from these quotas, the INA did establish the U.S. Border Patrol as a unit in the Bureau of Immigration, which was itself a division of the Department of Labor.

As the INA restricted the immigration of certain workers in the Eastern Hemisphere, workers from Mexico were excluded from quotas on the grounds that they provided much needed cheap labor to the U.S. economy. During the Bracero Program, an estimated five million Mexican workers came to the United States to work in agriculture, construction, and manufacturing. This large-scale importation of Latin American workers was punctuated by large-scale deportation efforts during times of economic contraction, like the Great Depression, and as a means to regulate bracero labor, such as Operation Wetback of 1954.

In 1965, the quota system was "equalized," and workers from Latin America, the Caribbean, and Canada became subject to numerical quotas for the first time. The number of visas available to people in the Western Hemisphere dropped from an unlimited number to just 20,000 per country per year by 1976. Because these new restrictions coincided with the end of the Bracero Program and the visas that it had provided, as well as economic crises throughout Latin America in the latter quarter of the twentieth century, the incidence of unauthorized immigration from Latin America rose rapidly from the 1970s onward.

Government spending on immigration enforcement accelerated rapidly throughout the 1980s, 1990s, and the first decade of 2000, with an overwhelming focus on the U.S. border with Mexico. The Reagan administration (1980–1988) increased funding for the Border Patrol by 130 percent, while the IRCA of 1986 increased Border Patrol personnel by 50 percent. Spending on detention and removal increased by 64 percent after the passage of IIRIRA in 1996, which made the detention of large numbers of immigrants with criminal convictions mandatory. In all, between 1985 and 2002, government spending on immigration enforcement quadrupled, from $1 billion to $4.5 billion annually. The share of this funding for detention and removal grew even more rapidly, expanding 806 percent in the same period, compared with a more modest 11 percent for interior investigations.

In the period of heightened concerns over national security following September 11, 2001, immigration enforcement again increased sharply. The government agencies charged with immigration enforcement were reorganized and came under the auspices of the Department of Homeland Security. While a majority of immigration enforcement activity continues to take place at the U.S.-Mexico border, immigration enforcement measures in the U.S. interior roughly quadrupled between 2006 and

2010. Between 2007 and 2010, ICE removals jumped 25 percent, from 291,060 to 392,862, and came close to reaching ICE's stated goal of four hundred thousand deportations annually. Although ICE states that it prioritizes the removal of criminal aliens or those who pose a threat to security, about half of those deported are non-criminal.

Increases in enforcement under ICE are largely attributable to two programs that engage local police agencies in immigration enforcement: 287(g) and Secure Communities. 287(g) empowers state, county, and local law enforcement agencies to petition for training by ICE in a partnership initiative that subsequently enables local police to enforce immigration law. As of July, 2011, 69 law enforcement agencies in 24 states have 287(g) agreements with ICE, and they are credited with the identification of over 200,300 "potentially removable aliens" at local jails.

The Secure Communities program is also a collaboration between ICE and local, state, and county systems. Through this program, funded by DHS since 2008, a memorandum of agreement allows fingerprints of those booked in the criminal system to be run through FBI and DHS records, recalling any history of past crimes and, if the accused has a record with DHS, his or her immigration status as well. ICE is automatically notified if the fingerprints have a "hit," even if the individual has not been convicted of any crime. Secure Communities has expanded from fourteen jurisdictions in 2008 to more than 1,300 jurisdictions in 2011, and ICE would like to extend the program nationwide by 2013. These collaborations between ICE and local police forces extend the immigration enforcement arm of the federal government deep into the U.S. interior.

For unauthorized immigrants, widespread collaboration between ICE and local law enforcement reduces the ability to travel within the United States, even to and from work, and to be in public spaces without fear of deportation. This has ramifications for work, social life, consumption practices, and overall quality of life of unauthorized people. For example, unauthorized immigrants in highly policed areas are more likely to accept a job with poor working conditions that is close to their home, rather than risk traveling to search for a better job. Unauthorized immigrants may also concentrate in relatively safe spaces, such as urban communities, rather than in suburban or rural areas in which local police actively cooperate with ICE. As ICE pushes to make Secure Communities mandatory across the United States, these effects are likely to multiply.

In spite of the increased fear associated with accelerated immigration enforcement, leaders in the immigrant rights community also credit these measures with galvanizing the immigrant rights movement. As immigration enforcement affects not only unauthorized people, but also their legal friends and family members, immigration enforcement measures have catalyzed voting drives and political campaigns, as well as marches and protests.

Ruth Gomberg-Muñoz

See Also: Detention Centers; Sanctuary Cities and Secure Communities; U.S. Customs and Border Protection (CBP); Workplace Raids.

Further Reading

Migration Policy Institute Web Site. 2013. MPI Resources on U.S. Immigration Reform, Border Enforcement and Security. http://www.migrationpolicy.org/pubs/US_Immi gration_Resources.php#security.
National Network for Immigrant and Refugee Rights Web Site. 2012. http://www.nnirr.org/
U.S. Immigration and Customs Enforcement Web Site. 2013. http://www.ice.gov/index.htm.

Immigration and Nationality Act (The McCarran-Walter Act) (1952)

The 1952 Immigration and Nationality Act, more commonly known as the McCarran-Walter Act, represented the most comprehensive piece of U.S. immigration legislation since the Johnson-Reed Act of 1924. Proponents of the McCarran-Walter Act considered it a reaffirmation and amplification of the limits on immigration set by Johnson-Reed (also known as the 1924 Immigration Act). In 1924, Congress passed the Johnson-Reed Immigration Act, an immigration law that severely restricted immigration from Eastern and Southern Europe *and* barred immigrants from Asia. The 1924 Immigration Act also made Asian immigrants ineligible for citizenship and excluded contract laborers, certain criminals, persons who did not meet certain moral standards, persons with various disabilities and diseases, paupers, some radicals, and illiterates. Finally, the Johnson-Reed Immigration Act established, for the first time in U.S. history, a permanent annual quota of 165,000 admissible immigrants and divided it according to country of origin. While Britain, for example, was allowed to send 34,000 immigrants a year, Italy could only send 3,845. The imbalance in numbers had favored the immigration of Western Europeans and was considered to be driven by the desire to exclude non-white populations. The battle between those arguing for more restrictions to immigration and those advocating for more inclusion would last more than forty years.

Although the McCarran-Walter Act retained many of the nativist provisions of the Johnson-Reed Act, the 1952 law also introduced some liberalizing elements that paved the way for the emergence of the multicultural society that characterizes the United States today. The combination of nativist and liberalizing elements of the 1952 Immigration and Nationality Act revealed the new role that immigration policy would play for the United States. While the 1924 Immigration Act was the product of the nation's post–World War I isolationism, the 1952 Immigration Act reflected in part the United States' geopolitical role in the world during the Cold War and the connection between immigration and foreign policy that this world position entailed.

A brief look at the number of legal immigrants who arrived in the United States between 1952 and 1965 shows how ineffective the McCarran-Walter Act ultimately was in restricting immigration. According to the annual immigration ceiling of 158,000 established by the law, just over 2 million immigrants should have entered the country from 1952 to 1965. In reality, 3.5 million immigrants came, far exceeding the quota limits. Of these 3.5 million immigrants, only about one-third were admitted under the quota system. During every year during which the act was in place, nonquota immigrants outnumbered quota immigrants. Moreover, although the participants in the debate on immigration continued to discuss and look at the impact of immigration from Europe, European immigrants exceeded immigrants from other parts of the world only during two of the 13 years during which the McCarran-Walter Act was in effect. Between 1953 and 1965, for the first time, European immigrants arriving in the United States did not represent the bulk of all immigrants entering the country. Foreshadowing things to come, immigrants from Latin America, the Caribbean, and Asia slowly began to replace them.

The law also unintentionally provided for the entry of a substantial number of refugees. Although the term *refugee* was completely absent from the law itself, an obscure provision in the act that gave power to the attorney general to grant temporary admission to an unlimited number of aliens "for emergency reasons or for reasons deemed strictly in the public interest" helped refugees enter the country outside the quotas as well. Through this loophole, Presidents Eisenhower, Kennedy, and Johnson all facilitated the entry of certain groups, mostly refugees from the Communist bloc. In particular, the executive branch allowed the entry of groups of Hungarians, Cubans, Tibetans, and Vietnamese whose status Congress later regularized through legislation.

Finally, the McCarran-Walter Act also made deportation easier and incorporated provisions that specifically targeted immigration from Mexico. The law, in fact, extended the range of the Border Patrol on the Mexican border from a "reasonable distance" to 25 miles from the U.S.-Mexico border and authorized Border Patrol agents to carry on searches without warrants of any vehicle and on private property. Although the law did not provide for warrantless searches of dwellings, it did prescribe severe penalties for harboring undocumented immigrants.

Contradicting growing border enforcement powers came with the introduction and ratification of the "Texas Proviso," in response to the continued use of guest workers from Mexico under the Bracero Program and the powerful influence of agribusiness in policy making. The Proviso established that employment of undocumented immigrants did not constitute harboring. Because of the proviso, if the police apprehended Mexicans who were in the country illegally at the workplace, they simply sent them back across the border without any legal repercussions for the immigrants or the employers.

The 1924 law represented the triumph of American nativism. Long-time supporters of more liberalized immigration reform considered the passage of the McCarran-Walter Act a stifling defeat. Its combination of the nativism of the 1920s with the anticommunist xenophobia of the 1950s led many to conclude that its repeal—potentially perceived as unpatriotic—would be impossible. Yet much had changed, and the different geopolitical conditions of the 1950s as well as the rise of civil rights movements of the 1960s paved the way for the passage of a more humane immigration policy in 1965 with the Hart-Celler Act. More importantly, the McCarran-Walter Act itself contained provisions that slowly caused the immigration system it sought to reaffirm and protect to lose legitimacy and created the preconditions that would necessitate a new immigration policy. In addition to abolishing racial discrimination for admission criteria and giving priority to family reunification, both of which allowed more immigrants to enter the country than the quotas allotted, the law also created a cumbersome system of appeals and a wide array of exceptions that ultimately made the immigration regime it sought to maintain untenable.

Maddalena Marinari

See Also: Bracero Program; Emergency Quota Act of 1921; Expedited Removal; Guestworker and Contract Labor Law; Hart-Celler Act (1965); Johnson-Reed Act (1924); U.S Border Patrol.

Further Reading

Daniels, Roger. 2004. *Guarding the Golden Door: American Immigration Policy since 1882.* New York: Hill and Wang.

Divine, Robert A. 1957. *American Immigration Policy, 1924–1952.* New Haven, CT: Yale University Press.

Graham, Otis L., Jr. 2004. *Unguarded Gates: A History of America's Immigration Crisis.* Lanham, MD: Rowman and Littlefield.

Marinari, Maddalena. 2009. "Liberty, Restriction, and the Remaking of Italians and Eastern European Jews (1890–1965)." PhD dissertation, University of Kansas.

Ngai, Mae. 2004. *Impossible Subjects: Illegal Aliens and the Making of Modern America.* Princeton, NJ: Princeton University Press.

Reimers, David M. 1992. *Still the Golden Door: The Third World Comes to America,* 2nd ed. New York: Columbia University Press.

Tichenor, Daniel J. 2002. *Dividing Lines: The Politics of Immigration Control in America.* Princeton, NJ, and Oxford, UK: Princeton University Press, 2002.

Zolberg, Aristide. 2006. *A Nation by Design: Immigration Policy in the Fashioning of America.* New York: Russell Sage Foundation.

Immigration and Naturalization Service (INS)

The United States Immigration and Naturalization Service (INS), a government agency, had the responsibility of managing immigration, border crossings, and naturalization: the process of becoming an American citizen. In 1932, the federal government merged the Bureau of Immigration and the Bureau of Naturalization to form the INS. In 1940, the INS moved to the Department of Justice as immigration became a matter of national security given the onset of war. The INS disappeared in 2003 when the state created new offices: the Customs and Border Protection (CBP), the U.S. Citizenship and Immigration Service (CIS), and the Immigration and Customs Enforcement (ICE). The CBP office handled terrorist, trade, drug, and foreign travel issues. It also addressed national security and public safety concerns. The CIS managed immigration and naturalization services, whereas ICE attended to immigration and customs investigations, deportation, and law enforcement. These new agencies fell within the Department of Homeland Security, the federal agency responsible for national safety that formed after the September 11 attacks.

To protect the nation from unlawful entrants, the Bureau of Immigration (later known as the INS) managed various ports of entry. Ellis Island in New York City and

Angel Island in San Francisco housed processing centers that managed millions of immigrants. The former primarily handled European immigration whereas the latter primarily oversaw Asian immigration. From 1910 to 1940, immigration officials at Angel Island interrogated, detained, and/or deported many Asians. The INS supervised restrictive and exclusionary immigration policies, such as the 1882 Chinese Exclusion Act that banned Chinese immigration and subsequent acts that stiffened travel affairs for U.S. citizens of Chinese descent. Likewise, the Quota Act of 1921 and the Immigration Act of 1924 nearly excluded all Asians.

Management of border crossings belonged primarily to the United States Border Patrol—formally established with the Johnson-Reed Immigration Act of 1924. With the restrictive and exclusionary immigration laws of 1921 and 1924, the government found the role of the Border Patrol especially important. What is important to note is the codification of racial profiling that the INS enabled. The governing statute of the Immigration Nationalization Act provides that any officer of the then INS "shall have the power without warrant to interrogate. . . any alien or person believed to be an alien as to his right to be or to remain in the United States. . . ." This mandate was later legally challenged, but upheld by the U.S. Supreme Court Ruling in *U.S. v. Brignoni-Ponce* (Perez, 2011). The enforcement powers thus granted to the INS that were carried out in the way of the Border Patrol inspection of the documents of citizens, immigrants, and foreign visitors entering the country. Its responsibilities included examination of visas and passports, collection of head taxes, fees to cross the border, and the power to arrest individuals crossing the border without authorization. Nearly eighty years later, in 2010, the court case brought against Arizona for its enactment of SB 1070 would continue to raise these issues.

Most scholars have conceded that this INS strategy did not effectively reduce undocumented migration from Mexico to the United States (Brownell, 2001). Consequences for unauthorized border crossings stiffened in 1929 when Congress made unlawful entry into the country a misdemeanor. Further still, in March 1999, INS announced a new "interior enforcement strategy" consisting of a five-year plan to oversee the deportation of undocumented immigrants as a means of solving local problems. Part of this plan was to conduct "threat assessments" in areas where immigration activity was present, which presumed criminal activity as well (Khokha, 2001).

The INS did not limit its daily operations to the border region, but extended them into the nation's interior (Belenchia, 1980). With offices stationed throughout the nation, the INS unevenly enforced immigration law. Agents managed and processed immigrants and foreign visitors at ports of entry. The INS also determined the issuance of visas. Additionally, officials penalized employers who hired undocumented workers. The INS officers conducted neighborhood and workplace raids throughout the country. They primarily targeted Latina/o communities because the INS often profiled brown bodies as "illegal." This reflected how mainstream media and U.S. society overall racially constructed "illegal aliens" as Mexican. In spite of the fact that looks did not and could not determine whether people were undocumented, reliance on racial appearances drove the INS to disproportionately apprehend and question those who looked Mexican. Racial profiling often led to the unjust deportation of American citizens, as was the case during the Great Depression and with Operation

Wetback of 1954, an INS campaign designed to deport the undocumented. Especially during these times, the INS focused its operation primarily on Latinas/os and even Filipinas/os.

Key federal legislation bolstered INS efforts. For example, under the Immigration Reform and Control Act of 1986, the state granted conditional amnesty to qualifying individuals, but it also allocated increased border enforcement funding to halt undocumented immigration. Moreover, the government approved various INS initiatives to halt undocumented immigration. It established Operation Blockade—renamed Operation Hold the Line—in El Paso, Texas (1993), Operation Safeguard in Tucson, Arizona (1994), Operation Gatekeeper in San Diego/San Ysidro (1994), and Operation Rio Grande in McAllen and Laredo, Texas (1997). Operation Hold the Line and Operation Gatekeeper militarized the busiest international ports of entry in Texas and California respectively. The programs significantly increased the number of Border Patrol agents. The names of these INS initiatives underscored alarmist preoccupation with national security. They also channeled attention to the southern border, and not the U.S.-Canada border. Furthermore, increased resources and the utilization of a wide variety of military strategies significantly strengthened Border Patrol projects in these southern regions. The INS integrated hardware and technological surveillance, such as night vision devices and sensors, to detect and capture smugglers and other people who crossed without authorization. It used helicopters to patrol the border. It installed bright lighting to help the Border Patrol guard the national boundary from unlawful entrants. These initiatives also added and toughened extensive barriers along the United States–Mexico border.

Under Operation Gatekeeper, the INS instituted an immigration court at the border. INS agents served multiple roles, such as guard and prosecutor, while working on their cases before an immigration judge. In 1996, INS agents gained more power with the Illegal Immigration Reform and Immigrant Responsibility Act (IIRIRA). IIRIRA instituted expedited removal, intended to speed up a deportation hearing by giving INS agents the power to review the case and make a decision accordingly. It established technology to improve access to a database that bridged immigration and criminal records. It erected barriers across a span of 14 miles, from the Pacific Ocean into the interior. This, however, did not halt undocumented immigration because people kept crossing to escape dire situations in their home countries. Instead, it pushed immigrants to cross the border in dangerous terrain, especially in the deserts and mountains. Many have lost their lives in the isolated and hostile landscapes of Arizona and California. Crosses adorn the Tijuana–San Diego border wall to remind people of the deaths caused by Operation Gatekeeper. In 2009, the American Civil Liberties Union estimated more than five thousand deaths. The high number of border deaths mobilized human rights activists on both sides of the border to denounce various INS projects.

Myrna García

See Also: Border Crossing; Illegal Immigration Reform and Immigrant Responsibility Act (IIRIRA); Johnson-Reed Act (1924); Operation Wetback; Ports of Entry; "Undocumented" Label; *United States. v. Brignoni-Ponce;* U.S.–Mexico Border Wall.

Further Reading

Belenchia, Joanne M. 1980. "Cowboys and Aliens: How the INS Operates in Latino Communities." *Peace & Change* 6.3:16–26.

Brownell, Peter B. 2001. "Border Militarization and the Reproduction of Mexican Migrant Labor." *Social Justice* 28.2:69–92.

Khokha, Sasha. 2001. "Community and Labor Relations: The INS Plays the 'Good Cop.'" *Social Justice* 28.2:93–95.

Magaña, Lisa. 2003. *Straddling the Border: Immigration Policy and the INS*. Austin: University of Texas Press, 2003.

Nevins, Joseph. 2002. *Operation Gatekeeper: The Rise of the "Illegal Alien" and the Making of the U.S.-Mexico Boundary*. New York: Routledge.

Perez, Javier. 2011. "Reasonably Suspicious of Being Mojado: The Legal Derogation of Latinos in Immigration Enforcment." *Texas Hispanic Journal of Law & Policy* 17.1:99–123.

Immigration Reform, 2013–2014

On April 16, 2013, a bipartisan group of eight senators chiseled out an 844-page proposal for overhauling the nation's "broken" immigration system. The so-called gang of eight were Charles Schumer (D-NY), John McCain (R-AZ), Dick Durbin (D-IL), Lindsey Graham (R-SC), Robert Melendez (D NJ), Marco Rubio (R-FL), Michael Bennet (D-CO), and Jeff Flake (R-AZ). The proposal, the *Border Security, Economic Opportunity, and Immigration Modernization Act* (S. 744), was a first attempt since 2005 when an enforcement-only measure passed the U.S. House of Representatives (Govtrack, 2013). Unlike the failed 2005 proposal, the 2013 bill included a path to citizenship and represented a move towards the political accommodation of a growing Latino constituency that made its voice heard with the 2012 presidential election (Rodriguez, 2012). In 2013, S. 744 was unveiled. A total of 301 amendments were proposed by Senate Judiciary Committee members, of which 92 were incorporated into the bill. On May 21st, S. 744 passed out of the Committee on a vote of 13–5 and it was introduced in the Democrat-controlled Senate. Debate on the Senate floor began on June 7, 2013 where senators filed more than 500 amendments. Although very few of these were voted on, a notable exception was the "border surge" amendment introduced by Senators Bob Corker (R-TN) and John Hoeven (R-ND), and supported by opponents of immigration, which proposed a record level of funding for border security spending. In the end, the bill sent to the House for consideration included a proposed $46.3 billion of initial funding to implement the Act. In the end, all Democrats in the Senate voted in favor of the bill. The 14 senators who opposed were all Republican.

Pro-immigrant groups (such as the American Immigration Lawyers Association) were initially cautiously optimistic about some of the provisions included in S. 744. as they apply to undocumented immigrants. In brief, according to a summary provided by the American Immigration Lawyers Association, these are:

- A proposal to provide those individuals here unlawfully to adjust their status to a new legal status category called "Registered Provisional Immigrant (RPI) Status." RPI status would last for a six-year term and could be renewed with payment of the application fee. A criticism of this provision was that this is not a Legal Permanent status (LPR). Instead, LPR will be issued if certain conditions are met after ten years.

- Except for DREAM Act–eligible students, applicants would be required to pay a $500 penalty fee.
- H-1B visa high-skill workers visa holders would be prevented from undercutting the wages paid to American workers by requiring employers to pay significantly higher wages for H-1B workers than under current law (and to first advertise the jobs to American workers at this higher wage before hiring an H-1B worker).
- Individuals with removal orders would be permitted to apply as would those immigrants currently in removal proceedings.
- The Agricultural Job Opportunity, Benefits, and Security Act (AgJOBS) would allow current undocumented farm workers to obtain legal status through an Agricultural Card Program.
- Young adults who qualify for DREAM Act Status and the Agricultural Card Program would be on the fast track to get their green cards (LPR) in five years and would be eligible for citizenship immediately after they get their green cards.
- Agricultural workers who fulfill future Agricultural Card work requirements in U.S. agriculture, show that they have paid all taxes, have not been convicted of any serious crime, and pay a $400 fine are eligible to adjust to legal permanent resident status. Spouses and minor children would receive derivative status.
- A new agricultural guest worker visa program would be established to ensure an adequate agricultural workforce. A portable, at-will employment-based visa (W-3 visa) and a contract-based visa (W-2 visa) would replace the current H-2A program. The H-2A program would sunset after the new guest worker visa program is operational.

Criticism of 2013 S. 744 by immigrant rights groups has been made on several points, especially for the implications for undocumented immigrant populations:

- It would mandate that all employers will be required to use the E-Verify system, and as part of the E-Verify system, every non-citizen will be required to show their "biometric work authorization card," or their "biometric green card."
- Individuals who have been granted RPI status would not be eligible for any publically funded welfare benefits.
- The total time it would take to become a citizen would be thirteen years.
- Applicants would have to pay all back taxes, per adult applicant.
- The original bill would have appropriated $3 billion to implement greater border enforcement (the Comprehensive Southern Border Security Strategy and the Southern Border Fencing Strategy) to acquire among other things: more surveillance and detection equipment to be developed or used by the Department of Defense, additional Border Patrol agents, and more unmanned aerial systems (drones). However, the Hoeven and Corker amendment would make this allocation 46 billion dollars.
- No out-of-status immigrant would be able to adjust to RPI status until the U.S. Congress received a notice from the Department of Homeland Security Secretary that the Comprehensive Southern Border Security Strategy and the Southern Border Fencing Strategy are in place.

- An immigration enforcement effectiveness rate of 90 percent or higher would be required for all high risk border sectors, and this goal must be reached during the first five years after the bill is enacted.

It is widely believed that this bipartisan effort at immigration reform that included a path to citizenship was a response to a record voter turnout by Latinos in the recent presidential election. The 2013 proposal came on the heels of a particularly contentious 2012 presidential campaign that resulted in the re-election of Barack Obama. A notable demographic shift in electoral behavior was especially apparent with 71 percent of the Latino electorate casting their vote for President Obama, according to an analysis of exit polls by the Pew Hispanic Center (Lopez and Taylor, 2012). During the months of campaigning, news pundits and political analysts had grown increasingly sensitive to some of the views about immigration that were expressed by the candidates. Those more closely aligned with the right wing of the Republican party and the Tea Party generally expressed their desire for greater, if not extreme, measures for immigration enforcement and border control. The amendment to S. 744 that added funding for border enforcement is a result of this view.

Months of media coverage made it increasingly difficult for Latino voters to ignore acrimonious views from those candidates who only promised to bring about only greater disrespect (such as using the term "illegals" to refer to undocumented immigrants) and harsher treatment of Latinos. For example, Republican presidential candidate Herman Cain became famous for his proposal for border enforcement which was to "electrify the [U.S.-Mexico] fence" (Huisenga, 2011). Texas Republican Governor Rick Perry was sharply criticized by the more restrictionist-leaning Republican candidates for a state law he supported that allowed undocumented students to enroll in Texas colleges and universities as in-state residents. In much the same way, former Republican House Speaker Newt Gingrich was criticized for expressing that deporting elderly grandmothers who were undocumented was unrealistic and unwise. Republican governor Mitt Romney's answer to the immigration issue during the primary debates was that, by preventing undocumented workers from obtaining a job, they would "self deport." Later news reports divulged that Romney had on his campaign staff as his advisor Kansas secretary of state Kris Kobach, the architect of Arizona's anti-immigrant "Papers Please Law," SB 1070, and other similar anti-immigrant state laws mushrooming throughout the country (Rodriguez, 2012). Ignored by these Republican candidates were polls conducted throughout the entire election cycle on the issue of immigration. These polls consistently found that immigration was an important issue for most all Latinos, with most in favor of offering undocumented immigrants a chance to earn legal status and few in favor of drastic measures such as deportation and resources for greater border enforcement (Lopez and Taylor, 2012).

In contrast, while campaigning in 2008, candidate Barack Obama made comprehensive immigration reform (CIR) one of his central campaign promises. And although on record as the administration with the greatest number of deportations—more than any other president, in June of 2011, the Obama administration issued its Morton Memo, directing immigration enforcement agents to use special consideration by not removing undocumented students, undocumented immigrants with long-standing family ties to the United States, undocumented immigrants who have contributed to their communities or served in the military, family members of veterans, those immigrants with serious health issues, caregivers, or victims of crime and those who had a strong basis for remaining in the United States. Then in June of 2012, President Obama issued the executive order, Deferred Action for Childhood Arrivals (DACA), a memorandum directing agencies that form part of the U.S. Department of Homeland Security (U.S. Customs and Border Protection, the U.S. Citizenship and Immigration Services, the U.S. Customs Border Protection, and U.S. Immigration and Customs Enforcement), to practice prosecutorial discretion towards those who as children immigrated to the United States without proper authorization. By October, 2012, Latino registered voters preferred Obama over Republican challenger Mitt Romney by 69 percent to 21 percent (Lopez and Gonzalez-Barrera, 2012). It is widely held that although Latino voters may have been disappointed with the great number of deportations that came with the Obama administration, they most probably feared a worse fate that might have resulted with the election of a Republican candidate for the office (Rodriguez, 2012).

While an immigration reform bill has passed the Senate, it has encountered much more push back in the House. By late summer of 2013, Republican Bob Goodlatte (R-Va), who as Chair of the House Judiciary Committee would be the first to examine the Senate version of the immigration bill, was reported to explain that the Republican-dominated House would take a piece-meal approach to immigration reform with separate bills, rather than the comprehensive route. The first individually addressed components would consider border security, immigration enforcement, and workplace verification. A key disagreement with S. 744 is its inclusion of so-called "special" pathways to citizenship for DREAM Act–eligible immigrants who were brought to the United States as children.

With the prospects of the Senate-proposed immigration reform advance in the House weakening, on September 20, 2013, Rep. Raúl Grijalva, D-Ariz., together with Filemon Vela of Texas, introduced a comprehensive immigration reform bill to serve as an alternative to what the Senate passed in June. Predictably, with the "border surge" amendment in S. 744, the bill has lost support among Democrats. The Grijalva-Vela bill, *The Comprehensive Immigration Reform for America's Security and Prosperity Act of 2013,* parallels a 2009 version of comprehensive immigration reform that had more than 100 co-sponsors but failed to advance.

Although the more progressive Grijalva-Vela bill has a remote chance of passing the Republican-controlled House, there are several significant differences compared to S. 744 that reflect wider public concerns about immigration. First, instead of limiting eligibility to those who entered the country before Dec. 31, 2011, as the Senate's reform does, the Grijalva-Vela proposal extends the cut-off date to the day the bill is introduced. The bill proposes to suspend the Operation Streamline program pending review of the goals, impacts and cost-benefit analyses, and it removes state and local enforcement from immigration enforcement efforts.

Finally, on October 2, 2013, House Democrats introduced an immigration reform bill, H.R. 15, *The Border Security, Economic Opportunity, and Immigration Modernization Act.* In essence, this proposal eliminates the Corker-Hoeven "border surge" amendment to the bipartisan senate bill passed on June 27, 2013 (S. 744). H.R. 15 replaces the border surge amendment with a bipartisan House border security bill,

H.R. 1417, which was passed unanimously by the Homeland Security Committee in May 2013.

With the U.S. Congress stalemated, several thousand people rallied for immigration reform in the nation's capital by blocking traffic in front of the Capitol building. For their act of civil disobedience, more than 100 activists were arrested, including eight Democratic members of Congress, including civil rights activist John Lewis (GA), Luis Gutiérrez (IL), Raúl Grijalva (AZ), Keith Ellison (MN), Joseph Crowley (NY), Charles Rangel (NY), Al Green (TX), and Jan Schakowsky (IL).

Anna Ochoa O'Leary

See Also: Deferred Action for Childhood Arrivals (DACA); DREAM Act; Morton Memo; Obama Administration; Operation Streamline; Policy and Political Action; Protests; Special Agricultural Workers (SAW)

Further Reading

American Immigration Lawyers Association. 2013. Outline of the Border Security, Economic Opportunity, and Immigration Modernization Act of 2013, April 16. Available at: http://www.aila.org/content/default.aspx?docid=44052.

Govtrack.us. 2013. S. 744: Border Security, Economic Opportunity, and Immigration Modernization Act. April 17, 2013. Available at: http://www.govtrack.us/congress/bills/113/s744/text.

Huisenga, Sarah. 2011. "Herman Cain acknowledges his electric border fence idea isn't a joke after all." *CBS News*. October 17. Available at: http://www.cbsnews.com/8301-503544_162-20121695-503544.html.

Linkins, Jason, and Sam Stein. 2012. "Mitt Romney, Newt Gingrich Spar over Immigration During CNN 2012 GOP Debate In Florida." *Huffington Post,* Jan. 26. Available at: http://www.huffingtonpost.com/2012/01/26/mitt-romney-newt-gingrich-immigration-florida-debate_n_1235344.html.

Lopez, Marc Hugo, and Ana Gonzalez-Barrera. 2012. "Latino Voters Support Obama by 3–1 Ratio, But Are Less Certain than Others about Voting." Pew Hispanic Research Center. October 11, 2012. Available at http://www.pewhispanic.org/2012/10/11/latino-voters-support-obama-by-3-1-ratio-but-are-less-certain-than-others-about-voting/.

Lopez, Marc Hugo, and Paul Taylor. 2012. "Latino Voters in the 2012 Election." Pew Hispanic Research Center. November 7, 2012. Available at: http://www.pewhispanic.org/2012/11/07/latino-voters-in-the-2012-election/.

Rodriguez, Cindy Y. 2012. "Latino vote key to Obama's re-election." *CNN,* November 9. Available at: http://www.cnn.com/2012/11/09/politics/latino-vote-key-election.

Immigration Reform and Control Act (IRCA) (1986)

During the 1970s, politicians crafted different forms of immigration reform legislation. Immigrant rights activists contested many of the proposed laws while politicians debated them. None had successfully passed the house and senate until Senator Alan Simpson of Wyoming and Representative Peter Rodino of New Jersey introduced a bill

President Reagan signs the Immigration Reform and Control Act (IRCA) of 1986. In this legacy piece of legislation, nearly 3 million undocumented immigrants were set on a pathway to citizenship, and a life out of the shadows. (Ronald Reagan Library)

in 1985. President Ronald Reagan signed this bill known as the Immigration Reform and Control Act of 1986 (IRCA). The legislative act provided conditional amnesty and instituted policy designed to curb undocumented immigration. IRCA enacted four major provisions. First, the act implemented sanctions on employers who knowingly hired undocumented workers. Second, IRCA instituted the Legally Authorized Workers (LAW) program. It granted amnesty to long-term undocumented residents who met the outlined criteria. The third provision created the Special Agricultural Workers (SAW) program to provide a pathway for legalization to qualified undocumented agricultural workers. Lastly, IRCA increased funding allocated to the United States Immigration and Naturalization Services (INS).

Under IRCA legislation, employers had to complete an Employment Eligibility Verification I-9 form for each employee hired after November 6, 1986. The form ensured that employers had reviewed the documentation showing their employees' legal authorization to work. Some forms of acceptable documentation included: U.S. passport, Native American tribal card, temporary residence card, driver's license, federal or state identification card, social security card, and school identification card with a photograph. Under law, employers could not suggest or prefer one document over another. Instead, new hires determined what documents to submit. Any worker hired who did not complete I-9 paperwork faced termination. Employers had to keep photocopies of the I-9 form along with the documents on file for every new employee. If not, the state penalized employers with fines ranging from $100 to $1,000 per employee. Furthermore, IRCA allocated money for workplace inspections. If the state discovered that employers had hired any unauthorized workers, it would deport these workers. Additionally, the state would fine employers anywhere from $250 to $10,000 per unauthorized employee. Repeat offenders faced possible imprisonment and stiffer fines.

IRCA also established provisions to prevent discrimination in employment practices. In theory, employers had to extend job opportunities to all those authorized to work in the United States. However, activists worried that these imposed sanctions would adversely affect Latinas/os in particular. Since mainstream society viewed Latinas/os, especially Mexicans, as undocumented, many activists feared that employers would hesitate to hire them. The state forbade employers from discriminating against prospective employees on the basis of citizenship or immigration status. To enforce this antidiscrimination provision, the government established the Office of Special Counsel for Immigration- Related Unfair Employment Practices. The agency is responsible for upholding the ban on the differential treatment of prospective and current employees based on citizenship or immigration status. The office extends its protection in recruitment, hiring, and firing practices. It also offers workshops to provide education on IRCA-related issues. The state instituted the office to address some of these concerns and provide some recourse. However, the effectiveness of the office is another question.

IRCA granted approximately 3 million people amnesty under the LAW and SAW programs from 1987 through 1989. The state adjusted the status for about 1.7 million LAW candidates and roughly 1.3 million SAW applicants. The bill granted approximately 2.3 million Mexicans amnesty or 70 percent of those granted amnesty. LAW applicants had to prove uninterrupted residency in the United States since January 1, 1982. As the government reviewed the case, the state issued LAW applicants temporary residence. Meanwhile, candidates had to remain in the United States. Applicants waited approximately eighteen months to learn of their fate. SAW applicants had to have worked on farms at least ninety days a year over a span of three years.

The government conditionally granted amnesty. Under IRCA, both LAW and SAW applicants had to enroll in civics courses and English as a Second Language classes. Otherwise, the state could revoke their permanent resident cards, or green cards. The government also held the discretion to revoke the legal residence status of any individuals who left the United States and failed to report to the United States on a yearly basis.

IRCA allocated $400 million in funds, a 75 percent increase, to the INS. It used the money to hire additional Border Patrol officers and to enhance enforcement along the United States–Mexico border in the two years that followed. This, however, did not halt undocumented immigration. Unauthorized immigrants continued to cross the border without apprehension. IRCA did not solve the problem of undocumented immigration for various reasons. Instead, it produced a new generation of undocumented people. Though IRCA imposed employer sanctions, it did not require employers to determine the authenticity of the documents. This loophole produced an aggressive surge in false documentation. Unauthorized workers presented counterfeit green cards, passports, driver's licenses, and other documents. And employers hired workers with these phony documents. Employers could bypass state discipline and continue to hire undocumented workers.

Since the state monitored the international movement of those granted amnesty, many family members and friends, especially women and children, joined their loved ones in the United States. Some of the undocumented children from this generation are the ones leading the Development, Relief and Education for Alien Minors (DREAM) Act, proposed legislation that would adjust the status for qualifying undocumented youth contingent on enrollment in higher education or honorable completion of military service.

Many people continue to immigrate to the United States without government authorization because their lives depend on it. Some flee war, political unrest, and state repression. Despite intense human rights violation by the government in Guatemala, El Salvador, and other countries, the United States offers no state-sponsored refuge. Others immigrate without a visa in order to escape persecution based on their sexual orientation. Some escape poverty sometimes produced by U.S. intervention. For instance, the North America Free Trade Agreement (NAFTA), a policy opening trade and investment between Canada, Mexico, and the United States, exacerbated poverty in Mexico. People prefer to risk their lives by crossing the border without authorization rather than endure these dire conditions.

Myrna García

See Also: Amnesty; Citizenship Education; Counterfeit Documents; Family Reunification; Laws and Legislation, Post-1980s; Special Agricultural Workers (SAW).

Further Reading

Calavita, Kitty. 1989. "The Contradictions of Immigration Lawmaking: The Immigration Reform and Control Act of 1986." *Law and Policy* 11.1:17–47.

Jones-Correa, Michael, and Els de Graauw. 2013. "Looking Back to See Ahead: Unanticipated Changes in Immigration from 1986 to the Present and Their Implications for American Politics Today." *Annual Review of Political Science* 16.

Powers, Mary G., Elen Percy Kraly, and William Seltzer. 2004. Migration Information Source.

Zolberg, Aristide R. 1990. "Reforming the Back Door: The Immigration Reform and Control Act of 1986 in Historical Perspective." *Immigration Reconsidered: History, Sociology, and Politics* 315–38.

Inadmissibility

In U.S. legal terms, *inadmissibility* is used to refer to any of several conditions that make a noncitizen ineligible to enter the United States. The term "inadmissible alien" was adopted with the Illegal Immigration Reform and Immigrant Responsibility Act (IIRIRA) of 1996. Before this act, the term was "excludable alien." IIRIRA provided the criteria that can be used to deny a petitioner entry into the United States. Currently there are 46 grounds for inadmissibility (Waits, 2009). A petitioner who is an "inadmissible alien" cannot be granted a visa to enter the United States if any of the conditions for inadmissibility apply. The list includes:

- The petitioner has a communicable disease, such as tuberculosis
- The petitioner has a mental disorder
- The petitioner has committed a serious crime (aggravated felony), or crime of moral turpitude, including prostitution
- The petitioner has committed a crime involving controlled substances (such as drugs), or firearms
- The petitioner is a spy or terrorist
- The petitioner is a voluntary member of a communist party
- The petitioner is a Nazi
- The petitioner is a polygamist
- The petitioner has falsely claimed U.S. citizenship
- The petitioner is present in the United States without authorization
- The petitioner reentered or attempted to reenter the United States without inspection
- The petitioner is an alien who had been ordered removed and who reentered or who attempted to reenter the United States without inspection
- Individuals who did not show up at their removal proceedings and who try to re-enter the country within five years of their removal
- Persons who knowingly committed fraud in order to obtain certain benefits under the INA

Depending on the circumstances, petitioners may qualify for a waiver of inadmissibility. However, some conditions, such as falsely claiming U.S. citizenship, cannot be waived.

The term "inadmissible alien" has been used to classify individuals who are not allowed to enter with authorization by the United States government. Under current law, individual U.S. Border Patrol agents have the right to deny entry or remove individuals deemed as inadmissible at their discretion. If an individual is found within the United States without authorization, or attempting to enter without inspection, agents are not required to further investigate any other aspects of inadmissibility. However, if an immigrant is already present in the United States, some of the conditions listed above may be grounds for deportation or may prevent him or her from applying for any adjustment of their status in the future. Deportable aliens are those immigrants found within the United States. Thus, those who reside in the United States without legal status may both face deportation and be found to be inadmissible.

For those undocumented immigrants residing in the United States, there are other consequences that come with deportation in terms of being inadmissible. For those deported after residing in the United States for a continuous period of more than 180 days but less than a year, they are inadmissible for three years. In other words, they are barred from applying for legal entry for three years. For those deported after having lived unlawfully in the United States more than a year, they are inadmissible for ten years. For those in this last category, if they reenter the United States without authorization, they are permanently inadmissible. Knowing that the opportunity of having legal status is increasingly out of reach may encourage undocumented immigrants to live in the shadows rather than risk deportation and separation from the families and communities that surround them in the United States. For this reason, the undocumented population grows with every passing year.

It is also important to note that inadmissibility also applies to individuals seeking asylum in the United States. They too can be deemed inadmissible according to the following guidelines laid out by the U.S. government in the Illegal Immigration Reform and Immigrant Responsibility Act of 1996. The reasons for denying asylum are:

- The petitioner has ordered, incited, assisted, or otherwise participated in the persecution of another on account of race, religion, nationality, membership in a particular social group, or political opinion;
- There are serious reasons to believe that the petitioner alien has committed a serious nonpolitical crime abroad before arriving in the United States; and
- The petitioner has engaged in terrorist activities.

Having a condition that potentially makes a petitioner for admission inadmissible makes it more difficult for legal permanent residents or citizen family members to petition for reunification through the family visa program under the Immigration and Nationality Act. These visas are available for immediate relatives: spouses, unmarried children, parents, and siblings.

The 1996 IIRIRA also made inadmissible those individuals that are likely to become "public charges." Immigrants in the United States petitioning for a family member to immigrate to the United States must sign a legally-binding affidavit of support to ensure that the new arrival will not fall into poverty and therefore be a burden to the state. The affidavit predisposes the sponsor to further hardship if, for example, the sponsor is a husband who is later divorced resulting in poverty conditions for the ex-spouse. In addition, before any application is finalized, the family member waiting to come to the United States to join his or her family (the "beneficiary") must prove that they are not inadmissible. The growing backlog of family reunification applications has made this wait time longer over the years and this adds to the number of potentially inadmissible immigrants. Potential beneficiaries are not allowed to travel and enter the United States while they wait for the application to be finalized. The combination of uncertainty and the desire to be together may tempt those waiting to immigrate to enter the country without documents. This would result in their inadmissibility. In recent years, these conditions have been at the center of litigation challenging the criteria for inadmissibility, especially with more immigration violations being increasingly categorized as felonies, making more of them grounds for inadmissibility (Cruz, 2010; Waits, 2009).

Yesenia Andrade

See Also: Deportation; Exclusion; Expedited Removal; Illegal Immigration Reform and Immigrant Responsibility Act (1996); Ports of Entry; U.S. Border Patrol.

Further Reading

Cruz, Evelyn H. 2010. "Because You're Mine, I Walk the Line: The Trials and Tribulations of the Family Visa Program." *Fordham Urban Law Journal* 38.1:155–181.

The Illegal Immigration Reform and Immigrant Responsibility Act of 1996 § 301(a), Pub. L. No. 104–208. 1996. Reprinted in 1996 U.S.C.C.A.N. (110 Stat. 3009).

Thronson, Veronica Tobar. 2012 "'Til Death Do Us Part: Affidavits of Support and Obligations to Immigrant Spouses." *Family Court Review* 50.4:594–605.

Waits, Michael M. 2009. "In Like Circumstances, but for Irrelevant and Fortuitous Factors: The Availability of Section 212 (C) Relief to Deportable Legal Permanent Residents." *Arizona Law Review* 51.2:465–501.

Incarceration

Since 2004 when more laws began to be introduced in state legislatures across the United States, the trend has been to increasingly police undocumented populations. Research on the policing of minority populations has already shown that an outcome of more policing is more numbers of arrests and incarceration. And although many of the anti-immigrant bills being introduced in state legislatures address a range of issues, laws intended to help police and other officials determine the status of a presumed immigrant upon a lawful stop or arrest represent one of the largest categories of laws being proposed or enacted at state and municipal levels of government. An example of such laws was brought to national and international attention in April of 2010 when Arizona's SB 1070 was signed into law. This law requires that state and local law enforcement agents investigate the immigration status of those detained for other violations. The law was challenged by the U.S. government in federal court later that same year (in July of 2010) by the U.S. Justice Department and several organizations including the National League of United Latin American Citizens (LULAC) and Mexican American Legal Defense Fund (MALDEP). The suit alleged that the Arizona law usurped the U.S. federal government's jurisdiction over the enforcement of immigration laws. In the fall of 2010, a federal district judge ruled against several provisions in SB 1070. This ruling was later appealed at the Ninth Circuit Court of Appeals in San Francisco. In the broadest of terms, SB1070 promotes a growing scrutiny and policing of immigrants, and more specifically of those whose appearance and activities might invite prejudice and speculation as to their immigrant status, in a phenomenon known as racial profiling, to increase the number of arrests. Statistics released in June of 2011 reveal that nearly half of all people sentenced for federal felony crimes are Latinos, and as a result of this trend, one out of every six Hispanic males and one out of every forty-five Hispanic females can expect to go to prison in his or her lifetime.

According to a report by The Sentencing Project, *Uneven Justice: State Rates of Incarceration by Race and Ethnicity,* Hispanics are incarcerated twice as often as non-Hispanic whites. The over-representation of Latinos in the total number of sentencing for federal felony crimes is apparent considering that Hispanics in 2011 made up 16 percent of the total United States. The increase is in part attributed to the fact that many arrests and incarcerations are for immigration-related offenses. According to U.S. Sentencing Commission data, sentences for felony immigration crimes that include entering into the United States without inspection as well as smuggling, accounted for about 87 percent of the increase in the number of Hispanics sent to prison since 2000. Expedited court hearings along the border are a major force driving a dramatic shift in who is being sent to federal prison. This trend is epitomized by the *en masse* hearings intended to deter illegal immigration, known as Operation Streamline, that began in 2005 in Del Rio, Texas, and soon spread to other Border Patrol sectors. This system is a departure from the expedited removal policy used by the U.S. Border Patrol and is intended to deter undocumented immigrants along the U.S.-Mexico border. Before 2005, unauthorized border crossers were only intermittently charged with federal felony offenses and more often simply driven back to the border, especially for first-time offenders. The progressive adding of federal charges to what was in many cases before 2005 a misdemeanor or administrative offense is referred to as criminalization. This also contributes to the popular perceptions that equate immigrants with criminals. Moreover, prejudice is fomented by the upsurge of drug-smuggling related violence in the border region. More frequently, Latinos arrested for a drug-related crime are referred to by officials and the media as cartel members. Experts in the analyses of drug-related violence in Mexico have refuted recent reports such as the one produced by the National Drug Intelligence Center that hundreds of U.S. cities have a Mexican drug cartel presence. Misinformation is thus responsible for proliferating images of immigrants as criminals who merit and justify increased surveillance and harsher penalties via the legal system, and indirectly contributes to the increase in the inmate population that is Latino and or immigrant.

Many policy makers question whether systems of accelerated legal proceedings such as Operation Streamline deter immigrants from crossing the border without authorization and instead distract prosecutors and police from pursuing offenders of more serious and often violent crimes. Ultimately, such fast-track programs speed immigrants through the legal system and contribute to the numbers of incarcerated immigrants and prejudice. Tucson federal defenders Jason Hannan and Saul Huerta challenged Operation Streamline's legality in 2009, in *United States v. Roblero-Solis,* where a federal court ultimately deemed the process to operate in violation of constitutionally protected due process. However, its continued practice in spite of the ruling and in spite of an overburdened and costly federal court system has contributed to the growing number of immigrants sent to federal prison for the primary crime of unlawfully entering or remaining in the United States after their visa has expired (visa overstayers), jumping from 6,513 in fiscal year 2000 to 19,910 in fiscal year 2010.

Meanwhile, miles away from the border, interior policing has also resulted in record number of immigrants who have been deported under the Obama administration, many of which are a result of workplace raids. The deportation of unauthorized immigrants by the federal government has roughly quadrupled in the last half-decade. The blame for this is routinely placed on the post-9/11 political climate in the United States that relies on the fear that terrorists may be sneaking into the country through a porous border with Mexico, even though such concerns have historically been disproven by a U.S. State Department report in 2011. Case studies of such communities under intense surveillance as Prince William County (Va.), Farmer's Ranch (Tex.), and Hazelton (Pa.) have recently been highlighted in the media and in documentaries such as *9000 Liberty.* Such "crackdowns" on immigrants resulting in deportations are disruptive of families and entire communities, resulting in family separation and trauma, especially when carried out by untrained, understaffed, and underfunded local governments.

Other laws contributing to the trend towards the increased incarceration of Latinos and immigrants include cooperative agreements between local law enforcement agencies and the U.S. Government such as those provided by a federal statute known as Section 287(g) of the Immigration and Nationality Act (INA) of 1996, and the Secure Communities program of 2005. Section 287(g) programs permit the federal government to delegate immigration enforcement power to state and local authorities. In January of 2011, the 287(g) program was operating in 72 jurisdictions through the United States. The program is similar to the later (2005) Secure Communities program of the Department of Homeland Security's Immigration and Customs Enforcement (ICE). Under the Secure Communities program, ICE and the Federal Bureau of Investigation (FBI) form an information-sharing partnership intended to assist federal immigration authorities identify and deport immigrants who have committed serious crimes, many of whom may be found in U.S. prisons. The Secure Communities program authorizes state and local police agencies to screen people for their immigration status, submit to the FBI the fingerprints of all suspects they detain, and hold them until federal government authorities take custody and begin the process for their removal from the United States.

Some communities throughout the United States have expressed concerns that the 287(g) program would link their police departments with immigration enforcement and undermine the trust they have built within their communities. This concern has been validated by findings contained in a Migration Policy Institute Report in 2011 that shows immigrants are more likely to avoid public spaces when 287(g) agreements are in place and thus are driven into the shadows—making them more vulnerable to crime, exclusion, and reluctance to report crimes that would bring interaction with police. Indeed, such agreements have resulted in higher rates of arrests and incarceration for misdemeanors (such as shoplifting, disorderly conduct, driving without a license or trespassing) rather than for serious crimes as was the intent. This has also resulted in a financial burden for local and state governments and growing resistance to them. Although there are great political pressures placed on local law enforcement agencies to participate, some California cities such as San Francisco, Santa Clara and Berkeley have attempted to opt out of such agreements, and are thus popularly referred to as Sanctuary Cities. For example, in May of 2011, California assemblyman Tom Ammiano (D-San Francisco) cosponsored a bill, AB1081, to "honor the rights" of local governments to "opt out" of the 287(g) program. By opting out, undocumented immigrants arrested in San Francisco for non-felony crimes or petty crimes will not be held in jail longer awaiting federal immigrant officials to take fingerprints or detain them for possible deportation. Instead, they will be released with a court date just like any other U.S. citizen.

In the end, stepped-up mechanisms to enforce immigrant law, such as 287(g) agreements, have benefited for-profit prisons. Privately-run prison facilities used to hold immigrants until deportation hearings, and to incarcerate them to serve their sentences, are a multibillion dollar industry dependent on immigration policies that emphasize the policing of immigrants. The over three billion dollars in revenues of the nation's two largest private prison operators, the Corrections Corporation of America

(CCA) and the GEO Group doubled from 2005 to 2011. The private prison industry has insured that detention beds are filled because of generous campaign contributions of $45 made to politicians at the state and federal level, some of whom have played key roles in shaping immigration policies, such as Senator Bob Corker (R-TN), co-author of the "border surge" amendment to the 2013 immigration reform proposal, S.744. The amendment provides funding of over 46 billion dollars for immigration enforcement. Republican Senator John McCain (R-AZ) reportedly received $32,146 from CCA, and fellow member of the bipartisan "Gang of Eight" that is working to draft S.744, Marco Rubio (R-FL), ranks among the top recipients of contributions from the Florida-based GEO Group, having received a reported $27,300 in donations over the course of his career. Both of these senators also sponsored a bill in 2011 to expand Operation Streamline, which would certainly provide more undocumented immigrant inmates for greater private prison profits (Chavkin, 2013).

Anna Ochoa O'Leary

See Also: Exclusion; Expedited Removal; Governance and Criminalization; Immigration and Customs Enforcement (ICE); Obama Administration; Operation Streamline; Overstayers; Sanctuary Cities and Secure Communities; Workplace Raids.

Further Reading

Capps, Randy, Marc R. Rosenblum, Cristina Rodriguez, and Muzaffar Chrishti. 2011. "Delegation and Divergence: A Study of 287(g) State and Local Immigration Enforcement." Migration Policy Institute, available at www.migrationpolicy.org.

Chavkin, Sasha. 2013. "Immigration reform and private prison cash." *Columbia Journalism Review.* February 20, 2013. Available at: http://www.cjr.org/united_states_project/key_senators_on_immigration_get_campaign_cash_from_prison_companies.php?page=all.

De Genova, Nicholas, and Nathalie Peutz, eds. 2010. *The Deportation Regime: Sovereignty, Space, and the Freedom of Movement.* Durham, NC: Duke University Press Books.

Goldsmith, P., M. Romero, R. R. Goldsmith, M Escobedo, and L. Khoury. 2009. "Ethno-Racial Profiling and State Violence in a Southwest Barrio." *Aztlán: A Journal of Chicano Studies* 34.1:93–124.

Hagan, Jacqueline, and Nestor Rodriguez. 2001. "Resurrecting Exclusion: The Effects of 1996 U.S. Immigration Reform on Communities and Families in Texas, El Salvador, and Mexico." In *Latinos: Remaking America,* ed. Marcelo M. Suarez-Orozco and Mariela M. Páez, 190–201. Berkeley, Los Angeles and London: UC Press.

Lydgate, Joanna. 2010. "Assembly-line Justice: A Review of Operation Streamline." The Chief Justice Earl Warren Institute of Race, Ethnicity and Diversity. University of California Berkeley Law School. Available at http://www.law.berkeley.edu/files/Operation_Streamline_Policy_Brief.pdf.

Mauer, Marc, and Ryan S. King. 2007. "Uneven Justice: State Rates of Incarceration by Race and Ethnicity." Washington, DC: The Sentencing Project. Available at: http://www.sentencingproject.org/doc/publications/rd_stateratesofincbyraceandethnicity.pdf

Milovanovic, Dragan, and Katheryn K. Russell, eds. 2001. *Petit Apartheid in the U.S. Criminal Justice System.* Durham: Carolina Academic Press.

Indigenous People

In general, the term *indigenous* refers to a person and/or one's ancestors who are and were the original inhabitants of a region. For this work, indigenous people are from the Americas, which includes Canada, and North, Central, and Southern regions of the American continent. Like most other immigrants to the United States, indigenous peoples from the Americas immigrate for political and financial reasons, in hopes of obtaining improved political freedom and to create economic opportunities that are not available in their country of origin or home country. Mexico has the largest indigenous population in North America. Indigenous migrants face similar issues as those of other migrants, but being undocumented and indigenous in the United States presents a specific set of challenges.

Approximately 10 percent of Mexico's population is comprised of indigenous peoples. However, they have been treated as insignificant both within Mexico and the United States. In both Mexico and United States they are often stigmatized and exploited, relegating them to impoverished conditions. In Mexico, the ten states with the largest share of indigenous population are Oaxaca (18.3 percent), Veracruz (13.5 percent), Chiapas (13 percent), Puebla (9.42 percent), Yucatán (8.2 percent), Hidalgo (5.7 percent), state of Mexico (5.6 percent), Guerrero (5.2 percent), San Luis Potosí (3.2 percent) and Michoacán (2.9 percent). Not surprisingly, these states are those considered to be among the less economically advantaged in Mexico, according to Mexico's *Instituto Nacional de Estadísticas y Geografía e Información* (INGEI). (INEGI is the equivalent to the U.S. Census Bureau.) Not surprisingly, populations from these states suffer from high poverty rates, poor health and living conditions, and low educational attainment. For example, Oaxaca, home to many indigenous groups including the Zapotec, has a significantly high illiteracy rate: 27 percent of the population is reportedly illiterate. Teenage males between the ages of fifteen and older had an illiteracy rate of 34.4 percent, while females ages fifteen and older had an illiteracy rate of 65.7 percent. High school dropout rates also minimize their employment opportunities.

It is estimated that more than one in ten Mexicans speaks an indigenous language. For the indigenous whose first language is their native dialect, knowing how to communicate in Spanish is critical for finding jobs where few speak their native language. Indigenous immigrants from Mexico travel north to the United States from areas such as Michoacán, Oaxaca, the Yucatan, Chiapas, and Hidalgo. Some of these indigenous peoples include the Purépechas from Michoacán, and the Triqui from Oaxaca. Many of them speak any of Mexico's 56 recognized languages. However, another well-known group of indigenous migrants are the Maya from Guatemala who fled their country during the civil war in Central America and have since settled in North America. A large number of those arrested in the Postville, Iowa, meatpacking plant raid in 2008 were undocumented Mayan immigrants from Guatemala. The precise number of indigenous peoples who have immigrated to the United States in order to work and live is unknown. However, the number is most likely in the hundreds of thousands, especially since the mid-1990s when the North American Free Trade Agreement (NAFTA) negatively impacted traditional subsistence agricultural economies in the south-central parts of Mexico. In 2010, the U.S. Census Bureau attempted to calculate for the first time those who are from Maya, Nahua, Mixtec, or Purepecha groups. The U.S. Department of Labor estimates indigenous migrants make up about 17 percent of the nation's farm workers, and may represent up to 30 percent of California's farm worker population. In addition, Florida also has a large indigenous immigrant population. In 2012, the Mexican Consulate in New York reported that approximately 250,000 of the city's 320,000 Mexican-born population is of indigenous origin.

For example, Michoacán is a state located in the west-central region of Mexico. The indigenous peoples of Michoacán immigrate from communities such as Chavinda, Cherán, and Santiago Tangamandapio. Many Michoacán immigrants send remittances to their families and home communities as well as participate in local community organizations that collaborate with transnational emigrant associations.

Indigenous peoples have politically organized both within their country of origin and in their receiving destinations, that is, the location to which they have immigrated. For instance, they have established home town organizations, they unite in order to celebrate their home community festivities, and they also send remittances to help sustain their home community festivals. Access to the internet has made their transnational communication possible and enabled them to remain connected to their home community.

Indigenous peoples have established social and political organizations such as the *Frente Indígena Oaxaqueño Binacional* (FIOB), a transnational Oaxacan association; migrant and local organizations in Baja California, and in Fresno and Los Angeles, California and in a number of cities in Oregon.

There are a number of destinations within the United States that these indigenous peoples have predominantly chosen to relocate to. These include indigenous people from the Yucatan, the Maya, and various indigenous people from Chiapas (such as Tzotzil Maya who have relocated to San Francisco). Many Purépechas have immigrated to the rural Midwest; many Triquis have migrated to Greenfield, California, and many Mexican Zapotec and Guatemalan Kanjobales have settled in and near Los Angeles. There is also a community of Kanjobal Mayans in Florida (Burns, 2010) Considering their common impoverished conditions upon arriving in the United States indigenous immigrants have proven to be quite inventive and persistent and successful in their goal to improve their circumstance, thrive and survive in the United States.

Dina Barajas

See Also: Central American Civil Wars; Globalization; Home Town Associations; Kanjobal Mayans; Midwest; Postville, Iowa Raid; Refugee Act (1980); Refugees; Zapotec People (Oaxaca).

Further Reading

Burns, Allan F. 2010. *Maya In Exile: Guatemalans in Florida.* Philadelphia: Temple University Press.

Fox, Jonathan F., and Gaspar Rivera-Salgado. 2004. *Indigenous Mexican Migrants in the United States.* La Jolla, California: Center for U.S.-Mexican Studies, UCSD/Center for Comparative Immigration Studies, UCSD.

Kemper, Robert V., and Ryan M Fisher. 2006. "Comings and Goings: The Multiple Faces of Latin American Diaspora." *Revista Europa de Estuios y del Caribeabril* 2083–89.

Lopez Castro, Gustavo. 2006. *Diáspora michoacán.* Zamora, Michoacán: El Colegio de Michoacán.

Individual Taxpayer Identification Number (ITIN)

ITIN stands for Individual Taxpayer Identification Number, and it is a number that can be issued by the Internal Revenue Service (IRS) to individuals who wish to file federal income taxes but who do not have, and cannot get, a social security number. The ITIN is a 9-digit number like a social security number. The ITIN does not confer employment eligibility, and although unauthorized workers can legitimately pay income taxes using their ITIN, they cannot use it to obtain a job. Dependents of U.S. taxpayers who are foreign nationals (that is, citizens of another country and not of the United States) may also be issued ITINs.

Because many unauthorized immigrants in the United States do not have a valid social security number, they can elect to use an ITIN to pay their income taxes. That is, ITINs allow unauthorized workers to pay their federal income taxes in a lawful manner despite their unauthorized status. ITINs do not confer eligibility to work in the United States or to receive Social Security benefits such as retirement, health (Medicare), and disability or other government benefits. In 2013, however, it will be more difficult for undocumented immigrants to receive an ITIN partly because of concern about abuses by some undocumented immigrants who may be claiming tax credits illegally. As of January 2013, the IRS instituted stricter procedures in order to apply for and receive the ITIN. Application will now need to include original documentation such as passports and birth certificates, or certified copies of these by the issuing agency.

Approximately three quarters of unauthorized workers in the United States pay taxes on their incomes, while the other quarter pay informally, i.e. unreported and/or outside the regulated economy. Of those unauthorized workers who pay income taxes, most use a social security number that either belongs to someone else, has never been issued by the IRS, or was issued to the immigrant but is not for employment purposes. When unauthorized workers pay taxes using an assumed or invented social security number, these tax revenues go into an "earnings suspense" file at the Social Security Administration (SSA). The SSA estimates that it receives more than five billion dollars in income taxes annually from workers whose name and social security number do not match SSA records. These wage contributions are assumed to come from workers earning income in the informal economy, and are assumed to be undocumented. Unlike workers who are authorized and whose wages are reported and regulated, undocumented workers are unlikely to apply for the benefits that these wage contributions would bring. These workers do not receive any social security benefits when they reach retirement age, nor can they claim refunds from the IRS if they have overpaid, even though these are monies that they are entitled to because they earned them and are getting nothing in return.

Because of this, many unauthorized workers have applied for an ITIN. The ITIN allows unauthorized taxpayers to claim overpayments, and thus to claim a tax refund, even though it does not make them eligible for social security benefits.

However, beyond the difficulties that undocumented immigrants will encounter after the new IRS procedures are in place, even Latinos who have no problem satisfying documentation requirements to establish and strengthen their relationship with banks or institutions such as the IRS will likely struggle. Latinos already face systematic barriers from fully participating in U.S. financial markets, such as low financial literacy, distrust of financial institutions, poor credit, and cultural norms related to saving. As a result, Latino borrowers are driven into areas of the financial marketplace and "fringe" financial agents to gain access to money, impacting their dependents (Ibarra and Rodriguez, 2005/2006). For example, during the period of high demand for home loans in the mid-2000s, some banks allowed immigrants to obtain a home mortgage using an ITIN even if they did not have a social security number, and this provided the opportunity for unscrupulous lenders who charged them higher fees to determine their credit-worthiness (McConnell and Marcelli, 2007).

Because the ITIN is a legitimate government-issued number, it has appealed to unauthorized immigrants who are uncomfortable using a fake or assumed social security number. An additional benefit of using an ITIN is that it leaves a record of federal tax payment which may be helpful to unauthorized immigrants who are trying to adjust their immigration status. Many undocumented immigrants may also want to contribute tax payments for the benefits they receive.

Ruth Gomberg-Muñoz

See Also: Identification Cards; Mortgages; Shadow Population; Small Business Ownership; Taxes.

Further Reading

Ibarra, Beatriz, and Eric Rodriguez. 2005/2006. "Closing the Wealth Gap: Eliminating Structural Barriers to Building Assets in the Latino Community." *Harvard Journal of Hispanic Policy* 18:25–38.

IRS. 2013. IRS.gov. http://www.irs.gov/individuals/article/0,,id=96287,00.html.

McConnell, Eileen Diaz, and Enrico A. Marcelli. 2007. "Buying into the American Dream? Mexican Immigrants, Legal Status, and Homeownership in Los Angeles County." *Social Science Quarterly* 88.1:199–221.

Informal Economy

Although it has been forty years since Hart's (1973) seminal essay first introduced the term "informal sector," this term remains a fuzzy and contradictory concept. (Note: While most scholars cite this 1973 essay as the publication where Hart introduced the term "informal sector" to the academic community, others suggest that Hart originally articulated his findings of the "formal" and "informal" income opportunities in Accra, Ghana, at a conference at the University of Sussex in 1971.) We can find numerous terms commonly used in the literature and popular culture that refer to the informal sector, including the following terms: *the informal economy, underground economy, unregulated economy, irregular, shadow economy, dark economy, hidden sector, black market, invisible sector,* and *cash economy.*

Based on this brief list, we can clearly see some ominous words, like "shadow," "dark," and "hidden," where we can easily infer an illegal activity, such as the sale of street drugs or prostitution. There's also a racist association regarding some of these words, like "black" and "dark" to connote illegal behavior.

In essence, the terms cover all income-generating activity, including labor, that is not reported for taxation. Because of so many restrictions on the hiring of undocumented workers in the United States, the informal economy is a sector of the economy that offers one of the few ways that these workers can earn a living and support their families. Examples of informal economy work may include domestic work, child care, selling food items and handicrafts, and yard cleaning. Often, informal economy work is incorporated and combined with formal economy sectors, such as construction and homebuilding. Although this practice may help contractors save labor costs, it becomes difficult to attain an accurate accounting as to how income and wages and other financial transactions take place, and therefore they go unregulated.

This doesn't mean that the informal sector or informal economy concept does not have any merit or applicability in a technologically advanced society like the United States, despite the lack of consensus on terminology in the literature. On a more profound level, the actual term may not necessarily be as important as the actual phenomena scholars are attempting to identify and describe both in developed and developing countries.

During the past two decades, for instance, scholars have documented the existence and vitality of the informal economy in advanced countries. Debunking the notion that the informal economy will wither away with the rise of advanced capitalism, for instance, scholars have documented the existing and growing nature of informal economic activity in the United States and other Western countries. Major research has been conducted on key informal sectors with direct links to the formal economy, such as construction, transportation, footwear, electronics, street vending and retail (Sassen, 1994; Zlolniski, 1994).

Although many definitions exist on the informal economy, Portes and Castells (1989) provide an oft-cited definition, emphasizing its unregulated characteristics. "The informal economy," they write, "[is] a process of income-generation characterized by one central feature: *it is unregulated by the institutions of society, in a legal and social environment in which similar activities are regulated* [authors' italics]."

In addition to this definition, scholars have identified informal activities as "those income-generating activities occurring outside the state's regulatory framework" (Sassen, 1994), such as individuals or companies who do not report income, or underreport income, evade taxes, violate zoning rules, ignore work-site protections, abuse minimum wage laws and disregard occupational health/safety standards. For example, the garment industry represents a commonly researched case, where workers (mostly women) work in sweatshops and engage in industrial homework accompanied by piece-rate wages.

While these definitions sound similar to illegal forms of generating unregulated income, such as the sale of street drugs and prostitution, as noted above, scholars who study the informal economy differentiate between licit and illicit goods and services (Portes et al., 1989). For example, there is a major difference between a street vender who sells corn (i.e., licit goods) on the corner and the drug dealer who sells crack cocaine (an illegal commodity) in the alley (an unregulated sale). Although both actors engage in informal economic activities outside of the regulatory framework where they will earn unreported income, we can clearly distinguish between the nature of the goods (i.e., licit versus illicit) and how the consequences associated with each activity may play out. In addition, the informal and formal sectors of the economy converge when wages earned in the formal economy are used for transaction in the informal economy (for example if a worker buys drugs), and in turn, the money made in the informal/illicit economy is used to buy goods and services in the formal economy (for example if the drug dealer buys a car from a regulated car dealership in the formal economy).

Of interest here is a 2005 snapshot of workers in Los Angeles' informal economy. Since the U.S. Census Bureau does not provide data specifically on paid gardeners, the authors of this study used the U.S. Census Public Use Microdata Samples (PUMS) combined with other sources such as the U.S. Immigration and Naturalization Service (INS) to report on landscaping service workers, focusing on those who are employed with a licensed landscaping company. Overall, the authors find a significant number of workers in Los Angeles's informal sector:

> Our best estimate is that on a typical day in 2004 there were 679,000 informal workers in the county and 303,800 in the city. These workers are estimated to account for 15 percent of the county's labor force and 16 percent of the city's labor force. Undocumented workers are estimated to make up 61 percent of the informal labor force for the county and 65 percent for the city (Flaming, Haydamack, and Joassart 2005, 1).

The informal economy does not offer the same legal protections that most workers enjoy in the formal sector, such as minimum wage guarantees, occupational safety regulations and prohibition against labor exploitation. Nevertheless, for those who lack legal status in this country or viable employment opportunities due to limited educational background, the informal economy provides a viable means of survival for many immigrant workers and emerging petty-entrepreneurs.

Alvaro Huerta

See Also: Domestic Work; Employment; Enclaves; Family Economics; Garment Industry; "Undocumented" Label; Workers' Rights; Workplace Injury.

Further Reading

Bromley, Ray. 1978. "Introduction: The Urban Informal Sector: Why Is It Worth Discussing?" *World Development* 6.9/10:1033–1039.

Hart, Keith. 1973. "Informal Income Opportunities and Urban Employment in Ghana." *The Journal of Modern African Studies* 11.1:61–89.

Portes, Alejandro, Manuel Castells, and Lauren A. Benton, eds. 1989. *The Informal Economy: Studies in Advanced and Less Developed Countries.* Baltimore: The Johns Hopkins University.

Sassen, Saskia. 1994. "The Informal Economy: Between New Developments an Old Regulations." *The Yale Law Journal* 103.8:2289–2304.

Valenzuela, Abel, Jr. 2003. "Day Labor Work." *Annual Review of Sociology* 29:307–333.

Zlolniski, Christian. 1994. "The Informal Economy in an Advanced Industrialized Society: Mexican Immigrant Labor in Silicon Valley." *The Yale Law Journal* 103.8:2305–2335.

International Students/Student Visas

The term "international student" generally refers to students that come from foreign countries with some form of student visa to pursue higher education in the United States. Under this definition, the number of international students at colleges and universities in the United States increased by 6.5 percent to 764,495 during the 2011/12

Erika, a 20-year-old student at Phoenix College who declined to provide her last name for fear of deportation, is shown in the college's library in Phoenix in 2007. It is not known how many of Arizona's 120,000 university students and 380,000 community college students are undocumented immigrants, but a 2008 law bars them from paying in-state tuition, receiving state-provided scholarships, and fee waivers if they cannot prove legal residency status. (AP Photo/Tom Hood)

academic year, according to the "Open Doors Report 2012," published by the Institute of International Education. International students consistently represent approximately 3.5 percent of total U.S. higher education enrollment every year.

Management of student visas has been increasingly controlled after September 11, 2001, as several of the terrorists involved in the attack on the World Trade Center had entered the country on student visas which they had overstayed. With the resulting implementation of the Student and Exchange Visitor Program (SEVP) and internet-based Information System (SEVIS), it is now nearly impossible to be entirely "undocumented" and at the same time enrolled as an international student at an accredited institution of higher education. However, there are many situations that produce and allow for the real possibility of undocumented international students.

Access to Higher Education for Undocumented Immigrants

While the U.S. government and American academic institutions actively promote U.S. higher education opportunities to potential international students abroad, undocumented immigrants already in the United States often fall through the cracks. They sometimes have less access to appropriate information and financial support for higher education than those in their countries of origin. In particular, in some states students without proof of lawful presence are classified as "international students" for the purpose of charging them out-of-state tuition to attend colleges and universities, even though in practice, such students may have lived most of their lives in the United States.

K-12 public schools in the United States are mandated to provide education to children regardless of immigration status, although other legal and economic factors, as well as migration itself, present barriers that marginalize them. Youth who have grown up in the United States despite their undocumented status often speak only English, are only familiar with American history and culture, and have no legal identity/documentation (permanent address, voter registration, driver's license, passport, etc.) in their country of origin. For political and bureaucratic reasons, along with the aforementioned ones, it is extremely difficult for them to (re-) integrate into the educational system of their country of origin and/or apply for opportunities extended to students in their home countries, including applying for a student visa.

As undocumented students advance in the K-12 public education system, the dilemma comes to a head when promising undocumented students wish to continue their studies after high school graduation. While most institutions of higher education require no proof of citizenship or legal residency in order to apply and be admitted as a regular, non-international student, documentation is necessary in order to access financing options normally provided to U.S. citizens and permanent residents, including federally subsidized student loans and many scholarships. Nor do undocumented migrants have access to the opportunities extended to potential international students in their countries of origin. Therefore, economic limitations become the primary barrier to higher education of undocumented migrants.

The DREAM Act

In recent years, advocates have organized to make financial aid and tuition discounts available to undocumented students who have been raised as Americans and have graduated from public high schools in the United States. Specifically, they argue that it is unfair to provide out-of-state tuition waivers to international students (as many states do) and not do the same for those who have grown up in the United States, which was not necessarily of their own choosing.

The DREAM (Development, Relief, and Education of Alien Minors) Act identifies approximately sixty-five thousand undocumented youth in this situation. The Act was first introduced in the Senate in August 2001, later re-introduced in the House of Representatives in March 2009, and subsequently blocked in a Senate filibuster in December 2010. "This bill would provide conditional permanent residency to certain illegal and deportable alien students who graduate from U.S. high schools, who are of good moral character, arrived in the United States illegally as minors, and have been in the country continuously for at least five years prior to the bill's enactment, if they complete two years in the military or two years at a four-year institution of higher learning. The students would obtain temporary residency for a six-year period. Within the six-year period, a qualified student must have 'acquired a degree from an institution of higher education in the United States or [have] completed at least two years, in good standing, in a program for a bachelor's degree or higher degree in the United States,' or have 'served in the uniformed services for at least two years and, if discharged, [have] received an honorable discharge." ("Dream Act Portal," 2013).

A similar bill has been proposed at the state level in California and Florida. In California, three versions were passed by both houses of the legislature and vetoed by the governor, before it finally passed in 2011. California, Illinois, Kansas, Maryland, Nebraska, New Mexico, New York, Texas, Utah, and Washington are extending in-state tuition to undocumented students, sometimes on the condition that they prove physical residency in the state for a given number of years.

Student Visas: A Legal Alternative to Undocumented Immigration?

In recognition that youth from sending countries are often motivated to illegally migrate to the United States due to limited opportunities for them in their communities, the U.S. State Department promotes more temporary, limited, and controlled migration for the purpose of formal study as an alternative to undocumented migration in these regions and to stimulate development upon their return. Acceptance in a formal program of study at U.S. institutions is contingent on the student's ability to obtain one of three types of student visas—F or M for "non-immigrant students," or J for "exchange visitors"—and usually on academic English language competence as demonstrated by the results of the Test of English as a Foreign Language (TOEFL) exam.

While each of the visa types varies in terms of the restrictions it places on international students, all severely limit their right to seek (off campus) employment and length of stay. In this way, even while having entered the country legally, international students may enter into quasi-legal status when violating the terms of their student visa. Depending on the type of visa, family members may or may not have permission to work. Other youth may enter the United States on a tourist visa in order to study (English) in private or informal settings, an activity which is not in accordance with this type of document. In either case, international students essentially become "undocumented" when they overstay their visas.

Incidentally, U.S. immigration and education policy is equally marginalizing to migrants that do not reside in the country: American-born children (often to undocumented migrants) who were raised or studied in high school abroad are by-and-large ineligible for international student scholarships, as are foreign-born citizens of other countries (e.g. a Guatemalan citizen living in Mexico).

Implications of Undocumented Migration for International Education: A Complex Relationship

Undocumented migration can indirectly affect potential international students' possibilities for studying in the United States in three ways. First, although student visas are rarely denied since the visa application process comes after the funding application and academic admissions processes, a request may be denied if the applicant has previously been detained, deported, and/or charged with a felony (which is not an uncommon correlate to undocumented migration). Second, some scholarships for international students prohibit consideration of people with relatives (illegally) residing in the United States. Third, *remesas* (cash remittances sent back to the country of origin) from large-scale migration (both documented and undocumented) from primary sending countries such as Mexico have played a role in increasing access to formal education there. As changing policies make undocumented migration more and more difficult, youth are unable to continue their studies (primary, secondary, and post-secondary) in order to meet the prerequisites for International Student programs, creating an emerging paradox between foreign education policy and immigration policy.

Katherine Careaga

See Also: Adult Education; Colleges and Universities; Deferred Action for Childhood Arrivals (DACA); DREAM Act; Education; Student Visas; Undocumented Students.

Further Reading

"Advising Undocumented Students." 2012. College Board. http://professionals.college-board.com/guidance/financial-aid/undocumented-students.

"Dream Act Portal." 2013. http://dreamact.info.

"For International Students. EducationUSA: Your Source on U.S. Higher Education. http://www.educationusa.info/for_international_students.php.

Feder, J. 2010. "Unauthorized alien students, higher education, and in-state tuition rates: a legal analysis." RS22500. Congressional Research Service.

"Financial Aid and Scholarships for Undocumented Students." 2013. FinAid. http://www.finaid.org/otheraid/undocumented.phtml.

Lee, Y. 2006. "To Dream or Not to Dream: A Cost-benefit Analysis of the Development, Relief, and Education for Alien Minors (DREAM) Act." *Cornell Journal of Law and Public Policy* 16:231–258.

"Open Doors 2012." 2012. Institute of International Education. http://www.iie.org/en/Research-and-Publications/Open-Doors.

Irish

Most Irish immigrants who reside in the United States do so legally, but in recent decades, many arrivals from Ireland have overstayed their visas and become undocumented immigrants, in part because the U.S. government is issuing fewer work visas (Lentin, 2007). In 2013, there were an estimated fifty thousand undocumented Irish immigrants in the United States (Novacic, 2013). Most Irish immigrants are concentrated in eastern regions of the United States, and in particular, in the states of New York and Massachusetts.

Although there were Irish immigrants to the United States before then, between 1846 and 1854 more than 1.75 million people emigrated from Ireland, an unprecedented number. The direct cause was the Irish Famine, which began in 1845, killing more than one million people. By the end of the nineteenth century, more than three million Irish immigrants had entered the United States. Irish immigrants faced a strong anti-Irish and anti-Catholic sentiment in America, which was predominantly an Anglo-Saxon Protestant nation at the time. Between 1820 and 1920, some three out of four Irish immigrants were Catholic, though the Scotch-Irish Protestants from Ulster were also well-represented. "No Irish Need Apply" was a slogan on some employment advertisements. Worse, there were waves of anti-Irish violence, with mobs assaulting immigrants or burning Irish homes and churches.

In the twentieth century, the creation of the Irish Free State in Ireland in 1921 came with a bitter civil war, economic recessions, conservative religious and political policies. For the poor in particular, there was little economic opportunity. Daughters and younger sons rarely inherited the family farm but instead served as unpaid labor for their fathers or elder brothers if they had no dowry or source of income. Thus, for the majority of the population, emigration remained one of the few available options, and America was the "golden land of opportunity" (Kenny, 2000: 183).

Rates of emigration from Ireland to the United States between World War II and the beginning of the twenty-first century fluctuated broadly based on economic cycles of stagnation and affluence. Nearly 27,000 Irish immigrants came to the United States in the 1940s, while 48,362 arrived between 1951 and 1960 due to the 1952 McCarran-Walter Act. This upward trend became even more pronounced with the passage of the Hart-Celler Act in 1965, which abolished the discriminatory U.S. national-origins quota system that had been in place since 1924. With the new law, Ireland's quota increased from 17,000 to 20,000 immigrants per year, but preference for admission also changed to those who had immediate family ties or possessed needed skills. Irish immigrants rarely met these qualifications, so only 37,500 came in the 1960s. The number plummeted even further to 6,559 in the 1970s, due to improving economic conditions back home.

In the 1980s, the United States reclaimed its popularity as a destination for Irish immigrants due to a major economic recession in Ireland and Great Britain. Emigration totaled 216,000 during the decade, with one in seven emigrants leaving for the United States. Many were undocumented immigrants who entered the country on temporary tourist visas and stayed, working in the informal economy to support themselves.

By the 1980s, the resurgence of Irish immigration created vibrant new Irish communities, often in old Irish neighborhoods in Boston, New York, and San Francisco. Many of the "New Irish" were middle-class university graduates of legal status who sought careers with American corporations. A larger percentage entered the country on temporary tourist visas and stayed indefinitely, working as undocumented laborers in construction, restaurants and bars, and domestic service. The New Irish were also different from even the most recent generation of immigrants in that they had left an independent, changing, modern Ireland that had seen at least some period of prosperity. They had never envisioned needing to emigrate and were thus resentful of their situation. In addition, the New Irish lacked tangible connections with Irish Americans, who associated Ireland with song, Catholicism, and physical-force nationalism. Immigrants did not join ethnic associations and were critical of U.S. foreign policy, politics, and lifestyles. While most could find a distant relative in Boston, New York, or Chicago and might look them up upon arrival, settlement depended much more on networks of friends, bar culture, and work availability. Their uncertain status prevented them from putting down roots, and, as a result, many remained more Irish than American. A group that emerged to respond to the needs of undocumented Irish population was the Emerald Isle Immigration Center. The center's work in the late 1980s focused its efforts on helping immigrants obtain bank accounts, driver's licenses, housing, medical insurance, education, and legal protection for undocumented immigrants.

Still, many undocumented Irish were determined to legalize their status. Irish-American politicians, members of the Irish Immigration Reform Movement (IIRM, a grassroots organization of undocumented Irish), and the publishers of the newly founded *Irish Voice* newspaper began to agitate for changes in U.S. immigration law. In 1987, the IIRM, with the help of Senator Edward Kennedy and Congressman Brian Donnelly of Massachusetts, attached a provision to an Immigration Reform and Control Act. The Immigration Act of 1990 was one of only two major immigration bills in the country's history to increase legal immigration. The legislation increased the focus of immigrant admission toward highly skilled workers. The bill also included a provision that became known as the Morrison visa program, named after Democratic Congressman Bruce Morrison of Connecticut, one of the Act's authors. Immigrants from the Republic of Ireland and Northern Ireland were allotted 40 percent (16,239) of the visas. The IIRM also established centers to help guide immigrants through the process of getting green cards, becoming citizens, and registering to vote.

In the 1990s and 2000s, Ireland experienced a period of unprecedented economic prosperity, creating a new demand for workers from the country's highly educated population. Subsidies from the European Union in Irish infrastructure, low tax rates, investment from American high-tech companies, and increased consumer spending allowed for yearly growth rates of 7 percent. Ireland's expanding economy was dubbed the "Celtic Tiger," leading to lower emigration rates, return migration from those abroad, and unprecedented immigration from Eastern Europe, South America, and Africa. Yet, while the tourism, construction, pharmaceutical, and technological industries boomed, opportunities in manufacturing and farming grew more slowly. By the end of the first decade of the new century, as the economy slowed and the government's attempt to bail out the banks led to the need for loans from the European Union, many Irish experienced a drastic reversal of fortunes. Again, emigration rates rose in response. During the 1990s, somewhat more Irish-born persons had been admitted by the United States than the number who had last resided in Ireland (1990–1999: 67,975 versus 65,400). However, the softening of the economy and the resumption of emigration after 2000 were apparent not so much in the total number admitted by the United States (which had dropped since the 1990s), but in the dramatic difference between the number who had been living in Ireland when applying for admission to the United States (2000–2009) and the number who had been born in Ireland but had not been living there when seeking admission to the United States (2000–2009: 28,239 versus 15,312). More recently, with hopes of immigration reform in the air, and given the latest economic crisis in Ireland, the IIRM has been working on the forefront of the push by the Irish lobby to secure a visa program for the Irish.

Meaghan Dwyer-Ryan and Daniel Kanstroom

See Also: Hart-Celler Act (1965); Immigration and Nationality Act (The McCarran-Walter Act) (1952); Overstayers; Student Visas; Work Visas.

Further Reading

Almeida, Linda Dowling. 2006. "Irish America, 1940–2000." In *Making the Irish American: History and Heritage of the Irish in the United States,* edited by J. J. Lee and Marion R. Casey, 548–73. New York: New York University Press.

Corcoran, Mary P. 1993. *Irish Illegals: Transients between Two Societies.* Westport, CT: Greenwood Press. Irish Immigration Reform Movement (IIRM) Website. 2012. http://irishlobbyusa.org/.

Kenny, Kevin. 2000. *The American Irish: A History.* New York: Longman.

Kenny, Kevin, ed. 2003. *New Directions in Irish-American History.* Madison: University of Wisconsin Press.

Lentin, Ronit. 2007. "Illegal in Ireland, Irish Illegals: Diaspora Nation as Racial State." *Irish Political Studies,* 22.4:433–453.

Meagher, Timothy J. 2005. *The Columbia Guide to Irish American History.* New York: Columbia University Press.

Novacic, Ines. 2013. "How Irish Immigrants in New York City See Immigration Reform." *The World,* April 17. http://www.theworld.org/2013/04/how-irish-immigrants-in-new -york-city-see-immigration-reform/.

O'Hanlon, Ray. 1998. *The New Irish Americans.* Dublin: Roberts Rinehart Publishers.

J

Johnson-Reed Act (1924)

The Johnson-Reed Act is also known as the Immigration Act of 1924. This act included two others: the National Origins Act and the Asian Exclusion Act. Sponsored by Albert Johnson in the House of Representatives and David Reed in the Senate and signed into law by President Calvin Coolidge, the act set immigration quotas at 2 percent of the U.S. residents originally from a given country as counted in the 1890 census. The 1924 National Origins Act superseded the 1921 Emergency Quota Act, which had for the first time provided limits on the number of immigrants to the United States based on nationality and race. Like previous enactments, it was a product of the desire to keep the United States as racially and culturally homogeneous as possible. It barred entry to those who were ineligible for naturalized citizenship (i.e., who were not "white"), thus cutting off what remained of Asian immigration after nearly fifty years of anti-Asian exclusion legislation. It is commonly accepted that the 1890 census was chosen in an effort to restrict further immigration by southern and eastern Europeans (particularly Jews, Slavs, Russians, and Italians) who were represented in larger numbers in later counts. At that time, the concepts of nationality and race were considered to be the same, and the national origins quota has largely been viewed as a deliberate and successful attempt to keep out those who were not of Anglo Saxon or Nordic derivation. Great Britain was given the largest quota, set at over 65,000. The lowest was one hundred.

Because "national origins" were defined according to the geopolitical boundaries as they existed in 1920 and because Western Hemisphere countries were not subject to the quota system, those inhabitants in the continental United States that came from those regions were not entitled to quotas. The law stated that it did not include "(1) immigrants from the [Western Hemisphere] or their descendants, (2) aliens ineligible for citizenship or their descendants, (3) the descendants of slave immigrants, or (4) the descendants of the American aborigines." Furthermore, the Act facilitated the immigration of those with close blood relations to naturalized citizens. In these ways, non-white and non-Europeans were discounted from being legally represented as part of the American nationality. By excluding non-whites from the quota system, European countries were entitled to larger quotas. Moreover, the national origins quota system conveyed a potent and enduring message: that white Americans and European immigrants had national origins and people of color did not.

Racial delineations and subsequent classifications were being codified across the political landscape, and immigration policy was a critical mechanism for this enterprise. The 1924 Act solidified racial hierarchies and classifications, perhaps even more than the 1917 Immigration Act. This was in large part due to the increased participation of eugenicists in these policy debates. Eugenicists believed that everything from poverty to intellect to crime to political orientation to sexuality was attributable to heredity and that the United States could and should control the character of the nation by controlling who entered and who procreated. They tended to believe in the superiority of the Nordic and Anglo-Saxon people and agitated for immigration policy that reflected this belief. As such, for the first time, the concept of racial unassimilability was introduced into thinking about American identity that excluded those persons deemed ineligible for citizenship. Whereas eugenicists indirectly influenced the 1917 law, they were more directly involved in the 1924 legislation. Madison Grant, author of *The Passing of the Great Race* and founding member of the American Eugenics Society (AES), was a framer of the 1924 National Origins Act. Grant was not a member of Congress, but Albert Johnson, the bill's sponsor in the House, was. He, too, was a member of the AES. Business-led campaigns against quota proposals were highly visible. As Chair of the House Immigration and Naturalization Committee Congressman Johnson (R-Washington State) was adept at getting his viewpoint across divisions in the business communities by both appealing to their desires for a plentiful, cheap, and compliant labor force, and reminding them of the difficulty of purging the Chinese from U.S. soil after enlisting them to build the railroads.

Prior to the National Origins Act and for nearly a decade, the debate over establishing a Mexican quota also developed. Mexican immigration had also inspired the similar fears expressed about admitting people from eastern Europe who were also perceived to be culturally and racially inferior. In debates about Mexican immigration, objections to their culture, health and religion were often raised. Policy makers had argued against Mexican immigration even before the quota system curbed the immigration from Europe. The American Federation of Labor president Samuel Gompers opposed their exclusion from the quota provisions, and his failure demonstrates how powerful the big-business lobby was in immigration matters. Cotton, fruit and vegetable growers and packers from agricultural states were organized labor's main opponents, and they were united and very vocal in their opposition to Mexico being included in the quota system. Unlike manufacturing, most forms of agriculture had not yet invested in cost-effective mechanization that would later displace labor, and agribusinesses were dependent on the success of large-scale manual labor operations. The pressure they exerted to exclude from the quota a readily available supply of cheap, "unassimilable," un-unionizable and un-American workforce proved effective (Allerfeldt, 2010).

When the numbers of European-born immigrants declined in the period after 1924, nearly 94,000 Mexicans entered the United States. State Department figures show that an average of nearly sixty thousand Mexican workers per year entered the United States between 1925 and 1930. Over five hundred thousand Mexicans emigrated to America in the decade so that the recorded numbers of documented Mexican immigrants reached to about 2.5 million by 1930. Greater numbers were suspected of entering illegally. In 1925, fourteen thousand Mexicans had reportedly been deported. The 1924 legislation also set down documentation requirements such as obtaining passports and visas. Enforcement of these provisions took a disproportionate toll on Mexicans north of the U.S. border, despite the fact that Mexico itself was not subject to quota restrictions. In 1929 the penalty for those attempting to help Mexicans enter illegally was raised from being a misdemeanor to a felony, while political pressure to include Mexico in quotas continued giving contradictory signals (Allerfeldt, 2010).

The national quota system was not eliminated until 1965.

Nancy Ordover

See Also: Assimilation; Chinese; Dillingham Report; Emergency Quota Act of 1921; *Strangers from a Different Shore; Strangers in the Land;* Xenophobia.

Further Reading

Allerfeldt, Kristofer. 2010. "'And We Got Here First': Albert Johnson, National Origins and Self-Interest in the Immigration Debate of the 1920s." *Journal of Contemporary History* 45.1:7–26.

Ngai, Mai M. 2004. *Impossible Subjects: Illegal Aliens and the Making of Modern America.* Princeton, NJ: Princeton University Press.

Ordover, Nancy. 2003. *American Eugenics: Race, Queer Anatomy, and the Science of Nationalism.* Minneapolis: University of Minnesota Press.

Zolberg, Aristide R. 2006. *A Nation by Design: Immigration Policy in the Fashioning of America.* Cambridge, MA: Harvard University Press.